Historiography
at the Court of Christian IV
(1588-1648)

Karen Skovgaard-Petersen

Historiography at the Court of Christian IV (1588-1648)

Studies in the Latin Histories of Denmark by
Johannes Pontanus and Johannes Meursius

MUSEUM TUSCULANUM PRESS

UNIVERSITY OF COPENHAGEN

2002

Karen Skovgaard-Petersen: Historiography at the Court of Christian IV
© Museum Tusculanum Press 2002
Design of dust jacket: Kim Broström
Set and printed in Denmark by Special-Trykkeriet, Viborg
ISBN 87 7289 703 1
ISSN 0902 9907

Renæssancestudier, 11.
Edited by *Forum for Renæssancestudier*

Published with support from
The Danish Research Council for the Humanities
Hielmstierne-Rosencroneske Stiftelse
The Norwegian Research Council

Museum Tusculanum Press
Njalsgade 92
DK-2300 Copenhagen S

www.mtp.dk

Contents

Chapter I

Introduction

The long reign of Christian IV (1588-1648) was a turbulent period. Around 1600 Denmark (united with Norway) enjoyed a certain prosperity, and economic and military expansion marked the new king's many projects. By the end of his reign prosperity had been replaced by economic crisis and widespread poverty, a development which was, of course, in part due to long-term structural changes. But the king's miscalculated intervention in the Thirty Years War in 1625, which resulted in a devastating occupation of Jutland in 1627-29 by the imperial army, also contributed to the misery, and so did the burdens of the so-called Torstensson War with Sweden 1643-45. Further, the Privy Council (*rigsråd*), which consisted of members of the highest nobility and which held sovereignty together with the king, seems to have blocked attempts at necessary reformation of the administrative system.

While Denmark in the early part of Christian IV's reign was recognized as the dominant Baltic power, this role was gradually taken over by Sweden in the course of the first half of the seventeenth century. The Danish-Swedish relationship had been one of rivalry ever since the breakdown of the Union of Kalmar between the three Scandinavian countries in 1523. In 1563-70 the two countries had fought the so-called Nordic Seven Years War, and a new war, the Kalmar War, was conducted in 1611-13. In both cases Denmark had retained her leading position. During the Thirty Years War, however, the scales turned, and the Torstensson War proved decisive. Denmark now had to surrender parts of Norway and the islands of Gotland and Øsel to Sweden, and was reduced to a second-rate power, while Sweden's era as a great power was just beginning.[1]

---

[1] For a survey in English of seventeenth-century European history which includes Scandinavian affairs, see Thomas Munck 1990.

Throughout his long reign Christian IV distinguished himself as a remarkable patron of the arts and sciences. He was well aware of the political potential of royal splendour, and numerous painters, architects, musicians and other artists were engaged at his court. They all contributed to creating an image of Denmark as a powerful, rich and culturally refined monarchy with long and glorious traditions.[2]

National history was an important ingredient in this presentation of Denmark and her king. Around 1620 the grand hall, *Riddersalen*, in the newly erected castle Frederiksborg was decorated with tapestries, depicting the king's own glorious deeds, culminating in the victories in the Kalmar war against Sweden 1611-13.[3] In 1637 Christian IV (probably inspired by the antiquarian Ole Worm and the chancellor Christen Friis) launched a new pictorial project of national history, a series of drawings of great scenes of Danish history from the earliest times up to the king's own day. A number of Dutch artists were commissioned to contribute. The drawings – eighty-four according to the plan – were to function as models for copper engravings intended for print and for paintings which were to decorate the great banqueting hall at the castle of Kronborg. In the end, however, the project failed. The copper engravings were never printed, and the paintings may never have been hung in accordance with the original plan. Their dispersion began soon after Christian IV's death. Today forty-eight drawings and fifteen paintings survive.[4]

National history was not, of course, a pictorial matter only. In fact, one of the cultural projects to which the king paid most attention was the publication of a new and comprehensive history of Denmark in Latin.

---

[2] A modern standard biography of Christian IV, where the king's use of art as an ideological instrument is a main theme, has been written by Steffen Heiberg (1988). A survey of the king's cultural activities and their ideological implications is found in the comprehensive exhibition catalogue, published on the occasion of the celebration of Christian IV's 400-year jubilee (his accession to the throne is traditionally dated 1588 when his father died, but he was not crowned until he reached maturity in 1596). The catalogue also contains a bibliography of the rich literature on culture and learning in the reign of Christian IV. More specialized studies are Kongsted 1988, on music at the court of Christian IV, and Schepelern & Houkjær 1988, which deals with the series of paintings ordered by Christian IV in 1637 (see below). The political message of the grand wedding in 1634 of Christian IV's son Christian (1603-47) and the Saxon princess, Magdalena Sibylla (1616-68) has been studied by Mara Wade (Wade 1992).

[3] Charlotte Christensen 1988, 313-14.

[4] The series and its artistic and intellectual context is the subject of a recent monograph by Schepelern & Houkjær (1988).

The result, or results, of Christian IV's (and his chancellor Christen Friis's) engagement in this project were the works which are the subject of this book, the *Rerum Danicarum historia* (1631) by Johannes Pontanus and the *Historia Danica* (1630-1638) by Johannes Meursius. Both Pontanus and Meursius were of Dutch extraction. It is a notable indication of the close cultural ties between the northern part of the Low Countries and Denmark in the first half of the century that Christian IV turned to Dutch artists and intellectuals in both these great enterprises of national history. One of the immediate functions of Pontanus's and Meursius's works was to provide literary material for the Kronborg Series.[5]

Pontanus's work dealt with the time up to 1448, while Meursius in his first part, published in 1630, covered the period 1448-1523, and in the second the preceding period up to 1448 (1448 was an important year in Danish history, since this was the year in which Christian I ascended the Danish throne, and all the following kings, including Christian IV himself, belonged to his family, the Oldenburg family). At his death in 1639 Pontanus left behind in manuscript an account of Danish history from 1448 to the death of Christian IV's father, Frederik II, in 1588. Likewise, Meursius set out to cover the later history and left behind him a manuscript account of the period 1523-50.

The most recent history, then, after 1588, was left untold, and accounts of the period 1523-88 were only available in manuscript, but apart from this deficiency the two men fulfilled a long-cherished wish, inasmuch as ever since the 1550s historians had been engaged, more or less officially by the Danish government, in the task of providing a Latin history of Denmark.

The Lutheran Reformation in Denmark was carried through in 1536 by Christian IV's grandfather, Christian III (1536-59). Great wealth and power now became concentrated in the hands of the kings and made it possible for them to spend considerable sums of money on representative cultural projects. Though Christian IV surpassed both his grandfather and his father, Frederik II (1559-88) in this respect, they, too, had realized the political potential of artistic splendour and the value of a national Latin history.

It was a common practice in early modern Europe for governments to engage men of learning to compose works of national history. A printed comprehensive national history would serve several purposes. To put it

---

[5] Schepelern & Houkjær 1988, 33.

Pieter Isaachs: Christian IV, c. 1611. In connection with the Kalmar War 1611-13 Pontanus's brother, Pieter Isaachs, celebrated Christian IV as martial hero in this picture. (Museum of National History, Frederiksborg).

generally, it would, by testifying to the glorious history of a given nation as nation, exercise a legitimizing function which would not only have an effect on foreigners but also serve the internal purpose of building up a national identity; it would represent current national interest in concrete issues such as territorial questions and, more particularly, it would put forward arguments in favour of the present ruler's right to be in power. Its representative value would further lie in its display of erudition, an indication of the present state of learning of the country.

The story of the many frustrated attempts in Denmark in the last half of the sixteenth century and the final achievement of Arild Huitfeldt, who published an impressive chronicle in Danish around 1600, has often been told in surveys of Danish literature and historiography. But it was due to Pontanus and Meursius, not Huitfeldt, that the old dream of a comprehensive Latin history of Denmark was finally fulfilled. During the seventeenth century and well into the eighteenth the histories of both men enjoyed the status of standard works of reference on Danish history, in Denmark as well as abroad.[6]

Unlike Huitfeldt's work, however, their histories have led a shadowy life in later literary and historiographical research, off-handedly dismissed as unimportant and rhetorical. This lack of interest stands in glaring contrast to the king's own attention to the promotion of national history. There is no doubt that the official historiography is the part of his cultural programme which has received least attention in the last 200-250 years. Let us take a brief look at the most important literature.

At the request of the Florentine librarian Giovanni Lami, who in the years 1741-63 published Meursius's collected works in Florence, the distinguished Danish historian and philologist Hans Gram (1685-1748) provided Meursius's *History* with a copious and immensely learned commentary. He here corrects a number of factual errors and he often regrets Meursius's failure to include a given subject; some of his comments amount to small treatises, and his own excellent grasp of the sources of Danish history is evident throughout. But Gram also fully appreciated

---

[6] Ellen Jørgensen 1931, 122. E. Seaton cites a number of examples of learned Englishmen's acquaintance with Pontanus's and Meursius's *Histories* in the seventeenth century (Seaton 1935). Helge Kongsrud points out that Hugo Grotius, in a revised edition of the *De iure belli ac pacis* of 1642 (1st ed. 1625), derived his information on Norwegian affairs from Pontanus (Kongsrud 1984, 77), and H.F. Rørdam likewise points to Grotius's use of Pontanus's *History* (Rørdam 1896, 302).

Meursius's lucid Latin style, as he makes clear in another context.[7] On the whole, though, Gram definitely had more respect for Pontanus's achievement, which he often finds occasion to praise in his notes to Meursius's work. This evaluation also comes out in a survey of historiography dealing with Denmark, where Gram while preferring Meursius's style, praises the greater learning of Pontanus's work.[8] His plan of publishing a collection of texts pertaining to Danish history (*Monumenta patriæ*), to be introduced by an essay on Danish historiography, came to nothing; a survey of contents of this essay has, however, been preserved, and it appears that he would here have given a substantial treatment of Pontanus's *Rerum Danicarum historia*.[9] In fact, a letter from Gram reveals that he planned to prepare a new edition of the work, which the historian Fr. A. Reinboth (d. 1749) in Schleswig had offered to furnish with a biography of the author. Reinboth had, it seems, for some time been collecting material on Pontanus, which is now to be found in the Royal Library in Copenhagen (cf. below, Chapter III). Gram was forced to give up the plan, and Reinboth, too, (judging from this manuscript) left his biographical project in an incomplete state.[10] Gram's high opinion of Pontanus was shared by another scholarly eighteenth-century Danish historian, P.F. Suhm (1728-98), who praised Pontanus's erudition and judgement, and regretted that Meursius had not learned more from him; but Meursius's style, he adds, is very good.[11]

H.F. Rørdam published a highly valuable biography of Pontanus in 1898, in which he also made some sound observations on his *History of Denmark* and its affinity with Pontanus's earlier historical works. He grants some originality to the early part of Pontanus's work, but regards the rest as a rhetorical reworking of various historical writings, first and foremost Arild Huitfeldt's *Danmarks riges krønike* (1595-1604).[12] This view is shared by Ellen Jørgensen in her classic survey of Danish historiography of 1931; Meursius's *History* she regards as an uninteresting adap-

---

[7] In the preface to his edition of Niels Krag's *Christianus III* (Krag 1737), 35.

[8] *Historici Daniæ et Norvegiæ præcipui* (Ms. in Jena, *Cod. Jen. Bud.* fol. 341 (photocopy in the Royal Library of Copenhagen)). On Gram's authorship, see Ellen Jørgensen 1924.

[9] The survey of contents is quoted in J. Langebek's preface to the first volume of his edition of *Scriptores rerum Danicarum* (1772).

[10] Extracts from Gram's letter are quoted in Rørdam 1898, 470-71.

[11] P.F. Suhm (1792): *Tanker om de Vanskeligheder, som møde ved at skrive den gamle danske og norske Historie*, 95-96.

[12] Rørdam 1898, 451-55; cf. also Rørdam 1896, 301f.

tation of Hans Svaning's Latin *History of Denmark* (from around 1570), of which the greatest part is now lost. Her interest in both Pontanus and Meursius is limited, since neither of them in her eyes contributed in any significant way to research in Danish history.[13]

Until recently, then, Pontanus's and Meursius's *Histories of Denmark* did not arouse much interest among historians for the simple reason that they did not provide any information which was not available from older sources. More sympathetic is Torben Damsholt, author of the latest account of early modern Danish historiography, where the notion of representative, official historiography is taken seriously and not dismissed with automatic contempt. But Damsholt does not go into any more detail than his predecessors. The same is true of the most recent history of Danish literature, though it does adopt, like Damsholt, a positive attitude towards the whole idea of rhetorical history.[14]

Two students of Scandinavian intellectual history form notable exceptions to this relative lack of interest. The Icelandic scholar Jakob Benediktsson has analyzed a section of Pontanus's *History of Denmark* in his study of the dispute between Pontanus and the Icelandic historian Arngrímur Jónsson on the question of the identification of ancient Thule.[15] H.D. Schepelern has not only translated into Danish a number of letters between Pontanus and the Danish antiquarian Ole Worm (on whom, see below), but also, as already mentioned, pointed out that Pontanus's and Meursius's *Histories* were used as sources for the Kronborg Series.

The Scope of the Present Book

The present book has been written from the conviction that the two *Histories* have other claims to our interest than simply as sources for older Danish history. It is an attempt to read them as literary products in their own right, to investigate the notions, conscious or unconscious, which shaped them.

Two closely interrelated questions will be basic to the investigation. What is the relation between the two works and why were both Pontanus

---

[13] Ellen Jørgensen 1931, 155-59.

[14] Torben Damsholt 1992, 59-61; Erik V. Rasmussen 1983, 155-59.

[15] Arngrímur, ed. Benediktsson, 1950-57, XII, 419-27. I shall return to this dispute in Chapter VI.

and Meursius engaged as royal historiographers? I shall describe this problem in more concrete terms, and suggest a preliminary answer, in the following survey (Chapter II) of the various attempts during the reign of Christian IV to have the project carried out. This survey and the biographies of Pontanus and Meursius (Chapter III) focus on the interplay between the government and the authors. In the Conclusion I shall discuss this subject from another angle: to what extent is it possible, on the basis of the preceding analyses of the two *Histories*, to form an opinion of the instructions given to the authors by the Danish government? I have chosen to conduct the analyses within this overall perspective, because I believe that the material – the *Histories* themselves viewed together with earlier works on Danish history and letters written in connection with their production – allows us to study in some detail one instance of a general phenomenon, viz. the interplay between politicians and intellectuals in the formation and presentation of national ideology in the early modern period.

The analyses themselves (Chapters V-IX) will (in broad terms) focus on three main areas. One is ideological and political: the two authors were engaged by the Danish king to write Denmark's history, and obviously the general picture of Danish history is a favourable one, but what is it like more precisely? How are Denmark's relations with Sweden, the contemporary rival, described during the course of history? What picture of the Danish monarchy is drawn?

Another main area is historiographical: what are the general underlying values in the works, what kind of subjects are included, how typical or untypical are they when seen in relation to contemporary historiography? This last question is, perhaps, over-ambitious, and I do not at all claim to have answered it sufficiently. The quantity of European Latin historiography from the period 1550-1650 is enormous, and modern surveys are few.[16] Only to a limited extent have I been able to point out direct influence from contemporary works; my aim has rather been to place Pontanus's and Meursius's contributions within some broad historiographical categories, and in this endeavour I have profited from re-

---

[16] As a *Repertorium* of early modern historiography, Eduard Fueter's *Geschichte der Neueren Historiographie* from 1911 is still highly useful. An inspiring and learned presentation of the study and theory of history in the early modern period is given by Donald R. Kelley in his recent *Faces of History* (1998) (which though covering the history of historiography from antiquity up to c. 1800, has its main focus in the early modern period).

cent works on the development of the study of history, notably by Donald R. Kelley who traces the roots of historicism in humanist historiography.[17]

Pontanus's and Meursius's *Histories of Denmark* are strikingly different – striking because the circumstances under which they were created are so alike. They were written during the 1620s and 1630s for the same employer on the same subject by authors of about the same age who had a common background in Dutch humanism. Briefly stated, we are dealing with the persistent historiographical distinction between, to put it schematically, learned antiquarianism and elaborate style, the former being represented by Pontanus, the latter by Meursius; another notable difference is the Christian moralism pervading Meursius's interpretation of Danish history, an element which is much more in the background in Pontanus's work.

Finally, I shall discuss questions of style – details of vocabulary and syntax as well as longer narrative units. My interest is here focused on the interplay between form and content, on the way in which linguistic and literary phenomena contribute to shaping the overall "message" of the works. Indeed, it has been my aim, as far as possible, to point to connections between all these three areas. For the sake of clarity, however, I have treated style in a separate chapter, Chapter VIII, while the thematic analyses are presented in Chapters VI (Pontanus) and VII (Meursius).

Since the objects of analysis are the texts themselves, questions of sources have only secondary importance. Whatever the source may have been of a given judgement put forward by one of the authors, he made it his own, endowed it with his own authority, by including it in his text. Obviously, though, questions of sources are highly relevant in an attempt to understand the works along the above-mentioned lines. As the sources used by Meursius and Pontanus are to a considerable extent known to us, it is possible to obtain some knowledge of their strategy of adaptation and reworking. If, for instance, it can be demonstrated that one of them added a piece of information or inserted a judgement on a given event himself, that he did not simply follow his main source, this is a significant indication of what he regarded as important. In both the thematic and the stylistic analyses I have therefore paid some attention to Pontanus's and Meursius's use of sources.

---

[17] Donald R. Kelley 1970. Cf. also Ulrich Muhlack 1991.

It would be unrealistic to assume that Pontanus's and Meursius's *Histories of Denmark* will ever be available in another language than their original Latin. Even a new edition is not likely to appear. I have therefore seen it as one of the purposes of this book to offer a guide to the works, to go into some detail about their contents in order to provide a general impression of the material to be found there, particularly in the case of Pontanus's work, which is by far the more comprehensive of the two.

A theme on which the book will not have much to say is the achievement of Pontanus and Meursius with respect to the factual side of the study of Danish history. I seldom venture into discussions of whether a given insight or fact presented by one of them corresponds to established views among historians today. To go into these factual matters in any satisfying degree would amount to writing another book. My concern has been less with the facts presented than with the underlying principles and values.

Even within this limited area my treatment is not exhaustive. The scarcity of earlier scholarship combined with the huge quantity of material – the *Histories* themselves, their sources, Danish and foreign contemporary historiography, letters to and from the authors – has often made me realize in the course of my studies that many more stones could be turned. On the other hand, since the works themselves have never been investigated along the lines sketched above, let alone compared with each other, and since the authors' engagements at the court of Christian IV have not received more than superficial treatment, my study is able to present a number of fresh findings on the process of composition and publication and, first and foremost, to offer the first comprehensive reading of the two texts. These monumental *Histories of Denmark* certainly deserve a more prominent place within Danish intellectual history and within the cultural programme of Christian IV than they have hitherto been given.

Editions

I shall here briefly survey some facts about the editions of the two *Histories*. Meursius's *Historia Danica* falls into four parts, the three first of which were published together in 1638. The first (pp. 1-118) begins with King Danus and ends with Valdemarus I (1157-82); it is separated into five books. The second part (separately paginated, 1-133) stretches from Canutus VI (1182-1202) to Christophorus III (*Christoffer af Bayern*, 1440-

48), and likewise consists of five books. The third part (1-87) covers the reigns of the three first Oldenburg kings, Christianus I (1448-81), Johannes (1482-1513), and Christianus II (1513-23), whose reigns are allotted one book each; this part of the work had been published separately in 1630. The fourth part deals with the years 1523-50, i.e. the reign of Fredericus I (1523-33), an interregnum, and the first part, up to 1550, of the reign of Christianus III (1536-59). Meursius left this last part behind in manuscript. It was not printed until 1746, when the whole work was published as Volume IX of the *Opera omnia* edition of Meursius's works (1741-63). Here this part takes up cols. 791-992, and it is presented as Books IV-VIII of Part III. In the present book, though, I shall refer to this part as Part IV.

While the overall editor of the *Opera omnia* was a Florentine librarian, Giovanni Lami, it was the Danish historian, Hans Gram (1685-1748), who on Lami's request took care of the edition of Meursius's *Historia Danica*. The commentaries with which he furnished it are in many cases essays on historical topics rather than commentaries on Meursius's text. In the same volume, following Meursius's *Historia Danica*, Gram published several related works: Stephanius's continuation of Meursius's history of Christianus III (1st ed. 1650) (cols. 993-1056), Meursius's edition of Ailnothus's *De vita et passione S. Canuti Regis et Martyri* (previously published 1631) (cols. 1057-1104) and his edition of an anonymous *De passione S. Caroli Comitis Flandriae S. Canuti Regis Daniae F.* (previously published 1631) (cols. 1105-14); further an anonymous nobleman's commentary on Meursius's *History*, entitled 'Anonymi auctoris in Historiam Danicam Io. Meursi priusquam publici iuris fieret observationes' ('Observations of an anonymous author on the History of Johannes Meursius, before it became common property', cols. 1115-30) (cf. Chapters III, VII), Meursius's answer, 'Ioannis Meursi ad adnotationes viri illustris a Domino Cancellario sibi communicatas Responsio' ('Reply of Johannes Meursius to the comments of a nobleman, which were communicated to him by the Lord Chancellor', cols. 1131-40), and Meursius's notes to Pontanus's *Rerum Danicarum historia*, entitled 'Ioannis Meursi animadversiones in Historiam Danicam Ioannis Isacii Pontani' (Criticisms of Johannes Isaksen Pontanus's Danish History by Johannes Meursius', cols. 1141-48) (cf. Chapter IX).

The edition of Pontanus's *Rerum Danicarum historia* of 1631 comprises 812 paginated pages, excluding the comprehensive indexes (in some copies the indexes are also paginated). The chronologically organized part of the work takes up pp. 1-636 and is divided into ten books. Then follows the geographical description of Denmark, taking up pp. 637-801, and notes to the work, 802-12. After the indexes, two pages of *addenda* and *errata* finish the work. It was originally furnished with five copper-engraved maps. In most extant copies they have been removed, but the University of Lund possesses a copy in which all five maps are found (cf. below, Chapter V).

Pontanus left behind in manuscript an account of the six first Oldenburg kings, from Christianus I to Fredericus II (1448-1588). It was brought from Harderwijk to Copenhagen, probably in the early 1650s, where it was preserved in the University Library.[18] From time to time transcriptions of parts of the comprehensive manuscript were made, and in 1729 the life of Christianus III (1536-59) was published in Hanover by Johannes Hübner; in 1735 followed an edition (in Flensburg) of the life of Fredericus II by G. Kryssing. In its entirety the second part of Pontanus's *History* was finally edited by E. J. v. Westphalen in his *Monumenta inedita rerum Germanicarum*, Vol. II, cols. 713-1230 (Leipzig 1740). It is based on a transcription made of the whole of the second part on the initiative of Frederik Rostgaard (1671-1745) in 1689; Rostgaard's manuscript is now in the Royal Library (*Gl. Kgl. S.* 839, fol.). Here also another transcription is preserved, which seems on some points to present a more reliable text (*Gl. Kgl. S.* 840, fol.).

Westphalen's edition came as a surprise to Hans Gram. Gram, who had much admiration for Pontanus's achievement, had planned to publish both Parts One and Two of Pontanus's *Rerum Danicarum historia*, as he wrote to an acquaintance in 1744. He had already prepared a transcription of Pontanus's own manuscript of the second part and sent it to a Dutch publisher, when the publisher changed his mind; and, he adds, since the work has now appeared in Westphalen's edition, he is forced to give up his plan, although the published version is based on a transcription inferior to the one he had prepared.

Finally a few words on the editorial practice adopted in the present book. In my transcriptions of early prints and manuscripts I have retained the

---

[18] On the fate of the second part of Pontanus's work I rely primarily on Rørdam 1898, 469-71.

original orthography and punctuation with the following exceptions: Accents have been left out, e with cedilla has been rendered with æ, and œ with oe, and abbreviations have been expanded. Obvious errors have been corrected without comment. I have retained the Latin names of the Danish kings when they are referred to as literary figures. I normally follow Pontanus's and Meursius's spellings of names.

Latin letters of the period are sometimes dated in the Roman fashion (*Kalendae, nonae, idus* etc.) and sometimes in the modern way (number of day). I have "translated" the Roman datings throughout. Another confusion arises from the fact that in this period both the Gregorian and the older Julian system were in use. I have simply adopted the date given in each letter and refrained from trying to establish which system is referred to except when it is explicitly indicated.

Chapter II

The Promotion of a New History of Denmark in the Reign of Christian IV

The first person in Denmark to receive official appointment as royal historiographer was Niels Krag in 1594. As noted by Ellen Jørgensen, the term *historicus regis* was common among contemporaries.[1] This attachment to the king is characteristic of the office. As we shall see, it is also reflected in the works of Pontanus and Meursius. Krag was told to finish a Latin history of Denmark within six years and to begin with recent history, the history of Christian III (1536-59) and Frederik II (1559-88). He was to receive 500 *daler* a year and 100 extra for assistants.[2] Krag only survived until 1602, having merely covered a fragment of Danish history, viz. the period 1533-50. His successor, Jon Jacobsen Venusin, was even less productive. He was a professor of rhetoric at the University of Copenhagen when he was appointed royal historiographer by Christian IV, but he died in 1608 and does not seem to have written more than notes for a history of Denmark. Then in 1616 Claus Christoffersen Lyschander (1558-1623/24), vicar and author of several historical poems in Danish, was appointed. According to his letter of engagement his salary amounted to 500 *daler* a year and another 100 *daler* were reserved for two assistants. Like Krag he was to write in Latin and complete the work within six years. Whereas Venusin, it seems, was to begin with the earliest times, Lyschander, like Krag, was told to start with recent history after the Reformation, that is, the reigns of Christian III and Frederik II.[3]

Later in the same year, 1616, Christian IV appointed a new chancellor, Christen Friis of Kragerup (1581-1639). He served in this capacity until

---

[1] Ellen Jørgensen 1931, 103.

[2] This account of Krag's appointment is based on Harald Ilsøe 1984. Krag's letter of engagement (*bestalling*) is published in A. D. Jørgensen 1884, 232-33.

[3] The letter is dated September 4, 1616 and printed in Rørdam 1868, 60-61.

Unknown artist (c. 1635): The chancellor Christen Friis. (Museum of National History, Frederiksborg).

his death in 1639 and came to play a key role in engaging the king's interest in literary and historical projects. Before we continue the survey of royal historiographers in the reign of Christian IV, I shall give a brief presentation of this important figure.[4]

In keeping with the contemporary ideal of the well-educated nobleman, Friis had studied at several foreign universities in Germany, France and Italy, and later in his work as chancellor he was particularly engaged in cultural, educational, and ecclesiastical affairs. It was at his suggestion that the poet and clergyman Anders Arrebo (1587-1637) set out to produce around 1630 a reworking in Danish verse of the French poet Du Bartas's sophisticated religious epic *La première Sepmaine* of 1579.[5] This poem was hugely admired in its day and had been translated more or less freely into several European languages. No doubt Friis saw the prestige attached to a Danish version; Arrebo's work was to place Danish in the group of refined vernacular languages.

Friis also promoted the antiquarian studies of Ole Worm (1588-1654), physician and professor at the University of Copenhagen, whom we have already met as the most likely originator of the plan of the Kronborg Series.[6] It was through the chancellor that Worm, in 1622,

---

[4] In his biography of Christen Friis, Ole Degn gives a useful survey of Friis's engagement in learned and educational matters (1988).

[5] Arrebo's poem, which is composed in alexandrines, is a pioneering work in Danish poetry. It was not printed until 1661. The standard biography of Arrebo was written by H.F. Rørdam (1857). Arrebo's and Du Bartas's poems are compared in Sørensen 1983, 109-13.

[6] Carl S. Petersen devotes ample attention to Worm's achievement as an antiquarian, and to antiquarian studies in Denmark in the seventeenth century (Petersen 1929, 554sqq). On the *Museum Wormianum*, see H.D. Schepelern 1971.

prevailed upon the king to order the bishops in Denmark and Norway to obtain information from their vicars about local antiquities, that is, archaeological objects, documents, local customs, and oral traditions. The reports of the vicars were sent to the chancellery and handed over to Worm. Aware of Worm's knowledge of runic inscriptions, Friis commissioned him to study a runic calendar from the fourteenth century, and the result was Worm's first antiquarian work, the *Fasti Danici* (1626), dedicated to Christian IV.[7] Worm's subsequent studies were concentrated on runes. He believed that runes had been a common form of handwriting and furthermore that the Icelandic language spoken in his day was close to the language of the runic inscriptions, and with great enthusiasm he established contacts with learned Icelanders in order to obtain Old Norse writings from Iceland. The chancellor's engagement in these studies of runes and Old Norse, which in his and Worm's eyes threw light on the high level of culture in the early Danish past, is evident from Worm's letters. Worm also dedicated a theoretical work on runes to the chancellor.[8]

The composition of a national history was a project that particularly engaged Friis. Throughout his period as chancellor there was always one and usually more than one man engaged in writing a new history of Denmark. There is no doubt that Christian IV's concern for the promotion of national history was considerably influenced by Friis.

As we shall see, he took an active interest in Pontanus's and Meursius's writings. A number of letters survive in which Pontanus addresses Friis about particular historical problems, and the chancellor saw to it that samples of their works were read and commented upon by himself or his assistants. Friis must be regarded as the driving force behind the organization of the historiographers' work. As Pontanus himself described it,

---

[7] If we may believe Worm's own description of the matter in a letter dated July 18, 1629, to the English antiquarian Henry Spelman, the work was produced to please some prominent men, as he says, rather than written out of a personal wish (Worm 1751, no. 426; Worm 1965-68, I, no. 284). In a letter to Johs. Cabeljavius in Bremen dated September 7, 1633, Worm says that it was the chancellor who persuaded him to concentrate on Danish antiquities (Worm 1751, no. 412; Worm 1965-68, I, no. 489). (Worm's letters have been published in Danish translation by H. D. Schepelern (Worm 1965-68). A less comprehensive Latin edition was prepared by Hans Gram and published in 1751 (Worm 1751). Worm's correspondence with Icelanders was published in 1948 by Jakob Benediktsson (Worm 1948)).

[8] *Runir seu Danica literatura antiquissima* (1636). Worm's main antiquarian work was a collection of all the runic inscriptions known by that time in Denmark and Norway, *Danicorum monumentorum libri sex* (1643).

he wrote "under the auspices of His Most Serene Royal Majesty, but by the direction of the most noble and distinguished Christen Friis, Lord High Chancellor".[9] Although he had not yet taken up his post as chancellor by the time of Lyschander's appointment, Friis seems to have instigated that, too.[10]

Lyschander, who had been engaged as royal historiographer in 1616, soon proved to be an unsatisfactory choice, and in 1618 Pontanus entered the scene. It seems that one year earlier, in 1617, another prominent Dutch scholar, Daniel Heinsius (1580-1655), had been appointed historiographer to the Swedish king, Gustav Adolf; in view of the current political rivalry between Sweden and Denmark this may have been a contributing factor to the decision of the Danish government to replace Lyschander with Pontanus, a scholar of international reputation. The Danish government proved more willing than the Swedish to provide its historiographer with salary and material. Heinsius was frustrated in his requests for both, and in the end nothing came out of his engagement as Swedish historiographer (cf. Chapter IV, 10).[11]

There is, however, some uncertainty as to the date of Heinsius's engagement, which may not have taken place until 1618,[12] in which case it can hardly have influenced the appointment of Pontanus. Nor is it known whether the Danish government was in fact aware of Heinsius's new role. But it is a reasonable assumption that the re-publication in 1617 of Johannes Magnus's violently anti-Danish History of Sweden was noticed in Denmark (it was first published in 1554, cf. Chapter IV, 2), and Pontanus's appointment may have been inspired, in part, by this circumstance.

Apparently Lyschander managed to keep his title and salary as royal historiographer, and it was agreed that he should go on writing, though not, as stipulated in the employment letter, in Latin but in Danish.[13] Pontanus was to take care of the Latin version. In 1622 Lyschander was able to publish a huge and rather confused work of history in Danish, *Synopsis historiarum Danicarum*. It was intended, however, only as a prelude to his

---

[9] *auspiciis Serenissimæ Regiæ Majestatis, ductu vero Nobilissimi ac Magnifici viri Christiani Frys, magni Cancellarii* (letter to Claus C. Lyschander, dated August 25, 1622 (Matthæus 1695, no. 101)).

[10] Rørdam 1868, 60 (cf. *ibidem* 63).

[11] On Heinsius's relations with Sweden, see Paul R. Sellin 1968, 52-60.

[12] The date is discussed by Bo Bennich-Björkman 1970, 208n.

[13] Rørdam 1868, 71-75.

main work, a history and description of Denmark in 116 books, of which only scattered parts seem to have been completed.[14]

Pontanus, then, took over the task from Lyschander. The terms of his appointment bear close resemblance to those of his predecessor. He, too, was to receive a salary of 500 *rigsdaler* a year himself and 100 *rigsdaler* for two assistants, and complete his work, covering the whole of Danish history from the beginning to Christian IV, within six years. Unlike Lyschander, however, he was to begin with the oldest history and then proceed chronologically.[15] In his case it is fairly certain that the chancellor was instrumental in bringing about the employment,[16] as he may also have been behind Lyschander's appointment two years earlier, although he did not become chancellor until later in 1616.

But Pontanus's work did not proceed as smoothly as his employers had hoped. In 1622 he received an impatient letter from Christian IV (dated February 14), urging him to speed up,[17] and two years later, in 1624, they must have realized that it would take too long if Pontanus were to complete the whole of Denmark's history himself. In that year another Dutchman, Johannes Meursius, was appointed historiographer to the Danish king, and he was told to concentrate on recent history, beginning in 1448, when the kings of the Oldenburg line made their appearance on the Danish throne. His original task was to write an account of all the Oldenburg kings, including Christian IV himself.[18] As I shall argue below, there seems to have been a change of plan soon afterwards, the celebration of Christian IV being left to others. Unlike Pon-

---

[14] On the title page of Lyschander's *Synopsis*, or *Slectebog* as it is often called, one reads: *Synopsis historiarum Danicarum. En kort Summa offuer den Danske historia fra Verdens Begyndelse til* [...] *Christian den Fierdes Konningstid oc Regimente, forfatted vdi de Danske Kongers Slectebog*. See further below, Chapter IV, 8.

[15] The letter is dated March 28, 1618 and printed in Rørdam 1898, 447-48 (it is summarized in *Kancelliets Brevbøger 1616-20*, 352-53 (*Sjællandske Registre* 16, 325)).

[16] Rørdam 1898, 446-47.

[17] Printed in Rørdam's biography of Pontanus (Rørdam 1898, 454; summarized in *Kancelliets Brevbøger 1621-23*, 253 (*Sjællandske Tegnelser* 22, 15)).

[18] This is clear from Johannes Grundtvig's survey of persons serving at the court of Christian IV, based on the accounts of the royal treasurers. From there Grundtvig gives a quotation showing that the king has called in Meursius from Leiden to Sorø "to be professor and Historicus, to describe the reigns of the Danish kings from King Christian and also what has happened during the life of His Majesty" (*Dr. Johannes Meursius har Kongen ladet forskrive fra Leyden i Holland herind til Soer Kloster, (eller: det kgl. Academi i Soer), at skulle være Professor og Historicus, at beskrive de Danske Kongers Historier fra Kong Christian, saa og hvad sig tildrager i hs. Maj.s Levetid*). (Grundtvig 1872, 182).

tanus, who stayed in the Low Countries, Meursius moved to Denmark and was engaged both as royal historiographer and as a professor at the newly established Academy for young noblemen at Sorø. It appears from the letter in which he accepts the offer that he was to receive 600 *rigsdaler* (*unciales*) as historiographer, apart from his salary as professor.[19] He was, like Pontanus, given two assistants.[20]

In the early years of the 1620s there is evidence of the keen attention with which the Danish government followed Swedish historiographical activities. It was one of the tasks of the Danish legate in Stockholm, Peder Galt, to inform the government in Copenhagen about these matters. Among his reports to Christen Friis is a transcript of the preface to the Swedish translation of Johannes Magnus's history, which had been published in 1620.[21] He commented on the Swedish runological studies,[22] and in January 1623 he sent Friis a history of the Swedish king, Gustav Vasa (1523-60), written by Erich Jörensson Tegel and published in 1622.[23] One month later Christen Friis complained to the Swedish legate in Denmark about some opprobrious claims in the work: Tegel had suggested that the Swedish realm in former times had comprised the province of Scania, and Friis declared that a similar claim against Sweden would never have been allowed by the Danish king.[24] While these interchanges do not seem to be directly connected with the engagement of Meursius,

---

[19] Letter from Meursius to Christian IV dated September 10, 1624 (Meursius 1741-63, XI, no. 573). – As to Meursius's salary as a professor there seem to have been attempts to reduce the sum originally promised. According to a letter from his Danish friend Holger Rosenkrantz (dated January 26, 1625), he could expect a salary of 500 *kurantdaler* as professor: [...] *quingentos nummos, singulo exaequante marcas duas, quas nominant Lubecenses cum dimidia, nostrates Courant Daler dicunt, id quidem ex literis vocationis tuae te percepisse arbitrabar* (Meursius 1741-63, XI, no. 580). This amount is confirmed by Tauber who quotes from a report (from 1623) on the organization of the future Academy that the professor of history was to receive 500 *kurantdaler* (Tauber 1827, 9). Before Meursius came to Denmark however, he received a letter from Niels Eggebrecht, secretary in *Tyske Kancelli*, in which he was informed that his salary as professor would be 400 *kurantdaler*. He confessed his confusion to Holger Rosenkrantz when he arrived in Denmark in May 1625, and Rosenkrantz wrote to the chancellor advising him to stick to the 500 *kurantdaler*, which he himself had originally promised Meursius (this letter is printed in Rosenkrantz 1887-89, 6, 305-7). According to M. Mackeprang's survey of Christian IV's Academy of Sorø, Meursius received 400 *rigsdaler* a year in his capacity of professor (Mackeprang 1924, 388).

[20] Grundtvig 1872, 182.

[21] *Peder Galts Depescher 1622-24*, ed. Nils Ahnlund 1920, VIII.

[22] *Ibidem* 15, 25.

[23] *Ibidem* 51.

[24] Harald Ilsøe 1973, 49.

they certainly form part of the framework within which the Danish historiographers' work should be seen. They not only bear witness to the general sensitivity in leading circles regarding historical statements, but also to Friis's view that such claims should not be put forward by a historian;[25] as we shall see, he later told Meursius to hold to a cautious line in his depiction of Danish-Swedish relations.

In the following years remarkable efforts were made by the Danish government to have older texts concerning Danish history published – efforts which took place regardless of the fact that Pontanus and Meursius were now both at work. After Claus Lyschander's death in 1623/24 his collection of historical manuscripts was transferred to the University. This was presumably the occasion for the letter in which the king, on March 1st 1625, ordered the professors of the University to go through the historical documents in the University Library and prepare those that seemed suitable for print. Rumours had apparently reached Copenhagen that Johann Kirchmann in Lübeck had found some texts concerning Danish history, and in a letter written the same day Christian IV ordered his *Rentemestre* that they should be obtained (at a decent price) and published.[26] The following day Jesper Brochmand was told by the king to see to a new edition of Huitfeldt's *History of Denmark* together with Lyschander's Danish history of Frederik II (since Huitfeldt, likewise in Danish, had covered the period up to Frederik II).[27] In the same period the possibility was even considered of having parts of Hans Svaning's unfinished *History of Denmark* made ready for print.[28] This work had been written in the 1560s and 1570s but it had been rejected for publication by the University professors who functioned as censors (cf. Chapter IV, 3).

None of these plans were realized at the time, but they do suggest that the government in the mid-1620s was highly impatient. The idea of pub-

---

[25] As underlined by Harald Ilsøe 1973.

[26] *Och efftersom nogle Fragmenta aff dansche historier schal findis til Lybeck, efftersom oss elschelige Doctori Arnisæo derom schall were beuist, da wille wi i lige maade, at i handler med den, som denum haffuer, om en billig foræring, som och i lige maade schulle forferdigis til trych.* (Miss. to *Rentemestrene* from Christian IV, dated March 1st, 1625, printed after a copy in *Konsistoriets Arkiv*, 189 in Rørdam 1868, 156. See also *Kancelliets Brevbøger 1624-26*, 346-47). There can hardly be any doubt that these fragments were the two medieval texts found in a manuscript in Lübeck Stadtbibliothek c. 1620 by Johann Kirchmann, viz. Theodericus's history of Norway (c. 1180) and the crusade account *Historia De Profectione Danorum* (c. 1200), as also suggested by Ole Degn 1988. They were not published until 1684.

[27] *Kancelliets Brevbøger 1624-26*, 348.

[28] Rørdam 1868, 111-13, 155-60.

lishing Svaning's previously rejected history is particulary surprising, considering the present engagements of Pontanus and Meursius. It seems reasonable to assume that some of these initiatives should be ascribed to Christian IV himself rather than to his chancellor. Since c. 1620 Christian IV had been increasingly involved in the ongoing European war, culminating in his martial engagement in the years 1625-29, and the almost desperate efforts to have works dealing with Danish history published in the spring of 1625 should perhaps be seen in this light.[29]

Let us return to the royal historiographers. In this sphere, too, we find high activity. In fact it seems that not even two were enough.[30] In the years 1626-29 at least one and probably two attempts were made to have a third man join the ranks. There is some evidence to suggest that a Danish delegation in 1626 addressed the Swiss theologian and polyhistor Johann Jacob Grasser (1579-1627) in Basel and asked him to accept the task of writing about Christian IV's own deeds; but the legate, Joachim Kratz, realized, it seems, that Grasser was too ill to undertake the task, and Grasser died shortly afterwards. At least the *Oratio funebris* of Grasser, written and delivered by Georgius Müller in 1627, mentions that Joachim Kratz visited Grasser shortly before his death in March 1627 on behalf of his king and asked him to accept the task of becoming royal historiographer. The king is not mentioned by name but described as the foremost leader of the Protestant cause, who has fought with the utmost bravery though not with equal fortune.[31] This in itself fits well with

---

[29] I owe this suggestion to Harald Ilsøe.

[30] It is sometimes assumed that Johannes Stephanius was appointed historiographer after Lyschander's death around New Year 1623/24 (he died briefly afterwards). There is, however, no evidence to confirm this theory. He is briefly mentioned in Rørdam's biography of his son, the later editor of Saxo's *Gesta Danorum* Stephanus Johannis Stephanius, on whom see Chapter III. (Rørdam 1891, 4-5).

[31] *Non possum* [...] *quin fidei caussa magni illius Regis, qui patrocinium Orthodoxiæ Euangelicæ et avitæ Sacri Romani Imperii tanto Majorum sanguine et virtute partæ libertatis, quæ sub jugo Hispanico ingemiscens animam agere videtur, in se suscepit et spiritu Heliano manus suas in hiantes hasce rimas immisit, magni inquam illius Regis judicium de Beato nostro Grassero in medium producam, utpote qui hunc inter omnes alios dignissimum præconem eligere dignatus est, a quo res ab ipsius Majestate, summa virtute, etsi non pari felicitate, adhuc quidem, gestæ prædicarentur et omnium seculorum memoriæ consecrarentur. Ex quo tanti Regis, vere Patris Patriæ, judicio clementissimo τόν μαχαριστόν nostrum, tanquam ex ungue Leonem, in proclivi est agnoscere et æstimare* [...] *nuper adeo ejusdem Regiæ Majestatis Legatus, Nobilissimus Dominus Joachimus Cratz Eques Divi Marci, ad hunc nostrum Beatum diverterit, eique expositis Serenissime Majestatis mandatis acta omnia obtulerit; sed quia Nobilissimus Vir facile poterat animo prospicere vires* τοῦ μαχαριστοῦ *corporis impares huic labori futuras, immo ipsum quoque vitæ spatium, promissa nihilominus Regiæ Majestatis in hunc nostrum benevolentia, vacationem eidem permisit* (Müller: *Oratio funebris de vita atque obitu* [...] *Grasseri,* 1627, 30-32).

Christian IV in 1627. We know further that the German Joachim Kratz functioned as a Danish diplomat, and that he was sent on a mission to Venice by Christian IV at the end of October 1626. The instructions Kratz received from Christian IV in October 1626 and his report of the mission, written in May 1627, are found in *Rigsarkivet*, Copenhagen (*TKUA A II, 6, Italien*). Here, however, no mention of Kratz's visit to Grasser in Basel is found.

Grasser was an old friend of Pontanus, who may have been the one who established the contact with the Danish government. He had recently, in 1624, published two historical works, one a historical presentation of Swiss and Italian towns (*Itinerarium politico historicum*), the other (written in German) a series of portraits of important men in Swiss history (*Schweitzerisch Heldenbüch*). His historical interests are thus well documented, but there is nothing in these works, as far as I have seen, to suggest any knowledge of or interest in Danish affairs. In the absence of supportive evidence I prefer to let it remain a suggestion that he was offered an engagement as historiographer by the Danish government.[32]

About two years later a new man, the Dutch Nicolaes van Wassenaer was asked to serve the Danish king as his historiographer. His employment is dated August 9, 1629, in a register of *Krigsbestallinger* (in *Rigsarkivet*, Copenhagen).[33] Rørdam, who first noted this, draws attention to the volumes of contemporary European history which Wassenaer published from 1622 until his death. Danish affairs are here treated amply and positively, and Rørdam suggests that this may be the reason that he was offered the post as historiographer. I think we could go one step further and claim that Wassenaer's literary merits in the field of contemporary history suggest that he, like – perhaps – Grasser, was asked to write about Christian IV himself. In fact it seems reasonable to connect his engagement to Christian IV's involvement in the European war since 1625, which had come to a (temporary) conclusion with the peace treaty in Lübeck in 1629. The treaty was signed in May and Wassenaer engaged in August – no doubt to celebrate the king as martial leader.[34] But again nothing came out of it, since Wassenaer died soon after. Not prepared to wait for Meursius to reach that far (which, eventually, he never did), the

---

[32] On Pontanus's friendship with Grasser (with whom he studied in Basel, 1600-1), see Rørdam 1898, 21.

[33] See Rørdam 1898, 471-73, where a short biography of Wassenaer is found.

[34] I am grateful to Harald Ilsøe for this suggestion.

Danish government asked first (as it seems) Grasser and then Wasse-naer.[35]

It seems, then, that Pontanus was to take care of the oldest history, Meursius of the Oldenburgs, and Grasser/Wassenaer of Christian IV himself. This implies a change of plan some time after Meursius's arrival, since apparently he had also been told at first to write of Christian IV, as we saw. Perhaps plans had already been changed once before with Meursius's own engagement, inasmuch as Pontanus, according to the original scheme, was to write a complete history of Denmark. However, contradicting this assumption is a letter from Pontanus, written in 1626, in which he apparently still sees himself as writing a complete history of Denmark. Declining an offer to become Professor of History and Greek in Groningen, he refers to his burdens as Danish historiographer. He says that much material has been handed over to him, "from which a full history of Denmark can be created and completed, and now I am totally occupied with preparing the first volume for print".[36] Not only does he refer to the work about to be printed as the first part, but he also describes the project as a history to be written *ad plenum*, "in full", which perhaps means "covering the whole of Danish history".

It is possible, then, that he was to adhere to the original plan of composing a complete history, while the other two would just write histories of shorter periods. We cannot know. But what we do know is that at some point it was decided that both Meursius and Pontanus should write a complete history of Denmark each – since this was what they eventually set out to do in the 1630s. After the publication of his own history of the three first Oldenburg kings (1448-1523) in 1630 and of Pontanus's history of the period up to 1448 in 1631, Meursius did not, as one might have expected, go on with the remaining Oldenburg kings up to his own time. Instead he wrote his own version of the time before the Oldenburgs. Nor did Pontanus make up for the deficiency of recent history. He

---

[35] Like Grasser, Wassenaer was an old friend of Pontanus, and the latter may, also in this case, have been consulted by Friis on the question of whom to engage as writer of contemporary affairs. His acquaintance with Wassenaer is documented in a poem written by Pontanus on the occasion of Wassenaer's death, where Wassenaer is referred to as an *amicus vetus*. The poem celebrates Wassenaer for his famous writings on contemporary history (Pontanus 1634, 87).

[36] *ex quibus historia rerum Danicarum ad plenum educi ac perfici queat, et nunc primo tomo typis describendo totus desudem* (letter from Pontanus to Franciscus Gomarus, dated July 15, 1626 (Matthæus 1695, no. 94)).

went on to write about the Oldenburg kings from the beginning, that is including the period 1448-1523, already covered by Meursius.

In other words, I think we are entitled to conclude that in the 1630s two complete Latin histories of Denmark were aimed at. But when this idea was formed is uncertain. It may have been right from the time of Meursius's engagement in 1624. Or it may be, as suggested above, that by that time only Pontanus was to write a full-scale history and Meursius and (later) Grasser/Wassenaer just smaller portions. This view receives support from an interesting letter written by Meursius in 1632 to his friend, the famous theologian and humanist scholar, Gerardus Vossius (1577-1649), in Amsterdam. Meursius here seems a little surprised at the decision to have him cover the period already treated by Pontanus:

> I am now writing a continuation of Saxo [i.e. the period after c. 1185], right up to the Oldenburg House with which I began, and (God willing) the goal is not far away. The noble lord, the royal chancellor, wanted me, although Pontanus's *History* has been published, to carry out that work once more. When I have finished that, I will then carry on with what I have begun on the Oldenburg House.[37]

The same discreet surprise on Meursius's side is apparent in a later letter to Vossius, where he mentions his ten books of Danish history, "in which I was ordered to go over (*retractare*) the whole of Pontanus's work".[38]

Although we know next to nothing about the plans for Grasser's and Wassenaer's work as historiographers – and in Grasser's case, his contact with the Danish government must remain a suggestion – it seems likely that in the last half of the 1620s the Danish government strove to obtain, and was prepared to pay, three foreign historiographers at the same time, in order to secure the completion of a comprehensive history of Denmark in Latin. In the 1630s it was willing to keep two historiographers on its payroll when one would have sufficed to take care of the period not

---

[37] *versor nunc in continuatione Saxonis, usque ad Domum Oldenburgicam, a qua inceperam, pertexenda, et non multum (Dei gratia) a fine absum. Illustris Dominus Cancellarius Regius, etiamsi edita Pontani Historia, operam repetere me istam voluit: qua finita, quae in Domo Oldenburgica inchoavi, etiam deinceps persequar* (letter from Meursius to Vossius, dated November 3rd, 1632 (Meursius 1741-63, XI, no. 695; Vossius 1691, II, no. 155)).

[38] *quibus totum Pontani opus retractare iussus fui* (letter from Meursius to Vossius, dated June 7, 1637 (Meursius 1741-63, XI, no. 755; Vossius 1691, II, no. 244)). The letter may belong to 1635 rather than 1637, cf. p. 75.

yet covered, 1523-c. 1630. It is a curious fact, which has not, I think, been noticed before, that by this time the Danish government seems to have wanted two separate versions of Danish history. What might be the point of that? I would suggest that the answer, or part of the answer, lies in the works themselves. Pontanus's work is considerably longer than that of Meursius. Probably part of the idea was to have Danish history presented in two versions, a longer and a shorter. In 1629, Jesper Brochmand (professor of theology, later bishop, 1585-1652), on the chancellor's order, wrote to Meursius to inform him of the chancellor's opinion of Meursius's account of the period 1448-1523, which he had seen in manuscript, and Brochmand here singles out two qualities of Meursius's work which had particularly pleased the chancellor, its stylistic elegance and its small scale: "What is immensely pleasing in your Danish History is the stylish diction and succinct description".[39] Thus, if the chancellor had not already told Meursius to write an abridged history – which he may very well have done – at least he was pleased with the idea when reading Meursius's draft of the period 1448-1523. It is a reasonable assumption that when he told Meursius to go on with the earlier history, he explicitly wanted him to go on writing "succinctly".

There are, however, as suggested in the Introduction, other significant differences between the two works. Whereas Pontanus's *History* is full of learned discussions and quotations, the succinct work of his colleague contains no quotations and few discussions; rather it is marked by moral reflections. Perhaps the chancellor had realized these differences when he told them both, probably in 1630-31, to write separate full-scale histories. He may have realized that their productions would be too different to function as parts of a whole, and consequently have persuaded the king of the advantages of having two versions, one long and learned, the other brief, elegant, and moralistic.

In the present book I shall try to demonstrate in further detail how different the two works are, despite all the features they have in common, written as they are at the same time for the same employer, on the same subject, by authors with a common background in Dutch humanism. The assumption that the difference was to some extent planned, that they were meant to be complementary, and that this design was con-

---

[39] *Immane quantum placeat et concinnior dictio, et compendio descripta Historia Danica* (letter from Brochmand to Meursius, dated January 4, 1629 (Meursius 1741-63, XI, no. 639; original in the Royal Library of Copenhagen, ms. *Thott* 1843, 4to)).

ceived by the chancellor must remain a hypothesis. Some further evidence will be given in the course of the book, and we shall take up the question again in the Conclusion.

After Meursius's death there seem to have been attempts to have the French classical scholar Claudius Salmasius (Claude de Saumaise, 1588-1658) engaged as his successor.[40] August Buchner (d. 1661), professor at Wittenberg, also seems to have been approached.[41] However, these plans came to nothing. Instead, Meursius's colleague at the Academy of Sorø, Stephanus Johannis Stephanius (1599-1650) took over the post as historiographer in 1639, and in this capacity he wrote the last part of Christian III's life, covering the years 1550-59, which had been left unfinished by Meursius. Apart from that there are signs that he was also told to prepare an account of contemporary history.[42]

---

[40] At least a somewhat cryptic letter from Salmasius, who by this time lived in France, suggests as much. The letter is addressed to André Rivet and dated August 15, 1640. See Leroy & Bots 1987, 231. Salmasius had been professor in Leiden since 1632.

[41] In his biography of Stephanius, Rørdam quotes a passage from one of Buchner's letters: he had received an exhortation from one of the professors at the Academy of Sorø, Johan Raue, to take up the vacant post after Meursius. Buchner goes on to declare his unwillingness to leave "this little nest of mine." The letter is not dated, but must belong to the autumn of 1639, before Stephanius was appointed as Meursius's successor (Rørdam 1891, 194).

[42] Rørdam 1891, 193-202.

Chapter III

The Authors

Johannes Pontanus

1. Pontanus's Career before his Appointment as Danish Historiographer

Before we embark on our discussion of the two histories of Denmark, I shall give a presentation of their authors. There are no modern comprehensive biographies of either Pontanus or Meursius. Sufficient material exists, though, to provide the basis for relatively detailed accounts of the two men's lives: their own scholarly works, various biographical notes in encyclopedias of the seventeenth and eighteenth centuries, and not least, the large number of letters to and from them both which have been preserved in various collections and which provide much valuable information about the Dutch and Danish intellectual milieus. However, I have not attempted to write full-scale biographies, but only to give an outline of their personal and scholarly background and then to go a little deeper into the circumstances under which they produced their histories of Denmark.

As already noted, Dutch-Danish cultural ties were particularly close by the time of Christian IV. The Dutch universities, especially the one in Leiden, by then enjoying a status as one of the main centres of learning in Europe, had taken over the role of German Protestant universities as the most important goal in the academic grand tour of young Danes.[1]

Johannes Isaksen Pontanus embodied this connection.[2] He was born

---

[1] Learned relations between the Protestant part of the Low Countries and Denmark in the sixteenth and seventeenth centuries are surveyed by Kay Schmidt-Phiseldeck (1945).

[2] In 1640, the year after Pontanus's death, an anonymous description of his life, which I shall refer to as *Vita et obitus* (1640), was published in Harderwijk. It was probably, as Rørdam notes, based on Pontanus's autobiographical notes (Rørdam 1898, 7, 466-67). (Pontanus also inserted a very brief autobiography in the *History of Denmark*, 728). Westphalen follows the *Vita et obitus* in his biography of Pontanus, prefaced to his edition of the second part of Pontanus's *History* (Pontanus, ed. Westphalen 1740, Preface 48-52).

Isac Isaachs (nephew of Pontanus): Johannes Pontanus. (Copper engraving in Pontanus's Rerum Danicarum historia 1631).

in 1571 in Helsingør in Denmark of Dutch Protestant parents who had fled from Haarlem in the 1560s. The family also had a Danish branch, the mother of Pontanus being the granddaughter of a notable governor (*lensmand*) in Bergen, Norway, Jørgen Hansen, who served the Danish king, Christian II (1513-23).[3] His father's name was Isaach Pietersz, and when Johannes later adopted the name Pontanus, it was probably an allusion to his birthplace close to the sea (*pontus*), the narrow Øresund that nowadays separates Sweden from Denmark (until 1658 Scania was Danish). It is not unlikely that Pontanus also had another allusion in mind, viz. to the famous Italian humanist and poet, Giovanni Pontano (1426-1503).

The father seems to have established contacts with a number of noble families and with the king, Frederik II; it was as the latter's agent that Isaach

---

The *Vita et obitus* also exists in a transcription in the Royal Library in Copenhagen (*Thott* 1957, 4to). This manuscript contains much additional information on Pontanus's life and works, collected in the 1730s by Fr. A. Reinboth (d. 1749), a historian from Schleswig. Apart from the *Vita et obitus* he also transcribed other biographies and letters to and from Pontanus. Besides this, the manuscript contains Reinboth's draft of a biography of Pontanus. As mentioned in the Introduction, there is evidence that the historian Hans Gram (1685-1748) intended to prepare an edition of Pontanus's *Rerum Danicarum historia*, and it appears that Reinboth had offered to furnish the edition with a biography of Pontanus. Gram abandoned his editorial project (cf. the Introduction) and Reinboth's biography was apparently never finished.

In 1898 H. F. Rørdam published a comprehensive biography of Pontanus, giving special attention to his work on Danish history. Rørdam based his work on the *Vita et obitus* from 1640, on Reinboth's notes in the ms. *Thott* 1957, 4to, and on the somewhat shorter biographies by Niceron from 1735 and by Bodel Nyenhuis from 1840. The latter, Nyenhuis 1840, is in its turn based on Westphalen, Niceron, and Pontanus's *Stammbuch*.

The first part of the present sketch, dealing with Pontanus's life up to his engagement as Danish historiographer in 1618, is primarily built on Rørdam and Reinboth. I have further consulted the *Vita et obitus*, the biographies of Niceron and Bodel Nyenhuis, and the biography found in *Nieuw Nederlandsch Biografisch Woordenboek* (ed. P. C. Molhuysen and P. J. Blok 1911ff), I, cols. 1417-20. In the latter part, which is about his work on the *History of Denmark*, my account is based mainly on letters to and from Pontanus. Pontanus's letters were edited by his grandson, Ant. Matthæus (1635-1710), in two collections, one from 1695 and one from 1698-1710 (2nd ed. 1738, to which I refer). Besides that, Rørdam found a number of important letters from Pontanus to Chr. Friis in *Rigsarkivet*, Copenhagen, written while he was engaged in composing the *History of Denmark*. They are published as an appendix to Rørdam's biography of Pontanus.

References to other biographies are found in Rørdam's biography, *passim*. Cf. also the brief biography and survey of his works in Haitsma Mulier & van der Lem 1990, 333-36.

[3] In his *History of Denmark* Pontanus takes care to refer to the man and their relationship, in connection with Jørgen Hansen's leaving Bergen, in 1523 or shortly afterwards, to follow Christian II in his exile: *Per idem tempus apud Norvagos arcis atque oppidi Bergensis præfectus Georgius Hansenius aviæ meæ maternæ parens, ubi accepisset Regem suum regnis relictis ad Cæsarem concessisse, arcem atque oppidum dioeceseos præposito, Johanni Canuto Regis ac domini sui nomine commisit, ipse herum secutus in Hollandiam quoque sive Brabantiam abiit* (col. 1081).

Pietersz, at some point during Pontanus's childhood, moved back to the Low Countries with his family and settled in Amsterdam (later he returned to Helsingør as agent of the States General of the United Provinces). His two sons, our Pontanus and his brother Pieter Isaachs (1569-1625), maintained the connections with the Danish royal family. Both went into the service of Frederik II's son, Christian IV, the brother Pieter Isaachs being one of the most significant painters at the court of Christian IV.

In 1592 Pontanus matriculated in Leiden, where he studied philology, medicine, philosophy and mathematics. After a visit to Italy he went back to Denmark in 1593, where he stayed for two years. Here he became attached to the astronomer Tycho Brahe (1546-1601), with whom he seems to have studied both astronomy and chemistry. Moreover he made two other aquaintances, which would prove valuable for his later historical studies. One was Arild Huitfeldt, an influential politician of the high nobility, whose impressive *History of Denmark* (1595-1604) (written in Danish) would later be the main source for Pontanus's own *History*. The other was Jon Jacobsen Venusin, who, by that time a vicar, later became royal historiographer. We shall return to both Huitfeldt and Venusin in the chapter on the historiographical background in Denmark (Chapter IV).

During the next nine years Pontanus studied in several places.[4] In England in 1595-96 he seems to have devoted himself to the philological and historical studies that would later become his main field. It was during this stay that he made acquaintance with another man whose historical works would influence his own, namely William Camden (1551-1623).[5] He studied in Leiden for the second time in 1597-98 and published an edition of Macrobius, which he dedicated to Huitfeldt. A copy of this book, found in the Royal Library in Copenhagen, has a handwritten dedication from Pontanus to Venusin and thus bears witness to his friendship with both these prominent Danish historians. Huitfeldt also wrote in Pontanus's *album amicorum*. Besides that, the edition of Macrobius is evidence of the friendship existing by that time between Pontanus and

---

[4] Pontanus's *stambuch* or *album amicorum*, which mainly contains entries from this period, is extant in Paris, Bibl. Nat., Coll. James Rotschild no. 3371. Microfilm in the Royal Library, Copenhagen, ms. micro 2027.

[5] Camden wrote in Pontanus's *album amicorum*. Their friendship is further attested by a letter from Pontanus to Camden, dated July 12, 1607, in which their earlier correspondence is mentioned. Pontanus here discusses various historical matters and sends with the letter a copy of his work, *Iter Galliæ Narbonensis* (1606). (Camden 1611, 90-91).

Johannes Meursius. The book was furnished with Pontanus's notes to Macrobius's text, and as an appendix there followed another set of notes, mainly textual, made by Meursius, who, in his dedicatory letter to Professor Bonaventura Vulcanius, notes that his young learned friend Pontanus had asked him to publish them in this book.

At Huitfeldt's manor house, Dragsholm, Pontanus now spent some time assisting him in his work on Danish history. He also went to Rostock to study with the renowned teacher and historian David Chytræus (1530-1600), and in 1601 in Basel he graduated in medicine. Here he made acquaintance with Johann Jacob Grasser (1579-1627), who many years later seems to have been asked by a Danish delegation to write the history of Christian IV; it is not known if this offer had anything to do with the connection between Pontanus and Grasser, but it may well have been the case (cf. Chapter II).[6] Shortly before, in Marburg, Pontanus had met the young Christen Friis, who later on became chancellor and was the driving force in promoting the production of the new Latin histories of Denmark. After some further travelling he spent two years in Denmark, and from 1604 (or 1606)[7] to his death in 1639 he served as a professor in Harderwijk in Gelderland in the Low Countries, where he taught a variety of subjects.

He was a hard-working scholar, combining philological and historical studies like many of his learned contemporaries in the Low Countries. His numerous works include editions and commentaries on classical authors, such as Martial, Sallust, Curtius, and Tacitus, and a thorough knowledge of classical literature pervades his historical works. His first major accomplishment in this field was a history of Amsterdam, *Historia urbis et rerum Amstelodamensium* (1611), which he later felt it necessary to defend against critics who found it too full of digressions[8] – a feature also notable in his *History of Denmark*. Other impressive historical treatises came from his pen before he was engaged as Danish historiographer in 1618. A work on early Frankish history from 1616, *Originum Francicarum libri VI*, was, like the history of Amsterdam, put on the Index, on account of the author's outspoken attacks on the Catholics and because

---

[6] Their friendship in Basel is attested by two poems, one written by Pontanus and found in Grasser's *album*, and one by Grasser addressed to Pontanus on the occasion of his degree. Both poems were included by Pontanus in his collected poems (Pontanus 1634, 34, 240-42). Their friendship is mentioned in Rørdam 1898, 21.

[7] Nyenhuis 1840, 96.

[8] Pontanus 1628, 1634. Cf. Rørdam 1898, 443-44.

of his opinion, stated in the Frankish history, that the religious beliefs of
the early Franks were close to those of the Reformed Church, to which
Pontanus himself belonged.[9] In the same period he involved himself in a
dispute with the geographer Philipp Clüver (1580-1622), whose treatise
on the earliest peoples living at the mouths of Rhine had provoked Pontanus's criticism in his *Geographical Discussions (Disceptationes chorographicae)*
of 1614. Clüver hit back in the work *Three Books concerning Ancient Germany*
(*Germaniæ antiquæ libri III*) of 1616, which in turn prompted Pontanus to
answer with another treatise, *A New Collection of Geographical Discussions in
Answer to Philippus Cluverus (Disceptationum chorographicarum adversus Phil.
Cluverum nova sylloge)* of 1617.[10]

A number of qualifications, then, would seem to have pointed to Pontanus as the right man to supersede Lyschander as historiographer. He
was a recognized authority on the migrations and settlements of the
German peoples in late antiquity. He had close connections with Denmark and the royal family; his father had served as Frederik II's agent in
Amsterdam and his brother Pieter Isaachs had taken over this position at
their father's death in 1615 and at the same time served as both artist and
art dealer at the Danish court.[11] Pontanus, moreover, was able to read
Danish, and he had even occupied himself with Danish history when as
a young man he assisted Arild Huitfeldt. Exactly which factors ranked
highest in the estimation of his future employers we cannot know, but it
seems reasonable, with Rørdam,[12] to point to Pontanus's expert knowl-

---

[9] Rørdam 1898, 444. Pontanus's Calvinistic views are expressed in an undated letter to one
Georgius Pannekokius, in which the main differences between Lutheranism and Calvinism
are summed up (Matthæus 1695, no. 121). The letter is couched in a conciliatory tone. Less
tolerant, judging from Westphalen's description, are three epigrams written by Pontanus in
1617, in which he argues against the Remonstrants on the question of predestination (the
Remonstrants were the more moderate Dutch Calvinists, see the biography of Meursius,
Chapter III). Westphalen writes: *Siquidem ex tribus ipsius epigrammatibus anno 1617. scriptis constat,
quod dogmata rigidissima de prædestinatione adversus confessionem ministrorum coetus Campensis Remon-
strantium strenue satis et aculeate defenderit* (Westphalen in Pontanus 1740, Præfatio, 48n).

[10] Rørdam 1898, 445-46. Pontanus himself refers to the dispute in the *Rerum Danicarum historia*, 764-65. Apart from that it is mentioned in his correspondence. In a letter of 1616 Hugo
Grotius does his best to comfort Pontanus: Clüver is a polemical character, he writes, who
does not even abstain from attacks on Caesar and Strabo, so Pontanus is in good company
(the letter is printed in Matthæus 1695, no. 47). Many years later, in 1633, Pontanus in a letter
to his young friend Marcus Z. Boxhorn regrets that some of Clüver's errors are repeated in
Angelus Werdenhagen's work *De Rebuspublicis Hanseaticis Commentarioli* (Matthæus 1695, no.
150).

[11] Charlotte Christensen 1988, 320.

[12] Rørdam 1898, 446.

edge of the early migrations and settlements (as demonstrated in the controversy with Clüver), since the chancellor, like Pontanus, was particularly interested in this subject. The fact that he had met the young Friis in person eighteen years earlier makes it likely that Friis had followed his career, either by personal letters or at least through his publications.

In 1618 Pontanus was summoned to Copenhagen, probably in connection with his appointment as historiographer. His letter of employment, signed by Christian IV, is dated March 28, 1618.[13] A poem from Pontanus to the chancellor written in the same year contributes to the impression that the initiative had come from Friis. Having compared his concern for the history of his country to that of the Danish chancellor Absalon, the patron of Saxo Grammaticus (who wrote the first full-scale Latin history of Denmark, the *Gesta Danorum*, around 1200), Pontanus inserts a reference to himself: "[...] while you wanted me to follow in the footsteps of earlier writers and make the deeds of previous generations the subject of my writing and transmit them to posterity".[14] In 1619, on May 13, his salary for the first year was paid to his brother, the painter Pieter Isaachs, who lived in Copenhagen.[15]

It was agreed that he should complete his work within six years. But it would take thirteen years before the first part appeared in print. For one thing he did not dedicate himself fully to the new task. Rather than settle in Denmark he kept his position as professor in Harderwijk. Besides that, he was involved in other projects, including the production of yet another grand-scale historical work, a history of Gelderland, where Harderwijk is situated.[16] As his numerous letters testify, he was constantly engaged in various philological studies.

---

[13] It is printed in Rørdam 1898, 447-48 (summarized in *Kancelliets Brevbøger* 1616-20, 352-53 (*Sjællandske Registre* 16, 325)). Evidence that Pontanus went to Copenhagen in 1618 is a poem, published in Pontanus's *Poemata* (1634), which is dated Copenhagen 1618 (as noted by Rørdam 1898, 447).

[14] [...] *Dum nos priorum subsequi vestigia / Voluisti, et illa gesta maiorum stilo / Nostro notari prodierque posteris.* The poem was printed both in the *History of Denmark*, 126, and in Pontanus's collected poems, Pontanus 1634, 99. Rørdam draws attention to this poem (Rørdam 1898, 448).

The biography of Pontanus, written shortly after his death, is also unambiguous as to Friis's role: *Quam eandem dignitatem* [as official historiographer] *cum regio salario acceperat jam ante a Serenissimo Daniae Rege Christiano quarto, adnitente, quem superius nominavi, magno regiae majestatis ejusdem Cancellario Christiano Frisio* (*Vita et obitus*, 1640, 10).

[15] Grundtvig 1872, 182.

[16] He was engaged as Geldrian historiographer on May 15, 1621 (Haitsma Mulier & van der Lem 1990, 333).

But let us now, on the basis of these letters, follow the long-winded process that led to the publication of the first part of his *History of Denmark* in 1631 and the completion of the second part shortly before his death. This survey will be more detailed than the one presented in Chapter II, and focus on the author, not on his Danish employers.

2. Preparations for the 1631 Edition

As stipulated in the contract Pontanus started with the oldest history. This is clear from a letter to Claus C. Lyschander, his colleague as historiographer to the Danish king (on whom, cf. Chapters II and IV,8). In a letter written in August 1622[17] Pontanus informs Lyschander that he has now covered more than thirteen centuries; as his work starts around 100 BC he seems to have worked his way steadily through the centuries up to 1200.

Throughout he kept the chancellor informed about his progress.[18] The first of these interim reports to have been preserved dates from March 1621. He is now working on the history of Canutus (1182-1202) and about to embark on his successor Valdemarus II (1202-41). It would seem, then, that he had by this time completed about one third of the work that eventually appeared in 1631 (Canutus's history is found on pp. 275-96 of the 812 pages). Along with the remaining history he now intends to start working on a geographical description of Denmark, and for that purpose he repeats an earlier request for material.[19]

Already at the beginning of the following year, however, Pontanus, as we saw in Chapter II, was told in a letter from Christian IV to finish the work as soon as possible. Pontanus was worried. The plan of the work would not allow him to finish it within a short time, he confessed to the chancellor. From the same letter it appears that he had just sent Friis a sample of his work, stretching from the history of Canutus Magnus to Valdemarus I (1018-1157), that is, part of what he had already finished the year before according to the earlier letter. He now wants to hear Friis's

---

[17] The letter is printed in Matthæus 1695, no. 101.

[18] In his biography of Christen Friis Ole Degn has made use of Pontanus's letters to Friis (Degn 1988, 116sqq).

[19] He asks for a poem by the Danish poet Erasmus Lætus (1526-82), which is probably Lætus's account of Danish history, *Res Danicæ* (1574), and for an unfinished geographical description of Denmark, *Daniæ chorographia*, by the Danish historian Anders Sørensen Vedel (1542-1616), the latter to be used in connection with his own geographical section. The letter is edited in Rørdam 1898, 476-77 (original in *Rigsarkivet* (Copenhagen)).

opinion.[20] Rørdam has shown that in August the same year he was told by Christian IV to perform another duty in his capacity as royal historiographer. Existing maps of the Baltic Sea were not precise and the names were in Dutch. Pontanus should now see to it that better maps with Danish names were printed. Unfortunately nothing further is known of this project.[21] This new task alloted to him must be seen as a sign that his excuses regarding the delayed *History of Denmark* were accepted.

But the royal command was a spur, he assured the chancellor. Probably he was referring to his work on this project when four months later, in August 1622, he regretted, in the above-mentioned letter to Lyschander, that he had not had time to read much of Lyschander's own history of Denmark, *Synopsis historiarum Danicarum*, 1622, which the author had sent him. Pontanus did however in a postscript find time to take up some points of eleventh-century Danish history which Lyschander had got wrong. Having received Lyschander's protests, he expanded his criticisms in a long letter to Lyschander in March 1623.[22] Though the tone is polite, it is clear that Pontanus found his colleague's work full of mistakes.

Friis's active interest in Pontanus's writings is manifest from the next letter we know of from Pontanus to the chancellor, written in December 1623. Friis's corrections and suggestions apparently were of an ethnographical nature, and Pontanus promises to do his best to follow them, but as we shall see, he also felt free to disagree at some points. The tone of this letter is optimistic. Apart from some corrections to be made, only the last two kings, Ericus Pomeranus (1412-39) and Christophorus Bavarus (1440-48) are now left, and Pontanus will then concentrate on the geographical part.[23] It is, by the way, clear from this and other letters – and from the printed work itself – that Pontanus had intended this geographical section to introduce the work. In the end it was decided to print it as the final part.

---

[20] Regarding the salary, Pontanus suggests that the money, *sub specie dalerorum imperialium*, should be handed over to a trustworthy courier, as had been done the year before. The letter is dated April 12, 1622, and printed in Matthæus 1695, no. 111 and in Rørdam 1898, 478-79.

[21] Rørdam 1898, 455-56, who quotes the letter from Christian IV to Pontanus, dated August 10, 1622 (it is summarized in *Kancelliets Brevbøger 1621-23*, 400).

[22] Letter from Pontanus to Lyschander, dated March 11, 1623 (Matthæus 1695, no. 103).

[23] Letter from Pontanus to Friis, dated December 10, 1623 (Matthæus 1695, no. 98; Rørdam 1898, 479-81).

In spring 1624 Pontanus told the chancellor that he felt he was near the goal. He had now finished the first part and collected material for the geographical section, which he thought would benefit from his paying a visit to Denmark. What is more, he informs Friis that he has also begun working on the Oldenburg kings.[24] At this time he betrays no knowledge of the government's intention to have Meursius write about the Oldenburg kings. But then we do not know exactly how far these plans had developed. Meursius's letter of employment dates from the summer of 1624. And, as mentioned in Chapter II, there may never have been any change in Pontanus's project.

By the time of Pontanus's next letter to Friis (October 1624), one would expect him to have learned about his new colleague, to whom an official letter of employment was written in July 1624 – especially since it appears that the chancellor had written to Pontanus in September. But there is no mention of Meursius, at least not directly. "I was glad to receive your letter", Pontanus writes, and he goes on:

> Since from that I understood that Your Magnificence is now in better health than you have been for some time, and that you are concerned to remember me, especially because you take care to mention, with such friendliness and enthusiasm, those matters which have to do with Danish history, a province which has been entrusted to me, and because you exhort me to publish an edition of some of the earlier parts, thereby applying the spur, as they say, to a horse which is already running. For I shall do my best to rise to the occasion.[25]

The rather solemn and elaborate wording *earum præsertim rerum, quæ ad Danicam historiam, cujus nobis provincia demandata* and the assurance that he will do his best, may suggest that Pontanus knows that he shares the task with somebody else, and that he now needs to define his task again. In the earlier letters he just refers to *historia nostra Danica, nostrum opus*, or simply *nostra*, when introducing the subject.

---

[24] Letter from Pontanus to Friis, dated March 19, 1624 (Matthæus 1695, no. 112; Rørdam 1898, 481).

[25] *Ex iis enim Magnificentiam tuam meliori valetudini post tenuem illam, qua aliquamdiu est usa, esse restitutam intellexi, tum et nostri colere memoriam, cum earum præsertim rerum, quæ ad Danicam historiam, cujus nobis provincia demandata, spectant, tam amice tamque sedulo mentionem injiciat, nosque ad editionem priorum aliquot partium cohortetur, et animum, quod dicitur, currenti addat. Nam ego, quantum in me erit occasioni haud deero* (letter from Pontanus to Friis, dated October 18, 1624 (Matthæus 1695, no. 95; Rørdam 1898, 482-84)).

From this letter we also learn that Friis had told Pontanus to make sure that the work was printed decently, with type-settings which would give it an attractive look. Pontanus now expresses his doubts whether any of the local printers in Harderwijk will be able to deliver a satisfying product, and he declares his intention of contacting "the Elzevirs and (other) publishers in Leiden" (*Elzevirios ac bibliopolas Leidenses*). In the end, though, the work was printed in Harderwijk. Though (as we shall be able to follow in more detail in Meursius's case) the practical arrangements with respect to the publication of the *Histories of Denmark* were left to the authors themselves, the chancellor had evidently given instructions about the exterior design of the book.

Pontanus further informs the chancellor that he would have sent him a new sample, comprising the kings Christophorus II (1320-32) and his son Valdemarus (*Valdemar Atterdag*, 1340-75), but no reliable messenger was found.

In this letter we also find Pontanus acting as Friis's book furnisher. Accompanying the letter was a collection of *scriptores Gothicarum rerum*. Likewise he had promised, in the letter of March 1624, to have a particular edition of Procopius, for which Friis had asked, sent by ship as soon as possible. These books further point to the chancellor's interest in history, particularly that of late antiquity and the early middle ages. He seems to have raised more questions on migrations and etymologies in relation to Pontanus's work, since Pontanus now, in the October letter, refers to points made by the chancellor. We shall return to them, since they have left their traces in the work itself.

In spite of the optimistic reports from Pontanus, his employers had not become any less impatient to see the results of his efforts. At the end of 1626 he received a new admonition from the chancellor telling him (in German) to hurry up with the publication.[26] He seems to have felt a certain pressure by that time. In the summer of the same year he had refused an offer to become Professor of Greek and History in Groningen – referring to his duties as Danish historiographer: "The king and his chancellor have engaged me to write a full-scale history of Denmark,

---

[26] Letter from Christen Friis to Pontanus, dated November 27, 1626; facsimile in Degn 1988, 117 (original in Hamburg Staats- und Universitätsbibliothek). In addition the letter is found among Reinboth's collections of material pertaining to Pontanus (Copenhagen Royal Library, *Thott* 1957, 4to, 31). (Printed in Pontanus 1909, 43 and in Jørgensen 1931, 157, but here ascribed to the king and not to Chr. Friis).

47

and just now I am busy finishing the first volume", he explains, adding as a further reason for his refusal that the Estates of Gelderland have opened the archives for him in order that he should also write a history of Gelderland.[27] As earlier pointed out, this letter suggests that Pontanus still regarded his task as one of writing the whole of Denmark's history, in spite of Meursius's being by this time engaged to write the history of the Oldenburg kings (cf. Chapter II).

Soon afterwards he must have sent Friis his draft of the geographical description, the *Chorographica regni Daniæ descriptio*, including his account of the earliest migrations (which is part of the geographical description). In 1627 he expresses his gratitude upon receiving the chancellor's notes, taking up some of his suggestions for discussion. Again it is a question of etymological deductions and early migrations, subjects that seem to have fascinated the chancellor no less than Pontanus himself. With the same letter he also sent a genealogical tree of the Danish kings in the eleventh and twelfth centuries.[28]

Far from having completed the whole of Danish history within six years, as had been agreed originally, he must have more or less finished only the first part, including the geographical description, which would eventually appear in 1631.

But why would it take another four years for the book to be published? Apparently Pontanus did not regard the work as completed. His Danish friend Stephanius (who was by that time in Leiden) had asked him to send three works on Denmark, Holstein and Iceland, respectively – the *Daniæ descriptio* by Jonas Kolding (1584, enlarged version 1594), the *De Holsatia* (1592) by Jonas von Elverfeldt and the *Islandia* (1607) by Dithmarus Blefkenius – but at this moment he needs them himself, he tells his friend in May 1629.[29] As Rørdam has shown, Pontanus went to Copenhagen in 1628, probably to obtain his salary and perhaps to gather further information on Danish geography as he in 1624 had wanted to do; this journey

---

[27] Letter from Pontanus to Franciscus Gomarus, rector at the Academy of Groningen, dated July 15, 1626 (Matthæus 1695, no. 94). As earlier mentioned, Pontanus had in 1621 accepted the task of writing a history of Gelderland.

[28] Letter from Pontanus to Friis, dated 1627 (Matthæus 1695, no. 90; Rørdam 1898, 484-85).

[29] Letter from Pontanus to Stephanius, dated May 17, 1629 (Matthæus 1695, no. 78). Similarly, in a letter to Ger. Vossius dated November 5, 1627, he asks for a biography of the French abbot Guilielmus (Vilhelm of Æbelholt), mentioned by Vossius in connection with Saxo Grammaticus in his book on Latin historians. Probably he had in mind the possibility of finding more material for his Danish history (Matthæus 1695, no. 93).

must have retarded the publication.[30] Besides, Pontanus's family was hit by the plague, and three of his children died in 1628-29.[31] All along he was engaged in other projects as well, not least the history of Gelderland.[32]

Final preparations for the press seem to have taken place in 1629-30. In a letter to the chancellor of January 1st 1630 he assures him that the *Chorographica descriptio* has now been delivered to the printer, adding that Friis must let him know soon if he has particular views about the title page and other exterior matters.[33] Pontanus invited a number of acquaintances to write laudatory poems – some of them are mentioned in letters to him[34] – at the same time producing the many indexes with which the book is furnished. The production of the maps to be included in the work apparently delayed the process, and in September 1630 he was about to give up the idea of maps altogether.[35]

3. Pontanus's Activities as Danish Historiographer in the 1630s

The chancellor was pleased with the book when it finally appeared. So at least he told the author.[36] And the enthusiasm seems to have been general, judging from a letter to Pontanus from his young relative Marcus Z. Boxhorn:

> Your Danish annals have recently met with such applause from everybody that I really cannot find fitting words.[37]

---

[30] Rørdam 1898, 457-58. Pontanus mentions that he visited the chancellor on this journey, in a letter to Stephanius dated March 16, 1629: *Memini me apud illustrem Cancellarium Frisium, cum in Dania nuper essem, vidisse Islandica Biblia in Islandia impressa* (Matthæus 1695, no. 76).

[31] Rørdam 1898, 458. Pontanus mentions the plague in letters to Johs. Lydius, 1629 (Matthæus 1695, no. 134) and to Chr. Friis, dated January 1st, 1630 (Rørdam 1898, 485-87) (original in *Rigsarkivet*, Copenhagen).

[32] *Historia Danica confecta, Geldrica te nunc totum occupat*, Johs. Smith, professor in Nijmegen, wrote to Pontanus on May 7th, 1629 (old style) (Matthæus 1695, no. 68).

[33] Letter from Pontanus to Friis, dated January 1st 1630 (Rørdam 1898, 485-87) (original in *Rigsarkivet*, Copenhagen). In a postscript he takes up the issue of his salary; for the past two or three years, the annual amount has not been paid to his relative Johannes Ettersenius, who used to receive the money in Pontanus's place.

[34] Matthæus 1695, nos. 70, 78, 82.

[35] Letter from Pontanus to Stephanius, dated September 20, 1630 (Matthæus 1695, no. 135). His work on the indexes is known from the same letter.

[36] *Gratum acceptumque fuisse opus nostrum historicum ex literis tuæ Magnificentiæ, quas mihi tradidit Christianus Weiner, Regiæ Maiestati ab epistolis, oppido lubenter intellexi*, Pontanus wrote to Friis on September 29, 1631 (Rørdam 1898, 487-88 (original in *Rigsarkivet*, Copenhagen)).

[37] *De Annalibus tuis Danicis, qui tanto nuper omnium applausu excepti sunt, quod satis pro merito dicam, non habeo* (letter from Boxhorn to Pontanus, dated April 1st, 1632 (Boxhorn 1662, 17)).

Also Caspar Barlæus wrote to express his admiration:

> Just recently you delighted me, brilliant Pontanus, with that outstanding work of yours, in which I believe you have matched the greatness of historical events with comparable diligence and toil. You are worth the patronage of kings, since your writings are worthy of kings, and you deliver to the light incidents far removed from people's recollection.[38]

Pontanus sent three copies to Stephanius in Sorø for which Stephanius thanked him heartily. He praised the "divine" work and assured Pontanus of the general appraisal among all learned men; Denmark had not seen anything so elegant since Saxo, he declared[39] – a praise which must have delighted Pontanus. In the Preface of the 1631 edition he is at pains to cast himself in the role of the new Saxo (cf. Chapter V).

The price of the work was five *rigsdaler* (*thaleri imperiales*), as Ole Worm informed his Icelandic friend Arngrímur Jónsson in 1631, adding that Arngrímur's own work on Icelandic history, *Crymogæa* (1609), could be bought for three *mark*.[40]

Amid the general praise Arngrímur Jónsson found cause for criticism. He was displeased with Pontanus's assertion in the *Chorographica descriptio* (the geographical part of the *History of Denmark*), that the name of Thule in classical texts referred to Iceland, the more so since the opinion was put forward as a polemical refutation of Arngrímur's theory in the *Crymogæa*. Some years later, in 1638, Pontanus was worried about rumours that the learned Icelandic historian intended to publish a refutation of his discussion of Thule – which he did but not until after Pontanus's death (cf. Chapter VI).[41]

---

[38] *Iam nuper præclaro illo tuo opere me beasti, clarissime Pontane, in quo magnitudinem rerum gestarum pari industria et labore mihi æquasse videris. Dignus et Regum favore, qui regibus digna scribis, et luci asseris res ab hominum memoria remotissimas* (letter from Barlæus to Pontanus, dated June 24, 1631 (Barlæus 1662, 401-2)). Some years later, in 1639, Gerardus Vossius, having also obtained a copy of Pontanus's *History of Denmark*, assured Pontanus of the great fame in store for him (letter from Vossius to Pontanus, dated July 23, 1639 (Vossius 1691, no. 360)).

[39] *Quaenam fuerit Bonorum omnium et Eruditorum de divino isto opere tuo censura, quaeris? Verbo dicam; omnes acclamarunt: καλῶσ καί σοφῶσ. Nihil etenim rerum gestarum, saltem literis consignatum, post coelestem Saxonis eloquentiam, Daniam vidisse elegantius* (letter from Stephanius to Pontanus, dated April 16, 1632, printed in *Archief voor kerkelijke geschiedenis* 1833,185-88).

[40] Letter from Ole Worm to Arngrímur Jónsson, written between May 6 and May 22, 1632 (Worm 1751, 314; Worm 1948, 26-27; Worm 1965-68, I, no. 440 (Danish trans.)).

[41] Letter from Pontanus to Stephanius, dated July 1st, 1638 (Matthæus 1695, no. 122).

At the end of his Preface, addressed to Christian IV (dated January 25, 1631), Pontanus declares his intention to go on writing about the Oldenburg kings including the king himself, and he asks the king to provide him with material. He does not refer to the fact that Meursius had already, in 1630, published an account of the first three Oldenburg kings. He simply seems to regard his task as the same as originally laid out, namely to write a history of Denmark from the earliest times to Christian IV himself. And the chancellor, in the letter in which he expressed his satisfaction with Pontanus's achievement, apparently said nothing to alter this impression. When Pontanus answered this letter in September 1631, he again stated that he would now continue his *History of Denmark* by writing of all the seven Oldenburg kings, that is from Christian I to the ruling Christian IV (the latter included), and then have the whole thing printed in one volume, with smaller type face than the 1631 edition.[42] Again Meursius's work (and Meursius himself) is left unmentioned. Whereas Meursius in his letter to Vossius from November 1632 (quoted above, Chapter II)[43] seems to have been surprised at the idea that he should cover the period already treated by Pontanus, the latter apparently regarded it as a matter of course that he should write a second volume on the Oldenburg kings, of whom the first three had already been treated by Meursius. Perhaps we may here see a confirmation of the theory put forward in Chapter II, that Pontanus's instruction had remained the same, namely to write a history of Denmark from the earliest times up to the present day, in spite of Meursius's appearance on the scene in 1624.

Apart from the praise of Pontanus's *History of Denmark* the chancellor in his letter had also suggested some corrections and additions, and Pontanus assured him, in the letter of September 29 1631, that he would include these suggestions in the next edition. Amid various other tasks he now worked on the second part of the *History of Denmark* until his death in 1639. In a letter to Friis of November 1633 he assured him that he was now totally occupied with this work.[44] One and a half years later he briefly informs Friis that he is working on the second volume of his *History of Denmark* (referring to a fuller report in a previous letter) and considers having it published either as a separate volume or together with the

---

[42] Letter from Pontanus to Friis, dated September 29, 1631 (Rørdam 1898, 487-88) (original in *Rigsarkivet* (Copenhagen)).
[43] Letter from Meursius to Vossius, dated November 3rd, 1632 (Meursius 1741-63, no. 695).
[44] Letter from Pontanus to Friis, dated November 8, 1633 (Matthæus 1738, II, 377-78).

first (printed with smaller type faces than the 1631 edition). The publishers (*bibliopolae*) prefer the first solution, he says, and their opinion carries weight because they will take care of the distribution of copies.[45] But three months later he informed Stephanius that he had decided to have the two volumes printed together with smaller type faces.[46] His work did not proceed at a great pace. In the summer of 1637 he declared that he was close to having completed his history of the Oldenburgs, but still it appears that he has not yet written the history of Frederik II (1559-88), for which he asks for material.[47] A few months later, in October 1637, this request is repeated.[48] Whether he eventually did receive material on Frederik II is not known (Chapter VI, below).

Meanwhile Pontanus had other projects on his mind to distract him from the *History of Denmark*. In fact, apart from his duties as professor, his main occupation in the 1630s must have been the grandiose history of Gelderland, *Historiæ Gelricæ libri XIV*, which was published in 1639.

Moreover he served the interests of Christian IV by another piece of writing during this period. In 1637 he published a refutation of the English historian and politician John Selden, who in a treatise named *Mare clausum* had claimed English right to the surrounding seas. Selden had written the work around sixteen years earlier as a response to Hugo Grotius's *Mare liberum* (1609), in which the right to free access to the sea for all nations is defended. At first Selden's work had been suppressed for political reasons but now, in 1635, it was published with a dedication to the king.[49] Pontanus's treatise argues that the North Sea in earlier times was ruled by other nations, Romans, Franks, Danes, and Norwegians. The work is a new demonstration of the author's knowledge of Danish and Norwegian history, and he himself, describing the contents in a letter to the chancellor (written June 1637 after the work's publication), draws attention to his already published *History of Denmark*, in which the same arguments about the historical rights to the sea in question can be found.

---

[45] Letter from Pontanus to Friis, dated March 25, 1635 (Rørdam 1898, 488-89) (original in *Rigsarkivet* (Copenhagen)).

[46] Letter from Pontanus to Stephanius, dated July 1st, 1635 (Matthæus 1738, II, 401-3).

[47] Letter from Pontanus to Chr. Friis, dated June 1st, 1637 (Matthæus 1738, V, 988-89; Rørdam 1898, 490-91).

[48] Letter from Pontanus to Chr. Friis, dated October 12, 1637 (Rørdam 1898, 491-92) (original in *Rigsarkivet*, Copenhagen).

[49] I here rely on the *Encyclopedia Britannica*. Pontanus's work is entitled *Discussionum historicarum libri II, quibus præcipue quatenus et quodnam mare liberum vel non liberum clausumque accipiendum, dispicitur expenditurque* (1637).

Pontanus clearly feels that he has acted in the interest of the Danish king by writing this refutation, since, as he explains to the chancellor, Selden even claimed English sovereignty over the Norwegian coastline. His presentation, in this letter to the chancellor, of Selden's *Mare clausum* and of his own line of argument suggests that he wrote the work on his own initiative.[50] Indeed more than one year earlier, in April 1636, he had already mentioned to the chancellor that he planned to collect evidence from Danish history to confute Selden; according to this letter it was a meeting in Utrecht with the chancellor's son which had inspired him to take action against Selden, the young Friis being also annoyed with Selden's book. Pontanus here describes to the chancellor the various historical arguments he had put forward in the conversation with his son.[51] – Around the same time, however, the Estates-General of the Dutch provinces had been sufficiently provoked by Selden's work to engage a scholar to write a refutation, as we learn from a letter to Meursius from Gerardus Vossius in Amsterdam.[52] Perhaps this was another inspiration for Pontanus to write a refutation from a Danish-Norwegian point of view.

Pontanus dedicated the work to the chancellor's son, referring in the dedicatory letter to their meeting in Utrecht. Naturally, he was also eager to hear the opinion of the father. He sent copies to him (and to the royal treasurers, using a courier named Martin Schulz),[53] and when the chancellor apparently failed to react, Pontanus once more, in a letter of October 1637, where he also repeats his request for material on Frederik II, discreetly asked for his opinion of the refutation.[54]

---

[50] Letter from Pontanus to Chr. Friis, dated June 1st, 1637 (Matthæus 1738, V, 988-89; Rørdam 1898, 490-91).

[51] [...] *in me recepi promisique, sive coram sive per literas, dato otio, ac retextis ex historia Danica, quæ huc pertinent, ordine id monstraturum* (letter from Pontanus to Friis, dated April 21, 1636 (Matthæus 1738, III, 744-45)). In two letters from the summer of 1636, Pontanus mentions his plans to refute Selden's work; the letters are addressed to a friend Wilhelmus Willichius, secretary to the Swedish *legatus* in the Low Countries (*Camerarii Suecorum apud Ordines Belgii foederatos Legati Secretarius*) and to Pontanus's younger relative Marcus Boxhorn; apparently the latter had suggested that Pontanus ought to react against Selden (Matthæus 1738, III, 746-49).

[52] *Grotii Mari Libero responsum a Seldeno Iureconsulto Anglo* [...] *Illustres Ordines nostri in mandatis dedere Graswinkelio Iureconsulto meo ante annos viginti discipulo et convictori ut opus hoc refellat* (letter from Vossius to Meursius, wrongly dated July 5, 1631 (Meursius 1741-63, XI, no. 676; Vossius 1691, I, no. 145). This dating must be an error for June 3, 1636, cf. below).

[53] As he told Friis in the letter of June the 1st, 1637, in which he informs him of his refutation of Selden and asks for material on Frederik II (Matthæus 1738, V, 988-89; Rørdam 1898, 490-91).

[54] Letter from Pontanus to Chr. Friis, dated October 12, 1637 (Rørdam 1898, 491-92) (original in *Rigsarkivet*, Copenhagen).

The payment of his salary did not always go smoothly. In 1630 Pontanus had not received his salary for two or three years, and in a letter to the chancellor of January 1st 1630 he now asks that a portion of this amount should be sent to him. In 1631, in the letter where Pontanus promises to follow the chancellor's suggestions in the next edition, Pontanus also thanks him for his promise to send two years' salary – an indication that his employers expected him to continue fulfilling his task as royal historiographer after the 1631 edition. In 1635 he again wrote to Friis to ask for two years' salary, suggesting the above-mentioned Martin Schulz as a courier (in the letter mentioned above, in which he discusses possibilities of publication).

Two years later, in 1637, he again instructed Martin Schulz to act on his behalf and find out whether a portion of his salary could be sent to Harderwijk, as he told Friis in the letter written in June 1637, and in October the same year he again made a polite request for money.[55]

However, there is evidence that no salary was paid to him after the summer of 1636.[56] But this circumstance should not, I think, be taken to indicate that he was no longer regarded as historiographer by his employers. In preceeding years also, he had received his money at irregular intervals. He kept working on the *History of Denmark* right up to his death in 1639, which he would hardly have done without some kind of encouragement from the chancellor. But I have not been able to find any allusions to such encouragement.

In 1637, as we saw, Pontanus had written most of the second volume of his *History of Denmark*, but something was still left to be done; various occupations probably kept him from working more than occasionally on this project. It seems that his friend Stephanius, Meursius's colleague at the Academy of Sorø, asked him about the progress of his work at some point during 1637, since Pontanus in a letter to Stephanius referred to this request, stating, in a highly interesting passage, the main reason for the delay:

> My Danish history, or more precisely its second volume, is not yet quite
> finished, although the printer keeps demanding it from me. But I hesi-

---

[55] These are the letters in which he also asked Friis for his opinion of Selden and for material on the history of Frederik II.

[56] Grundtvig 1872, 182.

tate, and the more so because of other people's utterances, people who, though not Danish themselves, encroach upon my Danish territory too, applying their scythe to my crops. And I have already seen before what they have given us about the first kings called Christian (there are four kings by that name). Several, not to say innumerable, errors are found here which deserve reproach, and they are due simply to lack of knowledge of Danish history. I mention this in passing and between us, lest someone should take offence. But I could not suppress it, and it may also serve as an answer to your letter written to me not this year but last year.[57]

The object of this assault, foreign persons who have expressed themselves on the subject of Danish history and who have earlier written so badly about the first Oldenburg kings, can hardly be anyone but Meursius. Stephanius (who will be introduced in a separate chapter below) would of course understand, being a friend of both of them.[58]

Pontanus wrote this letter on July 1st, 1638. Meursius's work, comprising the whole period from the legendary king Danus to the end of Christianus II's reign in 1523, does not seem to have appeared in print before September, judging from the letter which Gerardus Vossius wrote to inform Meursius of the publication.[59] Pontanus cannot have seen Meursius's account of the period up to 1448 – in fact a letter from Vossius to Pontanus informs us that Pontanus had not seen Meursius's 1638 edition as late as July 1639[60] – so his reference to it (*obnunciationes*, utterances) must concern the work about to appear. Pontanus is afraid that

---

[57] *Historia nostra Danica, aut ejus saltem tomus alter, nondum ad umbilicum est perductus, licet flagitet eum identidem typographus; Sed cunctamur, et cunctantes etiam reddunt obnunciationes aliorum, qui in Danica quoque nostra, nostramque hanc messem, licet haud Dani, falcem injiciunt. Et vidi jam pridem, quæ primos Christianos (quo nomine Regum quatuor censentur) nobis exhibent, sed ejusmodi, in quibus perplura, ne sexcenta dicam, occurrunt, quæ reprehensionem mereantur, idque ex sola rerum Danicarum ignoratione. Quod tamen obiter et inter nos, ne fortasse in noxam cuiquam cedat. Reticere interim haud potui, ut vel esset responsi vice ad ea, quæ non horno sed anno ad me scripsisti* (letter from Pontanus to Stephanius, dated July 1st, 1638 (Matthæus 1695, no. 122)).

[58] Reinboth was probably the first to note this passage and he does not hesitate to identify Meursius as the object of Pontanus's attack (*Thott* 1957, 4to, 94, 99). Curiously enough, Rørdam, who also quotes the passage, refuses to attempt an identification (Rørdam 1898, 464-65).

[59] Letter from Vossius to Meursius, dated September 29, 1638 (new style) (Meursius 1741-63, XI, no. 769; Vossius 1691, I, no. 340).

[60] *Danicam Meursij historiam necdum videris, ea intra dies paucos distrahetur publice. Hactenus soli amici, quibus donavit, exemplar habent, iique perpauci* (letter from Vossius to Pontanus, dated July 23, 1639 (Vossius 1691, I, no. 360)).

Meursius's forthcoming work will be as full of errors as his earlier account of the Oldenburg kings of 1630. And if we may believe his explanation to Stephanius, this fear was a reason for his own delay.

Pontanus's contempt is to some degree mirrored in what he eventually wrote, since he included some criticisms of his colleague, although not by name (below, Chapter IX). Pontanus's use of Meursius's nationality as an argument against him, in implicit contrast to his own Danish background, is also reasonable enough, his own primary source, Arild Huitfeldt's Danish *History of Denmark*, being more detailed and informative than the Latin history of Hans Svaning on which Meursius had to rely.

What I should like to stress here, however, is the rather hostile tone of Pontanus's judgement. Danish history is *his* field, and Meursius is an intruder. One would have thought that Pontanus after fourteen years would have grown accustomed to the idea of a colleague, but this letter does not give us reason to think so.[61] As we shall see, Meursius on his side was no great admirer of Pontanus's history either. Far from collaborating, the two men, by this time, seem to have regarded each other as rivals (cf. below).

In spite of the reluctance caused by Meursius's work, Pontanus did complete an account of the Oldenburg kings, which he left behind him in manuscript. The life of Christian IV, which in 1631 he had planned to include in the second volume, is absent, however. Whether he then intended to go on with a third volume, containing the life of Christian IV, we do not know. The biography written in 1640 states that he worked on the *History of Denmark* until shortly before his death on October 7, 1639.[62]

The only scholar who has cared to consider the relationship between Pontanus and Meursius in their capacity as Danish historiographers, is, as far as I know, F.A. Reinboth (d. 1749), who left behind him a huge manu-

---

[61] In 1630 Meursius had published his history of the period 1448-1523. Curious to see it, Pontanus asked his friend Petrus Scriverius if he might borrow Scriverius's copy at the beginning of 1631. Scriverius, however, unable to get hold of the book, confines himself, in an apologizing letter, to emphasizing that Pontanus need not fear any rivalry, since they are not dealing with the same periods. (This was hardly news to Pontanus, as Scriverius obviously thought). Scriverius's words *Quod autem concursum existimes, fugit te ratio*, could be taken to mean that Pontanus himself had expressed fear of rivalry. The letter from Scriverius to Pontanus is dated February 13, 1631 (new style) (Matthæus 1695, no. 71).

[62] *In manibus tum habebat alteram partem Historiae Danicae, quam ut perficeret, magno enitebatur studio et cura: nec defuit labori successus. Paucis enim ante mortem diebus eam perduxit ad primordia gubernationis Christiani IV* (*Vita et obitus*, 13).

script, rather confused but very informative, with drafts of a life of Pontanus and transcriptions of Pontanus's letters and biographies of him (above, note 2). On the basis of the passage quoted above from Pontanus's letter to Stephanius, Reinboth emphasizes the hostile rivalry between Meursius and Pontanus. As this passage indeed might be taken to suggest, he even ventures to see their rivalry as the reason that Pontanus never himself published his account of the Oldenburg kings.

This is, however, in my view not likely to be the case. Another letter from Pontanus to Stephanius written in 1639 not long before Pontanus's death clearly indicates that he intended to publish the second part; he regarded it as finished and only awaited the necessary preparations on the part of the publisher (*bibliopola*) before it appeared in print.[63] Reinboth is aware of this letter and simply regards the publisher as a convenient excuse on Pontanus's part: the real cause for his not having published the second part, Reinboth declares, was Meursius, who had published the whole of the history from Danus to Christianus II in 1638; he even advances the theory that Pontanus had asked his relatives not to publish his Oldenburg part after his death.[64] But then, why did Pontanus keep working on the second volume right to his death? Although the poor quality (in his eyes) of Meursius's 1630 edition does seem to have discouraged him somewhat from publishing his own account of the same period, he would hardly have gone on writing if he had given up the idea of publication. While rightly emphasizing the strained relationship between the two, Reinboth seems to forget that they were both engaged by the Danish government. Pontanus must have counted on his employers insisting on the publication of his work. Therefore I am inclined to believe Rørdam's theory, that the reason that no one cared to publish the second volume of Pontanus's *History of Denmark* after his death was the death shortly before, on October 1st 1639, of the chancellor Christen Friis, who had been the driving force in the administration of Pontanus's and Meursius's engagements.[65]

---

[63] *Nunc ad te mitto historiam meam Gelricam. Danicam, sive tomum secundum istius historiæ, paratum quoque habemus, emittendum, volente Deo, ubi parata omnia habuerit, quæ ad tantum opus emoliendum spectant, bibliopola* (letter from Pontanus to Stephanius, dated 1639 (Matthæus 1695, no. 80)). Since he only finished the *History of Denmark* shortly before his death, the letter was probably also written in his last days. He refers to his being seriously ill.

[64] Reinboth in *Thott* 1957, 4to, 97.

[65] Rørdam 1898, 469.

Reinboth further points out that Pontanus did not receive the documents concerning the Oldenburg period which he had asked for in the preface to the 1631 edition and in a letter to the chancellor, and Reinboth supposes that Meursius had taken possession of the relevant documents first. In Reinboth's view it was as a consequence of the lack of archival material that Pontanus included fewer transcriptions of documents in the second part than in the 1631 edition. But as far as I can see, Pontanus's knowledge of documents from Danish archives derives from Arild Huitfeldt's *History of Denmark* (1595-1604). Huitfeldt's account of the Oldenburg kings is much fuller than his treatment of the previous period, and in preparing his adaption of this part of Huitfeldt's work Pontanus now had to abbreviate more extensively than before. This is, I would suggest, the reason that he did not include as many documents from Huitfeldt as he had done in the first part.

Pontanus and Meursius died within a few weeks of each other. Soon afterwards, in November 1639, Stephanius was appointed Meursius's successor both as historiographer and as professor at the Academy of Sorø. Stephanius was told to complete Meursius's unfinished life of Christianus III (1536-59). No one, it seems, thought of publishing Pontanus's account of the period 1448-1588, a negligence which, as just mentioned, was surely related to the death of Christen Friis. In a letter to Arngrímur Jónsson from 1641, Ole Worm mentioned that Pontanus had died and left his *History of Denmark* in an incomplete state.[66]

Two years later followed the publication of Arngrímur's *Specimen*, in which he refuted Pontanus's theory that Thule mentioned in ancient texts should be interpreted as Iceland. This work had been under its way for some time.[67] Already in 1633 Arngrímur sent from Iceland a first draft to Worm in Copenhagen, and having received encouragement from Worm he had sent him a new copy ready for publication in 1637. It is not clear why the *Specimen* was not published soon afterwards. Worm showed the manuscript to Stephanius and Meursius, who both recommended it

---

[66] Letter from Worm to Arngrímur Jónsson, written May 19, 1641 (Worm 1751, no. 341; Worm 1948, 64-65; Worm 1965-68, II, no. 932 (Danish trans.)).

[67] On the dispute between Pontanus and Arngrímur on the identification of ancient Thule, see Jakob Benediktsson's introduction to his edition of Arngrímur's *Specimen* (Arngrímur, ed. Benediktsson, 1950-57, XII, 419-27), on which the present survey is built. Cf. also below Chapters III and VI.

for publication. Apparently Worm then, in 1638, handed it over to the chancellor, Christen Friis, and by his death in 1639 it was still in his possession, though it was not found among his papers until some years later. It is not impossible, then, that he tried to hold back the publication of this correction of Pontanus's history. The new chancellor, Christen Thomesen Sehested, however, did not have such scruples. He wanted the *Specimen* published, and Arngrímur then prepared a new manuscript, dedicated to Sehested.

In the early 1650s the manuscript of Pontanus's account of the period 1448-1558 was, it seems, brought to Denmark by Christen Ostenfeldt (1619-71),[68] who travelled in the Low Countries during this period. It was stored in the University Library, and allowed to remain unprinted until Westphalen's edition of 1740. Meanwhile it was occasionally consulted and transcribed.

One of its readers was the staunchly Lutheran professor in Copenhagen, H.G. Masius (1653-1709), renowned for his polemical attitude towards Calvinism. In a dispute with another theologian S. Andreæ (1640-99), professor in Marburg, who belonged to the Reformed Church, Masius argued that Denmark had always adhered to true Lutheranism.[69] One of the issues was Frederik II's rejection of the orthodox Lutheran *Book of Concord*. Masius claims that this story is told in several mutually contradictory versions, which in itself makes it unlikely to be true. Furthermore one of the witnesses is Pontanus, who in his history of Frederik II praises the king for the *moderatio* he displayed by not accepting the *Book of Concord*. But Pontanus is not to be believed here, Masius argues, inasmuch as he was himself a Calvinist (14). Later, in connection with Christian III, he also makes use of Pontanus's history to demonstrate that even a Calvinist could recognize that Christian III was not being unreasonably severe when he expelled some Calvinist fugitives from Denmark (29).[70] Masius even claims (15) that Pontanus's Calvinistic sympathies also come out in the first volume, without, unfortunately,

---

[68] Ostenfeldt's role is noted by Reinboth (*Thott* 1957, 4to, 99), who had found this piece of information written in the margin of a copy of Hans Svaning the Younger's *Chronologia Danica* (1650). In 1661 Ostenfeldt became a librarian at the University Library.

[69] Masius 1691. The dispute is mentioned by Westphalen in Pontanus 1740, Preface 48n, and by Rørdam 1898, 469.

[70] Pontanus on the *Book of Concord*, col. 1230; on Christian III's expulsion of the fugitives, col. 1186.

giving any examples. I have not been able to find such traces, but Protestant views are expressed in some places.[71]

Masius no doubt exaggerates the Calvinistic element of Pontanus's work. I have mentioned the dispute because it reminds us that Pontanus, as briefly touched upon above (note 10), seems to have belonged to the more rigid branch of Dutch Calvinists, the Counter-Remonstrants, or Gomarists, so named after the theological professor Franciscus Gomarus (1563-1641). (The fact that Gomarus, in the 1620s, offered Pontanus a post at the university of Groningen also points in this direction). In Denmark the reign of Christian IV was in many respects marked by a rather rigid Lutheranism and intolerance of Calvinistic tendencies. In this light it is noteworthy, I think, that the Danish government did not abstain from appointing a historiographer whose Calvinistic sympathies cannot have been unknown.

---

[71] This is a much stronger issue in Meursius's work, and I have made a brief mention of Pontanus in connection with a treatment of Meursius's Protestant themes (Chapter VII).

Johannes Meursius

1. Meursius in Leiden

Unlike Pontanus, Meursius had no family connections with Denmark. Born in 1579 in Loosduinen, near the Hague, he matriculated at the University of Leiden in 1591 at the age of twelve.[1] Even before the age of twenty he had published several editions and studies of classical texts.

For about a decade, from 1599, he was engaged by Johan van Olden-barnevelt (1547-1619), by this time the leading statesman of the province of Holland, and of the Dutch Republic, consisting of the seven northern provinces of the Low Countries. As a tutor for his employer's two sons Meursius travelled extensively and saw, as he himself notes, "the courts and libraries of the greatest princes in the Christian world",[2] and from these libraries he collected material for future studies and editions. In 1608, in Orléans, he also obtained a doctoral degree in Law. From 1610 to

---

[1] In 1625 Meursius's brief autobiography appeared as part of the *Athenæ Batavæ*, a work published on the occasion of the 50th anniversary of the University of Leiden in 1625 and containing, among other things, autobiographies of most of the professors who had been engaged at the University since its foundation. Shortly after Meursius's death in 1639 Adolphus Vorstius (1597-1663), professor in Leiden, gave a brief but panegyrical account of his life in a consolatory letter to his son (1640). A fuller biography was written by Daniel G. Moller (1642-1712), who served as a professor at the University of Altdorf from 1674 to his death and in that capacity composed a number of brief dissertations on various historians. It was later used by Johannes Schramm in his biography of Meursius of 1715. Both Moller and Schramm draw affectionate portraits of Meursius. Schramm is more informative, bringing in, among other things, Meursius's various conflicts with his colleagues, a subject on which Moller is silent. Vorstius's letter and Moller's and Schramm's biographies were all included in the first volume of Meursius's *Opera omnia*, 1741. A short biography is found in Tauber's study of the Academy of Sorø (Tauber 1827, 41-43).
Apart from these older works, I have, in the present outline of Meursius's life, made use of the recent biographical article by Chris L. Heesakkers (1994), which focuses on Meursius's time in Leiden. I have further consulted two articles on Meursius's historical work during his time in Leiden, Fruin 1900-5 (1st ed. 1872) and Sepp 1872, and the biography of Meursius found in *Nieuw Nederlandsch biografisch woordenboek* (ed. P. C. Molhuysen and P. J. Blok 1911ff), VII, cols. 872-73. Cf. also the brief biography and survey of his works in Haitsma Mulier & van der Lem 1990, 287-91.
The latter part of this biographical sketch, which deals with Meursius's time in Denmark, is primarily based on the valuable collection of letters to and from Meursius published in Vol. XI (1762) of Meursius's *Opera omnia* (1741-63), supplied with letters to and from Meursius's friend Gerardus Vossius (published in Vossius 1691), and with a collection of letters to and from Meursius in The Royal Library of Copenhagen (ms., *Thott* 1843, 4to).
[2] [...] *maximorum totius orbis Christiani principum aulas vidit, et bibliothecas* (Meursius 1625, 193).

Johannes Meursius. (Copper engraving in Meursius's Historia Danica. 1638).

1624 he served as a professor in Leiden, in History and Greek, as he writes in his autobiography; his special field was Greek history under the emperors of Constantinople.[3]

During his fourteen years as a professor in Leiden, his activity both as editor and as a writer on Greek antiquities was astonishing. He also seems rather impressed with himself in the autobiography he published in the *Athenæ Batavæ* (1625) (it is written in the 3rd person): "[...] not only did he always conduct the ordinary lectures with the same diligence and reliability as his other colleagues; but in writing and editing books – and this is the basis of the reputation of a university – his achievement was so significant, that while he may have had equals among his colleagues, surely no one surpassed him. And if that should not be reason enough for honour and esteem, at least this must be regarded as sufficient reason, that he alone, in his short period as professor, has edited more Greek authors, previously unpublished, than all the other professors, whatever their number, have done since the birth of the university fifty years ago".[4] – Modern readers, tempted to smile at such straightforward self-praise, must bear in mind that it probably did not have the comical ring to it that it has today.

He even found time for more academic activity than he mentions here, combining, like Pontanus, his duties as professor with a lucrative employment as historiographer. In 1611 he was appointed official historiographer to the Estates-General, and published as early as the following year the *Rerum Belgicarum liber unus*, on the Twelve Years' Truce in 1609 between Spain and the United Provinces.[5] It was followed by *Rerum Belgicarum libri quatuor* (1614), on the regime of the duke of Alba 1567-73, to which was attached a fifth book containing a revised version of the

---

[3] Heesakkers 1994, 16.

[4] [...] *ut et lectiones omnes ordinarias pari cum collegis reliquis diligentia, atque fide, semper obierit; libris vero conscribendis, et edendis, qua re fama Academiarum constat, tam insignem operam dedit, ut hic quoque nullum sibi e collegis, si non parem, certe superiorem habeat. quod si laude, ac favore, dignum esse non videbitur, saltem hoc videri possit, quod Auctores item Græcos, nunquam antea vulgatos, unus ipse plures dederit, brevi hoc Professionis suæ tempore, quam a primis Academiæ incunabulis, quinquaginta retro annis, cæteri Professores omnes, quoquot isthic exstiterunt* (Meursius 1625, 194).

[5] The circumstances of Meursius's appointment – he competed with his colleague Dominicus Baudius (1561-1613) – are the subject of Fruin 1900-5 (1st ed. 1872).

Rerum Belgicarum liber unus.[6] His last work for the Estates-General, a biography of William of Orange, *Gulielmus Auriacus*, came out in 1621.

By this time, however, Meursius was facing problems. From 1620 the Estates-General stopped paying him his salary as historiographer,[7] although he begged them to be allowed to continue and even dedicated to them his newest book, *Graecia feriata*. Likewise his position at the University deteriorated; among other things, a commission criticized him for neglecting his teaching.[8] It seems a reasonable assumption that these adversities were related to the fall of Meursius's old mentor, Oldenbarnevelt, who was taken prisoner by Maurice of Nassau in 1618 and executed in May 1619.[9] The power struggle between the two men was bound up with the religious controversy between two groups of Dutch Protestants, the sternly Calvinistic Counter-Remonstrants (or Gomarists, so named after Franciscus Gomarus, 1563-1641) and the more moderate and tolerant Remonstrants (or Arminians, so named after their theological leader Jacob Arminius, 1560-1609), to whom Oldenbarnevelt belonged.[10] Since 1617 Maurice had sided with the Counter-Remonstrants. At the synod of Dordrecht in 1618-19, which took place while Oldenbarnevelt was imprisoned, the Counter-Remonstrants had won a total victory.

There are, on the other hand, indications that Meursius took a less friendly attitude towards the Remonstrants in the early 1620s than he had done before. When in 1625 he published the *Athenae Batavae*, which was a revised version of an earlier edition of 1613, he had removed some of the laudatory remarks about prominent Remonstrants like Arminius and Hugo Grotius (1583-1645).[11] These observations were made in 1872 by Christiaan Sepp, who on that basis doubted whether the adversities experienced by Meursius during his last years in Leiden had to do with his former ties to Oldenbarnevelt.[12] However, there can be no doubt of his

---

[6] See the *Repertorium van geschiedschrijvers in Nederland 1500-1800*, eds. Haitsma Mulier & van der Lem 1990, 287.

[7] *Ibidem.*

[8] Chris Heesakkers 1994, 17-18.

[9] This is also the view of Meursius's most recent biographer, Chris Heesakkers 1994, 17.

[10] The conflict centred on the doctrine of predestination and the authority of the state in Church matters (Meyjes 1984, 56-57).

[11] On Grotius's relations with the Remonstrants, see G.H.M. Posthumus Meyjes 1984.

[12] Christiaan Sepp 1872.

relief at having finally escaped persecution in Leiden, when, in 1625, he wrote from his new home in Sorø, Denmark, to his friend, Gerardus Vossius (1577-1649), who from 1622 to 1631 was Professor of History and Eloquence in Leiden: "so that I ought not to be sorry at having replaced so hostile and unloving a stepmother with such a kindly mother".[13]

In a much later letter (from 1640) to Claudius Salmasius, Vossius himself hinted at Meursius's having been victim of some kind of persecution in Leiden. Deploring the fact that Salmasius's enemies are still spreading malicious lies about him, Vossius continues: "they would not stop, even if they could persuade you to go to the same place where they forced Meursius to go".[14] As we have already seen, Christian IV had apparently offered Salmasius the post as Meursius's successor in Sorø; Vossius seems to imply that Meursius was forced to leave Leiden by the same men who now persecuted Salmasius. Among the enemies of Salmasius referred to by Vossius may well be Daniel Heinsius (1580-1655), whose persecution of Salmasius, when the latter served as a professor in Leiden at the beginning of the 1630s, is well attested.[15] Vossius's letter, then, may be taken to suggest that Heinsius was involved in Meursius's misfortunes. At the synod of Dordrecht Heinsius had supported the Counter-Remonstrants actively, in opposition to the Arminian Vossius. If he was indeed active in driving away Meursius, this would be a further argument in favour of connecting Meursius's troubles with his ties to the Remonstrants. There are signs that relations between the two were strained – Schramm notes in his biography of 1715 that Meursius used to deplore the fact that Heinsius, earlier on, had tried to break the ties of their friendship,[16] and two of his letters to Vossius suggest some kind of bit-

---

[13] *ita ut poenitere non debeat, quod Novercam tam iniquam, neque mei quidquam amantem, cum benigna adeo matre commutaverim* (letter from Meursius to Vossius, dated July 15 (old style), 1625 (Meursius 1741-63, XI, no. 582; Vossius 1691, II, no. 67)). Here and elsewhere I follow the orthography of the Meursius edition, when a letter has been published among both his and Vossius's collected letters.

[14] *Quanquam nec illud si foret, desinerent follibus immensis de te mendacia spirare. Imo ne quidem si persuadere possent ut eo ires, quo Meursium fugarant* (letter from Vossius to Salmasius, dated August 28, 1640 (Vossius 1691, I, no. 391)).

[15] Sellin 1968, 43-51.

[16] [...] *semperque in Epistolis ad Amicos indoluit, quod Dan. Heinsius magnum illud illo tempore Bataviæ orbisque eruditi sidus simultate amicitiæ vincula rumpere conaretur* (Schramm 1715, Ch. 11).

terness against Heinsius.[17] On the other hand, Heinsius and Meursius kept in friendly contact in the first years after Meursius's settling in Denmark, which clearly speaks against Heinsius's being actively involved in driving Meursius away.[18]

Whatever the role of Heinsius, I find it likely that Meursius's adversities from around 1619 had to do with his Remonstratensian connections in spite of his apparent attempts to approach their opponents. But even if the precise reason for the unfriendliness surrounding Meursius is difficult to grasp, it remains certain that in the early 1620s he decided to settle in Denmark. Among the Danish students in Leiden was the young nobleman, Gunde Rosenkrantz (1604-75). Meursius became acquainted with his father, the influential and learned Holger Rosenkrantz (1574-1642), to whom he dedicated his *Peisistratus* (1623) – and with the benefit of hindsight one wonders whether he did that in the hope of preparing the way for a career in Denmark. Rosenkrantz, in a letter of July 1623, merely thanks him for the dedication and for taking care of his son. But before December they seem to have come to an understanding that Rosenkrantz should use his influence to find a suitable position for Meursius in Denmark. In a letter to Meursius from December 1623, he writes: "I wish I could demonstrate to you and your family how fond of you I am, not so much in words and letters, as in deed and practice, and God knows I hope that my native country, as well as I, will very soon of its own accord furnish you with the proof you deserve."[19]

From his letter it would appear that Meursius had confessed to Rosenkrantz his current troubles at home, and that Rosenkrantz then promised to see what he could do. Apparently nothing concrete had been decided in the Danish government about a position for Meursius by this time. Rosenkrantz only hints that something is under way. Still, Ro-

---

[17] In a letter to Vossius, Meursius refers to a canonry recently bestowed on Vossius by the English king, adding that now "our friend is no doubt jealous, he who never ceases to criticize his own friends out of envy and malice". The editors of both Vossius's and Meursius's letters have added: "Dan. Heinsius probably". Letter from Meursius to Vossius, dated March 5, 1630 (Meursius 1741-63, XI, no. 815; Vossius 1691, II, no. 109). Cf. another letter from Meursius to Vossius, dated May 27, 1637 (Meursius 1741-63, XI, no. 829; Vossius 1691, II, no. 243).

[18] Chris Heesakkers 1994, 21.

[19] *Animum vero, qui in te propendet valde, quum ego non tam verbis et literis, ut facto et opere ipso comprobare tibi tuisque desiderem, spero cum Deo bono, Patriam ipsam meam propediem mecum, argumentum te dignum, sua sponte tibi subpeditaturam* (letter from Holger Rosenkrantz to Meursius, dated June 23, 1623 (Meursius 1741-63, XI, no. 535)).

senkrantz had probably hatched more definite plans than he told Meursius. Less than two months before, the Academy of Sorø had opened, one of Christian IV's most conspicuous achievements within the field of education. It was an institution devoted to the higher education of young noblemen, combining academic studies with traditional noble activities such as riding and fencing.[20] As one of the promotors of the project Rosenkrantz seems to have been entrusted with the task of finding suitable teachers. So if Meursius had in fact suggested the possibility of settling down abroad, the idea of engaging him in Sorø must have come readily to Rosenkrantz's mind. The new academy needed competent and renowned teachers to enhance its reputation and attract other able, international figures. Meursius easily met these demands, and his engagement here would clearly be in the interest of both parties.

Christen Friis was no doubt involved in the appointment of Meursius at the Academy, too. Meursius himself suggests as much in the dedicatory letter to his *Athenæ Batavæ* (1625) (see below). The idea of combining the task as professor with that of historiographer may very well go back to the chancellor. He was the one who knew that it would still take some time before Pontanus finished the first part of his history, let alone the second on the Oldenburg kings.

Meursius's prime qualification as historiographer was his three earlier works on Dutch history. They even dealt with recent history, which may have further qualified him for treating the Oldenburg kings in the eyes of his Danish employers. Compared to Pontanus it must have been regarded as a setback that he would not be able to read Danish. On the other hand, the manuscript of a Latin history of Denmark by Hans Svaning (c. 1500-84), which included the early Oldenburg kings, was available in the University Library.[21]

---

[20] The Academy of Sorø, founded by Christian IV, existed from 1623 to 1665. In medieval times there had been a monastery, and in 1586 the school was reorganized by royal decree. After 1665 the school continued, and in the eighteenth century the Academy was revived. The history of this educational institution is surveyed by Kai Hørby (1962). The standard work on the history of the institution in Sorø as a whole, including the medieval monastery, is *Sorø. Klostret, skolen, akademiet gennem tiderne* by M. Mackeprang *et al.* (1924), in which a number of thorough articles deal with the Academy of Christian IV. Much useful material on the Academy is also found in Tauber 1827.

[21] However, a letter from Jacob Fincke to Meursius from December 1626 perhaps suggests that the idea of letting Meursius base his work on Svaning had only recently been formed; see below.

These were probably the motives that prompted the Danish government to have Meursius engaged both as Professor of History and Politics and as historiographer. On July 15, 1624, the official letter of his employment was signed by Christian IV. Meursius, who received the letter on September 1st, 1624, wrote to express his gratitude and ask for permission to delay his departure owing to diverse obligations.[22]

Ironically, the last work he found time to publish before his escape-like departure from Leiden was the above mentioned *Athenæ Batavæ*, celebrating the first fifty years of the University of Leiden. Meursius, as he himself makes clear, is to be regarded as an editor more than an author of this work, since he has chiefly collected autobiographies of the professors. And Meursius added to the irony by dedicating the book, not to the Estates-General nor to the supervisors (*curatores*) of the university,[23] but to the Danish chancellor Christen Friis. The contents of the dedicatory letter mirror Meursius's future occupation in Denmark, not his past in Leiden. The military glory and intellectual achievements of the Danes during the course of history, he argues, have not received the praise they deserve. Proving this thesis in a brief survey, Meursius demonstrates his knowledge of Danish history and men of learning. Turning, towards the end, to the many learned kings, he singles out, not surprisingly, Christian IV and his marvellous foundation of the Academy of Sorø. This brings him, appropriately, to the relationship between his addressee and himself, and he celebrates Friis as one of the promoters of the Academy and of his own engagement there.

2. Meursius in Sorø. The Publication of the First Volume of his History of Denmark

He now moved to Sorø with his family in 1625 and served in his double position as professor and historiographer until his death in 1639. He found himself enthusiastically greeted, and was at the same time, as we have seen, relieved to have escaped the enemies back at home. Five years later he was no less enthusiastic: "I'm well off in Denmark, by the grace of God; the nobles befriend me, the learned are fond of me, and I

---

[22] Letter from Meursius to Christian IV, dated September 10, 1624 (Meursius 1741-63, XI, no. 573).

[23] To whom earlier versions of the work of 1613 and 1614 had been dedicated, see Heesakkers 1994, 18-20.

wouldn't heedlessly change my situation".[24] Judging from his letters to Vossius, he generally enjoyed his years in Sorø, during which he also found time to publish several works on Greek antiquities.

Although the Academy was firmly based on Lutheran orthodoxy, the professors were not obliged to embrace the Augsburg Confession, only to refrain from promoting any other religion or religious practice.[25] Nevertheless, in 1630, the theological professor, the strictly Lutheran Christian Matthiæ, accused Meursius of leading his pupils astray with Calvinistic doctrines, but the king soon intervened in favour of Meursius.[26] In a letter to Vossius (April 1631), Meursius assures him that Matthiæ is an exception among the Danish theologians; they are in fact very moderate and peace-loving, far from *ferocia germanica*.[27] Even if Meursius's personal stance in the dispute between Remonstrants and Counter-Remonstrants is not quite clear, it does seem, as suggested above, to have been closer to the moderate Remonstrants. In this context it is perhaps significant that another staunch Lutheran in Denmark, Jesper Brochmand (1585-1652), wrote to Meursius in 1635 to express his admiration of Meursius's interpretation of three of the Psalms in the work *Meditationes sacrae* from 1604. In this work, dedicated to Oldenbarnevelt, Meursius throughout stresses the general Protestant theme of man's inferiority and sinfulness and God's sublimity. We may take it from Brochmand's praise that he had not been provoked by any strictly Calvinistic doctrines in this work from Meursius's youth.[28]

He does not seem to have started working on the *Historia Danica* immediately. From a letter written at the end of 1626 by Prof. Jacob Fincke (1592-1663) in Copenhagen it is evident that Meursius had not asked for material for the history until recently, and that he only now, together with the letter, obtained his main source, Svaning's manuscript on the Oldenburg kings. Fincke acts on the chancellor's behalf, as he makes clear; it was on his order that Fincke sent Meursius the last of the three volumes of Svaning's *History of Denmark*, which dealt with the three first Olden-

---

[24] *Mihi bene est in Dania, Dei gratia; favent proceres, amant docti, nec mutare temere velim* (letter from Meursius to Vossius, dated June 3rd, 1631 (Meursius 1741-63, XI, no 819; Vossius 1691, II, no. 130)).

[25] Mackeprang 1924, 387.

[26] Norvin 1924, 613; Tauber 1827, 37.

[27] The passage from Meursius's letter is quoted in Tauber 1827, 37.

[28] Letter from Brochmand to Meursius, dated April 2nd, 1635 (Meursius 1741-63, XI, no. 733; original in the Royal Library of Copenhagen, ms. *Thott* 1843, 4to).

burg kings. But Fincke also suggests that the choice of Svaning's work, being the only one in Latin, was his own.[29] Anyway, whether the idea was Fincke's or Friis's or someone else's, this was a choice which, as we shall see, determined the shape of Meursius's own history to a considerable degree.

From now on Meursius worked fast. Already at the beginning of 1629 he had received an encouraging note from Jesper Brochmand, ensuring him of the pleasure with which the chancellor had read his manuscript. This draft consisted of more than one book – Brochmand refers to *libri* – and since the edition of 1630, which covers the years 1448-1523, only consists of three books, Meursius had probably sent the complete manuscript of this period to the chancellor in the last half of 1628. But something had to be changed, as Brochmand informed Meursius, since the chancellor had found his treatment of the Swedes too unfavourable (cf. Chapters IV, 3 and VII).[30]

In the summer of 1630 the small work had gone to press, as Meursius told Gerardus Vossius in a letter, adding that some leading men had urged him to publish this *specimen* of his work. Probably he just wanted to make clear that it was not his own idea to edit a volume of only three kings.[31] All the same, his discreet surprise at this idea confirms the impression, already noted in connection with Pontanus, that the "leading men" – among whom was no doubt Friis – rather impatiently awaited the results of the historiographers' efforts.

Meursius's *History* was published by one of the prominent publishers and booksellers in Copenhagen, Joachim Moltke. A royal letter, dated September 10, 1630, grants him privilege on the work and forbids re-edi-

---

[29] [...] *sæpius cogitavi qvid tibi potissimum mittendum esset ex tot quasi adversariis et collectaneis vernacula lingua ut plurimum conceptis præter unicum Svaningium, qvi videtur historiam nostram in ordinem redigere voluisse. Ex cujus tribus tomis* [...] *tertium hunc ex mandato et traditione Domini Cancellarii transmitto* (letter from Fincke to Meursius, dated December 5, 1626, printed in Rørdam 1891, 278-79 (original in the Royal Library of Copenhagen, ms. *Thott* 1843, 4to)).

[30] Letter from Brochmand to Meursius, dated January 4, 1629 (Meursius 1741-63, XI, no. 639; original in the Royal Library of Copenhagen, ms. *Thott* 1843, 4to). In April 1629 Meursius also declared to Ger. Vossius that he had finished his history of the first Oldenburg kings (letter from Meursius to Vossius, dated April 12, 1629 (*ibid.* no. 643; Vossius 1691, II, no. 102)).

[31] *Ego nunc Historiam trium Daniae Regum edo Hafniae impellentibus Viris aliquot Primatibus; qui ut me ac mea amant; æstimantque* [aexistimatque Meursii epist.: corr. ex Vossii epist.], *sic vulgari specimen istud operae meae plane cupiunt. Vbi Typographus absolverit, mittam exemplar* (letter from Meursius to Vossius, dated June 21, 1630 (Meursius 1741-63, XI, no. 660; Vossius 1691, II, no. 114)).

tions in Denmark within ten years, in order to further his chances of having his expenses covered. But the work turned out not to sell very well. From a survey made in 1666 of the stock of books which Moltke had left behind at his death in 1664, it appears that 187 copies of the 1630 edition of Meursius's *Historia Danica* were still unsold, in spite of repeated advertisements in the catalogues of the book fairs in Frankfurt and Leipzig in the 1630s. This does seem to indicate a rather poor interest, although the total number printed is not known. Perhaps the publication in Amsterdam in 1638 of Meursius's account of the whole of Danish history up to 1523 lessened the demand for this first small *specimen*.[32]

Meursius was quick to distribute this first result of his efforts as Danish historiographer. He sent a number of copies to his friend Vossius and asked him to distribute them to their common friends.[33] Reactions to the work are found in letters to him from the following years. He himself informs Vossius of the applause it has received in Denmark;[34] from the Hague Cornelius van der Mylen assured him that the work was well received by *des hommes d'estat, et des lettres*,[35] and Vossius wrote an enthusiastic letter, favourably comparing the style of Meursius's *History* with Daniel Heinsius's latest historical work, the *Rerum ad Sylvam-Ducis atque alibi in Belgio aut a Belgis anno 1629 gestarum historia* (Leiden 1631).[36] From Copenhagen Christian Thomesen Sehested wrote to congratulate the author, although by his own admission he had not yet read it,[37] and Petrus Cunæus similarly thanks him heartily for the copy he has received

---

[32] The royal privilege to Moltke is summarized in *Kancelliets Brevbøger*, 1630-32, 230 (*Sjællandske Registre* 18, 509). I owe my information on Moltke to Ingrid Ilsøe's survey of his activities as publisher and bookseller (Ingrid Ilsøe 1979-80).

[33] *Edidi hic Historiae meae Danicae Libros III. operae maioris specimen. Mitto aliquot exemplaria, tibi et amicis reliquis, quae te distribuere velim: Riveto, Cunaeo, Heinsio, Vorstio, Barlaeo, Scriverio, quanquam nostri nihil amplius memori. Vorstio vero etiam alterum addi cupiam, pro avunculo Buchelio, ad quem ille recte mittet. Literis vero ad Mylium quas inclusi, adde exemplaria quatuor* (letter from Meursius to Vossius, dated September 19, 1630 (Meursius 1741-63, XI, no. 817; Vossius 1691, II, no. 120)).

[34] *Certe hic cum summo plausu est accepta* (letter from Meursius to Vossius, dated March 25, 1631 (Vossius 1691, II, no. 125)).

[35] Letter from Cornelius van der Mylen to Meursius, dated May 2nd, 1631 (Meursius 1741-63, XI, no. 673).

[36] Letter from Vossius to Meursius, dated May 12, 1631 (Meursius 1741-63, XI, no. 674; also printed *ibidem* no. 654 wrongly dated 1630; Vossius 1691, I, no. 119).

[37] Letter from Chr. Thomesen Sehested to Meursius, dated January 8, 1631 (Meursius 1741-63, XI, no. 670).

without commenting further on the work.[38] Points of criticism were also raised. Rosenkrantz praised Meursius's "felicitous style of writing" (*felicitas in scribendo*), but he also suggested that some errors might have crept in.[39] The English antiquarian and historian Henry Spelman, to whom Meursius had sent a copy, wrote to inform him of his own and his friends' positive judgement; but one thing displeased them, and that was the lack of reference to other authors (a feature of the work to which we shall return in Chapter VIII on style).[40]

3. The Publication of the Second Volume

Shortly after the publication of the first part of his history, Meursius was able to publish another fruit of his studies in Danish history. In 1631 – the dedicatory letter to the nobleman Frantz Rantzau (1604-32) is dated February 1631 – appeared his edition of the earliest piece of Danish historiography in Latin, the English monk Ailnothus's *De vita et passione S. Canuti* (written about 1120).[41] Still, he must have worked intensively on the next part of his own history, on the period up to 1448. About two years after the publication of the first part, in November 1632, he announces to Vossius that he has now almost finished the preceeding period, and after that he will go on with the remaining Oldenburg kings.[42]

---

[38] Letter from P. Cunæus to Meursius, dated April 30, 1631 (Meursius 1741-63, XI, no. 672).

[39] Letter from Holger Rosenkrantz to Meursius, dated December 13, 1630 (Meursius 1741-63, XI, no. 668).

[40] *probavimus omnes, uti par erat, et laudavimus, sed Auctores tuos obiter te non laudasse increparunt nonnulli* (letter from Spelman to Meursius, dated July 31, 1632 (Meursius 1741-63, XI, no. 692)). In June 1633 Adolphus Vorstius in Leiden wrote to thank Meursius for the copy he had received (*ibid.*, no. 703).

[41] *Ælnothus Monachus Cantuariensis, De Vita et Passione S. Canuti, Regis Daniæ. Item, Anonymus, De Passione S. Caroli Comitis Flandriæ, eius F. Ioannes Meursius Ex Codice Bibliothecæ Hafniensis descripsit, edidit, et Notas addidit. Hafniæ, apud Joach. Moltkenium M. DC. XXXI.* Ailnothus's work had been edited earlier, in 1602. In the preface Meursius explains that he only became aware of this edition after having decided to make his own, and in view of the many errors in the 1602 edition, he did not consider a new edition superfluous. The most recent editor of Ailnothus, M. Cl. Gertz, drily notes that although Meursius did correct a number of the errors found in the 1602 edition, his own edition contains even more (Ailnothus, ed. Gertz 1908-12, 48).

[42] *Quod Historiam autem adtinet: versor nunc in continuatione Saxonis, usque ad Domum Oldenburgicam, a qua inceperam, pertexenda, et non multum (Dei gratia) a fine absum. Illustris Dominus Cancellarius Regius, etiamsi edita Pontani Historia, operam repetere me istam voluit: qua finita, quae in Domo Oldenburgica inchoavi, etiam deinceps persequar* (letter from Meursius to Vossius, dated November 3, 1632 (Meursius 1741-63, XI, no. 695; Vossius 1691, II, no. 155)).

Soon after he must have sent the pre-1448 manuscript to the chancellor for examination. Brochmand informed him, in September 1633, that Friis, though not having read all of it, was very pleased with what he had seen so far.[43] Friis did not have much time for reading, as he himself explained to Meursius in a letter written almost a year later, in June 1634; he had still just read part of Meursius's draft, but "with the utmost pleasure", and he now looked forward to seeing Meursius's account of the remaining Oldenburg kings. He was concerned, however, that some passages might be offensive to the neighbouring countries and had asked the royal secretary, Niels Eggebrecht (1580-1638), to go through the whole work. His comments were sent with the letter.[44]

The engagement of Niels Eggebrecht is another sign of the seriousness with which the composition of a Danish history was viewed. In this case Friis did not have the time to examine the work himself, and let his trusted secretary do it. Interestingly, a set of commentaries has actually been preserved, made at the request of Friis by an anonymous author. It would have been tempting to ascribe them to Eggebrecht, had not their author been termed a nobleman, a *vir illustris*, in the headings of the three preserved manuscripts; and Meursius in his answer greets him *illustris et generose domine* ("noble and eminent lord"), as he would hardly have greeted the German commoner Eggebrecht.[45] It would seem, then, that Friis entrusted both Eggebrecht and the nobleman with the task of looking into this part of Meursius's work.

Both editions of Meursius's *Historia Danica*, the one from 1630 and the one from 1638, are dedicated to Christian IV, as was Pontanus's *Rerum*

---

[43] Letter from Brochmand to Meursius, dated September 19, 1633 (Meursius 1741-63, XI, no. 712; original in the Royal Library of Copenhagen, ms. *Thott* 1843, 4to).

[44] Letter from Chr. Friis to Meursius, dated June 23, 1634 (Meursius 1741-63, XI, no. 723 (here dated June 13 1634); original in the Royal Library of Copenhagen, ms. *Thott* 1843, 4to).

[45] The nobleman is even, in one of the manuscripts (The Royal Library of Copenhagen, ms. *Thott* 1552, 4to), identified as Palle Rosenkrantz (1587-1642), a Danish nobleman who in the 1620s served Christian IV in various diplomatic negotiations. Since the identification is based on another text in the manuscript, a letter, and not on the commentary to Meursius's history, I think it needs further corroboration before we can declare Palle Rosenkrantz to be the author of the commentary. But it is noteworthy that the letter is also found in the two other manuscripts which contain the commentary (The Royal Library of Copenhagen, mss. *Gl. Kgl. S.* 2930, 4to; *Gl. Kgl. Saml.* 2429, 4to). A link between the two men exists, inasmuch as Meursius dedicated his *Regnum Atticum* (1632) to Palle Rosenkrantz.

Danicarum historia from 1631. Originally, however, Meursius had intended to dedicate his second volume to the chancellor. The dedicatory letter he had written to Friis was examined by Brochmand who found nothing to correct, as he wrote to Meursius, also in June 1634. But nine months later, in March 1635, the plan was cancelled. Brochmand wrote to Meursius that the chancellor, apparently so far unaware of Meursius's intention of dedicating the work to him, was utterly disapproving, ordering instead that Meursius should dedicate his work to the king in order to secure for himself the royal favour, and in order to make it easier for the chancellor to obtain for Meursius's son an ecclesiastical benefice (*beneficium*).[46]

Meanwhile Meursius was engaged in having his works published in an *Opera omnia* edition. Vossius, who in 1631 moved from Leiden to Amsterdam to become Professor of History at the new *Athenaeum Illustre* there, acted as mediator between him and the Dutch printers, and the correspondence between Vossius and Meursius provides interesting glimpses into the production and trade of books. In the autumn of 1632 Vossius informed Meursius of the intention of the famous printer in Amsterdam, Blaeu (Blauwius), to edit both Meursius's and others' work on Danish history.[47] From Meursius's answer in November it appears that he had previously asked Vossius to negotiate with another publisher in Amsterdam, Johannes Janssonius, about editing the history of Denmark and apparently also some other of his works, but since he had received no answer he would gladly use Blaeu instead.[48] In January 1633 Meursius learned from his friend that both Janssonius and Blaeu wanted to publish his and Pontanus's *Histories of Denmark*, though in separate volumes (Janssonius had published Pontanus's *History of Denmark* in 1631). Vossius recommended Blaeu, whose types were finer (*venustiores*), and warned Meursius against paying attention to their remarks about

---

[46] The two letters from Brochmand to Meursius are dated June 23, 1634 & March 4, 1635 (Meursius 1741-63, XI, nos. 725 & 732; the original of the first is in the Royal Library of Copenhagen, ms. *Thott* 1843, 4to).

[47] Letter from Vossius to Meursius, dated September 25, 1632 (Meursius 1741-63, XI, no. 694; Vossius 1691, I, no. 238). Willem Blaeu (1570-1638) was the founder of the printing house which was carried on by his sons Johannes and Cornelis. From Vossius's letters it appears that he also conducted the negotiations with one of the sons before the father died.

[48] Letter from Meursius to Vossius, dated November 3rd, 1632 (Vossius 1691, II, no. 155; the letter is also printed in Meursius 1741-63, XI, no. 695, but a substantial passage has been left out without indication, containing *inter alia* the instructions about the printers).

each other. Moreover Blaeu wanted to publish Meursius's collected works.[49]

No further mention is made of the first of these projects, but Meursius was highly interested in the idea of an *Opera omnia* edition. He soon wrote back to Vossius with details about the arrangement of the single works which Vossius was to convey to Blaeu. His writings on "Attic things" should be collected in Volume I, his historical works in Volume II, Volume III should be taken up with works of various kinds, while Volume IV should contain authors of whose works he had made the *editio princeps*.[50] A few months later followed material for the first volume.[51]

Blaeu's printing made slow progress. In April 1634 he had not even started, as Vossius informed Meursius. Between him and Janssonius a bitter rivalry had developed, and Vossius assumed this to be part of the reason for his delay;[52] four months later he blamed Janssonius more directly for harassing his rival.[53] Meursius was annoyed but nevertheless sent the material for Volume II in October 1634; this was not the historical works as originally planned but, as it seems, works on Greek antiquities.[54] Nothing apparently happened in the first half of 1635 – in March Meursius informed Vossius that his *History of Denmark* should be dedicated to the king and not to the chancellor, and he promised to send a preface dedicated to the king soon[55] – and Meursius, clearly impatient, now threatened to have the pre-1448 part of his *History of Denmark* published separately in Denmark.[56] In another letter, which perhaps belongs

---

[49] Letter from Vossius to Meursius, dated January 8, 1633 (Meursius 1741-63, XI, no. 697; Vossius 1691, I, no. 189).

[50] Letter from Meursius to Vossius, dated April 10, 1633 (Meursius 1741-63, XI, no. 701; Vossius 1691, II, no. 166).

[51] Letter from Meursius to Vossius, dated August 20, 1633 (Meursius 1741-63, XI, no. 822; Vossius 1691, II, no. 175).

[52] Letter from Vossius to Meursius, dated April 30, 1634 (Meursius 1741-63, XI, no. 721; Vossius 1691, I, no. 222).

[53] Letter from Vossius to Meursius, dated September 5, 1634 (Meursius 1741-63, XI, no. 726; Vossius 1691, I, no. 236).

[54] *Mitto interim quae 11. Tomi erant, et in illis Cretam meam* (letter from Meursius to Vossius, dated October 27, 1634 (Meursius 1741-63, XI, no. 728; Vossius 1691, II, no. 208)). Meursius did not send the historical works until the end of 1636.

[55] Letter from Meursius to Vossius, dated March 11, 1635 (Meursius 1741-63, XI, no. 824; Vossius 1691, II, no. 212).

[56] Letter from Meursius to Vossius, dated June 23, 1635 (Meursius 1741-63, XI, no. 825; Vossius 1691, II, no. 221).

to the same period, Meursius launches the same threat, hinting at the impatience with which his employers awaited the publication: "My superiors", he declares, "may force me to find a Danish printer".[57]

In January the following year, however, Meursius was confident that he would be able to send his historical works to Vossius at the beginning of spring and now wanted them to be placed in the first volume.[58] Still he apparently expected Blaeu to begin printing some of the works already sent, and three months later he has learned from a friend in Amsterdam that nothing has happened so far. He is now ready to give up the idea of an *Opera omnia* edition and asks Vossius to return his unprinted works if the printer does not begin now.[59] By the time of his next letter, Vossius had not been able to get hold of Meursius's unprinted works, since Blaeu was away; but his brother had assured him that now everything would turn to the better.[60] Meursius was willing to give him another chance but would postpone the delivery of his historical works, until he had seen proof of the printer's seriousness.[61] Shortly afterwards, in August 1636, Vossius assured him that now finally, frightened by Meursius's letters, Blaeu had begun to print his *Opera omnia*.[62] But Vossius's optimism seems

---

[57] Letter from Meursius to Vossius, dated June 7, 1637 (Meursius 1741-63, XI, no. 755; Vossius 1691, II, no. 244). I am inclined to regard the date as an error for 1635, since the letter treats of the same topics (diverse works by Vossius and Grotius published in 1635) as the other letter (of June 23, 1635) in which he threatens to have the work printed in Denmark. Moreover in June 1637, the printing of the *History of Denmark* had in fact begun, and Meursius in a letter dated May 27, 1637, informs Vossius that he has now received a specimen of the *History of Denmark* (see note below). It seems highly unlikely that he should have written the threatening letter just a week later.

[58] This seems to be the meaning of Meursius's words: *Si id fieri commode queat, Tomo historico primum locum dari velim: quem transmittam, volente Deo, primo vere* (letter from Meursius to Vossius, dated January 6, 1636 (Meursius 1741-63, XI, no. 743; Vossius 1691, II, no. 228[b])).

[59] Letter from Meursius to Vossius, dated April 22, 1636 (Meursius 1741-63, XI, no. 826; Vossius 1691, II, no. 230). Cf. also a letter from Meursius to Vossius of April 19, 1636 (Meursius 1741-63, XI, no. 827; Vossius 1691, II, no. 234).

[60] Letter from Vossius to Meursius, wrongly dated July 5, 1631, *III. Non Iulii*, (Meursius 1741-63, IX, no. 676; Vossius 1691, I, no. 145). The letter clearly belongs to the early summer of 1636, and the correct date is presumably June 3, 1636; Meursius in his next letter (see next note) refers to Vossius's letter written on this day, *iii. Non. Jun.*

[61] *Ubi videro Typographum serio manum operum editioni admovere, mittam Danicam Historiam* (letter from Meursius to Vossius, dated June 18, 1636 (Vossius 1691, II, no. 233; the letter is also found in Meursius 1741-63, XI, no. 746, but without the postscript, which contains the passage quoted)).

[62] *NVnc demum forte territus, literis tuis, excudere omnia tua Blavius coepit* (letter from Vossius to Meursius, dated August 14, 1636 (new style) (Meursius 1741-63, XI, no. 747; Vossius 1691, I, no. 286)).

to have been premature. In a bitter and pessimistic letter of December 1636 Meursius urges Vossius to persuade Blaeu to fulfil his promise, repeating his wish to begin with the historical works, because of the impatience of his Danish employers; together with this letter, it appears, he sent his *Historia Danica*.[63]

In April 1637 even Vossius's patience was apparently coming to an end. In a letter to Meursius, he went through all the troubles inflicted on his friend because of the procrastination, stressing the economic aspect, in that Meursius could now have received tokens of gratitude from those to whom the works were dedicated. Still, he was confident that Blaeu, who had now received Meursius's *History of Denmark*, would begin with this work, and that he would procure the necessary Greek type from Frankfurt, which he had lacked so far and needed for the other works: "Meanwhile his press will not toil as much with any other work as with your *History of Denmark*", Vossius ends reassuringly.[64]

The news that Meursius's *History of Denmark* was now in print was brought by Vossius later in April 1637 to Mericus Casaubonus, Professor of Theology at Oxford,[65] and one month later Meursius himself expressed his joy at having received a specimen of his *History*.[66]

But his optimism was premature. In July 1637 the *History of Denmark* was still unprinted, Vossius told Hugo Grotius. He further informed him that Blaeu's excuse for not having printed the work, which he had received a year ago, was that the German-Swedish war made delivery of paper difficult – "and meanwhile Meursius is highly annoyed that he has been fooled like that for five years".[67]

---

[63] *Mitto tandem, si quid forte hominem exstimulare istud possit, Historiam Danicam, quam praeverti, ceteris sepositis omnibus, maxime velim* (letter from Meursius to Vossius, dated December 20, 1636 (Meursius 1741-63, XI, no. 828; Vossius 1691, II, no. 240)). Presumably the preface to the whole of the *Historia Danica* and the preface to its Part II were sent together with the history itself; in the printed work they are dated Sorø, December 7, 1636.

[64] *Interim nullo aeque opere praelum eius fervebit quam Historia tua Danica* (letter from Vossius to Meursius, dated April 6, 1637 (Meursius 1741-63, XI, no. 750; Vossius 1691, I, no. 250, dated April 7, *sine anno*)). Already the year before, in a letter to Hugo Grotius, Vossius had complained that Meursius's relations with his Danish dedicatees would suffer from the procrastination (letter from Vossius to Grotius, dated March 17, 1636 (Vossius 1691, I, no. 278)).

[65] *Excuditur hic Historia Danica Meursii* (letter from Vossius to Casaubonus, dated April 20, 1637 (new style) (Vossius 1691, I, no. 298)).

[66] *Accepi etiam specimen Historiae Danicae, quod per Elzevirium ad me mittebas* (letter from Meursius to Vossius, dated May 27, 1637 (Meursius 1741-63, XI, no. 829; Vossius 1691, II, no. 243)).

[67] *Interim ringit Meursius, sic se quinquennio habitum ludibrio* (letter from Vossius to Grotius, dated July 10, 1637 (Vossius 1691, I, no. 305)).

From Vossius's indignant letter to Meursius in September 1637 it appears that things were again at a standstill; but now he has at least succeeded in making Blaeu realize the impropriety of his behaviour.[68] And in October Meursius optimistically told Vossius to whom he wanted to send copies of the printed edition of the historical works: Mylius and Rivetus in the Hague, Heinsius, Cunaeus and Vorstius in Leiden, and of course to Vossius himself. In addition Meursius wanted at least 20, or if possible 24, copies sent to himself.[69]

As late as May 1638 Meursius regrets that the king and the *rigsråd* (*senatus*) have waited such a long time to see the work which has not yet been published.[70] But at long last, in September, Vossius announces to his friend that his works on Dutch (*Belgica*) and Danish history have now appeared in print in one volume.[71]

With this, Blaeu had only fulfilled part of the agreement. The idea had been to produce an edition of Meursius's collected works, but now that the *History of Denmark* had appeared in print, Blaeu was in no hurry to continue with the rest of Meursius's works. Vossius vents his anger in a letter to Grotius, advancing the interesting theory that Blaeu had printed the historical works first, contrary to the original agreement, presuming that they would sell better: "It is now almost six years ago that Meursius, on Blaeu's request, sent him everything, published as well as unpublished, with the sole exception of the *History of Denmark*, which he wanted to be published last. But he, on the contrary, began with this work, because he assumed that it would be easier to sell than the rest of this man's works".[72] Vossius perhaps exaggerates Blaeu's unreliability. As we have seen, Meursius originally wanted the historical works to occupy Volume II of his *Opera omnia*, which probably reflects the intended order

---

[68] Letter from Vossius to Meursius, dated September 10, 1637 (Meursius 1741-63, XI, no. 757; Vossius 1691, I, no. 309).

[69] Letter from Meursius to Vossius, dated October 12, 1637 (Meursius 1741-63, XI, no. 758; Vossius 1691, II, no. 257).

[70] Letter from Meursius to Vossius, dated May 21, 1638 (Meursius 1741-63, XI, no. 764; Vossius 1691, II, no. 259).

[71] *Danica ac Belgica tua Historia tandem ad finem perducta: quo nomine gaudeo. Deinceps, ut cetera maturentur, urgere Blauwios non desistam* (letter from Vossius to Meursius, dated September 29, 1638 (new style) (Meursius 1741-63, XI, no. 769; Vossius 1691, I, no. 340)).

[72] *Jam prope sexennium est, quod postulato ipsius Meursius transmisit omnia, edita, inedita, sola excepta Historia Danica; quam postremo excudi volebat. Ille contra, ab hac orsus est, quia cæteris ejus viri vendibiliorem fore arbitrabatur* (letter from Vossius to Grotius, dated October 14, 1638 (Vossius 1691, I, no. 344)).

of appearance. And then, as we saw, he seems to have changed his mind, since he sent the printer some works on Greek antiquities to be included in Volume II. In this phase he may, as Vossius suggests, have wanted the historical works to be published after the others. But in January 1636 Meursius himself declared that he now wanted the historical works in Volume I (even though he did not send the *Historia Danica* to Blaeu until December 1636). Nevertheless, whether justified or not, Vossius's suspicion that Blaeu had economic motives for printing the *History of Denmark* first is interesting in itself.

The Blaeus never published an *Opera omnia* edition of Meursius's works. In a letter to Hugo Grotius, Vossius complains that he does not know what will become of this project.[73] The main problem now was that the older Blaeu had died and the sons had problems in coming to a mutual understanding. (It was, it seems, with one of the sons, who was apparently more or less in charge of the business for some years before the father's death, that Vossius had conducted the negotiations over Meursius's works). Besides, as Vossius explained to Meursius, they had to wait for the completion of the printing of one of Vossius's own works before they could go on with Meursius's, since they did not have enough Greek type to print them simultaneously. He also informed Meursius that he had ordered the Blaeu brothers to see to it that Meursius could have at least thirty-six copies of the Danish history at his disposal.[74]

But Meursius had had enough. In spite of weak health he wrote to Vossius on June 1st 1639, asking him to inform Blaeu that if he did not now hurry along with the rest of his works, he would take revenge by having the *History of Denmark* republished by Joachim Moltke in Copenhagen, including his account of the years 1523-50 which had not been printed so far, and he would see to it that import of Blaeu's edition into Denmark would be prohibited.[75]

---

[73] Letter from Vossius to Grotius, dated December 15, 1638 (new style) (Vossius 1691, I, no. 345).

[74] Letter from Vossius to Meursius, dated March 21, 1639 (new style) (Meursius 1741-63, XI, no. 778; Vossius 1691, I, no. 350 likewise dated but *St. V.*, "old style").

[75] *Blavio vero, illud ut denunties velim, ni deinceps gnaviter in excudendis meis pergat, me iniuriam ulturum esse; et Moltkenio Historiam Danicam recudendam traditurum, cum Auctario rerum Friderici Primi, Interregni, atque Christiani III. tum et curaturum ei privilegium, quo in Regnum hoc importari Blavii editio prohibeatur. Itaque serio secum reputet, quid hic sibi faciendum esse putet. Ego certe non diutius sum passurus me deludi etiam porro, neque patientiam meam ultra laedi* (letter from Meursius to Vossius, dated June 1st, 1639 (Meursius 1741-63, XI, no. 831; Vossius 1691, II, no. 282)).

Sepulchral painting of Meursius and his family in the church of Sorø. (Photogravure in The Royal Library, Copenhagen).

The threat was never carried out. Meursius, who had been ill for some time, died on September 20, 1639. Around the same time, it seems, Vossius finally managed to obtain a clear answer from the Blaeus to the effect that they were no longer interested in printing Meursius's works; they would return his manuscripts to Vossius.[76]

It is noteworthy that all these protracted negotiations with the printer do not seem to have involved the Danish government. It was Meursius himself who conducted the negotiations with Blaeu (though mostly through Vossius). The arrangement may seem surprising in view of the chancellor's efforts, out of concern for national reputation, to have the contents of Meursius's *History* checked. But indirectly we may perceive a certain governmental supervision over the process of publication. The 1638 edition of Meursius's *History* was, as I said, published together with his works on Dutch history in one volume. Apart from this, however, there were also printed copies which only contained the *Historia Danica*. Meursius explains in the Preface (which is the same in both groups of the 1638 edition) that these separate copies were made in order to fulfil the wish of the king and "those who wanted to have the edition of this work completed".[77] The Danish government, it would seem, had insisted that the *Historia Danica* should be found in a separate volume, not only as a part of Meursius's *Opera omnia*. Furthermore, the chancellor, as we saw, insisted that the *History of Denmark* should be dedicated to Christian IV and not to himself. And Meursius was aware of the impatience of his employers; he decided (as mentioned above) to change his original plan and have his historical works printed first, because he feared that his employers would insist that he should find a Danish printer if Blaeu did not speed up.

I have not found any suggestions to the effect that the Danish government supported the publications financially. We saw how in 1630 the publisher Joachim Moltke in Copenhagen took upon himself the financial risk of the publication of Meursius's account of the period 1448-1523, and Blaeu's considerations concerning profits likewise suggest that the risk was his.

After having sent off the manuscript of his pre-1448 history, Meursius did not consider his *History of Denmark* completed. He went on with the

---

[76] This is clear from a letter from Vossius to Grotius, dated January 1st, 1640 (old style) (Vossius 1691, I, no. 372), in which he also mentions that he informed Meursius of this development shortly before his death, and informs Grotius of Pontanus's death. In a letter to Meursius, written a few days after his death, Vossius told him that he had tried to find other printers, but so far they had refused (letter from Vossius to Meursius, dated September 25, 1639 (Meursius 1741-63, XI, no. 790; Vossius 1691, I, no. 365)).

[77] *Inter quæ cum tua Historia classem ducat, separatim dare statui: quo et Majestatis tuæ, et eorum, qui promotam cuperent editionem, desiderio satisfacerem* (Meursius 1638, preface to Christian IV).

remaining Oldenburg kings, i. e. the period after 1523. At the time of his death he had reached 1550, basing his account of the history of Christian III on Niels Krag's unprinted *History of Christian III* (written c. 1600), which covered the period 1533-50.[78] He even planned to embark on the history of Frederik II – or more likely, the chancellor wanted to push him onwards. Friis saw to it that a German version of Lyschander's Danish *History of Frederik II* was produced by the secretary Niels Eggebrecht and sent to Meursius; Friis was convinced, he told Meursius in the letter accompanying the translation, that Latin or German accounts of Frederik II's wars in Ditmarsken (1559) and against Sweden (1563-70) could be found, but warned him that Chytræus's account (i.e. in the *Saxonia*) was full of errors.[79] Meursius, it seems, never found the opportunity to make use of Eggebrecht's translation, since it was sent to him only a month and a half before his death. But the engagement of Eggebrecht to produce this translation for Meursius is another piece of evidence of the chancellor's enthusiasm to have the history of Denmark made public in Latin.

Meursius also left behind him a rich collection of printed books and manuscripts. Two of the most dedicated collectors of books in Denmark at the time, Stephanus Johannis Stephanius and Jørgen Seefeldt, purchased parts of it, and the rest was inherited by his son.[80] A catalogue of his printed books, or rather of a selection of them, is extant in the Royal Library in Copenhagen. It is furnished with prices in Dutch guilders (*floreni Hollandici*) and stuivers (*stuferi*), and is clearly made in connection with a sale. Walde points out that Meursius's collection of printed books must have been considerably larger than what is mentioned in the catalogue, and he assumes that the catalogue reflects a sale arranged by Meursius himself of a selection from his library.[81] Another sale from his collection of books was

---

[78] Both Meursius's account of the period 1523-1550 and Niels Krag's *Christianus III* were first published by Hans Gram, in 1746 and 1737 respectively. A fine copy of Meursius's account 1523-50 of which most is written in Meursius's hand and the rest in Stephanius's is found in the Swedish Skokloster (ms. 52,4) (Ellen Jørgensen 1917, 25). According to the younger Svaning's preface to his edition of Stephanius's account of the last part of Christian III's reign (1650), Meursius's manuscript was found, in 1650, in the nobleman Laurids Ulfeldt's library (Rørdam 1891, 253).

[79] Letter from Chr. Friis to Meursius, dated August 9, 1639 (Meursius 1741-63, XI, no. 785).

[80] Meursius's letters (both his own and those he received) came to Seefeldt's library, where Seefeldt's librarian, Zacharias Lund, made a copy of them. Hans Gram later based his edition of the letters on Lund's transcription (Meursius 1741-63, XI).

[81] The Royal Library of Copenhagen, ms. *Gl. kgl. S.* 2120, 4to. On Meursius's library and its destiny, see Walde 1916-20, 432-38 and Walde 1917, 58-65.

arranged in Leiden in 1642, for which a printed catalogue exists. It states explicitly that only a part of Meursius's books are included.[82] Here the theological works predominate, while the number of historical works is considerably smaller than in the catalogue from Copenhagen.

4. The Personal Relationship between Meursius and Pontanus

Towards the end of the biographical sketch of Pontanus above, we saw that Meursius found a severe critic in his colleague Pontanus, who in a confidential letter to Stephanius expressed his negative opinion of Meursius's account of the three first Oldenburg kings. I mentioned that the eighteenth century historian F. Reinboth seems to be the only scholar who has considered the relationship between Meursius and Pontanus in their capacities as Danish historiographers. I think he is right to emphasize that their relationship was one of jealous rivalry, even though he probably exaggerates its effects.

Reinboth focuses on Pontanus. But we also happen to know something – in fact more – about Meursius's opinion of Pontanus's work, and it seems that the low esteem was mutual. Naturally, Meursius consulted Pontanus's *History of Denmark* of 1631, when he himself was given the task of writing about the same period (up to 1448). He made some interesting notes when reading Pontanus's work and they have been preserved. We shall deal with them later (Chapter IX), and here just observe that they are exclusively concerned with Pontanus's shortcomings. Nothing positive is mentioned. We must not conclude from this that Meursius did not admire Pontanus's achievement, but other circumstances do suggest a rather negative attitude on his part. During his work he several times attacks views held by Pontanus, although he does not mention his name (examples are given in Chapter IX).

Besides, Meursius was remarkably willing to support the publication of the *Specimen* written by the Icelandic historian Arngrímur Jónsson, in which Arngrímur refutes Pontanus's opinion, put forward in the *Chorographica descriptio* of the *History of Denmark* that Iceland was identical with the Thule in classical texts (see further Chapter VI). On Worm's sugges-

---

[82] *Pars Librorum Rarissimorum tam Græcorum, quam Latinorum Viri Nobilissimi D. Joannis Meursii, Quorum auctio habebitur Lugd. Batav. in ædibus Francisci Hackii, die ultimo Septemb. stilo novo, hora octava matutina. Lugd. Batavorum, anno* MDCXLII.

tion,[83] Stephanius (who was Meursius's colleague in Sorø) asked Meursius to recommend the publication of Arngrímur's work to the Amsterdam printer Janssonius. Stephanius wrote back to tell Worm that Meursius had recommended that Worm should have a copy made, which could then be handed over to Janssonius's assistant, whom Meursius expected to come to Denmark soon.[84] Some months later, Worm reported to Arngrímur in Iceland that his treatise had pleased Stephanius and Meursius, who strongly desired to have it published.[85] It is tempting to interpret Meursius's active interest in the publication of Arngrímur's treatise as another piece of evidence of rivalry between the two men.

However, I do not want to press the point about their personal relationship. It must be emphasized that Pontanus and Meursius not only had very similar educational backgrounds, but also belonged to the same circle of Dutch humanists. The fact that Pontanus's edition of Macrobius of 1597 was furnished with commentaries by Meursius points to their having by this time established some kind of friendship (cf. above). It is also interesting that Vossius in a letter to Meursius concerning the publication of Meursius's *De Atticae regibus* suggests that if the printer, Janssonius, chooses to print the work in Harderwijk (where Pontanus lived), he will ask Pontanus to assist in the process.[86]

Nevertheless I would like to make two points. For one thing they did not collaborate. There are no signs that they exchanged information and points of view on Danish history; in view of the fact that so many of both men's letters are extant,[87] this observation may be significant as an indication *e silentio* of mutual rivalry. Rather, and this is the second point, each was critical of his colleague's achievement. Their mutual criticism may well have been an expression of personal jealousy, but it was also, I think, rooted in divergent conceptions of a work of national history.

---

[83] Letter from Worm to Stephanius, dated February 7, 1638 (Worm 1751, no. 190; Worm 1965-68, II, no. 699 (Danish trans.); extract in Worm 1948, 345).

[84] Letter from Stephanius to Worm, dated February 27, 1638 (Worm 1751, no. 191; Worm 1965-68, II, no. 703 (Danish trans.); extract in Worm 1948, 345-46).

[85] *D. Meursio, M. Stephanio omnia arrident, qvi editam percuperent* (letter from Worm to Arngrímur Jónsson, written May 1638 (Worm 1751, no. 334; Worm 1948, 48-49; Worm 1965-68, II, no. 714, Danish trans.)).

[86] Letter from Vossius to Meursius, dated January 8, 1633 (Meursius 1741-63, XI, no. 697; Vossius 1691, I, no. 189).

[87] Apart from a letter from Meursius to Pontanus of 1598 on Macrobius (Matthæus 1738, III, 751) I have not seen any letters between them.

A Note on Stephanus Johannis Stephanius

Mapping out Meursius's and Pontanus's intellectual milieu is not within the scope of the present book. But one man deserves special attention, since he plays a role in both men's preoccupation with Danish history. Symptomatically, he too mirrors the close contacts between Danish and Dutch intellectuals. This is Stephanus Johannis Stephanius (1599-1650).[1] He studied in Leiden twice, in 1623-24 and in 1626-30, and among others he made acquaintance with Vossius and Heinsius, to whom he dedicated his first commentary on Saxo Grammaticus's *Gesta Danorum* of c. 1200, *Breves notæ ac emendationes in [...] Saxonem Grammaticum* (Leiden 1627). Among the men to whom he sent a copy of the book was Christen Friis, who, in line with his interest in promoting studies of national history, encouraged him to continue his studies in Saxo – studies that eventually materialized in his edition of Saxo (1645) and his massive commentary *Notæ uberiores in Historiam Danicam Saxonis Grammatici* (1645).

In Leiden he also formed a friendship with Pontanus. Saxo was a common interest, being one of the main sources for Pontanus in his work on Danish history. A number of letters from Pontanus to Stephanius dealing with textual questions and Saxo's literary models have been preserved.[2] Stephanius, in the *Notæ uberiores*, often draws attention to his friend's merits within the field of Saxonian scholarship.[3] Another indication of their closeness was the anthology of texts concerning Denmark edited by Stephanius in 1629, as part of a series of descriptions of various countries published by the Elzevirs.[4] Not only did Pontanus advise him on which texts to print, he also allowed him to include chapters from his own forthcoming *History of Denmark*.[5] Stephanius duly acknowledged his debt to him in the preface. He also contributed a laudatory poem to Pontanus's *History of Denmark*.

---

[1] The basic biography of Stephanius was written by H. F. Rørdam (1891). For a survey of his achievement in the study of Danish history, see Ellen Jørgensen 1931, 127-32.

[2] E.g. in Matthæus 1695, nos. 40, 41, 78, 135, 141, 163.

[3] Stephanius 1645, 58, 78 etc.

[4] Stephanius 1629. See Rørdam 1891, 26.

[5] The anthology came in two versions, both in 1629. The second version was enlarged with extracts from two chapters of Pontanus's forthcoming history: *Cæli solique qualitates et regni Daniæ dotes* (*Rerum Danicarum historia*, 1631, 773-75), and *Mores, ingenia et instituta Danicæ gentis* (*ibidem* 775-92), and with a *Chorographica Daniæ descriptio compendio e Jona Coldingensi et Isacio Pontano, aliisque excerpta*. Both versions contain Pontanus's chapter *Regni Danici status politicus* (*ibidem* 765-67). A closer description of Stephanius's edition is found in Rørdam 1891, 26-29.

In 1630 Stephanius, to his own relief, succeeded in obtaining a post in Denmark, promoted among others by Pontanus, who, in a letter to the chancellor, took care to recommend the young man and his studies in Saxo.[6] It so happened that Stephanius now became Meursius's colleague as professor at the Academy of Sorø, and the two men seem to have struck up a friendship of mutual profit, also in the literal sense that Stephanius, whose financial problems are well attested, borrowed money from Meursius. Meursius on his part benefited from Stephanius's knowledge of Danish history and historical sources[7] – and, most likely, also from his knowledge of the Danish language. Though it is not known how much Danish Meursius learned during his years in Sorø, the fact that the chancellor, as late as 1639, had Lyschander's Danish history of Frederik II (1559-88) translated into German for him, indicates a rather poor grasp of the language. Still, there are traces in Meursius's *History of Denmark* of his acquaintance with Danish texts (in his notes to Pontanus, furthermore, he refers several times to Huitfeldt's *History of Denmark*, which was written in Danish), and it is reasonable to assume that he received assistance from Stephanius when consulting Huitfeldt's work.

Stephanius took care to pay tribute to the memory of Meursius in his commentary on Saxo, the *Notæ uberiores* of 1645, just as he did to the memory of Pontanus. He refers to several of Meursius's books, including the *Historia Danica*. His repeated presentation here of Meursius as "my very close friend" (*amicus meus conjunctissimus*) confirms the impression of a genuine friendship.

In the learned controversy between Pontanus and Arngrímur Jónsson concerning the identification of ancient Thule, Stephanius, like Meursius, sided with Arngrímur. In Meursius's case, as suggested above, one may suspect baser motives of rivalry behind his eagerness to see to the publication of Arngrímur's defence. Stephanius, however, was probably more engaged with the scholarly question itself. He was impressed with Arngrímur's work, which he had read in manuscript, and, in a letter to Ole Worm, expressed his doubts as to Pontanus's ability to uphold his

---

[6] Letter from Pontanus to Friis, dated January 1st, 1630 (Rørdam 1898, 485-87 (original in *Rigsarkivet*, Copenhagen)).

[7] An example, also mentioned by Rørdam 1891, 39, is found in Meursius's preface to the reader in his edition of Ailnothus (1631), where he acknowledges his debt to Stephanius for having drawn his attention to an earlier edition of the text (1602). Cf. above, p. 72.

point of view; but discussions between men of such learning, he continued, will always increase our knowledge.[8]

On the other hand, as we saw above, he was also the addressee of the letter in which Pontanus attacked Meursius's account of the first Oldenburg kings. Pontanus obviously felt free to confide in him, perhaps even expecting him to share his view of Meursius's work. To Meursius's critical notes on Pontanus's *History of Denmark*, Stephanius also in a few places added arguments in support of Pontanus. Both these circumstances may be taken to confirm the impression from his studies in Saxo that he himself felt closer to the antiquarian kind of historiography pursued by Pontanus.

In Sorø he carried on his work on Saxo's *Gesta Danorum*, which formed the centre of his research activities. Eventually, he was able to publish a new edition[9] and a highly learned commentary, the above mentioned *Notæ uberiores in Historiam Danicam Saxonis Grammatici* (Sorø 1645). He here discusses Saxo's work not only in the light of classical and medieval literature, runic inscriptions, and archeological evidence, but also in the light of the Old Norse literary tradition, to which Ole Worm had drawn his attention. Stephanius and Worm were pioneers in this field among Danish historians. In Meursius's *History of Denmark* no traces of acquaintance with Old Norse literature are found, whereas Pontanus made use of Mattis Størssøn's *Norwegian Chronicle* from the 1540s which consists of extracts of the medieval kings' sagas, translated into Danish.[10]

There is no reason to doubt Ellen Jørgensen's statement that Stephanius's main interest lay in older Danish history.[11] In the course of the 1640s he was engaged in preparing a collection of historical writings on Danish history.[12] Though he himself did not carry through this project, his collec-

---

[8] Letter from Stephanius to Worm, dated February 27, 1638 (Worm 1751, no. 191; Worm 1965-68, II, no. 703 (Danish trans.); extract in Worm 1948, 345-46).

[9] *Saxonis Grammatici Historiæ Danicæ Libri XVI*. Although the year of publication was 1644 according to the title page, it cannot have come out until the following year, since the dedication to Christian IV is dated 1645 (Rørdam 1891, 225).

[10] On the initiative of Arild Huitfeldt it was printed in 1594 in Denmark, and this is the version which was used by Pontanus. Størssøn's chronicle has been edited in 1962 by Mikjel Sørlie. Mattis Størssøn (d. 1569) formed part of the humanist circle in Bergen in the middle of the sixteenth century; they made several such extracts from the kings' sagas which they translated into Danish; see J.G. Jørgensen 1993.

[11] Ellen Jørgensen 1931, 159-60.

[12] Rørdam 1891, 198-99, 234-35.

tion proved useful to J. Langebek (1710-75) and his successors, who eventually published a collection of *Scriptores rerum Danicarum* (1772-1834).

However, the only piece of historiography which Stephanius himself composed was about the more recent past. Shortly after Meursius's death in September 1639 he was appointed his successor both as Professor of History at the Academy of Sorø and as royal historiographer.[13] In this capacity he wrote a continuation of Meursius's uncompleted account of the history of Christian III, covering the last years of his reign, 1550-59. A testimony of Stephanius's and Meursius's common work on Christian III's history is a fine copy of the last part of Meursius's *Historia Danica* (the period 1523-50). Most of it is written in Meursius's own hand and the last part in Stephanius's.[14]

It seems that Stephanius had been told to continue and write also the history of Frederik II (1559-88) and of the ruling Christian IV himself. In 1646 he informed Worm that he would go on to Frederik II after the completion of the last nine years of Christian III's reign. Already around New Year 1640-41 he asked one of his friends, the poet Zacharias Lund, who had been in Sweden as tutor to a young nobleman, for news of contemporary Swedish-Danish affairs, apparently intending to include such information in a historical account.[15] These preparations did not, however, result in any history of Frederik II and Christian IV from Stephanius's pen. As far we know, Stephanius never went further than the death of Christian III in 1559.

He did not himself live to see this little work in print. It was published shortly after his death, in 1650, by Hans Svaning (the younger).[16] But before his death Stephanius had made arrangements for publication.[17] Like Meursius, he experienced certain problems at this stage. From a letter from him to Ole Worm it appears that he had originally made a deal with a publisher in Copenhagen, Jørgen Holst, and a printer in Sorø,

---

[13] No letter of appointment has been preserved, but a royal letter, dated November 5, 1639, orders the head of the Academy, Justus Høg, to appoint him *Historiographus Regius* and Professor of History (Rørdam 1891, 196, 266).

[14] Ellen Jørgensen 1917, 25; cf. above p. 81.

[15] Rørdam 1891, 200-2.

[16] Stephanius's work was re-edited by Hans Gram in his edition of Niels Krag's *Christianus III* (Krag, 1737, 331-401), and in his edition of Meursius's *History of Denmark* (Meursius 1741-63, IX, cols. 993-1056). A brief presentation of the work focusing on ideological values is given by E. V. Rasmussen in the most recent history of Danish literature, Rasmussen 1983, 157-58.

[17] Rørdam 1891, 245-53.

Henrik Kruse; but when the latter demanded some of the money in advance, Stephanius apparently found it necessary to ask Worm to help him find another publisher in Copenhagen, perhaps Joachim Moltke.[18] Worm's answer is not known, but it must have been dissuasive, since Stephanius in his next letter complained over the reluctance of the printers in Copenhagen; had he not been in such a hurry, he adds, he would have had no problem in having the work published in the Low Countries.[19] (When the work finally came out, in Hans Svaning's posthumous edition, the publisher and printer were Jørgen Holst and Henrik Kruse). Stephanius's difficulties thus confirm our impression from the letters of Meursius that the practical arrangements concerning publication were left to the royal historiographers themselves.

It is a curious fact that Meursius's unprinted account of the first part of the reign of Christian III (up to 1550) was not published along with Stephanius's continuation (covering the king's last years, 1550-59). Rørdam ascribes this negligence to the chancellor, Christen Thomesen Sehested,[20] and in more general terms it may be seen as an indication of the diminished enthusiasm for the whole historiographical project in Danish governmental circles compared to the days of Christen Friis, who had died in 1639. The chancellor's death, as earlier mentioned, was probably also the reason that Pontanus's account of the whole of the Oldenburg period up to Frederik II's death in 1588 was allowed to remain unprinted and apparently forgotten in the first decade after Pontanus's death. One may wonder why Stephanius did not, as far as we can see, do anything to get hold of Pontanus's manuscript, since he knew from Pontanus himself that he had completed the second part of his *History*.[21] Whatever the reason for that, it is clear that Stephanius was engaged to replace Meursius both as Professor in Sorø and as Royal Historiographer. It was Meursius's work which he was told to continue, not Pontanus's.

---

[18] The letter (which is written in Danish) is dated January 23, 1650 (the relevant parts are printed in Rørdam 1891, 247-48; paraphrased in Worm 1965-68, III, no. 1673).

[19] Letter from Stepanius to Worm dated January 30, 1650 (Worm 1751, no. 312; Worm 1965-68, III, no. 1675 (Danish transl.); parts of it are printed in Rørdam 1891, 249).

[20] Rørdam 1891, 253.

[21] Letter from Pontanus to Stephanius, dated 1639 (Matthæus 1695, no. 80).

Chapter IV

Pontanus's and Meursius's Predecessors. Danish Historiography after the Lutheran Reformation

1. Introduction

The attempts in the latter half of the sixteenth century to produce a new history of Denmark have not lacked scholarly attention. My discussion of these historians will be justified, I hope, by my viewing them as predecessors of Pontanus and Meursius and not of Huitfeldt. Huitfeldt's *Danmarks riges krønike* (1595-1604) is usually seen as the crowning achievement of early modern Danish historiography, while Pontanus's and Meursius's *Histories of Denmark* are dismissed as derivative. But as earlier suggested, I believe that this disregard of Pontanus and Meursius is anachronistic. I shall here take up subjects which presented themselves as important to the sixteenth-century historians as well as to Pontanus and Meursius: the religious dimension, the problem of the oldest history, the treatment of Sweden, and the proper subject matter of national historiography.[1]

A full-scale Latin history of Denmark had in fact existed since about 1200, when Saxo Grammaticus wrote his monumental *Gesta Danorum*, stretching from the mythical King Dan to his own times, ending in c. 1185. Saxo's work, printed already in 1514 in Paris, enjoyed considerable fame among intellectuals in the sixteenth century, not least on account of

---

[1] A comprehensive study of these aspects does not exist, though many observations on the individual authors and works have of course been made. The attempts in the sixteenth century to produce a Latin history of Denmark are surveyed in the histories of Danish historiography by Ellen Jørgensen 1931, 85-106, and by Torben Damsholt 1992, 53-61, and in the histories of Danish literature by Carl S. Petersen 1929, 374-416, and Oluf Friis 1945, 404-44. Harald Ilsøe has in a number of articles from the 1960s onwards thrown light on both the individual historians and their work and governmental interest in the project. References to these and other more specialized works will be given below.

its unique style – a highly classicizing vocabulary in combination with mannerist features.[2]

Since the time of Saxo, a number of annalistic chronicles had appeared, but no work of history on a grand scale, with the exception of the *Chronica regnorum aquilonarium*, a history of Denmark, Sweden, and Norway written in the early years of the sixteenth century by the German historian and diplomat, Albert Krantz (1448-1517), from Hamburg. This work was published posthumously, first in a German translation in 1545, and three years later in the original Latin, both dedicated to the Danish king, Christian III, who had also supported the publication financially.[3] But Krantz's work did not fulfil the demands of a new history of Denmark. Danish historians in the latter half of the sixteenth century, though frequently consulting him, regarded Krantz's knowledge of Danish affairs as highly insufficient, just as they found his attitude towards Danish points of view unreasonably unfriendly.[4] Besides, Krantz's work did not cover the period after 1504.

When in the latter half of the sixteenth century the composition of a new Latin history of Denmark, covering not only the period after Saxo but the whole of Danish history, became a matter of governmental engagement, it was due to several mutually dependent factors. A Latin national history would, as mentioned in the Introduction, bear witness to the long and glorious monarchical traditions of Denmark and present concrete political issues which accorded with the interests of the ruling king. The image of the nation thus created would not only impress foreigners but also serve the internal purpose of building up a national identity. Besides, a Latin history would, by its very existence, testify to the present state of Danish learning and culture. Important, too, was the simple fact that other European countries had had their history treated in major Latin works in recent times, such as Paolo Emilio's *De rebus gestis Francorum* (1516sqq), Polydore Vergil's *Anglica historia* (1534), Hector Boethius's *Scotorum historia* (1526), Albert Krantz's *Saxonia* (1520) and *Van-*

---

[2] On the ideological background to the edition of Saxo of 1514, see Karsten Friis-Jensen 1988-89. On the use of Saxo by two early sixteenth-century writers of Scandinavian history, Albert Krantz and Johannes Magnus, see Karsten Friis-Jensen 1991.

[3] According to the title page the year of printing was 1546, while 1548 is the date of the colophon. V.A. Nordman, who discusses the various editions of Krantz's work, regards 1548 as the correct year of publication (Nordman 1936, 9-22). Christian III's financial support is mentioned by Jørgensen 1931, 85. On Krantz's work, see also Grobecker 1964.

[4] Harald Ilsøe 1984, 236.

dalia (1519).[5] Moreover, from a political point of view there was a need for historical arguments in negotiations with other foreign countries. The trained diplomat Jørgen Rosenkrantz frequently regretted the lack of a modern account of Danish history, not least the most recent part.[6]

Of major importance was the political rivalry with Sweden in the sixteenth and seventeenth centuries. As noted at the beginning, Danish-Swedish relations had been tense ever since the days of the Union of Kalmar between the three Scandinavian countries (1397-1523), and three times between the Reformation and the death of Christian IV it came to open warfare, in 1563-70 (The Nordic Seven Years War), 1611-13 (The Kalmar War) and 1643-45 (The Torstensson War). The tensions were reflected in ongoing literary polemics. A multitude of various kinds of literature appeared in print, in many cases meant to serve the double purpose of stimulating hostile feelings against the neighbour and of denigrating the neighbour country in the eyes of foreigners. During the Seven Years War and the period preceeding it the strained relations found expression in a number of defamatory writings between the two neighbours.

2. Johannes Magnus's Historia de omnibus Gothorum Sveonumque regibus

Seminal in this so-called literary feud was the great Latin history of Sweden by Johannes Magnus (1488-1544), first published in 1554 (but written in the 1530s).[7] The work is ardently patriotic and imbued with hatred of everything Danish. Not only did Magnus paint the Danes in black colours, he also took up concrete matters of dispute, such as the national status of Scania (since 1658 the southernmost part of Sweden, until then part of Denmark).

---

[5] The most comprehensive survey of early modern historiography is Eduard Fueter 1911. Most of these works were reprinted more than once, but here and elsewhere I only give the year of their first appearance in print, unless otherwise stated.

[6] Harald Ilsøe 1984, 256 (referring to Peder Hegelund's preface to his *Epigrammata Philippi Melanchtonis* (1583)).

[7] Johannes Magnus, who was Catholic archbishop, left Sweden in 1526, by which time the new king Gustav Vasa (1521-60) was beginning to carry through a Lutheran reformation. Magnus never returned. His *History of Sweden* was completed in 1540 during his stay in Venice. On Johannes Magnus and his brother Olaus and their literary productions, see Kurt Johannesson 1982 (English trans. 1991).

In astonishing detail Magnus tells the history of the Swedes and their Gothic ancestors from the earliest times. Eighty-eight years after the Deluge, Noah's grandson Magog settled in Sweden and founded the Gothic community. The following centuries saw the dawn of a Gothic Golden Age, flourishing long before Greece and Rome. It was only much later that the obscure islands south of Sweden (i.e. Denmark) were colonized by a band of criminals expelled from Sweden. Magnus then tells the history of the heroic Goths and Swedes up to the sixteenth century, creating an unbroken list of Gothic/Swedish kings and depicting his heroes as superior, both physically and morally, to the Greeks and Romans, whose defeats at the hands of the Gothic heroes figure prominently.

In itself the idea of regarding peoples mentioned in ancient sources as ancestors of modern Europeans and linking them with the biblical origins of mankind was quite uncontroversial. Also the idea of tracing the Goths back to Magog, son of Japhet, had old roots. Isidore of Seville (d. 636) is the first to expound it in a historical work, the *Historia Gothorum* (1, 66).[8] What is remarkable in Magnus's version is his number of details from these remote times in combination with his aggressive patriotism. Magnus had to rely on his own imagination. Not afraid of deliberate falsifications, he claims support from sources he does not know and manipulates those he does know.

Magnus's calumnies did not escape his Danish readers, who were eager to point out the weak foundations of this piece of anti-Danish propaganda.[9] There is no doubt that this work made the need for a Danish counterpart acutely felt in Denmark. Though Magnus wrote his work in conscious emulation of Saxo, it also bore the stamp of humanist historiography. In some respects Saxo was not a match for Magnus, not only because he only dealt with the time up to c. 1185 but also because his work did not measure up to the standards of sixteenth-century historiography regarding the earliest history. Magnus had provided the connection with the Old Testament, which was lacking in Saxo.

It so happens that we possess a concrete piece of evidence for the Danish concern with the effects abroad of Magnus's work.[10] From Lon-

---

[8] Ed. Th. Mommsen, MGH AA 11, 2, 267-304. Berlin 1894.

[9] Some of Magnus's falsifications are mentioned in Svaning 1561, *passim*, and in Lætus 1574, 39, 42-43, 69. A general rejection of this *fictorum sycophanta* is found in a poem by the Danish poet Johannes Amerinus (1576), CBr.

[10] Ellen Jørgensen 1931, 87-88.

don the Danish professor and diplomat Hans Münster reported home to Caspar Paslick in 1559 the popularity of Johannes Magnus's *History*; he advised Paslick to persuade the king to see to the publication of a history of Denmark written in an elegant style, in order that foreign people could acquire a better knowledge of Danish affairs and the stain which Magnus had put on Denmark's honour could be washed away. "I have written about this in such detail", Münster ends, "because I now realize how important it is that princes support learned and eloquent men who can pass on the knowledge of past events to future generations by writing in a polished manner".[11] Eventually, eighty years later, the works of Pontanus and Meursius would fulfil Münster's wish. And as we shall see, Magnus's work had not ceased to exercise its influence. Reactions to his points of view can be detected in both Pontanus's and Meursius's *Histories of Denmark*.

3. Hans Svaning[12]

By the time of Münster's report from London, Hans Svaning (c. 1500-84) had already been working at some time on the composition of a full-scale Latin national history. A former student of Melanchthon's[13] he had been tutor to Christian III's son Frederik (II) in the 1540s, and from the 1550s he is known to have been working on his *History of Denmark*, in agreement with the Danish government. He himself, in his *Refutation of Johannes Magnus* (1561, see below), informs us that the chancellor Johan Friis (1494-1570) kept exhorting him to write a history of Denmark, and a poem by Hans Frandsen addressed to Svaning in 1561 seems to confirm the impression that he was expected to compose a national history.[14] But he was never officially appointed Royal Historiographer.[15]

---

[11] *De quibus rebus ideo ad te diligentius scribo, quod nunc re ipsa comperiam, quanti referat principes apud sese alere eruditos et disertos homines, qui polite scribendo rerum gestarum memoriam ad posteritatem possint transfundere.* (Extracts from Münster's letter are printed in Ellen Jørgensen 1931, 221-22 (original in *Rigsarkivet*, Copenhagen)).

[12] The basic biography of Svaning, including a survey of his literary production, was written by H.F. Rørdam (Rørdam 1867, 66-101).

[13] He had already come to Wittenberg in 1529 and studied there for several years.

[14] See Rørdam 1867, 89, where both passages are quoted.

[15] He has often been presented as Royal Historiographer, e.g. by Kr. Erslev 1928, vii, and Carl S. Petersen 1929, 380. Ellen Jørgensen, however, cautiously stressed that nothing is known of such an engagement (Jørgensen 1931, 88), and Harald Ilsøe has later demonstrated that Svaning was never officially engaged as historiographer (Ilsøe 1972, 22-34, cf. Ilsøe 1984).

He did, however, compose various minor historical pieces at the request of the government. The most important of these was a defence against some of the accusations put forward in Magnus's work; it was published in 1561 along with a sample of his *History of Denmark*, the life of King Johannes (*Hans*, by Svaning spelled *Ioannes*, 1481-1513), *Chronicon Ioannis*.[16] The choice of this king was no doubt determined by the ongoing polemics. Hans was one of the kings of the Union of Kalmar between Norway, Sweden, and Denmark, during which Sweden again and again tried to gain independence. Magnus tells the history of the Union as a clash between Danish thirst for power and Swedish love of liberty, while Svaning's history of King Johannes is designed to bring about the opposite idea. In his description the untrustworthy, sly Swedes governed by ambitious and greedy leaders broke their solemn oath time and again and betrayed Johannes, who was prone to think too well of them.[17]

The government's engagement with this work is well attested. In December 1559 the king issued a letter ordering the professors of the university to read it before publication. Svaning himself, in an afterword, mentions that he wrote the work at the instigation of the chancellor, Johan Friis, and Christian III. Johan Friis's active interest in Svaning's work – he served in practice as its supreme censor – inaugurated the close collaboration between leading politicians and historiographers which culminated in Christen Friis's supervision of Pontanus and Meursius. The publication of works of national history was a political concern at the highest level.[18]

The life of Johannes was for a long time the only part of Svaning's *History of Denmark* to be published. Only much later, in 1658, did another minor part come out, the life of Christianus II (1513-23). But in fact Svaning had almost certainly composed a more or less complete history of Denmark, stretching from King Dan to the end of Christianus II's reign in 1523, when in 1579 he was ordered by the chancellor, Niels Kaas,

---

[16] I here rely on Harald Ilsøe's study of Svaning's *Refutatio* and *Chronicon Ioannis*, Ilsøe 1972.

[17] The book containing these two pieces was published under the pseudonym Petrus Parvus (the name of a recently deceased professor in Copenhagen), and according to the title page the year of printing was 1560 instead of the correct 1561. The reasons behind these manoeuvres are discussed by Harald Ilsøe 1972.

[18] Formally censorship was exerted by the professors of the university. In the case of historiography, however, the chancellors themselves took an active part and they had the last word. This theme is treated in further detail in Harald Ilsøe 1973, 46-51.

to submit it to the university professors for examination. Since it was not published, they must have rejected it, and it was stored in the University Library, where eventually it was burned in 1728.

But Svaning's successors had access to his manuscripts, and in Meursius's case it even constituted the main source, at least for his account of the three or four first Oldenburg kings. On the whole, though, the preserved fragments of Svaning's history before the Oldenburg kings do not justify the epithet *Svaningius Redivivus* given to Meursius by Svaning's grandson. It seems fairly certain that Meursius only made limited use of his predecessor's manuscript for the period c. 1157-1448; to what extent he used him in the earliest history is more difficult to establish, but it does seem reasonable to regard him as the main source for this part (see Chapter VII).

Not much is known of Svaning's huge work today. Apart from the two printed parts, only the history of Christianus I (1448-81) has been preserved in manuscript (with some lacunas), along with scattered notes and excerpts concerning the older history; otherwise we can still gain an impression of its disposition from the table of contents preserved among Stephanius's papers.[19] Enough survives, though, to make possible an investigation into the literary and ideological aspects of Svaning's history, but with the notable exception of Ilsøe's treatment of the *Refutatio* and *Chronicon Ioannis*, no such study has, as far as I know, been conducted. Nor is this the place for any detailed discussion of these matters – the analysis of Meursius's work (Chapter VII) will entail some observations on Svaning's presentation of the material – but I shall briefly take up three of the four aspects mentioned above: the religious dimension, the problem of the oldest history, and the treatment of Sweden.

---

[19] The table of contents is published in William Christensen 1913, 5-8, 176-77. Svaning's history of Christianus I (1448-81) is found, although with a major lacuna, in a ms. in the Royal Library, Copenhagen (*Gl. Kgl. S.* 2444, 4to), which also contains passages from the period 1332-1448. Another manuscript in the Royal Library, Copenhagen (*Bartholiniana, Tome J, E don. var.* 1, fol.) contains excerpts of Svaning's *History of Denmark* from the eleventh to the fifteenth centuries. Further, an annalistic chronicle, preserved in ms. in the Royal Library, Copenhagen (*Ny kgl. S.* 561, fol.), seems to be based on Svaning's work. Other transcriptions of these annals exist, see Mohlin 1960, and *Annales Danici,* ed. Ellen Jørgensen 1920. Extracts are printed in Mohlin 1960, in *Archiv für Staats- und Kirchengeschichte der Herzogthümer* II, 227-52 (ed. J. M. Lappenberg), and in *Scriptores rerum Suecicarum* III, 1, 120sqq (ed. C. Annerstedt). Quotations from Svaning's work were also incorporated by Stephanius in his comprehensive commentary on Saxo's *Gesta Danorum* (1645). Apart from that an extract composed by Svaning in Danish and dealing with the period 1241-82 is extant. It was published by Kr. Erslev in 1928. (This survey of the preserved parts of Svaning's history is based upon Erslev's introduction and Harald Ilsøe's biography of Svaning in *Dansk biografisk leksikon,* 3rd ed.).

Svaning's *History of Denmark* seems to have been characterized by a strongly Christian, or, more precisely, Melanchthonian outlook. One of the preserved fragments suggests an attempt to place Danish history within the frame of universal history. The fragment, which is known from Stephanius's notes to Saxo, is devoted to the subject of the heathen gods. Starting out with a matter-of-fact presentation of the heathen gods worshipped by the Danes, Svaning bursts into a long lamentation of the ignorance and darkness that governed the human race after the appearance of original sin, or as Svaning says, "the sin of our first parents", before God in his mercy sent His word. And then he goes on: "This immense favour of God should be counted as more than all the riches of the world by all pious people, and particularly by kings, princes and public authorities [...] they have recently been liberated from those errors and idolatrous cults to which their predecessors once in their blindness adhered, by means of the Divine Word, which God in these last days of the world in His unspeakable goodness towards the human race again has revealed to the world".[20]

Svaning describes the Danish development from idolatry to Christianity and from depraved Christianity, that is Catholic abuse, to the Lutheran Reformation, and places this development in a universal perspective. In these latter days God has again revealed the Divine Word to man, i.e. through the Reformation.

Melanchthon's conception of world history is most elaborately set forth in his reworking of Johann Carion's chronicle, which kept the name of Carion also in Melanchthon's version. In its complete form the chronicle tells the history of the world from the Creation up to the present times. It is a universal history in the Christian sense that the whole of world history is described as God's design for human redemption.[21] Melanchthon allots a fixed span of years to the world, 6000 altogether,

---

[20] *Hoc ingens Dei beneficium, pluris æstimare, quam totius mundi opes, pij omnes debebunt; maxime autem omnium, Reges, Principes ac, Magistratus [...] quod ijs erroribus atque idololatricis cultibus modo liberati sint, in quibus olim illorum prædecessores excæcati hæserunt, idque beneficio verbi divini, quod Dominus sub extrema hæc mundi tempora, pro ineffabili sua bonitate erga humanum genus mundo denuo patefecit* (Extract from Svaning's *History of Denmark* in Stephanius 1645, 140).

[21] The original German version was first published in 1532. Melanchthon's Latin reworking of the period from the beginning of the world up to Charlemagne was first published in 1558-60. Melanchthon did not himself complete the reworking of the chronicle. His son-in-law, Casper Peucer, took care of the period from Charlemagne to Charles V. The whole work was first published in 1572. I have used an edition from 1580. On the interpretation of the chronicle I follow Fraenkel 1961, 52-107, and Klempt 1960, 17-33.

divided into three periods of 2000 years. The first 2000 years "before the Law" (*duo millia inane*) were followed by 2000 years "of the Law", that is from Abraham to the birth of Jesus; the last period of 2000 years is, seen from the sixteenth century, approaching its end – the more so, since it is going to be shortened as a result of increasing human sinfulness.

Melanchthon thus, like Svaning, refers to the notion of living in the last days, most forcefully in a passage about his own time, the old age of the world. He combines this notion with his sense of belonging to God's chosen few and with polemics against Catholics and other non-Lutherans. In the midst of the confusion created by idol-worshipping popes and monks, Turks and other Mohammedans, the true Church is protected by God, he assures his reader (cols. 900-2; cf. cols. 719-20).[22]

Much later in his work, in the history of Christianus II, Svaning again refers to Luther's appearance in these last days of the world. Having drawn a parallel between the contemptuous reception in Denmark of an early German Lutheran and the persecutions of the pious in the early days of the Church, he prays: "may God not extinguish the light sent to us in these last days of the ageing world [...]".[23] The comparison itself is very much in the vein of Melanchthon's reworking of *Carion's Chronicle*. The *vera ecclesia* is here depicted as a small group of true believers, a group which has always been persecuted throughout history. In the above-mentioned passage Melanchthon draws a similar parallel between two phases of ecclesiastical history, the persecuted Church at the time just before the birth of Christ and the Church (i.e. the Lutherans) of his own time (col. 900). Even closer to Svaning is Melanchthon's parallel between the period of Lutheran reform and the time of the apostles, where the true doctrine had to fight against error.[24]

---

[22] I have discussed the Melanchthonian character of the above quoted passage from Svaning in another context, Skovgaard-Petersen 1998a. On Melanchthon's influence on historical and political discourse in sixteenth-century Denmark, see further Skovgaard-Petersen 1998c.

[23] *Hæc fuit tum illa gratia, quam pro repurgata Ecclesiæ doctrina, a tot idolatricis cultibus, a tot crassissimorum errorum tenebris, Deo optimo Maximo nostri referebant. Non ei absimilis gratiæ, quam olim in primordio primitivæ Ecclesiæ, suis piis Regibus exhibuerunt, quorum alios interfecerunt, ac martyrio coronarunt, alios Regno ejectos in exilium exegerunt, alios aliis modis excruciatos e medio sustulerunt. Faxit omnipotens Deus noster, ut hanc lucem quam postremis hisce senescentis mundi temporibus post tantas tenebras nobis accendit [...] agnoscamus, ut diu, verbi ipsius lux, nobis nostrisque successoribus luceat, nec permittat propter nostram ingratitudinem, atque negligentiam, eam extingui [...]* (Svaning 1658, 141-42). It is not clear to me which kings Svaning here refers to as persecuted Christians; perhaps it is simply a metaphor for leading Christians.

[24] *Carion's Chronicle*, cols. 922-23.

These are ideas which are also found elsewhere in Melanchthon's writings.[25] But even if we cannot claim with certainty that it is *Carion's Chronicle* that lies behind the passage quoted from Svaning, I think it is true to say that Svaning here places national history within the frame of Melanchthonian universal history, which is synthesized in his reworking of *Carion's Chronicle*.

Judging from the preserved parts, Svaning's *History of Denmark* shares another characteristic with Melanchthon's chronicle: events are often interpreted in terms of punishments or rewards from God. The course of history as described by Svaning is fundamentally governed by divine justice.[26]

In this respect, and in his Melanchthonian overall view of world history, Svaning's *History of Denmark* resembles other contemporary historical writings of Danes who had studied in Wittenberg, including his successor Anders Sørensen Vedel.[27] Though to the next generations of historians Christian moralism and Protestant world history is a less important issue, Meursius's *Historia Danica*, strongly moralistic as it is, also bears some resemblance to the work of Svaning in this respect.

If Christian moralism came to play a smaller role in the works of later historians, the same cannot be said of the two other topics to be discussed here in relation to Svaning. Both the earliest history and the proper treatment of Sweden presented recurrent problems to historians of the following generations.

In the case of Danish origins the problem was two-fold. In the traditional account related by Saxo the Danes were an autochthonous people. Danish history begins with the eponymous King Dan, son of Humble

---

[25] In his exposition of Melanchthon's view of history Fraenkel includes many earlier writings of Melanchthon's (Fraenkel 1961, 52-109).

[26] A point in question is the history of Christianus II, which Svaning throughout sees as an example of God's wrath against the arrogant tyrant, culminating towards the end, where the imprisoned king at last realizes that kings should always fear God, lest His anger cause their downfall, and expresses his newly acquired humility towards God in a repentant speech (Svaning, 1658, 488-89).

[27] In his history of Danish literature Oluf Friis stresses the strong influence of the Melanchthonian view of history on Danish humanists in the sixteenth century. He talks of a Melanchthonian school, in which he no doubt counts both Svaning and Vedel. The present survey owes much to Friis's suggestions (Friis 1945, 404-36). Examples of such Melanchthonian historical works are Erasmus Lætus's history of the birth and baptism of Christian IV, written 1577 (Lætus, edd. Skovgaard-Petersen & Zeeberg 1992), and Anders Sørensen Vedel's prefaces to his translation of Saxo (1575) and to his edition of Adam of Bremen (1579). Cf. further Skovgaard-Petersen 1998a & 1998c.

and that is all we learn about Dan's origin.[28] No attempt is made to connect Dan and the Danes with other peoples known from classical texts or with the Bible. But already in the late Middle Ages this missing link between Dan and the Bible was considered unsatisfactory. For instance, in the fifteenth-century Rhymed Chronicle (*Den danske Rimkrønike*) Dan's father is presented as a descendant of Japhet, son of Noah. In the sixteenth century this was an established view not only in Scandinavia. Melanchthon for one had, in the *Carion's Chronicle*, depicted modern Scandinavians as descendants of the Goths and the Cimbrians, whose roots, along with other peoples known from classical sources, went back to Noah.

It appears from the preserved table of contents of Svaning's *History* that he adhered to the list of kings as found in Saxo. His history began with King Dan. But apparently he combined the kings from Saxo with accounts of diverse peoples which were known from classical and early medieval sources and were regarded, in the sixteenth century, as Scandinavian ancestors: *Saxones, Vandali, Cimbri, Gothi, Longobardi*. He included a number of small chapters on these peoples, such as *De migratione Gothorum ex Dania et Svecia in Hungariam, Thraciam, Italiam*. With this he established a connection with the Graeco-Roman world. And in the light of Melanchthon's procedure I think we can be fairly sure that Svaning also furnished the Danes, probably through the Cimbrians, with biblical origins (one of the introductory chapters is entitled *De origine Danorum*).

Having thus made up for one deficiency in Saxo's *Gesta Danorum*, he was still faced with another problem concerning its account of the early past. During the sixteenth century the credibility of the first part of Saxo's work had become a matter of dispute among both Danish and foreign intellectuals, who pointed to the many magical elements and fantastic episodes, such as the travels of one Torkil to regions beyond the human world (VIII, Ch. xiv-xv) or the virgin who was raped by a bear and later gave birth to a son (X, Ch. xiv, 15).[29] This scepticism was a general trend in the studies of the various national pasts in Europe. Already at the beginning of the sixteenth century Polydore Vergil had called into question the mythical past of England, as it was related in Geoffrey of

---

[28] The ideological implications of the autochthonous origin are discussed in Mortensen 1987.

[29] Stephanius prefaced his commentary to Saxo, the *Notæ uberiores* (1645) with a catalogue of quotations from such critics of Saxo, among others Ludovicus Vives and Jean Bodin.

Monmouth's *History* (written c. 1130). Similarly the Trojan origins of France received only lukewarm attention in Paolo Emilio's *History of France*. The English historian William Camden (1551-1623) summed up the new orientation:

> Nevertheless in our era, which has escaped from those deadly shades of ignorance, the French have disclaimed their progenitor Francio as a fabrication, the Scots of sounder opinion have scorned their Scota, and Truth herself has also put to flight Hiberus, Danus, Brabo and all the remaining insubstantial heroes of that grain; therefore let others show us why Britons should cling to their Brutus, but I myself see no reason whatever why I should support a character whom Vives, Adrianus Junius, Buchanan, Polydore, Bodin and other men of deep penetration reject with unanimous judgement, and a very large number of our native scholars refuse to acknowledge, as being a counterfeit.[30]

A forceful rejection of the early legendary part of Saxo (the period before c. 800 AD) is found in an interesting letter by Anders Fos (1543-1607), bishop of Bergen in Norway, in which he declares that "Saxo is an ocean of fables and lies". At least the part of Saxo's work dealing with the period before c. 800 AD is in his view completely untrustworthy. His point of view deserves particular attention here, since it was voiced in connection with Svaning's *History of Denmark*. One of the censors who were to determine its fate around 1581-83, was Anders Fos's relative Desiderius Fos (who died c. 1599).[31] Asked for advice as it seems, Anders Fos in the letter suggests that only the part of Svaning's history that continued Saxo ought to be published. It seems likely, though it cannot be proved, that Anders Fos's arguments actually influenced the censors' decision not to have Svaning's work printed.[32]

---

[30] *Sed cum nostra ætate, quæ e fatalibus illis ignorantiæ tenebris emersit, Franci suo Francioni tanquam ementito patri renunciauerint, Scoti sanioris iudicij suam Scotam reiecerint, Hiberum etiam, Danum, Brabonem, et ejus farinæ cæteros vmbratiles heroas veritas ipsa fugauerit: cur Britanni suo Bruto adhæres-cant doceant alij, ego vero nihil video, quomodo illum suffulciam, quem Viues, Hadrianus Iunius, Buchananus, Polidorus, Bodinus, et alij magno iudicio viri coniunctis sententijs denegant, et ex nostratibus quamplurimi eruditi, vt supposititium non agnoscunt* (Camden 1590 (1st ed. 1586), 7).

[31] See Rørdam's preface to his edition (1875) of Fos's letter, entitled *Censura de Saxone Grammatico*. It appears from the royal letter in which Svaning was ordered to submit his writings and material that his *History* was to be scrutinized by the chancellor, Kaas, and other members of the Privy Council. The censure of the university professors, among whom was Desiderius Fos, probably followed that of the councillors (Ilsøe 1984, 246).

[32] As argued by Rørdam in the preface to his edition (1875) of Fos.

The tension between the legendary tradition from Saxo and the scattered information to be dug out from classical and early medieval texts is also evident in the works of Pontanus and Meursius. Although other Danish historians such as Vedel, Huitfeldt and Venusin shared Fos's distrust in Saxo, it was left to Pontanus to produce an alternative version of the early part of Danish history, based on classical and early medieval testimonies. Meursius, on the other hand, though leaving out the obviously fantastic elements of the *Gesta Danorum*, kept to the tradition from Saxo.

Svaning's inclusion of the oldest kings may have contributed to the rejection of his work, as we saw. So may his treatment of the Swedes. Recognizing the many polemical pamphlets as one of the causes of the Seven Years War between Sweden and Denmark (1563-70), the authors of the peace treaty of 1570 had included a prohibition against writings insulting the neighbour country. The prohibition remained in force (although not in times of war) until 1675,[33] and may well have been a primary motive for the Danish government not to engage itself officially in the production of a new national history in the first decades after 1570.[34] In one case, however, the highly anti-Swedish epic poem *Margaretica* (1573) by Erasmus Lætus (1526-82), the government was probably involved, since the author, who had been ennobled by the king in 1569, enjoyed the status of a kind of court poet.[35] But if the poem was indeed the result of some sort of agreement with members of the government, the author did his utmost to hide this circumstance. He published the work during travel abroad with a dedication to Elizabeth of England, not to a Dane; in glaring contrast to his practice in the other poems published on the same journey, he avoided all mention of the king and other prominent Danes in the Preface.

Cautiousness seems, in short, to have marked the Danish government's handling of relations with Sweden. Seen in this light, Svaning's rather aggressive treatment of Sweden may well have caused concern, judging from the preserved parts of his history, which concern mainly the three first Oldenburg kings. After all, a substantial part was probably written in the aggressive atmosphere before or during the Seven Years

---

[33] On this topic, see Harald Ilsøe 1973.

[34] As suggested by Harald Ilsøe 1984, 252-53.

[35] The *Margaretica* (Frankfurt a.M. 1573) celebrates the Danish victory over Sweden in 1389 which led to the formation of the Union of Kalmar in 1397, alluding at the same time to the Seven Years War, so that it is thereby depicted as a much more convincing Danish victory than in fact it was. See Skovgaard-Petersen 1987 & 1988.

War, when the prohibition had not yet been made; his *History of Johannes* was, as we saw, published as a counterpart to Magnus's attacks.

This theory gains support from Christen Friis's objection in 1629 to Meursius's first draft of his Oldenburg history. The chancellor, so Meursius was informed by Jesper Brochmand, found the description of the Swedes too fierce, that is, potentially insulting.[36] Now, since this part of his work was a close adaptation of Svaning, it is reasonable to assume that Friis's fears were shared by the censors of Svaning's work fifty years earlier. Meursius no doubt softened the tone. In the printed version of 1630 much of Svaning's polemic has been left out, probably as a result of the chancellor's intervention.

As I shall argue in more detail later (Chapter VII), Svaning's *History of Denmark* as a whole was presumably written as a counterpart to Magnus's work.

4. *Anders Sørensen Vedel*[37]

When Svaning submitted his *History* for censorial examination in 1579, he did not act on his own initiative, but on an order from the chancellor, Niels Kaas. Probably he did not regard it as finished yet. Anyway, a younger man, Anders Sørensen Vedel (1542-1616) had already been striving for some time to obtain an agreement with the government to the effect that he should compose a history of Denmark.

After studying, among other places, in Wittenberg with Caspar Peucer (Melanchthon's son-in-law), Vedel served in 1568-81 as a court preacher in Copenhagen, during which period he published a number of religious and historical works, the most important being his Danish translation of Saxo's *Gesta Danorum* (1575) and his *editio princeps* of Adam of Bremen's *Historia ecclesiastica* (1579). In the prefaces to both works he betrays the influence of Wittenberg. Danish history is, in the Saxo-Preface, described in much the same terms as in the quotation from Svaning above:

---

[36] Letter from Jesper Brochmand to Meursius, dated January 4, 1629: *Libros rerum Danicarum, quos Illustris Regiae Maiestatis Cancellario commisisti legendos, mea opera tibi remitti voluit. Immane quantum placeat et concinnior dictio, et compendio descripta Historia Danica. Subveretur tamen Illustris ipsius Magnificentia, ne Sveci alicubi paulo mordaciore dictionis sale perfricentur* (Meursius 1741-63, XI, no. 639).

[37] The basic biography of Vedel is C.L. Wegener's *Historiske Efterretninger om Anders Sørensen Vedel*, published as an appendix to his edition of Vedel's translation into Danish of Saxo's *Gesta Danorum* (1851). On Vedel in English see Mortensen 1995.

initial piety (with the advent of Christianity) gradually degenerated into papal and monkish depravity, but has recently, in these last days of the world, been restored by the Lutheran Reformation.[38]

Like Svaning, Vedel was never officially appointed historiographer, but he worked in agreement with the government. In his case also, a crucial role must be assigned to the chancellor, Niels Kaas (1534-94), successor of Johan Friis. It was to him that Vedel in 1578 addressed the elegant treatise entitled *Commentarius de scribenda historia Danica*, in which he outlined his ideas for a new history of Denmark, thereby indirectly applying for a post as royal historiographer.[39] Kaas then, it seems, presented the matter to the king and the Privy Council in 1578, and though the result was not the official engagement as historiographer that Vedel had probably hoped for, his project at least obtained some support from the authorities. Svaning's forced surrender of both his own manuscripts and his collection of documents in the following year is an indication of Kaas's support of Vedel; the documents were to be handed over to Vedel. He then settled in Ribe in 1581 in order to dedicate himself to the writing of his history of Denmark.

Also like Svaning, however, he was obliged, thirteen years later, in 1594, to submit whatever he had written together with the documents he had in his possession. But unlike Svaning next to nothing seems to have come of his project. Only his preface and the history of the king, *Svend Tveskæg* (d. 1014), both written in Danish, are known to have been completed. Both survive today along with a detailed plan of the work. In his

---

[38] I have discussed Vedel's preface to Saxo in further detail in Skovgaard-Petersen 1998a, and his preface to Adam of Bremen in Skovgaard-Petersen 1998c.

[39] It has usually been assumed, by Wegener, Ellen Jørgensen and others, that Vedel wrote the work *after* he had been asked by representatives of the government to take upon himself the task of writing Denmark's history. This was what Vedel himself wanted the world to believe, when in the early 1590s he wrote the preface to his Danish history (on which see below). But as Ilsøe has shown, Vedel in the late 1570s played an active role in outmanoeuvring Svaning in order to take over the historiographical project; the treatise is to be read as Vedel's application to become historiographer (Ilsøe 1984).

The *commentarius* has been preserved in two versions, both in Vedel's own hand, the Latin one from 1578 (the Royal Library, Copenhagen, ms. *Gl. kgl. S.* 2437, 4to) and a revised and slightly enlarged Danish translation from 1581 (*ibidem* Ms. *Gl. kgl. S.* 2435, 4to). The relation between the two versions has been discussed by Lars Boje Mortensen (1991). While clearly influenced by the many contemporary theoretical works on historiography, the so-called *artes historicæ*, especially that of François Bauduin, Vedel's work is of a more practical nature, concerned with the concrete problems of writing a national history (Mortensen 1998a & 1998b). The Danish version has been published by Rasmus Nyerup in 1787 and by Gustav Albeck, *Humanister i Jylland*, 1959, 130-52.

case, then, we are not dealing with a direct influence on Pontanus or Meursius. Rather he deserves attention here for his visions and ideas, pointing both back to Svaning and forward to Pontanus.[40]

Vedel's above-mentioned treatise, the *Commentarius de scribenda historia Danica* from 1578 is an interesting piece of historical theory. It bears witness to the author's knowledge of contemporary historical theory as well as to his own ambitions. Here I shall just single out a few points for discussion.

The conflict between national, legendary tradition (i.e. Saxo) and foreign testimonies is also evident in Vedel's considerations. Well aware, apparently, of the widespread scepticism towards Saxo, he wants to leave all fabulous elements out:

> and we barely have one Saxo, so that whenever I think to myself how much is contained in him which we would rather were not, and how much is lacking which we would rather were there, I cannot reflect on this without groans and sighs,[41]

is his somewhat resigned judgement of Saxo. In line with this distrust he firmly states that only after the arrival of Christianity and literacy can Danish history be written on a solid basis; the first historical epoch of Danish history, he says, begins c. 700 AD (13v-14r). This is the first chronologically fixed point of Danish history. Vedel, in short, expresses much the same view of Saxo as Anders Fos was to do a few years later.

Does this mean that Vedel here recommends the drastic procedure of beginning a new Danish history from 700 AD, leaving out everything preceding this date? That seems to be the case, but it is perhaps significant that he does not explicitly take up the problem of what to do with Saxo's early history.

The reliability limit of 700 AD only concerns the national tradition, however. The various peoples known from classical and early medieval sources to have migrated from Scandinavia are also given a place in Vedel's ideal history. Their Danish origin should in fact be clear from the start. After a geographical description and an account of Danish ways of life (*mores*), Vedel wants the historian to turn to the first inhabitants:

---

[40] Pontanus did make use of some of Vedel's other writings. In his *History of Denmark* he refers to Vedel's translation of Saxo (216) and to his collection of old Danish ballads (310-11). In a letter to Lyschander of August 1622 (Matthæus 1695, no. 101) he also refers to a genealogical work by Vedel, which may be an unprinted piece of writing.

[41] *et nos vix vnum Saxonem habemus, cui quantum insit, quod abesse, quantum desit, quod inesse mallemus, quotiescunque mecum cogito, non possum sine gemitu et suspiriis recordari* (Vedel, *Commentarius*, 7r).

> Moreover a close enquiry should be made as to the identity of these lands' first inhabitants and the reason for their being here.[42]

– No doubt, these considerations would involve an establishment of the biblical connection. Further, the language of these first Danes should be discussed and their various migrations outlined, with particular focus on the motives behind them (12v-13r). But their history in their new homes should be treated elsewhere and separately, not as part of the historical account proper (16r). Exact chronology was another of Saxo's weak points, Vedel notes. (A reference to the birth of Christ and one to Charlemagne is really all there is). This was a point also raised by Anders Fos, and it is related to the two men's general dissatisfaction with the few points of contact between Saxo's account and foreign traditions. Vedel announces his intention to provide a chronological survey at the end, and also to include references to years in the narrative, though discreetly, for stylistic reasons. He also recommends that genealogical relations should be made clear.

The most important object of historical writing, he declares, is to give a trustworthy explanation and account of the dissemination of the true religion. Again the influence from Melanchthon is clearly to be seen; nations (*respublicæ*) are established by God in order that He can protect His flock (14v-15r). This is a recurrent idea in Melanchthon's *Carion's Chronicle*: "[God] wishes realms to be lodgings for the Church" (*vult [Deus] imperia esse hospitia Ecclesiae*)[43]– "the Church" denoting the group of true believers found throughout history.

Further information about Vedel's ideal history of Denmark is to be found in his detailed plan outlined some years later, in the mid-1580s probably, when he was engaged in writing his Danish history. This is a document which bears ample witness to Vedel's high-flying ambitions. The work outlined here was to be divided into twenty-two books, to which was to be added a separate account of the history of the Danish Church and Danish learning in seven books.[44] In line with the recommendations of the *Commentarius*, he intended the first books to give a geographical description of Denmark, present Danish ways of living,

---

[42] *Atque inquirendum est studiose, qui, et qua occasione primi extiterint harum terrarum incolæ* (Vedel, *Commentarius*, 12v).

[43] Melanchthon 1844 (1st ed. 1558), 718.

[44] The plan has been published by Wegener in his *Historiske efterretninger om Anders Sørensen Vedel*, 140-44 (see note above), after a ms. in the Royal Library of Copenhagen (ms. *Gl. Kgl. Saml.* 824 fol).

and to discuss the first inhabitants of Denmark, their language, origins and migrations. This treatment, we learn, was to provide the link with the Bible; the ancestors of the Danes were to be traced back to Noah.

As we saw, Svaning also apparently started with a description of Denmark, Norway and Sweden. But the meticulousness with which Vedel intended to describe the country in the first three books is remarkable. It seems that he planned to take up much the same topics as Pontanus later included in the huge *Chorographica descriptio* of his *History of Denmark*.

Interestingly, Vedel does not seem to have adhered to his rigid rejection in the *Commentarius* of the first part of Saxo's *Gesta Danorum*. According to his plan the fourth book should go briefly through the pagan Danish kings, from Dan to Gorm the Old. He may of course, as Pontanus would do later, have intended to express his own scepticism regarding these traditions; nevertheless in the light of his remarks in the *Commentarius*, it is noteworthy that he did not simply leave them out.

While Svaning, it seems, inserted chapters on the migrations and conquerings of the various peoples in the course of his narrative, Vedel in the *Commentarius* recommended another strategy, namely that these foreign events should be treated separately, in order not to confuse the reader and divert his attention from the history of the Danes in Denmark. When writing the plan he seems to have gone one step further and left out the foreign history, limiting the account of the migrations to the introductory chapter where the focus would be on their background in Denmark. Pontanus would later adopt the opposite strategy, emphasizing the deeds of the various peoples in their new homes in Italy, Spain, England and France.

In the *Commentarius* Vedel had declared, with Melanchthonian echoes, the dissemination of Christianity in Denmark to be the most important theme of such a history. From the plan it appears that he intended to devote five books, apart from the twenty-two books of political history, to the history of the Church in Denmark. According to the preserved description they would have been strongly reminiscent of *Carion's Chronicle*, dealing first with the period from the creation of the world to the settlements of Noah's progeny, then with Satan's dominion over the Northern countries until God in his mercy liberated them from darkness, then with the first healthy period of Christianity and the ensuing increase of papistic abuse, and finally with the restoration of God's holy Word and the true doctrine. – Again, as in the fragment from Svaning, Danish history is placed within the perspective of Melanchthonian universal history.

But it was not in the spirit of *Carion's Chronicle* that Vedel chose to separate ecclesiastical history from the main account; at least this division
suggests that the focus of the rest of the work would have been on secular matters. When writing the preface to his Danish history (which he
probably did in 1590 or 1591[45]), Vedel made clear that universal history
and national history are two different types of historiography, observing
different rules.[46] Perhaps he here implied, among other things, that a
national history should not take over the concept of history of *Carion's
Chronicle* where all history is seen as sacred history.[47]

Ecclesiastical history is not the only topic which is singled out for special treatment in the plan. Cultural history was to be the subject of the
third book, *Ethographia gentis Danicæ*, encompassing the manners and customs of the Danes and the common man's way of living from the earliest
times. Intellectual history, that is, a survey of the most learned men in
Danish history, was to be treated in a book appended to the five books of
Church history.

Vedel was probably the first Danish exponent of the opinion that the
proper subject matter of history was not only politics, wars and religion
but the whole sphere of human life. It was a view held by French
philosophers and jurists such as Jean Bodin and Fr. Bauduin, with whose
theoretical writings on history Vedel was familiar.[48] In Germany intellectual history was emerging as a branch of history. Reiner Reineccius in his
introductory lecture in Helmstedt in 1583 divided history into three
parts, ecclesiastical, political, and intellectual.[49] No less important, prac-
tising historians were beginning to include such antiquarian, or, in a
broad sense, cultural, matters when writing national histories, influenced

[45] The dating is Wegener's in his *Historiske efterretninger om Anders Sørensen Vedel*, 171 (see note above).

[46] *Og hvad ville vii sige om den ordden og Skik, som enhver historie effter Sin art udkrefver? Thi ligesom alle historier er ikke en Slaus, saa kunde de ikke heller alle Skrifvis effter en form og Maneer, ikke mindre end som alle Skoe kunde giøris ofuer Een læst* [...] *Derfaare fattes og dannes verdsens og de fire Monarchiers his-torie udi Sin form for Sig, og Et Enligt Kongerigis historie udi Sin fadson for Sig* (150). Vedel's Preface was published by P. F. Suhm in 1779.

[47] It has been claimed that *Carion's Chronicle* treats secular and sacred history as to some extent independent areas. Against this Peter Fraenkel has convincingly argued in favour of the view, that "Melanchthon knew only one kind of history and [...] this was essentially sacred history" (Fraenkel 1961, 59-61).

[48] For the accomplishments of this French school within law, philology and historical theory, see Donald R. Kelley 1970. Vedel's knowledge of these authors has been studied by Lars Boje Mortensen 1998a & 1998b; cf. also Harald Ilsøe 1984, 240-41.

[49] Adalbert Klempt 1960, 69sq.

by contemporary thematic descriptions of national antiquities, the Renaissance prototype being Flavio Biondo's *Italia illustrata* (1474). We shall return to this subject in connection with Pontanus, since (as already suggested) in this respect Vedel may be said to anticipate what Pontanus eventually carried out; in his *Chorographica descriptio* attention is paid to manners and customs along with national character, and a survey of Danish men of learning is also found.

Separate books (21 and 22) of Vedel's planned history were to be devoted to genealogical and chronological surveys. These ancillary disciplines of history were developing rapidly in Vedel's day, and his teacher in Rostock David Chytræus (1530-1600) had emphasized their importance both in teaching and in writing.[50] Vedel intended to provide his readers with information on the family relations of the individual Danish kings and to relate Danish history to the history of the four world monarchies. Again the resemblance with Pontanus is noteworthy. He has not, as Vedel planned to do, separated genealogy and chronology from the historical account proper. But throughout, Pontanus dates the events of Danish history not only in relation to the birth of Christ but also to the history of the four world monarchies; and genealogical tables are frequent.[51]

5. Niels Krag[52]

In 1594, when Vedel was forced to submit all his documents and manuscripts to the Danish government, a new man was already waiting to take over. This was Niels Krag (c. 1550-1602), a professor of Greek at the University of Copenhagen with diplomatic experience. Unlike Svaning and Vedel, Krag was officially appointed Royal Historiographer. The

---

[50] Detloff Klatt 1908, 39-45, 50sq.

[51] Though no doubt originally planning to write in Latin, Vedel changed his mind and composed his history (the part(s) he actually completed) in Danish. This is clear from the preface; he has written the work in Danish, he explains, on the advice of "those who have most influence", in order to improve the possibility of making corrections before it was translated into another language (Vedel, ed. Suhm 1779, 158). Cf. Harald Ilsøe 1984, 244, and Lars Boje Mortensen 1991.

[52] In the copious preface with which Hans Gram furnished his edition of Krag's *History of Christianus III* he also included a detailed biography of the author with particular attention to his literary production (Krag, ed. Hans Gram 1737, 3-32). Rørdam, in his much shorter life of Krag, supplemented this with further biographical information (Rørdam 1868-77, III, 522-41). See also Ellen Jørgensen 1931, 101-6.

architects behind the new post of Royal Historiographer were prominent members of the government, and apparently it was the rather pro-Swedish point of view put forward by David Chytræus in his *Saxonia* (1st ed. 1585) that now convinced them of the necessity of an active historio-graphical strategy. Krag was given the official support that Vedel had lacked, both in terms of money and assistance and in terms of access to the archives. He was told, as mentioned in Chapter II, to finish a history of Denmark within six years (like Lyschander and Pontanus later), and (also like his successors) he was to receive 500 *daler* a year and 100 extra for assistants.[53]

He was ordered to begin with recent history, that of Christian III (1536-59) and of Frederik II (1559-88), and then to work his way back-wards as far as King Frotho, that is until the birth of Christ. Christian III's accession to the throne was regarded as an important event, the beginning of the Protestant era, and the lack of historical accounts of his reign and the Lutheran Reformation in Denmark had often been re-gretted. Besides, Chytræus's above-mentioned *Saxonia* also dealt with recent times. The appointment letter explicitly mentions a Latin history.[54]

But for all his official support, Krag did not get any closer to the goal than his predecessors. The expiration of the (somewhat optimistic) six years' term – during which Krag was also sent on several diplomatic mis-sions by the Danish government – was followed by his death in 1602, and all he left was an unfinished *Historia regis Christiani III*, covering the period 1533-50.[55] The manuscript was, like Svaning's, preserved in the University

---

[53] Krag's letter of appointment is printed in A.D. Jørgensen: *Udsigt over de danske Rigsarkivers Historie* (1884), 232-33.

[54] The account given here of the motives behind Krag's appointment is based on Harald Ilsøe 1984, who notes (251) that Krag had the personal qualifications that Vedel lacked, prac-tical experience as a diplomat and a more thorough classical training. In pointing to Chytræus's *Saxonia* as the most likely incentive for the government's official involvement, Ilsøe argues against the hitherto prevailing view (going back to Hans Gram, see next note) that Krag's engagement was connected with George Buchanan's treatment of Danish-Scot-tish matters in his *Rerum Scoticarum historia* of 1582, notably with regard to the Orkneys; but Krag was told to begin with Christian III's and Frederik II's reigns, which would not offer any opportunity to take up these matters. Chytræus's work, on the other hand, deals with recent history.

[55] Published by Hans Gram in 1737. Krag also made preparations for the remaining part of his history. He collected sources for medieval and earlier history (Ilsøe 1963-66), and also received material from the Icelandic historian Arngrímur Jónsson (Arngrímur, ed. Jakob Benediktsson, 1950-57), e.g. IV, 14.

Library.[56] Though not printed until 1737, the work was used by historians in the seventeenth century, primarily Meursius and Stephanius.

Merely a torso though it was, Krag's *History of Christianus III* broke new ground. Krag had been given access to the royal archives (and other private and public archives), and his account is to a considerable extent based on original documents. Also noteworthy is its classicism. I think it is fair to say that Krag's *History of Christianus III*, more than the works of Pontanus and Meursius, belongs to the tradition of humanist historiography established by Leonardo Bruni's *Historiarum Florentini populi libri XII* (completed around 1440; 1st printed ed. 1516). The language and style is close to that of the great Roman historians, and like them he focuses almost exclusively on politics. Krag does not share Vedel's interest in cultural and ecclesiastical history. Unlike Meursius he only rarely interprets events as results of God's interference.

With Krag we approach the world of Pontanus and Meursius. Like them he combined classical scholarship with national historiography. The publication in 1589 of his description of ancient Sparta, the *De republica Lacedaemoniorum* had secured him international fame, and among his admirers was the young Meursius whose interests went in the same direction. In 1599, when Meursius himself, young though he was, had already gained a certain scholarly reputation, Krag made a short stop in Leiden on his way home from a diplomatic visit to England. Meursius tried to have a meeting arranged, but in vain. Shortly afterwards Meursius, regretting the failed opportunity of meeting the famous author of the Spartan description, dedicated his *Exercitationes criticae* to him.[57] – By this time, it seems, Krag had also made the acquaintance of Pontanus in Copenhagen.[58]

6. Arild Huitfeldt[59]

The period 1595-1604, when Krag and later his successor Venusin were at work as royal historiographers, saw the publication of a history of Denmark in ten volumes, covering the whole of Danish history up to the

---

[56] It did not burn in the great fire of 1728 and is still extant in the Arnamægnean collection in Copenhagen (AM 26, fol.), with marginal notes made by Meursius and others.

[57] Krag, ed. Hans Gram 1737, 15sq (Gram's preface).

[58] Cf. the contemporary biography of Pontanus, *Vita et obitus*, 1640, 8.

[59] Huitfeldt's life is the subject of an informative monograph by H.F. Rørdam (1896), which also deals with his *History of Denmark*. More recently Harald Ilsøe has thrown new light on many aspects of this work in various articles.

Arild Huitfeldt. (Copper engraving by Albert Haelwegh 1652 based on a now lost painting). (Museum of National History, Frederiksborg).

death of Christian III in 1559. The author was the nobleman Arild Huit-feldt (1546-1609), member of the Privy Council and chancellor of the realm (*Cancellarius regni*). Based upon original documents, foreign histori-ography, both medieval and more recent, Danish medieval annals, and his sixteenth-century predecessors, Huitfeldt's work provided a huge increase in knowledge of the Danish past. In the following centuries it was widely read, exerting a considerable influence not only on the study of history but also more generally on Danish cultural life.[60]

Denmark had gained its up-to-date national history, but it was written in Danish, not in Latin, and was stylistically imperfect. While fulfilling some of the requirements, it was still not designed to impress foreigners and convince them of Danish points of view; nor was it satisfying from a rhetorical point of view. Huitfeldt himself was well aware of these deficiencies. In the preface to the first of the volumes, *Christian III*, of 1595, he presents his work as material collected in order that others could then compose a more refined work in Latin. No doubt he had the recently appointed Krag in mind, who had been told to begin with the history of Christian III. In fact, when already in about 1580 Huitfeldt had started collecting material for a history of Denmark, it was presum-ably solely to assist Vedel. Apparently Krag's entering the scene promp-ted Huitfeldt to publish this material, thereby indicating that it was to be seen as a work of history in its own right; but he did so knowing (in Ilsøe's words) that Krag would get the last word, in Latin. He intended his work to be a help for the production of the Latin history, as he keeps reminding his readers not only in the first preface, but in the prefaces to most of the following volumes.[61]

The full-scale Latin adaptation of Huitfeldt eventually turned out to be composed not by Krag, but, twenty to thirty years later, by Pontanus. He followed Huitfeldt closely from about 1200 AD and also consulted him, though less extensively, in the preceeding period. Huitfeldt's ar-rangement of the material was strictly annalistic, with notes on diverse events listed in a rather haphazard order. Another prominent feature is the multitude of documents quoted *verbatim*. True, quotations of docu-ments were found in much contemporary historiography, but in Huit-feldt's work their dominant position definitely marks the work as a col-

---

[60] Ilsøe 1967.

[61] In this account of the relationship between Huitfeldt and the contemporary historians, I rely on Harald Ilsøe 1984, 247-48, 256-58.

lection of material rather than as a finished history itself. In these respects, among others, Pontanus often adhered very closely to his source. He, too, quoted a considerable number of documents, and he kept to the annalistic arrangement, though occasionally rearranging the order of events within a year in order to achieve a higher degree of internal coherence. It is, then, an open question whether Pontanus's treatment of Huitfeldt's work was in fact the stylistic elaboration that Huitfeldt himself had had in mind. Arguably Pontanus's text with its high proportion of quotations would not have fulfilled Huitfeldt's demand for "a more refined and perfect history in Latin", as he puts it in one place.[62]

Stylistically imperfect, Huitfeldt was a pioneer not only in his grasp of the enormous material and the use of original documents, but also in his interpretations of the past. He shares the didactic view of history with earlier humanist historians. History repeats itself. But the lessons to be learnt from his account are mostly of a concrete, political nature. The Christian moralism of Melanchthon and his pupils is not very pronounced. Being himself a member of the high nobility, he was a firm supporter of the Danish constitution after the Reformation with its division of power between the king and the Privy Council, and he also interpreted older history in this light, stressing that Denmark was an elective, not a hereditary kingdom and that the right to elect the king belonged to the nobility.[63]

He does not seem to have shared Vedel's ambitions regarding separate treatment of cultural and intellectual history. He concentrates on politics, especially diplomacy, with occasional notes on such matters as new buildings, unusual weather conditions, important foreign events, fire, etc. Only ecclesiastical history is dealt with separately; no other topics, such as Danish topography or intellectual history, are singled out for separate treatment, as Vedel had planned to do.

As to the beginning of Danish history he makes quite clear that it is all very uncertain. He himself starts with Dan, and then follows (with minor alterations) the list of kings found in Saxo. And though he does discuss various attempts to date the reign of Dan in relation to the beginning of the world (*annus mundi*) and biblical history, he refrains from any solution.

---

[62] Preface to *Christianus III* (1595).

[63] These ideological aspects of Huitfeldt's history are discussed in Oluf Friis 1945, 433sqq, in Harald Ilsøe's article on Huitfeldt in *Dansk biografisk leksikon* (1980), and, along with stylistic remarks, in Harald Ilsøe 1967.

Nor does he try to establish a certain connection between biblical and Danish history, no doubt realizing the impossibility of finding the truth of these matters. Saxo, then, forms the backbone of his early history. But everything that seemed too fabulous has been cut out, he assures us in the preface to this volume, and the whole account of the early period, corresponding to the first half of Saxo, is heavily abbreviated. From around 700, when Denmark is mentioned in foreign sources, these are included together with Saxo. Huitfeldt regarded Saxo's lack of chrono-logical indications as one of his grave shortcomings. Throughout he has himself sought to make up for this deficiency by referring to computa-tions of sixteenth-century chronologers; but he cautiously abstained from putting precise dates to the pre-Christian kings.

7. Jon Jacobsen Venusin[64]

That Huitfeldt had not met the demands of a new history of Denmark in the eyes of the Danish government was clearly demonstrated by the appointment of a successor to Krag in 1602, Jon Jacobsen Venusin (d. 1608). Though the tangible results of his studies in Danish history were more meagre than any of his predecessors' – nothing is known from his hand except a collection of notes[65] – he stands out as an interesting the-oretician. Along with his work as historiographer, he was Professor of Rhetoric at the University of Copenhagen. Two collections of theses survive, *De historia* (1604) and *De fabulis* (1605), which point to his interest in contemporary discussions of historical theory and give some hints as to how he might have tackled the problems of the earliest history.[66]

The primary theme of his historical writings was the need to exclude all fabulous elements.[67] In the *De historia* he argues that it is not possible to obtain certain knowledge of the past before written sources exist, since oral traditions are not to be trusted. In the *De fabulis* both Saxo and foreign instances of fabulous historiography, especially Johannes Mag-

---

[64] Venusin has also been the subject of a comprehensive biography by H.F. Rørdam (Rør-dam 1874-77).

[65] The Royal Library of Copenhagen, Ms. *Ny Kgl. Saml.* 467 fol. The contents are summarized by Karsten Christensen 1978, 49-50.

[66] The *De historia* and its relation to contemporary theory of history is discussed in Skov-gaard-Petersen 1996.

[67] His appointment letter has not been preserved. Judging from his own activities he was to begin with the earliest history.

nus's Gothic fables, are criticized. He found Saxo unacceptable as the basis for early Danish history, and collected, as is evident from the surviving notes, a considerable number of testimonies from ancient and medieval authors on this period, probably with the intention of rewriting early Danish history on this basis.

Again, it was Pontanus who eventually realized his predecessor's intentions. As already mentioned, he actually managed to rewrite early Danish history on a classical basis, and also in other respects he seems to have shared views held by Venusin. While depriving Denmark of the long list of kings found in Saxo, both historians make up for this reduction by underlining the Danish origin of many peoples of the early Middle Ages. Both display a marked fondness for etymological deductions, finding the earliest mention of Denmark in the Roman geographer Pomponius Mela's *Sinus Codanus* (1st cent. AD). Ellen Jørgensen has suggested a direct influence of Venusin on Pontanus, who takes up some of the problems discussed by Venusin in the preserved notes.[68]

With Venusin's death, his rich collections of documents and historical accounts, which went back to Svaning, Vedel, and Krag, were placed in the University Library. This material (later supplemented) was regarded as national property and placed at the disposal of the royal historiographers.[69] Meursius, as we know, received the manuscript containing Svaning's *History of Denmark*. In the preface to his edition (1631) of Ailnothus's life of Canutus Sanctus he refers to his going through some writings (*monumenta*) from the "Copenhagen Library" (*Hafniensis Bibliotheca*), among which he found Ailnothus's work. Pontanus asked the chancellor, in a letter written in March 1621, to send "the topographical description that Vedel once began to outline", a reference, probably, to a draft of Vedel's introduction to his history of Denmark.[70] He may have received it and made use of it in his own *Chorographica descriptio*. In another letter he expresses his debt to Vedel on the subject of genealogy,

---

[68] Ellen Jørgensen 1931, 155.

[69] A survey of the accumulation of the historiographers' collections in the University Library (Copenhagen) is found in Birket Smith 1882, 22sqq. The material is known from lists made when the historians' collections were given to their successor or (from 1608) submitted to the University Library. Lists of Vedel's, Krag's, Huitfeldt's and the Norwegian historian Henrik Høyer's collections are found in Birket Smith 1882, 106sqq. A list of manuscripts which Stephanius had borrowed from the University Library is published by W. Christensen 1913.

[70] The letter (whose original is found in *Rigsarkivet* in Copenhagen) is printed in Rørdam's biography of Pontanus, Rørdam 1898, 476-77.

which perhaps may be taken to suggest that he had had access to Vedel's notes.[71] It is tempting to assume that he paid a visit to the University Library when he went to Copenhagen in 1618 and again in 1628. The points of agreement between him and Venusin might be explained by his having consulted notes by Venusin preserved in the University Library; at least one finds that the library possessed a treatise by Venusin arguing that the Normannic leader Rollo was Danish – and this is, as we shall see, a point of view shared by Pontanus (cf. Chapter VI).[72] Otherwise though, I have not been able to find concrete evidence in Pontanus's work for his having consulted the collections in the University Library. It is reasonable, with Birket Smith, to assume that neither Pontanus nor Meursius made extensive use of the historiographical collections.[73]

8. *Claus Christoffersen Lyschander*[74]

If Venusin in some ways prefigured Pontanus, the intervening historiographer Claus Christoffersen Lyschander (1558-1623/24) may well be labelled his contrast. As mentioned earlier (Chapter II), he was appointed historiographer in 1616 on terms similar to those of Krag; but after only two years Pontanus took over the task of writing a Latin history. The reason was probably sheer distrust on the part of the chancellor, Christen Friis, as to his ability to fulfil the task. He was allowed to keep his salary, however, maybe, as Rørdam suggests, in order that he could finish the studies on which he was working.

---

[71] Letter from Pontanus to Lyschander, dated August 25, 1622 (Matthæus 1695, no. 101).

[72] Birket Smith 1882, 145.

[73] Birket Smith 1882, 30n. Birket Smith, however, does seem to regard Pontanus's request, put forward in the preface to his *History of Denmark*, for archival material (i.e. material from the historiographical collections) as evidence of actual use, which it is not. In another context Pontanus refers to the *monumenta* placed at his disposal. This may simply refer to his having received a number of printed works from Copenhagen, perhaps a copy of Huitfeldt's *History of Denmark* (letter from Pontanus to Franciscus Gomarus, dated July 15, 1626 (Matthæus 1695, no. 94)). In the same context Pontanus refers to the *ampla seges* given to him by the king and the chancellor. I am not sure whether it refers to money or material. Anyway, since he here uses his historiographical obligations to explain why he is unable to accept an offer to become professor in Groningen, he underscores the binding and demanding character of the task. I do not think this letter provides an argument for Pontanus's having received much handwritten material from the University Library.

[74] In Lyschander's case also, H.F. Rørdam wrote the basic biography (1868). Lyschander's letter of appointment is printed here, 60-61. Together with the biography Rørdam edited Lyschander's survey of Danish authors and their work, the first of its kind (though unfinished).

The result of his studies, at least the only result printed in his own time, was the *Synopsis historiarum Danicarum* (in Danish), or *Slectebog*, which appeared in 1622.[75] In this huge work he provided Denmark with an early past like the one Johannes Magnus had given Sweden. Lyschander here goes back to Adam in his search for Danish roots. In establishing a connection between an early Danish past and the Bible he is not content with general theories of peoples, such as Cimbrians and Goths. No, he knows the names and accomplishments of all the Danish rulers from Noah onwards, and he depicts a veritable Cimbrian empire in these early days before Saxo's first kings.[76] This work, then, is the real Danish parallel and answer to Johannes Magnus's *History of the Swedish Kings*. But, written in Danish, it never had the foreign appeal which Magnus's work had. Nor did this romantic historical fantasy influence domestic opinion in the way Magnus's work did in Sweden, where Gothicism coloured royal propaganda as well as academic historical studies during the Swedish "Age of Great Power" (*Stormaktstiden*) in the seventeenth century.[77]

On the contrary, the book gave Lyschander a singularly bad reputation among later historians, at least in the eighteenth century. Pontanus had already noted, politely, in two private letters to Lyschander, some genealogical errors in the latter's account of Danish medieval history.[78] P.F. Suhm found in it "everything that foolhardiness and stupidity together can produce".[79] His contemporary, Ludvig Holberg (1684-1754), wondered in his own history of Denmark, *Danmarks riges historie* (1732-35), how anyone could ever have believed Lyschander's fantasies,[80] and he devoted one of his *Epistles* (no. 193) to an amusing parody on the whole

---

[75] The work is treated in Rørdam 1868, 82-103, Carl S. Petersen 1929, 385-87, and Oluf Friis 1945, 440-43.

[76] He built on a small treatise, *Umbra Saxonis*, written in the 1570s by the Danish vicar Niels Pedersen (c. 1522-79). Pedersen claims support in a document (obviously a forgery) of unspecified antiquity. Whether Lyschander realized the spuriousness of this so-called "gullandic" document, is not clear. Anyway he reproduced it in his *Synopsis*. See further Carl S. Petersen's treatment of this Danish branch of Gothicism (Carl S. Petersen 1929, 381-89).

[77] On Magnus's influence in *Stormaktstiden*, see Nordström 1934.

[78] Their extant correspondence, two letters from Pontanus and one from Lyschander, belongs to the years 1622-23. It is printed in Matthæus 1695, nos. 101-3. See also Rørdam's biography of Lyschander, Rørdam 1868, 87-89.

[79] P.F. Suhm (1792): *Tanker om de Vanskeligheder som møde ved at skrive den gamle danske og norske Historie*, 94.

[80] I, 34 (1856 ed.).

Gothicist line of thought, with special attention to the Swede Olaf Rud-
beck's *Atlantica* (1679).[81]

Lyschander, like Vedel, outlined an ambitious plan for a new history of
Denmark, a plan which is of some interest as an expression of the same
ideals as Vedel. Lyschander wanted to write an *histoire totale* of Denmark,
dealing not only with political history, but also with language, laws,
clothes, manners, ways of living, religion, schools and universities etc.[82]
In this ambition he resembles Pontanus, who, less high-flying, included
some of these subjects in his history.

Lyschander left behind the introduction to this history of Denmark,
in which he included a geographical description of the country.[83] It is less
detailed than the one written by Pontanus (the *Chorographica Regni Daniæ
descriptio*, which takes up pp. 637-812 of his 1631 edition), and unlike Pontanus's description it contains a fair amount of legendary lore. On the
basis of Suhm's partial edition of Lyschander's geographical part of the
introduction I have not been able to trace any borrowings in Pontanus's
Chorographica descriptio; but he may well have acquainted himself with
Lyschander's geographical studies in Copenhagen in 1628, since
Lyschander's notes on Danish provinces were found in the University
Library.[84]

9. Poetical History

While it was left to Pontanus and Meursius to fulfil the old demand of a
national history in Latin, a number of poetic accounts in Latin of Danish
history saw the light in the latter half of the sixteenth century. Erasmus
Lætus (1526-82) stands out as the author of two huge epics on Danish
history, the *Res Danicæ* (dealing with the whole course of history from
Noah to the wedding of Fridericus II in 1572) and the above-mentioned
Margaretica (about the battle in 1389 between the Swedish King Albrecht

---

[81] In his discussion of Lyschander, Carl S. Petersen draws attention to Holberg's parody
(Petersen 1929, 388-89).

[82] The plan is preserved in a manuscript in the Royal Library of Copenhagen (*Ny kgl. Saml.*
585, fol.); it is paraphrased in Rørdam's biography, 68-71.

[83] Preserved in the mss. *Ny Kgl. S.* 887, 4 and *Thott* 1545, 4 (the Royal Library in Copenhagen);
extracts of the geographical description were edited by P.F. Suhm in 1780. Cf. Rørdam 1868,
95sqq. I have only had access to Suhm's edition.

[84] *Lyschandri notitia provinciarum Daniæ etc.* (Birket Smith 1882, 138). I am grateful to Harald
Ilsøe for this suggestion.

and the Danish Queen Margrethe). Herman Chytræus wrote an epic on Danish history since the advent of Christianity, and Hans Jørgensen Sadolin published, in 1569, a collection of epigrams about the Danish kings from the legendary Dan to Fridericus II and his son Christianus (IV). Many others could be mentioned.

Such poems may be said to have served the same purposes as the desired Latin history. Written in Latin they could be read by foreigners, they depicted the past from a pro-Danish point of view, and they were in themselves indications of the level of humanistic culture in Denmark. The government encouraged and probably also supported the publication of Erasmus Lætus's works abroad in 1573-74. He seems to have enjoyed the status of court poet, just as Sadolin earned the title *poeta laureatus* for his epigrams on the Danish kings. But still the historical poems could not make up for the absence of a history of Denmark in prose, as the continuous efforts to procure such a work make clear. The relation between humanist historiography in prose and poetry is a complicated one, and to my knowledge it has not been an object of thorough study. But I think it is true to say that the poems enjoyed greater freedom as to composition and selection of events and that there was a sense that their authors were not committed to any particular degree of research. Consequently they did not possess the same authority as a work of history in prose.

10. Swedish Historiography after Johannes Magnus

The strained Danish-Swedish relations in the sixteenth and seventeenth centuries were, as will have appeared above, mirrored in contemporary historiography. Johannes Magnus's *History of the Swedish Kings* from 1554 made its impact on historiography in Denmark. Svaning's *Refutatio* (1561) was a direct response, and his *magnum opus*, the unprinted *History of Denmark*, should probably be interpreted in the light of Magnus's accusations (cf. below, Chapter VII). Erasmus Lætus's two historical poems, *Margaretica* (1573) and *Res Danicæ* (1574), are both, in part at least, reactions against the Swedish historian. Lyschander's huge *Slectebog* (1622) is perhaps, as we saw, the work which comes closest to being a Danish parallel to Magnus. But, on a smaller scale, reactions to his accusations are also found in Huitfeldt and Venusin.

Interestingly, reactions to Magnus's *History of the Swedish Kings* can also be traced in Pontanus's and Meursius's works; as late as about 1630, then, some of its most provocative claims had to be refuted, directly or indirectly – a reflection of its status as the Swedish national history in the Swedish Great Age of Power. More recent Swedish historiography, however, did not leave many traces in the works of the royal Danish historiographers, with the partial exception of Johannes Messenius (c. 1579-1636).[85] As professor in Uppsala he wrote a number of treatises on subjects of Swedish history and topology, which reveal his admiration for Johannes Magnus. Besides, he was the author of a polemical answer to Svaning's *Refutatio*, named *Retorsio imposturarum* (*A Retort to Impostures*) (1611). It is not this pamphlet, though, but some of Messenius's other historical writings which, on a few points, left their mark in the works of Pontanus and Meursius.[86]

Swedish historiography in the first decades of the seventeenth century was of modest proportions.[87] In 1622 Erich Jörensson Tegel published a history of Gustav Vasa (1523-60) in Swedish, which was in part a reaction against Huitfeldt's work and written at the request of Gustav Vasa's son, Karl IX (1599-1611), as Tegel himself explains in the preface.[88] Royal historiographers were not officially engaged until the 1640s – except, that is, the Dutchman Daniel Heinsius, whom we have already met as an acquaintance of Meursius. He was engaged as royal Swedish historiographer in 1617/18 and was commissioned to write the *res gestae* of the ruling king, Gustav Adolf. Despite his repeated requests for documentary material, he never received either that or salary. After the death of Gustav Adolf in 1632 negotiations between him and the Swedish government were renewed but still without result. Of particular interest in our context is a letter written by Heinsius to the Swedish chancellor, Oxenstierna, in December 1625; once again he here asks for the necessary documents, drawing the chancellor's attention to Meursius's recent engagement as historiographer to Gustav Adolf's rival, Christian IV, in which capacity, Heinsius points out, he received a handsome salary and access to material.[89]

---

[85] On Messenius and his works, see Henrik Schück 1920.

[86] Messenius also wrote an extensive history of Sweden, *Schondia illustrata* (from the Deluge up to 1616), which remained unpublished until the beginning of the eighteenth century.

[87] Henrik Schück 1927, 109-14, 282-86.

[88] Quoted by Rørdam in his biography of Huitfeldt (1896, 174).

[89] Heinsius's complicated involvement with the Swedish government is treated by Paul R. Sellin 1968, 52-60.

In 1636 the bishop of Strängnäs, Laurentius Paulinus, published his *Arctoæ historiæ libri III* (*A History of the North in Three Books*). The first book deals at length with the creation of the world, after which there follows a geographical survey of Sweden including a description of the contemporary political situation, legislation, and national character. The second (and longest) book surveys Swedish history from the Creation up to the death of Gustav Adolf in 1632, and the third deals with the "external Goths", that is Gothic feats in southern Europe in late antiquity and the early Middle Ages. Paulinus's work is thoroughly influenced by Magnus; indeed he set out, he explains in the preface, to write a compendium of Magnus's Swedish history, and as far as Magnus's work goes, it forms the basis of Paulinus's account. Nevertheless, the plan of his work is rather different, not only because it covers the most recent history of the sixteenth and early seventeenth centuries, but also because world history is narrated parallel to Swedish, arranged in a separate column on each page.

The publication of Paulinus's *History* may well owe something to the appearance in 1631 of Pontanus's *Rerum Danicarum historia* and in 1630 of Meursius's *Historia Danica* (on the three first Oldenburg kings). However, I have not been able to find references in Paulinus to his Danish counterparts, either direct or indirect. His treatment of the Danes certainly in some ways resembles that of Magnus with emphasis on the Danes being a younger people than the Swedes and their inferior strength and morals, particularly in the earliest history and again later in the period of the Kalmar Union in the fifteenth century. But in other respects Paulinus's tone is considerably more friendly and respectful. Scania, which according to Magnus rightly belonged to Sweden and was only illegally in Danish hands, is in Paulinus's introductory geographical survey presented as part of Denmark without further comment (105). Denmark as a whole is here acknowledged as a well-ordered and flourishing society (148-50).

The rather modest historiographical activity in Sweden in the first four decades of the seventeenth century forms a striking contrast to the situation in Denmark, where one historian after the other, in collaboration with the government, strove to compose a new Latin account of the Danish past. Presumably Johannes Magnus's history played a role in both cases. In Sweden its existence must have limited the need for yet another national history (in spite of Magnus's criticism of Gustav Vasa whose descendants occupied the Swedish throne). From a Danish point of view, however, it formed a challenge. Svaning's history particularly, closest in time to Magnus, seems to have been marked by this provocation. It is probably correct to say of all the attempts surveyed in this chapter to produce a new Latin history of Denmark, that Magnus's work served as one of several inspirations, albeit a negative one. Even in the works of Pontanus and Meursius, as I have said, his influence is felt.

Chapter V

Opening the Books

1. The Title Pages

Pontanus's *Rerum Danicarum historia* is in all respects an impressive work. It presents itself as a stately folio. The copper-engraved title page represents a building. On a broad column in the middle a carpet is hung, on which contents and author are announced:

> RERUM DANICARUM HISTORIA, LIBRIS X Unoque Tomo ad Domum usque Oldenburgicam deducta, AUTHORE IOH. ISACIO PONTANO Regio Historiographo. Accedit Chorographica REGNI DANIÆ tractusque eius universi borealis Urbiumque DESCRIPTIO eodem Authore. Cum Indicibus locupletissimis.

> (A HISTORY OF DENMARK, In One Volume of TEN BOOKS, brought right down to the House of Oldenburg, By THE AUTHOR, JOHANNES ISAKSEN PONTANUS, Royal Historiographer. Added to this is a Geography of THE DANISH KINGDOM and A DE-SCRIPTION of that whole Northern region and its Cities, by the same Author. With very substantial Indexes).

At the base, information on place and year of publication is found, together with the name of the publisher:

> AMSTELODAMI, Sumptibus Ioannis Ianssonii. ANNO 1631.

> (Published AT AMSTERDAM by Johannes Janssonius, 1631).[1]

The column is flanked by two statues, placed in niches and standing slightly back from the column. Their names are written above. To the left is Danus, the first Danish king according to Saxo (who calls him Dan), and to the right is another Danish king, Gotricus. The selection of the

---

[1] The name of the printer is found in the colophon, Nicolaus à Wieringen in Harderwijk (*Hardervici Gelrorum, Excudebat Nicolaus à Wieringen. Anno M.DC.XXXI*). Some copies bear the name of another publisher, Henricus Hondius, cf. the illustration on the following page. Other copies have an unillustrated titlepage where only author and title are mentioned: *Ioannis Isaacii Pontani Regis Historiographi RERVM DANICARVM HISTORIÆ LIBRI DECEM*. There seem to be no other differences between these copies than the title page.

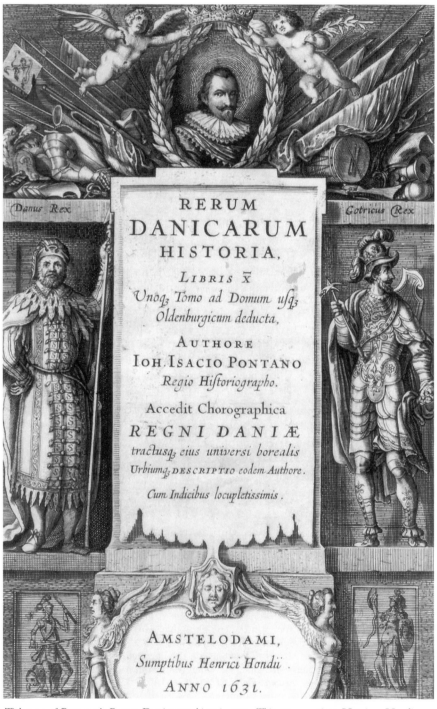

Danus Rex ... *Gotricus Rex*

RERUM
DANICARUM
HISTORIA,
LIBRIS X̄
Unoq₃ Tomo ad Domum usq₃
Oldenburgicum deducta,

AUTHORE
IOH. ISACIO PONTANO
Regio Historiographo.

Accedit Chorographica
REGNI DANIÆ
tractusq₃ eius universi borealis
Urbiumq₃ DESCRIPTIO eodem Authore.

Cum Indicibus locupletissimis.

AMSTELODAMI,
Sumptibus Henrici Hondii.
ANNO 1631.

Title page of Pontanus's Rerum Danicarum historia 1631. This copy mentions Henricus Hondius as publisher. (The Royal Library, Copenhagen).

latter seems to agree well with Pontanus's treatment in the book, Gotricus being the first of Saxo's kings whom he recognizes as historical (dating, in Pontanus's view, from the beginning of the ninth century), since he is mentioned in foreign accounts (38, 92-94). More surprising is Danus's presence on the title page, in view of Pontanus's explicit scepticism regarding the first legendary part of Saxo's *Gesta Danorum*. But as we shall see, his scholarly scepticism did not prevent him from stressing the continuity of the Danish monarchy ever since King Danus. On the title page itself, Danus was not to be discarded as the first Danish king. Below the statues two figures from classical mythology are found, one, presumably Hercules, under Danus and another, Minerva, under Gotricus, symbols of strength and wisdom to be associated with the Danish monarchy. Above the column we find a portrait of Christian IV himself surrounded by imperial symbols: laurels encircle the portrait and on both sides drums, trumpets, banners and various pieces of armour are found, while two angels hold a crown above his head. This title page, in short, befits an official work of national history, depicting the modern king as a powerful ruler of an age-old monarchy, as symbolized by his two predecessors; the author of the work is presented as royal historiographer.

Who designed this title page? It may have been Pontanus in collaboration with Christen Friis, since it is clear from a letter from Pontanus to Friis that Pontanus expected Friis to put forward his points of view regarding the publication and the design of the book.[2] But to what extent Friis actually did give concrete instructions is not known. For all we know, the composition of the title page may well have been a matter between author, printer and publisher.

The metaphor used on this title page, the book as a building, was not uncommon on title pages in the seventeenth century. Nevertheless, the close resemblance between the title page of Pontanus's history of Denmark and the title page of his other grand-scale history, the *Historia Gelrica* of 1639 is noteworthy. Here we also find the title and the name of the author written on a carpet hanging down the central column and the

---

[2] *Sed de re tota amplius cogitabo, expectaturus simul quid tua porro Magnificentia faciendum statuat* (letter from Pontanus to Friis, dated October 18, 1624 (Matthæus 1695, no. 95; Rørdam 1898, 482-84)). In 1630, when the work was in the press, Pontanus again asked for Friis's opinion: [...] *ad tuam mihi recurrendum Magnificentiam identidem video, orans resecransque, ut si quid operi universo ornando esse, et maxime si quid ipso in limine ac frontispicio dicendum addendumque tua Magnificentia e re existimet, eius ut certior fieri prima quaque occasione possim* (letter from Pontanus to Friis, dated January 1st, 1630 (Rørdam 1898, 485-86; original in *Rigsarkivet*, Copenhagen)).

name of the publisher, and in this case also the name of the printer, written together with place and date of publication on the base of the column; and significantly, we also here see two important figures from the national history, both liberators of the *patria*, Claudius Civilis (the Batavian rebel in the first century AD, known from Tacitus's *Histories*) and William of Orange (1533-84), flanking the central column.[3] The *Rerum Danicarum historia* and the *Historia Gelrica* were printed by the same printer, Nicolaus à Wieringen, in Harderwijk; Janssonius in Amsterdam, who is named as the publisher on some of the copies of the *Rerum Danicarum historia*, also figures as such on the title page of the *Historia Gelrica*. It seems likely that the close similarity was due to a wish on the part of Pontanus and perhaps the publisher and the printer to have his two main historiographical works appear in the same style.

The *History of Denmark* begins with a dedicatory letter, taking up six pages, addressed to the king, and a preface to the reader of one page, both by Pontanus. Then follows a portrait of the author, painted by his nephew, Isac Isaachs, and engraved in copper by J. V. Velde; on the frame Pontanus is presented as historiographer to the Danish king and to the duchy (*ducatus*) of Gelderland. Below is a poem of eight hexameters, written in the first person singular; the author, addressing himself to Denmark, presents himself as writer of a history of the country and stresses his personal ties to Denmark. Then follow, as the last of these introductory elements, thirteen dedicatory poems. Two of the authors are Danes, Jacobus Matthias and Stephanus Johs. Stephanius, and the rest belong to the circle of Dutch humanists, Adrianus Hofferus, Caspar Barlæus, Daniel Heinsius (whose Greek poem is followed by a Latin translation made by B. Faber), Jacobus Zevecotius, Janus Gruterus, Jacobus Revius (one of his two poems being in Greek), Marcus Suerius Boxhorn, Petrus Scriverius, and S. Ampzing (who added a Dutch translation of his Latin poem).[4] In Pontanus's letters it is possible to follow some of his efforts to procure these poems from his friends and colleagues.

---

[3] No monarchical symbols are found on the title page of the Geldrian history, unlike the title page of Pontanus's history of Denmark, a difference which reflects the governmental difference between the Danish monarchy and Gelderland, whose sovereignty lay in the estates.

[4] The introductory part of the Geldrian history has been arranged along the same lines. After the preface, addressed to the fathers of the *ducatus Gelriæ et comitatus Zutphaniæ*, come ten laudatory poems, the first being an epigram by the famous learned woman Anna Maria von Schurmann, and then we find the same portrait of the author from 1630, although with another poem printed below written by Jacobus Zevecottus.

In Pontanus's *History of Denmark* a number of copper-engraved maps were found, five according to Pontanus's 18th century biographer, F.A. Reinboth, namely of Denmark, Holstein, Sweden and Norway, Funen, and Iceland.[5] In the Royal Library of Copenhagen a copy with three maps (*Daniae Regni Typus, Ducatus Holsatiæ, Islandia*) is found (this copy bears Henricus Hondius as the name of the publisher). In the copy of Pontanus's work found in the University of Lund (published by Janssonius) five maps agreeing with Reinboth's description are found. In the other copies I have consulted (University Library in Bergen and a private copy) no maps are extant.

While Pontanus's work thus presents itself as an official national history, the first edition of Meursius's *History*, from 1630 (in quarto) is very modest. The text of the title page simply announces:

> IOANNIS MEVRSI HISTORIÆ DANICÆ Libri III. In Quibus Res commemorantur gestæ a CHRISTIANO I; ac IOANNE, eius filio: et nepote, CHRISTIANO II. Cum Gratia et Privilegio. HAFNIÆ, Apud IOACH. MOLTKENIVM, Bibliopolam ibidem. Anno M. DC. XXX.

> (Three Books of DANISH HISTORY by JOHANNES MEURSIUS. In Which the Accomplishments of CHRISTIANUS I are remembered; of JOHANNES, his son; and of his grandson, CHRISTIANUS II. With Licence and Privilege. Published at COPENHAGEN by JOACHIM MOLTKE, who is Bookseller there. 1630).

Apart from a frame, the title page is unillustrated. In this book there is no portrait of the author and there are no laudatory poems, only a preface addressed to the king. Meursius's official role as royal historiographer is indicated in the preface.

Again, as far as I know, we have no information about the designer of the title page. Our information about the circumstances surrounding this edition of the first part of Meursius's *History* amounts to the royal letter which grants Joachim Moltke privilege on Meursius's *History*, and to

---

[5] I quote Reinboth's words on this topic: *Adiectae illi sunt mappae geographicae vel topographicae manu Gerhardi Mercatoris in aes incisae. Expectavit clarissimus autor a Joanne Laurenbergio præstantissimo Mathematico et mathematum in Sorana academia Professore mappam Zelandiae curatius ac antea delineatam, quam, quia non impetrare potuit operi nec inseruit. An in conficiendis reliquis istius viri opera fuerit usus me latet. Sunt vero tabularum numero quinque – 1. Totius Daniae, 2. Holsatiae, 3. Sveciae et Norvegiae cum confiniis, 4. Fioniae, 5. Islandiae, quae Georgum Carolum Flandrum auctorem habet* (Ms. Thott 1957, 4to, 62).

Meursius's remark, in a letter to Vossius, that the "leading men" wanted him to publish this work as a specimen of the future full-scale history (cf. Chapter III). This latter circumstance seems to explain the remarkable difference between the 1631 edition of Pontanus's *History* bearing the marks of an official history of Denmark, and the modesty of Meursius's 1630 edition.[6]

More surprising, in fact, is the relative modesty of the next edition of Meursius's *History*, when compared to that of Pontanus's 1631 edition. The title page is not illustrated, and there are no laudatory poems. Before I go into that, let me give a brief description of the book's design. The 1638 edition came in two versions, both in folio: one which contains Meursius's collected historical works and one which only contains the *Historia Danica*. The former has been given a title page which ambitiously proclaims this volume to be the first of Meursius's collected works:

> IOANNIS MEVRSI HISTORICA; Danica pariter, et Belgica; uno Tomo comprehensa: Quorum seriem pagina post præfationem ad Lectorem indicabit. Operum Omnium TOMVS PRIMVS. AMSTELO-DAMI, Apud GVILIELMVM et IOANNEM BLAEV; M D C XXXVIII.

> (THE HISTORICAL WORKS OF JOHANNES MEURSIUS; both Danish and Dutch, contained in one Volume; their sequence is indicated on the page after the Preface to the Reader. VOLUME ONE of the Complete Works. Published at AMSTERDAM by WILLEM AND JOHANNES BLAEU. 1638).

After the title page follows another title page, likewise unillustrated, to the first part of the history (from Danus to 1182);[7] then comes a preface dedicating the whole volume, indeed the whole forthcoming *Opera omnia* edition, to Christian IV and an address to the reader (also repeating the optimistic statement that this is the first part of Meursius's collected works). A list of contents follows next and finally a copper-engraved portrait of the author, made by the royal Danish engraver Simon de Pas (c. 1595-1647). On the frame of the portrait Meursius is presented as his-

---

[6] Meursius's 1630 edition was, according to *Bibliotheca Danica*, reprinted in 1631 and furnished with a new title page. I have not had access to this print.

[7] *IOANNIS MEVRSI HISTORIÆ DANICÆ, SIVE, DE REGIBVS DANIÆ, Qui familiam Oldenburgicam præcessere, eorumque rebus gestis, a DANO ad CANVTVM VI, in quo desinit Saxo, LIBRI QVINQVE PRIORES. AMSTELODAMI, Apud GVILIELMVM et IOANNEM BLAEV, M D C XXXVIII.*

IOANNIS MEVRSI
HISTORICA;
Danica pariter, & Belgica;
uno Tomo comprehenfa:

*Quorum feriem pagina poft præfationem
ad Lectorem indicabit.*

Operum Omnium
TOMVS PRIMVS.

AMSTELODAMI,
Apud GVILIELMVM & IOANNEM BLAEV,
cIɔIɔcXXXVIII.

Title page of Meursius's Historia Danica 1638. (The Royal Library, Copenhagen).

toriographer to the Danish king and professor at the Academy of Sorø. Parts II (covering the period 1182-1448) and III (1448-1523) also have separate title pages[8] and prefaces addressed to Christian IV's son Christian (Part II) and to the king himself (Part III), the preface of the third part being the same as in the edition from 1630.

The prefaces and title pages to the single parts are also found in the other version of the 1638 edition, which only contains the *Historia Danica*; this version begins with the title page announcing Part I, then follow the same prefaces as in the other version, a list of contents, and the same portrait of the author with the same presentation on the frame.

As mentioned above it is difficult to determine the role of the chancellor in the exterior design of the books. While Pontanus, in his letters to Friis, wanted his employer's opinion on these matters, they are not a subject of discussion in Meursius's correspondence with the chancellor and his representatives. It is tempting to see the difference between the title pages – the grand style of Pontanus's title page where the king himself is represented above the central column, and the unillustrated title pages of both editions of Meursius's work – as reflections of governmental instructions. The government may have wished to mark the difference between Meursius's modest compendium and Pontanus's comprehensive work of national history. The lack of laudatory poems to introduce Meursius's *History* should perhaps be explained similarly. On the other hand it is quite possible that these were matters between author and publisher/printer (who in Meursius's case were identical). Meursius apparently did not want laudatory poems for his *Opera omnia*, and since he planned the *Danish History* to be published as part of the *Opera omnia* edition, he may not have considered it necessary to procure either laudatory poems or an illustrated title page specifically for the *Historia Danica*. When he was told to have this work printed also in a separate version, he did not even furnish it with a title page introducing the whole *History*; these copies simply begin with the title page introducing Part I. This circumstance may be taken to suggest that the separate version was planned

---

[8] (Part II): *IOANNIS MEVRSI HISTORIÆ DANICÆ CONTINVATIO. SIVE, DE REGIBVS DANIÆ, Qui familiam Oldenburgicam præcesserunt, et eorum rebus gestis, a Canuto VI, in quo Saxo desinit, usque ad Christianum I, LIBRI QVINQVE POSTERIORES. AMSTELODAMI, Apud GVILIELMVM et IOANNEM BLAEV, M D C XXXVIII.*

(Part III): *IOANNIS MEVRSI HISTORIÆ DANICÆ LIBRI III. In quibus res commemorantur gestæ a CHRISTIANO I; ac IOANNE, ejus filio: et nepote, CHRISTIANO II. AMSTELODAMI, Apud GVILIELMVM et IOANNEM BLAEV, M D C XXXVIII.*

in a hurry and perhaps also that Meursius's Danish employers did not express any strong opinion regarding the exterior design of Meursius's *History*, not even of the separate 1638 version, which, according to Meursius's preface, was produced at their request.[9]

When Vossius recommended that Meursius should use the Blaeu's printing-house rather than that of Janssonius, where Pontanus's *History of Denmark* was published, his main argument was that Blaeu's types were finer (*venustiores*). There is no denying that Meursius's work in the 1638 edition is typographically a more attractive piece of work than that of Pontanus, not only because of the types but also because each page in Meursius's work has been arranged in two columns, while Pontanus's text is printed in a single wide column. Apart from that, there are not a few misprints in Pontanus's text.

2. Size

The difference in size between the two works will be illustrated by a few figures, based on a rough estimate of characters. The whole of Pontanus's 1631 edition (including the geographical description) is around three times as long as the whole of Meursius's 1638 edition. The difference is partly due to the simple fact that, unlike Pontanus, Meursius did not write a geographical description of Denmark. His work is simply a chronological narrative. On the other hand, Meursius's 1638 edition covers the history up to 1523, whereas the chronologically organized narrative of Pontanus's 1631 edition only goes up to 1448.

More telling is a comparison between their accounts of the period up to 1448. Again Pontanus's version turns out to be around three times as long as that of Meursius. This considerable difference must of course be accounted for in our examination of the two works. Here let me just mention one important factor which leaps to the eye when you open the books: Pontanus's account is full of quotations (typographically marked as such), whereas not a single one is found in Meursius's work. In fact, the quotations included in Pontanus's account of the period preceding 1448 take up about 130 of the 636 pages (we shall return to Pontanus's quotation practice in Chapter VIII). But even so, excluding the quotations, Pontanus's narrative is more than twice as long as Meursius's.

---

[9] Cf. the passage from Meursius's Preface, also quoted above (p. 81): *Inter quæ cum tua Historia classem ducat, separatim dare statui: quo et Majestatis tuæ, et eorum, qui promotam cuperent editionem, desiderio satisfacerem* (Meursius 1638, Preface to Christian IV).

3. The Dedicatory Prefaces

A reading of Pontanus's and Meursius's dedicatory prefaces of their *Histories of Denmark* suggests some of the characteristic features of the two works – and the differences between them. Addressing the king, Pontanus here combines royal praise with a presentation of his own treatment of Danish history. He takes his point of departure in the statement that a king earns particular glory if he can point to a long series of ancestors on the throne, and declares that Christian IV surpasses other kings in this respect. This claim, he goes on, is not based on Saxo's fables but on the highly trustworthy classical author Strabo. Moving forward in time he points out (still in the first paragraph) other foreign authors (Gregory of Tours, Paul the Deacon, Albert of Stade) in whose works information on Danish kings can be found; the focus shifts from authors to medieval Danish kings, whose royal virtues reflect the virtues of the divine ruler himself. It is God who bestows power on the kings and deprives them of their power if they are not worthy of it. Right from the beginning, then, Pontanus distances himself from Saxo's account of the earliest past and suggests how he himself will base his account on foreign classical and medieval authors. Another main theme of the work, as we shall see, is also touched upon in these introductory lines; this is the suggestion that Danish kings in the course of history have belonged to very few families.[10]

In the next paragraph Pontanus explicitly compares his own work with Saxo's *Gesta Danorum*. Having first emphasized the qualities of Saxo's work (its rich subject matter and copious style), he goes on to list its shortcomings, viz. the many fabulous anecdotes in the earliest part, its lack of precise chronological references, and its disregard of the Danes' achievements abroad in the course of history. These are shortcomings, though, for which Saxo can be forgiven, Pontanus declares, and which he now himself sets out to amend: he will supply precise chronological references, he will make the Danes' achievements abroad, their "colonies" and conquests from the Cimbrians' march against Rome onwards, a main theme; furthermore, he is able to base his account on many more texts than Saxo, and finally he notes that his account will also cover the 300

---

[10] *At tua tuorumque prosapia, Rex potentissime, domui tuæ propria nec aliunde accersita* (Pontanus 1631, Preface to Christian IV, fol. 2r).

years after c. 1200, where Saxo's work ends, thus reaching Christian I (the year 1448), the ancestor of Christian IV.[11]

Having thus described his own work, Pontanus now lists his predecessors who since the middle of the sixteenth century have been charged by the Danish kings with the task of writing a history of Denmark. Beginning with Petrus Parvus Rosefontanus (the alleged author of Svaning's *Refutation of Johannes Magnus* and *Chronicon Ioannis*) he goes on with Svaning, Vedel, Krag, Venusin, and Lyschander. Finally Arild Huitfeldt is singled out for praise. Pontanus makes it clear that he holds a special position (*Sed præter hos omnes* [...]), no doubt because he did not belong to the group of royally appointed historiographers, writing as he did as an independent nobleman. More space and praise is devoted to him than to the other historians, which clearly reflects the importance of Huitfeldt's work for Pontanus in his own work (cf. Chapter VI).

Interestingly, Meursius is not mentioned in Pontanus's catalogue of royally appointed historiographers. But perhaps one might detect a hint at Meursius's engagement immediately afterwards, where Pontanus, in the last third of the preface, turns his attention to his own person: even though there are many men, also in Denmark, who could execute this work better than I and write in a more dignified and copious manner, he begins, Your Majesty nevertheless wanted me to undertake the task.[12] This emphasis on *his* being the royal historiographer is noteworthy, coupled as it is with the omission of Meursius's name. It is tempting to see in this omission a refusal, as we have noted in Pontanus's letters (cf. Chapter III), to recognize Meursius's status as royal Danish historiographer.

It is appropriate, Pontanus goes on, that he who has spent his first years and also later periods of his life in Denmark, should now be called back to his origins, so to speak, (*quem* [...] *ad sua, ut sic loquar, primordia revocas*); the king, moreover, has demonstrated his kindness by allowing him to stay in Harderwijk, where he was bound by his engagement to compose a history of Gelderland. God has bestowed upon the king a concern for learning – and, Pontanus adds, He has blessed him with

---

[11] [...] *ad atavum usque tuum, Rex serenissime, Christianum II* (fol. 3v) – which must be an error for *Christianum I.*

[12] *Atque hisce demum insignibus oppido viris, fato suo cum laude perfunctis, cujusmodi et alij, ingenio atque eloquentia præcellentes, hodieque nec domi desint indiesque succrescunt, qui istam multo fortasse quam ego exornare spartam melius, atque exsequi copiosius ac gravius potuissent, me tamen ante decennium, et quod excurrit, tua Majestas postliminio surrogatum, hancce accipere provinciam clementer voluit* (Pontanus 1631, Preface to Christian IV, fol. 4r). I owe this suggestion to Minna Skafte Jensen.

excellent advisers, particularly the chancellor Christen Friis, who has provided Pontanus with help and support throughout; as a prominent politician Friis has been to Pontanus and to Denmark what the archbishop
Absalon, another leading statesman, once (around 1200) was to Saxo
Grammaticus.

Pontanus here (towards the end of the preface) presents himself as a
new Saxo, writing in close collaboration with the Danish governmental
representative of his day. The preface is very much about his relation to
Saxo. He is at pains to define his work in relation to the *Gesta Danorum*, to
underline in which respects his treatment of Danish history is superior to
that of his predecessor, while at the same time casting himself in the role
of the new Saxo. The preface ends with Pontanus's promise to publish a
continuation which will deal with the Oldenburg kings, a project which
will benefit from further supplies of material, he adds (cf. above p. 51).
The preface is dated Harderwijk, January 26, 1631.

In the preface to the period 1448-1523 (the part which was first published
separately in 1630), Meursius in the first half strikes a religious note.
Addressing the king, he views Christian IV's recent deeds as an expression of divine providence. He begins, as Neo-Latin writers often do, with
a reference to classical literature, viz. a saying ascribed to the Roman
emperor Titus: "Imperial power is the gift of fate".[13] Interpreting this
sentence in a Christian sense, he takes as his examples the three first Oldenburg kings of Denmark (1448-1523) who form the subject of the
1630 edition. While the two first (Christian I, 1448-82, and Hans, 1482-
1513) were blessed with God's grace, the third (Christian II, 1513-23) lost
his power and was sent in exile, since God wanted to punish him as a
result of his arrogant and impious rule. Kings owe their power to God,
and He deprives them of their power if they abuse it. God protects
kings, Meursius goes on, taking as his example the addressee of the
preface himself, Christian IV, whose realm has recently suffered from
severe threats, Jutland and Holstein having being occupied by a foreign
enemy. On account of Christian's great piety, however, a piety which
makes him the David of his age, God would not allow the enemy to go
further and instead saw to it that the king could benefit from a favourable
peace arrangement. It was this piety which prompted the king to enter
the war in defence of German liberty and religion. The cause was just,

---

[13] *Principatus fato dari* (Suetonius, *Divus Titus*, Ch. 9,1).

but the outcome, the defeat at Lutter am Barenberg, sad, since God wanted to punish the sins of Germany and Denmark. Divine providence sometimes postpones its support of a good cause. It is most appropriate that the king has chosen as his motto the sentence *Regna firmat pietas*, "the realms are strengthened by piety". Just as his piety makes Christian IV loved by God, it also secures him the affection of his people.

In this first half of the preface, the theme is the relationship between kings and God. The theme enables Meursius to offer a flattering interpretation of Christian IV's intervention into the Thirty Years' War, his defeat at Lutter am Barenberg in 1626, the imperial army's subsequent occupation of Jutland, and the Peace of Lübeck in 1629. He manages to present these events as a demonstration of Christian IV's concern for the Protestant faith, for peace and justice. As we shall see, it is a dominant theme of Meursius's *Historia Danica* itself, that kings owe their power to God, who bestows His rewards and punishments upon them. Meursius's work is pervaded by the same Christian moralism which he here brings to bear on Christian IV. Pontanus, too, as we just saw, touches upon this theme in his preface, but only in passing; similarly events are only rarely interpreted in Christian terms in his *History of Denmark*, though the theme is not entirely absent.

At this point Meursius introduces his own person as being one of Christian IV's devoted subjects. He goes on to present himself as royally engaged historiographer and ask the king to receive the present specimen of his *History of Denmark* kindly. The king's insistence that his sons should benefit from a Latin education clearly shows his own concern for learning as does his institution of the newly founded academy of young noblemen at Sorø. His reputation abroad is built just as much on his support of learned studies as on his triumphs in war. In fact, the latter is dependent on the former, since great men need writers to praise them in order to be remembered, a topos which Meursius now develops: having produced a number of classical examples, he ends with two recent kings who have demonstrated their interest in letters, the French kings Francis I (1515-47) and Henry IV (1594-1610); the latter, wanting to equal Francis I in this area, planned to institute a new academy in Paris, but never carried through the project.[14] Christian IV, who in other respects is

---

[14] Meursius refers to personal contact for this information (*cum Perronius Cardinalis, ut narrantem ipsum audivi ...*, Preface 1638, fol. A3v). As for his knowledge of Francis I, he refers to Jacobus Thuanus's *Historia sui temporis* (1604sqq).

on a par with Henry, is superior to him in that he has managed to establish the Academy of Sorø. The preface is dated Sorø, August 7, 1630.

The preface to Meursius's account of the preceding period 1182-1448
(addressed to Christian IV's son and designated successor, Christian),
likewise takes up the theme of rulers' dependence on historiographers. It
enables Meursius to pay homage to his own predecessors as royally
appointed historiographers and, towards the end, to remind the addressee of their personal contact when the prince listened to Meursius
lecturing on Tacitus.

Having first mentioned a number of medieval and Renaissance rulers
who have distinguished themselves by their concern for history, Meursius then turns his attention to the many Danish kings whose historical
interests are well known, beginning, however, not with a king but with
the archbishop Absalon. Next comes Ericus X (Erik of Pomerania,
1412-39), to whom Meursius ascribes a work of history,[15] and now he
lists the names of the men who have been royally appointed historiographers in the sixteenth and seventeenth centuries: Petrus Parvus, Svaning,
Vedel, Krag, Venusin, Lyschander, Pontanus, and Meursius himself.

Interestingly, Meursius includes his colleague, Pontanus, who, as we
saw, does not list Meursius among the Danish historians in *his* preface.
Pontanus's unwillingness to recognize Meursius as his colleague was not
mutual, then, which is natural enough inasmuch as Meursius only entered
the scene when Pontanus's position as Danish historiographer was a *fait
accompli*. Besides, the mention of Pontanus is noteworthy in view of the
fact that Meursius does not mention his name in the *History* itself,
although Pontanus's work served as one of his main sources. Huitfeldt's
name, however, is absent from Meursius's lists of Danish historiographers, since Meursius here deals with the Danish historiographers who
were paid by Frederik II and Christian IV, the overall subject being good
rulers' interest in historical writing. But as we saw, Pontanus nevertheless
added Huitfeldt's name after having surveyed the royal historiographers.
This difference reflects the simple fact that Huitfeldt's work served as
Pontanus's main source, while it was of little importance to Meursius (cf.
Chapter VII.2).

---

[15] The work is nowadays known as *Rydårbogen* and dated in the latter half of the thirteenth
century. After its first appearance in print in 1603, it was commonly held to have been
written by Erik of Pomerania. Cf. Chapter VI, p. 184.

From these Danish examples Meursius returns to general remarks on his main theme, good rulers are eager to have their deeds commemorated in writing. The point of view is then expressed with a quotation from Tacitus.[16] The reverse is true as well – bad rulers fearing to have their wicked deeds made known to posterity are no friends of historiography. Meursius mentions three Roman emperors (Tiberius, Caligula, Domitian) as instances of this general rule (his material being taken from Tacitus and particularly Suetonius). Virtuous princes love history, and the dedicatee himself, the Crown Prince Christian, is a living example. As documentation of his historical interests Meursius reminds him of his wish to hear Meursius himself lecture on Tacitus with a class of young noblemen at Sorø. On this personal note ends the preface to Part II, which is dated Sorø, December 7, 1636.

The brief preface (also dated Sorø, December 7, 1636) to the earliest period of Danish history (up to 1182) serves as preface to the whole 1638 edition; it introduces both the group of copies which contain Meursius's works of Danish and Dutch history, and the group of copies which only contain the *Historia Danica*. It is addressed to Christian IV. Meursius here strikes a personal note from the beginning: it has now been thirteen years since the king offered him a position in Denmark. Among his reasons for accepting the offer was his wish to be able to serve Christian IV, who is superior to all other kings of his age in a number of respects, including the most important virtue of all, piety. Now that the printer has suggested publishing his collected works, Meursius has wanted to place the *Historia Danica* as the first in this edition in order to demonstrate that just as he has humbly served the king, he now places all his works under Christian's protection, in other words he dedicates this whole (projected) *Opera omnia* edition to the Danish king. Further he adds (as already quoted, Chapter III) that in order to comply with the wish of the king and "those who wanted to have the edition of this work completed", he had also wanted to print the *History of Denmark* in separate volumes.

---

[16] *Cætera principibus statim adesse; unum insatiabiliter parandum, prosperam sui memoriam: nam, contemtu famæ, contemni virtutes* ("Rulers receive instantly everything else they want. One thing only needs to be untiringly worked for – a fair name for the future. Contempt for fame means contempt for goodness", Tac. *Ann.* IV, 38, trans. Michael Grant).

4. Dates

A glance through Pontanus's 1631 edition and either of the two Meursius editions reveals another difference. Throughout the narrative part of Pontanus's work, at the bottom of each page, the contemporary ruler of the Roman empire is indicated. Beginning with the consuls of the Roman republic, Pontanus continues with the Roman emperors, and then, from Charlemagne (768-814) onwards, the Western emperors.[17] There is a significant exception to this practice, however, and that is the part of the work where Saxo's legendary history is paraphrased (12-41). As he makes clear from the outset, Pontanus did not regard this part of Saxo as real history, and he thus marks his scepticism by omitting to relate it to Roman history. Apart from that, the history of Denmark is throughout linked to the rulers of Rome and their German successors.

This strategy is probably related to the traditional division in the Christian universal histories into four world monarchies, the last of which was the Roman including the succeeding German empire. This structure of world history had been given its canonical form in *Carion's Chronicle* (1532, German; reworked in Latin by Melanchthon and Caspar Peucer 1572, cf. Chapter IV). Here the eschatological aspect, the notion of the impending end of the world, is strongly present. But *Carion's Chronicle* also came to serve as the basis of many, more secularized world chronicles. As late as 1733 Ludvig Holberg (1684-1754), professor in Copenhagen, based his compendium of world history on the model of the four world monarchies. In Pontanus's work Danish history is related to the main course of universal history, though with no eschatological suggestion.

Meursius did not establish this connection with world history. No contemporary Roman rulers are indicated in his work. That reflects a significant difference to which we shall return: whereas Meursius deals almost exclusively with the Danish past, Pontanus's work is filled with references to foreign history. Danish history in his version is seen as part of a more comprehensive history.

One of the repeated criticisms of Saxo in the sixteenth century was his lack of chronological references, and both Pontanus and Meursius have indicated in the margin the beginning of each new year with Roman

---

[17] In Westphalen's edition of the second part of Pontanus's work from 1740 this practice has not been followed.

letters. Interestingly Meursius did not put any dates in the first part of the work (the period up to 1182, which had been covered by Saxo). This omission displeased the anonymous nobleman whom the chancellor had entrusted with the task of reading the work in manuscript. But Meursius, in his answer to the nobleman's criticism, first points to the considerable uncertainty of the earliest chronology, and then goes on to say that no doubt Saxo could have given chronological references in the later part of his history, but his fine sense of style forbade him to destroy the unity of his work by putting dates in the last part of the work when he had not done so from the beginning.[18] This is a strategy, we infer, of which Meursius approves. He himself chose to avoid indications of years in the first part (up to 1182). His own stylistic concern is further to be observed in that he only brings a few chronological references into the text itself, including the later part. Whereas in Pontanus's work years are also frequently inserted within the text, Meursius has by and large reserved them for the margins.

---

[18] *Potuisset sine dubio Saxo noster in nonnullis postremorum etiam annos indicare, uti factum a Pontano. Sed profecto vir egregii iudicii, quod non posset in principio, illud nec in fine voluit: arbitratus, faciem historiae decoram magis, si a se differret nusquam, et ubique similis foret. Et hoc puto in Praefatione mea ad Lectorem dici posse.* ('Ioannis Meursi ad adnotationes viri illustris a Domino Cancellario sibi communicatas responsio' (Meursius 1741-63, IX, col. 1131. The nobleman's comment is found *ibidem*, col. 1115)).

Chapter VI

Pontanus's
Rerum Danicarum historia

The Chorographica Regni Daniæ Descriptio

The *Chorographica Daniæ descriptio* (*Geographical Description of Denmark*) takes up more than one fifth of the whole of 812 folio pages of the 1631 edition (637-801). It follows after the ten books of chronological narrative, though Pontanus himself originally wrote it as an introduction. This original disposition corresponded to that of other national histories. It was an established feature of regional histories, as it had been in classical and medieval historiography, to open with a geographical presentation of the region whose history was to be told. For reasons unknown – though presumably it was just a matter of length – he was prevailed upon to have it printed as an appendix instead. The change was clearly not decided until the whole work was written, as is clear from several references in the chronological history to the *Chorographica descriptio* as preceding the work. Since, then, Pontanus wrote the work with the intention of introducing it by the *Chorographica descriptio*, and since it presents characteristic features of his work as a whole, I shall here deal with this part first.

Many works were consulted by Pontanus in the process of writing the *Chorographica descriptio*. Among the important recent works was Jon Jensen Kolding's *Daniæ descriptio nova* (1594), which, brief as it was, furnished Pontanus with material on Danish localities. Another modern inspiration was David Chytræus's *Saxonia* (first ed. 1585), of which he made use in his treatment of Norway and Sweden.

1. Survey of Contents

After an introductory chapter on the name of Denmark, the *Chorographica descriptio* falls into two main parts, first a survey of Denmark and then a general description of social structures (form of government, classes, law) and of natural assets (crops, national character, famous men of learning).

The survey is by far the longer section. Starting with Jutland, it goes on with Scania and the Scandinavian peninsula, the Baltic Sea and its islands, and finally the rest of the Danish islands. A town or a region is typically described in terms of buildings, history, famous men, civil and ecclesiastical status, and surrounding landscape.

The total picture is one of a rich, beautiful, and well-organized country. The abundant fertility of Danish soil is a recurrent theme, as is the highly productive stockbreeding and fishing. It all provides a basis for a flourishing trade, as emphasized in this passage about Århus and its neighbouring towns on the east coast of Jutland:

> these individual towns have bays lying on that sea-coast, where, as though into their bosom, they very comfortably receive vessels carrying foreign merchandise, which put in from Scania, Zealand, Funen, the Wendish towns and, lastly, Sweden and Norway.[1]

Denmark is a modern centre of North European trade, receiving foreign ships into her bosom, or, to use Jordanes's tag about Scandinavia, a sort of reversed "womb of nations" (*vagina gentium*). Also Elsinore at the entrance to the Sound and the Baltic Sea is visited every day by foreign ships:

> Foreigners from all over, Friesland, Holland (Hollanders especially), Flanders, France, Spain, England, Scotland, Prussia, Sweden, Norway, Muscovy, Pomerania and the whole of Wendland, not counting others who call there daily in their swarms[...][2]

A characteristic feature of Pontanus's Denmark is the many historical monuments and memories attached to particular localities. Castles and churches provide tangible evidence of the long history recounted in the main part of the work. Famous men and events are also connected to certain places – the small island Hven occasions a long presentation of the astronomer Tycho Brahe (728-29), another island was the native place of the theologian Niels Hemmingsen, whose life is briefly told (722), and

---

[1] *Sinus habent singula [oppida] ejusdem maris patentes, quibus veluti gremio ex Scania, Sælandia, Fionia, urbibusque Vandalicis ac denique Suecia ac Norvegia appellentia navigia mercesque peregre advectas commodissime recipiant* (661).

[2] *Exteri, et præsertim Hollandi, ceterique e Frisia, Hollandia, Flandria, Gallia, Hispania, Anglia, Scotia, Borussia, Suecia, Norvagia, Moschovia, Pomerania, totaque Vandalia aliique eo confertim quotidie appellentes* [...] (726). Likewise, the town of Køge is *negotiatione præsertim frumentaria florens* (730) and Nykøbing *frugum abundantia aliisque mercimoniis celebrata* (731).

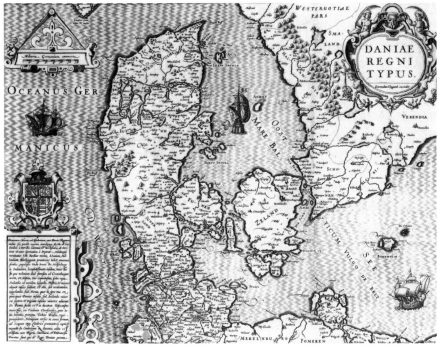

Map of Denmark. Copper engraving in Pontanus's Rerum Danicarum historia 1631.

the founder of the school Herlufsholm, the nobleman Herluf Trolle, is honoured with a rather far-fetched theory of the origin of his name (732). The rich Danish past is present everywhere.

Nor does Pontanus forget to commemorate his own past. In connection with the long presentation of Elsinore, where he himself was born, he inserts a brief autobiography, which turns into a lamentation over his recently deceased brother, Pieter Isaachs (1569-1625), who is regarded, as he is by modern art historians, as one of the outstanding painters at the court of Christian IV (728).

The last part of the *Chorographica descriptio* (765 sqq) deals with the political and legal organization and with the national character of the Danes and their intellectual achievements.[3] Again, an impression of harmony and stability is conveyed, and the long monarchical traditions, going back

---

[3] As mentioned in connection with Stephanius, some of these last chapters of the *Chorographica descriptio* – on the political organization, on the natural gifts, the national character – had already been published by Stephanius in his anthology of writings about Denmark, the *De regno Daniæ et Norwegiæ, Insulisque adjacentibus* [...] *tractatus varii* (Leiden 1629). See further Rørdam 1891, 26-29.

to the Cimbrians, are emphasized. In fact, right from Gotricus at the time of Charlemagne, the kings have belonged to the same family. Pontanus here inserts a rejection of the French philosopher Jean Bodin's description of Denmark as a principate (*principatus*) and not a proper monarchy because of the coronation charter to which the kings had to submit.[4] In Pontanus's eyes, Denmark is a mixture of the two, but closest to being a monarchy. This leads him to a rejection of another dishonouring claim of Bodin's, namely that Denmark in the twelfth century was subject to the German emperor. No, says Pontanus, and having gone through the course of events, he concludes that the emperors Lotharius (1125-37) and Fredericus Barbarossa (1152-90) in vain tried to make the Danish kings acknowledge their dependent status.[5] As we shall see, Meursius also takes up this point. Apparently, it was important to refute any suggestions of Danish dependence on Germany, perhaps as a consequence of Bodin's influence.

Having then described the economic and administrative conditions of the five estates (767-69), Pontanus emphasizes the ideal balance between elective and hereditary monarchy:

> From this I think it sufficiently clear that the constitution of the Danish kingdom is exceedingly well established: there is an open election of the king, but it is executed only from members of the royal family.[6]

The general support of the king from high and low, he concludes, forms an effective bulwark against both internal and external wars.

The legal system also has old roots. The number of laws is small, which Pontanus finds particularly healthy, referring to Lipsius's *Politica* (1589) for support of this point of view. The chapter ends on a patriotic note:

> [Denmark] has firmly kept the laws and decrees of our forefathers, once they were passed; and having employed them successfully right up to our

---

[4] Bodin 1572 (first ed. 1566), 212b.

[5] In the chronological narrative Pontanus does in fact declare that Valdemarus I in 1162 accepted the Emperor as his lord in return for receiving Wendland (*Vandalia*): *Eaque pollicitatione ad obsequium suum regem pertraxit* (241). But he then adds that this subjection was in name only (*sola specie non re*). Pontanus here follows Saxo closely (*Gesta Danorum*, XIV, Ch. xxviii, 16), who attempts to play down the event, cf. Karsten Friis-Jensen 1993a, 201.

[6] *Ex his liquere sat puto, regni Daniæ politiam peroptime constitutam: dum ita sit libera regis electio, ut ea non nisi ex regia familia perficiatur* (769).

own time, at any rate with the addition of small 'recesses', as they are called, she has not tied herself up with ambiguities and the wiles of the advocate,[7]

and while recognizing the inspiration from Roman and canon law, he stresses the singular smoothness and effectiveness of the Danish judicial system.

Before embarking on the subject of the Danish national character, Pontanus once again draws attention to the rich crops and fertility of Danish soil. Most of this chapter on natural assets (773-75), however, is taken up with a discussion of the word *øl* (beer) and a rejection of a textual conjecture in Tacitus's *Germania* made by Beatus Rhenanus (see below).

With regard to the national character, he stresses the Danes' desire for conquest. Far from being rude and ignorant, as the Romans often depicted Scandinavians, they were always remarkable fighters who defeated their enemies time after time. Their brilliance as sailors is seen nowadays in their vigorous trade all over the earth – Pontanus particularly notes the friendship recently struck with the king of Ceylon.

Danish traditions of learning, while not equalling the Italian, are certainly among the second best (779sqq). It appears clearly from Saxo, Tacitus and Ammianus that the Muses have been cultivated from the earliest times in Denmark. Saxo tells of how King Hjarne (one of the legendary kings) was elected because of his gifts as a singer, and this, Pontanus points out, is a mark of the Danes' appreciation of culture, which overshadows the celebrated liberality of the Roman nobleman Scipio towards his poet Ennius. He then proceeds chronologically, offering a survey of Danish men of learning from the twelfth century to the seventeenth. Around 1200, we learn, Danish letters were in a flourishing state. Pontanus celebrates the three archbishops Eskil, Absalon, and Anders Sunesen, the first for his connection with Bernard of Clairvaux, the second for his combined activity as military and ecclesiastical leader, and the third for his literary works, a Latin paraphrase of *Skånske lov* and a *poema heroicum*, the *Hexaemeron* (a didactic theological poem on the creation of the world).[8] There were other great intellects at that time. It is in

---

[7] *Leges et decreta majorum semel lata firmiter retinuit* [i.e. *Dania*]: *iisque in hoc usque tempus, brevibus saltem, quos vocant, adjectis Recessibus, feliciter usa, ambagibus se atque artibus caussidicinæ non innexuit* (773).

[8] It was still unpublished when Pontanus wrote, as he himself mentions. It was first published by M. Cl. Gertz in 1892.

fact astonishing, Pontanus observes, that elegance and literary glory could reign in these remote Northern parts at a time when barbarism occupied the rest of Europe (781). These considerations are followed by a long presentation of Saxo Grammaticus. Having noticed the admiration which has surrounded Saxo since the end of the Middle Ages (or as he says, since the introduction of a more refined kind of learning, *doctrina cultior*, 781), Pontanus now evaluates his achievement along the same lines as in the Preface: rich and varied in subject-matter and style as it is, Saxo's history can only be blamed for its lack of chronological references and its too many fabulous elements. Pontanus further quotes Gerardus Vossius's praise of Saxo in his work on Latin historians (*De historicis Latinis*) (781) and even includes the letters accompanying the 1514 *editio princeps* of Saxo between Lage Urne and Christian Pedersen (782-83).

After this great age of learning Denmark declined into the same state of barbarism as the rest of Europe, Pontanus declares, displaying the humanists' scathing attitude towards medieval letters. A few exceptions are found, though, but Pontanus primarily focuses on the fifteenth and especially the sixteenth centuries in the following biographical survey of distinguished Danish men of learning.[9] The whole chapter concludes with catalogues of chancellors (from 1539), rectors of the University (1479-1619), and professors of the University (1539-1619) (788-92), to which is appended praise of the nobleman and politician, Arild Huitfeldt. Though not himself a professor, he deserves to be remembered here, says Pontanus, because of his remarkable achievements within Danish historiography. Pontanus does not conceal his own previous position as Huitfeldt's assistant: "at one time I, too, was a member of his household and his secretary".[10]

---

[9] This survey of humanist letters in Denmark deserves closer study. I will here limit myself to listing the men of learning each given a brief presentation by Pontanus: Peder Låle, Matthæus Delius, Erik of Pomerania, Claudius Niger, Petrus Parvus Rosæfontanus, Peder Palladius, Paul Madsen, Jakob Madsen, Erasmus Lætus, Johannes Pratensis, Peder Svave, Hans Frandsen, Anders Sørensen Vedel, Niels Hemmingsen, Tycho Brahe, Henrik Rantzau, Christianus Cilicius Cimber, Peder Sørensen, Anders Krag, Niels Krag, Jon Jacobsen Venusin, Isak Grønbæk, Johannes Machabæus, Christian Machabæus (783-87). Names of contemporary men of learning are added without further presentation (787-88).

[10] *cui et nos aliquando domestici et ab epistolis fuimus* (792). In the case of Venusin, who had also been engaged as Royal Historiographer, Pontanus likewise mentions their friendship: *Ab hoc eadem scribendæ historiæ provincia est demandata elegantissimi ingenij viro Ionæ Iacobæo mihi dum viveret amicissimo, Venusini cognomine, quod in insula Porthmi Danici Venusia, vulgo Venam dicimus, esset progenitus* (786).

The last chapter (792-801) is about the Danish language. The relationship between the Scandinavian languages, German, Flemish, and English is illustrated by quotations of the Lord's Prayer in all these languages. Apart from this, Pontanus focuses on the names of the months and weekdays.

2. The Antiquarian Tradition

Language, letters, geography, monuments, crops, trade, political and judicial administration – the Danes and their country are presented thoroughly. Besides this, Pontanus has also found room for discussions of e.g. the identification of the *Thule* mentioned in classical literature, the original home of the Normans, and the *Getae* and the Goths in late antiquity.

The reader has been prepared for this broad range of subjects in a short introduction to the *Chorographica descriptio* (638), emphasizing the importance of knowledge about the origins of peoples, names, situation, nature and size of the individual localities, the founders of the towns and their situations, and the character, ways of living, and institutions of the people. Pontanus supports this point of view with several authorities.[11] Not that it could be said to be controversial. As mentioned before, a geographical survey normally introduced the chronological narrative of a national history. In the last half of the sixteenth century the range of subjects treated in these introductions tended to increase. Although Pontanus's treatment may be somewhat more detailed than usual, several recent works of national history were introduced by similar descriptions of early settlements, language, and manners; examples are George Buchanan's *Rerum Scoticarum historia* (1582), Johs. Mariana's *Historiae de rebus Hispaniae libri XX* (1592), Ubbo Emmius's *Rerum Frisicarum historia* (1616). And as we saw, Vedel also intended his history to begin with a broad presentation of Denmark.

---

[11] By declaring that geographical knowledge is the eye of history, he re-used a metaphor employed by David Chytræus in his *De lectione historiarum recte instituenda* (Rostock 1563), B8v. He then mentions a division of history into four branches, *Topicon, Pragmaticon, Chronicon, Genealogicum*, a division which went back to the *Methodus legendi cognoscendique historiam tam sacram quam profanam*, 1579, by Reiner Reineccius, professor in Helmstedt (cf. Uwe Neddermeyer 1988, 291). The topical part, Pontanus explains, has been reserved for separate treatment in order not to distract the reader from the historical events, and Lucian's warning against such distractions is mentioned (*How to write History*, Ch. 19).

This interest in taking up a variety of subjects and describing a country from many angles is related to the rise of antiquarian studies in the sixteenth and seventeenth centuries. In a survey of the antiquarian tradition A. Momigliano traces the division between historical and antiquarian studies back to Thucydides, whose work became a model for the chronological narrative of political and military events. Other aspects of the past – laws, institutions, customs, genealogy – were relegated to the domain of the antiquarians. These were engaged in collecting and organizing material, and their presentation took the form of synchronical descriptions. This classical division of historical research was given new life in the Renaissance and the next centuries. The object of antiquarian investigations was now not only the classical past, but also the national past of the various European countries. Here Flavio Biondo (1392-1463) was an important figure. His description of Italy, *Italia illustrata* (1474), became the model for antiquarian treatment of other countries. The antiquarian descriptions are systematically organized and deal with a variety of subjects. The past is not only described in terms of wars and heroic deeds. Customs, language, traditions, political and legal institutions, and inventions are typical subjects.[12] This widening of the subject of history, the historicizing of more and more areas of human life, is one of the major characteristics of historical studies in the early modern period.[13]

Examples of such thematic treatments of a country are Wolfgang Lazius's *Vienna Austriae* (1546), and William Camden's *Britannia* (1586), and in this group should also be counted the *Res Germanicæ* (1531) by

---

[12] Arnaldo Momigliano has discussed the antiquarian approach to history in two illuminating essays, Momigliano 1966 (first ed. 1950) and Momigliano 1990.

[13] This is a point emphasized by Ulrich Muhlack in his study of the prehistory of historicism in the nineteenth century (Muhlack 1991, 196-268). The same point is made by Donald Kelley (1970) in his study of the sixteenth-century French historians who combined the study of history with the study of law and insisted that cultural matters belonged to the field of historical research. Antiquarian studies in England in the late sixteenth and seventeenth centuries are the subject of Chapter 4 in F.S. Fussner 1962. Danish antiquarian studies receive ample attention in Carl S. Petersen's learned history of Danish literature. Having pointed to the inspiration from Renaissance Italy and Biondo in particular, Petersen treats of the study of runic inscriptions in Denmark around 1600, which was conducted in an atmosphere of rivalry with Sweden. Then follows his discussion of Ole Worm (1588-1654), the most important Danish representative of the antiquarian branch of history (Carl S. Petersen 1929, 554-97). Antiquarian studies and Ole Worm also figure prominently in the recent survey of Danish historiography by Torben Damsholt, who stresses (like Momigliano and Fussner) the importance of antiquarian studies for the development of historical methods (Damsholt 1992, 61-70).

Beatus Rhenanus.[14] Others combine the thematic approach with a chronological narrative, and in this group belong the national histories I mentioned earlier, by Buchanan, Mariana, and Emmius, together with Pontanus's *History of Denmark*. To term the thematic parts of these national histories antiquarian is perhaps misleading, since they present primarily a contemporary description, and a more adaequate term would perhaps be "cultural history". Still, the very idea of describing the country systematically in a variety of facets is related to antiquarian studies, and the historical aspect is present throughout these descriptions of the contemporary situation.

This is very much the case with Pontanus's *Chorographica descriptio*, not only in the many references to old buildings and to historical events connected with particular places, but also in the treatment of single subjects. The presentations of each of the major parts of the country and its neighbours are introduced by quotation of the classical texts supposedly referring to the area in question; and the subjects of the following essays (on the political and judicial organization, on the national character, on learning, on language) are all seen in a historical perspective. In this way the *Chorographica descriptio* functions as a supplement to the chronological narrative. In addition to providing a description of contemporary Denmark, it also made room for historical treatment of more subjects than those taken up in the main narrative.

Pontanus's inclusion of the Danish history of learning breaks new ground. Reineccius, whose division of history he refers to in the introduction to the *Chorographica descriptio*, had, in a lecture of 1583 entitled *Methodus legendi cognoscendique historiam tam sacram quam profanam* (*A Method*

---

[14] The *Res Germanicæ* deals with ancient Germany, up to the eleventh century. The first book is, within an overall chronological structure, organized geographically and rendered in terms of tribes. The second book, which focuses on the Franks, likewise gives a chronological account but then, in the latter half, concentrates on ethnographical subjects, such as religion and language. The third book is about Rhineland cities. Surveys and discussion of the contents are found in Paul Joachimsen 1910 (rep. 1968), 132sqq and John F. D'Amico 1988, 185sqq (where further references to studies on the *Res Germanicæ* are given). D'Amico's study deals with Beatus Rhenanus's achievement as a textual critic and the influence of these studies on his historical works. Beatus Rhenanus's antiquarian approach is also connected to his philological work in Hentschke & Muhlack 1972, 14-59, and placed within the context of the history of the study of German history in Muhlack 1991.

On Camden's historical works, see Chapter 9 of F.S. Fussner 1962; on the *Britannia* in particular, see W.H. Herendeen 1988, who underlines the historical and learned aspects of the work (with further references to modern studies of the *Britannia*). Paul Joachimsen gives a brief presentation of Lazius's works (Joachimsen 1910 (rep. 1968), 150-54).

of Reading and Understanding Both Sacred and Secular History), treated the history of learning as one of the three kinds of pragmatical history, the other two being political and ecclesiastical history, and this inclusion of intellectual history was an innovation.[15] In Denmark, Jon Jacobsen Venusin, in his treatise *De historia* (1604), following Reineccius, had also presented intellectual history as a branch of historiography. Vedel and perhaps Lyschander had planned to include a survey of the Danish history of learning in their histories (cf. Chapter IV). It seems to have been on its way to general recognition, both in theory and practice, when Pontanus composed his survey of Danish men of learning.

3. Etymology and the Classics

Among the important works of national antiquarianism were Beatus Rhenanus's *Res Germanicæ* (1531) and William Camden's *Britannia* (1586). These works must be counted among Pontanus's main sources of inspiration – as it will be recalled, he was a personal friend of Camden. He refers to both with respect.[16] Like both of them he takes a keen interest in the early migrations of the European peoples and in etymological deductions. It is also in line with their viewpoints when Pontanus rejects the traditional explanation of the name of Denmark (*Danmark*) as going back to the eponymous first king, Dan.

Camden had, like many others of the time, drawn attention to Plato's recommendations in the dialogue *Cratylos* that etymologies of words which had been borrowed from other languages should be established from their original language, and that name and thing should correspond.[17] These principles are followed by Pontanus in a number of cases where he points to a resemblance between a place-name and a Danish word. Ridiculing those who derive *Scandinavia* from the Latin words *conscendant* and *naves* (supposedly referring to the fact that travels to and

---

[15] I rely on Adalbert Klempt 1960, 69sqq.

[16] Camden is mentioned 640 (in the *Chorographica descriptio*) and 105, 129, 150, 193, 361 (in the chronological narrative). Rhenanus is mentioned 774 (in the *Chor. descr.*).

[17] In the preface to his *Britannia*, Camden states his view of etymology: *Plato in Cratylo iubet vt nominum origines ad Barbaricas linguas, vtique antiquiores reuocemus: ego ad Britannicam siue Wallicam (vt iam vocant) linguam, qua primæui, et antiquissimi huius regionis incolæ vsi sunt in etymis, et coniecturis semper recurro. Iubet ille vt rei nomen, nomini rei consonet: si dissonet, ego minime admitto,* (Camden 1590, *Ad Lectorem.* (Cf. Plato, *Cratylos* Ch. 409; 389sqq)). On etymology in the sixteenth and seventeenth centuries, see George J. Metcalf 1974.

from the region were often conducted by boat), he argues that the name is derived from *Skåne* (*Scania*) in the local language (the *gentis idioma*), which is related to the Danish word *skøn* (beautiful) (670). The name of Skanderborg, a town in Jutland, has the same root in Pontanus's view.[18] Similarly, he derives *Fyn* from *fin*,[19] Elsinore (in Danish *Helsingør*) – on account of its position at the narrowest point of the Sound – from *hals* (neck, 726), Faffuerlandt from *fager* (beautiful),[20] Zealand (*Selandia*, in Danish *Sjælland*) from *sejen/sajen* (sow) and *sæd* (crops) (724); *Amager*, which delivers many kinds of food to Copenhagen, is related to the Italian word *magasino*, *-mag-* denoting storing place (725), while *Korsør* indicates that superstitious (i.e. pre-Protestant) inhabitants had once placed an unusual number of crosses (*kors* in Danish) in this area (730).

In most cases, however, Pontanus is not concerned with the meaning of a name but with its resemblance to a name mentioned in a classical text, since this, in his eyes, suggests a historical connection. The name of the town of Køge, south of Copenhagen, bears witness to the presence in this area of the *Cogeni* (a people mentioned by Jordanes) (675, 730). *Bergi*, a Northern island according to Pliny (IV, Ch. 16), is easily identified with Bergen on the Norwegian west coast (671), in Pontanus's day the largest town in Norway. In the case of Århus (661) he prefers to reject the traditional derivation from *Åre* (oar) and *hus* (house) in favour of the *Harudes*, a people living in Jutland (*Cimbrica Chersonesus*) according to Ptolemy.[21] Sometimes he combines the two kinds of etymological deductions. On a few occasions he derives a place-name from a historical person, Ottesund and Otby from Emperor Otto, Tyrholmia from Thyra (663).

It is easy to laugh at such speculations, and there is no denying that they do have a ring of arbitrariness and opportunism about them. This was a common feature of etymology around 1600. It was left to scholars in the course of the seventeenth century to formulate rules for phonetic changes, for what could legitimately be compared and what could not.[22] Pontanus himself seems to be aware of this uncertainty, since he often

---

[18] [...] *Scanderburgum, quasi Schonderburgum a pulchritudine et amoenitate dictum* (661).

[19] *Fionia tam formæ quam situs amoenitate conspicua est. Unde et vernacule loquentibus id nominis pulchrum notat* (721).

[20] [...] *a pulchritudine sic dicta* (664).

[21] They are called *Kharoudes* by Ptolemy (*Geographia* (ed. Mullerus 1883), II, Ch. 11,7).

[22] George J. Metcalf 1974, 244sqq.

ascribes an etymological explanation to others without giving his own opinion. On *Hamburg*, for instance, he says: "They believe it is a name given to it from the forest owned by the lords of Ham".[23] And though his interest in etymology is manifest, most of the place-names mentioned are not subjected to etymological dissection at all.

Before archaeology had been established as a reliable method of achieving knowledge of the past, etymological deductions provided a link with literature, and literary evidence was by far the most important source of historical information (although the value of inscriptions was increasingly noted by historians, including Pontanus, as we shall see).

4. Written Sources

Written sources, i.e. classical and (less prominently) medieval texts supposedly referring to Danish localities, are brought forward on almost every page of the *Chorographica descriptio*. They constitute the point of departure for Pontanus's presentation of each of the larger parts of Denmark. Let us as an example go through the main points of the presentation of Jutland (643-53).

In Pontanus's view, one of the earliest authors to refer to Jutland was the Greek geographer Strabo (1st century BC & AD), from whom he quotes a number of passages,[24] demonstrating that Strabo's *Cimbrica Chersonesus* is to be identified with Jutland. Pontanus then engages in a debate with contemporary historians on the interpretation of Strabo. Two points are on his mind. First, the notion put forward by the Frisian historian Suffridus Petri (1527-97) in his *De origine Frisiorum* (1590) that the Cimbrians never lived in Jutland must be thoroughly rejected. No doubt Pontanus's motives were patriotic and scholarly at the same time, the established view of early Danish history being based on the identification of the Cimbrians as ancestors of the Danes; like the Goths they had been formidable opponents of the Romans on several occasions, and their biblical origin was regarded as an established fact. Secondly, as he himself says (645), he wants to avoid accusing the ancient geographer of ignorance, as Philipp Clüver had recently done. This is a good illustration of his attitude towards classical authors. Though by no means regarding them as sacrosanct, he starts from the assumption that they make sense.

---

[23] *Nomen inditum existimant a silva* [...] *quam possiderunt domini de Ham* (666).
[24] By far the longest is Strabo, *Geography*, VII, Ch. 2.

Shortly afterwards he does in fact himself dispute an assertion of Strabo's (645-46). While agreeing with him that the reason for the Cimbrians' migration was not the normal tides, as earlier geographers before Strabo had claimed, he doubts whether Strabo had understood them correctly; they may have referred to the occasional very violent tides in this area which are also frequent nowadays, he suggests; this kind of violence might well have caused the inhabitants to migrate. He then argues against the assumption, which according to Strabo was common among Greek authors, that the Cimbrians and the Cimmerians (known from Homer) were one people.

Moving forward in time, Pontanus calls Pliny as his next witness. Here we find references to the first Roman naval expedition to these remote places at the time of Augustus. In passing, Pontanus notes how Velleius Paterculus, eager to glorify his patron Tiberius, makes him the leader of the venture when it was in fact, as Suetonius tells us in his life of Claudius, Drusus Germanicus (646-47).[25] Characteristically he does not confine himself strictly to Danish matters. An observation on Roman history is not outside the scope of his work.

Having discussed various interpretations of Tacitus's praise of the Cimbrians in the *Germania* (Ch. 37,1), Pontanus embarks on a philological discussion (647) on Pliny's division of German tribes.[26] While approving of two textual corrections made by the German philologist and historian Beatus Rhenanus (1485-1547), whom we have already met as the author of the *Res Germanicæ* (1531), he disagrees with Rhenanus's suggestion that the group of Germans to which the Cimbrians belong according to Pliny should be *Vigevones* and not *Ingevones*.[27] No, says Pontanus, the form *Ingevones* is right, since Tacitus clearly had this passage from Pliny in mind, when, in his enumeration of Germans (*Germ.* Ch. 2), he named the northern Germans *Ingevones*, and Pliny himself, in the preceding chapter (IV,13), mentions the *Ingevones*. Philology and history thus go hand in hand. In order to gain a clear picture of the early Danish past, the classical texts must be understood correctly, and this entails, in Pontanus's practice, discussions with modern scholars.

Further, he provides an etymological argument for the form *Ingevones*, analyzing the word as a German compound made up from the elements

---

[25] Pliny, *Hist. Nat.*, II, Ch. 67; Velleius Paterculus, *Hist. Rom.*, II, Ch. 106; Suetonius, *Diuus Claudius*, Ch. 1.

[26] Pliny, *Hist. Nat.*, IV, Ch. 14.

[27] Rhenanus 1531, 114-15.

eng (narrow) and *wohnen* (live), that is, people who live in a narrow area, which applies to the Cimbrians (648).

Next in his chronological presentation of classical authorities is the Greek geographer and astronomer Ptolemy (2nd century) (648-50), who lists a number of peoples living in *Cimbrica Chersonesus*.[28] Northernmost live the Cimbrians, that is, as Pontanus explains, in modern Vendsyssel; their name is retained in the name of the region, Himmersyssel (south of Vendsyssel, today *Himmerland*), the K-sound being left out. The same phonetic development can be observed in other Jutland place-names, Pontanus notes, such as Horsens and Harboe which both go back to another people mentioned by Ptolemy, the *Charudes* whom he identifies with the *Harudes* mentioned by Caesar.[29] While Ptolemy simply lists the Cimbrians as one of the peoples inhabitating the peninsula, Pontanus apparently regards the other peoples as various branches of the Cimbrians.[30] In one case he admits to having trouble with reconciling Ptolemy's names with modern place-names, suggesting as one possibility that there may be errors on Ptolemy's part (650).

Pontanus also calls attention to Ptolemy's attempt at locating the peninsula by degrees of longitude and latitude (II, Ch. 11,2). A similar attempt at precise location, though in *stadia*, was made by the Greek geographer Marcianus Heracleotes (4th-5th cent.), whom Pontanus mentions briefly (650-51). The last author to be quoted and discussed is the eleventh-century historian Adam of Bremen, who was, Pontanus notes, among the first to use the name Jutland (651-53).

Thus classical authors provide information on the early Danish past. It is what they have to tell that constitutes our knowledge about this remote period. Throughout it can be observed how Pontanus struggles to harmonize the information of classical texts with modern realities. He does not call attention to the geographical distance or to other factors which might have hampered their access to reliable information. Intertwined with this search for information is the patriotic effect of listing the numerous classical texts in which Denmark is mentioned. Denmark is made part of the classical world. This may actually be said to be one of

---

[28] Ptolemy, *Geographia*, II, Chs. 11, 7.

[29] Caesar, *Bellum Gallicum*, I, Chs. 31, 37, 51.

[30] *Maxime omnium septentrionales Cimbri referuntur* [...] *ita tamen ut omnis interim ipsorum fuerit regio, quæ Cimbrica Chersonesus dicitur, distincta in civitates seu populos plures, quorum præter Cimbros septem Ptolemæus enarravit* (649).

the fundamental messages of the *Chorographica descriptio* and indeed of Pontanus's *History of Denmark* as a whole: Scandinavia was not unknown to the classical authors.

In the same way, other historians before Pontanus had presented their countries as parts of the classical world, by digging out from classical texts references to the areas in question. Camden for one built his description of the early Britons' ways of living, customs and national character on classical sources – very much like Pontanus. Buchanan, in the third of the introductory books of his history of Scotland, collected a number of classical quotations – from Caesar, Tacitus, Orosius and others – pertinent to Scottish history. Rhenanus and Lazius in their descriptions of Germany and Vienna, respectively, took classical authorities as their starting point. These historians shared with Pontanus an extensive knowledge of classical texts, a firm (but not unshakable) belief in them,[31] and a predilection for etymological deductions.

After the publication of Pontanus's *History of Denmark* the identification of ancient Thule became a matter of heated dispute between Pontanus and the Icelandic historian Arngrímur Jónsson (1568-1648). Pontanus, in the *Chorographica descriptio*, objects to Arngrímur's view (put forward in earlier works, primarily the *Chrymogæa sive rerum Islandicarum libri III* of 1609) that the Thule mentioned in classical texts does not correspond to modern Iceland. Pontanus argues at some length that ancient Thule is indeed identical with Iceland (741-63); to this he appended large parts of the fantastic account of a journey to the fabulous islands Frislandia, Estlandia, and Entgrovelandia undertaken, so the text claims, by the Venetian Zeni brothers around 1380 (755-65). Pontanus vaguely states that the work is of relevance in connection with Iceland, but he does not comment further upon it.[32]

In response Arngrímur wrote a treatise in the course of the 1630s, entitled *Specimen Islandiæ historicum*, which was not, however, published until 1643 in Amsterdam, that is, after Pontanus's death.

---

[31] As illustrated by the following passage from Camden's *Britannia*: *Quia vero et locus exigere videtur, et sequenti mentioni lux maxima inde exoriatur, liceat mihi Romanorum in Britannia historiam non e fabellis nostris quas vani esset scribere, et stulti credere: sed ex incorruptis priscæ antiquitatis monumentis summatim, et carptim hic perstringere* [...], (Camden 1590, 38).

[32] *Quorum conatus ac pericula cum literis tradita sint et Islandiam quoque eique vicinas terras præcipue spectent, nec omnium hodie manibus habeantur, cujusmodi ad nos, ex Italico reddita Latine, fuerunt delata, his subjungere operæ pretium existimaui, æquo lectori judicium relinquens* (755). The account of the Zeni brothers' journey is now regarded as purely fictive, composed by a younger member of the Zeno family and published for the first time in 1558.

Arngrímur's point of view (which was shared by Stephanius and Ole Worm) reflects his interest in defending Icelandic historical sources as the chief testimonies on Icelandic affairs, sources which he blamed Pontanus for neglecting. According to them Iceland was not permanently inhabited until the Norwegians came in the ninth century. Pontanus, on the other hand, referred (753-54) to two letters by the emperor Ludovicus Pius and Pope Gregorius IV, dated 834 and 835, concerning the establishment of an archbishopric in Hamburg and Ansgar's vocation as archbishop there; in these letters, which he quotes *verbatim* in the chronological narrative (97-98), Iceland is mentioned as belonging to Ansgar's province. He takes this as an indication that Arngrímur cannot be right in asserting that Iceland was not settled until 874.[33]

Pontanus's opinion may be said to reflect his firm belief in the relevance of classical texts; they treat of things identifiable today. In a letter to Stephanius of 1638, he made it clear that here in his view real glory was to be found for the Icelanders; he did not understand, he said, why Arngrímur would not accept his point of view, which implied that Iceland was known by the Greeks and Romans; the island would thus gain considerable glory "from that antiquity on which almost all of us usually pride ourselves".[34]

5. The Influence of Tacitus's Germania

Of special importance among Pontanus's classical sources is Tacitus's *Germania*. Ever since this small ethnographical treatise had become known to German humanists in the last half of the fifteenth century, it had served as an inspiration for feelings of national pride.[35] Against the

---

[33] See Jakob Benediktsson's thorough account of the dispute in the introduction to his edition of Arngrímur's *Specimen* (Arngrímur, ed. Benediktsson, 1950-57, XII, 419-27). In a survey of the concept of Thule in the sixteenth and seventeenth centuries M. Mund-Dopchie 1992 notes that Pontanus's identification of Thule with Iceland was indeed the *communis opinio* at the time. She gives credit to Arngrímur for his attentive reading of the *Landnamabók* and notes Pontanus's somewhat selective use of classical texts in this discussion.

[34] *At id cur obsecro optimus ille doctissimusque Arngrimus agere tantopere urgereque identidem constituit? Quid decedat ipsi Islandiæ hoc si adstruatur? imo quid non accedat ex ipsa antiquitate, qua gloriari fere cuncti solemus, si hoc admittatur, et maxime cum tam diserte, quod toties totiesque hanc in rem adduxi, ex Norvagia navigari solitum in Thulen Plinius memoret?* (Letter from Pontanus to Stephanius, dated July 1st, 1638 (Matthæus 1695, no. 122)).

[35] The ideological impact in Germany of Tacitus's *Germania* is a subject which has, in the course of the last century, received considerable scholarly interest. Many central authors are

Italian humanists' contemptuous accusations of barbarity, drunkenness, rapaciousness, their German counterparts, with this new literary weapon in their hands, were able to describe the ways of living and the moral habits of the ancient Germans in positive terms. Unlike contemporary Romans, German tribes in the first century AD had been freedom-loving, honest, proud, noble, and so on; these ancient Germans described by Tacitus were, it was broadly agreed, the ancestors of modern Germans. The heyday of this, at times, hysterically patriotic movement was the first half of the sixteenth century. This was the period of political exhortations, when German humanists, such as Conrad Celtis (d.1508) and Ulrich von Hutten (1488-1523), expressed their hope in forceful terms that Germany could again achieve its ancient glory.[36] But although this direct political exploitation of Tacitus's *Germania* waned, it still remained one of the basic texts of German historical scholarship.[37] A central theme was the moral purity of the ancient Germans in that golden age, excelling as they did in such virtues as charity and hospitality.[38]

Pontanus's description of the Danes and their country has in many respects been shaped by Tacitus's *Germania* and the Germanistic movement. The *Germani* of Tacitus was, he noted, a collective term including the *Cimbri, Sueones, Fenni and Venedi*,[39] who were the ancestors of modern Scandinavians (642).[40] Like his German predecessors he regarded Tacitus as an eyewitness to German affairs, on the assumption that he had been travelling in the region: "As procurator he was an eye-witness in Belgic Gaul".[41] We shall here look at some of his Tacitean themes, with retrospective glances at the procedure of the German humanists of the previous century.

---

presented in Joachimsen 1910 (rep. 1968). Even more thorough is the modern standard work by Jacques Ridé (1977). Valuable, too, is Frank L. Borchardt's monograph (1971), which discusses the various theories of the German past from the fifteenth and sixteenth centuries in the light of the sources from antiquity and the Middle Ages. Another recent, but less detailed, treatment is found in Chs. 2 and 3 of K.C. Schellhase's work on Tacitus's influence on Renaissance political thought (1976).

[36] K.C. Schellhase 1976, 31-49.

[37] K.C. Schellhase 1976, 60.

[38] Jacques Ridé 1977, II, 1167sqq.

[39] Tacitus deals with these peoples in *Germania*, Chs. 37, 44, 46. Pontanus later discusses at length the identity of the *Venedi*, concluding that they were of the same German origin as the *Vendeli* and the *Vandali* (708-13).

[40] Later he notes again: [...] *septentrionales, quos suam etiam intra Germaniam conclusit Tacitus* (688).

[41] *autopa Galliæ Belgicæ procurator fuit* (684). Cf. Jacques Ridé 1977, I, 162, III, 67.

The notion of indigenousness is a central point in the *Germania*. The Germans are depicted as unmixed with other peoples.[42] The German humanists had seized upon this idea with enthusiasm, claiming to have here the explanation of native German military strength and virtues and the astonishing ability of the Germans to remain untainted by foreign vice.[43]

Pontanus follows suit. He introduces the *Chorographica descriptio* with a discussion of the origin of the Danes, taking as his starting point the name of Denmark (639-43). Numerous theories have been put forward, we learn. According to one of them, the Danes were descendants of the *Dahae*, a people mentioned by various classical authors as living beyond the Caspian Sea. Interestingly, Pontanus had been approached with this idea, while working on his *History of Denmark*, by the chancellor Christen Friis himself. Friis had apparently pointed out some resemblances between the Danish and Persian languages (*lingua Parthorum*), and in his reply Pontanus politely refuses to accept the theory; the idea is interesting, he says, and if we only had proof of a migration to our part of the world, it might convince the sceptics. In the *History of Denmark* itself, however, he reveals himself as one of these sceptics (640).[44] – Not only do we have here another indication of the chancellor's active engagement in Danish history, it is also notable that Pontanus felt free to argue against his employer. The idea of the Persian origin of the Germans was also rejected by Ubbo Emmius in his history of Friesland of 1616.

Among the various theories about the name of Denmark, Pontanus prefers to derive the name from *Danschiones*, a people who, according to Ptolemy, lived in Scandinavia.[45] Whereas the other theories make it necessary to assume that migrations, unmentioned in classical literature, took place from the south to Scandinavia, Ptolemy actually locates the *Danschiones* in Scandinavia. And that is the point: the Germans – to whom, as we saw, the Scandinavians belong – have lived where they live now ever since Japhet. This is the meaning of Tacitus's famous dictum

---

[42] Tacitus, *Germania*, Chs. 2, 4.

[43] A point of view suggested by Tacitus himself: *Ipse eorum opinionibus accedo, qui Germaniae populos nullis aliis aliarum nationum conubiis infectos propriam et sinceram et tantum sui similem gentem extitisse arbitrantur* (*Germania*, Ch. 4). Cf. Jacques Ridé 1977, II, 1056-1119.

[44] Pontanus's reply to Friis (dated 1627) is found in Matthæus 1695, no. 90, and in Rørdam 1898, 484-85.

[45] *Geographia*, II, Ch. 11,16; in the edition by Mullerus 1883, they are called *Daukiones*. I have not had an opportunity to examine older editions in order to check whether the form *Danschiones* is used.

that the Germans were *indigenae*, Pontanus declares; there have been no immigrations from south to north since Japhet (642). Whatever Friis thought of Pontanus's theory of the *Danschiones*, he could hardly complain about its patriotic spirit, implying as it did an unbroken settlement in Denmark since the generation after Noah.

On Tacitus's evidence Pontanus now states that the Germans have never been affected by Greek or Asian or other exotic customs, and have been able to maintain their own hospitable ways of living.[46] This is quite in agreement with earlier German humanists, such as Andreas Althamer (d. 1564) who, in his influential commentary on the *Germania*, emphatically rejected the idea of a Greek, Roman or other foreign origin of the Germans.[47] The ideological impact is clear. Not only does Pontanus establish the important link between Danish history and the Bible and provide the Danes with a very long history as an independent people, he also stresses the moral purity of the ancient Germans.

The identification of ancient and modern Germans as the same people led to the assertion among early German humanists that Germans of the sixteenth century still possessed the qualities of their ancestors. "Our best claim to honor and glory, however, is founded upon our superior virtue, a trait in which we excel all the other nations of mankind", declared the German humanist and poet Heinrich Bebel (1472-1516) in the first decade of the sixteenth century in an oration to the emperor Maximilian I.[48]

---

[46] Having quoted *Germania*, Ch. 2 Pontanus goes on: *Quibus in verbis Tacitus cum indigenas facit Germanos, indicare voluit, eos qui jam ante innotuerant Romanis, et tum indies ijsdem innotescerent, hominum fuisse genus qui non aliunde venerint, sed ibi nati essent, utpote sui tantum similis gens. Ut ita indigenarum vocem accipiamus non quasi autochonem esse aut terrigenam hunc populum velimus, sed qui sedes istas, in quas a primis suis archegis Iapetho et Gomero deductus fuerat, continenter incoluerit, nullis exinde Asiæ aut Græciæ aut gentium similium exoticis, sed sui tantum soli moribus hospitijsque assuefactus* (642).

[47] The following passage is from Althamer's commentary on Tacitus's *indigenas* (*Germ.*, Ch. 2): *Frivolum itaque comentum est, nullaque firma authoritate fulcitum, eorum, qui finxerunt, quosdam Germanorum a Græcis aut Romanis, aut aliis peregrinis gentibus ortos [...] Ast ego [...] malo [...] dicere, Germanos gnæsios, hoc est, vere germanos, sinceros, indigenas, in ipsa Germania genitos, ab nulla exotica natione derivatos* (Althamerus 1609 (first ed. 1536)). This commentary, which had already appeared in a shorter form in 1529, was reprinted several times, and Pontanus also refers to it in the *Chorographica descriptio* (647). On Althamer, see Paul Joachimsen 1910 (rep. 1968), 146-50 (with further references).

[48] Heinrich Bebel: *Oratio ad Maximilianum I Caesarem de ejus atque Germaniae laudibus*. Here quoted (in G. Strauss's trans.) from Donald R. Kelley's anthology: *Versions of History* [...](1991), 346-49. Cf. also the title of a poem by Ulrich von Hutten from 1511: *Quod Germania nec virtutibus nec ducibus ab primoribus degeneravit* (*Opera omnia* III, 331-40; I owe this reference to Schellhase 1976, 40). Celtis likewise recognized the physical and mental characteris-

But the chorus of patriotic German historians in the first half of the sixteenth century was not entirely in unison. Beatus Rhenanus deplored, in the *Castigationes* to his edition of Tacitus's works (Basel 1533), the sad moral degeneration since the time of the ancient modern Germans, and he was echoed by Andreas Althamer in his commentary on the *Germania* (1536).[49]

In one case Pontanus seems to adopt the idea of a moral degeneration, introducing at the same time an important distinction between Scandinavians and other Germans. The famous German hospitality praised by Tacitus,[50] indeed the general moral habits of the ancient Germans, he says, now only survive in Scandinavia.[51] Pontanus knew both Rhenanus's edition and Althamer's commentary and may very well have been inspired directly by them.[52] At any rate Pontanus turns the idea of degeneration into praise of the Scandinavians. They have preserved the old moral standards, the *prisci mores*, better than other Germans.

The hospitality of the Scandinavians was evidently a quality which Pontanus wanted to stress. He returns to it twice – the first time in his short presentation of Norway (to which we shall return), the next time in his description of the Danish national character:

> Tacitus, speaking of the Germans, asserts that no other people is as prone to festivity and feasting and that they regard it as a crime to exclude anyone from their house.[53]

---

tics of the ancient Germans in his own contemporaries, as emphasized by Joachimsen 1910 (rep. 1968), 111. – The same reasoning, but to the opposite effect, was made by the Italians who transferred the defects of the ancient Germans to their modern counterparts. Jacques Ridé notes that the Italians' fundamental assumption was that the moral and the cultural level of a people go hand in hand (Ridé 1977, I, 122).

[49] *Jam virtus languescere coepit. flagitia laudari, probitatem proscribi, et omnia pessum ire cernimus* (Althamerus 1609, 265). Rhenanus deplores the modern moral decline in his commentary to *Germania*, Ch. 19 (Rhenanus 1542 (first ed. 1533), 162). His comment is quoted by Althamer in his commentary to the *Germania* and also by K.C. Schellhase 1976, 63 & 195. See also Jacques Ridé 1977, II, 1185.

[50] Tacitus, *Germania*, Ch. 21.

[51] *Non quod hodie adhuc apud Germanos eum durare morem velim innuere, sed ut pateat potius quantum hic illi a prisca consuetudine recesserint, quamque soli septentrionales, quos suam etiam intra Germaniam conclusit Tacitus, eum hodieque morem ac priscæ ingenuitatis simplicitatem, toti olim Germaniæ familiarem, constanter retineant* (688).

[52] He refers to Beatus Rhenanus's edition of the *Germania* on p. 774, and to Althamer's commentary on p. 647.

[53] *Tacitus de Germanis loquens asserit haud aliam gentem convictibus atque hospitiis effusius indulsisse, et nefas apud eos habitum mortalium quenquam tecto arcuisse* (777). Cf. Tacitus, *Germania*, Ch. 21: *quemcumque mortalium arcere tecto nefas habetur*.

Tacitus's Germans also had their faults, such as excessive drinking. Beatus Rhenanus deplored the German habit of drinking, which he found flourishing among his contemporaries.[54] But others tried to belittle the problem in diverse ways. Johannes Nauklerus, for instance, author of a *Weltchronik* (1516), drew attention to a passage in Caesar to the opposite effect.[55] Others diminished the importance of the habit. Thus Hutten, in his dialogue *Inspicientes* (1520), in which the interlocuters are Apollo and his son Phaethon, let Apollo himself dispose of the problem by emphasizing that they only drink at night.[56]

Pontanus also finds a solution. He is able to make a happy combination of Tacitus and Saxo. "As to Tacitus's assertion that the Germans drink and feast excessively", he says, "we learn from Saxo that this vice was only introduced much later in Denmark".[57] Caesar tells us, he goes on, that wine was unknown or at least unused among the *Nervii* (in Belgic Gaul); from Italy the use and abuse of wine spread to Germany during the centuries after Caesar. Danish innocence, in other words, lasted longer than that of other Germans; when Scandinavians finally did learn to drink, the teachers were their southern neighbours. Finally Pontanus (with a quotation from Pliny) notes that even the Romans were prone to drinking. This is his way of minimizing the whole problem (778).[58]

In this case, then, the Scandinavians are not "super-Germans" more close to their ancient fathers than other Germans. On the contrary, the

---

[54] Luther also deplored this habit of his fellow countrymen with reference to Tacitus (Jacques Ridé 1977, II, 1189).

[55] Paul Joachimsen 1910 (rep. 1968), 97 (cf. Caesar, *Bellum Gallicum*, IV, Ch. 2). The same procedure was adopted by Franciscus Irenicus in his *Germaniae exegesis*, II, 18 (1518) (Jacques Ridé 1977, II, 1188-91).

[56] U. v. Hutten, *Opera omnia* IV, 269-308 (I owe the reference to K.C. Schellhase 1976, 44).

[57] *Alias de Germanis quod addit iterum Tacitus, convivia effuse et armatos subinde agitare eos, nec ulli probro fuisse diem noctemque continuare potando, id mali etiam Danos, sed serius, afflasse ex Saxone est intelligere* (778). Cf. Tacitus, *Germania*, Ch. 22. Pontanus goes on to quote two passages from Saxo, one on King Ingellus who allowed luxurious German habits at his court (VI, Ch. viii, 7) and one on Sveno (in the twelfth century) who likewise preferred foreign sumptuousness to domestic simplicity (XIV, Ch. ix, 1).

[58] Jacques Ridé goes through a whole number of strategies adopted by the German humanists, some of which resemble that of Pontanus:
   a. Other peoples also drink. **b.** Warlike peoples are particularly prone to drinking. **c.** It was an effect of the German climate. The need for alcohol increases the farther north one comes. **d.** Since wine was unknown to the Germans, they drank a fruit juice weak in alcohol. **e.** They only drank rarely and in order to celebrate the gods. **f.** The vice was imported, since only the Germans close to the Roman empire had the possibility of consuming wine. Others simply chose to disregard Tacitus on this point. (Ridé 1977, II, 1188-91).

reader is here asked to accept that Tacitus did not have the Scandinavians in mind when he criticized the drinking habits of the Germans. Pontanus does recognize the existence of beer in ancient Denmark, to which, in another context, he ascribes their occasional drunkenness.[59]

The war-like spirit of Tacitus's Germans was perhaps the most constant topic of the patriotic writings of the German humanists, who also eagerly noted the occurence of this virtue in later periods.[60] Heinrich Bebel expressed this aspect of German history forcefully: "The Germans surpass all other peoples in bravery", he declared.[61] Again Pontanus follows suit. In the *Chorographica descriptio* he supports the notion that the word *Cimber* is related to the modern Danish verb *kæmpe*, fight, (776), and in the chronological narrative the victories and plunderings of the Cimbrians, the Goths, the Angles, and later the Normans are all treated as parts of Danish history – and very noteworthy parts. Some of these events had also been important as examples of German heroism in German historians,[62] but Pontanus emphasizes that these heroes were specifically ancestors of the Danes.

At the same time Pontanus is at pains to demonstrate the high cultural level of the Danes, both in ancient and recent times, and devotes a long section to the treatment of *Danorum ingenia, studia, mores* (775-92). As a matter of fact, Tacitus did not have much to say about the cultural life of the Germans. It amounted to a brief reference to the songs in which they commemorated past events and songs before battle.[63] But Pontanus makes the most of these few lines. Having boldly declared that the learning of the Danes is not far from being on a par with that of the Italians, he then goes on to criticize the Italian historian Paolo Giovio (1483-

---

[59] He objects to a correction suggested by Beatus Rhenanus. Tacitus's words *ut inter vinolentos* (*Germania*, Ch. 22) about the Germans' quarrels after having been drinking, Beatus, in his commentary on the *Germania*, wanted to change to *ut inter violentos*, because the Germans did not have wine (Rhenanus 1542 (first ed. 1533), 163). No, says Pontanus, Tacitus means that they behaved as if they had been drinking wine – because the effect of beer is the same (774-75).

[60] Jacques Ridé 1977, II, 1119-63.

[61] *Germani fortitudine cunctis gentibus excellunt.* From Bebel's *De laude veterum Germanorum* (1509), quoted from Ridé 1977, II, 1121. Another example is Johannes Cochlaeus's emphasis on the German *bellica virtus* in his *Brevis Germaniæ descriptio* of 1512 (Cochlaeus, ed. Langosh 1960, II, 14). Jacques Ridé 1977 quotes Celtis to the same effect (II, 1124).

[62] Jacques Ridé 1977, I, 446, II, 837, 1126, 1135, III, 392.

[63] *Celebrant carminibus antiquis, quod unum apud illos memoriae et annalium genus est, Tuistonem deum terra editum* (Tacitus, *Germania* Ch. 2) and *sunt illis haec quoque carmina, quorum relatu, quem barritum vocant, accendunt animos futuraeque pugnae fortunam ipso cantu augurantur* [...] (*ibidem* Ch. 3).

1552), who had expressed his surprise that the modern Germans had risen to such cultural excellence in view of their previous barbarity (779). No, says Pontanus. If Giovio had only cared to consider the history of the Danes, he would have realized how they have always combined their love of Mars with their love of the Muses. Again Pontanus is able to point to an agreement between Saxo and Tacitus. Saxo tells us, he says, that the Danes used to commemorate their glorious deeds both in the composition of oral poetry and in inscriptions on rocks, just as if he wanted to explain to us what Tacitus meant by his reference to the commemorative songs of the Germans.[64]

His final argument in favour of a sophisticated culture in ancient Denmark is (as earlier mentioned) about the successor of Frode Fredegod, Hjarne the Poet (*Hjarne Skjald*). He made his way to the throne solely by means of his songs, which created such an impression on the people and the nobility that they instantly chose him as their king. This was a small effort and a huge reward – which far surpassed the respect that Scipio paid Ennius by honouring his statue and, after he had died, his grave. The implicit message of this comparison (which Pontanus borrowed from Saxo's *Gesta Danorum* VI, ch. i), is, of course, that the ancient Danes outdid even the Romans in their respect for cultural activities (780).

Among the earlier German humanists some like Pontanus emphasized the high cultural level of the ancient Germans.[65] Others, among whom was Andreas Althamer, had accepted the Italian picture of the rude ancient Germans and contrasted it with the immense progress in German culture since Tacitus.

Pontanus, as we saw, proudly points out (773) that only few laws were in existence in Denmark, referring to Lipsius's recommendation in his *Politica* (1589). This was also a favourite topic of the Germans, who were particularly fond of Tacitus's phrase: *plusque ibi boni mores valent quam alibi bonae leges* ("and good habits carry more weight there than good laws elsewhere").[66]

---

[64] Cf. Saxo, *Gesta Danorum*, Preface.

[65] Jacques Ridé 1977, I, 236-45.

[66] *Germania*, Ch. 19. See Jacques Ridé 1977, II, 1168sqq.

6. *Gothicism Dismissed*

The Germanistic ideology has many points in common with the Swedish Gothicism of Johannes Magnus; both must be seen against the background of the Italian humanistic contempt of northern European barbarity.[67] Magnus's Goths are noble and brave, just as the Germanistic Germans, and they are culturally highly advanced. Remarkable, too, is their hospitality, another topos of the Germanists.[68] But Magnus's fabrications are considerably more daring than those of his German colleagues. As will be recalled, he depicts a heroic and learned Gothic golden age, older and more refined than the classical world, and exclusively Swedish. The Danes have no share in Magnus's Gothic glory; on the contrary, he is throughout vehemently anti-Danish. Only the Swedes were descended from the Goths, who in turn were the off-spring of Noah's son Japhet.

The notion of Gothicism was based on various favourable descriptions of the Goths from late antiquity, primarily Jordanes's history of the Goths, *Getica*, which dates their emigration from the island Scandza before the Trojan war and describes their conquests in heroic terms. There is medieval evidence both from Sweden and the Continent that Sweden was regarded as the original home of the Goths. In the fifteenth century, in connection with the national movement in Sweden against the Union of Kalmar, which was dominated by Denmark, Gothicist sentiments began to be seriously cultivated in Sweden, as is clear from a number of works still extant. Eventually, Johannes Magnus in his *History of the Swedish kings* of 1554 delivered the canonical version of Swedish Gothicism.[69]

While also clearly inspired by the Germanistic trend, as we have seen, Pontanus has (not surprisingly) no sympathy with Magnus's construc-

---

[67] See Kurt Johannesson 1982, 114-20. Jacques Ridé 1977 also notes the similarity and refers to Gothicism as "germanistique scandinave" (II, 928; III, 332).

[68] Magnus describes how the Swedish king Carolus once, in the legendary past, decreed that his subjects should always excel in hospitality: [...] *constituit ut Gothi ac Sueci inter se, et maxime in omnes advenas et peregrinos hospitalitatem observarent, summumque nefas ducerent, quicumque viatorem a tecto coerceret* [...] (153; I refer to the edition of 1617). Cf. Tacitus: [...] *quemcumque mortalium arcere tecto nefas habetur* (*Germania*, Ch. 21), the same passage from Tacitus's *Germania* that we have seen Pontanus allude to. Magnus concludes from this that the Swedes must be the most hospitable people in Europe in his own time: *Hinc ego deductum puto, quod vix alibi in tota Europa promptior liberaliorque hospitalitas quam apud Sueones et Gothos hodie inveniatur* (153).

[69] On the history of Gothicism, see J. Svennung 1967 and Johan Nordström 1934.

tions, whose basis he sets out to destroy. His main point is that the Goths and the Getae are not the same people, although they have been regarded as such since the fourth century; from earlier authors, such as Herodotus and Strabo,[70] he argues, it is clear that the Getae were a Thracian people; but the Goths were Germans. It is the false identification with the Getae, he goes on, that enabled Jordanes (in the sixth century) in his history of the Goths to describe their early past in such detail. In fact we know nothing of their history before the second century AD, Pontanus declares; they settled in Dacia after 160 AD, and this caused the following generations to identify them with the Dacians, the Getae, and Scythians; authors such as Jerome, Orosius, and Claudianus (all writing around 400 AD) use *Gothi* and *Getae* indiscriminately (675-76).

This is actually an impressive piece of scholarship – set forth in more detail than suggested here; *inter alia* Pontanus also enters into a dispute with Joseph Scaliger, in whose notes to Eusebius the identity of Goths and Getae had also been claimed (677-79). While he was not the first to draw this distinction between the Goths and the Getae,[71] Pontanus does seem to have been the first to recognize its undermining effects on the notion of Gothicism. Modern scholarship agrees: in the standard work on Swedish Gothicism J. Svennung (who betrays no knowledge of Pontanus) also makes it clear that it was the confusion of Goths and Getae that provided the basis for the development of Gothicism.[72]

Having established his fundamental error, Pontanus is now in a position to give the deathblow to Magnus's Gothicism; not only did Magnus repeat the error of Jordanes, he enlarged it by his numerous inventions.

---

[70] Herodotus, *Histories*, IV, Ch. 93; Strabo, *Geography*, VII, Ch. 3,2.

[71] Paul Joachimsen mentions that Beatus Rhenanus had distinguished between the two peoples, (Joachimsen 1910 (rep. 1968), 153). Pontanus himself in a letter of 1632 refers to the geographer Philipp Clüver's (1580-1622) arguments in favour of such a distinction. This letter, addressed to Constantin Huygens (poet and diplomat 1596-1687) and written in October 1632, criticizes Daniel Heinsius for the confusion of *Gothi* and *Getæ* in his recent and otherwise praiseworthy panegyric of the Swedish king (Gustav Adolf). Pontanus supports Clüver's point of view by various arguments, among which is the testimony of Ptolemy (Matthæus 1695, no. 52). In the *History of Denmark* Pontanus, in one of the following chapters, also finds occasion to give credit to Clüver for his distinction between *Gothi* and *Getae*, but here it only serves as an introduction to a lengthy rejection of Clüver's theory that the *Gothi* are identical with the *Gothones* (679-82). Clüver's theory localized the Goths in the region around Danzig (Clüver's own homeland, as Pontanus points out) and thus removes them from Scandinavia altogether, a point of view with which Pontanus has no sympathy.

[72] J. Svennung 1967, 1-10.

Pontanus is rather sarcastic in making the point that, once the basis is removed, all that remains of Magnus's constructions is what he has got by "begging" from Saxo, that is, a Danish historian.[73]

The unusual aggressiveness of this passage must be seen in the light of Magnus's influence on contemporary Swedish propaganda. His Gothic fantasies provided material for extolling Swedish triumphs against the Catholics in the Thirty Years War as yet another expression of Gothic bravery against Rome.[74] This popularity of Magnus's *History of the Swedish Kings*, hostile to everything Danish as it is, must have caused concern in Danish government circles and Pontanus's rejection was probably highly welcomed. It is important to note that Magnus, not Sweden, is the target. Pontanus simply points to the fundamental error of his constructions, without giving any hint of anti-Swedish polemics. This agrees well with the cautiousness in relation to Sweden displayed by the chancellor when he asked Meursius to treat the Swedes in a more friendly fashion in his history of the Oldenburg kings (cf. Chs. IV,3, VII). While in fact demolishing the whole basis of Gothicism, Pontanus's strictly scholarly arguments could not be said to violate the prohibition of 1570 against defamatory writings. Magnus is here defeated with learned weapons.

Still, Pontanus did not reject a kind of moderate Gothicism. In the chronological history he depicts Gothic triumphs in late antiquity at length. Shortly after his rejection of Magnus, he sums up the achievement of the Goths in these words:

> So much so that, after this noblest and bravest of peoples, the Gothic race, had made Germany, Gaul, Spain and Italy obedient to its word, the Emperor Charles V was quite right when he was accustomed to say, as Levinus Lemnius testifies, that the entire aristocracy in the whole of

---

[73] *Quod idem secutus etiam superiori seculo Ioannes Gothus archiepiscopus Upsalensis, non tantum, quæ Iornandes est prosecutus Getica et Scythica, suam in rem vertit, ac Suedicam istis calamistris exornavit aut potius oneravit historiam, sed et tredecim præterea Gothorum reges ante Bericum, Iornandi primum, producit, qui omnes in Scandia Gothis imperitarint ante ipsorum e peninsula egressum. Egressum autem eum in annum rejicit a diluvio octingentesimum septuagesimum quintum, qui fuit ante natum Christum millesimus quadringentesimus trigesimus; quo tempore filij Israelis a Iudice Othoniele regebantur. Quas si demamus ex illo opere, Geticas inquam Scythicasque res, exiguus profecto reliquus erit ab eodem ex Saxone Grammatico Danorum historiographo emendatus rerum Suedicarum acervus. Et ausus idem non Gothos tantum in Scytas transformare, sed fucum insuper lectori incauto faciens, affirmare historiæ suæ libro I capitulo 23 non erubuit, quasi Strabo libro XI Massagetas orientales esse Gothos asseruerit: Cum Strabo ne per somnium quidem Gothorum uspiam meminerit (676).*

[74] Johan Nordström 1934.

Europe had been propagated from the regions of Scandia and Goth-
land.[75]

Pontanus, then, limits his account of the Goths to classical and medieval
times, basing it on Isidore of Seville's *Historia Gothorum* and other late
classical works. But its ideological impact is still considerable. For one
thing, Pontanus makes it clear that the Goths were not a Swedish
monopoly. They had their original home in the whole of Scandinavia,
and not, as Swedish authors would have it, exclusively in Sweden. In a
chapter on the name of Jutland (653-54), Pontanus emphasizes the close
relationship between the roots *Got-*, *Gut-*, and *Jut-*, leaving the reader with
the impression that Jutland was also a home of the ancient Goths.

Interestingly, the chancellor, Christen Friis, had himself taken up this
theme in a letter to Pontanus in 1624. In his reply, Pontanus refers with
approval to the proposal put forward by the chancellor that the Goths
and the Danes were one people. Pontanus here produces the same arguments as in the *Chorographica descriptio* (653-54), some of which, as he
makes clear in the letter, had in fact come from Friis himself.[76] It is perhaps significant that in the printed work Pontanus did not put it as
bluntly as Friis had apparently done in his letter, that Goths and Danes
are one people. He or Friis or both may well have feared Swedish reactions to this idea which might be taken to suggest that the Goths were
forefathers of the Danes only. Pontanus did not want to deprive the
Swedes of their Gothic past, and in the chronological history he says
explicitly that the Goths emigrated from Scandinavia and the adjacent
islands (59). But he clearly wanted to claim a share of the Gothic glory
for the Danes – and in the letter we have evidence that he shared this
wish with the chancellor.

---

[75] *Adeo ut nobilissima hæc fortissimaque gentium, Gothorum natio, cum exinde Germaniam, Galliam, His-
paniam Italiamque sibi dicto audientem fecerit, haud immerito sit dicere solitus Imperator Carolus Quintus,
testante Levino Lemnio, universam totius Europæ nobilitatem e Scandia et Gothia tractibus fuisse prosem-
inatam* (682). This passage forms the conclusion of Pontanus's arguments against Philipp
Clüver who, as mentioned above, had suggested that the whole of this story of the Gothic
emigrations from Scandinavia was pure fabrication.
[76] The letter is dated October 18, 1624 and printed in Matthæus 1695, no. 95, and in Rørdam
1898, 482-84.

The Chronological Narrative of Pontanus's
Rerum Danicarum historia

The chronological narrative of Pontanus's *Rerum Danicarum historia* consists of two parts. The first covers the period from the earliest times up to 1448, when the Oldenburg kings ascended the throne. This part takes up pp. 1-636 of the 1631 edition. The second part, which Pontanus left behind in manuscript, treats the period 1448-1588, that is, the reigns of the Oldenburg kings from Christianus I to Fredericus II. It was published in 1740 by E. J. v. Westphalen in his *Monumenta inedita rerum Germanicarum*, Vol. II, cols. 713-1230.[1]

The first part of the present chapter, Sections 1-5, goes through the work from the beginning onwards, focusing on the challenges presented to Pontanus in reworking his source material into a history of Denmark. Most attention is devoted to the first five books, that is, the period up to 1157, which is treated in Sections 1-4. The rest of the work (Books VI-X and the Oldenburg Section) is presented more briefly in Section 5. The reason for this arrangement is that the early periods of Danish history up to c. 1200 posed special problems for Pontanus, inasmuch as he chose to base his account on a variety of classical and medieval texts and not simply to rewrite Saxo's *Gesta Danorum*. His use of sources for the period c. 1200-1588, on the other hand, is much more simple, since Huitfeldt's *History*, which he had also consulted earlier on, was now the unrivalled main source; throughout this part Pontanus's procedure is basically the same.

I have found it most purposeful to present this part of Pontanus's work (Books VI-X and the Oldenburgs) thematically. In the second part of the present chapter, Section 6, I have selected a number of themes for discussion, most of which belong to the political and ideological sphere, and we shall often have occasion to notice how Pontanus departs from Huitfeldt on such questions. Although focus in this thematical section is on Pontanus's treatment of the period 1157-1588, I have also, where it seemed natural, taken the earlier part into consideration.

It is a characteristic feature of Pontanus's *History* that he constantly refers to and quotes from other texts. In the ten books up to 1448 alone I have counted references to well over 200 different works and authors, to which must be added the numerous inscriptions either quoted or men-

---

[1] I refer to Pontanus's 1631 edition by pages and to Westphalen's edition by columns.

tioned; the total number of references and quotations in this first part comes close to 1000, excluding quotations of documents. We shall return to this in the chapter on style.

1. The Introduction

Like other historians of his time Pontanus in the *Chorographica descriptio* resorted to classical historians for information on the earliest national past. Traditional accounts of the early history were rejected. In the course of the sixteenth century many European historians – e.g. Paolo Emilio, Polydore Vergil, Beatus Rhenanus, George Buchanan, William Camden – had expressed their distrust of traditional tales of eponymous founders of a nation. When writing the chronological narrative, Pontanus was faced with the problem of the traditional legendary early history, as told by Saxo Grammaticus. The very first words of Pontanus's first book make clear his attitude towards Saxo's account of early Danish history:

> Those who have written about the first beginnings of the Danes – particularly Saxo Grammaticus and others who follow him – all agree that Danus was the founder of the people. I, however, putting these things aside or leaving them out for a short while, have found it better to begin with the migration of the Cimbrians from their home in their peninsula [Jutland]. These events are known from the greatest authors, whereas the other things – which are narrated instead, as being very old – largely resemble those traditions mentioned by the great author Livy, which belonged to the time before the foundation of Rome, or the time when it was about to be founded, and which were beautiful stories rather than facts based upon trustworthy historical proofs. Meanwhile, I have not wanted to omit to bring forward that which has historical worth, although these things so remote from our own time as well as antiquity in general have a right not only to our reverence but also to our tolerance.[2]

Here Pontanus manages to combine a thinly veiled distrust in Saxo with respect for the traditional, long and heroic Danish past. As he explains, his point of departure will instead be the solid classical accounts of the Cimbrians. Saxo's dubious stories will not be excluded, however, but follow later. They are, as Livy says of the early Roman myths, "rather beautiful stories than based upon trustworthy historical proofs". Still

[2] *QUI res Danorum a primis initijs ad posterorum memoriam literis consignatas tradiderunt, quos inter præcipue Saxo Grammaticus alijque eum secuti, Danum gentis conditorem uno omnes consensu memorant. Nos, sepositis aut omissis paulisper istis, auspicium potius ab ipsa Cimbrorum e sua chersoneso egressione*

quoting Livy, he then stresses the reverence and hence the tolerance with which these old myths should be regarded, and later, again using Livy's words, he declares that he will neither affirm nor refute these old stories.[3] Livy's elegant and shrewd reservations with regard to early Roman history are thus very appropriately adapted to Danish origins.[4]

Pontanus here echoes the English historian William Camden. Writing of the early English past, Camden was faced with the same problem, acknowledging the sentimental force of tradition in these words:

> In this matter everybody must form his own judgement; whatever the reader thinks is not a matter of great importance to me. Let it be the privilege of antiquity to mingle false things with true, divine things with human, and so to add dignity to the beginnings of cities.[5]

Camden here uses the same passage from Livy to confront the problem of the early myths. Livy provided a model for combining distrust and respect, and, notably, the allusion to Livy entailed a parallel between Roman past and English/Danish past. This scepticism regarding the remotest past was given a patriotic twist: great nations like Rome, England, and Denmark have a right to heroic myths.

2. Books I-III (The early history, up to c. AD 750)

An Alternative to Saxo

Pontanus now sets out to give an alternative version of early Danish history, building on material found in classical descriptions of the northern European peoples. Danish history in his version takes its beginning from

---

faciendum censuimus; Quod ea maximis authoribus prodita, ista vero, quæ vicem eorum, ut vetustissima recitantur, ejusmodi multa sint, qualia esse quoque illa, quæ ante conditam condendamque Romam a scriptoribus sunt memorata, decora magis relatu, quam incorruptis rerum gestarum monumentis tradita, summus authorum Livius retulit. Interim tamen in medium adduxisse, quæ historiam præsertim spectant, haud omittendum existimavi, quamvis et alias antiquitati, et rebus illis a memoria nostra remotissimis, sua debeatur ut reverentia, sic etiam venia (1).

Cf. Livy, Preface, 6-7: *Quae ante conditam condendamve urbem poeticis magis decora fabulis quam incorruptis rerum gestarum monumentis traduntur, ea nec adfirmare nec refellere in animo est. Datur haec venia antiquitati, ut miscendo humana divinis primordia urbium augustiora faciat.*

In translating the Pontanus passage I have borrowed from the Loeb translation of Livy when the two texts agree.

[3] *Quorum ego et nomina et facta etiam præcipua, secutus præsertim Saxonem, ita deinceps recensebo, non ut ea vel affirmare vel refellere sit animus* [...] (11). Cf. Livy, Preface 6.

[4] I have presented these observations on Pontanus's use of Livy in Skovgaard-Petersen 1994.

[5] *In hac re suum cuique liberum esto per me iudicium, quicquid existimarit lector, haud equidem in magno ponam discrimine. Detur hæc venia antiquitati, vt miscendo falsa veris et humana diuinis, primordia gentium, et vrbium augustiora faciat* (Camden 1590, 6).

the migration of the Cimbrians and the Teutones from their homes – Jutland and the adjacent isles – around 110 BC to Noricum, Helvetia, and finally Italy, where they were defeated by the Roman general Marius. Having related this in great detail (mostly based on Plutarch's biography of Marius), Pontanus surveys the Cimbrians' role in Roman literature up to Tacitus, after whom they are not mentioned until they occur in the poems of Claudianus around 400. The heroic nature of the Cimbrian expeditions is summed up at the beginning of Book Two: "they demonstrate the people's power and [...] their strength in war, which inspired great fear in the Romans".[6]

The Cimbrians were not only great warriors, they were also civilized. Having related how they released their enemies because they had fought so well, Pontanus exclaims: "This act on the part of the barbarians, as the Romans called them, was hardly barbarous. In their admiration of virtue, even the virtue of their enemies, they wanted to reward them with such an outstanding benefit".[7] Plutarch, in his account of Marius, more than once refers to the Cimbrians as barbarians, and Pontanus here explicitly distances himself from this designation. Towards the end of the Cimbrian chapter he refers to Tacitus's mention of the Cimbrians in the *Germania*:

> Tacitus, who lived under Trajan, tells us that their *civitas* was small but their fame great; by *civitas* he understands not a town or a city but a collected and organized group of citizens who live under jurisdiction and laws.[8]

Pontanus does not, like Tacitus, focus on the contrast between the small community and their great fame. This observation only serves as a point of departure. The central concept for Pontanus is *civitas*. The Cimbrians were a civilized people, he emphasizes, living in an organized society.[9]

Then follows (12-41) a heavily abbreviated version of the first half of Saxo's work, and after that an anthology (42-54) of passages from Roman historians (Livy, Florus, Orosius, Justinus) dealing with the invasions of Italy by Gauls and Germans which took place in the centuries before the Cimbrians' war against Marius. Pontanus wants his readers to realize,

---

[6] *quæ gentis potentiam, ac [...] formidabilem ejus Romano populo militiam summopere ostendat* (58).

[7] *Quod sane barbarorum, ut eos Romani appellabant, haud quaquam barbarum factum: qui virtutem admirati eam etiam in hoste tam insigni remunerandam beneficio voluerunt* (6).

[8] *[...] ut [...] Tacitus qui sub Trajano claruit, parvam eorum civitatem, sed gloriam ingentem fuisse commemoret: intelligens scilicet civitatis nomine non opidum aut urbem, sed collectam ac constitutam civium multitudinem, jure ac legibus viventium* (11, cf. Tac. *Germania*, Ch. 37).

[9] I have drawn attention to this passage in connection with a comparison between Pontanus's and Ludvig Holberg's *Histories of Denmark* (Skovgaard-Petersen 1996).

173

Crispin de Pas the younger (1639): In the Cimbrian camp, Scaurus, the captured Roman legate is slain by Bolus the Cimbrian leader. Pontanus's emphasis on the Cimbrians as Danish ancestors served as an inspiration to the creators of the Kronborg Series. This scene - known from Livy's epitome 67 – is included by Pontanus (p. 3). (Drawing from the Kronborg Series, cf. above, p. 10, and see further Schepelern & Houkjær 1988, 57). (Dept. of Prints and Drawings, The Danish National Gallery).

he says (42), that the designation *Galli* should be understood in a broad sense, often including the Germans, and sometimes also the Cimbrians and the Teutones. These texts, then, also throw light on the early history of the Danes.

The book closes with an antiquarian discussion (55-57) of giants, occasioned by an earlier reference to Teutobocus, king of the Cimbrians and Teutones, who is said to have been of huge stature. Pontanus, however, though acknowledging that many giants are known from both sacred and profane literature, will not accept, as had recently been claimed, that the old Northerners *en bloc* were giants. He especially refers to an "otherwise very learned man" who recently put forward the theory that the first inhabitants of Scandinavia were giants and descended from the Canaanites who were expelled by Joshua from the Holy Land. Pontanus here no doubt refers to the Icelandic historian Arngrímur Jónsson who had advanced this theory of the early Scandinavian giants and their biblical origin in his work of Icelandic history of 1609, *Chrymogæa* (I,4); he had claimed support in Gilbertus Genebrardus's *Chronographiæ libri IV*

Crispin de Pas the younger (after 1637): Captured Romans are set free having sworn an oath on a copper ox. This scene is celebrated by Pontanus (p. 6) as an illustration of the Cimbrians' high level of civilization. (Drawing from the Kronborg Series, cf. above, p. 10, and see further Schepelern & Houkjær 1988, 55). (Dept. of Prints and Drawings, The Danish National Gallery).

(Paris 1580), according to which some of the Canaanites had reached Germany and the neighbouring areas. But in Pontanus's view Arngrímur's and Genebrardus's ideas were nothing but fables. He produces a number of arguments, one of which is the lack of support in classical texts; much more sensible, he declares, is the established view that Scandinavians, and indeed all Europeans, were descended from Noah's son Japhet (on whom Pontanus refers to the *Chorographica descriptio* for further information).[10] No doubt, though, Scandinavians (apart from those living in the northernmost areas) are generally tall, strong and handsome, Pontanus declares patriotically at the end, ascribing this supposed fact to the climate.

Having paid his half-hearted respect to traditional Danish origins in his abbreviation of Saxo, he proceeds in the next two books with his

---

[10] In the *Chorograhica descriptio*, as we saw, Pontanus attacks Arngrímur's view (put forward in the *Chrymogæa*) that Iceland was not the Thule known from classical texts. In his comprehensive answer to this criticism, the *Specimen Islandiæ historicum* from 1643, Arngrímur concentrates on the question of Thule and does not take up the subject of giants.

Crispin de Pas the younger, after 1637. Cimbrian emissaries present Emperor Augustus with a copper vessel. The choice of this motive for one of the drawings of the Kronborg Series is likely to have been inspired by Pontanus's History of Denmark. The scene in Pontanus's interpretation (pp. 10, 22, 643) depicts the Cimbrians as a civilized and powerful people with friendly relations to Rome. (Drawing from the Kronborg Series, cf. above, p. 10, and see further Schepelern & Houkjær 1988, 58-59). (Dept. of Prints and Drawings, The Danish National Gallery).

alternative: the account of the migrations of the Goths, the Vandals, the Angles and others in late antiquity and the early Middle Ages, based again on the solid ground of classical authors, Jordanes, Isidore, Bede, and others. In Pontanus's view, these peoples were all descended from the Cimbrians – and therefore they belong to Danish history.[11]

Book II (58-78) begins by briefly mentioning the Lombards. From Paul the Deacon's account in the *Historia Langobardorum* (written c. 790), which was used by Saxo, it appears, says Pontanus, that they left Scandinavia around 500; but he prefers the testimonies of Strabo, Velleius Paterculus, Tacitus and Ptolemy, according to which they already lived by the Elbe in the time of Augustus.

After this the book concentrates on the Goths. Having left their homes in Scandinavia and wandered extensively, they settled by the

---

[11] Pontanus's focus on migrations and settlements abroad in the first four books later inspired Ludvig Holberg, whose *History of Denmark* (in Danish) from 1732-35 begins with a brief survey of the Cimbrians, Goths, Lombards, and Normans. On Holberg's use of Pontanus, see further Skovgaard-Petersen 1996.

Danube around AD 190 and divided themselves into Ostrogoths and Visigoths. Basing his narration on Jerome, Orosius and others, Pontanus then tells the history of both Gothic branches up to the time of the Emperor Justinian with special focus on their conquest of Rome in 410 under Alaric. The Vandals and the *Rugii* (under king Odoacer) are also briefly touched upon.

The brief third book (79-86) takes us to England. In the fifth century the Angles were summoned from their homes in Jutland to help the British king, Vortigernus, against the Scots, and they settled permanently in the British isles. The account goes up to 800 and is based primarily on Polydore Vergil's *Anglica historia* (first ed. 1534, enlarged 1555).

In these first three books, then, Pontanus manages to provide an impression of Scandinavia, and particularly Denmark, as an *officina gentium* ("manufactory of nations"), as Jordanes had put it. Pontanus echoes him at the beginning of Book Three:

> After the end of the period of fame and renown for the Goths, the Rugii, the Vandals, and the Lombards, there were sent out, from the very same womb, so to speak, and repository of peoples, but with other names, the Angles, the *Vithæ* and the Saxons.[12]

– All through this period, from c. 100 BC – AD 800, then, warlike peoples set out from their Scandinavian homes and burst into Europe, where they came to dominate in various parts.

The account is based on a large number of classical and medieval texts, and also later works, such as Polydore Vergil's *History of England*. Pontanus follows them closely, with an eye to the possibilities of extolling his Danish protagonists. Thus Polydore Vergil notes that the *Britanni* in the fifth century decided to ask the Anglo-Saxons, reputed to be competent warriors, for assistance against the aggressive Scots, and men were sent to Germany to invite them (55).[13] This favourable but brief introduction of the Anglo-Saxons was duly enlarged by Pontanus. He includes the *Vithæ*, mentioned by Bede, who, he says, are now called *Iutae*,

---

[12] *Post ergo Gothorum, Rugorum Vandalorum ac Longobardorum absolutam jam pene claritatis ac nominis periodum, emissi ex eadem hac veluti vagina ac promptuario gentium, sed alijs appellationibus, Angli, Vithæ et Saxones* (79). These three peoples, Pontanus adds, came from Jutland, the *Vithæ* being known from Bede, the Angles being mentioned by Tacitus, and the Saxons by Ptolemy.

[13] I have used an edition of Polydore Vergil's *Anglica historia* of 1570 (Basel) (first ed. 1534).

("from Jutland"), and he notes that the Angles came from the southern-most part of Jutland; thus the Danish origin of these people is established. As for the Saxons, he makes no attempt to furnish them with a Danish origin, but he applies to them Polydore Vergil's praise of the Anglo-Saxons as competent warriors.[14]

In some cases, though, his source displays a more or less unfavourable attitude towards the Danes, and Pontanus then discreetly makes the necessary adjustments. Polydore Vergil tells of the Angles' leader, Hengistus, who planned to conquer the whole of England after he had been invited to support King Vortigernus against the Scots:

> soon he began to ponder by which tricks or by which means of deception he could gradually obtain the sovereignty of the island for himself and his men.[15]

In Pontanus's version Hengistus's cunning and greed are replaced by the responsible leader's concern for the welfare of his own people:

> he regarded it as his duty to consider in which ways he could gradually secure a firmer possession and residence for himself and his men in this agreeable and pleasant region.[16]

Pontanus's distrust of the earliest part of Saxo's history was not new. Similar views had been put forward by Vedel, Huitfeldt, Venusin and others in the sixteenth century and at the beginning of the seventeenth. But unlike his predecessors, Pontanus does not simply air his scepticism and then proceed to retell the early history known from Saxo. He succeeds in producing an alternative version, which was, in his view, built on much more solid ground. He is at pains to emphasize that his account is based on trustworthy authors, assuring his readers of the sound basis of his chapter on the Cimbrians; it is built on "classical writers and particularly on those who have the highest authority in the opinion of all learned men" (*ex classicis, et ijs præcipue scriptoribus, quorum summa est apud*

---

[14] *vicinos e regione ad ortum borealem Anglos, ad collum Cimbricæ Chersonesi locatos, Vitasque Bedæ, nunc Iutas vocatos, una cum Saxonibus, qui tum præcipue rei militaris fama longe lateque illustres ac celebres habebantur, accersendos decernitur* (80).

[15] *protinus secum cogitare coepit, quibus dolis, aut artibus regnum sibi atque suis in insula sensim pararet* (55).

[16] *id sibi agendum putavit, quibus ipse modis sibi suisque possessionem ac sedem stabiliorem in regione tam commoda tamque amoena paulatim firmaret* (80-81).

omnes doctos authoritas) (58). His firm belief in the writings of the ancient Romans and Greeks, which we have met in the *Chorographica descriptio*, is no less evident in the chronological narrative. It was a belief which he shared with contemporary historians, such as Camden and Buchanan, who likewise set out to reconstruct their early national pasts on the basis of a high number of classical authorities.

The Abbreviation of Saxo's Earliest History

In his introductory remarks, quoted above, Pontanus notes that the whole of Saxo's first part must be regarded with scepticism, or as he himself puts it, with tolerance; he promises to tell only "what especially pertains to history" (*quæ historiam præsertim spectant*) and leave out all fabulous and mythological elements. This does not imply, however, that he selected only what he regarded as historically correct in his summary of Saxo. It just means that what he regarded as supernatural absurdities were left out.

His general distrust with regard to the early Saxo is also apparent in the introduction to the résumé of Saxo. He will not leave out domestic history entirely, he declares, but on the other hand he will neither confirm nor reject what he here puts forward from Saxo – again using a tag from Livy's preface, as mentioned above. In the summary itself (12-38) he keeps his promise of neither confirming nor rejecting, but his frequent resort to the indirect form: "Saxo says ..." (*memoratur, narratur, Saxo scribit, traditur, proditur* and more) discreetly suggests his distrust.

Still, this scepticism is not total. When events and names mentioned by Saxo are supported with etymological arguments, he seems to recognize them as historical facts. Thus, he calls attention to etymological relations between modern place-names and events or persons from the early Saxo. Humblus's name is found in Humlebæk (12), Roe's in Roskilde (17), Balderus's in Baldersundt (18), Hjarnus's in Hjarnø and Hjarnehøj (24) (these similarities, apart from the first, were already noted by Saxo himself and later by Huitfeldt). Similarly, he seems confident when a statement of Saxo can be supported by a reference to a classical author. One of the laws made by the great legendary Danish king, Frotho III (*Frode Fredegod*), contained a warning against flight from battle.[17] This, as Pon-

---

[17] Mentioned by Saxo V, Ch. v,2. According to Saxo, Frotho ruled at the time of the birth of Christ.

tanus points out, fits well with the moral code of the Germans, as described by Tacitus in the *Germania* (Ch. 14). He is willing to believe that the Danes were unusually tall and strong, since it agrees with descriptions of the Germans in Tacitus, Caesar and Hirtius.[18]

Pontanus's résumé of Saxo is a mere skeleton. Long stretches of narrative are reduced to a few lines. Thus the eventful reign of Hading, which occupies more than half of Saxo's first book (I, Chs. vi-viii) is described in 38 lines by Pontanus; he tells the story of Frotho III (*Fredegod*) in seventy lines (a little more than one page), while Saxo devotes the whole of Book Five of the *Gesta Danorum* to this king. Pontanus uses five lines to tell the romantic story of Hagebartus and Signe and its aftermath (29), which takes up eight pages in the modern edition of Saxo (VII, Chs. vii). He did, however, include some of the poetic passages from the first part of Saxo's work.[19]

But if the narrative is merely a summary, the amount of antiquarian material is notable. The story of king Svibdagerus's reign takes up just nine lines; but on this king, who had conquered Denmark as king of Norway, Saxo had not had much to say either. Saxo, however, included a brief presentation of the three kinds of superhuman magicians at that time, occasioned by his mention of two giants who took care of the old king's children during Svibdagerus's reign (I, Ch. v). Pontanus picks up the thread and delivers a long and learned dissertation (seventy-three lines), on giants, druids, and soothsayers in classical literature, concluding that the giants in Saxo's history, to whom the upbringing of the princes was entrusted, must be understood as druids (13-15). Similarly, the story of Hjarnus, who was proclaimed king on account of his funeral poem on the late King Frotho, is in Pontanus's version mostly concerned with parallels in classical literature regarding the high esteem for poetry (23-24).

---

[18] *Et ne longe abeamus, hoc decus ac robur corporum boreæ populis, quod hic Saxo injicit, præ reliquis contingere et olim fuisse, præter Tacitum, qui magna Germanorum corpora agnoscit, etiam Cæsar oculatus testis de Gallis quoque illis primis et antiquissimis fateatur* [...] *Et Hirtius de bello Africo Gallis Germanos jungens, Gallorum Germanorumque corpora mirifica specie amplitudineque exstitisse refert* (15). Cf. Tacitus, *Germania*, Ch. 4: *magna corpora et tantum ad impetum valida*, and later; Caesar, *Gall.*, II, Ch. 30; *Bell. Afr.*, Ch. 40.

Pontanus also notes the tall stature of the Danes in the *Chorographica descriptio*, again referring to Caesar and Hirtius (776-77).

[19] Saxo VI, Ch. i, Ch. iv,6-7 & VI, Ch. ix,19 (vv. 17-19), VIII, viii,9, & 11. Another exception to the narrative brevity is a long speech (19-20) made by Amlethus, which Pontanus took *verbatim* from Saxo IV, Ch. i,2-7. It is, in fact, by far the longest of the direct speeches (which are few and mostly short remarks) in the whole work.

In his treatment of Frotho III (*Frode Fredegod*), the greatest king in these remote times, if we are to believe Saxo, Pontanus says very little about his numerous wars (22-23). Instead he quotes Saxo's description of the Finns and their way of living,[20] and then focuses on Frotho's legislation. Since Frotho was a contemporary of Augustus, Pontanus here includes a reference to Strabo, who tells how the Cimbrians sent a sacred kettle to Augustus as a sign of friendship,[21] a story which Pontanus has already told earlier in the book. Pontanus underlines that the present is not a sign of subjugation; rather he uses the episode to illustrate Cimbrian civilization and relations to Rome (cf. illustration above).

Arild Huitfeldt's *History of Denmark*, which served as Pontanus's main source for the later history (cf. below), also gives a summary of the earliest Danish history, as told by Saxo. In fact his version is even briefer than Pontanus's. Not only did Pontanus include more of the events narrated by Saxo, he also, as we just saw, presented a number of antiquarian observations based on classical literature, which are not found in Huitfeldt. Huitfeldt, on the other hand, devotes some attention to chronology, attempting to date most of the early kings in relation to the Creation and to the birth of Christ. Pontanus only once, in the chapter on the first king, Danus (12), relates these early events to world history, distancing himself from this consideration by the words *referuntur a quibusdam*. Otherwise he refrains from any attempt to relate the events known from Saxo's first part to universal chronology. As earlier noted he here departs from his practice elsewhere of giving the name of the contemporary world ruler at the bottom of each page (cf. Chapter V). This lack of dates indicates that the events narrated here are not necessarily historical realities, while Huitfeldt by his many chronological references implies the opposite. Huitfeldt presents the material of Saxo's first part as the earliest Danish history, and as such it can be dated in relation to world history. Pontanus, having already presented what he believed to be a more trustworthy version of the early Danish past, can afford to refrain from relating Saxo's stories to world history.

Thus Pontanus adopted a different strategy from Huitfeldt in the handling of the first part of Saxo's work. But even if he does not mention Huitfeldt here, there is no reason to doubt that Pontanus also consulted Huitfeldt in this part. His sole chronological consideration seems

---

[20] Saxo, V, Ch. xiii,1.
[21] Strabo, *Geogr.*, VII, Ch. 2.

inspired by Huitfeldt, as does his brief but indignant rejection (17) of Johannes Magnus's claim that a Swedish king once placed a dog on the Danish throne[22] (we shall return to this claim later in the chapter).

It may have been on Huitfeldt's authority, too, that Pontanus included a poem in (a strange kind of) Danish (36-37), which deals with the emigration from Denmark in the reign of Snio. But Pontanus may also have found the poem in Cl.C. Lyschander's *Synopsis historiarum Danicarum* (1622), which, as we know from his letters, Lyschander had sent to him.[23]

The poem, however, was a fake – a fact which perhaps neither Huitfeldt, Lyschander nor Pontanus realized. Purporting to be of very old age, it was probably fabricated by the Danish vicar Niels Pedersen (c. 1522-79), who claimed to have found it during his stay in Gotland (1547-56) as part of a spurious "Gullandic" document (on which see Chapter IV, 8). Pontanus welcomed the poem. It referred to the emigrants as *Vinnilender*, and Pontanus here saw a confirmation of his point of view, that the emigration from Scandinavia was not undertaken by Lombards, as stated by Paul the Deacon, since they were already settled in northern Germany by Augustus's time.

Another already-existing adaptation of Saxo's early history was to be found in Albert Krantz's account of the history of the Scandinavian kingdoms, the *Regnorum Aquilonarium, Daniæ, Sueciæ, Noruegiæ chronica*,[24] an account which is much fuller and much more loyal to Saxo than Huitfeldt's, although Krantz occasionally states that he omits some of Saxo's absurdities. It was possibly the inspiration from Krantz (*Dania*, I, Ch. 3) which made Pontanus quote Lucan on Romulus and Remus in connection with the two sons of the first king, Dan (12). Pontanus's familiarity with Krantz's work also shows itself negatively, in that he draws attention to Krantz's shortcomings (12, 16, 22, 35); sometimes he lumps him together with Saxo (22, 31).

At the end of the summary Pontanus has arranged the fifty-two kings he has taken over from Saxo in three trees or *stemmata* (39-41). The first includes the kings from Danus to Rolvo (*Rolf Krage*), the last of the male line from Danus. After him Hotherus reigned, and he was related to the

---

[22] Huitfeldt, *Fra Kong Dan* [...], 8.

[23] Cf. above, Ch. III. The poem is edited and commented on in the recent edition of Lyschander's poetry by Fl. Lundgreen-Nielsen & E. Petersen (1989), I, 391-92, II, 318-19. Huitfeldt's edition of the poem is found in *Fra Kong Dan* [...], 25-26.

[24] First published in Latin in 1548. I shall refer to the edition of 1583 (Frankfurt am Main).

earlier kings through his father's mother Suanhvida, sister of Frotho I. The second tree starts with her and ends with King Haldanus II. He left no children behind and was followed on the throne by his father-in-law, Unguinus, with whom the third tree begins, and this takes us up to Gotricus. His successors, says Pontanus, ruled until the kings of the Oldenburg line took over (in 1448).[25]

Considering his scepticism regarding the early part of Saxo, Pontanus surprisingly makes much of these genealogies. Indirectly these detailed trees bear witness to an old and stable kingdom, and this ideological point was apparently too important to fall victim to Pontanus's own version of the earliest history based on classical texts (cf. below, Sections 6).

3. Book IV

Sources

Book IV (87-125), covers the period c. 500-900. Pontanus now organizes the narrative according to kings. Except for the summary of Saxo in the first book this has not been the case so far. Although he treats the history of the Cimbrians and the other emigrating peoples as foreign Danish history, the kings of these peoples belonged by convention to the national histories of the geographical areas in question. But Pontanus lists both the Spanish kings, descendants of the Goths, and the English kings, whose ancestors were the *Angli*. In this way he suggests the ramifications of Danish influence on the history of Europe.

The narrative is based primarily on foreign sources, especially Frankish and French. The first Danish king known from these sources is Gotilacus whose plunderings are mentioned by Gregory of Tours. He is not found in Saxo. The next to mention the Danes – and again it is about plunderings – is a contemporary of Gregory, Venantius Fortunatus, at the end of the sixth century, and then there is a gap until the period of Charlemagne, when the *Frankish Annals* and other texts tell of King Sigefridus (89-92) and of his brother Gotricus. Pontanus identifies this Gotricus with Saxo's King Godefredus, whom he had mentioned as the last king in the summary of Saxo's legendary first part.

---

[25] *Cuius postea stirps adusque Christophorum III. omniumque ex hac prosapia ultimum continuata, suo exhibebitur loco* (39).

The foreign and the domestic traditions are in fact only superficially merged. The domestic history, built on Saxo, with supplements from the *Annales Ryenses*,[26] is related separately. But the main narrative is based on a multitude of medieval and later foreign accounts; important are (in chronological order) the *Frankish Annals* (8th-9th centuries), Regino of Prüm's *Chronica* (c. 900), Dudo of St. Quentin's *De moribus et actis primorum Normanniæ ducum* (before 1017), Adam of Bremen's *Gesta Hammaburgensis ecclesiae pontificum* (c. 1070), William of Jumièges's *Gesta Normannorum ducum* (final version c. 1070), Helmold's *Chronica Slavorum* (1160s), Albert of Stade's *Annales Stadenses* (c. 1260), the *Ypodigma Neustriæ* ascribed to Thomas Walsingham (d. c. 1422), Polydore Vergil's *Anglica historia* (1534), Albert Krantz's *Regnorum Aquilonarium, Daniæ, Sueciæ, Noruegiæ chronica* (1548), George Buchanan's *Rerum Scoticarum historia* (1582) and the *Chronicon Norwegiæ* (1594).[27]

The result is that this period, the ninth and tenth centuries, is treated quite differently from the way Saxo had done it. The numerous expeditions undertaken by the Danes form the main theme, while domestic history is reduced to a minimum. The agents of Danish history in this part of Pontanus's work are not individuals, but the collective *Dani* and *Normanni*.

There is a close similarity between Huitfeldt's and Pontanus's strategies. Huitfeldt, too, based his account on information found in foreign works of history, while retaining, with some exceptions, the framework of Saxo's kings. Pontanus no doubt made himself familiar with Huitfeldt's treatment of the period. But the differences between Pontanus and Huitfeldt should not be overlooked. Their selections of material often differ, and Pontanus's account is generally much fuller. And what is particularly noteworthy, he gave his account of Danish and Norman expeditions a heroic touch which is absent from Huitfeldt.

---

[26] *Rydårbogen* or, as Pontanus refers to it, *Chronicon Regis Erici*. This small but influential annalistic work was written in a Cistercian monastery in Ryd, south of Flensburg, in the latter half of the thirteenth century. Its first editor, Erpold Lindenbruch, who published it in 1603, regarded the Danish king, Erik of Pomerania (1412-39) as the author, and so did Stephanius, who included the work in his anthology of texts on Denmark, (Stephanius 1629). (Modern ed. by E. Kroman 1980).

[27] As mentioned in the biography of Stephanius (Chapter III), this was a collection of extracts of the medieval kings' sagas, translated into Danish, which had been made by Mattis Størsson in the 1540s and printed in 1594.

The Reign of Ericus Barn

As an example of Pontanus's procedure, I shall go briefly through his long account of the reign of Ericus Barn (103-14) in the latter half of the ninth century (Pontanus does not date it precisely). Saxo had not had much to say of this king. Ericus inherited the throne as a small child (*barn* in Danish), whereupon his uncle seized power. After the latter's death Ericus proved himself a competent warrior and an enemy of Christ, who persecuted the Christianized Danes; but towards the end of his life, the missionary Ansgarius put an end to this blameworthy behaviour (IX, Ch. v, 8-vi). In Huitfeldt's and Pontanus's versions, however, the Norman conquests have been incorporated, and this is a period full of dramatic events.[28]

Huitfeldt (*Fra Kong Dan* [...], 55-83) lets his account of Ericus Barn's reign cover the period 856-901. He begins by referring to Erik's persecutions of the Christians and Ansgarius's salutary influence. He declares that he finds it hard to believe that as many kings ruled in Denmark in the ninth and tenth centuries as Saxo states. Instead he prefers the smaller number found in Adam of Bremen (57-58). Most of the rest of his account of Ericus Barn is taken up with various conflicts in England known from English historians (Huitfeldt mentions Polydore Vergil and Florence of Worcester, cf. note below) and from Danish annals; Norman invasions in France and Frisia are also mentioned. But Huitfeldt had more to say of this period. He concluded this first volume of his history with an appendix on the Norman invasions and settlement in France in the period c. 850-1066, based on Thomas Walsingham and other English chronicles, as he himself informs us.

Pontanus does not take over Huitfeldt's dating of Ericus Barn's reign. Not only does he omit to date its beginning, he also ends the account as early as 891. He accepts the tradition from Saxo that Ericus's son, Canutus (*Lodneknud*), followed his father on the throne, while Huitfeldt regards Canutus as a minor prince, not as a king (*Fra Kong Dan* [...], 73).

Pontanus begins, like Huitfeldt, by noting Ansgarius's influence on Ericus and the latter's development from persecutor of the Christians to believer (103). He then discusses the relationship between Saxo's account of the sons of one of the previous kings, Regnerus (*Regner Lodbrog*), and various names of Danish kings and leaders mentioned by foreign au-

---

[28] Krantz, on the contrary, merely summarizes Saxo in twenty lines. He treated the Norman conquests in the Norwegian part of his *Regna Aquilonaria* (cf. below).

thors, and compares, again like Huitfeldt (60-61), Saxo's description of his death to that of English historians (103-4). The rest of the chapter relates events abroad. Pontanus first follows some of the sons of Regnerus. One of them, Ivarus, waged war against the Angles, and Pontanus now deals with the conflicts between Danes and Angles. His treatment differs considerably from Huitfeldt's account. The latter covers a longer period and mentions several battles in the 860s and 870s, while Pontanus focuses on one battle near Chippenham at the beginning of the 870s. Pontanus here gives an abbreviated version of the account found in Polydore Vergil's *Anglica historia*. He makes some ideological adjustments, leaving out Polydore Vergil's praise of the English king Alfredus and some of his less flattering descriptions of the Danes. Thus, Polydore had written of a battle so hard and equally matched that the Danes, who had often before been beaten, now seemed to be an altogether different people:

> [...] adeo anceps fuit, vt non cum Dacis sæpe antea fusis, fugatis, atque etiam victis, sed cum aliqua noua gente videretur dimicatio esse (101, 1570 ed.)

> ((the struggle) [...] was so equally matched that the contest did not seem to be waged against the Danes, whom they had often previously routed and sent fleeing, and vanquished, too, but with some unheard-of foe).

Pontanus just makes a small change:

> [...] adeo anceps fuit ut non cum Danis aut notis adversarijs sed cum gente aliqua nova videretur esse dimicatio (105)

> ((the struggle) [...] was so equally matched that the contest did not seem to be waged against the Danes or any well-known opponents but with some unheard-of foe)

– thereby avoiding the degrading reminder of earlier Danish defeats. In this respect, too, he differs from Huitfeldt who makes no attempt to heroize the Danes and depicts them as cruel and pagan robbers. But, as the quotation shows, Pontanus to some degree retains the English perspective. The Danes are seen as the enemies.

Pontanus then embarks on a discussion of the identities of the various examples of Danes named Ericus from the same time; among them was a son of Regnerus who made several attacks on England and France (105). This Ericus, Pontanus goes on, was followed by Hastingus, a nobleman in the service of yet another son of Regnerus, named Biorno

(*Bjørn Jernside*). Hastingus went to Italy in order to conquer Rome, for which, unfortunately, he mistook the town of Luna. Pontanus writes in some detail about Hastingus's stratagem (105-6). Pretending that he was weak and now wanted to be baptized, he and his men were hospitably received by the local bishop and used the opportunity to get acquainted with the town. Next day his men pretended that Hastingus was dead and a solemn funeral was arranged in the town, during which he suddenly rose from the bier and together with his men started plundering the town and slaughtering its inhabitants. Hastingus then returned to France where he went into the service of the French king, Carolus Calvus (Charles the Bald).

This story of Hastingus goes back to Dudo's Norman history (I, Chs. 5-7). He and William of Jumièges (I, Chs. 8-9) (both writing in the eleventh century) depict him as an example of pagan evil and cruelty against Christians.[29] Albert Krantz, however, in his *Norvegia* (II, Chs. 2-4), retold the story but toned down the almost superhuman cruelty of Dudo's and William's Hastingus. It was Krantz's version which Pontanus chose to follow, making only minor alterations.[30] Pontanus, like Krantz, makes no attempt to conceal the fact that Hastingus, in this case, behaved cruelly: "Not only the bishop himself but also clergymen and laymen alike were all slaughtered", he says.[31] Nevertheless, shortly before, as an introduction to this episode, he made a significant alteration in Krantz's presentation of Hastingus. Krantz had written:

---

[29] Dudo: *De moribus et actis primorum Normanniæ ducum* (modern ed. by J. Lair, 1865). William of Jumièges: *Gesta Normannorum ducum* (modern ed. by E. M. C. van Houts, 1992). Pontanus was familiar with both Dudo and William of Jumièges, both of whom are quoted in the *History of Denmark* (Dudo 123-124, William 132-35). This tradition is also represented by English historians, e.g. in the *Flores Historiarum* (publ. under the name of Matthias Westmonasteriensis in 1567, 1570, 1601; Pontanus refers to MW on pages 79, 179, 183).

[30] As an example of the close similarity between Krantz and Pontanus I quote the description of Hastingus's entrance into the town in front of the naive inhabitants:
Krantz, *Norvegia*, II, Ch. 4: *Igitur magno apparatu lauacrum in ecclesia præparatur, circumstant primarij vrbis viri et foeminæ. Spectaculum gerebatur, cernere virum barbaræ nationis principem, ad sacra Christi properantem. Vbi cuncta ex sententia constiterant, prodibat auro fultus et ostro princeps Haddingus, baculo innixus, vix debilem (vt simulabat) gressum trahens.*
Pontanus (106): *Hinc magno apparatu lavacrum jussu pontificis instruitur, accurrentibus ad novum spectaculum omnis sexus atque ordinis hominibus simulque admirantibus virum Barbaræ gentis principem ad Sacra Christi festinantem. Omnibus rite præparatis prodibat auro ostroque insignis Hastingus innixus baculo ac debilem (ut videbatur) gressum trahens.* – Pontanus's tendency to reuse the words and syntax of his source will be discussed in Ch. VIII.

[31] *Ipse non tantum Episcopus, sed et clerus laicique sine discrimine cuncti trucidati* (106).

[...] Haddingus quidam regio sanguine, sed feroci animo vir, natus ad arma, fortem exercitum dux fortis in Galliam exponebat, prædabundus incedens quocunque se verteret. Ecclesiarum incendia, matronarum stupra, puellarum raptus, virorum neces sine numero peregit (*Norvegia* II, Ch. 2).

(Haddingus, a man of royal blood but a fierce character born to fight, landed in France, the strong leader of a strong army. He intended to plunder wherever he went. Innumerable churches were burned by him, women violated, girls raped, men murdered).

Pontanus turned Hastingus into a warlike hero. He only took over the reference to his royal origin and then celebrated his military triumphs:

Eum proxime secutus Hastingus alijs Haddingus regio similiter sanguine vir, magnumque nomen domi militiæque cum ob animi promptitudinem, tum res præclare gestas adeptus ... (105).

(After him [i.e. a son of Regnerus] followed Hastingus (others call him Haddingus), a man likewise of royal blood, who had achieved a great reputation both at home and on the battlefield, on account of his resoluteness as well as his outstanding exploits).

These events are not mentioned in Huitfeldt's chapter on Ericus Barn. But they do occur in his appendix on the Normans in France. Here again there is a notable difference in Huitfeldt's and Pontanus's attitudes. Huitfeldt sees Hastingus as "an unspeakably sly and deceitful man" (*en wsigelig tredsk oc vnderfundig Mand*). He and his men are cruel and aggressive pagans who plunder innocent Christians and burn their homes.

Pontanus now has more to say of Regnerus's son Bjorno, whom he knew from Saxo. Identifying him with the Buerno mentioned in George Buchanan's *History of Scotland*, he describes Bjorno's expedition to Scotland in 874, where he fought succesfully against the Scottish King Constantinus. He here simply transcribes Buchanan's account word for word – with the exception of Buchanan's *Danorum desperationem* which he changes into *Danorum virtutem* (106; on this passage, cf. Chapter VIII). This episode is not mentioned by Huitfeldt.

The rest of Pontanus's chapter on Ericus Barn is taken up with accounts of numerous Norman plunderings and battles with the locals in the last twenty years of the ninth century (107-14). Some of it had also been related by Huitfeldt, but in a less detailed manner – e.g. the bishop

Rembertus, who advised the Frisians to trust in God and thereby prepared them for the impending attack of the Normans (Pontanus 108-9;
Huitfeldt, *Fra Kong Dan* [...], 69-70).

Pontanus's account is marked by the view-point of the foreign
sources, that is, of the victims. Thus, when the imperial troops learn that
the Normans are close, they are frightened:

> Unde panicus quidam terror omnium mentes invasit. Duces convocata
> militari concione, ut solet in re trepida ac dubia, inter se anxij deliberare
> [...] (114).

> (A panic fear seized everybody. The leaders summoned a military
> meeting, and as is common in dangerous and uncertain situations, in
> their alarm they now discussed [...])

— as Pontanus says, using the words of the German annalist Regino of
Prüm. This perspective is also retained when Pontanus occasionally portrays the Normans as aggressive plunderers, describing their actions with
expressions such as *incendijs ac direptionibus cuncta commiscuit* ("they mingled
everything with arson and plundering", 108); likewise he does not conceal their hatred of Christians (*ob Christiani nominis odium*, "owing to their
hatred of the name Christianity", 106).

However, he does not explicitly condemn the Normans as robbers
and murderers, as Huitfeldt does again and again. The difference in their
attitude may be illustrated by their descriptions of the Normans' preparations for new attacks after having suffered defeat from the Frisians (the
result of bishop Rembertus's exhortations mentioned above):

Huitfeldt:

> De Normend vilde heffne den Skade de finge vdi Frisland / paa det
> gantske Romerske Rige / Da drager de met deris Konger / Sigefred oc
> Godefred / paa Rijn / Massen / oc Skalden. Vdi Franckerige ynckelige
> mørder oc røffuer de huad faarekom / oc haffde K. Karl kun for en
> Abefuel. (*Fra Kong Dan* [...], 70).

> (The Normans wanted to take revenge on the whole Roman empire for
> the harm they suffered in Friesland. They set off with their kings Sige-
> fred and Godefred, travelling on the Rhine, the Maas, and the Schelde.
> In France they commit miserable murders and robberies wherever they
> come, and they made King Karl look like a fool).

Pontanus:

Nam Godefridus et Sigefridus, intellecta suorum clade, magno studio magnisque animis in ultionem exsurrexere, nec Frisiam modo sed universas Francorum provincias nomenque Christianum vindictæ, destinabant. Itaque majore quam unquam antea exercitu coacto et in naves imposito e Dania alacres solverunt, maximo ubique adventus sui fama excitato terrore, Galliamque agmine tripartito per Rhenum, Mosam, ac Schaldim subeuntes, classe sua infestam habuerunt (109).

(For Godefridus and Sigefridus, having learned that their men had suffered defeat, were seized by a violent desire for revenge. And they did not aim at Friesland only, but at all the Franks' provinces and at Christian people. So having collected an army that was bigger than ever before and made it ready to sail, they set off from Denmark, briskly and energetically. Everywhere the news of their arrival aroused great fear. Having divided the army into three forces and travelled on the Rhine, the Maas, and the Schelde, they rendered France insecure with their fleet).

– The two accounts both build on Adam of Bremen (or Krantz, who here transcribes Adam almost *verbatim*).[32] Huitfeldt retains Adam's emphasis on the Normans' cruelty in France, while Pontanus simply notes that they attacked. Instead he adds a positive touch by means of the adjective *alacres*, denoting energy and activity, and he gives an impression of Norman power – they collected an army bigger than ever. Shortly afterwards Adam declares that Frisia and England are said to have been subject to Danish rule from that time. Unlike Huitfeldt, Pontanus takes over this statement, rendering it more powerful by means of small adjustments:

Adam:

Atque ex illo tempore Fresia et Anglia in ditione Danorum esse feruntur (I, Ch. 39).[33]

(And from that time Friesland and England are said to have been subject to the Danes' rule).

---

[32] *Nortmanni plagam, quam in Fresia receperunt, in totum imperium ulturi cum regibus Sigafrido et Gotafrido per Rhenum et Mosam et Scaldam fluvios Galliam invadentes miserabili cede christianos obtruncarunt, ipsumque regem Karolum bello petentes ludibrio nostros habuerunt* (Adam of Bremen, *Gesta Hammaburgensis ecclesiae pontificum* I, Ch. 39). Cf. Krantz, *Norvegia* II, Ch. 8.

[33] Again Krantz uses Adam's words (*Norvegia*, II, Ch. 8).

Pontanus:

Atque ex illo tempore [...] et Angliam et Frisiam sub Danorum constitisse imperio, præter Albertum Stadensem etiam Adamus Bremensis testatum facit (109).

(And from that time [...] both England and Friesland were subject to Danish rule, as not only Albert of Stade but also Adam of Bremen testify).

Both formulate the statement as a report. But while Adam uses the *feruntur* to make a reservation as to its truth, Pontanus, by referring to two authorities, seeks to convince his readers. Besides, he has replaced Adam's *ditione* by the more powerful *imperio*, and stressed the extent of the Danish rule by the *both-and* construction. The widespread terror the Normans inspire serves in Pontanus's account to emphasize their power.

The Origin of the Normans

The Norman expeditions (or Viking raids) form the main theme of the fourth book. In the first three books, as we saw, Denmark is portrayed as the motherland of the conquering peoples that swarmed over Europe in late antiquity and the early Middle Ages. This perspective is to some degree retained in Book IV. At the beginning Pontanus makes clear that the Normans' raids are to be seen in the tradition of the Goths, the Angles and the other peoples who swarmed out from Scandinavia in early medieval times. They were, in fact, inspired by the *virtutis exempla*, the valorous examples, of their forefathers, says Pontanus, giving a propagandist twist to the old argument on the use of history, the force of example.

Pontanus treats the Normans as Danes. Initially he states that the Danes and the Normans were of the same origin and it further appears that he regards the Normans as a collective term, denoting Scandinavians; they came not only from Jutland, but also from the northern part of Scandinavia and the islands of the Baltic Sea (86).[34] Similarly, he argues in a separate chapter of the *Chorographica descriptio* that even though Adam of Bremen and Albert Krantz reserve the term *Normannia* for Norway, it must be understood in a broader sense; he shows that Adam himself also used the term *Normanni* to denote Scandinavians and

---

[34] [...] *Dani mox Normannique, eadem origine sed alijs nominibus gens, ejusdem inquam chersonesi partim indigena, partim vicinus, versus boream Scandinaviæ et insularum Balthici maris populus* [...] (87).

Crispin de Pas the Younger (?): Duke Rollo is enfeoffed with Normandy. As in Pontanus's History, Rollo is also depicted as a Danish hero in the Kronborg Series. This event suggests his importance as an-cestor of William the Conqueror, and the choice of this motive may have been influenced by Pontanus. (Drawing from the Kronborg Series, cf. above, p. 10, and see further Schepelern & Houkjær 1988, 75-76). (Dept. of Prints and Drawings, The Danish National Gallery).

quotes passages from Einhard to demonstrate that *Dani* and *Normanni* to him were synonyms (691-92). It is clear that he disapproves of Krantz placing the Norman expeditions in the part of his work dedicated to Norwegian history, and his own strategy in Book IV thus forms a correc-tive to Krantz. The Norman expeditions also form part of Danish his-tory.

As for the most famous of the Norman leaders, Rollo, Pontanus is at pains to demonstrate his Danish origin, as opposed to the claim of the *Chronicon Norwegiæ* that Rollo came from Norway. On the authority of Dudo and William of Jumièges, Pontanus argues that he was Danish and only happened to seek refuge in Norway (118). This was evidently an important issue. Pontanus added an appendix to the fourth book (123-25) in which he quoted the relevant passages from Dudo and William of Jumièges. Here he states once again that Krantz is wrong in taking the term *Normanni* to denote only Norwegians; it must be understood in a broader sense as Scandinavians.

Moreover Pontanus follows the history of Rollo's successors, the Norman dukes, who also became kings of England, and from whom the English kings of Pontanus's day, James and Charles (James I, 1603-25, and Charles I, 1625-49), are descended (117). Rollo's descendants, whose careers Pontanus depicts as a branch of Danish history, are even presented in a schematic family tree ending with William the Conqueror (119-20). Later Pontanus wonders why William should nourish unfriendly feelings towards the Danish king Sueno (*Sven Estridsøn*, 1047-74) in view of his own Danish origin (but then he realizes that there were other reasons for hostility, 189).

The Normans have, in other words, left their mark on English history up to the present day. And not only on English history. Another appendix to the fourth book (120-21) goes briefly through the establishment in the eleventh century of the Norman rule in Sicily – another instance of Danish influence on European history.

Pontanus was not the first to boast of the Danish connections with the Normans. Hans Svaning included a chapter on the subject, as the preserved list of contents testifies.[35] Huitfeldt also regarded Normans as a common denominator for Scandinavians (*it samlet Folck / aff alle disse 3. Riger*, (*Fra Kong Dan* [...], 35-36)). In the supplement on the Normans in France he concludes with the following statement on their common origin, very similar to Pontanus's introduction to Book IV:

> I have wanted to relate these things briefly from Thomas Walsingham and other English chronicles in order that the reader may see and understand that the Normans in France and the Danes who earlier on ruled in England originate from one people and are compatriots.[36]

Huitfeldt, like Pontanus, noted that Rollo became the ancestor of the royal family which ruled England in his own day (*Fra Kong Dan* [...], 75).

---

[35] Ed. W. Christensen 1913.

[36] *Dette haffuer ieg saa korteligen vilde fortelle aff Thoma Valsinghami, oc andre Engelske Krønicker / Oc det fordi / at mand kand see oc skionne / at de Normend vdi Franckerige / oc de Danske / som før haffde Engeland inde / ere kommen aff it slags Folck / oc ere Landmend sammens* (*Fra Kong Dan* [...], Appendix).

4. *Book V*

Sources

In the first part of the fifth book (126-231), which covers the period c. 900-1157, wars in foreign countries still loom large. Rollo is mentioned once more on the occasion of his death in 918, and again praised for his ability to establish a new realm on foreign soil (128).[37] Huitfeldt just mentions his death (*Fra Kong Dan* [...], 89).

The Danish conflicts in England are treated at length, based primarily on Polydore Vergil, but again duly modified in order to tone down Vergil's rather hostile attitude towards the Danes. Other sources used by Pontanus for events in England are William af Malmesbury's *De gestis regum Anglorum* (c. 1130), and the above-mentioned works of William of Jumièges and Florence of Worcester. Among the many other works consulted by Pontanus in this book, are Adam of Bremen, Albert of Stade, Helmold, and the *Chronicon Norwegiæ*. Special importance is attributed to the contemporary, anonymous *Encomium Emmæ*, which had recently been printed for the first time, in 1619. This work clearly appealed to Pontanus, being a contemporary source and giving a favourable account of Danish rule in England under Canutus Magnus. In fact Pontanus appended two of the work's three books to his chapter on Canutus Magnus (163-72).[38]

In the course of the book the Danish kings and their domestic rules stand out with increasing clarity. From the end of the eleventh century Saxo forms the backbone of the narrative, but much of his material has been left out; on the other hand important supplements are taken from foreign authors and Huitfeldt.

The reign of Canutus Magnus

In order to illustrate Pontanus's handling of his sources, I will go a little deeper into his description of the reign of Canutus Magnus (c. 1014-1036; modern historians date his reign 1019–35) (147–63). Canutus managed to bring several nations under his rule, and the imperial greatness of Denmark is a main theme in Saxo's account (X, Ch. xiv–xx). This thread was enthusiastically picked up by Pontanus, but not by Huitfeldt.

---

[37] *vir profecto belli laudibus clarissimus: quippe quo vix alius in hostili solo sibi ac posteris suis majore virtute principatum non modo paravit, sed ita præterea constituit, ut ceteris quibusque maximis regibus ac regnis par viribus fuerit* (128).

[38] The *Encomium Emmæ* was written 1041-42 at the request of Emma, Canutus's widow, by a monk in Flanders. It also deals with the period after Canutus's death in 1035. Modern edition by Campbell 1949 (rep. 1998).

Saxo briefly mentions his conquest of *Slavia* and *Sembria*, and then turns to his fighting and victory in England. Then follows an account of the origin of a Swedish warrior Ulvo in Canutus's army, whose grandfather was a bear. The Norwegian King Olaus reconquers Norway from Canutus and his piety is the object of Saxo's praise. Ulvo now, out of hatred for Canutus because of his virtue and courage, organizes an attack on the Danish king, in collaboration with the Norwegian and the Swedish kings. Having finally defeated this force, Canutus is the ruler of six countries.

After some minor episodes Saxo tells of the death of Ulvo. He was killed on the order of Canutus himself at a Christmas party, after having bragged about the death of some of Canutus's men in their fighting against his own army. This leads to a long account of Canutus's law-making, which was designed to create discipline among his warriors. It turns out that Canutus himself becomes the first to break the law by killing one of his men on one occasion when drunk. Saxo's point, however, is Canutus's praiseworthy handling of this affair. He bids his men judge him, declaring himself ready to undergo any punishment. The men, however, realizing that they need Canutus as king, give him the power to judge himself, and he sentences himself to pay a price nine times higher than has been fixed by the law. He then sails to Normandy to take revenge on his brother-in-law, Richard of Normandy. The latter flies to Sicily, but Canutus himself is taken ill and dies. On his own order his body is carried around among the Danish warriors, giving them the spirit to fight successfully against the French.

Huitfeldt tells the story of Canutus quite differently (*Fra Kong Dan* [...], 132-56). His main source for Canutus's reign is Adam of Bremen, and he found his material on the wars with England in English historians and on Norway in the *Chronicon Norwegiæ*. None of Saxo's episodes reappear in his version. On the other hand he includes events not mentioned by Saxo, most conspicuously Canutus's visit to the Pope in Rome; he even quotes Canutus's letter (in Danish translation) to the English bishops about the results of his journey (150-53).The letter was to be found in William of Malmesbury's *De gestis regum Anglorum* (II, Ch. 183) and in Florence of Worcester's *Chronica*.[39]

---

[39] Florence of Worcester (d. 1118) was regarded as the author of a history, *Chronica chronicarum*, which is nowadays attributed to John of Worcester (d. after 1140). (I rely on R. Sharpe (1997), *A Handlist of the Latin Writers of Great Britain and Ireland before 1540*).

Pontanus begins by pointing out that the *Annales Ryenses* and the *Encomium Emmæ* both acknowledge Canutus's brother Haraldus as king between Sueno (*Svend Tveskæg*) and Canutus Magnus. He then turns to the conflicts in England, which he, like Huitfeldt, treats in much more detail than Saxo, on the basis of English histories, among them the *Encomium Emmæ*, which Huitfeldt had not had access to.[40] But no trace is found in his version of the tradition, represented by William of Malmesbury (II, Ch. 180) among others, that Canutus sent the sons of the late English king, Edmundus, to the Swedish king asking him to have them killed (cf. Pontanus 152). No doubt his concern for the reputation of the Danish king made him conceal this act of cruelty – whereas Huitfeldt speaks of Canutus's "impious request" (*wgudelig Begæring*, (*Fra Kong Dan* [...], 143)). Pontanus also pays some attention to Saxo here by quoting his version of the events after the fighting had stopped (151).

After the English affairs follows a brief survey of the years 1018-22, which is partly translated from Huitfeldt (Pontanus 152, Huitfeldt 144); the mention of episcopal affairs is based on Adam of Bremen, but Pontanus concludes by praising, in Saxo's words, Canutus's concern for the Church.[41] The Norwegian King Olaus's death is told simply as a result of internal strife, without mention of Saxo's Ulvo and his alliance with Olaus against Canutus nor of Canutus's subsequent role in the killing of Olaus. In the following brief account of Canutus's conquest of Norway, though, Pontanus builds on Saxo in combination with the *Chronicon Norwegiæ* (154).

It is at this point that Saxo observes that Canutus now ruled six countries (X, Ch. xvii,1). Pontanus, not missing this opportunity to stress Danish power and influence abroad, enlarges Saxo's observation by reminding the reader of their names, adding, too, a correction of Krantz, who in his view had misunderstood Saxo (154).[42] From William of Mal-

---

[40] In his commentary on Meursius, Hans Gram expressed his admiration of Pontanus's handling of Canutus Magnus's conquest of England: *in quibus laudandam prorsus operam, ita ut vix aliquid ultra desideretur doctissimus Pontanus posuit* (Meursius 1741-63, IX, col. 177). More generally, Gram later praises Pontanus for having understood that Denmark's history in the ninth, tenth, and eleventh centuries could not be written without the use of English historians (*ibidem*, col. 190).

[41] *Adeo ut de ipso vere dici possit, eum sanctitate et fortitudine instructissimum non minus religionem, quam regnum proferre curæ habuisse* (153). The praise is taken from Saxo's obituary of Canutus: *siquidem sanctitate ac fortitudine instructissimus non minus religionem quam regnum proferre curæ habuit* (X, Ch. xx,3).

[42] According to Krantz, Canutus only ruled five countries, since he leaves out (as Pontanus disapprovingly notes) *Sembia* and *Slavia* and includes Normandy (*Dania* IIII, Ch. 28).

mesbury Pontanus now inserts a description of Canutus's son Sueno's expedition against the Scots, which, although it turned out to be fruitless, is here depicted as yet another attempt to enlarge the realm.

He now, like Huitfeldt, tells of Canutus's visit to the Pope, quoting (in Latin) his letter to the English bishops (155-57), known from the works of Florence of Worcester and William of Malmesbury. Various foreign affairs are mentioned (157), and Pontanus in one case distances himself from Saxo and chooses to follow Adam of Bremen and Albert of Stade. Most attention is paid to the marriage and subsequent divorce of Canutus's daughter and Henricus, son of the emperor Conradus (157-58), based on English historians and concluded by a quotation from Jacob Meyer's *History of Flanders* (1531; later enlarged) (Adam of Bremen, Saxo, and Huitfeldt just briefly mention the marriage).[43] The flight of Sueno, Canutus's son who had been placed as vice-ruler in Norway, leads to a brief discussion of his origin, in which Pontanus presents the conflicting versions of the English Florence of Worcester and the *Chronicon Norwegiæ*.

On Canutus's death Pontanus follows Saxo, agreeing, though, with the English tradition and Huitfeldt that he was buried in England rather than in France, as Saxo has it. Again Pontanus adopts the favourable image of Canutus depicted by Saxo, here by quoting Saxo's panegyrical obituary (159). To this account of Canutus's death he now adds an argument to the effect that Canutus did not set out to fight Richardus of Normandy, who had died by this time; instead Pontanus suggests, on the basis of William of Jumièges, that Canutus died during fights in England with Richard's son Robertus.

Pontanus, then, collected material from various foreign sources, just like Huitfeldt; it is reasonable to assume that he consulted Huitfeldt for inspiration, but his familiarity throughout with the older sources is clear, and he usually gives a much fuller relation of the events than Huitfeldt. Unlike Huitfeldt, he pays attention to Saxo. Sometimes he simply notes that Saxo's account differs from the one he has presented himself. But more fundamentally, he recreates Saxo's image of Canutus as the powerful and pious king who ruled over six countries.

This is particularly clear in the last part of the chapter (160-63). So far Pontanus has not touched upon those events of Canutus's reign which in

---

[43] Hans Gram devotes a long note (in his commentary on Meursius) to the demonstration that the "most learned" Pontanus (and his Dutch sources) were wrong in believing that Canutus's daughter spent the last part of her life in Bruges (Meursius 1741-63, IX, col. 183).

Saxo's version were the most important: the episodes involving Ulvo, including his death on Canutus's order, his lawmaking, his own breaking of the law by killing one of his men, and the severe sentence he subsequently passed on himself. But now, having given a chronological account of Canutus's reign, he takes up these matters (which Huitfeldt, as we saw, left completely untouched), and he does so in a way clearly designed to add extra dimension to the greatness of Canutus.

First, however, he tells a story about Canutus's piety, related neither by Saxo nor by Huitfeldt. As an answer to some flattery, the king once, on an English beach, demonstrated his inability to stop the waves, concluding that only God should be recognized as a *rex potentissimus* (160) (a story known from medieval English historians). The anecdote does not, though, simply serve as an illustration of royal piety. It also attributes to Canutus the status of a classical ruler; Pontanus points out that Canutus's rejection of his men's praise put him on a par with Augustus, who likewise tried to bring an end to empty flattery and would not tolerate being called *dominus*.[44] – Similarly, in connection with the mention of Canutus's dead body on the battlefield shortly before (159), Pontanus reminds his readers of another Roman emperor Vespasian, who on his deathbed had declared that an emperor ought to die standing.[45]

Canutus's lawmaking in Denmark and England, which is now presented (160-61), is of course seen as an indication of his concern for his countries.[46] Then follows a discussion of the character of Ulvo (*Ulpho* in Pontanus) – beginning with his death. Saxo had passed over this incident rather quickly, making clear that Canutus's order to have him killed because of Ulvo's bragging was absolutely justified. Pontanus, on the contrary, is able to use even this incident to make a panegyrical point; again he draws a parallel with a classical ruler, this time Alexander the Great, who had similarly killed one of his own men, provoked by his drunken talk at a party.[47] That the parallel is meant to emphasize Canutus's power is spelt out by Pontanus in his presentation of Alexander as *cognomento similiter Magno* (161).

---

[44] Cf. Suetonius, *Divus Augustus*, Ch. 53.

[45] Cf. Suetonius, *Divus Vespasianus*, Ch. 24.

[46] *Tali Canutus animi altitudine ac modestia vere Christiana insignis, ut regnum insuper laudatissimis statutis ornaret, civilia etiam jura sibi curæ ac cordi esse ostendens* [...] (160). From Saxo's long description of the single laws, Pontanus quotes excerpts, which are, however, printed as one single passage (161, cf. Saxo X, Ch. xviii,4sqq).

[47] Cf. Plutarch, *Alexander*, Ch. 51.

Canutus is the equal of the mightiest rulers of antiquity. Pontanus, in fact, makes many such comparisons between Danish history and antiquity. They do not all concern rulers, but even so, they have the effect of raising Danish history to the level of the classical world. Thus, when the murderers of King Ericus V (1241-50) are compared to the murderers of Caesar (337), Danish history is presented as equivalent to Roman history. We shall return to this in the chapter on style.

Pontanus now turns to a discussion of Saxo's description of Ulvo's fantastic origin as the grandson of a bear, comparing it with other sources (Adam of Bremen, *Rydårbogen* and some 'English chronicles'), according to which Ulvo was an English nobleman. Pontanus, while leaving his reader in no doubt as to the absurdity of Saxo's anecdote, adopts a tolerant position; we must allow antiquity, he says, to invent fabulous stories in order to make origins more spectacular; this is a common phenomenon; the Greeks maintained that snakes were created from the blood of Titans and blood from Medusa's head, and the Romans that their founders Romulus and Remus were sons of Mars and raised by a wolf. Therefore, he goes on, the Danish annals should not be blamed for wanting to make the birth of the great king Sueno (*Sven Estridssøn*, d. 1074, who was son of Ulvo) more majestic.

This is the same Livian tolerance which Pontanus applied to the first, legendary part of Saxo's work. Old myths designed to magnify the origins of spectacular persons or phenomena must be allowed. Thus Sueno, nephew of Canutus, whose history follows shortly afterwards, is dignified also in Pontanus's account by this explanation of the function of the myth – and Pontanus again draws a parallel between Danish and classical history.

Pontanus also briefly mentions Krantz's rationalistic theory that Ulvo's grandfather had had the name of a wild animal, *Lupus* (wolf, in Danish *Ulv*), and that this name had given rise to the story of the bear. In the introduction to his commentary on Saxo (1645), Stephanius takes a similar view of the affair. In an earlier chapter he quotes a number of critics of Saxo (*Saxomastiges*), and two of these (the authors of the *Centuriæ Magdeburgenses* and the Danish historian Jon Jacobsen Venusin) refer to the story of the bear as an example of the fantastic character of Saxo's work. Stephanius's rationalistic answer may well be seen as a response to such statements – and so indeed may Pontanus's exhortation to tolerance.

Instead of rewriting Saxo's *Gesta Danorum*, Pontanus, as we have seen, chose to build his narration of early Danish history (from antiquity up to c. 1200) on a large number of various sources, classical, medieval and almost contemporary. His version is very much about Danes (including Cimbrians, Goths, Anglo-Saxons, and Normans) outside Denmark. Huitfeldt had followed the same strategy but in a less comprehensive fashion, and Vedel and Venusin had also realized the necessity of supplementing Saxo with foreign sources for early medieval history. This insight reflects the increased availability of printed texts in the latter half of the sixteenth century.[48] Pontanus's treatment of the early Danish past is a conspicuous example of the new possibilities within the field of historical studies after the spreading of the use of printing. Historical studies could now be conducted on the basis of a multitude of various sources which could be compared and found to supplement or contradict each other. Saxo's work was no longer the only version of the early history of Denmark.

5. Books VI-X and the Oldenburg History (up to 1588)

Sources

Book VI (232-324) covers the period 1157-1241, the reigns, that is, of Valdemarus Magnus (1157-82), Canutus (1182-1202), and Valdemarus II (1202-41). For the first part, up to c. 1185, Saxo still forms the basis, but other authors, primarily Helmold (from whose *Chronica Slavorum* Pontanus often quotes), Krantz, and the *Chronicon Norwegiae* have also left their traces. Many details and episodes from Saxo's rich narrative of this period have been left out. The role of Archbishop Absalon (c. 1128-1201), crucial in Saxo, is much less important in Pontanus's version. Here the focus is rather on the kings.

As Pontanus notes (279), Saxo only goes up to c. 1185. From now on Huitfeldt's *History of Denmark* becomes by far the most important source for Pontanus's work. His dependence on Huitfeldt, however, is not as total as has sometimes been maintained. Ludvig Holberg, in his own *History of Denmark* (1732-35), passes an unkind judgement on Pontanus (after having noted Huitfeldt's wish to let others write a more perfect history

---

[48] The consequences of the invention of printing for various branches of learning is the subject of the classic study by Elizabeth Eisenstein (1979). Historical studies, though, are not taken up for discussion in her book.

on the basis of his own): "It may well be said that Pontanus's history is simply a translation [of Huitfeldt], without the slightest attempt at criticism or correction".[49] Already in 1650 Hans Svaning the younger had named Pontanus a *Huitfeldius Latinus* in the preface to his *Chronologia Danica*. This nickname has since then stuck to Pontanus, though Carl S. Petersen and Ellen Jørgensen seem to acknowledge his independence in the early history (that is, as far as Saxo goes); and H.F. Rørdam rightly notes that even in the later part of the work where Huitfeldt is the main source, the nickname is somewhat exaggerated.[50]

In the history up to c. 1185 Pontanus often consulted Huitfeldt's work and no doubt received inspiration here to include events, which he then retold on the basis of older sources. It is true that from the point where Saxo stops, Pontanus's use of Huitfeldt increases dramatically, and Huitfeldt's work is his unrivalled main source up to the death of Christianus III in 1559. But the *Huitfeldius Latinus* label must be qualified. For all the closeness of his adaptation of Huitfeldt, Pontanus made considerable additions, expansions, and omissions.

In many cases he abbreviated Huitfeldt's account heavily. This is most striking in his unprinted Oldenburg section, where Huitfeldt had presented a rich amount of material, but it is also notable in the previous history. Pontanus also supplied material from many other authors. Krantz's history of the Scandinavian countries figures throughout, up to the point it reaches. Other important sources are Albert of Stade, Helmold, and the *Chronicon Norwegiæ*. In the history of Johannes (1481-1513) Pontanus made use of Hans Svaning's account of this king, and for the three first Oldenburg kings he also consulted Meursius's history.

Pontanus's history of Fridericus II (1559-88) is shorter and less detailed than his treatment of the preceding kings (cols. 1192-1230). Lyschander had written a Danish account of this king, a work which was later published in 1680 by Peder Hansen Resen. In August 1639 a German version of Lyschander's work was sent to Meursius by the chancellor.[51] Already in June 1637 Pontanus had asked the chancellor for

---

[49] *Ja man kand sige, at Pontani Historie er en puur Oversættelse deraf uden ringeste Critiqve eller Emendation*, Holberg (quoted from the edition of 1856), I,1.

[50] In his unfinished biography of Pontanus, Reinboth explicitly distances himself from this description of Pontanus, his main argument being their different handling of the early history (Ms., *Thott 1957, 4to*, 72-74). Cf. also Carl S. Petersen 1929, 611; Ellen Jørgensen 1931, 158; Rørdam 1898, 453.

[51] Letter from Chr. Friis to Meursius, dated August 9, 1639 (Meursius 1741-63, XI, no. 785).

material on Frederik II,[52] but whether he, too, received a version of Lyschander's *History of Frederik II* (either in Danish or in Eggebrecht's German version) is not known. It is clear that the work later edited by Resen is much fuller than Pontanus's rather lapidary account, which makes it unlikely that he had received a full copy of Lyschander's *History of Frederik II*. But extracts may have been made from Lyschander's work and sent to him. Anyway, a comparison with Cilicius Cimber's description of the war in Ditmarsken in 1559 (*Belli Ditmarsici descriptio*) and Caspar Ens's account of the Seven Years War (1563-70) (*De Bello Svecico commentarii*) reveals that Pontanus used these works as his primary sources for the two wars.[53]

It is one of the aims of this chapter on the chronological narrative of Pontanus's *History* to demonstrate in what respects Pontanus's *History* differs from Huitfeldt's. Observation of differences between the two will contribute to our understanding of the special character of Pontanus's approach. So far we have seen that Pontanus's presentation of Denmark as a powerful and influential nation in the earliest history has no counterpart in the work of his predecessor. In the following section (5.2) I shall briefly try to show that the theme of Danish influence abroad is also present, though in a very moderate form, in Pontanus's later history.

Danish Influence Abroad

Danish history from the twelfth century onwards could not be painted in such bold strokes as to convey the impression of Denmark as an *officina gentium*. But some traces remain. Once Pontanus came to the period when Danish expeditions abroad no longer made up the bulk of his account, his most important means of creating the impression of Danish influence abroad were explanations of the genealogical ramifications of the Danish royal families. Moreover he furnished his readers with notes, often quite brief, on episodes involving Danes, or suggesting Danish

---

[52] Letter from Pontanus to Chr. Friis, dated June 1st, 1637 (Rørdam 1898, 490-91; Matthæus 1738, V, 988-89).

[53] Extracts from Cilicius's work were published by Caspar Ens together with his history of the Seven Years War in 1593. Pontanus does not mention these works, but he refers in passing to some others, such as Jacob Ulfeldt's *Hodoeporicon Ruthenicum* (1608) (col. 1220), and a description of the nomination of Christian (IV) in 1584 (col. 1225).

influence, in foreign countries. As already suggested, this is a theme which Huitfeldt had not taken up, just as, in the early history, he did not make a point of celebrating Denmark as an *officina gentium*. None of the examples mentioned below are found in his work.

In the *Chronica majora* of Matthew Paris (d. 1259) Pontanus found a reference to the Pope's offering the Emperor's throne to the Norwegian King Haquinus after the emperor Gulielmus's death in 1256. Pontanus even quotes Matthew's words because, as he says, Denmark and Norway are mentioned (347-48).[54] In fact only Norway is mentioned in the quotation, but Pontanus gives Denmark a share in the Norwegian honour, even though the countries were not united by that time. In connection with the Emperor's death, Pontanus draws attention to another testimony of Danish influence in Matthew Paris's work (550) (admittedly a detail), namely that the Frisians in their fight against the emperor Gulielmus in 1256 used weapons called *gesa Danica*, Danish javelins (347).

Similarly, in Johannes Aventinus's *Annales ducum Boiariae*,[55] he came across a reference (VII, Ch. 21) to a *rex Cimbrorum*, who in 1364 (the dating is Pontanus's) acted as a mediator after an attack on Noricum. Identifying the king as Valdemarus III (*Atterdag*, 1340-75), Pontanus did not omit to draw attention to this piece of hitherto unknown Danish history (495).

From the Swedish Johannes Messenius's *Theatrum nobilitatis Svecanæ* (1616) he learnt of an offer of marriage in 1444 made by the Turkish sultan, Balthazar, on behalf of his daughter to the Danish king, Christophorus III (1439-48) (624-25);[56] though Pontanus openly declares his own distrust, he nevertheless devotes considerable space to the story and even quotes the sultan's letter from Messenius. Further, he deals at some length with the mediation of Christianus I (1448-81) in a conflict between Fridericus, *dux Brunsvicensis*, and Maximilianus, *dux Austriæ ac Burgundiæ* (later Emperor Maximilian I), in 1479 (cols. 837-38).

Pontanus does not confine himself to crowned heads. In Jacob Meyer's *History of Flanders* he found several references to Danish affairs,

---

[54] In the modern edition of Matthew Paris, the Pope's address is dated 1251, following shortly after the death of the emperor Fridericus II (*Matthæi Parisiensis [...] Chronica Majora*, ed. H. R. Luard, vol. V (1880; rep. 1964), 201.

[55] Written 1519-21, this work was not published in its entirety until 1580. Aventinus died 1534.

[56] Messenius 1616, 122-23.

such as the distinguished career of Balduinus Danus in the French army in the 1350s (488).[57]

The German humanists of the sixteenth century had unanimously extolled recent German triumphs within the cultural sphere, the invention of the printing press and gunpowder. Pontanus follows suit. As to the printing press, he observes how different parts of Germany all lay claim to the honour of the invention, and he comments dryly: "Everybody is, as we know, a supporter and admirer of his own country".[58] But then he reveals himself as precisely such a patriot, since his main point turns out be the introduction of yet another possible inventor, Nicolaes Jensen, whose very name, says Pontanus, points to his Danish origin.[59] His discussion of the invention of gunpowder is just as evidently written from a Danish point of view. From the material Pontanus refers to, it seems clear that the Danes were among the first to make use of this invention, around 1350. We even learn that the chancellor himself had drawn his attention to the early use of gunpowder in Denmark and consequently advised him to pursue this topic. But then, as Pontanus notes, the Arabs may also lay claim to the title of inventors, and finally he wonders whether the honour of both inventions does not rightly belong to the Chinese (507-8).[60]

Nevertheless, with their suggestion of the crucial role of Danes, these discussions also contribute to the picture of the Danes' influence abroad throughout history. This picture is, however, primarily produced by a rich royal genealogy.

---

[57] *Reperio eodem hoc tempore illustrem militia ac celebratissimum fuisse Balduinum Danum. Qui apud regem Galliarum Iohannem stipendia merens in eo bello, quod adversus Eduardum Anglorum regem sævissimum gerebatur, magister ballistariorum Quintini Fanum defendendum susceperat, attestante Annalium Flandricorum scriptore Mejero* (488). Other examples of Danes abroad: 339-40, 493. The first of these, dealing with a Dane in Poland in the 1250s, is also found in Huitfeldt, *Chron. I*, 211-14.

[58] [...] *ut est suæ quisque nationis studiosus ac admirator* (621).

[59] [...] *haud debet omitti, qui ipso se nomine Danum prodit Nicolaes Jensen, quem Gallicum alii faciunt. Hic initio præstantissimæ hujus artis celeberrimus fuisse apud Venetos typographus memoratur. Et exstat ac commendatur præcipue ejus Plinii Naturalis Historia, elegantibus, ut tum res erant, typis excusa sub annum Christi, qui sequetur, 1472, elapsis ab hoc qui supra est positus, annis circiter triginta* (621). Huitfeldt confines himself to a brief note on the invention of the printing press in 1440, *Chron. III*, 648. Nicolas Jensen (c. 1420-80) was a French printer working in Venice.

[60] His source for this consideration is a number of recent reports from Danish and foreign seafarers.

6. Selected Themes

The Royal Family

Pontanus displays a keen interest in genealogical questions. Like other auxiliary disciplines of history the study of genealogy enjoyed widespread interest in the sixteenth and seventeenth centuries. David Chytræus, for one, the influential historian in Rostock with whom Pontanus had studied for a while, had not only stressed the importance of genealogy in his teaching but also in his own works delivered contributions to the study of genealogy.[61] Another scholar in the field was Elias Reusner (1555-1612), who published several works on the subject, and whose information Pontanus corrects more than once (e.g. 201, 461). Huitfeldt also endeavours to give a clear account of the intricate family connections of Danish kings. But Pontanus devotes considerably more space to the subject.[62]

Throughout the work, he inserted schematic representations of Danish royal genealogies. Apart from one, they all include both the kings and their wives and siblings, and the individual family members are presented in a few words.[63] Royal or princely houses related to the Danish – the Normans (119-20, 122-23), the Norwegians (385-87), the Holsteiners (461-62), the Mecklenburgers (512), the ancestors of Ericus Pomeranus (1412-39) (529-31) – are also thus presented. The explicit purpose of these genealogies is to create clarity. Besides, they have the important effect of emphasizing that Danish kings constitute the central theme of the book.[64]

---

[61] Detloff Klatt 1908, 50.

[62] Pontanus recognizes his debt to Huitfeldt and Anders Sørensen Vedel on this subject in a letter to Lyschander, dated August 25, 1622 (Matthæus 1695, no. 101). It probably means that he had had notes from Vedel's hand placed at his disposal.

[63] At the beginning of the work, after the summary of Saxo, Pontanus inserted a genealogy of the early Danish kings according to Saxo, the fifty-two kings from Danus to Gotricus (39-41). This is followed by detailed surveys, also presented in the form of family trees, of the kings from Gotricus to Sueno (*Svend Estridssøn*, d. 1074) (178-80), from Sueno to Valdemarus I (d. 1182) (231), from Valdemarus I to Valdemarus II (d. 1241) (323-24), from Valdemarus II to Christophorus III (355-56), and again after Christophorus III, at the end of the chronological narrative in the 1631 ed. (636). Finally, the ancestors of Christianus I are presented graphically at the beginning of the Oldenburg section (cols. 717-18).

[64] Huitfeldt, too, included a number of family trees. At the end of the first volume he presents a genealogy of the Christian kings treated there, that is from Gorm to the death of Voldemar I (d. 1182). Moreover the descent of the Danish Princess Ingeborg is depicted

Such presentations only form a minor part of Pontanus's genealogical material, though. The work abounds with expositions of royal relationships, often in the form of discussions with other historians.[65] Some of these notes do not involve Danes at all, or only marginally, such as one about the family of the emperor Ludovicus Bavarus (Ludwig of Bavaria) on the occasion of his death in 1347 (476) and another about the wedding between the sister of the English king, Eduardus IV, and the son of Philippus, *Burgundiæ dux*, in 1467 (col. 802). None of these are found in Huitfeldt.

But Danish royal genealogy is naturally of central importance. Pontanus follows the branches of the Danish royal family in wide ramifications. At the beginning of the chapter on King Nicolaus (1104-34) he discusses Flemish relations with the Danish royal family (205). So does Huitfeldt (*Fra Kong Dan* [...], 202), and Pontanus may well have been inspired by his account (to which he actually refers, though only in order to point out that he disagrees on some aspects). After the death of Canutus Magnus in the mid-1030s he seeks to clear away the confusion about Emma, the mother of Canutus Durus (*Hardeknud*, d. 1042).[66] The birth of Jacobus IV of Scotland in 1473 prompts him to insert a piece of Scottish dynastic history (cols. 821-23), pointing out the relations with Denmark and celebrating the ruling king and his father, who united Scotland and England (col. 822). Another example is the Danish Rollo, who, although not royal himself, became ancestor of the English royal family (117).[67] – Reflecting a contemporary interest as they do, the numerous

---

graphically (*Chron. I*, 54-55). She was disowned by her husband, Philippe Auguste of France, who claimed that they were too closely related. Huitfeldt argues that this was not the case, and Pontanus follows him closely, even reproducing the family tree (289). At the end of Huitfeldt's *Chron. II* is found a *Genealogia ducum Slesvicensium*, beginning with Abel (1232), and a *Genealogia comitum Holsatiæ*, beginning with Adolph (1030). Furthermore, Huitfeldt introduced his Christian I with a table of the king's ancestors and descendants down to Christian IV.

[65] Examples of genealogical discussions: presenting the second queen of Valdemarus II, Berengaria, Pontanus argues that she was of Portuguese, not Flemish, origin; the confusion has arisen, he points out, because her brother Ferdinandus carried the title of *Flandrensium Comes* due to his marriage to Johanna Constantinopolitana, heiress to Flanders (302). Later he corrects Huitfeldt as to which lady of the Norwegian royal family Duke Ericus of Langeland married in 1295 (380).

[66] *Postmodum Emmam Richardi II, Normanniæ Ducis sororem, Regis Ethelredi, ut meminimus modo, viduam, legitimis sibi nuptijs copulavit. Ex hac Canutus cognomento Durus, et Gunilda procreati. Quod vel ideo repetere visum, quia Emmam confundi cum Alvina et Durum Canutum non Emmæ, sed Alvinæ tribui apud auctores, præter Vigorniensem, etiam domesticos, quamquam perperam, traditum reperi* (159).

[67] Other examples of genealogical notes are found on pages 129-30, 175, 177, 190, 373.

genealogical discussions contribute to creating an impression of greatness; Danish royal connections, being widely diffused, testify to the influence and importance of Denmark throughout history.

An important genealogical point is the demonstration that the Danish kings right from the beginning and up to the present day have belonged to very few families. As an appendix to his summary of Saxo's early history, which comprises fifty-two kings, Pontanus depicts the family connections between these kings (39-41). It is made clear that normally son followed father on the throne; even when that was not the case, some kind of family connection existed between a king and his successor (as noted earlier, Pontanus does not question Saxo's early history when dealing with this subject). Further we learn that all the kings from Gotricus, king number fifty-two, to Christophorus Bavarus (1440-48) belonged to the same family:

> Thereafter his [i. e. Gotricus's] lineage brought these first primeval kings
> down in an unbroken sequence as far as the last, Christophorus Bavarus,
> where it fixed an end to this whole royal pedigree, and after him came a
> new house and family, namely that of Oldenburg.[68]

He takes up the theme in the final paragraph of the 1631 edition. With the death of Christophorus in 1448, says Pontanus, the age-old stock of Denmark's kings became extinct, a stock of kings who had ruled from the very beginning.[69]

Particular attention is of course paid to the Oldenburg line. Both Huitfeldt and Pontanus include an account of the family background of the first Oldenburg king, Christianus I, in connection with his accession to the throne in 1448. But Pontanus is by far the more meticulous. He points out that the Oldenburgs were related to both the old Danish royal family and to the Saxon Prince Widukind and argues at length against several historians, including Huitfeldt (cols. 718sqq). Later, on the occasion of the death of Christianus I's wife in 1495, Pontanus takes the opportunity to connect her with the present king: "the royal house [...]

---

[68] *Cujus* [i.e. *Gotrici*] *exinde progenies primos et aborigines hos reges, quorum Christophorus Bavarus postremus fuit, ad domum usque novam ac stemma aliud, Oldenburgicum nimirum, serie nusquam interrupta deducit finemque prosapiæ huic universæ statuit* (39).

[69] *Atque ita defuncta sine liberis non modo, de qua diximus, Christophori sorore sed et ipso quoque Christophoro, extincta est illa vetustissima [atque] aboriginum Daniæ regum prosapia, clausitque agmen omnium <ultimus> Christophorus* (635). The period seems syntactically flawed. I take *aboriginum* as an adjective to *regum*.

whose descendants control the reins of the kingdom successfully even today" (*regiam domum* [...] *cujus hodieque posteritas regni habenas feliciter moderatur*, col. 884).

The Monarchy

Royal genealogy is only one aspect of the celebration of the Danish monarchy in Pontanus's work. Kings and queens are often endowed with dignity, power and splendour, much more than in Huitfeldt's *History of Denmark*. Here follow some examples.

Queen Margareta (1387-1412) spent most of the year 1391 in Norway and Sweden, but not much is known about her doings there, Huitfeldt regrets. So does Pontanus, advancing however his own opinion that she accomplished many things, especially with regard to establishing a mutual affection between the peoples of the three countries which were to be united in a short while.[70]

In 1474 Christianus I went to Rome. On his way he came to Milan, and Pontanus, like Huitfeldt, tells of the splendid welcome offered him by Duke Galeaceus (Galeazzo), who wanted him to put a word in for him with the Emperor on his way back to Denmark. "And so he did", says Huitfeldt (*Christian I*, 239). Pontanus, not content with this simple statement, took the opportunity to praise Christianus's diplomatic skills: "And he did that with the utmost care and the utmost prudence, as I shall tell later", he declares (*Quod et ipse summa cum cura, summa prudentia præstitit, ut inde dicetur*, col. 824).

The Pope's reception of Christianus I in Rome is described by Huitfeldt in some detail (*Christian I*, 239). But Pontanus is more emphatic, declaring that the great honour with which the Pope received him was only appropriate to such a powerful king.[71] When meeting the Danish king, Huitfeldt further tells us (*Christian I*, 240), the Pope was astonished

---

[70] [...] *res* [...] *varias multasque peregisse, et in uniendis regnis animisque subditorum conciliandis, tum et armis, quæ Alberti nomine erant excitata, componendis totam fuisse vero est simile* (522). Cf. Huitfeldt, *Chron.*, III, 87.

[71] Pontanus here consulted Meursius, who had written: [...] *qui regnorum trium regem potentissimum, cujus fama jam adventum anteverterat, obviam misso Cardinalium senatu, summo cum honore excipit, et hospitium in palatio suo tribuit* (III, 18).

Pontanus: *Ipse cum reliquo patrum ac purpuratorum senatu, eum, ut par erat, tantæ potentiæ Regem summa cum honoris demonstratione Romæ excepit ac ipsi suo in palatio metari hospitium præcepit* (cols. 824-25).

Meursius on his side built on Krantz: *Is trium regnorum potentissimum regem, cuius fama venientem longe præcesserat* [...] *hospitaliter excipit: secum collocat in palatio* (*Dania*, VIII, Ch. 37).

at his ignorance of Latin.[72] Pontanus, however, manages to place this embarrassing circumstance in a flattering light. He says nothing of Christianus's lack of learning or the Pope's surprise until some years later when the king receives the Pope's permission to found a university in Copenhagen. *Now* we hear of the Pope's surprise – his admiration, that is, of such piety and enthusiasm for the promotion of learning in an uneducated man.[73]

Pontanus strives to convey an impression of the Danes' love of their kings. In connection with royal celebrations Pontanus virtually always stresses the unanimity of the people or at least the nobility – everybody supported the king. As when Valdemarus II had his son designated as successor in 1215:

> His son Valdemarus III was hailed as successor to the realm by the votes of all the magnates, and afterwards he went to an assembly held in Viborg in Jutland, where he was met with the same affection and favour from everybody.[74]

Huitfeldt had said nothing either of the noblemen's unanimity or of public joy.[75] The same tendency makes itself felt in Pontanus's abbreviation of the early part of Saxo. Of one king, Butlus, Saxo (followed by Krantz, *Dania* II, Ch. 15-16) had only noted that he was forced to abdicate on the arrival of the lawful king, Jarmericus (VIII, Ch. x,5). Pontanus suggests that a more fitting ceremony was celebrated on Jarmericus's return, when everybody agreed that he should be king:

---

[72] Krantz, too, mentions the Pope's surprise at the uneducated king: *Multa sæpe cum pontifice per interpretem locutus, multa cum illo pontifex: miratur in tanto principe nullas literas* (*Dania*, VIII, Ch. 37).

[73] *Egitque per interpretem omnia Rex, mirante hoc magis summo Pontifice hunc in Rege non admodum litteris ac linguis exculto pietatem ac litteras bonaque studia promovendi animum* (col. 829). Cf. Huitfeldt, *Christian I*, 253-54, where the Pope's permission to found the university is mentioned but not a word of his admiration. – Meursius, like Pontanus, tried to reduce the embarrassment. He said nothing of the Pope's surprise but simply let Christianus I himself, when visiting Rome, "ponder over the dignity of learning, although he was not a learned man himself", and seek permission to found a university (III, 18).

[74] *Hic filius ejus Valdemarus tertius procerum omnium suffragijs regno inauguratus, atque inde profectus ad concionem quæ habebatur Viburgi Cimbrorum, eundem affectum ac favorem erga se cunctorum expertus est* (305).

[75] *Der lod hand hans Søn Woldemar hyldis / Siden førde hand hannem til Viborg Landsting Aar 1216. Oc lod hannem der hyldis / for Herre oc Konge / at bliffue effter hans Død* (*Chron. I*, 102-3).

When he had given his nephew Jarmericus a friendly and splendid reception, the magnates embellished him with a diadem and he was unanimously pronounced king.[76]

He also sees to it that royal ceremonies are surrounded by befitting splendour. The funeral of the king's mother in 1300 was celebrated "with
remarkable pomp and solemnity; her body was transferred to Ringsted
where it was buried in the presence of the king and the magnates of the
realm next to the royal monuments".[77] Huitfeldt merely records her
death and place of burial (*Chron. II*, 40).

Another royalistic touch is found in Pontanus's modification of Huitfeldt in the following passages, which explain the background to an out-
break of internal violence in 1256 (both have just recorded the king's
friendly relations with foreign princes):

> *Huitfeldt:* But otherwise King Christoffer was a burden to the people and
> the clergy. The common man of the country rebelled against him, perhaps
> instigated by the archbishop. They gathered together with their clubs and
> destroyed many castles and fortresses along with many manor houses.

> *Pontanus:* Only the ecclesiastical order and the indiscriminate crowd,
> which was believed to have been instigated by the ecclesiastics, caused
> him not a little trouble. Harbouring hostile feelings towards both castles
> and the fortresses of the country and the noblemen's manor houses,
> they gathered together and took pleasure in destroying them and razing
> them to the ground.[78]

– Pontanus here shifts the origin of the trouble from the king to the
clergy and the people. Moreover, by the suggestion that the common
people took pleasure in the destruction (*ludo ducebat*), Pontanus underlines the absurdity of their action.

---

[76] *Iarmericum vero nepotem ejus amice magnificeque exceptum proceres diademate ornarunt omniumque suffragijs regem proclamarunt* (33).

[77] *Ejus funus insigni cum pompa ac solennitate Ringstadiam delatum ibidem juxta regia monumenta, comi-
tante principe ac regni proceribus, honorifice est conditum* (388).

[78] Huitfeldt: *Men ellers vaar K. Christoffer Almuen / oc den Geistlige stand / fast Besuærlig / At den
Menige mand vdi Riget sætte sig op imod hannem / Maa skee aff Erchebispens Tilskyndelse / Oc løbe
tilsammens met deris Kølffuer / Oc brøde mange Slaatte oc Feste neder i Grunde / met mange Herregaarde*
(*Chron. I*, 250).
   Pontanus: *Tantum ordo ecclesiasticus, et, cujus ille incentor credebatur, promiscua multitudo, haud
parum ei negotij facessijt. Nam et arces et regni propugnacula prædiaque nobilium infesta habens, ea, facto
concursu, diruere ac solo æquare ludo ducebat* (347).

In the years 1332-40 Denmark had no king. Huitfeldt (*Chron. II*, 405), followed by Pontanus (456), complains of the miserable state of affairs when Denmark was in the hands of Holsteiner counts; in both texts we learn that the Danes now regretted that they had sent the king and his son into exile. But instead of Huitfeldt's concluding commonplace that we should realize the consequences of our actions, Pontanus added extra emphasis on the indispensability of a king:

> Septennium exinde tenuit, priusquam regno rex et patriæ, ut sic dicam, pater est redditus (456)

> (It was then a full seven years before a king was given back to the kingdom, and a father, so to speak, to the fatherland)

– thus ending on a note of monarchical pathos, strengthened by the alliterations *regno rex* and *patriæ pater*.

Compared to the historical court poetry of Erasmus Lætus around 1570, it is notable how seldom members of the nobility are singled out in Pontanus's history.[79] Lætus's long catalogues of leading noblemen, his addresses to them one by one, his careful references to the long histories of their families – all this is absent (with the exception of a list of noble families in the *Chorographica descriptio*, 771). While in Lætus's case such praise of the influential members of society naturally reflects his own dependence on these persons, it is noteworthy that nobody apparently, not even the high-born chancellor, saw the modest role assigned to the nobility in Pontanus's work as a defect. It seems that a work of a royal historiographer was expected to focus almost exclusively on the kings.[80] This royal focus is even stronger in Meursius's work.

We have seen how Pontanus, in the *Chorographica descriptio*, while praising the present Danish political system for its balance between elective and hereditary monarchy, nevertheless finds it closer to being a *monarchia* than a *principatus*, since the kings are only chosen from one family – an arrangement which he regards as particularly beneficial. He here explicitly

---

[79] The role of the nobility in the works of Lætus's contemporary, Anders Sørensen Vedel, has been discussed by Karsten Friis-Jensen (1993b).

[80] Huitfeldt's nobleman's point of view comes out with particular force in his praise of Frederik I (1523-33) for having given noblemen power of life and death over their peasants (*Frederik I*, 35-36). Pontanus mentions this point, but without Huitfeldt's praise (col. 1078). Nor did he include Huitfeldt's censure of Valdemarus III (1340-75; Huitfeldt calls him Valdemar IIII) for his persecution of the nobility (*Chron. II*, 627, cf. Pontanus 502).

Chapter VI

refutes the criticism put forward by Jean Bodin that Denmark, on account of the coronation charter, was not a truly sovereign monarchy. Apparently, this was regarded as an allegation which had to be countered.

Furthermore, in the chronological narrative, Pontanus comes close to presenting Denmark as a hereditary monarchy. The many genealogical trees not only serve to give clarity and to mark the ramifications of Danish royal families throughout history. They also underline the hereditary character of the Danish monarchy. Pontanus seeks to demonstrate that the throne has been occupied by very few families. Significantly, as we have also seen above, in this connection he treats the legendary material from Saxo without reservations; there is no need to air his scholarly scepticism in the ideological question of proving the continuity of the Danish royal families. All the kings from Gotricus to Christophorus III (d. 1448, the last king before the Oldenburgs), he claims (39, 41, 635), belonged to one and the same family.

In this respect he differs markedly from Huitfeldt, who nowhere attempts to demonstrate how the Danish throne has been occupied by just a few families. On the contrary, Huitfeldt, as a firm supporter of the balance of power between king and Privy Council, often stresses Denmark's status as an elective monarchy and points to the dangers of a hereditary system.

After the death of Valdemarus II in 1241 Denmark was ravaged by internal discord between his heirs. As a prelude to this period Huitfeldt spells out the benefits of one man's rule, and Pontanus follows him closely in this abstract praise of monarchy; just as there is only one sun, there should be no more than one ruler, they both claim. But Pontanus left out Huitfeldt's argument that the small size of Denmark makes the country particularly vulnerable to rival princes.[81] For one thing he no doubt found it unnecessarily degrading; in the *Chorographica descriptio* his readers were in fact to gain the opposite impression – of a country consisting of many diverse provinces, of which the biggest, Jutland, was almost as long as the whole of Italy, if Holstein was included (654-55). But the primary reason for Pontanus's omission was probably his awareness that Huitfeldt here points to the risk of quarrels between the heirs of the king, one of Huitfeldt's repeated criticisms of hereditary rule.

Later, when summing up the disastrous reign of Ericus VIII (1412-39), Huitfeldt reproaches the king for having tried to have his own rela-

---

[81] Huitfeldt, *Chron. I*, 164-65; Pontanus 325.

212

tive Bugislaus designated as his successor; this was a design, Huitfeldt argues, which went against the fundamental elective principle of the Danish monarchy.[82] The passage was left out by Pontanus (615).

One of the key passages in Huitfeldt's *History of Denmark* is his defence of the dethroning of Christianus II in 1523. Against the theocratic view that the subjects must be completely obedient to the temporal authorities ordained by God, he argues that the public authorities are obliged to get rid of tyrants (*Christian II*, 272-78). He lists a number of similar cases of revolts, among them three revolts against Danish kings.

Pontanus left out most of this discussion. He takes his point of departure from Huitfeldt's Melanchthonian conclusion that God transfers power to another ruler on account of sins and crimes (col. 1073). Christianus II's successor was his uncle, Fredericus I, and Pontanus now draws attention to the earlier revolts against Danish kings mentioned by Huitfeldt.[83] The parallel he sees, however, does not simply concern the revolts, but the fact that these kings were all succeeded on the throne by relatives:

> The realm, however, was transferred to Duke Fridericus, who was of the same Oldenburg extraction, although of another line – just as had also been the case in Denmark earlier on, when King Christophorus, son of Ericus, and his son, and also Valdemarus (whom several people count as the fourth of that name), and finally Ericus Pomeranus had been deposed by the senate and removed from power; in their place it did not put any others apart from relatives.[84]

Instead of Huitfeldt's justification of the overthrow of tyrannical rulers, Pontanus here focuses on the genealogical continuity of the Danish monarchy.

---

[82] *Det meste hannem skilde ved Rigerne / vaar / at hand vilde trenge dennem paa for Konge / hans Fader-broderson / Hertug Bugislaff / imod dette Rigis fundamental Low / som er it Valrige / huilcket Rigens Raad icke vilde / oc der met vilde hand giøre dette Rige til it Arffuerige / oc allehaande Forandringe vndergiffuen som metfolger Arffueriger / huor den ene Arffuing fortrycker den anden* (Chron. III, 625).

[83] Huitfeldt: *Vdi lige maade er tilforn skeed her vdi Danmarck / met Kong Christoffer Erickssøn desligest hans Søn / oc Kong Valdemar den fierde / oc Kong Erick aff Pomern / imod huilcke Landsens Indbyggere haffuer dennom opsæt / deris Priuilegier, Friheder oc Rigens Beste at forsuare* (Christian II, 273).

[84] *Translatum autem regnum in Ducem Fridericum, qui alterius quidem lineæ, sed ejusdem est domus prosapiæ Oldenburgicæ, haud secus, quam etiam olim in eadem hac Dania factitatum, cum Rex Christophorus Erici, ejusque filius, tum et Woldemarus, quem quartum nonnulli faciunt, et Ericus denique Pomeranus, postquam a regni senatu depositi amotique imperio essent, haud alios in locum eorum quam similiter agnatos surrogaverat* (col. 1076). (Valdemarus's (*Valdemar Atterdag*, 1340-75) presence in Pontanus's list seems to be a mistake. Revolts occurred against him, as Huitfeldt has it, but he was not removed from power).

Earlier in the history of Christianus II, Pontanus briefly touches upon the status of all the three Scandinavian countries, on the occasion of the recognition of the hereditary rights of Christianus II to Sweden. He builds on Huitfeldt. Huitfeldt observes that until the Union of Kalmar (1397) both Sweden and Norway were hereditary monarchies; afterwards they became elective like Denmark, until Sweden was again made hereditary by the provision of Gustav Vasa (in 1543):

> Her aff er vel at see / oc forfare / at Suerig saa vel som Norge / aff fordum tid / effter begge Rigers beskreffne Lowe / haffuer værit Arffue Riger / indtil den venlige Sammenbinding / som skede vdi Drotning Margrettis tid / met Danmarck / **Siden erre de bleffuen Val Riger / som Danmarck** / Indtil Kong Gustaff atter haffuer giort Suerig met almindelig Beuilning til it Arffue Rige (*Christian II*, 147).

> (From this it is easy to see and understand that Sweden as well as Norway since ancient times according to the written laws of both kingdoms have been hereditary kingdoms until the friendly union which was formed with Denmark in Queen Margrethe's day. Since then they have become elective kingdoms like Denmark, until King Gustavus by general consent again made Sweden a hereditary kingdom).

In Pontanus's adaptation of this passage, the change brought about with the Union of Kalmar only concerned Sweden. He does not refer to either Denmark or Norway as elective monarchies (we shall return to this passage in the section on Norway below):

> Ex quibus præter alia hoc quoque est cognoscere Sveciæ regnum non minus quam Norvegiæ esse ac fuisse antiquitus hereditarium, ad tempus usque Reginæ Margarethæ, quo is rerum status nonnihil est immutatus, **ac factum Sveciæ regnum electivum**, donec idem ad vetustissimum vicissim morem ac modum reduxerit Rex ejus nominis primus Gustavus, qui omnium consensu fecit hereditarium (col. 1032).

> (Among other things we can learn from this that the Swedish kingdom no less than the Norwegian is and was from ancient times hereditary, right up to the time of Queen Margaretha, when this state of affairs was considerably altered and the Swedish kingdom was made elective, until King Gustavus, the first of that name, led it back again to its age-old habit and usage, when he, with the approval of everybody, made it hereditary).

– Note also how Pontanus underlines the old traditions of hereditary rule in Sweden.

The suggestion of the hereditary nature of the Danish monarchy is also found on the church portal of Frederiksborg, Christian IV's most ambitious castle in ornament and design (built 1600-20). The two statues portray two of Christian IV's remote predecessors, Ericus Infans, the first Christian Danish king, according to Saxo, and his son Canutus – an indication of the Christian as well as the hereditary nature of the Danish monarchy (Cf. Heiberg (1988), 74).

Pontanus and Huitfeldt both wrote as government spokesmen under Christian IV, Huitfeldt as a former member of the government and still active as a politician, Pontanus engaged by the king. He was the *regius historicus* and this attachment to the king is reflected in his work. His emphasis on the quasi-hereditary character of the Danish monarchy is noteworthy in view of the fact that Denmark was an elective monarchy. In this respect he differs significantly from Huitfeldt, who repeatedly underlines the elective character of the Danish monarchy, a point of view closely connected with his social position as a member of the high nobility, where the formal right to elect the king was placed.

But Pontanus was not the first to strike this theme. It was one of the central purposes of Jacob Madsen's versification of the first book of Saxo's *History*, from 1568, to demonstrate that Denmark had always been a hereditary monarchy.[85] In 1577 Erasmus Lætus in his description of the birth and baptism of Christian IV argued in favour of hereditary rule, even to the point of listing its benefits as opposed to an electoral system.[86] The church portal of Frederiksborg, Christian IV's most ambitious castle in ornament and design (built 1600-20), is flanked by two statues, of Ericus Infans, the first Christian Danish king, according to Saxo, and his son Canutus – indicating that the Danish monarchy is both Christian and hereditary.[87]

Though Pontanus displays a stronger royalism than Huitfeldt, both praise the present state of affairs. It must also be emphasized that Pontanus does not consistently leave out Huitfeldt's references to the elective character of the Danish monarchy. Mentioning the discussion among the Danish magnates about the successor of Valdemarus III (1340-75), he refers, *en passant* and following Huitfeldt, to the "law of election" (*jus electionis*) by which the Danish kings acceded to the throne.[88] Likewise he took over Huitfeldt's reference (*Christian III*, Qq1v) to the elective character of the Danish monarchy in connection with the hereditary arrange-

---

[85] See Karsten Friis-Jensen 1996.

[86] Lætus, ed. Skovgaard-Petersen & Zeeberg 1992, 80-92 (Lætus's work remained unprinted until Rørdam's edition of 1875).

[87] Heiberg 1988, 74-77, who also notes that such artistic symbols of hereditary monarchy had been used already by Christian IV's father, Frederik II (1559-88).

[88] [...] *Danmarck / som vaar it frit Valrige* [...] (Huitfeldt, *Chron. III*, 1). [...] *Daniæ regnum, quod jure electionis Regem sumebat* [...] (Pontanus, 503). It might be objected that Huitfeldt and Pontanus are here just presenting the arguments of some of the magnates. But since they do not distance themselves from the statement, they do seem to accept it as a fact.

ments of the Swedish king, Gustavus Vasa in 1544 (dated 1543 by Huit-feldt and Pontanus). But he left out Huitfeldt's subsequent observation of the dangers of a hereditary system and explained instead the rules of hereditary succession laid down by Gustavus Vasa.[89]

In this section we have come across some examples of Huitfeldt's theoretical political observations, which form an interesting and characteristic feature of his work. The accounts of Christophorus II (1320-32) and Christianus II (1513-23), for instance, give rise to reflections on a people's right to revolt against tyrants;[90] the Swedish revolts against Ericus Pomeranus make Huitfeldt consider the benefit of having many castles, and he concludes that it is much more important for the king to be loved by his subjects (*Chron. III*, 528-29); from the example of Christianus I (1448-81) he draws the lesson that a king should not leave his country in times of war (*Christian I*, 33).

   Pontanus, characteristically, took over Huitfeldt's declarations of the benefits of monarchy after the death of Valdemarus II in 1241, as we saw. But by and large such abstract considerations made on the basis of events narrated are few in Pontanus's *History of Denmark*.[91] In this respect it differs significantly not only from Huitfeldt's work but also, as we shall see, from that of Meursius, where general observations on power, morals, and religion form a recurrent feature.

Norway

By the time of the publication of Pontanus's first volume in 1631 Norway had been united with Denmark for 251 years, since 1380 (and would continue to be so until 1814). From 1397 to 1523 all the three Scandinavian countries were united under one ruler in the Union of

---

[89] In fact the version of Pontanus's text printed in Westphalen's edition (col. 1174) does leave out the reference to Denmark as an elective monarchy. But the syntax is flawed, and a check in the two preserved manuscript versions reveals that the reference, while left out in the manuscript on the basis of which Westphalen made his edition (*Gl. Kgl. S.* 839, fol.), was included in the other (*Gl. Kgl. S.* 840 fol.).

[90] *Chron. II*, 401-5, *Christiern II*, 275-78, cf. Kanstrup 1973.

[91] Two other exceptions may be mentioned: Pontanus draws from Abel's murder of his brother, Ericus V (1241-50), the conclusion that internal strife is most damaging to a country, especially if the bishops and the clergy are involved, as they were by that time (337, cf. Huitfeldt, *Chron. I*, 205-6). The sad fate of Albrecht of Mecklenburg, who ruled Sweden from 1363 to 1389, makes Huitfeldt observe that native princes are generally to be preferred to foreign (*Chron. III*, 104-6), a theme which Pontanus briefly touches upon (524).

Kalmar. In 1536, with the accession to the Danish throne of Christian III, the grip was tightened. Norway now became, in theory, reduced to the status of a Danish province, but in practice the incorporation was never as complete as prescribed in the coronation charter of the new king. Norway would always occupy a peculiar status within the Danish monarchy.[92]

This status is mirrored in Pontanus's work.[93] Norway is neither treated as a foreign country nor as an integral part of Denmark. In the *Chorographica descriptio* Norway is, together with Sweden, relegated to an "addition", *brevis attextus*, the two of them occupying the same status in relation to Denmark, as neighbouring countries.

Nevertheless Pontanus tells us considerably more about Norway than about Sweden in the *Chorographica descriptio*. The chapter on Norway takes up five pages (697-702), that on Sweden itself only two (702-4), followed, though, by two pages on the Swedish colonies Finland and Estonia (704-5). Norwegian regions are treated in single chapters with a heading each, whereas the chapter on Sweden is not divided into smaller units. It is mainly concerned with names and positions, with an occasional note about mining and crops. The Norwegian regions are described in a more lively fashion – as regards the fief of Oslo, for instance, we hear of the many ships, bound for diverse countries loaded with timber, we hear of the mines near Tønsberg and of Oslo as the centre of jurisdiction. In the section on Bergen – by that time the largest town in Norway – Pontanus tells of the winding streets, the Hanseatic merchants, its lively trade and fishing, and a certain game invented by the Hansa merchants. Nidaros (*Nidrosia*, modern Trondhjem) is famous for its cathedral, and we hear of its central administrative position. In short, these descriptions bear more resemblance to those of the Danish regions than does the rather laconic presentation of Sweden.

In the section introducing Scandinavia as a whole, Pontanus takes his point of departure from classical literature, as is usual in the *Chorographica descriptio*. He believes that he has found a remarkable reference in Pliny to Norway, and indeed to its most important town Bergen:

---

[92] On the interpretations of "Norgesparagraffen" in Danish historiography in the sixteenth century, see Erling Ladewig Petersen 1973.

[93] This section on Norway is an enlarged version of my treatment of Pontanus in Skovgaard-Petersen 1995.

> In these words of Pliny it is worth noticing that Norigon is the name (only slightly different in form and pronunciation) of the country which is also today normally called Norrige, and in a contracted form Norge, by the inhabitants; further that these age-old authors regarded it as an island or a peninsula; and that the very famous port of this kingdom, which is still today called Bergen, in Pliny's day, or even before, was likewise called Bergos, although it was believed to be an island.[94]

This was of course an important sign of the old age and prosperity of the country. Pontanus has more in store. In the chapter on Norway he singles out the Norwegians as the prime upholders of the old German virtue (according to Tacitus) of hospitality:

> The inhabitants are honest people, total strangers to intrigues and deceit, fond of foreigners, and as hospitable as any.[95]

– Again, a comparison with Sweden is enlightening. Pontanus says nothing either of classical testimonies of Swedish localities or of the Swedish national character. All these features contribute to give Norway a special position in Pontanus's work.

Thus, though presented as a neighbouring country, Norway is, so to speak, encompassed by Danish patriotism. Perhaps there is also an element of defence in this praise of Norway. A hundred years earlier, in 1532, the German geographer, Jacob Ziegler, had published a description of the Nordic countries, *Schondia*. Ziegler, who was an acquaintance of Johannes Magnus and apparently much influenced by his view of Denmark, makes the most of Danish tyranny in Norway:

> [This country], then, is under Danish rule. The Danes not only collect lawful and tolerable taxes, they rake together all goods and take them to Denmark, that is, they strengthen the durability of their power by weakening the subjects.[96]

Ziegler's *Schondia* came out again in 1575, 1583, and 1587 together with

---

[94] *Notandum autem in verbis Plinij, Norigon, quam proximo flexu ac sono id regnum dici, quod hodieque vulgo incolis Norrige, et contracte Norge, appellatur; atque idem insulæ aut peninsulæ nomine accepisse illos vetustissimos: ut et celeberrimum ejusdem regni emporium Bergos, hodie adhuc Bergen dictum, ætate similiter Plinij, vel ante, vero insula habitum* (671; cf. Pliny, *Nat. Hist.*, IV, Ch. 16).

[95] *Incolæ sunt probi, sine fuco ac fallacia, exterorum amantes, et si qui alij, hospitales* (697).

[96] *Itaque est hoc tempore sub potestate Danorum. Hi non legitimos modo redditus et tolerabilia vectigalia imperant: sed omnia commoda corradentes, transferunt in Daniam, videlicet diuturnitatem imperij constituentes in infirmitate subiectorum* (Ziegler ed. Wolf 1583, 483).

Krantz's history of Denmark, Sweden and Norway, the *Chronica regnorum aquilonarium*.[97] By the 1630s it was not forgotten, as Meursius's use of it shows (below, Chapter VII). Johannes Magnus himself had similarly painted a bleak picture of the Danish suppression of Norway. In the great speech *contra Danos* towards the end of his work, the previous prosperity of the Norwegians is contrasted with their miserable life under Danish rule.[98] – The distribution of such accusations should probably be seen as part of the background of Pontanus's emphasis on the prosperous state of contemporary Norway. (Unfortunately, though, there is no mention of Norway in Pontanus's correspondence with the chancellor).

The special position of Norway also comes out in the chronological narrative of Pontanus's *History*. Norway is first and foremost treated as another country. Pontanus, as we have seen earlier, is remarkably anxious to bring home the point that the Normans were not only Norwegian ancestors but Danish as well; he particularly seeks to demonstrate the Danish origin of their heroic leader, Rollo, both in the chronological narrative and in the *Chorographica descriptio* (118, 123sqq, 691). Indirectly, then, his zeal in this matter confirms the status of Norway as a neighbouring country, not as a part of Denmark. It was unacceptable to leave Norman honour to the Norwegians.

Still, Norway is not just any foreign country in the chronological narrative either. For one thing Pontanus inserted long stretches of Norwegian history before the union with Denmark; most of this, it is true, is connected to Danish history, but in some cases the reader is presented with Norwegian history in its own right, e.g. the death of a Norwegian nobleman in 1240 (320-21), the Norwegian king's death in 1262 in connection with a raid in Scotland (360-61), and Scottish-Norwegian dynastic relations around 1290 (377-78). All this was also mentioned by Huitfeldt, but only very briefly.[99] Pontanus's treatment, based on the

---

[97] Nordman 1936, 21.

[98] *Et si nulla alia exempla essent, quæ vos a Danica societate penitus avertere deberent, saltem illæ atrocissimæ injuriæ, quas Dani Norvegiano regno (postquam se illis infelicissimo fato conjunxit) irrogarant. Siquidem Norvegiani, qui pridem divites, locupletesque et felices fuerant, nunc ad Danicam societatem adducti, amissa prorsus libertate experiuntur quam miserrimum sit, sese miseris hominibus credidisse* (899-900). Laurentius Paulinus, who in 1636 published a Swedish history, *Historiæ Arctoæ libri III*, on the basis of Magnus (above, Ch. IV, 10), also mentions Danish suppression of Norway (I, 106-7).

[99] Huitfeldt, *Chron. I*, 157, 303, *Chron. II*, 13. – Pontanus also tells of the Norwegian King Harald Hardraade's travels to Greece, Byzantium, Jerusalem and other places in the middle

Chronicon Norwegiæ, is much more comprehensive. He even depicted their kings in three elaborate genealogical trees (385-87).

A significant detail is the comparison made by Pontanus between a dream in which the mother of the Norwegian King Harald Haarfagre (c. 872-930) saw a tree with many branches growing up from her bosom and Suetonius's account of a portent of Vespasianus's future dignity: an oak put forth a new branch on the three occasions when Vespasianus's mother gave birth to a child; each branch indicated the destiny of one of the children, Vespasianus's branch being like a whole tree (384).[100] As earlier mentioned, these parallels form a characteristic feature of Pontanus's style, serving to make Danish history appear as equal to the classical past. This device is here applied to Norwegian history with the reference to Vespasian.

Having written about the Norwegian King Sverre, Pontanus surveys Norwegian-Danish relations up to his time. Sverre and his successors ruled in Norway until Queen Margareta:

> and since that time Norway has constantly been attached to Denmark, using, however, her own laws and her own justice. This connection is still lasting and has now existed for about 240 years.[101]

Here Pontanus emphasizes the age of the existing arrangement, and consequently its legitimacy. He points out that Norway employs her own laws. That was also stressed by Huitfeldt, though in another context (*Frederik I*, 275), and it seems reasonable to connect this theme with the accusations, such as the one found in Ziegler's work, of Danish tyrannical rule in Norway.

Pontanus also follows Huitfeldt in his emphasis on the obligations of Norway when the union between the two countries was formed in 1380. In this year Margareta's son Olavus, king of Denmark, inherited Norway at the death of his father Haquinus, and the Norwegian council on this occasion committed itself to work for the union of Denmark and

---

of the eleventh century (193-94). He may have been inspired by Saxo (XI, Ch. iii), though he found his treatment of these events too fabulous. Before telling the episode as he had found it in the Norwegian chronicle, he quotes Saxo's account. Huitfeldt left this out.

[100] Cf. Suetonius, *Divus Vespasianus*, Ch. 5.

[101] [...] *perpetuoque deinceps cum ea* [Denmark] *cohæsit, sed suis legibus suoque jure usa. Durat illa conjunctio etiamnunc, continuata per annos plus minus* CCXL (261).

Norway under one king for ever. This is Pontanus's version and it comes from Huitfeldt.[102]

Huitfeldt's view of the Danish-Norwegian relationship during and after the Union of Kalmar has been analyzed by E. Ladewig Petersen.[103] He shows how Huitfeldt consistently stresses the obligations of the Norwegians to stay united with Denmark under one king and makes a point of demonstrating the illegal nature of the Norwegian revolts against Denmark (in the years 1501-2, 1531-32, 1534). Huitfeldt carefully notes that the revolt in 1501-2 was unjustified (*Hans,* 183, *Christian II,* 5), and that the Norwegians signed a letter declaring that they would never again rebel against Hans or his successors (*Hans,* 196). Two new revolts in 1531-32 and 1534 were in Huitfeldt's eyes strongly contributory to the harsh treatment of Norway in 1536, when the country was incorporated as a province of Denmark (*Frederik I,* 274-75). Elsewhere, too, he sees this event as a consequence of their earlier defections (*Hans,* 183).

Pontanus left out these reflections. He did not even paraphrase Huitfeldt's description of "the Norwegian paragraph" (*Norgesparagraffen*) in 1536, in spite of Huitfeldt's own indication of its importance.[104] Probably he lacked Huitfeldt's concern to create a consistent explanation of Norway's present status. What is more, he must have disapproved of Huitfeldt's description of Norway as an elective monarchy both in his rendering of *Norgesparagraffen* and in some of the other reflections mentioned. The hereditary nature of the Norwegian monarchy was given up, in Huitfeldt's eyes, when Norway entered into the union with Denmark,[105] as is clear from the passage quoted above in connection with Sweden. Since the Union of Kalmar Norway and, until 1543, Sweden have been elective monarchies like Denmark, he declares here (*Christian II,* 147). As we saw, Pontanus, in his adaption of this passage, only refers

---

[102] Huitfeldt: *Da holdis faare Dronning Margrete oc Rigens Raad i Norge / dennem igien til vilie i Danmarck / som tilforne vaare Eens at samtycke Kong Oluff til Danmarck / en Forplict at vere giort oc ganget imellem / at Danmarck oc Norge stedse skulle bliffue tilsammens / vnder en Konge (Chron. III, 27).*

Pontanus: *Et agi continuo cum Regina Margareta regnique Norvagici proceribus tum cæptum, ut ipsi in gratiam Danorum, qui Olavum ipsorum etiam suasu ad regni Danici diadema promovissent, id vicissim operam darent ut Dania Norvagiaque in perpetuum conjunctæ uno sub Rege haberentur (508).*

[103] Erling Ladewig Petersen 1973.

[104] *Dog findis i samme Første Recess, en Artickel / som ieg icke her haffuer villit gaa forbi* [...] (*Christian III,* Dd1v). Pontanus's treatment of the events 1536-37 is much briefer than Huitfeldt's (cols. 1157-64).

[105] Erling Ladewig Petersen 1973, 444-45, 452.

to Sweden as an elective monarchy, and simply leaves out Denmark and Norway. In fact he explicitly declares that the Norwegian monarchy is hereditary and has been so for a long time:

> Ex quibus præter alia hoc quoque est cognoscere Sveciæ regnum non minus quam Norvegiæ **esse ac** fuisse antiquitus hereditarium, ad tempus usque Reginæ Margarethæ, quo is rerum status nonnihil est immutatus, ac factum **Sveciæ** regnum electivum, donec idem ad vetustissimum vicissim morem ac modum reduxerit Rex ejus nominis primus Gustavus, qui omnium consensu fecit hereditarium (col. 1032).

> (Among other things we can learn from this that the Swedish kingdom no less than the Norwegian is and was from ancient times hereditary, right up to the time of Queen Margaretha, when this state of affairs was considerably altered and the Swedish kingdom was made elective, until King Gustavus, the first of that name, led it back again to its age-old habit and usage, when he, with the approval of everybody, made it hereditary).

The thread is picked up in the *Chorographica descriptio*, where, in the conclusion of the chapter on Norway, Pontanus firmly declares that Norway is a hereditary monarchy:

> It is a hereditary kingdom (*regnum*), which has been connected to Denmark for more than two centuries with an indissoluble tie, through the marriage between Queen Margareta and Haquinus.[106]

Huitfeldt, on the contrary, describing Norway's status after 1536, just as firmly declares that Norway is no longer a hereditary country (*Christian III*, Dd1v). The difference seems parallel to the difference noted above in relation to the Danish monarchy, whose quasi-hereditary nature is emphasized by Pontanus. But what does Pontanus's statement mean? Perhaps he simply refers to the traditional title of the younger brothers of the Danish kings since Christian III, heir to Norway. One should also consider, however, whether his point of view ought to be seen in connection with contemporary arguments to the same effect. The German political theorist, Henning Arnisæus, who served as Christian IV's personal doctor from 1619 to his death in 1636, is reported to have written a

---

[106] *Regnum est hæreditarium, Daniæ jam ante duo circiter secula per connubium, quod cum Haquino regina Margareta injit, nexu indissolubili adunitum* (698). – Pontanus included one of Huitfeldt's references to the non-hereditary nature of the Norwegian monarchy, but it is put in the mouth of a Norwegian bishop both in Huitfeldt's and Pontanus's accounts (Huitfeldt, *Frederik I*, 181; Pontanus, col. 1117).

treatise on the hereditary right to Norway.[107] And later, in the 1640s, attempts on the part of Christian IV to separate Norway from the control of the Danish Privy Council went hand in hand with propaganda for Norway's being a hereditary monarchy.[108] In light of the fact that the composition of Pontanus's work had been supervised by the chancellor Christen Friis, his straightforward declaration of the hereditary character of the Norwegian monarchy, short as it is, is certainly worth noticing.

Sweden

The conflicts between Sweden and Denmark during the Union of Kalmar (1397-1523) naturally occupy a significant position in Pontanus's *History of Denmark*. The subject, however, was delicate, on account of the tense relations between the countries ever since the dissolution of the union. The political rivalry was, as we saw, mirrored from the middle of the sixteenth century in a polemical branch of historiography in both Sweden and Denmark. Acknowledging the damaging effect of such writings, the peace negotiators after the Nordic Seven Years War in 1570 issued a prohibition against defamatory writings. Cautiousness then came to dominate the attitude to Sweden in Danish historical writing. Thus Huitfeldt managed to avoid this denigrating tendency, exhibiting, in the words of Harald Ilsøe, "a certain pro-Danish fairness."[109]

Some taunts remain, though, in Huitfeldt's work. Like his predecessors, notably Hans Svaning, though less often, he glorifies the Union of Kalmar, a tendency which must have been provocative in Swedish eyes, since the union had been dominated by Denmark, and Sweden had revolted against it time and again. When Denmark and Norway become united under King Olav in 1380, Huitfeldt writes:

> Men dette er siden meget herligere fuldbracht / oc kundgiort / effter Konning Oluffs død / da Dronning Margrete haffde fanget Suerige til / Oc alle disse tre Riger bleffue sammenbunden til Euig tid / vnder en Herre oc Konge at bliffue / som videre oc paa sit sted skal meldis. (*Chron. III*, 27).

---

[107] The work is not extant. It is mentioned by Herman Conring (1606-81), *De republica Danica* (*Opera IV* (1730), 400). (I here rely on Knud Fabricius 1920, 83 and Helge Kongsrud 1984, 66-68).

[108] Helge Kongsrud 1984, 181sqq, 245-47; Sverre Bagge & Knut Mykland 1987, 150; Steffen Heiberg 1988, 443-44.

[109] Harald Ilsøe 1973, 49.

(But this was carried through later, after the death of King Olav, and proclaimed with much more glory, when Queen Margrethe had taken hold of Sweden, and these three countries were united for ever, to remain under one lord and king, as we shall hear later).

Pontanus echoes him:

> Quod ipsum, Olavo quoque mox defuncto, repetitum multoque illustrius transactum, ubi Sueciam etiam sui juris Margareta fecisset, collectis tribus his Boreæ regnis unoque sub sceptro ac monarcha constitutis, ut suo exinde loco dicetur (508).

> (When also Olavus soon afterwards had died, this union was entered upon again and accomplished with much greater distinction, when Margareta had brought Sweden also under her authority, and these three Northern realms had coalesced and been fixed under a single rule and monarchy, as will be described later at the appropriate point).

Around 1440, when Erik of Pomerania, king of Denmark, Norway and Sweden, had gone into exile, the Swedes, according to Johannes Magnus, would not tolerate that a new foreign king, Christoffer of Bavaria, was thrust upon them by the Danes; deceived, however, by their astute neighbours they finally accepted (832-35). But after Christoffer's death in 1448, they realized that they would be much better off with their own king and Karl Knuttsøn was now proclaimed king of Sweden. This view had found its way into the 1593 edition of the influential *Chronicon Saxoniæ* (first ed. 1585) by David Chytræus, in which the history of the Scandinavian countries was also told.[110] In reaction, probably, to these foreign conceptions, Huitfeldt, while briefly admitting that the Swedes were not consulted in connection with the election of Christoffer of Bavaria in 1439, underlines that they broke the agreement between the three countries when Karl Knuttsøn was proclaimed king.[111] The Danes, in his account, did not offer the royal title to Christian of Oldenburg until the Swedish breach was known. Pontanus, closely following Huitfeldt in his account of the events after Christoffer's death, is just as unambiguous – the Swedes were to blame:

---

[110] Erling Ladewig Petersen 1973, 445-47.
[111] *Chron. III,* 627; *Christian I,* 1-4.

> Therefore, when the Swedes had withdrawn from the bond of the union
> of these three countries and taken their own king, the Danes, too, were
> forced to make their own decision about electing a king and master.[112]

– The Danes had even, Huitfeldt and Pontanus tell us, asked the Swedes
to take part in the election of a common king immediately after
Christoffer's death in 1448, but the Swedish separatists had nevertheless
persuaded the other Swedish councillors to elect Karl Knuttsøn, arguing
that the Danes had not consulted the Swedes when Christoffer of
Bavaria had been proclaimed king eight years before. Pontanus, who had
left out Huitfeldt's admission of this circumstance, now adds: "although
this was untrue, as appears from what has been said above"[113] – thus
making sure that this argument – and Johannes Magnus's version – is not
believed.

Similarly, both reproach the Swedes for their many protractions and
excuses for not keeping their promises.[114] This, however, is a theme much
more prominent in Hans Svaning's account of Johannes (*Hans*, 1481-
1513), and though Pontanus made use of Svaning from time to time in
his own history of Johannes, he did not take over these clearly offensive
passages. Similarly, the unreliability and greed for power of the Swedish
rebel leaders, very dominant in Svaning's account, were considerably
toned down by Huitfeldt and Pontanus, though traces remain.[115]

In some cases Pontanus sharpened the anti-Swedish tone compared to
Huitfeldt. He is unambiguous in condemning the Swedes for being insin-
cere when agreeing to a truce in 1471:

> This deceitful truce was accepted by the king, who hoped for peace, but
> it turned out to his own detriment, when food supplies were gone and
> his soldiers tired. Realizing that these last actions were no different from
> the first and that he could expect nothing from the Swedes [...]

Huitfeldt is not so outspoken:

> King Christian trusted this truce and agreement of peace. But later it

---

[112] *Cum igitur a vinculo unionis trium horum regnorum se disjunxissent Sueci, ac sibi seorsim Regem sump-
sissent, coacti etiam Dani de Rege ac domino eligendo secum statuere* (col. 715). (Cf. Huitfeldt, *Christian
I*, 4).

[113] *licet falso, quod docent præcedentia* (col. 715).

[114] Pontanus, col. 831; Huitfeldt, *Christian I*, 269.

[115] E.g. Pontanus, col. 859; Huitfeldt, *Kong Hans*, 59.

resulted in great trouble. When he saw that he could do nothing, and
that food supplies had disappeared [...][116]

The echoes of Svaning's hostile tone are heard in Pontanus's description
of Sten Sture's behaviour in 1495: *callide enim, ne dolose dicam, acta omnia*
("since everything was done cunningly, not to say treacherously", col.
884), which has no parallel in Huitfeldt.[117]

In general, though, it is fair to say that Pontanus retained the balanced
point of view of Huitfeldt. Evidently written from a Danish point of
view, their works lack the aggressive quality of Johannes Magnus and (on
a lesser scale) of Hans Svaning.

Both, however, found it necessary to mobilize a convincing defence
and reject some of the most aggravating claims launched by Johannes
Magnus. Thus, in the highly important issue of the right to Scania (which
eventually became Swedish in 1658), Magnus had tried to prove that the
Danes only possessed this province illegally, since the province had been
sold to Sweden in 1343.[118] Arguing that the old borders had later been
restored, Huitfeldt attacks this view, and Pontanus follows suit.[119]
Swedish claims to Scania were a recurrent issue in the tensions between
the two countries, in the days of Johannes Magnus as well as in the reign
of Christian IV. Soon after the publication in 1622 of Erich Tegel's history of Gustav Vasa, Christen Friis had complained to a Swedish agent
about assertions in the work that Scania had in former times been

---

[116] Pontanus: *Verum istæ dolosæ induciæ spe pacis a Rege concessæ, ipsi exinde absumto commeatu et milite defatigato per incommoda acciderunt. Etenim ultima primis respondere, nec a Svecis exspectandum quicquam videns* [...] (col. 818).

Huitfeldt: *Paa huilcken Anstand oc Syn til Fred Kong Christiern forlod sig / Men siden kom der offuer vdi stor Besuæring. Da hand saae sig intet at kunde vdrette oc Fetalien metgick oc fortæredis for hannem* [...] (*Christian I*, 217).

[117] Cf Svaning's characterization of Sten Sture in 1495: *Nec vnquam magis quam in eo, nihil sin-cere, aut ex animo, sed omnia astute insidioseque cum Ioanne Rege Stenonem egisse, palam factum est* (*Chronicon Ioannis*, R3v). Svaning's life of Johannes was the only part of his *History of Denmark* which had been printed (in 1561) when Pontanus composed his work.

[118] Johannes Magnus strongly emphasizes the binding character of the agreement in 1343. It was agreed, he says, that Skåne [...] *omni via juris, adeoque indissolubili pacto unitam esse debere regno Gothiæ, et de cætero perpetuis temporibus censenda esset regni Gothiæ, et non Daniæ pars, repositis terminis ejusdem regni Gothiæ, ut ab initio regnorum fuerant, in medio freto Eresundiano, quo Daniæ regnum ab Aquilonaribus terris, et regnis separatur* (766).

[119] *Quod autem eæ literæ in ipsum Oresundiæ fretum Suecia limitem videantur producere, atque idem hodieque ita habendum, quia tum pronunciatum, ut Gothus concludit, haud quaquam concedi debet. Nam postmodum ad Danici regni laciniam ubi redijt Scania, veteres et qui ante observati fuerunt, non Oresunda, Suecia ac Daniæ limites in usum revocati* (473, cf. 490. Huitfeldt, *Chron. II*, 467; cf. *ibidem*, 553-54). (*Gothus* was a conventional term for Johannes Magnus).

Swedish.[120] Huitfeldt's and Pontanus's rejections of Johannes Magnus's historical arguments are clearly to be seen in the light of contemporary politics.

Another recurrent theme in the Danish-Swedish polemics, admittedly without the concrete political implications of the Scanian issue, was Magnus's story about the legendary Swedish King Attilus, who placed a dog on the Danish throne in order to punish the arrogant Danes (282). The story went back to Saxo, who tells of a Swede Gunnarus who made a dog the ruler of Norway (VII, Ch. ix,4), but Magnus changed it, by giving the Danes the shame of being ruled by a dog and by letting the episode take place at an earlier stage.[121] In the great speech *contra Danos* put into the mouth of Hemming Gadh towards the end of the work, Magnus finds occasion to return to the story:

> What do you think he could have wanted to achieve by this action if not to make the highly insolent people [the Danes] realize that their arrogance was punished more openly, when they bowed their heads to a dog?[122]

The story, degrading in itself, was here presented with extra animus. No wonder, then, that the Danes reacted indignantly. Svaning delivered an answer in his refutation of Magnus (1561), and so did Erasmus Lætus, indirectly, in his epic poem *Margaretica* (1573). Both Huitfeldt and Pontanus (though not directly dependent on Huitfeldt here) are careful to mention it – and to reject it as absurd.[123] This was obviously a serious matter, and in 1640 Stephanius suggested to his friend Ole Worm that he, in his forthcoming *Regum Daniæ series duplex* ("The Twofold Line of

---

[120] Harald Ilsøe 1973, 49.

[121] Attilus rules Sweden many generations before Gunnarus, according to both Magnus and Saxo (who calls him Athislus). He is mentioned in Saxo's Book II. Magnus claims that he had several sources for his version (*plures antiquæ Danorum et Suecorum historiæ*, 103); he even lets Hemming Gadh refer to Danish sources older than Saxo in his grand speech *contra Danos* towards the end of the work: *Hæc etsi Saxo dissimulet, asseratque ista illi cani, quem Gunnarus* [ed. 1617: *Gunuarus*] *Sueticus Noricis præposuit, convenire, attamen verius de Racchone Danis præfecto affirmantur, qui juxta alias, et vetustiores Danorum historias, a canibus discerptus interijt* (889).

[122] *Quo facto quid alium eum* [Attilus] *assequi voluisse putemus, quam ut plenus superbiæ populus* [the Danes], *insolentiam suam manifestius puniri cognosceret, dum obnixos latranti vertices inclinaret?* (888-89). But the words came from Saxo. Magnus here reuses Saxo's indignant apostrophe to the reader, "he" being in Saxo the Swedish Gunnarus and "the insolent people" the Norwegians (VII, Ch. ix, 4).

[123] Huitfeldt, *Fra Kong Dan* [...], 8-9; Pontanus, 17.

Danish Kings", 1642), should make it quite clear that the story about the dog on the Danish throne was pure fable.[124]

Pontanus, however, takes up the theme of the dog ruler later, in connection with Saxo's story of the Swedish Gunnarus (29-30). He does not, as Saxo, suggest that Gunnarus had reasons for punishing the Norwegians in this way, but focuses exclusively on the brutality of the action, comparing Gunnarus to Caligula, the proverbially cruel Roman emperor, who, according to Suetonius, was said to have appointed a horse to the consulate.[125] Pontanus's stress on the Swedes' brutal treatment of Norway should perhaps be seen as yet another reaction to Magnus's (and Ziegler's) accusations of Danish tyranny in Norway; dealing with Gunnarus, Magnus not only declares that Saxo's story of his placing a dog on the Norwegian throne is highly exaggerated, but also adds that even if it were true, it would have been a "bite" much less serious than that inflicted by the Danes when the Orkneys were torn away from Norway[126] – a reference to the Danish King Christian I's surrender of the Orkneys to Scotland in 1468 by way of mortgage.

Pontanus also included other criticisms of Johannes Magnus. In 1332 Johan of Holstein sold Scania to Sweden after having received the province as security from the Danish king Christophorus II three years before. While Huitfeldt here confines himself to noting that the legitimacy of this sale was later called in doubt, Pontanus launches a firm rejection of Magnus's claim that Christophorus II in fact begged the Swedes, both by envoys and by letters, to let Scania return to Sweden; the claim is particularly suspect, says Pontanus, since Magnus does not quote his sources and since they are not otherwise known.[127] Similarly he is not content to tell his own version of Ericus VIII's (1412-39) settling down on the island of Gotland in 1439. A rejection – not found in Huitfeldt – of Magnus's disgraceful claim that Ericus took flight from an aborted meeting with the leader of the Swedes back to the island of Gotland is introduced with these harsh words:

---

[124] Letter from Stephanius to Worm, dated January 22, 1640 (Worm 1751, no. 197; Worm 1965-68, II, no. 826 (Danish trans.)).

[125] Suetonius, *Caligula*, Ch. 55.

[126] *Hic Saxo Danicus multis verbis exaggerat, quomodo Gunno iste devictæ gentis superbiam domiturus, canem Norvegianis in Regem præfecisset: quod si factum fuisset, profecto longe minus perniciosum morsum illi regno inflixisset, quam ille unus morsus erat, quo a Norvegia avulsæ fuere insulæ Orchadum* (Magnus, 282).

[127] Pontanus 455; Huitfeldt *Chron. II*, 393; cf. Magnus 765.

But it is beyond any doubt – as the domestic *acta* show, but this was left out or simply unknown to Johannes Magnus, like so much else – that king Ericus [...][128]

Magnus's description of Danish tyranny in the Union of Kalmar (1397-1523) also prompted Pontanus to include explicit objections. Following Huitfeldt (*Christian I*, 14), he relates how Danish envoys in 1449 asked the Swedish king to give up his siege of the island of Gotland, demonstrating by historical arguments its Danish nationality. Then he adds of his own accord:

... from the preceding account, then, it is easy to understand how much confidence we should have in Johannes Magnus, who claims the opposite and bombastically threatens to put forward arguments from Saxo to the effect that Gotland belongs to the kingdom of Sweden.[129]

Later, in connection with the election of Christianus I as Swedish king in 1457, Pontanus finds it necessary to correct Johannes Magnus: Christianus was not thrust upon the Swedes (*intrusus*), but warmly welcomed by the leading men of the country (*exceptum a præcipuis benigneque admissum*, col. 757).

On less sensitive issues Pontanus sometimes mentions Magnus without contradicting him. The Swedish king in 1335 passed a law forbidding slavery. Magnus, however, refuses to believe that there had ever been slavery in Sweden, says Pontanus (457) – clearly marking his scepticism by simply stating the law as a fact and then referring to Magnus's chauvinistic point of view.[130] There may well be an element of ridicule on Magnus's behalf here, as there certainly is later on when Pontanus makes

---

[128] *At certo certius est, quod acta domestica ostendunt, omissum aut ignoratum ut alia permulta Gotho, Ericum regem* [...] (611). Cf. Magnus, 831-32.

[129] [...] *ut facile ex hisce colligi possit, quid hic fidei Johanni Gotho debeatur contrarium asserenti ac multa minitanti se ex Saxone allaturum, quibus Svediæ regno Gothlandia asseratur* (cols. 725-26). Cf. Johs. Magnus's description of the meeting: *Neque deerat eis animus contra apertam veritatem loquendi, et affirmandi, quod Gotlandia ad suam Daniam jure pertineret. Quod quam veraciter dixerint, satis ostendit eorum historicus Saxo, qui Daniæ terminos describens, Gotlandiam inter eos ponere non audebat: immo in toto historiæ illius contextu sæpissime apparet, Gotlandiam Gothico regno, non Danico adscribi. Obstat etiam nominis etymologia, quæ dicit, Gotlandiam terram esse Gothorum* (844) (and more arguments follow).

[130] Pontanus probably refers to the proud speech of Engelbrecht, leader of the Swedish rebellion against Denmark in the 1430s, in which he contrasts Swedish liberty with Danish servitude (Magnus, 819). Huitfeldt, *Chron. II*, 406, mentions the law but says nothing of Magnus.

the following comment on Magnus's account of certain predictions of divine wrath which was to befall the Swedes because of their acceptance of the Danish King Christophorus (1440-48):

> These and similar things must be counted as no more than trifling anecdotes. I have decided to include them in order that I should not seem to have left anything out on purpose. But the author [i.e. Johannes Magnus] must answer for the truth.[131]

We have already seen how Pontanus's condemnation of the basis of Gothicism in the *Chorographica descriptio* deals a severe blow to the early part of Johannes Magnus's *Swedish History*. In the narrative history he also attacks the Swedish historian on several occasions, sometimes following Huitfeldt, sometimes on his own initiative. More than seventy years after its first appearance in print, Magnus's *History of the Swedish Kings* clearly still troubled the Danes. Though anxious to avoid insulting their Swedish neighbours, the chancellor apparently did not worry about the effect of Pontanus's corrections of Magnus. Well founded as they generally are, they give an impression of simply setting things right.[132]

Foreign Affairs
Foreign affairs loom large in Pontanus's *History*. Many events abroad, such as the Norman conquests, are presented as forming part of Danish history. But Pontanus frequently turns his attention to foreign events which are simply notable for their own sake. Sometimes he expands on a theme only briefly noted by Huitfeldt. The death of Carolus Crassus (Charles the Fat) (dated 888 by Huitfeldt and Pontanus) is simply noted by Huitfeldt (*Fra Kong Dan* [...] 76), but occasions in Pontanus's version a short biography including quotations of two memorial inscriptions (113).

---

[131] *Quæ aliaque ejusmodi ut nænias habenda, ne quid tamen omissum studio videretur, adjicere visum fuit, fide penes authorem relicta* (618; cf. Magnus, 835). Clearly sceptical, too, is Pontanus's comment on Magnus's statement that when Christophorus III entered Stockholm in 1441, people shouted that the Swedish Karl Knuttsøn was more worthy of the rule of Sweden: *qua vel fide vel authore non addens* (620; cf. Magnus, 837). None of these references to Magnus is found in Huitfeldt.

[132] It should not be overlooked that Pontanus also made extensive use of Magnus simply as a source of information. In the following instances he explicitly refers to him as such: 372, 391, 429, 481, 487, 492, 521, 610, 635, cols. 750, 753-4, 755, 816. The last time he mentions the Swedish historian it is about Magnus's own fate. The Catholic archbishop went into voluntary exile in Italy when Gustav Vasa introduced the Lutheran reformation in Sweden. Bringing much historical material with him, Pontanus writes, "he composed his *History of Sweden*, which I have at my disposal" (*ubi Gothorum, quæ est in manibus, historiam concinnavit*, col. 1109).

Likewise he has much more to say on the occasion of the deaths of Fredericus Barbarossa in 1190 (282, Huitfeldt, *Chron. I*, 31) and Fredericus II in 1250 (338-39; Huitfeldt, *Chron. I*, 209), and of the increasing power of the Ottomans around 1300 (382; Huitfeldt, *Chron. II*, 32); Huitfeldt's note (*Chron. I*, 104) on Cazimir of Pomerania, who went to the Holy Land in 1217 is included in Pontanus's larger account of a crusade which started out in that year (305-6). The death of Pope Eugenius in 1447, barely mentioned by Huitfeldt (*Chron. III*, 684), prompts Pontanus to go through his papacy, even quoting a passage by Baptista Mantuanus on the Englishman, Thomas Rhedonensis, who was unjustly sentenced to death by the Pope (628-29). He similarly expanded Huitfeldt's note on the capture of Byzantium in 1453 considerably (cols. 742-43, Huitfeldt, *Christian I*, 43), and he also mentions the attempt to reconquer the city in 1464 (col. 792).[133]

Moreover, Pontanus added foreign material not mentioned by Huitfeldt at all (or, in the earlier books, by Saxo). The story of the death of Emperor Otto III (dated 1001 by Pontanus) is told in order to demonstrate that ordeal by fire was in use not only in Denmark but also elsewhere (140-41). As a prelude to a Norwegian expedition to the Holy Land in 1104 he sums up the facts of the First Crusade (203). The death of Adolphus of Holstein in 1261, whose abdication Pontanus had recorded under the year 1239 (Huitfeldt says 1238), occasions a presentation of this prince and an excursus on other great regents in history who resigned voluntarily (359). Johan Huss is hailed as a Protestant *avant la lettre*. Dealing with events in the year 1400, Pontanus finds occasion to mention the celebration of the papal jubilee by Pope Bonifacius IX,[134]

---

[133] Other examples of foreign events related in more detail by Pontanus than by Huitfeldt: the European context of a conflict between Valdemarus II and Bishop Valdemarus of Bremen (P., 298-300, H., *Chron. I*, 83-87), the conflict between the emperor Fredericus II and the Pope in the 1240s (P., 328, H., *Chron. II*, 173-74, 178), the death of the emperor Gulielmus in 1256 (P., 347, H., *Chron. I*, 251); the death of the Swedish king, Magnus, in 1290 occasions a small obituary in Pontanus's version (377), which he did not find in Huitfeldt (*Chron. II*, 12). He says more than Huitfeldt about the destruction of the order of the Templars in 1311 (P., 405-6, H., *Chron. II*, 144), and expands on his predecessor's note about the year 1314 being without pope, emperor and king of France (P., 412, H., *Chron. II*, 194). The death of Pope Benedictus in 1342, also mentioned by Huitfeldt (*Chron. II*, 449), prompts Pontanus to tell an anecdote about Petrarch's hostility towards him, even bringing a quotation in Italian (468); likewise Pontanus tells at some length of a conflict between Hamburg and some Frisian pirates in 1450 (cols. 733-34), while Huitfeldt simply notes in one line that the Frisians were active as pirates (*Christian II*, 27).

[134] Huitfeldt briefly mentions the jubilee (*Chron. III*, 160).

the scope of which, he declares, was simply to sell indulgences; but it was by this time that Huss proclaimed that the Gospel and faith itself provided indulgence at any time (533). Pontanus's own connections with Harderwijk and the Dutch province of Gelderland are evident in several places. Sometimes it has to do with Danish history. Thus he has found out, he tells us, that there is in Harderwijk a document about an agreement in 1326 between Valdemar, king elect, and the burghers of the town, and the document is then quoted (442-44).[135]

To be sure, there were at least as many notes of foreign events in Huitfeldt's history which Pontanus left out. To mention just a few: episcopal matters in northern Germany in 1287 (*Chron. II*, 4), Pomeranian affairs in the 1290s (*Chron. II*, 27), England's war with France (*Chron. II*, 478), the foundation of the University of Erfurt in 1392 (*Chron. III*, 91), the death of Carl of Burgundy in the battle of Nancy in 1477 (*Christian I*, 269), a rebellion in Hamburg against the bishop of Bremen in 1483 (*Hans*, 43-55), the discovery of America in 1492 (*Hans*, 108).

It is difficult to see a clear strategy in Pontanus's omissions and additions of foreign matters in relation to Huitfeldt. Primarily it is reasonable to underline the similarity between the two in this respect. Both inform their readers of a multitude of events abroad, without claiming that they have a particular relevance to Danish history. But, as the examples mentioned above show, they are allowed a much broader treatment in Pontanus's version. Where Huitfeldt is often content with brief annalistic notes, Pontanus typically expands with details of background and course of events.

With his generous inclusion of foreign material Pontanus adopted a strategy radically different from Meursius, in whose work practically no foreign events are mentioned, unless they have a direct bearing on Danish affairs. We saw, in Chapter V, how at the bottom of each page Pontanus indicates the contemporary ruler of the Roman empire and its German successor. The multitude of foreign events mentioned in the text itself has the same effect, of presenting Danish history in the larger context of world history. This is a feature conspicuously absent from his colleague's account.

---

[135] A similar example, concerning Amsterdam, is found p. 623 (briefly in Huitfeldt, *Chron. III*, 664). Other examples of foreign affairs in Pontanus and not in Huitfeldt: having mentioned the inhabitants (*Stedingi*) of Stade in northern Germany, Pontanus, under the year 1214, tells how they were later put under a ban (304-5). Furthermore he deals with fights against the Turks in the mid-1450s (cols. 747-48).

Cultural Affairs

In the *Chorographica descriptio* Pontanus, as we have seen, takes up a variety of subjects which in a broad sense can be termed cultural, or antiquarian, such as language, customs, crops, institutions, laws, and learning. In the course of the chronological narrative, too, he found occasion to touch upon these and similar subjects (though, as a consequence of his annalistic scheme, in scattered notes). We have already taken notice of the discussions of the possible existence of giants in antiquity and of the inventions of gunpowder and printing; the many genealogical accounts may also be placed in the group of antiquarian subjects.

Huitfeldt, too, demonstrates a wide range of interests, not confined to the sphere of politics and wars. From him Pontanus took over notes on ways of living. Thus Huitfeldt had presented his readers with a survey of the daily income of Valdemarus II (1202-41) (*Claus Bille's Pergamentz Bulle, Chron. I*, 112), and this piece of economic history was included by Pontanus (309). Similarly he took over from his predecessor (*Christian I*, 274) a list of prices from 1478 (col. 835), and a little later he informs us of the unusually high prices of rye in 1492, again based on Huitfeldt (*Hans*, 108), including Huitfeldt's observation that nowadays this would not be regarded as expensive (col. 879). From Huitfeldt Pontanus also learned about some tradesmen who, in 1389, sailed to Greenland without permission. To this episode Pontanus adds his own reflection on the difference between seafaring then and now in these regions.[136]

In a number of cases Pontanus made a note on intellectual matters unmentioned or only briefly touched upon by Huitfeldt. He inserted, for instance, biographies of important intellectuals, some Danish (Anders Sunesen, 293-94, 315), and some foreigners (Bernard of Clairvaux, 265, Cardinal Bessarion, 627);[137] and he enlarged Huitfeldt's obituary of Ericus VIII (1412-39) by celebrating the chronicle believed to have been written by the king (615, cols. 773-74). As part of Canutus Magnus's history he tells a piece of Danish intellectual history not found in Huitfeldt's work: Canutus's daughter, says Pontanus, settled down in Bruges, where she eventually died in 1043, leaving to the canons of a local church many valuable books now lost, "except her psalter in Danish, as the distin-

---

[136] *Liquetque per ea tempora Gronlandicam navigationem minus fuisse periculosam, cum nondum coacervata esset ex Trollebottis glacierum ea copia, quæ nunc impedita ea omnia ac difficilia reddit; adeo ut vix nisi a parte insulæ, qua Libonotum Borealem spectat, terram hodie, quamvis et id subinde difficulter, detur contingere* (521). Cf. Huitfeldt, *Chron. III*, 81.

[137] The presentation of Abbot William (294) is taken from Huitfeldt (*Chron. I*, 70).

– Pontanus left out most of Huitfeldt's general political observations.
– Pontanus left out Huitfeldt's praise of the elective monarchy in Denmark and instead added a distinct royalist touch with suggestions of Denmark being in practice a hereditary monarchy.
– Pontanus followed Huitfeldt in his moderate criticism of the Swedes during the Union of Kalmar and he supplied further refutations of Johannes Magnus.

Chapter VII

Meursius's *Historia Danica*

1. Introduction

The present chapter on Meursius's *History* is organized thematically. After a survey of sources follows a discussion of a number of selected topics which I consider important in Meursius's presentation of Danish history; as in the case of Pontanus, I have chosen to focus on ideological and political themes.

Meursius's *Historia Danica* is throughout organized according to kings. The first part begins with the first Danish king, Danus, and ends with Valdemarus I (1157-82); it is separated into five books. The second part, likewise consisting of five books, stretches from Canutus VI (1182-1202) to Christophorus III (*Christoffer af Bayern*, 1440-48). The third part covers the three first Oldenburg kings, Christianus I (1448-81), Johannes (*Hans*, by Meursius spelled *Ioannes*, 1482-1513), and Christianus II (1513-23), whose reigns are allotted one book each. The fourth part deals with the years 1523-50, i.e. the reign of Fredericus I (1523-33), an interregnum, and the first part, up to 1550, of the reign of Christianus III (1536-59).[1]

We have already had occasion to note the considerable difference in size between Pontanus's and Meursius's *Histories of Denmark* (Chapter V); there is evidence that Meursius was told to write a compendium of Danish history (cf. Chapter II). As one important reason for this difference in size, I have mentioned the fact that Pontanus quotes extensively from other texts, unlike Meursius, who never brings in a quotation. We shall return to this subject in the chapter on style.

Another reason for the difference in size, also briefly mentioned in Chapter V, is simply that Meursius did not write a pendant corresponding

---

[1] References to Parts I-III (the history up to 1523) will follow the page numbering in the edition of 1638, while references to Part IV, the period 1523-50, will follow the column numbering of the *Opera omnia* edition.

to Pontanus's copious *Chorographica descriptio*. He confined himself to giving a chronological account, beginning like Saxo with King Dan (whom Meursius calls Danus). Contrary to Pontanus, Meursius displays no scruples about the early part of Saxo. He follows the historical tradition established by Saxo's *Gesta Danorum*, as far as it goes. No mention is found of the Cimbrians, the Goths, the Anglians, the Lombards, or the Normans (except a reference to the inhabitants of Jutland as *Cimbri*, before Danus united the various provinces, 1,1, and another to the migration of the Lombards in the reign of Snio, 1,35). From the very start, as I said, Meursius's account is arranged according to kings, whereas Pontanus only adopts this organizing principle from around 800 AD.

As a third important factor accounting for the briefness of Meursius's *Historia Danica* compared to his colleague's work, I shall point to his limited range of subject matter. But before we go more deeply into that, let me say some words about Meursius's sources.

2. Meursius's Sources

A striking difference between Pontanus's and Meursius's *Histories* is the small number of references in Meursius's text to other works. Altogether they amount to about fifty, and the total number of works and authors he mentions scarcely exceeds fifteen. By contrast, Pontanus, as earlier mentioned, constantly refers to other works and authors. In the ten books covering the period up to 1448, more than 200 different works and authors are referred to, and the total number of references and quotations in this first part comes close to 1000, excluding quotations of documents.

The frequency of references is primarily a stylistic question (and will be treated as such later). I have mentioned it here to point out that in most cases it is a fairly straightforward (but time-consuming) task to map out Pontanus's sources, although he clearly felt no obligation to document every single piece of information. In Meursius's case things are a little complicated, owing to the facts that he rarely gives any clue to his sources and that the greater part of one of his main sources, Hans Svaning's *History of Denmark*, is lost.

Most of the Oldenburg part of Svaning's work has, however, survived, and a comparison reveals that Svaning clearly formed the basis of Meursius's *History*, at least to the death of Christianus II in 1523 and probably to the death of his successor, Fredericus I, in 1533.[2] We even know from a letter that the third part of Svaning's history (it was divided into three main parts) was sent to Meursius in 1626 when he set out to compose the first part of his history.[3] Besides, Meursius also made use of Krantz's *Regnorum aquilonarium, Daniæ, Sueciæ, Norvagiæ chronica* (1548) in the histories of Christianus I (1448-81) and Johannes (1481-1513), and in the history of Christianus II he supplied his description of the massacre in Stockholm (1520) from the German geographer Jacob Ziegler's account of this event, which had been appended to his work on Scandinavia, *Schondia* (1532).[4] This is a surprising choice, since Ziegler's work is decidedly anti-Danish.[5] From 1533 onwards, Meursius relied on Niels Krag's *Historia*

---

[2] I here follow Hans Gram in the preface to his edition of Krag's *History of Christianus III*, where he declares that Svaning completed the history of Christianus II (1513-23) and made a first draft of that of Fredericus I (1523-33): *extra omne dubium interque certissima haberi, Svaningium* [...] *absoluto CHRISTIERNO II. et vita FRIDERICI I. primis quasi lineis designata, plane cessavisse* [...] (Krag 1737, ed. Gram, Preface 103). Rørdam, however, referred to this passage for support that Svaning never went further than Christianus II (Rørdam 1867, 96); later he even claimed that since Svaning stopped here, Meursius could not have made use of Svaning in his treatment of Fredericus I (Rørdam 1891, 202). But I think Gram's words *primis quasi lineis* must be taken to mean that Svaning had made a rough sketch of a history of the reign of Fredericus I (the Danish translation (1776) of Gram's preface to Krag's *History of Christianus III* likewise translated these words into *et Udkast af Kong Friderich I. Historie*, 144). Gram also in his commentary on Meursius's account of Fredericus I's reign notes some instances where Meursius and Svaning disagree with Huitfeldt's version (cols. 795-96, 797 *et alia*), and apart from such factual disagreements the order of events is not always the same. I am inclined, then, to regard Svaning as the basis of Meursius's account of Frederik I, but of course he may also have consulted Huitfeldt's much more detailed account from time to time, perhaps receiving linguistic assistance from Danish friends, such as his colleague Stephanius.

Against this interpretation of Gram's *primis quasi lineis* weighs, however, the list of contents of Svaning's *History of Denmark* (published in Christensen 1913), which stops at Christianus II. If, then, as I think, Meursius did have some material from Svaning at his disposal for the reign of Fredericus I, it must have amounted to no more than notes.

Curiously, Lami, in the Preface to Meursius's *Opera omnia IX*, quotes Gram to the effect that Meursius simply left out an account of Fredericus I's reign, since Svaning never got as far and no other Latin account existed. Apart from the fact that Meursius did write an account of Fredericus I, this statement contradicts Gram's own statement in the edition of Krag's work and his references to Svaning in the commentaries to Meursius's Fridericus I.

[3] Letter from Prof. Jacob Fincke to Meursius, dated December 5, 1626 (Rørdam 1891, 278-79). See above, Chapter III.

[4] For Ziegler's authorship, I rely on V.A. Nordman 1936, 21 and Kurt Johannesson 1982, 38. I have used the edition of Ziegler's *Schondia* and the *Christierni Secundi* [...] *crudelitas* (on the massacre in Stockholm) of 1583 (published together with Albert Krantz's *Regnorum aquilonarium, Daniæ, Sueciæ, Norvagiæ chronica*); here the author of the *Christierni Secundi* [...] *crudelitas* is not named.

[5] Ziegler was a personal friend of Johannes Magnus, and he himself mentions in the *Schondia* that Magnus provided him with information on Scandinavian matters. See further Kurt Johannesson 1982, 25, 38.

regis Christiani III, which only went as far as 1550, however, as does Meursius's account (Christian III died in 1559).[6] Meursius also seems to have made use of Huitfeldt's history of Christian III; at least they agree in a number of details not found in Krag.[7]

More problematical is the assessment of Meursius's use of the early, pre-1448, part of Hans Svaning's work, of which only small fragments survive. It seems likely that the chancellor saw to it that the early part of Svaning's work was also sent to him, when he was told to go on with the pre-Oldenburg history. The nickname *Svaningius Redivivus*, given to Meursius by Svaning's grandson, furthermore suggests a strong dependence on Svaning during the whole work. But as earlier mentioned (Chapter IV), this epithet does not seem fully justified.

A comparison with Pontanus's *Rerum Danicarum historia* reveals that this work served as Meursius's main source for the period c. 1182-1448, i.e. Part II of Meursius's *History*. In fact, the last part of his account of Valdemarus I's reign (1157-82) is also primarily based on Pontanus (and even before this, from around the middle of the twelfth century, traces of his colleague's work are found in Meursius's version).[8] But enough fragments of Svaning survive to suggest that he, too, was consulted by Meursius in the course of his composing the account of the period c. 1182-1448.[9] This impression is supported by some passages which differ so

---

[6] Krag's manuscript of the *Historia regis Christiani III* is still extant in the Arnamagnæan Collection in Copenhagen. In it a number of notes are found, made by various hands. At least two are written by Meursius, both corrections of factual errors (363, 464).

[7] A few examples: the bishop Joachim Rønnow was captured in the house which then belonged to the bishop, says Krag, and Meursius follows him, and then adds: 'which has now been made a university' (col. 887). Huitfeldt makes the same addition (*Christian III*, Cciiiv). Shortly afterwards Meursius adds to the description from Krag of Rønnow's fate that he died in 1544 (col. 888). Huitfeldt does the same (*ibidem*). Before the battle at Øxebjerg in 1535, Meursius adds to Krag's presentation of the place that Øxebjerg was situated *medio ab urbe lapide* (col. 859), which is probably a translation of Huitfeldt's *en halff Mijl fra Assens* (*Christian III*, Piv).

[8] Some extracts from Svaning's *History of Denmark* concerning the reign of Valdemarus I (found in the Ms. *Bartholiniana, Tome J, E don. var.* 1, fol. (346-75), the Royal Library of Copenhagen), do not seem to have influenced Meursius's account. Meursius's primary sources for the life of this king were Saxo, Krantz, and Pontanus.

[9] In the following instances influence from Svaning on Meursius seems certain (the passages from Svaning's *History of Denmark* are preserved in the ms. *Bartholiniana, Tome J, E don. var.* 1, fol. (346-75)):
Svaning, 349, Meursius II, 8 (conflict between Adolphus of Holstein and Canutus VI). Svaning 349, Meursius II, 9 (the death of Valdemarus I's widow). Svaning 349-50, Meursius II, 13 (agreement between Otto of Braunschweig and Valdemarus II). Svaning 353-4, Meur-

much from Pontanus that it is best explained by Meursius's having used another source. But without question Pontanus forms the basis of Meursius's treatment of this period, and most of the preserved fragments of Svaning's work dealing with this period have left no trace in Meursius's work. As mentioned in Chapter IV, a fragment of Svaning's history written in Danish survives. It deals with the period 1241-82, and as the editor of the fragment, Kr. Erslev, has established, Meursius here follows Pontanus rather than Svaning.[10]

It is in the early history up to Valdemarus I's reign 1157-82 that it is most difficult to come to grips with Svaning's influence on Meursius. Here Meursius follows the domestic tradition from Saxo, including the earliest legendary part, with some additions from various medieval chronicles, especially the *Annals of Ryd*.[11] So did Svaning, as is clear from the list of contents and the preserved fragments, and the problem consists in determining when Meursius used Saxo (and the chronicles) directly and when he used Svaning as an intermediary.

Meursius's account shows many differences of various kinds from Saxo, in factual details as well as in narrative devices; he brings in a number of speeches (mostly indirect), which are either much briefer in Saxo or not found at all.[12] Judging from later parts of Meursius's work, where we can observe his strategy of adaptation, it appears that he would not himself insert a speech or make factual changes. All these deviations from Saxo, then, point to Svaning's influence. Moreover, Meursius himself, in his answer to the anonymous nobleman's comments, at one point reveals his dependence on Svaning.[13] Hans Gram, Meursius's eighteenth-

---

sius II, 48 (the murder of Ericus VII in 1286). Svaning 354, Meursius II, 65 (conflict between Archbishop Esgerus and Ericus VIII in 1317/18). Svaning 355, Meursius II, 73 (conflict between Bishop Tycho of Børglum and Christophorus II in 1329).

[10] Kr. Erslev 1928, XI. Erslev points to a few instances where Meursius seems to follow Svaning. Erslev claims that Meursius generally follows Huitfeldt (and Pontanus). I think it is more correct to say that he follows Pontanus and thus indirectly Huitfeldt.

[11] Meursius, like Pontanus, refers to this thirteenth-century chronicle as *Chronicon regis Erici* (above, p. 184).

[12] E.g. Meursius I, 22 (Saxo VI, Ch. iii,2). Meursius I, 23 (Saxo VI, Ch. iv,10), Meursius I, 49 (Saxo X, Ch. v).

[13] *De Othini oraculo, Vpsaliae consulto, sum Svaningium sequutus* (Meursius, 1741-63, IX, col. 1132). The nobleman had objected to Meursius's locating of Odin in Uppsala; he preferred Funen (*ibidem*, col. 1124). Meursius kept Uppsala in the printed edition (I, 29).

century commentator, refers *en passant* to Meursius's use of Svaning a number of times in his commentary on Meursius's early history.[14] And some fragments from Svaning on twelfth-century affairs reveal that Meursius made use of him for this period where Saxo also was available.[15] On this basis I find it most likely that Meursius did in fact use Svaning as the primary source for his Danish history up to 1157, though no doubt consulting Saxo throughout.

This is not to say that he did not make use of other sources in the early history. Indeed, most of his discussions and references – which are, as I said, few in all – are found here. We saw how Pontanus in the early medieval period, c. 700-1100, in his attempts to combine the domestic tradition from Saxo with the foreign sources, gives priority to the latter. Meursius, on the other hand, bases his account on domestic sources – and professes his preference for them as opposed to foreign works at

---

[14] In his comments on Meursius's account of Frotho II's reign, Hans Gram notes: *Possent quidem hic multa de Odino* [...] *in medio afferri; nec non summa Chronologiae negligentia in Saxone Grammatico (quem hic Meursius, post Suaningium exscribit,) indicari* (Meursius, 1741-63, IX, col. 35). In the legendary King Sigarus's history, Meursius lets a certain Haco send his ships to Roskilde, not to Kalundborg (another town in Zealand), as Saxo has it: *Hic noster* [sc. Meursius] *Io. Suaningium ducem habuit, non Saxonem,* says Gram (*ibidem,* col. 60). And a little later: *Hic iterum Suaningius, cuius verbis noster inhaeret* [...] (*ibidem*). To Meursius's statement that Haraldus III recaptured England, Gram again notes that Meursius *ex Suaningio suo desumsit* (*ibidem,* col. 67). From these and other similar references to Svaning's early history, it would seem that Gram had had access to Svaning's manuscript before it was burned in 1728. In his comments on Meursius's account of Christianus I he actually says that he has a manuscript of Svaning's work, though not an autograph (col. 657). But this does not necessarily mean a manuscript comprising the whole of Svaning's *History.* He may have known this part of Svaning's work from the manuscript *Gl. Kgl. S.* 2444, 4, which had come to the Royal library in 1732. His earlier references to Svaning may likewise be based on transcriptions of parts of the work, or on notes from pre-1728 acquaintance with Svaning's work. The only time, as far as I have seen, when he does quote Svaning, he has taken the words from Stephanius's commentary to Saxo: Meursius informs us (I, 2) that the Swedish King Sigtrugus trusts an omen from Odin that he cannot be conquered with *ferrum* (iron), and his Danish opponent, King Gramus, then uses a golden club. Saxo is less detailed and just says that Gram had learnt from some soothsayers that Sigtrugus could only be conquered with gold, whereupon he makes the golden club (I, Ch. iv, 12). (Gram's comment col. 8, cf. Stephanius 1645, 37).

[15] The first extracts from Svaning's *History* found in the ms. *Bartholiniana, Tome J, E don. var.* 1, fol. (346-75) concern the period 1056-c. 1157, and of them the following seem to have left their trace in Meursius's work:
1 Svaning, 346, Meursius I, 60-61 (Sueno III (1047-74) sees to it that the archbishop in Bremen is no longer the ecclesiastical head in Denmark, by Svaning dated 1056).
2 Svaning, 346, Meursius I, 84a (the nickname of Magnus, son of Nicolaus (1104-34)).
3 Svaning, 346, Meursius I, 80 (the battle of Fotevig (dated 1135 by Svaning); only Svaning's condemnation of the bishops who joined the fighting seems to have been taken over by Meursius, cf. below).

least twice in this part of the work (I, 37, 43). He refers to various Danish chronicles, primarily the *Annals of Ryd*, but also the small anonymous *Compendiosa historia*, nowadays ascribed to Povl Helgesen (c. 1485-1535).[16] Other works referred to are the *Encomion Emmæ*, Ailnothus's *Vita S. Canuti Regis* (on *Knud den Hellige*, 1080-86, written c. 1120),[17] Albert of Stade's world chronicle (thirteenth century), and Krantz's *Regnorum aquilonarium, Daniæ, Sueciæ, Norvagiæ chronica*. On the authority of the *Annals of Ryd* and the *Encomium Emmæ* Meursius even inserted a King Haraldus VII between Sueno II (*Svend Tveskæg*) and Canutus Magnus, against both Saxo and Svaning, basing his brief account (I, 53) totally on the *Annals of Ryd*.[18]

Even though discussions and references are even fewer in the later parts of the work (after c. 1157), it must be emphasized that Meursius, while clearly following one main source for a given period, i.e. Pontanus (c. 1157-1448), Svaning (1448-1533), and Krag (1533-50), consulted other authors throughout. His notes on Pontanus's *History of Denmark* (on which, see below Chapters VIII, IX) are evidence of his large knowledge of writings pertaining to Danish history, and so are the commentaries with which he furnished his edition (1631) of Ailnothus's above-mentioned work. Furthermore, judging from the catalogue of his printed books (above, Chapter III), he was the owner of an impressive amount of historiography, classical, medieval and Renaissance works alike.

It is a curious fact that Meursius never mentions his two main sources, Svaning's and Pontanus's *Histories of Denmark*, when after all, he does from time to time refer to other sources, especially in the early history. And there are other puzzles concerning his use of these two main

---

4 Svaning, 347, Meursius I, 86 (foundation of a monastery in Scania, dated 1144 by Svaning).

5 Svaning, 347, Meursius I, 88 (Canutus receives help from the bishop of Bremen, c. 1150).

6 Svaning, 347, Meursius I, 92 (Sueno receives help from the bishop of Bremen, c. 1155).

7 Svaning, 348, Meursius I, 93 (Duke Henricus of Saxony flees from Denmark allegedly because he feared a shortage of fish in Lent, c. 1155).

[16] Probably written in the 1520s, this small Latin chronicle was first edited by Erpold Lindenbruch in 1595 (Leiden). It covers Danish history from Dan to Christian II. In 1886 A.D. Jørgensen demonstrated that the author must be the Carmelite friar, Povl Helgesen (modern ed. by M. Kristensen & H. Ræder 1937).

[17] Meursius himself, as earlier mentioned, published an edition of Ailnothus (1631). (Modern ed. by Gertz 1908-12).

[18] The idea may have come from Pontanus, who did not give Harald VII his own chapter but mentions that the *Encomium Emmæ* and the *Annals of Ryd* recognize him as king. The preserved list of contents of Svaning's history shows that he did not count Harald VII among the kings.

sources. Why did Meursius not also use Svaning as his primary source for the period, c. 1157-1448? Why did he switch to Pontanus? Apparently Svaning's *History* was in some way deficient compared to that of Pontanus, but I do not think the few surviving fragments of this part of Svaning's work allow us to come closer to an answer.

The opposite question, why Meursius did not base the first part of his *History* on Pontanus, is perhaps easier to answer. I think it brings us back to the question of why both Pontanus and Meursius were asked to write a full history each. Meursius may well have been told by his employers to adhere to the traditional account of both the legendary past and the early medieval history, as Svaning had done. Pontanus's radical beginning of Danish history with the Cimbrians' march against Rome and the amount of foreign history in his work for the whole of the period up to around 1100 needed to be balanced by an account of the traditional early past. As a counterweight to Pontanus, Meursius may have been told to keep to domestic affairs according to the tradition from Saxo. In fact, he introduces his account by explaining why he does not say anything of the origin of the Danes, their earliest history, or of Denmark's geographical situation: "Others have given diligent accounts of the origin of the Danes, their old age, and the geographical situation of Denmark, and therefore I will not go into these matters; instead I will turn to the kings and their deeds at home and abroad", he declares.[19] This is no doubt a reference to Pontanus's 1631 edition. It is an important indication that the two works were planned to be complementary.

3. Survey of Subject-matter

In contrast to Pontanus, Meursius keeps within a rather limited area of topics. As he himself states in the passage just quoted, he confines himself to telling of "kings and their deeds at home and abroad". Kings, wars and state affairs form the contents, which are treated from the point of view of a general theme, namely the right exercise of power. As far as we can follow his reworking of sources, it is clear that he abbreviated them heavily throughout. We shall here take a quick look at his selection of material.

---

[19] *QVÆ origo gentis, quæ antiquitas, quive ipsius Daniæ situs, quia alii magna cura tradiderunt, prætermittam: et ad reges, atque res eorum gestas, domi pariter forisque, me convertam* (I, 1).

According to the list of contents of Svaning's history,[20] there were in its earliest part a number of chapters which have no parallel in Meursius's work. He did not, as already noted, write a geographical introduction, whereas Svaning seems to have begun with descriptions of Denmark, Norway and Sweden, an account of the origins of the Danes, and a presentation of two other neighbouring peoples, the *Saxones* and the *Vandali*. This was the sort of information provided by Pontanus, and in my view Meursius's omission should be seen in that light. Further, he did not take over Svaning's chapters on the migrations of the Cimbrians, the Goths and the Lombards, and again the explanation probably lies in Pontanus's *History of Denmark*, where the migrations form a main theme. Svaning, moreover, inserted a chapter on the pagan religion in Denmark, unparalleled in Meursius's work, from which such antiquarian material is totally absent.[21] Another antiquarian passage in Svaning's *History of Denmark*, known through Stephanius's notes on Saxo,[22] dealt with Cimbrian ceremonies when a new king was elected. It has left no trace in Meursius's narrative.

When it comes to the contents of the narrative in the early history, we have practically nothing left of Svaning, and we are left to compare Meursius directly with Saxo. We cannot say whether a given omission (or addition) is due to Meursius or Svaning. Compared to Saxo, Meursius abbreviated heavily. Among the many passages he left out may be mentioned: the poetic parts of Saxo's early history; episodes which do not include the kings themselves, episodes from their childhood and youth, and passages involving the heathen gods[23] and other super-natural events.[24]

Some such fantastic elements are found, though, e.g. the witchcraft which made King Haldanus's enemies immune to weapons of iron (I,

---

[20] Christensen 1913, 1-8; 176-77.

[21] Stephanius brings a substantial quotation from this chapter into his notes on Saxo (Stephanius 1645, 140-41; cf. above Chapter IV, 3). As I shall argue later, Svaning's Protestant interpretation of the development from heathendom to Christianity in this passage seems to have influenced Meursius.

[22] Stephanius 1645, 29.

[23] In some cases, though, the gods are mentioned. King Hotherus's rival Balderus is presented as son of Othinus (*Odin*, I, 10), and in the history of Frotho II, Meursius refers, with due scepticism, to the belief that the Norwegian king was son of Othinus (I, 15).

[24] A few examples of omissions of such events may be mentioned: the giants who raised the young princes in the reign of Svibdagerus (Saxo I, Ch. v,2-6), King Hadingus's travel to the realm of the dead (Saxo I, Ch. viii,14), King Fridlevus's liberation of a young prince captured by a giant (Saxo VI, Ch. iv,4-7).

26). In the earlier version of Meursius's work, which the chancellor asked the anonymous nobleman to go through, there may have been more fabulous ingredients than in the printed version. At least the nobleman found it necessary to warn Meursius to leave out such absurdities. The occasion was Meursius's mention (in the reign of Frotho I) of a dragon which guarded a treasure (I, 6). The nobleman suggested another more rational explanation, that it was simply a man, a pirate, called Draco. He recommended that Meursius also elsewhere left out all similar occurrences, "so that the whole work should not be regarded with suspicion".[25] In the nobleman's eyes, fabulous elements clearly formed a threat to the dignity of the work. Meursius saw the point (which is not a matter of course; he did not accept all the nobleman's suggestions). Instead of his original *auri custos draco*, the printed version has *auri custos Draco, quod piratæ excellentis nomen erat.*

Later in his work, when following Pontanus's *History of Denmark*, Meursius similarly skipped almost all passages which did not deal with kings. No documents or any other texts are quoted, discussions of sources are reduced to a minimum, foreign events which are not directly related to events of Danish history are left unmentioned, and genealogical and cultural subjects are only rarely touched upon. The same tendency makes itself felt in his adaption of Svaning, whose autobiographical passages he also left out, for obvious reasons, as well as Svaning's various digressions. Niels Krag's *History of Christianus III* is probably the source which Meursius follows most closely; his adaption has preserved most of the long paraphrases of letters and negotiations, characteristic of Krag's work. But his wish to summarize is also evident here. He left out various scenes, such as Krag's depiction of the joy of the inhabitants of Copenhagen when they were liberated by Christian III in 1536, and the coronation of Christian III in 1537 is merely mentioned by Meursius (col. 897), in contrast to Krag's careful description of its meaning (167-69).

In order to illustrate Meursius's procedure in the early history – and the difference between him and Pontanus – I shall here briefly follow up the survey, presented in Chapter VI, of Pontanus's account of the two early

---

[25] *Auri custos draco – Addendum auri custos Archipirata insignis Draco nomine; ita alii. Vbi vero alibi huiusmodi non verisimilia occurrunt, praetereunda potius, ne totam Historiam in subspicionem vocent* ('The anonymous nobleman [...]', Meursius 1741-63, IX, col. 1121).

medieval kings, Ericus Barn and Canutus Magnus. Meursius's history of Ericus (I, 45) is, like Saxo's (IX, Ch. vi), short and limited to domestic affairs, except for a reference to a war in Germany; by contrast, Pontanus's long account, as we saw, is almost wholly devoted to foreign expeditions. As in Saxo, the point of Meursius's version is Ericus's transformation from a pagan persecutor to a devout Christian under the influence of Ansgarius. But close to Saxo as he is, Meursius includes information not found in the *Gesta Danorum*, viz. Ericus's war in Germany, his destruction of the church in Schleswig and his later foundation of another in Ribe. I suspect Meursius is simply following Svaning, although I cannot account for the latter's source for the destruction of the Schleswig church.[26] Of the war in Germany Meursius says that Ericus sent an army there because they had accepted Christianity and because they had defected from Danish rule in the reign of his grandfather. As I shall argue later, this touch of organized politics, "sending an army", and the emphasis on the continuity of Danish supremacy over neighbouring countries are characteristic features of Meursius's early history, features which are likely to go back to Svaning.

Similarly, the much longer chapter on Canutus Magnus (I, 53-57) is by and large structured like Saxo's, although Meursius includes the anecdote, also found in Pontanus but not told by Saxo, of Canutus's pious rejection of flattery: On an English beach Canutus demonstrated that he was not the ruler of the sea, and pointed out that there was only one *rex potentissimus* (I, 56).[27] Meursius's familiarity with other traditions than Saxo also comes out in vague references in connection with the battles in England and the death of the Norwegian King Olaus. Nevertheless his narrative is strikingly different from that of Pontanus who, as we saw, found most of his material in foreign historians and left out the central episodes of Saxo's account.

---

[26] The war in Germany is mentioned in the *Annals of Ryd*. The building of the church in Ribe is referred to in the *Compendiosa historia*. Pontanus (103) and Huitfeldt (*Fra Dan* [...], 56) also mention the Ribe church, on the authority of Adam of Bremen (I, Ch. 29), whose work was first published in 1579, and thus, presumably, was unknown to Svaning; none of them mentions the destruction of the church in Schleswig. Both points were mentioned in Rimbert's *Vita Anskarii* (written c. 870), Ch. 31-32, which was not, however, published until 1642. See also Gram's discussion *ad loc.*, Meursius 1741-63, IX, col. 124.

[27] Meursius's version of the anecdote is more elaborated, with details not found in Pontanus. He lets Canutus address himself particularly to an envoy from the Emperor, and this person is not known from any other account of this episode according to Hans Gram (comm. *ad loc.*).

Like Saxo, Meursius draws attention to the fact that Canutus ruled several countries, but he does not add extra emphasis on the king's power, as Pontanus had done. Instead he focuses on Canutus's moral character. His legislation is seen as an indication of his wise and mild rulership. The severe sentence he passes on himself for the murder of one of his subjects is emphatically praised by Meursius: The world would be a better place if all kings behaved like Canutus.[28] But even Canutus committed grave faults. Having praised him towards the end as a great, pious, strong, and just king, Meursius proceeds to blame him strongly for the murders of the English King Eduardus and the Norwegian King Olaus (I, 56),[29] which "right-minded people will never forgive".[30] Such considerations are, as we shall see, typical of Meursius.

One of the dominant figures in Saxo's account of Canutus's reign is Ulfo (*Ulphus, Ulvo*), whom Saxo reports to be the great-grandson of a Swedish bear. Pontanus, as we saw, though favouring the information found in foreign historians that Ulfo was an English nobleman, argues that allowance must be made for such mythologizing of the origin of grand phenomena (in this case Ulfo's son, the Danish king, Sueno Esthritius). Meursius simply presents Ulfo as a highborn Englishman, thus departing from Saxo: *Vlfo, homo Anglus, loco sat illustri natus* (I, 54). However, a comment made by the anonymous nobleman who read the work in manuscript at the chancellor's request, reveals that Meursius had originally presented Ulfo as an influential man in Sweden, *summi inter Suecos loci*. The nobleman did not approve:

> I know that both Saxo and Swedish historians claim that Ulfo was born
> in Sweden, that his father was Torchetillus, or Trugellus Sprageleg, and
> that his father Biorno, was the son of a bear (which is Bjørn in our lan-

---

[28] *Factum admodum præclarum, et rege dignum, regibusque universis imitandum! quod si facerent, multo etiam felicius cum imperiis quibuscunque ageretur, ac virtutem subditi majore quoque studio amplecterentur, qui ad vitam principis componere suam fere amant* (I, 56).

[29] In the preceding account Meursius did not make it that clear that Canutus was guilty of these deaths. Eduardus died, he says, *sive scelere suorum, seu insidiis Canuti* (I, 53). In Olaus's case Canutus let his men bribe some of Olaus's men to kill him; Meursius adds that other writers explain Olaus's death differently (I, 55).

[30] [...] *apud bonos nusquam veniam impetrabunt* (I, 56). From the commentaries of the anonymous nobleman it appears that Meursius originally used the words *Machiavelli schola* in connection with his condemnation of Canutus's role in the deaths of the two kings. The nobleman objected that the name of Macchiavelli is below the dignity of a work of history (*Machiavelli Schola: Velim hac sublata, nec enim e dignitate Historiae hominis Scholastico-politici Machiavelli nomine hoc loco uti* (Meursius 1741-63, IX, col. 1126b).

guage). But these are pure fables, due to his friendship with the Swedish king and to his conspiring with the Swedes against Canutus. Ulfo was an Englishman. His father was born of Danish parents (no doubt of royal blood), and was called Trugel Spraclei. This is clear from the English historians, with whom, unless I am mistaken, Ericus Pomeranus agrees in his *History*. This explanation should be retained, then, and those fables rejected.[31]

The careful explanation of the animal origin of Saxo's Ulfo at the beginning suggests, I think, that it had not been mentioned by Meursius. Meursius, it would seem, in the first version avoided the fable and simply made Ulf a Swede. The nobleman here explains to him that that would not do: presenting Ulf as Swedish amounted to subscribing to the absurd theory of the bear; the English tradition must be accepted. Meursius, as we saw, obeyed.

4. Reflections on Power and Morals

The Influence of Justus Lipsius

The kings stand in focus throughout. From Danus to Christianus III we follow their doings, and the reign of each is rounded off by an evaluation of his personal character and achievements. The special position of rulers also constitutes the main theme of Meursius's many general reflections and morals. These reflections are found all through the work. Sometimes they form part of the evaluation of a king, in other cases they are inserted as comments within the narrative. They form a distinguishing feature of Meursius's history. Neither Pontanus nor Svaning provided him with more than a few such general political considerations, which must be regarded as an important contribution on Meursius's part.

A number of these reflections on the nature of power have classical roots. I shall give some examples. In Sallustian terms, Christianus III

---

[31] *Novi tam Saxonis, quam Historicorum Svecorum sententiam esse, Vlvonem natum esse in Svecia, patrem eius Torchetillum, vel Trugellum Sprageleg, avum Biornonem, Vrso, (qui Biorn nobis dicitur) procreatum. Sed merae sunt fabulae, ex eo ortae, quod Sveciae Regis amicitia fretus, in Sveciam se saepius recepit, et cum Svecis conspiravit in Canutum. Vlvo vero Anglus natione erat. Pater Danicis (procul dubio Regii sanguinis) ortus parentibus, vocabatur Trugel Spraclei. Haec ex Historicis Anglicis patent, quibus, ni fallor, adsentitur Ericus Pomeranus in sua Historia. Quam expositionem, fabulosa illa reiecta, retinendam censeo* ('The anonymous nobleman [...]', Meursius 1741-63, IX, col. 1126b). Meursius in his answer to the nobleman's comments ('Ioannis Meursi ad annotationes viri illustris a Domino Cancellario sibi communicatas Responsio') reformulated this passage (*ibidem*, col. 1140), but in the history itself he just presented Ulvo as an Englishman without further discussion.

(1536-59; Meursius counts the beginning of his reign from 1534) is pondering the benefits of internal unity:

> CHristianus, in hunc modum rex creatus, qui concordia crescere res parvas sciret, et discordia etiam dilabi maximas [...] (col. 841).

> (Christianus had now been appointed king in the way I have described. Knowing that concord makes small things grow while discord makes even great things fall apart [...]).[32]

This passage forms a supplement to Krag's laconic statement: *Tum a Christiano de concordia ordinum actum* ("Then Christianus saw to concord between the orders", 56).

Christianus II (1513-23) was once helped by a Swedish bishop in his fight against Sweden, but instead of reward he repaid him with death. Svaning notes his ingratitude in these words:

> sed pro his omnibus [...] malam postremo abstulit gratiam (Svaning 1658, 316).

> (But in return for all these things he [the bishop] was badly thanked in the end).

Meursius, however, sees in this behaviour an instance of a general phenomenon. He meditates on the dangers of rendering service to bad rulers, since they will not tolerate being bound by a debt of gratitude to anyone:

> sed malorum ita principum fert ingenium; ut, obnoxii subditorum beneficiis, cum se impares compensandis ob eorum magnitudinem esse videant, destrui fortunam suam per hæc ipsa arbitrentur: ideoque, ceu offensis asperati, odium pro gratia reddant; vindicentque, quod remunerare nequeant (III, 75).

> (It is a distinctive feature of the mentality of wicked princes that when they are indebted to their subjects for services rendered and realize their incapability to repay them because of the magnitude of these services, they assume that their own fortune is actually destroyed by them. And therefore, as if insulted by offence, their return is hatred instead of gratitude, and they avenge what they cannot reward).

The wording recalls Tacitus's comment on the ingratitude of Tiberius when realizing his huge debt to one of his subjects:

---

[32] Cf. Sallust, *Jugurtha*, Ch. 10,6: *nam concordia parvae res crescunt, discordia maxumae dilabuntur.*

> Nam beneficia eo usque laeta sunt, dum videntur exsolui posse: ubi multum anteuenere pro gratia odium redditur (Tac. *Ann.* IV, Ch. 18).

> (For services are welcome exactly as long as it seems possible to requite them: when that stage is left far behind, the return is hatred instead of gratitude).

From Tacitus's observation on Tiberius's behaviour, then, Meursius coins a general political maxim.

With this he reveals the influence of a contemporary trend normally (in modern scholarship) referred to as "Tacitism". A seminal work was Justus Lipsius's *Politicorum sive civilis doctrinae libri sex qui ad principatum maxime spectant (Six Books on Politics or Civil Doctrine, which Especially Pertain to Sovereignty*, 1589).This is a handbook of political wisdom, written for princes and their advisers and consisting of quotations from classical authors linked by Lipsius's short commentaries. Like Meursius in the above quoted passages, Lipsius extracts from classical authors eternally valid truths on the nature of power and the exercise of government.[33]

Tacitus is, as Lipsius himself makes clear in the Preface, by far the most quoted author. From the end of the sixteenth century numerous commentaries on his works were published, in which the authors sought to deduce general political rules from Tacitus's observations on the exercise of government in the early Roman principate. Peter Burke has described the movement of political Tacitism as a first attempt to establish a science of politics based on a set of generalizations. These generalizations were, in this first stage, to a large extent lifted from Tacitus. Burke, then, sees political Tacitism as "no more than a transition between moralized politics and scientific politics".[34]

Meursius shares this interest in formulating general political rules on the basis of particular historical events. He was very well versed in classical literature, and his observations may stem from his own reading of the classics. In the case of Tacitus's works, we even know that Meursius read them with his pupils in Sorø shortly after his arrival there.[35] In many

---

[33] I have discussed Meursius's debt to Tacitus and Lipsius at greater length in an article (1995). Many of the examples in this and the following sections (4.1-3) are taken from this article, but in the present context I discuss the moral values of Meursius's account in more detail.

[34] Peter Burke 1969, 168.

[35] Letter from Nicolaus Vismar to Meursius, dated July 30, 1626 (Meursius 1741-63, XI, no. 610).

cases, though, he probably gleaned them from a contemporary hand-book, such as Lipsius's *Politica*. The unwillingness of wicked princes to be bound by debts of gratitude is also a theme treated by Lipsius, who quotes several passages from classical authors to this effect, among them the one from Tacitus.

In one case I even think it can be demonstrated with reasonable certainty that Meursius made use of Lipsius's *Politica*. Some Danish kings made promising beginnings but did not live up to them later on. One of them is Nicolaus (*Niels*, 1104-34), who is, to some extent, modelled on Tiberius as he is portrayed by Tacitus in the *Annals*. In his final appraisal of him Meursius first notes his good beginnings

> Vbi regnum nactus esset, ut initia principatus fere bona, et ad famam componuntur, laudabiliter illud gessit, sed in fine vehementer inclinavit (I, 81).

> (Because the early days of a reign are for the most part good and contrived with a view to reputation, his actions were praiseworthy when he ascended the throne, but in the latter stages they declined dramatically).

This observation is of Tacitean origin:

> inde initia magistratuum nostrorum meliora ferme et finis inclinat (Tac. *Ann*. XV, Ch. 21).

> (Hence, the early days of our officials are usually the best; the falling off is at the end).

But Meursius probably borrowed it from Lipsius's *Politica*. It has nothing to do with Tiberius, and its Tacitean context is quite different from Meursius's use of it. It is part of Thrasea Paetus's speech in the senate against the increasing power of the provincials as opposed to that of the Roman governor. Moreover, Lipsius has devoted a chapter to the maxim that princes often deteriorate, where he also quotes this sentence from Tacitus. Here he has himself, by a small addition, pointed to its validity for princes as well as for public authorities in general (*magistratus*): *Initia magistratuum (aut principum) fere meliora sint, sed finis inclinet* – cf. Meursius's *initia principatus*. Besides, Lipsius's heading may have inspired Meusius to include the word *laudabiliter:*

> Initia principatuum plerumque laudabilia, sed id non satis, perseverandum esse (Lipsius, *Politica*, 30).

(The early days of a reign are usually praiseworthy; but that is not enough. This course must be kept).[36]

In the same chapter Lipsius brings in another quotation from Tacitus about deteriorating princes:

(peccare paullatim) indulgentia fortunæ et prauis magistris, discunt audentque –

(schooled by an indulgent fortune and wicked teachers they gradually learn and dare to sin).

and cf. Tacitus:

donec indulgentia fortunae et pravis magistris didicit aususque est (Tac. *Hist.* II, Ch. 84).

(but finally, schooled by an indulgent fortune and wicked teachers, he learned and dared the like).

This tag is also applied to King Nicolaus towards the end of the obituary. Meursius suggests that Nicolaus's deterioration should be ascribed to forces outside the control of the king rather than to his own nature:

sive etiam aliena [sc. vitia], a magistris pravis doctus, ac corruptus, ut interdum reges solent, indulgentia fortunæ, exercere ea coepit (I, 81-84a).[37]

(or his depravity was due to outside influence, when he had been schooled by wicked teachers and corrupted by an indulgent fortune, as kings sometimes are).

Again, since Tacitus does not use the phrase in connection with Tiberius but with a later emperor, Vespasian, and since, as we just saw, Meursius was probably inspired by this chapter in the *Politica* in his introduction to the obituary of Nicolaus, I also find it likely that Lipsius was the mediator in this case. What in Tacitus is a concrete description of Vespasian has the form of a general rule about the behaviour of princes in both Lipsius and Meursius.

Since princes, as we learned above, do not like to be under any obligation, their feelings towards those who help them by means of treason are

---

[36] One of Nicolaus's predecessors Olaus (*Oluf Hunger*, 1086-95) provides, in Meursius's account, another instance of this rule of good beginnings: *Olaus, regno jam potitus, ut initia fere principes, famæ suæ commendandæ, bona amant* [...] (I, 67).

[37] There is an error in the pagination in the 1638 ed. Two pages bear the number 84 and two the number 85, while no 82-83 are found. Hence I distinguish between the two 84-85s by a and b.

negative. Twice in the course of his *Historia Danica* Meursius finds occasion to point out that princes love treachery but hate traitors. A German prince bribes the leader of the Danish guard at Dannevirke to let him through, and then hangs him:

> illico in furcam agit: manifesto documento, amare quidem principes proditionem sed odisse proditorem (I, 92).

> (he hangs him at once – a clear lesson that princes, though loving treason, hate traitors).

The second time Meursius makes this observation concerns Fridericus I (1523-33). The castle of Kalundborg (in Zealand) is surrendered to the king by the prefect, and Fridericus later blames the prefect for his treachery. Meursius again points to the general lesson, this time, however, turning it into a princely virtue:

> Bonus princeps, gratam quidem se proditionem habere, sed ingratum (ut fit fere) proditorem ostendebat (cols. 796-97).

> (As a good prince he made it clear that he was grateful for the treachery but (as is often the case) ungrateful to the traitor).

Lipsius quotes four classical passages to this effect. Closest to Meursius's wording is one from Plutarch's *Moralia*, in Lipsius's translation:

> Ego [sc. Augustus] proditionem amo, proditores non approbo.
> (I like treachery, but I cannot say anything good of traitors).[38]

Interestingly, however, Huitfeldt makes the same general observation (in Latin) in connection with Frederik I's treatment of the prefect.[39] It may go back to Svaning, or Meursius may have been inspired by Huitfeldt on this point. Huitfeldt refers to it as a *Sprickuort*, a common saying, as indeed its occurrence in Lipsius's *Politica* confirms.[40]

It seems clear that the general rules Meursius deduced from the lives of the Danish kings were current in contemporary political theory. And we may be fairly certain that Meursius used Lipsius's *Politica* in the course

---

[38] Lipsius 1596, 123 (from Plutarch, *Moralia*, "Sayings of Romans").

[39] *Principes amare proditionem, non proditores* (Huitfeldt, *Frederik I*, 74; the surrender of the castle is mentioned *ibidem* 40-41).

[40] In his translation of Saxo, Anders Sørensen Vedel made a marginal note on the first episode, the killing of the leader of the guard: "A traitor's well-deserved reward and punishment" (*En Forræderis rette Løn oc Straff*). Less pungent than Meursius's observation, this comment illustrates the exemplary value of the episode (Saxo, trans. Vedel 1575, 340).

of composing his *History of Denmark*.[41] As to the contents of these generalizations, they highlight the special position of rulers, in line with Meursius's general focusing on kings, their characters and their achievements. But can we draw some conclusions about Meursius's view of history and politics? What lessons does Meursius want his readers to learn from Danish history?

The Realistic Trend

In view of the many borrowings from Tacitus, one would perhaps expect Meursius's observations to bear the same cynical stamp as that of the Roman historian. This is in general not the case, however, as we shall see in the next sections. But some are indeed simple and disinterested observations on the exercise of power, like the one about the reluctance of bad rulers to tolerate being under a debt to someone.

Echoing Svaning's *History of Johannes*[42] Meursius criticizes Johannes (1481-1513) for having placed non-Swedish men as governors in Sweden. And, characteristically, he adds a general lesson:

> A prince who wishes in future to keep firmly in obedience to him peoples who have been forcefully made his subjects should carefully ensure the following: let him appoint as their governors natives of those countries whose loyalty has been ascertained; or let him restrain the rule of his own men in such a way that by exercising their power according to the laws and treating agreeably and courteously those whose minds have been infuriated by the slaughter of their own folk, they may soon soften them. The result will be that he will have these peoples' goodwill continually at his disposal.[43]

– this piece of advice is in the interest of the prince's securing his own power.

In 1360 the Swedish king Magnus gave to Valdemarus III (*Valdemar Atterdag*, 1340-75) the province of Skåne (*Scania*), which had formerly be-

---

[41] The catalogue of Meursius's printed books which is extant in The Royal Library of Copenhagen (cf. above, Chapter III) lists both Lipsius's *Politica* (*Monita Politica*, Antwerpen 1613), and Tacitus's works with Lipsius's notes (*Tacitus cum notis Lipsij*, Leiden 1595).

[42] *Chronicon Ioannis*, z4v-Aar, Ff3r.

[43] *Itaque id curare sedulo princeps debet, qui subjectos armis populos retinere in constanti obsequio volet; ut præfectos aut indigenas illis ponat, quorum fidem sibi exploratam habeat; aut suorum dominatum sic coerceat, ut, imperium juxta leges exercentes, asperatos clade sua illorum animos, blande ac comiter habendo, mox demulcea<n>t. Ita demum est futurum, ut eorum voluntas in perpetuum sua sit in potestate habiturus* (III, 59).

longed to Denmark but had been in Swedish hands since 1343. Meursius notes the unusualness of such a gift, inasmuch as princes will normally do everything to keep what they have obtained, even if it was by illegal means:

> That is undoubtedly a rare instance among princes; they would rather lay claim to something with almost total unreasonableness, even though it has been unfairly gained, than restore it honourably; they value any kind of enlargement of their power in preference to leaving an illustrious reputation to posterity.[44]

This has no parallel in Pontanus (490), whom Meursius otherwise follows here, or for that matter in Huitfeldt (*Chron. II*, 553-54). – It turns out that Magnus's liberality was after all, in Meursius's view, guided by egoistical motives; he needed Valdemarus's friendship (II, 89).

Another insight into the greedy nature of most princes is found in the history of Johannes (1481-1513). The leader of the rebellious Swedes was Sten Sture. Meursius, closely following Svaning, tells of his refusal to give up the leadership in spite of Johannes's repeated attempts at persuasion, and then he rounds off with this general rule, which is not found in Svaning:

> Indeed, virtually no one surrenders power willingly to someone else, and the passion for mastery is hardly laid aside even with one's life.[45]

In the same vein princely egoism is demonstrated when in 1534 Maria, regent of the Low Countries, refused to help Christianus (III) against Lübeck. Otherwise following Krag, Meursius himself added this general lesson to be learnt:

> Thus Christianus obtained nothing from Maria but words at such a pressing time, which furnished a shining example here, too, that rulers more or less value treaties according to their advantage and do not abide by them except insofar as they believe it suits their interests.[46]

---

[44] *Certe rarum in principibus id exemplum est; et, injuste quanquam parta, vindicare summa fere cum iniquitate malunt, quam honeste restituere: potiusque incrementum potestatis quodvis ducunt, quam egregiam ad posteritatem famam* (II, 89).

[45] *Adeo nempe nemo fere imperio cuiquam unquam volens cedit: et cupiditas dominandi vix cum vita etiam ponitur* (III, 28).

[46] *Ita nihil Christianus tempore tam necessario a Maria praeter verba reportavit, claro etiam hic exemplo, foedera utilitate fere principes aestimare, nec servare, nisi quatenus rebus suis expedire arbitrentur* (col. 842).

Fear is a theme to which Meursius returns more than once. Fear may be of use to a prince as a weapon against rebellious subjects. After fighting for years with the Swedes, Johannes (1481-1513) should not, in Meursius's view, have started another war against Ditmarsken, since he gave the Swedes a chance to renew their rebellion. A wise prince will see to it that an old enemy whom he has no reason to trust is constantly kept in fear.[47]

There is also the kind of fear that must always haunt princes and make them excessively suspicious. The excellent Christianus I (1448-81) may in Meursius's view be reproached for only one thing, his readiness, caused by fear, to believe the false accusations against a Swedish archbishop. This is a common phenomenon, Meursius points out: people in high positions are prone to believe that crimes are being prepared against them:

> For the most part this is the fate of kings: since their circumstances are conspicuous, and they are thereby exposed to no small dangers, and a great many, too, they are often afraid of everything, even when all is safe, and easily give credence to their fears; moreover they rush to take vengeance on crimes which are not even contemplated.[48]

Dealing with one of the very first kings, Meursius notes that wicked rulers are particularly exposed to fear because of their (latent) bad conscience: "however, the mind that is uneasy over its sins is as a rule perpetually frightened of receiving its deserts" (*verum inquies scelere animus, uti fere, quæ meretur, semper timet*, I, 1), and again a little later: "And as malefactors with an uneasy conscience are generally afraid, because they know what they have earned [...]" (*Vtque mali, inquieti conscientia, metuunt fere, quod se meruisse sciunt* [...], I, 25). Similarly, the murderers of Ericus VII (1259-86) fled to Norway haunted by their own conscience: "owing to their consciousness of wrongdoing, they reckoned that nowhere in Denmark was safe for them" (*conscientia facinoris, nullum sibi locum tutum in Dania existimantes*, II, 48).[49]

---

[47] *Verum prudens rerum princeps, quisquis hostem debellatum, et imprimis, propter fluxam ante fidem, merito suspectum etiam, continere in officio deinceps volet, nunquam illi metum eripiet: sed parata ad formidinem arma habebit, quæ ostentet e propinquo* (III, 31). — Svaning merely blames Johannes for his boldness and greed (*Chronicon Ioannis*, X1r).

[48] *Sed hoc regum fere fatum est; ut, fortuna eminente, cum periculis non exiguis, plurimisque, sint expositi, omnia sæpe, etiam tuta, metuentes, facile, quod timent, credant: et præcipites crimina, nec cogitata, ulciscantur* (III, 20).

[49] Meursius follows Pontanus (373) closely in this passage, but he has himself provided the murderers with this motive for fleeing.

The excessive fear felt by princes was a standard theme in historical and political writings from classical antiquity onwards. It was cultivated by Tacitus, not least in his portrait of Tiberius, and Lipsius, too, devotes a chapter of the *Politica* to classical passages on the suspicions and fears of rulers. In this respect also, Meursius seems to reflect contemporary interest in the workings of power.

In one case I think Meursius has attempted a literary imitation of Tacitus on a larger scale. This is in his portrait of King Nicolaus (1104-34), which recalls the Tacitean tyrant Tiberius (*Annals* I-VI). We shall here just touch on the main points, since I have treated this passage in more detail elsewhere.[50]

The portrait of the king tells the story of an initially good king who gradually deteriorated. Like Christianus I (1448-81) later, but much more seriously, he is haunted by unfounded suspicions and prone to believe in malicious gossip – a feature typical of tyrants in both classical and later literature.

More particularly, Nicolaus shares with Tiberius a secret and patient waiting for revenge; when his nephew Canutus Slesvicensis (*Knud Lavard*) is accused (falsely) of trying to become Nicolaus's successor instead of the king's own son, Magnus, Nicolaus pretends not to care but plans to execute his revenge on Canutus later: "Although he kept the injury hidden for the time being, he was waiting for the appropriate time to reveal it" (*offensa quanquam in præsens occultata, tempus tamen, revelandæ opportunum, exspectaret*, I, 72), and later: "but in Nicolaus's mind this false accusation had rooted itself so firmly that he would admit no excuse at all" (*tamen animo Nicolai ita valide hæc calumnia inhærebat, ut omnino excusationem nullam admittere vellet*, I, 73). The wording itself is not particularly close to Tacitus's descriptions of Tiberius.[51] But since Meursius in his final summing up of Nicolaus's reign draws a clear parallel between Nicolaus and Tiberius, it is at least arguable that he also wants his reader to associate Nicolaus with Tiberius at an earlier stage.

We have seen previously how Meursius begins the obituary by using a Tacitean phrase (probably with Lipsius as intermediary) on the general good beginnings of rulers. Next Meursius praises the king's personal

---

[50] Skovgaard-Petersen 1995.

[51] Tiberius's reaction to Calpurnius Piso's denunciation of the corruption of public life bears some resemblance to the description of Nicolaus quoted above: *quae in praesens Tiberius civiliter habuit: sed in animo revolvente iras, etiam si impetus offensionis languerat, memoria valebat* (Tac. *Ann.* IV, Ch. 21).

modesty. However, these virtues gradually disappeared, or as Meursius says, Nicolaus divested himself of his virtues: *Sed paulatim exuit virtutes istas*, a metaphor which recalls Tacitus's description of Tiberius in the early part of his reign:

> erogandae per honesta pecuniae cupiens, quam virtutem diu retinuit, cum ceteras exueret (Tac. *Ann.* I, Ch. 75)
>
> (for, given a good cause, he was ready and eager to spend – a virtue which he long retained, even when he was divesting himself of every other),

– the more so, since in both cases the virtue in question is personal modesty.

Gradual deterioration is also the theme of Tacitus's obituary of Tiberius (*Ann.* VI, Ch. 51). The private life of both rulers is singled out for praise, and both finally reach depravity. In Tiberius's case those who had put restraint upon him earlier were now dead, and he was now (in the words of the Loeb translation) following his own bent: *suo tantum ingenio utebatur.*[52] So was Nicolaus, perhaps: "having soon slipped into vices, whether ones of his own that had long been cunningly concealed [...]" (*in vitia mox prolapsus, sive sua, diu callide celata* [...], I, 81), but Meursius then suggests, as an alternative explanation, that he had been led astray by his councellors:

> sive etiam aliena, a magistris pravis doctus, ac corruptus, ut interdum reges solent, indulgentia fortunæ, exercere ea coepit (I, 81-84a).
>
> (or his depravity was due to outside influence, when he had been schooled by wicked teachers and corrupted by an indulgent fortune, as kings sometimes are).

As noted above, these words stem from another Tacitean passage (*Hist.* II, Ch. 84). What is most interesting, however, is the fact that Meursius softened the verdict on Nicolaus compared to that on Tiberius by this last suggestion; perhaps he was not the only one to blame, since he may have been influenced by bad teachers. The verbal similarities between the

---

[52] R. H. Martin and A.J. Woodman suggest that *suo tantum ingenio utebatur* should be translated "he (sc. Tiberius) had only himself to rely on", that is, after the death of Sejanus. With this interpretation the passage does not say anything about the true character of Tiberius (Martin & Woodman (edd.): *Tacitus, Annals IV*, 27-29). If I am right that he is alluding to this passage in his obituary of Nicolaus, Meursius must have understood it as a statement about Tiberius's true nature.

two obituaries amount to a few significant words (*privatus, vita, mores*); but altogether I think there can be no doubt that Meursius wanted his readers to recall the Tacitean Tiberius.

Two circumstances may have inspired Meursius to make this connection. Saxo emphasizes Nicolaus's private modesty, the quality which Tacitus grants to Tiberius, and notes that Nicolaus did not change his ways of living after ascending the throne (XIII, Ch. i, 1). Further, the relation between Nicolaus and Canutus is not unlike that of Tiberius and Germanicus. The young prince is popular and successful, and the older ruler wants another less popular young prince (Drusus/Magnus) as his successor. These accidental parallels between the two rulers in Saxo and Tacitus may explain why Meursius, contrary to his practice elsewhere in his history, has made the effort to associate a Danish king with a particular figure of classical literature.

The features which in Meursius's account link Nicolaus with Tiberius, the gradual deterioration and the secretive suspiciousness, are not present in Saxo's description. Did Meursius take over the parallel from Svaning? I think not, since in the preserved parts of Svaning there are no traces of any familiarity with Tacitus; he wrote his work before the wave of Dutch political Tacitism with its interest in extracting general observations on the workings of power. In all probability Meursius himself saw and elaborated the parallel between Nicolaus and the Tacitean Tiberius.

The Moralistic Trend

The disinterested realism of the observations discussed in the preceeding chapter is not a dominant approach. Generally Meursius wants to advise the ruler to be aware of his duties and do what is morally right.

A king must constantly bear the safety of his subjects in mind. Both Valdemarus I (1157-82) and Johannes (1481-1513) are criticized for being too lenient towards their beaten enemies. Mildness is indeed a virtue, Meursius says towards the end of Valdemarus's reign, but not always recommendable to kings, since the safety of their subjects is at stake. A wise ruler will rather praise than practise mildness (I, 117-18).[53] Similarly, Johannes's patience with the many Swedish rebellions against the Union of Kalmar, was "a rare example, not to be imitated by princes": when a

---

[53] No such reflection is found in either Saxo, Pontanus, or Krantz.

prince displays such forgiveness, the victims will be his own subjects because they will have to fight the same enemy later on.[54]

The fate of Ericus X (1412-39) is discussed at length. His lack of consideration for his subjects was the decisive factor in his downfall, Meursius concludes:

> since in this matter he regarded his royal authority as much more important than his subjects' privileges, which he had sworn on oath to uphold, God soon plainly took revenge on his pride and treachery, and he was cast down from his throne.[55]

Sometimes the advice on good government is not given in authorial comments but attributed to the kings themselves. We have already seen how Christianus III is made to consider the benefits of national unity in Sallustian terms. Of one of his remote predecessors, Rolvo, Saxo narrates that once on a visit to the Swedish king he was asked by some guests which kind of bravery (*fortitudinis genus*) he valued most, and his answer was patience (or endurance).[56] His own patience is then put to test. Meursius left out this whole episode, but towards the end, in the summing up of Rolvo's reign he alludes to it:

> Once, when asked which virtue he thought surpassed all others, he replied, 'Patience,' since that was his belief; to govern a state a good prince needs nothing so much as patience.[57]

Again the theme of the good ruler is highlighted. Meursius ascribes to Rolvo a moral reflection about the necessity of patience in a good prince, where the discussion in Saxo concerns bravery and patience in general.

Another legendary king, Scioldus, realized that he had to set a good example himself if the luxurious habits of the people were to be restrained:

---

[54] *Vnde factum, uti totum ejus regnum nihil aliud quam perpetua quasi quædam lucta fuerit cum perfidia et Stenonis, et Suantonis, sociorumque, ac Lubecensium. Quibus, toties ignoscendo, animos, et vires, semper ad rebellionem novam confirmabat: raro exemplo, nec principibus imitando. Nam in talibus, ut non licet bis peccare, ita neque bis ignoscere: et crudelis est in subditos, quisquis hosti, postea non nisi illorum sanguine rursum coercendo, gratiam delicti ejusdem iterum facit* (III, 59). — This point is not found in Svaning's *Chronicon Ioannis.*

[55] *qua in re dum majestatem ipse suam subditorum privilegiis, in quæ jusjurandum dederat, multo potiorem habet, mox superbiam, ac perfidiam, clare ulciscente Deo, solio dejectus fuit* (II, 128).

[56] Saxo, II, Ch. vi,4.

[57] *Percunctanti aliquando, quam virtutem cæteris præstare duceret; patientiam, respondit. quippe sic existimabat: bono principi, ad rempublicam gubernandam, nihil magis patientia opus esse* (I, 10).

ratus, uti res se habet, populi in regem obsequium, et amorem æmulandi, poena, legibus constituta, multo potiorem esse (I, 2).

(He was of the opinion – which is also quite true – that the people's deference to the king and the love of emulating him is much stronger than legal sanctions).

A much later successor, Canutus Sanctus (1080-86), arrives at the same conclusion:

gnarus vero, obsequium in principem studiumque æmulandi, magis fere valida esse, quam propositam legibus poenam (I, 63).

(He was aware that deference to the sovereign and the desire to emulate him are more powerful than legal sanctions).

Tacitus uses the same words about Vespasian's ability to restrain the general luxury among his subjects by his own example:

obsequium inde in principem et aemulandi amor validior quam poena ex legibus et metus (Tac. *Ann.* III, Ch. 55).

(Thenceforward, deference to the sovereign and the love of emulating him proved more powerful than legal sanctions and deterrents).

– but then again, this maxim was also quoted by Lipsius in the *Politica* (36), and there is no telling whether Meursius was inspired by Lipsius or Tacitus in this instance.

As we have already seen, Canutus Magnus (1018-35) once when drunk, killed one of his men. He was also aware that he had to obey the laws if his people were to do so, and sentenced himself to severe punishment:

Moreover, he was aware that the greatest protection for the laws was the example set by the king; those which he had decreed for his subjects, he also let apply to himself.[58]

In another passage Meursius ascribes some reflections to the early medieval king, Gormo Anglicus. Gormo had previously ruled both Denmark and England; but when the English revolted, he did not attempt to re-establish his reign. Meursius suggests various reasons for this level-headedness:

---

[58] *quin et, gnarus, maximum legum munimentum principis exemplum esse, quas in subditos sanciverat, etiam in se admisit* (I, 55).

neque ille castigare est conatus: sive animi ignavia, et non vindicare ausus; sive etiam pacis studio, ac modestia: et quod, gnarus, maximo imperio fere maximam inesse curam, unus binis regnis impar, haud gravate, coerceri intra terminos imperium, ac regendi minui sibi onus, ferret (I, 46).

(Nor did he try to punish them, whether out of cowardice and lack of courage to take revenge, or out of concern for peace and modesty, and because he realized that a huge empire demands utmost attention; he did not mind that his realm became enclosed between narrower borders and his burden of ruling thereby reduced, since he, one man, was incapable of ruling two kingdoms).

This dictum originally comes from Sallust, though slightly different from Meursius's wording: *multa cura summo imperio inest* ("much anxiety lies in supreme power"). Lipsius, however, quotes Sallust thus: *maximo imperio maximam curam inesse* ("the greatest anxiety lies in the greatest power").[59] The agreement between Meursius and Lipsius suggests the latter as Meursius's source, although, again, the phrase may also have been a commonplace in political writings of the time.

After suffering defeat against the Swedes in a battle near Stockholm in 1471, Christianus I decides to give up his attempts to persuade them to rejoin the Union of Kalmar. Svaning makes him regret that he had been forced into this cruel war (fol. 65v-66r), and Meursius further suggests that he reflected on the duties of a good king and the fundamental condition of power:

> [...] either tired of fighting, and thinking that the blood of his subjects must henceforth be spared, for he knew that this was something a good prince should take account of above all; or reflecting to himself that every kingdom whatsoever is granted and removed by Fate; finally considering, too, that while his fortunes, which could clearly be ruined by some larger disaster, were still intact, he should deliver the rights to his kingdom unimpaired to his heir.[60]

All through history we find kings who are able to reflect on their position and moral duties. By ascribing such reflections to the kings themselves,

---

[59] Lipsius, *Politica*, 32. Sallust, *Hist. frag. Oratio C. Cottae*, 13.

[60] [...] *sive bellandi pertæsus; et parcendum deinceps sanguini subditorum arbitratus, cujus potissimum rationem bono principi habendam sciret: sive cum animo suo reputans, regna quævis fato dari, et auferri: denique etiam, ut, fortuna adhuc integra, quæ corrumpi clade aliqua majore plane poterat, jus in regnum illud suum hæredi illibatum traderet* (III, 18).

Meursius portrays them as wise, level-headed and pious. And the opposite is true as well. The villains omit to reflect on the fundamental conditions of this life, as in the case of Magnus, the murderer of Canutus Slesvicensis (*Knud Lavard*) (in 1131):

> yet the wretched fellow did not bethink himself that God avenges crimes sternly, or that the sceptres of kings are held in His hand.[61]

But let us return to the narrator's judgements on the characters and their actions. The moral obligations of the prince are in focus. For instance, the Swedish king's plan to murder one of the legendary kings, Hadingus, is followed by this comment: "by a very shameful plan, one unworthy of royalty" (*Turpi admodum consilio, et principibus indigno*, I, 5). The legendary King Frotho I is reproached in an authorial comment for disguising himself as a woman in order to gain access to a town which he has beleaguered for a long time. This was a trick "not to be used by a king", the narrator declares.[62] Other examples are found in the lives of practically all the kings. Each reign is rounded off by an appraisal of the king's achievement and moral character.

Meursius's universe is governed by justice. The morally good cause will finally win. In the following instance it can be observed how he transforms a cynical analysis of politics in Tacitus into a moral condemnation. In the first book of the *Annals* one of Tiberius's relatives has been killed. Tacitus more than suggests that the emperor himself was pulling the strings, but in order to remove any suspicion, Tiberius wants the matter discussed in the senate. This idea causes one of the accomplices to teach Tiberius some basic rules of autocracy:

> [...] neve Tiberius vim principatus resolveret cuncta ad senatum vocando: eam condicionem esse imperandi ut non aliter ratio constet quam si uni reddatur (Tac. *Ann.* I, Ch. 6).

> ([...] and also to watch that Tiberius did not weaken the powers of the throne by referring everything to the senate: it was a condition of sovereignty that the account balanced only if rendered to a single auditor).

Meursius alludes to this episode in his summing up of the reign of

---

[61] *verum miser, neque Deum scelera ulcisci rigide, aut in ejus manu esse regum sceptra, cogitabat* (I, 76).

[62] [...] *neque regi usurpanda*, I, 7. Svaning apparently had another version of these events, which is known from Stephanius (Stephanius 1645, 66); according to this the king let a soldier disguise himself as a woman and go into the town; so no judgement on the king is found here.

Ericus IV (*Erik Emune*, 1134-37), who made his way to the throne by killing his brother and nephews:

> Impii profecto reges, et omnino illaudati, qui a cæde propinquorum regnum suum inchoandum sibi putant; neque aliter constare rationem principatus arbitrantur, quam si eum abominando bonis omnibus consilio sanguine suorum firment (I, 84b).

> (Those kings are truly impious and entirely despicable who reckon that their reign should begin with the killing of relatives. They think that the account of monarchy will only balance if they, by a design abominable to all good people, strengthen it with the blood of their own relatives).

Where Tacitus's episode demonstrates that the prince must guard certain secrets, Meursius wants to point out that killing relatives is not uncommon among evil princes. In this case I find it likely that Meursius alludes to Tacitus's work itself. Not only the words, but also the circumstances – the king who kills a relative in order to secure his own power – are so similar that there can be no doubt that Meursius had the passage from the *Annals* in mind.

Kings who, like Ericus IV, obtained their power by illegal means will always be punished. The legendary king Svibdagerus likewise made his way to power by crime, and soon lost it again. Meursius points to the exemplary value of this course of events:

> parata scelere regna, cum non diu tenuisset, maxima cum ignominia, uti fere fieri solet, rursum amittit (I, 3).

> (After he had ruled for a short time the kingdoms which he had obtained by crime, he lost them again with the utmost disgrace, as usually turns out to be the case).

– and so did Abelus (1250-52), who after having killed his brother, King Ericus VI (*Erik Plovpenning*, 1241-50), tried to secure the throne for his own sons – but in vain:

> sat aperto documento, principatus fato dari; et facilius scelere parari regna, quam transmitti ad hæredes (II, 33).

> (giving quite clear proof that dominions are dispensed by fate, and that it is easier to acquire realms through crime than to transmit them to one's heirs).

The same lesson may be learnt from Lipsius's *Politica:*

nulla quæsita scelere potentia diuturna est.[63]

(no power that is obtained through crime is long-lasting).

Lipsius in fact, like Meursius, wants to demonstrate how the world is governed by justice. Both are thoroughly familiar with Tacitus's works, but neither of them retains his cynicism.

In this fundamental respect also, then, I think we should regard Lipsius's *Politica* as a possible source of inspiration for Meursius. In the Preface Lipsius, while praising Macchiavelli as a great political thinker, also regrets his deviations from the path of virtue. And he himself, in the quotations he introduces, highlights the moral obligations of the prince.

The admiration for Lipsius's *Politica* among the Dutch humanists is well attested in Meursius's friend Gerardus Vossius's warm recommendation of the work to a young friend who had asked for a list of contents. The *gnomæ* collected by Lipsius are about politics (*civilis prudentia*), and they are at the same time brief and morally laudable, in short, highly useful, Vossius declares, and they provide the best possible beginning for the young man, apparently about to enter upon a study of law (*studium civile*).[64]

It is worth noticing that precisely this quality of usefulness was emphasized in the description of the purpose of rhetorical lectures at the Academy of Sorø. Being closely connected to history, rhetoric should inform the students of "political and ethical counsels" (*monita politica et ethica*).[65]

5. The Christian Foundation

A distinctive feature of Meursius's moral view of history is its Christian basis. The fundamental justice of the world is due to the will of God. He bestows rewards and punishments throughout history. In this respect Meursius differs somewhat from Lipsius, who is primarily concerned

---

[63] Lipsius, *Politica*, 29 (from Curtius X, Ch. I, 6). Cf. also Meursius I, 1-2; I, 67.

[64] *Summi sane viri, cujus de civili prudentia libros initiis istis studii tui Civilis maxime accomodatos existimavi, idque non solum ob brevitatem atque ordinem, sed etiam ob tot laudabilia dicta, ex quibus, sedulæ instar apis, suum hoc mellificium confecit. Tuum nunc erit sæpius eos lectitare, quo tot aureæ sententiæ penitius animo inhæreant. Illustriores etiam gnomas et exempla præclara, quæ legendo deinceps observabis, vel ad oram, vel charta inserta, e regione suo quoque loco annotabis* [...] (undated letter from Vossius to Brianus Brounerius (Vossius 1691, I, no. 179)).

[65] Tauber 1827, 22.

with human affairs though emphasizing, in chapters on this particular subject, the importance of respecting and fearing God.[66]

The Christian interpretation of events is a characteristic feature of Meursius's work. More often than not he refers to the will of God in his appraisal of a king. Thus the Tacitean obituary of King Nicolaus ends with the Christian reflection that God avenged the murder of Canutus, to which Nicolaus was accessory, by the murder of Nicolaus himself (I, 84a).

Divine justice determines the course of history. In this respect Meursius stands firmly in the older Melanchthonian tradition, most forcefully represented by the world history, *Carion's Chronicle* (which was, as earlier mentioned, first published in German in 1532, and then later in Melanchthon's and Peucer's Latin adaptation), where God's recognition of virtue and punishment of sin determines the whole course of history; in both *Carion's Chronicle* and Meursius's *History of Denmark* we find ancient pagan history presented in terms of God's will. The legendary king, Frotho, killed his brother and thereby caused his own downfall, as Meursius points out:

> But God, who wills that crimes, particularly such terrible ones, should be neither hidden nor unpunished, ordained that he should first labour under the disgrace of detestable parricide, and then also be punished.[67]

Another example is that of Gramus, one of the very first kings, whom Meursius judges along these lines:

> He was a great king, in whom nothing can be censured except his matrimonial fickleness and the repudiation [of his wife]. This behaviour is disgraceful and forbidden also to kings, and God, who is both the author and the upholder of matrimony, will not leave it unpunished, though it is often practiced because of lust.[68]

We are here in the legendary, pagan past. Throughout the course of his-

---

[66] The first chapters of the *Politica* are about *Pietas*, which Lipsius defines as *rectus de Deo sensus, rectus in Deum cultus*. Later he urges that religion should be the primary concern of the prince, this time with several quotations from Lactantius (79-82).

[67] *verum Deus, qui flagitia, et inprimis tam horrenda, neque occultata cupit, neque impunita esse, voluit, ut infamia primum execrandi parricidii laboraret, inde etiam poenas daret* (I, 24).

[68] *Princeps magnus, et in quo nil reprehendas, quam amoris conjugalis inconstantiam, et repudia: etiam regibus indecora, et illicita; neque a Deo, ut auctore matrimonii, ita quoque assertore, impunita, quanquam sæpe per libidinem usitata* (I, 3).

tory, Meursius uses the same Christian values as the basis of his judgements. In this case the king's matrimonial infidelity is censured. The same sin was committed by the Danish king Valdemarus II (1202-41), who was also afflicted with divine punishment: "for adultery, of which he discovered God was a very clear avenger" ([...] *adulterio* [...] *cujus Deum satis manifestum ultorem est expertus*, II, 24).

Valdemarus III (*Valdemar Atterdag*, 1340-75) was another king who, like Gramus, repudiated his wife, claiming that she had been unfaithful. Meursius condemns this behaviour in unambiguous terms (II, 93), and points out that God demonstrated the innocence of the wife by His singular favour to their daughter Margareta, who eventually became ruler of Sweden, Norway and Denmark. Perhaps the best example of Meursius's condemnation of matrimonial infidelity is found in his discussion of the consequences of Sueno III's (*Sven Estridssøn*, 1047-74) many extra-matrimonial affairs, as we shall see below.

Time and again God's rewards to good kings and punishments for bad ones are emphasized, as in this final statement on the disastrous reign of Christophorus II (1320-32):

> [...] with obvious proof that, as God cherishes, exalts and strengthens good monarchs, so, conversely, He hates and overturns bad rulers, demolishing their schemes and their kingdoms.[69]

A long time before, when the legendary Buthlus ruled, the Danes were taught the same lesson:

> But when God has determined that he will punish the sins of kings and of the people they rule, he weakens and reduces their realms; on the other hand, when He has decided to bless them, he consolidates and enlarges their territories.[70]

– And much later Christianus II (1513-23) was punished by God, who saw to it that he finally brought about his own downfall:

> However, because God had resolved to overthrow his great dignity and power, He subverted his plans, as generally occurs in human affairs.[71]

---

[69] *manifesto argumento, Deum, uti bonos reges amat, evehit, ac confirmat, ita malos contra odisse ac dejicere; et consilia eorum, atque regna, dissipare* (II, 76).

[70] *Sed peccata regum Deus, populique his subjecti, cum decrevit castigare, regna infirmat, minuitque: uti contra, cum constituit beare, firmat ea, et adauget* (I, 32).

[71] *Verum deus, qui evertere tantam ejus magnitudinem, ac potentiam, apud se constituisset, consilia eius, uti fere in humanis rebus solet, pervertebat* (III, 84).

6. The Christian Element in Meursius's Sources

Above we have seen examples of some central themes of Meursius's Christian moralism. Surprisingly, at least for a reader who comes from his *History of Denmark*, Meursius's earlier historical works on recent Dutch history, the *Ferdinandus Albanus* (or *Rerum Belgicarum libri IV*) and the *Gulielmus Auriacus*, while loaded with moral judgements on concrete matters, are marked neither by general reflections on power nor by Christian moralism.[72] Tempting as it may be, it would be wrong to conclude that he simply took over these important features in the *Historia Danica* from his sources. I shall now argue that this Christian moralism must to a large extent be ascribed to Meursius himself. With the partial exception of Svaning he did not find it in his sources.

First it must be said that in Meursius's long history of Christianus III (covering the years 1533-50) instances of God's interference in human affairs are relatively few, although God is often mentioned by the king and other good men, whose piety is thereby made clear. In this respect Meursius's version resembles its source, Niels Krag's *History of Christianus III*, in which events are only rarely, in the authorial comments, seen as results of God's interference. The two instances I have noticed do not recur in Meursius's adaptation, appearing as they do in passages which Meursius has abbreviated heavily.[73]

On the other hand Meursius also made some significant "Christian additions" in his adaptation of Krag. In one case Meursius replaced Krag's political reflection with a specifically Christian one. On a friendly visit to Gustavus of Sweden in 1535, Christianus III was close to being captured by his host. Krag here points out that rulers who place themselves at the mercy of other men in power are subject to great danger, since, if the hosts are not by nature decent, their concern for their own

---

[72] I have found only six general reflections in the *Guilelmus Auriacus*, all brief and all reading more like short standard phrases, e.g.: *at Parmensi, ut in rebus lætis solet, crevit animus* (33). In the same work I have found only three authorial references to God, all of them explaining apparently miraculous events: *nec spes ulla miseris reliqua; cum tanquam e machina Deus subito casu oppressos liberat* (67), *jamque fere humanæ opis nulla amplius spes restabat, cum e machina deus juvit* (100), *ac postridie, ut præsentem opem suam Deus manifestam faceret, flans Vulturnus; aquas, ceu perfecto opere, rursum urbe summovebat* [...] (134).

[73] They are found in Krag's description, 140, of the sufferings of the inhabitants when Copenhagen is beleaguered in 1536 and in his summing up of Christianus III's reorganization of the Church in 1537 (172).

reputation is rarely strong enough to make them behave decently.[74] Meursius first notes a lesson similar to Krag's, that princely friendships are often best at a distance. Then he explains Christianus's salvation as God's design:

> Actual experience, too, has taught that meetings between the greatest princes are very hazardous; their friendship remains steadfast while they are apart, but is weakened when they are together. Nevertheless God, who holds all the purposes of evildoers in His hand, who wished Christianus's supreme virtue and probity to be respected as befits a king, and who had marked him out for the restoration and governing of Denmark, snatched him from danger and diverted Gustavus's mind from perpetrating a crime.[75]

In his reworking of Pontanus's *History* for the period c. 1157-1448, Meursius inserted a number of religious reflections, a feature which is almost absent from Pontanus's work. Meursius's conclusion (quoted above) of Christophorus II's reign, which states God's punishments of wicked kings (II, 76), is an example of his adding a Christian moral to a passage in which he otherwise follows Pontanus. In the following case we can observe how Meursius substitutes one moral lesson, made by Pontanus (who had found it in Huitfeldt), with another which is specifically Christian. In 1395 Albertus of Sweden was forced to give up the Swedish throne and return to Germany. His defeat makes Pontanus and Huitfeldt reflect on the many violent deaths among the Swedish rulers in the pre-

---

[74] *Salubre vero documentum Regibus et Principibus, ne temere alienæ fidei credentes, se in discrimen dedant. Qvotusqvisqve enim mortalium ita tenax recti, ut non probro exiguum præmium anteponat, nedum regni aliqva fides sit? Enimvero qvo qvisqve celsiore loco positus, tanto magis decoris sui et famæ prodigus facinus nefarium audebit. Ad fastigium enim regium pudor, si non indolis bonitate, certe metu infamiæ, raro pertingit: Et si qvæ est infamia facti, a paucis Regibus, qvanta ea sit, intelligitur. Æmulatio autem plerumqve magnis ingeniis est insita, Regum etiam comitatur fortunam, paribus invisam. Et qvidem vicinorum eo magis, qvo propior in oculis prosperitas, qvam sibi noxiam fore opinantur, suspicaces ipsi, et ex qvavis levicula rerum mutatione diminutionem sui formidantes* (Krag: *Historia regis Christiani III*, ed. Gram 1737, 104-5).

[75] *experientia quoque ipsa didicit, admodum periculosos maximorum principum congressus esse; tum eorum amicitiam in absentia constare, sed praesentia imminui. Verum Deus, qui consilia malorum cuncta sua in manu habet, ac virtutem, et integritatem summam Christiani, rege dignam, honoratam cupiebat, Daniaeque instaurandae, ac regendae destinabat, hunc eripuit, et a scelere patrando animum Gustavi avertit* (col. 864).

The fate of Christianus II (1513-23), who was imprisoned from 1532 until his death in 1559, provokes from Krag the following reflection on the changes of fortune: *Documentum vero, Regibus gloria ingentibus timendam fortunam, ne, qvum ferociant et subjectis intolerabiles fiant, ipsi se salutis suæ incautos evertant et pessundent* (287). Meursius, on his side, replaced fortune with God. From Christianus II's example kings may learn to fear God: *Magnum, regibus etsi maximis, documentum, ut timere Deum discant, ne si nimium ferociant, et intolerabiles subiectis fiant, perditum se ipsi eant* (col. 966).

ceding century. Pontanus (still following Huitfeldt) advances a general rule – as he rarely does – that rulers should always bear in mind the fickleness of fortune. Almost as an afterthought he then points out that Albertus's oppressive regime in Sweden had made him unpopular so that he had only himself to blame for his downfall:

> Yet apart from these factors it was this, too, that destroyed Albertus: summoned from his native Mecklenburg to the royal summit of Sweden, he neglected and scorned the inhabitants of that realm and, showing little concern for the statutes and laws of this people, appointed his own countrymen to the control of almost all public offices. Hence he was despised and rejected by the very folk he had himself despised, not only as a foreigner but also as someone inimical to their ways, so that after being held prisoner for seven years he was inevitably forced to return to his homeland.[76]

Meursius took this passage as a point of departure for a religious moral. At last Albertus, after his cruel tyranny over the Swedes, fell victim to God's wrath. Although divine revenge sometimes comes late, no one can escape it:

> So by the just judgement of heaven Albertus was compelled to surrender to Margareta the kingdom he had wrested from his uncle, Magnus. He had certainly held it for some time, while God closed His eyes to Albertus's extreme wrong; but divine vengeance, although slow, is sure, there is no man who can escape it, and as it generally moves with less speed, so it strikes all the more heavily. It was not simply his criminal usurpation of the Swedish realm which was perilous for Albertus, but even more so the fact that he had disdained those national laws he had sworn to uphold and treacherously spurned the native-born noblemen by dispensing high offices to his own countrymen. Undoubtedly it transpires in practice that those who take possession of others' dominions with outstanding wickedness and rule them as dishonourably as they acquired them are building a stair to their own ruin.[77]

---

[76] *Quamvis Albertum præter ista etiam hoc pessum dedit, quod e Megapoli sua ad regium Suecorum fastigium vocatus, posthabitis aut contemptis regni indigenis, tum et gentis statuta legesque parum pensi habens, muneribus fere omnibus populares suos præficeret. Unde non tantum, ut extraneum sed populi quoque moribus adversum, ab illis ipsis, quos contempserat, contemtum rejectumque ad suos regredi post annorum septem captivitatem necessitas adegit* (524). – Huitfeldt discusses in further detail the general benefits of indigenous rulers as opposed to regents of different nationality from their subjects (*Chron. III*, 105-6).

[77] *Ita Albertus, justo numinis judicio, regnum, quod avunculo Magno eripuerat, Margaretæ tradere coactus fuit. diu quidem, connivente ad injuriam summam Deo, id tenuerat: verum ultio divina, quanquam lenta, tamen certa est; nec evadere quisquam homo illam potest: ac, quo minus fere properat, eo gravius affligit. Et*

Unlike Krag and Pontanus, Svaning, in his history of the three first Oldenburg kings, displays a tendency to moralize along Christian lines. In his
lives of Christianus I (1448-81) and Johannes (1481-1513), though, most
of the references to God's judgement form part of anti-Swedish polemical attacks. These passages were left out by Meursius, due to his generally
less aggressive attitude towards the Swedes (cf. below), and he did not –
with one or two exceptions – insert other Christian reflections in his
accounts of these two kings.[78] By contrast, the history of Christianus II is
seen in a theological light both in Svaning and Meursius. The king's flight
from Denmark in 1523 and his long imprisonment from 1532 to 1559 is
described as a punishment inflicted by God because of the cruel massacre in Stockholm in 1520 and more generally because of his arrogance
and pride. On the other hand they both reduce the enormity of the crime
to a certain extent by pointing out that the massacre must be seen as a
divine punishment on the Swedes for their unfair treatment of the
Swedish bishop, Gustav Trolle. Within this framework Meursius displays
some independence. Not only did he place these moralizing passages at
other points in the narrative than Svaning, he also gave his own theological interpretation of a single episode (see below).

On this basis it is difficult to decide to what extent the many references to divine justice in the early part of Meursius's work are taken over
from Svaning. He shared with Svaning a tendency to interpret events as
the results of God's will, but judging from the three first Oldenburg
kings he did not follow Svaning slavishly in this respect. In fact, a brief
passage from the legendary part of Svaning's history, quoted by Stepha-

---

Alberto non duntaxat id perniciosum erat, quod per nefas regnum Sueciæ invasisset, verum magis etiam il-
lud, quod, contemptis regni legibus, in quas sacramentum dederat, perfide indigenas proceres aspernatus, mu-
nia, ac dignitates, inter populares suos distribuerat. nempe ita usu venit, ut, imperia aliena qui per nefas sum-
mum occupant, ea indigne, sicut nacti, gubernantes, ipsi sibi ad ruinam gradum struant (II, 99).

Some other examples: One of the murderers of Ericus VI, his brother Abelus, himself
becomes king, but only to be met with God's punishment, Meursius tells us. For one thing
his brother's riches, which he had hoped to find, did not exist, and then his son was kid-
napped: *Auxit hunc dolorem casus alius* (the kidnapping of the son)*, mox subsequutus; Deo regnum,*
parricidio paratum, ipso statim in principio sat aperte castigante (II, 32); Pontanus only speaks of
Abelus's grief at the discovery that his brother had left no riches behind (338), and then
wonders in secular terms why the boy was taken prisoner (339). Ericus Pomeranus (1412-39)
was once prevented from attacking Stockholm by a storm, Pontanus tells us (599); Meursius
sees the storm as a result of God's decision (II, 119). Examples are also found in Meursius's
discussions of the character and rule of the king at the end of each chapter.

[78] Here follow two examples of claims put forward by Svaning and not taken over by Meursius, to the effect that God supported the just Danish cause against the Swedes:

nius, provides us with evidence that Meursius was no stranger to inserting his own Christian moral conclusions. The passage is about the legendary king Gramus, whose matrimonial infidelity and repudiation of his wife Meursius criticizes in the passage (I, 3) quoted above. Stephanius first quotes Meursius's censure with approval: "For this reason [Gramus's infidelity] Meursius, of superlative renown, rightly concludes the life of Gramus with these words: [...]".[79] Then follows Stephanius's rendering of Svaning's commentary on Gramus's behaviour, which is rather an antiquarian and non-moralizing piece of information to the effect that polygamy was allowed in those days, though not to kings, who were, however, allowed to repudiate their wives, as many examples show.[80] The fact that Stephanius quotes from both Svaning and Meursius suggests that Meursius's censure of Gramus did not have a parallel in Svaning, in other words that Meursius did not simply take over his Christian condemnation of Gramus from Svaning. It seems to have been his own idea. Infidelity is a sin for which he blames several kings, and it seems likely that he himself supplied the moralizing on this theme.

The most conspicuous example of Meursius's censure of infidelity concerns Sueno III (*Sven Estridsøn*, 1047-74). Svaning's account of this period is not known today, and we shall now, dealing with Sueno and his sons, consider Meursius's Christian moralism in relation to Saxo.

Sueno III is condemned for his many love affairs by both Saxo (XI, Ch. vii, 1) and Meursius (I, 62). Five of his sons, all born outside marriage, followed him in turn on the throne, but whereas Saxo only makes short matter-of-fact references to this circumstance (XII, Ch. vii,6; XII, Ch. viii, 2),[81] Meursius sees the whole period as dominated by the effects of Sueno's sins. In his introduction to this era he admits that the singular phenomenon of the five sons was to some extent a reward for Sueno's piety; but primarily it must be seen as a punishment, since the reigns of

---

From the history of Christianus I: *Hæc inaudita et formidabilis clades, testatur deum periuria violationes pactorum, foederum et similia atrocia scelera, grauissime etiam in hac vita punire tam certo, ut raro ejuscemodi inulta abeant* [...] (Ms. *Gl. Kgl. S.* 2444 4to, 64r).

From the history of Johannes: *Deus enim ob hanc crudelitatem Suecis indignatus, omnem postea rerum bene gerendarum illis industriam, atque consilia ademit* (*Chronicon Ioannis*, Dd3r).

[79] *Quare recte concludit his verbis vitam Grami Clarissimus Meursius* [...] (Stephanius 1645, 40-41).

[80] *Svaningius permissa olim Regibus fuisse repudia commemorat:* "*Fuit autem in Borealibus hisce regnis in gentilitate olim polygamia libera vulgo, sed nequaquam Regibus, quibus tamen repudiare uxores permissum fuisse, multorum Regum exempla testantur*" (Stephanius 1645, 41).

[81] Huitfeldt and Pontanus do not mention it at all.

all these sons were, in various ways, unhappy (I, 62). Towards the end of the period, he passes a more explicit moral judgement:

> Indeed God's judgements are a subject of wonder. He abhors unlawful lusts, abhors adulteries, and takes revenge with the harshest severity. Yet illegitimate sons, even those born from an adulterous union, he makes into kings and invests with majesty; this is to shame the peoples whose sins He believes He must punish. Then He vexes the kings themselves and demonstrates to everyone that He exacts retribution on the parents through their offspring. So, in order to punish the nation for their sins and chastise Sueno's lust through his family, he ordains five kings in succession for Denmark, all bastards.[82]

– Sueno's debauchery, in short, was punished by his five sons' sad fates, and so were the crimes of the people by the disgrace of having five illegitimate sons as kings. This whole period of almost ninety years is thus interpreted, with no authority from Saxo, in the light of God's displeasure with Sueno's many love affairs.

Another example of Meursius's making a moral pattern cover a longer stretch of history concerns the murder of Canutus Slesvicensis (*Knud Lavard*) in 1131. After Canutus's death the king, Nicolaus, planned to have his nephew Ericus (brother of Canutus) killed with help from the Norwegian king Magnus, to whom Ericus had fled. Saxo condemns the Norwegian king's greed: "with the incitement of gain he became more unscrupulous than a brigand and from being hospitable turned hostile" (*lucri irritamento latrone corruptior hostisque ex hospite effectus*, XIII, Ch. xi,4). But Meursius further adds that the plan was not compatible with God's design for the future, inasmuch as God had destined Ericus to be king, and he deduces from this the general doctrine that when human beings try to oppose divine plans it is always in vain.[83] Later we learn that the reason that Canutus V, whose father was Magnus, Nicolaus's son, only ruled for a short time was his father's murder of Canutus Slesvicensis:

---

[82] *Admiranda certe Dei sunt judicia. Detestatur illegitimas libidines, detestatur adulteria, vindicatque severissime. natos tamen illegitime, etiam ex adulterio, reges facit, et circundat majestate; in opprobrium populorum, quorum sic peccata sibi punienda arbitratur. tum exercet ipsos reges; ac, parentes se ulcisci in progenie, omnibus testatum facit. ita Daniæ, ut peccata incolarum castigaret, et libidinem Suenonis, in prosapia, quinque ordine reges edit, omnes nothos* (I, 84a).

[83] *Facinus pudendum certe, et bonis omnibus detestandum! hinc occidi Nicolaus postulat nepotem patruus, inde patruum uxoris, et novercæ suæ virum, hospitemque, interficere animum inducit Magnus. verum Deus, qui et scelera semper quævis execratur, et Ericum Danis regem constituere proposuerat, eum eripit periculo, et conservat ad id tempus, quamvis postea morti tamen violentæ permissurus. Et ostendit hoc exemplum,*

Nor was he unfit to rule the whole of Denmark, if God had so wished. But it seems that the weight of his father's crime pressed heavily on him, and the murder of Canutus Slesvicensis, that finest of lords, which was recounted above, rendered him so provoking to the Deity that He determined the wrong should also be avenged on the son.[84]

Again, no such reflection is found in Saxo, not even an obituary. Of course, in these overall Christian interpretations, we cannot rule out the possibility that the inspiration came from Svaning. But in the light of Meursius's apparent independence of Svaning in his Christian censure of the legendary King Gramus's infidelity, I am, as earlier mentioned, inclined to regard his stress on the long-reaching effects of Sueno III's amorous affairs as his own idea; and this may very well be the case also with his interpretation of the effects of the murder of Canutus Slesvicensis.

But let us return to Saxo. He is like Meursius a Christian moralist, but the religious aspect is less pronounced than in Meursius. Where Saxo often refers to what is pleasing and displeasing to God, Meursius's God takes an active part, distributing rewards and punishments and steering the course of history according to His designs. Thus Saxo describes at some length how Haraldus (1074-1080) paid more attention to his own religious practices than to good government, which, he notes, displeases God (XI, Ch. x,8). In Meursius's version God acts by removing this unworthy king in order to make way for his worthier successor, Canutus Sanctus:

> It is apparent that God also wished to remove him so quickly from the throne, as someone unworthy of it, in order that Canutus, distinguished for his manifold virtues, should obtain it as his due. Be assured that, as He sometimes wrenches good kings out of their kingdoms because of their subjects' sins, so He wrests their kingdoms from bad ones because of their own sins.[85]

---

frustra hominum consilia summi numinis providentiæ adversari: ac noceri posse nulli quem tuendum idem sibi constituerit (I, 80).

[84] *nec indignus toti Daniæ imperare, si sic Deo placuisset. sed premebat, ut videtur, patris scelus: qui, Canuto Slesvicensi, principe optimo, uti supra memoratum, interfecto, ita numen irritavit, ut in filio quoque illud persequendum constitueret* (I, 95).

[85] *ac videtur etiam Deus solio eum, ceu indignum, adeo cito demovere voluisse, ut Canutus, varia virtute clarus, illo, velut sibi debito, potiretur. Certe Deus, ut interdum bonos reges ob peccata subditorum, regnis eripit, ita regna ob peccata sua, malis* (I, 63).

Another significant difference between Meursius and Saxo is their concept of God's role in the pre-Christian era. In Saxo's work God is not mentioned until the beginning of the Christianization of Denmark (except the reference to the birth of Christ, V, Ch. xv,3). By contrast Meursius, as we have seen, refers to God's judgements and interventions from the very beginning.

7. *The Protestant Outlook*

Meursius's Censure of the Worldly Bishops
We noted above how this feature, God's intervention all through history, is also characteristic of Melanchthon's influential *Carion's Chronicle*. In other respects, too, Meursius's *Historia Danica* bears a Protestant stamp. Between Valdemarus I (1157-82) and the archbishop, Eschillus, there was an ongoing conflict. At one point, Saxo tells us, Eschillus tried to reconcile himself with the king by giving him back some ecclesiastical property which previous kings had donated to the Church. Saxo condemns Eschillus's disrespect for the pious generosity of earlier kings; he regards the Church as the rightful owner of the property in question.[86] Meursius, however, changes the course of events. He has it that Valdemarus accepted Eschillus's request for reconciliation on the condition that the property was given back to the crown. This change has a Protestant ring to it. Meursius avoids blaming Eschillus for restoring property from the Church to the crown, and depicts Valdemarus's demand for the property as a just punishment of the arrogant archbishop. Powerful clergymen, he declares, are severely punished by God:

> [...] giving a sufficiently clear proof that God, who hates pride in every type of human being, particularly loathes it in the supervisors of His Church, including the highest ones, who, rightly and properly, should shine forth before everyone in devout humility and humble devoutness, with the result that He castigates them very harshly; and He does this all the more severely, the more lofty the station to which He has exalted such a person.[87]

---

[86] Saxo, XIV, Ch. xxvi,13, echoed by Krantz, *Dania*, VI, Ch. 13; Pontanus seems to join in their criticism (239).

[87] *manifesto sat exemplo, Deum, qui superbiam odit, in quocunque hominum genere, eam in ecclesiæ suæ administris, etiam summis, quos humilitate pia, humilique pietate, prælucere universis æquum erat, maximopere detestari, et punire severissime: atque eo quoque gravius, quo sublimius quem evexerit* (I, 101).

Similar censure of episcopal arrogance is found in a number of six-teenth-century Danish Protestant historians, such as Svaning (see below), Vedel,[88] and Huitfeldt.[89] Meursius is also emphatically on the side of the kings in the numerous clashes between Church and the monarchy during the thirteenth century. So are Huitfeldt and Pontanus. In Meursius's work, however, criticism of episcopal power and worldliness forms a recurrent theme, much more prominent than in Huitfeldt and Pontanus, and, as I shall argue here, I think he was inspired by Svaning on this point.[90] The idea of changing the course of events in the episode just mentioned probably goes back to Svaning. Judging from his strategy of adaptation elsewhere, Meursius was not prone to invent such changes himself.

One particular aspect of the medieval bishops' wordly activities is the object of Meursius's severe censure, viz. their active engagement in war-fare. This lamentable practice, we learn, began in the reign of Canutus Sanctus (1080-86), who gave the bishops the highest rank among the councillors (*senatores*) and invested them with the right to fight in wars. This was a bad arrangement, says Meursius, since war with all its horrors and atrocities is irreconcilable with ecclesiastical life; the primitive Church (*ecclesia antiqua*) does not offer any example of this kind.[91] Saxo, on the contrary, praises Canutus for his elevation of the bishops (XI, Ch. xi, 4-5), and Pontanus mentions it briefly with no hint of disapproval (197).

Meursius takes up this critique again after the battle of Fotevig in 1134, where King Nicolaus together with his son Magnus were slain by Ericus, brother of Canutus Slesvicensis (*Knud Lavard*), whom Magnus

---

[88] Vedel condemns medieval episcopal luxury in his prefaces to the translation of Saxo (1575) and in his preface to the edition of Adam of Bremen (1579).

[89] E.g. in the preface to his clerical history of Denmark, *Den geistlig Histori.*

[90] But Meursius does not seem to have made use of Svaning in his account of the conflicts between kings and bishops in the thirteenth century, judging from some fragments of Svaning's work dealing with the bishop Jakob Erlandssøn (d. 1274) and his conflicts with the king, (Ms. *Bartholiniana, Tome J, E don. var.* 1, fol., 351-2).

[91] *[Canutus] statuit, ut deinceps ducum instar, principumque, haberentur; ac supremum quoque locum inter regni senatores obtinerent. atque ita, antea limitibus inclusi suis, et sejuncti a civili potestate, nunc jus gladii accepere. quin, translata in alios sacrorum cura, bella etiam gesserunt: malo certe instituto, et omnino im-probando. nam consilia, reipublicæ recte et pie gubernandæ, maxime in iis rebus, quæ conjunctæ cum ecclesia, ab ecclesiæ antistitibus aliquando postulare, uti non iniquum fuerit, ita bellum illis ipsis, sanguinemque ef-fundendum, tum diripiendas urbes, populosque bonis suis exuendos, stupra etiam, et raptus, quæque alia comitari fere solent, demandare, plane impium: graviusque peccant ipsi, cum mandatum in se recipiunt, ac re-ceptum exsequuntur. nec exemplum istiusmodi in ecclesia antiqua ullum exstat* (I, 64).

had recently killed. In this battle many bishops (who fought with Nicolaus) were killed:

> Bishops fell, too; in registering their approval of such an intolerable murder and following the parricide, they were enveloped in a united punishment with him and shamefully expended in war lives which were responsible to the Church and peace, lives which should have been employed in the praiseworthy furtherance of each.[92]

Both Saxo and Pontanus (and Huitfeldt), mention the many fallen bishops,[93] but none of them with Meursius's condemnation. A fragment of Svaning, however, survives, which shows that he shared Meursius's view of the warrior bishops; almost all the bishops of the country died in defence of the unjust cause, Svaning states, and this was the first time that bishops in this country joined in a battle. Then he continues:

> And I think God then did this for the sake of the merits of King Canutus, by whose goodwill they had achieved the right to wield the sword (*jus gladii*); God saw to it that they defended, cruelly and with weapons in their hands, murder, false oath and other similar crimes committed by Magnus, his [Canutus Sanctus's] own nephew, crimes from which they ought to have kept him back and kept the people back by pious teachings; they broke the limits of their vocation, and since they took the opportunity to go to war from wicked beginnings, they were polluted by the same crimes as Magnus and had an unhappy death, recklessly wasting their life, which they owed to piety, on the battlefield.[94]

---

[92] *cecidere et episcopi: qui, patratum tam indigne parricidium approbantes, ac secuti parricidam, una cum eodem poena involuti debitas ecclesiæ, et paci, animas, ac cum laude in utraque occupandas, bello turpiter impenderunt* (I, 81).

[93] Saxo, XIII, Ch. 11,11; Pontanus 212; Huitfeldt, *Fra Kong Dan* [...], 205.

[94] I quote in Latin the whole of Svaning's outburst against the bishops who fought for Magnus at the battle of Fotevig: *Neque vero solus homicidij poenas dedit Magnus, sed Pontifices qvoqve regni prope omnes iniustam defendentes cædem, una cum Magno trucidati sunt, anno liberationis nostræ 1135. Ante hanc cladem nusqvam pontifices regni castra seqvutos fuisse aut bella gessisse legimus, qvi qvanto consensu Nicolao Regi adhæserint in causa hac iniqvissima, et qvanta pertinacia contra Ericum pugnaverint, testatur illorum miserabilis exitus, qvod simul omnes in hac pugna ceciderint. Ac existimo id tum dedisse Deum Canuti Regis meritis, cujus beneficio jus gladii adepti erant, ut homicidio, periurio, cæterisque id genus sceleribus Magni nepotis ipsius, a qvibus tum ipsum, tum populum, pia doctrina avocare, illorum fuisset, armis atrociter adeo patrocinati sint, qvi extra vocationem erumpentes, dum a malis initiis belligerandi sumunt occasionem, eodem scelere cum Magno polluti, infelicem sortiuntur vitæ exitum, et vitam, qvam pietati debebant, in acie temere profundunt.* (Ms. *Bartholiniana*, *Tome J, E don. var.* 1, fol., 346-47).

Svaning's somewhat intricate line of thought seems to be that since the bishops were morally to blame for defending Magnus's criminal cause and died a well-deserved death, Canutus's original fault in giving the bishops the *jus gladii*, the right to wield the sword, was diminished – and Svaning here suggests that God did this with Canutus's otherwise laudable rule in mind. Meursius has not attempted at such an *Ehrenrettung* of Canutus. But it is clear that Svaning and Meursius not only disapprove of the warrior-bishops but also both trace the root of the evil in Canutus Sanctus's elevation of the bishops, his giving them the *jus gladii*, an expression which they both use. Svaning's casual reference to this act of Canutus strongly suggests that he had already criticized it in his chapter on Canutus Sanctus, as Meursius does.

Meursius takes up this theme again, when Absalon becomes bishop at the beginning of the reign of Valdemarus I (1157-82), and again when Absalon's successor Anders launches an expedition to Estonia.[95] Again, Meursius disagrees blatantly with Saxo, who praises Absalon emphatically for his double defence of the faith as warrior and bishop (XIV, Ch. xxi, 3).

The Protestant nature of this censure becomes unmistakable, when Fridericus I in 1527 wants a synod to consider reforming the Danish Catholic Church:

> When they had all come together there, serious deliberations took place about changing the position of the Church, about reforming religion in accordance with the time of the apostles and leading it back to its old purity. In Denmark the bishops had neglected their proper task and involved themselves in worldly things, a habit which went back to the time of Canutus Sanctus, who had placed them among the magnates, thereby causing huge damage to the Church, and who had connected them with warfare, which is alien to the holy order.[96]

---

[95] On Absalon: *cujus clara, etiam in multis bellis, postea pro Valdemaro, ac Canuto, ejus filio, opera commemorabitur: maxime laudanda quidem; magis tamen, nisi, pridem Deo, et ecclesiæ ejus, consecratus, sagum postea vesti sacræ prætulisset: atque bella, quamvis justa, tamen plena sæpius impietatis, gerere duxisset prius, quam commisso sibi populo verbum Dei explicare, et exemplo quoque suo pietatem erudire* (I, 98).

On Anders: *quæ res uti reipublicæ quidem profuit, sic religioni nocuit. quippe illi quanto magis se negotiis civilibus, bellicisve, miscuere, tanto minus studiis religionis incumbentes, veluti profani facti, curam quoque ecclesiarum certe insuper habuerunt* (II, 12-13).

[96] *qui cum omnes convenissent, de mutando Ecclesiae statu, ac religione item ad Apostolorum tempora reformanda, et ad priscam puritatem reducenda serio deliberatur. Etenim in Dania sacrorum praesules, praeterhabito munere suo, rebus mundi se miscebant more dudum inveterato a Canuti sancti tempore, qui eos Ecclesiae maximo cum detrimento inter principes accensuerat, et ad bella, multum a sacrato ordine aliena, adplicaverat* (col. 801).

The worldly behaviour of the bishops is seen as Catholic abuse, a deviation from original religious purity, which is about to be restored by the Lutheran reformation. In the first occurrence of this theme (quoted above), where Meursius criticizes Canutus Sanctus for his elevation of the bishops among the worldly magnates, he also draws attention to the primitive Church, the *ecclesia antiqua,* the restitution of which was an important ingredient of Protestant discourse.

In view of Svaning's outburst against the bishops in his account of the battle of Fotevig, I think it likely that he also inspired Meursius to other attacks. In fact the same criticisms of medieval bishops were put forward by Anders Sørensen Vedel in the Preface to his translation of Saxo of 1575. Surveying Christianity in Denmark he describes how initial piety gave way to decline when "the bishops, forgetting their office and their vocation, grabbed the worldly sword and took on the colour of the Antichrist".[97] Vedel, like Meursius and Svaning, uses the sword as a symbol of worldly power, with which the bishops have nothing to do. Both Svaning and Vedel were imbued with Protestant historical thought. Both had studied in Wittenberg, Svaning with Melanchthon and Vedel with his son-in-law, Caspar Peucer, who also finished the reworking of *Carion's Chronicle* after the death of Melanchthon. In Peucer's part of the work we find outbursts against papal and episcopal worldliness, very much like those found in Svaning, Vedel and Meursius.[98]

If, then, we can here trace some influence from Svaning's *History of Denmark*, Meursius apparently made this point of view his own. In his notes to Pontanus's *History*, he criticizes Pontanus for his praise of Absalon's military achievements which had caused Pontanus (233) to compare him to the Roman emperors, who being also *pontifices maximi* ("chief priests"), likewise combined military and religious leadership. But Meursius objects:

> They were pagan pontiffs, not Christian. Warfare is not suitable to the latter, full of impiety as it is. For them it is more appropriate to take care

---

[97] *Biscoperne [...] forgætte deris rette Embede oc Kald. De grebe til det Verdslige Suerd, oc toge Antichristens Hofffarffue paa sig* (Vedel, Preface to trans. of Saxo, 7).

[98] Peucer e.g. deplores the depravity of the medieval church in these words: *Nil magis inimicum esse atque infestum nec perniciosum magis Ecclesiæ et Reipublicæ superba tyrannide Sacerdotum, cum discedentes a verbo Dei et suæ vocationis metis, transformant ministerium Euangelij in Monarchiam politicam, et falso ministerij prætextu abusuque rapiunt exercentque potestatem in quoscunque suo libitu, didicit orbis Christianus hisce annis quingentis post Henricorum bella, quibus vicit et regnauit tyrannis Pontificum* (Melanchthon 1580, 460).

of the Church, which has been entrusted to them by God. Saxo, whom Pontanus follows, says the same, but he commits the same error.[99]

Other Protestant Themes

In the description of the Lutheran Reformation itself in 1536-37, and the civil war which preceded it, Meursius follows Krag's thorough account, in which the Protestant outlook is also unmistakable. Both Krag and Meursius focus on Christianus, son of Fridericus I, in his fight for the Reformation and for royal power. They both portray him as the pious, prudent, mild, and generous champion of the good cause, concerned about the people and about "restoring the country" (*instaurare rempublicam*, as Meursius says, col. 887). His imprisonment of the Catholic bishops is seen as a prudent and necessary arrangement, supported by the *senatores* and well deserved by the bishops.[100]

Furthermore, Meursius twice refers to God's protection of Christianus III in his attempts to restore Denmark. In a passage also quoted above, Meursius ascribes Christianus's escape from the Swedish king, Gustavus I, to God's interference, a reflection not made by Krag:

> Nevertheless God, who holds all the purposes of evildoers in His hand, who wished Christianus's supreme virtue and probity to be respected as befits a king, and who had marked him out for the restoration and governing of Denmark, snatched him from danger and diverted Gustavus's mind from perpetrating a crime.[101]

The phrase *instaurare Daniam* no doubt includes Christianus's reformation of the Church. Later, when in 1536 Norway has finally been subdued by Christianus's men, Meursius concludes by emphasizing that these and other arrangements were favoured by God and were evidence of God's support of Christian:

---

[99] *Illi Pontifices ethnici erant, non Christiani; quos non decet militiam, impietatis plenam sequi: nam his magis convenit, commissam sibi a Deo Ecclesiam, curare. Idem dicit quoque Saxo, quem secutus est Pontanus, sed eundem errorem errat* ('Ioannis Meursi animadversiones in Historiam Danicam Ioannis Isacii Pontani [...]', Meursius, 1741-63, IX, col. 1143)).

[100] Meursius, col. 887, Krag 149.

[101] *Verum Deus, qui consilia malorum cuncta sua in manu habet, ac virtutem, et integritatem summam Christiani, rege dignam, honoratam cupiebat, Daniaeque instaurandae, ac regendae destinabat, hunc eripuit, et a scelere patrando animum Gustavi avertit* (col. 864).

> As all these affairs prospered according to Christianus's wishes through
> the kindness of the Deity, so God's manifest goodwill also showed itself
> in other places.[102]

Again Meursius himself added this reference to God in his adaption of
Krag.[103]

In the account of the organization of the new Church, however,
Protestant ideology is definitely more prominent in Krag's version (167-
72). This passage has been much abridged by Meursius (cols. 897-98), but
echoes of Krag's celebration of the Protestant cause are heard. Thus
Meursius makes it clear that in the ordination of the new superinten-
dents no rites were used which did not belong to the old Church.[104]

We saw above how Meursius in numerous cases censures, in religious
terms, the marital infidelity of the kings. It is a sin which is punished by
God. While not being an exclusively Protestant theme, it nevertheless
bears a Protestant stamp in Meursius's handling of it. Meursius's assertion in connection with the legendary king Gramus that God is both the
author and the upholder of marriage corresponds closely to Melanchthon's view put forward in several of his writings. "Both marriage
and the political order are things established by the everlasting God and
given approval by the voice of heaven", he declares in his influential *Loci
theologici*.[105] Melanchthon sees marriage as a divinely instituted foundation
of human society. Meursius's depiction of the wide-reaching consequences of Sueno III's marital infidelity even has a parallel in Melanchthon's warning in the *Loci theologici* that God punishes this sin with
public disaster (Melanchthon, though, does not deal with rulers specifically but with adultery in general, unpunished by the public authorities):

> Let them [the authorities] know that the strictest commands of God
> enjoin them to maintain the marriage laws and to punish adulteries and
> roving, impure lusts [...] for it is most sure that He is tremendously wrath

---

[102] *Haec ut cuncta Christiano ex sententia, Numinis benignitate, succedebant; ita aliunde quoque manifes-
tus Dei favor se ostendere* (col. 895).

[103] Krag simply writes: *Qvæ qvum Regi ad voluntatem affluerent, tum vero accessit ea insignis felicitas,
qvod* [...] (164).

[104] *In his autem ordinandis, nulli ritus sunt adhibiti, nisi Apostolis in Ecclesia primitiva usitati* (col. 898).

[105] *Et Coniugium et politicus ordo res sunt a Deo aeterno institutae et approbatae expresse voce divina* (col.
990). (The *Loci theologici* came out in several editions during Melanchthon's life. I have used
the edition of the *Corpus Reformatorum* XXI, cols. 601-1106, which is based on Melanchthon's
last edition of 1559).

with those uncontrolled lusts and the heedlessness of the governors who neither punish them nor eject the guilty from the community. And it is on account of these crimes that there range among the human race many public retributions, such as wars, devastations, the annihilation of men and women, and other mighty catastrophes, as the examples of Sodom and Canaan reveal.[106]

Meursius, too, in the summing up of the period when Denmark was ruled by Sueno III's sons, declares that God hates adultery and punishes it severely: "He abhors unlawful lusts, abhors adulteries, and takes revenge with the harshest severity", and public disaster followed: He made the illegitimate sons into kings "to shame the peoples whose sins He believes he must punish [...] In order to punish the nation for their sins and chastise Sueno's lust through his family, he ordains five kings in succession for Denmark, all bastards" [the Latin text is quoted in note 82 above].

As we saw, Meursius almost certainly inserted the reflection on divinely instituted marriage himself in the chapter on Gramus; whether he himself added the other censures on the marital infidelity of the kings, we cannot know, but it seems likely. In any case we can observe that he chose to emphasize this theme.

Leaving the sphere of kings we shall briefly consider Meursius's treatment of the episodes which in Saxo form part of the Danes' transition from heathendom to Christianity. Here, too, religious echoes from Svaning are probably to be detected.

A key juncture in the *Gesta Danorum* is Saxo's account of two expeditions to remote realms under the leadership of King Gormo and one Torchillus, who as a result of the travels recognizes the impotence of the heathen gods and vaguely perceives the existence of one God, *universitatis Deus* (VIII, Ch.s xiv-xv). The stories are filled with mythological lore, various strange beings trying in diverse ways to prevent the Danes from reaching their goal and so on. These fantastic elements had been completely suppressed by Krantz, Huitfeldt, and Pontanus. Krantz and Huit-

---

[106] *Sciant* [i.e. the authorities], *severissimis mandatis Dei praecipi, ut leges coniugiorum conservent et puniant adulteria, vagas et incestas libidines [...] quia certissimum est Deum horribiliter irasci et ipsis libidinum confusionibus et negligentiae gubernatorum, qui eas non puniunt, nec sontes e medio tollunt. Et propter haec scelera vagantur in genere humano multae poenae publicae, bella, vastationes, dissipationes hominum et aliae magnae calamitates, ut ostendunt exempla Sodomorum, Cananaeorum [...]* (Melanchthon: *Loci theologici* (*Corpus Reformatorum XXI*), col. 1072)

feldt both mention the fabulous nature of these anecdotes and refuse to go into further details.[107]

Meursius, too, objects to Saxo's account, expressing his wonder that he included these episodes. But Meursius also offers an explanation of how the stories should be understood: it was the devil himself, who, through the monsters Geruthus and Ugarthilocus (*Udgårdsloke*), deceived Torchillus and Gormo. In those heathen times the devil by means of such illusive tricks tried to strengthen his power over people:

> However, the stories that others relate about the dwelling and riches of Geruthus, the pagan god Ugarthilocus, and Gormo's journey thither, together with the mission of Torchillus, I shall here omit. Whoever wishes to know about these matters will find them in Saxo, whom I would prefer to marvel at rather than follow. Yet I must admit that such fables once found credence in the devil's kingdom when there was ignorance of the Christian faith. Certainly at one time the enemy of mankind, cheating the human race in its simplicity with illusions of this nature, was wont to mock the credulous and seek the strengthening of his realm with these tricks. Such an artifice was practised on Gormo and Torchillus by Geruthus and Ugarthilocus; but of these men Torchillus later became the first in all Denmark, as far as there is historical certainty, to embrace the Christian belief, as he did in Germany.[108]

This passage was apparently considerably different in the manuscript version which the anonymous nobleman saw. Approving of Meursius's omission of the diabolic delusions, he advised him to mention that the devil, to strengthen his power, used various kinds of magic on Gormo and Torchillus, further, to refer the curious reader to Saxo, and finally to mention that Torchillus was the first Dane to be Christianized:

---

[107] Huitfeldt and Pontanus both present Torchillus briefly as one who wants to convert his countrymen, and Huitfeldt adds that the rest is clouded in fables (*Fra Dan* [...], 28; Pontanus 38). Krantz refers the curious reader to Saxo, refusing to go into such unhistoric fables: *Ibi quæ ferantur esse comperta, fabulis deputanda, legant qui velint ex Saxone ista prosequente, ego ad historiam pertinere non arbitror. Somnia et monstra volitantia, quæ anilibus næniis propiora sunt, rerum gestarum ordini non putaui inserenda* (*Dania*, II, Ch. 24).

[108] *At quæ de Geruthi sede, opibusque, et Vgarthiloco idolo, tum Gormonis huc itinere, et Torchilli pariter legatione, alii tradunt, hic omittam. qui hæc scire tamen volet, apud Saxonem inveniet: quem mirari equidem, quam sequi, malim. quanquam fatear, in diaboli olim regno, fideique Christianæ ignorantia, talia fidem invenisse. Certe olim per ejusmodi præstigias generis humani hostis hominum simplicitatem circumveniens, et illudere credulis solet, et in illis regni sui confirmationem quærere. Hoc Gormoni, ac Torchillo, a Gerutho, et Vgarthiloco, factum: e quibus Torchillus tamen post id tempus, omnium Danorum primus, quantum ex Historia constat, fidem in Christum in Germania est amplexus* (I, 36).

> *On the dwelling of Geruthus* – our history has been managed in the best way, for the author leaves out those devil's tricks; nevertheless I should like him to put in an account of how Gormo and Torchillus were exposed to various magical shapes and illusions by the evil one and by those utter villains, Geruthus and Ugarthilocus, so that they might strengthen their kingdom and false beliefs in those regions. [Note:] the reader who is eager for information must go back to Saxo.

> *However, I omit the subject matter which is not far from fairy-tales*[109] – But the fact that afterwards Torchillus became the first Christian, of whom there is historical certainty, must plainly not be omitted.[110]

The last period of Meursius's passage, then, where he informs us that Torchillus became the first Dane to adopt Christianity, seems to have been inserted on the nobleman's suggestion. Apparently the same goes for the rest of the passage quoted except the beginning *At quæ* [...] *hic omittam*. Originally Meursius may just have written that he would not go into these episodes.

Among the surviving fragments of Svaning's *History of Denmark* is a long passage dealing with the heathen gods. Here, too, the cunning devil easily dominates the simple-minded human beings with his various tricks:

> None the less, amid such deep blindness of humankind and so many jests of Satan, by which people in this heathen zone of the North were mocked in different ways, he was worshipped in his own days instead of God.[111]

– Svaning then further elaborates this theme. Vgarthilocus (*Udgårdsloke*) also figures here, a horrible monster, apparently one of the shapes in which the devil appeared. Like Meursius, Svaning asks his reader to consult Saxo for more details on Vgarthilocus and the others. In view of

---

[109] These words (*Omitto vero illa, quae a fabulis propiora sunt*), which refer to Meursius's manuscript version, are not found in the printed edition.

[110] *De Geruthi sede* – *Optime Historiae nostrae consultum, quod diabolicas istas praestigias omittat auctor; vellem tamen, ita inseri hoc, variis, magicisque imaginibus, et elusionibus expositum Gormoni, et Torchillo a Cacodaemone, et sceleratissimis Gerutho, et Vgartiloco, quo regnum suum, superstitionesque hisce locis firmarent.* [Note:] *Ad Saxonem scire avens remittendus Lector.*

Omitto vero illa, quae a fabulis propiora sunt – *Plane vero non omittendum, quod Torchillus Christianus ex eo factus primus, de quo ex Historia constet* ('The anonymous nobleman [...]', Meursius, 1741-63, IX, col. 1125a).

[111] *Attamen in tanta hominum cæcitate, et in tot ludibrijs Sathanæ, quibus, varijs modis, in hac ora Boreali, in gentilitate, homines est ludificatus, pro Deo suis temporibus cultus est* (Stephanius 1645, 140-41).

these similarities, it is not unreasonable to assume that Meursius consulted Svaning's *History of Denmark* when reworking the passage on the nobleman's suggestion.

Svaning's chapter on the heathen gods is in its turn reminiscent of the view of world history presented in Melanchthon's *Carion's Chronicle*. The tyranny of the devil and the total darkness of those heathen times was a punishment for original sin, Svaning tells us. Along with the rest of the human race God has liberated the Danes from their ignorance of God and recalled them from error; and recently, in these last days of the world, God has renewed this call and liberated us from idolatry by the Lutheran Reformation. Danish heathendom is here given its place within universal history, outlined from original sin to the present "last days of the world". Meursius does not touch upon these grand perspectives. But his depiction of the diabolic tyranny before Christianity certainly seems to be reminiscent of Melanchthon's view of history.[112]

Later when summing up the reign of Regnerus (*Ragnar Lodbrog*), Meursius refers to another notion found in Svaning, the blindness of the heathens. When a heathen prince destroys sacred Christian objects, it is to be deplored rather than blamed; his restitution of the old gods was not caused by wickedness but by blindness; God will not, however, tolerate such contempt, not even by heathens, and He saw to Regnerus's punishment.[113] This reflection is not found in Saxo. Meursius may well be the author himself, or he may have been influenced by Svaning.[114]

The light-dark metaphor returns in Meursius's description of the beginning of the Reformation. Fridericus I (in 1527) wanted clergymen who "could teach the doctrine of the Gospel in an incorrupt form", and

---

[112] Another Danish Melanchthonian historian, Svaning's younger contemporary Erasmus Lætus (1526-82), also describes the devil as an active force cunningly exercising his power over human beings, though not in connection with heathendom but with medieval degeneration of Christian life in Denmark (Lætus, edd. Skovgaard-Petersen & Zeeberg 1992, 312sqq. Cf. Skovgaard-Petersen 1998c).

[113] *nam quod sacra Christiana, per Haraldum in regnum suum introducta, aboleverit, id in principe gentili deplorandum potius fuerit, quam culpandum. nam, qui Christum ignorabat, pie se putabat facere, si, quos credidisset deos, miseranda cæcitate, non malitia detestanda restitueret. verum Deus, qui nec a gentili quoquam, etsi maxime ignorante, minui honorem suum impune sinit, factam sibi contumeliam severissime vindicavit. Multo autem gravius peccatum Haraldi: qui cognitionem quanquam veri Dei nactus esset, plane tamen neque pietatem habuit in principio, nec constantiam in fine. ac videtur quoque Deus simulationem ejus castigare statuisse, cum dejectum a Regnero iterum voluit* (I, 43).

[114] This notion of heathen blindness is also found in Vedel's survey of Christianity in Denmark in the preface to his translation of Saxo (1575).

later "everybody rejoiced at having now gone from the darkness of errors into the clarity of light."[115]

A few more notes should be added on the Protestant outlook in Meursius's work in relation to Svaning and Pontanus. In Svaning's account of the three first Oldenburg kings, many digressions of a Protestant nature are found, which Meursius left out. But in one other respect we can definitely observe Meursius adopting a stricter Protestant line than his predecessor: he excludes all references to Catholic saints as indicators of dates. Both Svaning and Pontanus employ them frequently, but Meursius, in his reworking, consistently replaces them with month and day.

Pontanus does not, as already noted, share Meursius's interest in deducing general truths from single events. General rules are few in his work, religious and non-religious alike, and he only rarely ascribes a course of events to the will of God. In short, he does not, like Meursius, interpret Danish history in Christian terms.[116] Nevertheless, his own Protestant sympathies are clear. They come out in various digressions, e.g. attacks on the popes (533, 628-29), a celebration of Johan Huss (533), and a denunciation of the Jesuits (353). In particular the emphatic praise of Bernard of Clairvaux resembles the criticism of the worldly luxury of the medieval bishops, also found in Meursius. Pontanus here suggests that Eschillus's decision to give up his title of archbishop and settle down in Clairvaux was due to influence from Bernard himself; Bernard feared the increasing worldliness of the bishops would lead to superstition and neglect of *honesta studia* – a faint echo of Svaning's and Meursius's attacks on the politically ambitious medieval bishops.[117]

---

[115] [...] *Ecclesiae ministros aptos darent, qui doctrinam Evangelii incorruptam porro traderent* [...] *Laetis adeo universis, quod e tenebris errorum semel tamdem in lucis claritatem evasissent* (col. 801). The Catholic editor of Meursius's *Opera omnia*, Giovanni Lami, was not pleased with such passages. He here comments, "once and for all", that Meursius was a stranger to "sacred Roman doctrines", which is why he speaks against truth; these and other blasphemous ravings spring from a mind astray, he warns his readers in a note (cols. 801-2).

[116] But moral religious reflections are not totally absent. Towards the end of Christianus II's history (col. 1073) he has translated from Huitfeldt (277) the biblical reflection, so popular in Protestant writings, that God shifts power as a consequence of sin and crime (on this passage, see above p. 213).

[117] *Adeo ut haud dubio Eschillus divi Bernardi quoque, præter cetera, concionibus motus proposito suo perseverantius institerit. Nam illis temporibus videns pientissimus ille doctor episcoporum immoderatis reditibus extingui paulatim honesta studia, pietatem in superstitionem degenerare, ac velut in agro inculto vitiorum omnium suppullulare semina, acerbissimis invectivis seculi mores ac sacerdotum luxum perstrinxit. His inquam similibusque motum id temporis Eschillum se totum severiori vitæ, spretis mundi honoribus, addixisse verisimile habendum* (Pontanus 1631, 265).

Protestantism and Monarchy

Now let us return to Meursius's main theme, the Danish kings and their exercise of power. Here we shall consider it in the light of the Protestant character of the work. The sympathy with the kings at the expense of the Catholic bishops is not the only example in Meursius's *Historia Danica* of Protestant views supporting monarchical ideology. Another similarity between Melanchthon's *Carion's Chronicle* and Meursius's *History* is their focus on the ruler's person. The fates of rulers and monarchies are determined by God alone, who punishes sins and crimes and rewards virtue and piety. Melanchthon is particularly fond of this biblical formulation (*Daniel* 2,21): [*Deus*] *transfert regna atque constituit* ("God transfers kingdoms and establishes them").[118] This phrase and variants of it were used time and again in Protestant circles. Huitfeldt had it printed, in Danish, on the titlepage of the first volume of his *History of Denmark* (Christian III, 1595). It was a main theme of the coronation speech to Christian IV by Bishop Peder Vinstrup in 1596.[119] Meursius, too, uses it, e.g. when foreign magnates around 1340 tried to divide Denmark among them:

> ostendit illis Deus, unum se auferre regna, ac conferre (II, 77).

> (God showed them that He alone removes and bestows the power of rulers).[120]

Kings owe their power to God. Their special position in relation to other human beings is, as we know, a subject often touched upon in Meursius's *History*. Sometimes he makes it clear that they also adopt a peculiar position in relation to God, and in this respect, too, there are interesting similarities with Melanchthon's views.

The sword as a symbol of the divine origin of royal power is found in Meursius's account of Valdemarus I's (1157-82) reaction to threats from Archbishop Eschillus. In Saxo's and Pontanus's versions,[121] the king de-

---

[118] Ridé 1977, III, 243. Cf. e.g. Melanchthon's *Loci theologici*, col. 993.

[119] Vinstrup, *Coronation Speech*, ed. Olden-Jørgensen 1999 (previous edition by Jensen 1967). Cf. also Caspar Peucer's preface to Melanchthon's and his own version of *Carion's Chronicle*: *DEVS constituit et transfert Regna. Hoc dictum velut Epigraphe præfigatur voluminibus omnium historiarum, et nostras de imperiorum motibus cogitationes dirigat ac moderetur* (a3f) (Here quoted from the first edition, 1572).

[120] Other examples in Meursius: I, 32, 45, 63; II, 33, 76; III, 18.

[121] Saxo XIV, Ch. xxvi,8; Pontanus 238.

clares that Eschillus is now thirsting for his blood, as he had previously wanted that of Valdemarus's predecessors. Meursius added to this answer:

> sed a Deo gladium se accepisse, quo in ordinem rebellantes cogere possit: et hoc ipsum scire velle (I, 101).

> (but he had received the sword from God, so that he could bring rebels to order; and he wanted the archbishop to be aware of this).

The use of the sword as the symbol of royal power was not, of course, a Protestant invention. But there may be a Protestant ring to this reference to the god-given sword to be used against the proud archbishop. Both Luther and Melanchthon used the sword as a symbol of the worldly power of the *magistratus*, bestowed on him by God. In his commentary on St Paul's *Epistle to the Romans* Melanchthon defines the *magistratus* thus:

> Magistratus est minister Dei, nobis ad bonum, vindex ad defendendos recte facientes, et puniendos delinquentes gladio, id est, poenis corporalibus.[122]

> (The magistrate is a servant of God, there for our good, a protector for the defence of right-doers and for the chastisement of transgressors by the sword, that is, by capital punishment).

A poetic description of Frederik II's coronation in 1559 refers to the sword as the symbol of the king's power given by God to subdue the rebels, just as Meursius lets Valdemarus I do. The king receives the sword and the bishop explains:

> Sed Deus omnipotens [... / ...] magistratum custodes ordinis armat, / Vt sontes punire, bonos defendere possint (vv. 483-85);

> (But Almighty God arms the magistrates as guardians of order, so that they may punish the guilty and defend the good).

the king then raises the sword:

---

[122] *Corpus Reformatorum XV*, col. 1013; cf. Huschke 1968, 93. In St Paul's *Epistle to the Romans*, which formed an important authority for Melanchthon's doctrine of the *magistratus*, the sword also symbolizes worldly power: *Si autem malum feceris, time: non enim sine causa gladium portat. Dei enim minister est: vindex in iram ei, qui malum agit* (Ch. 13,4). Cf. also Melanchthon's words in the *Loci theologici: Ideo enim a Deo armatus est gladio*, about the magistrate who shall ensure that the laws are respected (*Corpus Reformatorum XXI*, col. 1011).

datum sibi vibrat lege mucronem, / Vt Gedeon, inuictus erit, sternetqve rebelles (vv. 488-89).[123]

(He brandishes the sword given to him by the law; like Gideon he will be unconquered and will overthrow rebels).

At the coronation of Christian IV in 1596, Peder Vinstrup declared that he was to hand over the sword to the king in God's place.[124]

Meursius's ideal king is a peace-loving, god-fearing, mild, and responsible ruler, concerned with the common good; numerous examples to that effect are quoted above. Although instances of an almost Machiavellian cynicism are also found, the Christian, moralizing view of government is definitely dominant.

This ideal had found an eloquent expression in Erasmus of Rotterdam's *The Education of a Christian Prince* (*Institutio principis Christiani*) of 1515, which in its turn influenced Melanchthon's doctrines of the Christian *magistratus*.[125] It came to dominate royal panegyrical discourse in Protestant Europe after the Reformation. In Denmark Erasmus Lætus's portraits of the Danish Queen Margrethe (1387-1412) in the *Margaretica* (1573) and of Frederik II (1559-88) in the *Res Danicæ* (1574) may be mentioned as examples of idealizations closely resembling the Erasmian prince.

Meursius's Valdemarus I (1157-82) also comes close to this ideal. He is well aware of the special position of kings in relation to God, and his only fault is, perhaps, that he is at times too mild. Once he forgave one of his men, Magnus, who had joined a conspiracy against him; but the king did take the opportunity to teach Magnus some basic Protestant doctrines; he warns him against joining the conspirators again, for even if the crime should not be discovered, God will take revenge, since all public executives (*magistratus*) have been instituted by God and are his vicars on earth; in other words, God will not tolerate any assault on Valdemarus:

> He warns him in earnest not to mingle with conspirators in future; unless he observes this, even if the offence remains hidden, God will

---

[123] Johs. Sascerides: *Historia de coronatione* [...] *Regis Friderici* (Kbh. 1559). Contemporary with Meursius's work is Jesper Brochmand's *Systema universæ theologiæ* of 1633, in which the sword is used to describe the king's power and duty to protect the worldly as well as the spiritual sphere (Fabricius 1920 (facs. 1971), 92).

[124] Peder Vinstrup, *Coronation Speech*, ed. Olden-Jørgensen 1999, 32.

[125] Bornkamm 1966, 291-315; Lausten 1987, 14-16.

avenge the crime, for by Him all public administrators are appointed and act as His deputies on earth.[126]

Meursius here lets Valdemarus refer to the concept of the *magistratus*, the public official, as instituted by God, which forms part of Melanchthon's teachings. It is the *magistratus* who upholds true knowledge of God, justice and peace, thus acting as God's vicar on earth, or as Melanchthon says in *Loci theologici*:

> God bestows on public officials an association with His name, with the intention that they should preserve heavenly institutions, that is to say, true knowledge of God, prayer to Him, justice and peace. How can they be called the vicegerents of God, if they neither recognize the Lord themselves nor make certain that He is recognized by others?[127]

Later, Meursius again refers to the concept of the king being God's vicar on earth. When the son of Christian II dies in 1532, Meursius explains that God did not want a son of the tyrant ever to return to his father's country; He punishes perfidy and cruelty particularly severely in princes, whom He wants to represent Him on earth.[128]

The exalted position of the king as the vicar of God here serves as an admonition to humility, not to arrogance. This special responsibility of the king as God's vicar is a main theme (of medieval inspiration) in Erasmus's above-mentioned *The Education of a Christian Prince*. There Erasmus at one point makes the following address to the prince:

> But when you who are a prince, and a Christian one, hear or read that you are God's picture, that you are God's vicar, take care not to let this make you arrogant; rather it should make you anxious to live up to your archetype [...] and that means, among other things, to try to work as hard as possible for the common good.[129]

---

[126] *serio monet ne deinceps conjuratis se misceret: nisi faciat, etiamsi crimen lateat, Deum, a quo magistratus universi constituti suam in terris vicem gerant, sceleris ultorem fore* (I, 113). In Pontanus's version, which Meursius otherwise follows in this episode, Valdemarus I simply forgives the conspirator because of their old friendship (and this is taken from Saxo, XIV, Ch. liv,35).

[127] *Impertit Deus magistratibus societatem sui nominis hanc ipsam ob caussam, ut res divinas, id est, veram Dei notitiam et invocationem, iustitiam et pacem tueantur. Quomodo dici possunt vicarii Dei, si Dominum nec agnoscant ipsi nec ab aliis agnosci curent?* (Melanchthon: *Loci theologici* (*Corpus Reformatorum* XXI), col. 1012).

[128] *Ac videtur certe Deus, qui perfidiam, et saevitiam, in principibus potissimum, quos in terris vicem gerere suam cupit, summopere detestatur, noluisse, ut e filiis tyranni unus saltem superesset, qui in patris aliquando solium reduceretur* (cols. 805-6).

[129] *At tu qui Christianus etiam es Princeps, cum audis aut legis te Dei simulacrum esse, te Dei vicarium*

The king's role as God's vicar is highlighted by the notion of monarchs being like "gods on earth", a phrase with biblical roots in Psalm 81/82. Melanchthon alludes to this psalm when arguing that the political order is divinely instituted.[130] Meursius takes up this theme twice, in both cases with the Erasmian emphasis on the special responsibility of the high office of the kings. Olaus Famelicus (*Oluf Hunger*, 1086-95) was one of the five sons of Sueno III (1047-74); having participated in the murder of his brother and predecessor, Canutus Sanctus (1080-86), he was deservedly punished inasmuch as his reign was a tragedy for himself as well as for the country. Meursius sums up:

> Although Olaus did not merit it because of his brother's murder, the Almighty nevertheless wished him to reign, so that He might chastise him more visibly and show that He felt the greatest possible detestation for such abominable outrages, even in the very persons He had set like gods on this earth.[131]

And Christianus II's sad fate demonstrates that God will not let rulers go free; he is particularly severe with them, since he wants them to be like gods on earth:

> He then demonstrated that He truly never fails to avenge perjuries, above all on those whom He has consented to raise to the highest rank of authority, so that they are like gods on this earth.[132]

Again, the emphasis on the king's quasi-divine status is here seen as a reason for humility rather than for pride.

The idea of the king as God's vicar also pervades Peder Vinstrup's coronation speech to Christian IV in 1596. Vinstrup's speech is thoroughly Melanchthonian. Here, too, the focus is on the responsibility of the king; because of his heavenly task, his exercise of just government by

---

esse, cave ne quid hinc intumescas animo: quin potius ea res te magis sollicitum reddat, ut respondeas arche typo tuo [...] *deinde ut quam maxime prodesse studeas omnibus* (Erasmus, ed. Christian 1968 (1st ed. 1515), 150-51).

[130] *Ego dixi, Dii estis, id est, divinum officium sustinentes* (Melanchthon: *Loci theologici (Corpus Reformatorum XXI)*, col. 994).

[131] *Eum Deus, quanquam indignum, propter interfectum fratrem, voluit regnare tamen, ut puniret evidentius: et ostenderet, se flagitia tam nefaria, etiam in illis ipsis, quos ceu deos in hac terra collocavit, quam gravissime detestari* (I, 67).

[132] *Tum ostendit, se perjuria semper quidem severissime vindicare; sed potissimum in iis, quos, ad summum dignitatis gradum evectos, in hac terra quasi deos esse voluit* (III, 61).

which peace is secured, God has, in the Scripture, given kings a share in his name, and called them gods and sons of the Exalted:

> Moreover, on account of this heavenly employment God gives them a share in His name; everywhere in the Scriptures He calls them gods and sons of the Most High, furnishing them and proclaiming them with a great many other majestic titles. By styling them 'gods' He makes known that they are His ministers, His living and breathing image on earth, for they act as His deputies and perform divine duties and functions.[133]

This and similar passages have given Vinstrup the reputation of inaugurating a new era of theocratic celebration of the Danish king, leading up to the introduction of absolutism in 1660. But as the recent editor of the speech argues, Vinstrup's speech is rather to be seen as conservatively Melanchthonian, and in fact similar words about kings being called gods in the Bible had already been spoken by Bishop Peder Palladius at the coronation of Christian IV's father, Frederik II in 1559.[134] Another example is found in the above-mentioned poetical description of the coronation of Frederik II in 1559, where the author, Johannes Sascerides, follows a line of thought very similar to Vinstrup in the passage quoted. Towards the end of the poem Sascerides describes the king, by means of various biblical and classical images, as the bestower of safety and peace on the people. One of his examples is this:

> Dij quoque psalmographo Reges a Rege vocantur, / Quando Dei præsint subiectæ nomine plebi (vv. 935-37).

> (Kings are also called gods by the psalm-composing king, since they govern the subject people in God's name).

This is simply a short version of Vinstrup's explanation of kings being referred to as gods in the Scripture. Royal panegyrics in Denmark after the Reformation were, as I said, very much coloured by Melanchthonian ideas of government, and references to the king as divine in such pane-

---

[133] *Propter hoc etiam munus coeleste, impertit ipsis Deus societatem sui nominis, dum eos in scriptura passim Deos et filios excelsi vocat, plurimisque aliis augustissimis titulis ornat et indigetat. Deorum namque appellatione, suos indicat esse ministros, qui imago ejus in terris viva et animata existentes, ipsius vices gerant, et officiis ac muneribus divinis fungantur* (Peder Vinstrup, *Coronation Speech*, 21). Note the verbal agreement with the passage from Melanchthon's *Loci theologici* quoted above.

[134] Olden-Jørgensen's preface to his edition of Vinstrup's speech (1999). Vinstrup's debt to Melanchthon is analyzed in more detail in Skovgaard-Petersen 1998c, 125-29.

gyrics were not unusual. These quotations are used in order to underline the king's duties: he has been given his high position in order to support the Church and his subjects – as both Melanchthon and his Danish followers stress.

These considerations have a bearing on our interpretation of Meursius's *History*. As we have seen, his celebration of the exalted position of kings is always uttered in connection with an emphasis on their duties. In this context it is important to note that Meursius (like Melanchthon) expresses his recognition of the right to rebel against a tyrant. At the end of Ericus X's (*Erik af Pommern*, 1412-39) history, Meursius considers whether his crimes were so serious that the Danes could have sent him into exile, if he had not left the country himself. Refusing to judge, he declares that there must be strong reasons if a king is to be exiled.[135] And in the case of the Danish arch-tyrant Christianus II, who was expelled, Meursius explicitly denies that the Danes had sufficient cause:

> Nor was that a good enough reason for expelling him from his realms. The Danes were distressed more by fear of him than by any danger from him; for he now felt keenly the punishment he had so cruelly received with Sweden, which, having shaken off its yoke, had now freed itself again; and this was able to keep him in check sufficiently to make him govern Denmark with a gentler hand in future.[136]

Meursius here clearly acknowledge the principle of the right of rebellion.[137]

In our evaluation of Meursius's view of royal power we must bear in mind that his work, like Pontanus's, enjoyed an official status. Meursius's *History* was controlled before publication both by the chancellor, Christen Friis, his secretary, Niels Eggebrecht, and the anonymous nobleman, engaged to perform this task by Friis (all three of them are known to have read the work in parts). The government wanted to be able to subscribe to what was said in the work. We have already seen that the chan-

---

[135] *ad reges solio dejiciendos, justum pondus omnia habere debeant* (II, 128). Meursius's long evaluation of the complicated figure of Ericus X has for the most part no close parallel in Pontanus's history (or for that matter in Huitfeldt or Krantz).

[136] *nec id causæ satis erat, quare regnis pelleretur. Et majore metu suo, quam periculo, angebantur; cum jam poenam Sueciæ tam crudeliter habita, quæ se denuo, jugo excusso, in libertatem vindicaverat, persentiret: idque eum, ad clementius gubernandam deinceps Daniam, satis coercere posset* (III, 86).

[137] In the case of Christianus II, Meursius's standpoint is the opposite of Huitfeldt's, who argues at length in favour of the justification of the banishment (*Christian II*, 272sqq).

Frederik II and his son, the future Christian IV, portrayed on one of the Kronborg tapestries. This was a series of 43 tapestries depicting the Danish kings from Dan onwards. Today fourteen are extant. The series was produced by Hans Knieper in the years 1581-85. The presence of the young prince, who in 1584 was hailed as successor to the throne, hints at the de facto hereditary status of the Danish monarchy. (The tapestries are also mentioned by Pontanus in his History of Denmark, p. 727). (The National Museum, Copenhagen).

cellor displayed a certain sensitivity on another political issue, viz. relations with Sweden; and the anonymous nobleman, in his comments on Meursius's work, discusses several other passages which have a bearing on contemporary politics. None of them apparently reacted against Meursius's Melanchthonian celebration of the kings, simply because, I would suggest, such phrases had belonged to the discourse about kingship since the Reformation.

Even so, there is reason to stress the strong royalism of Meursius's work. He focuses narrowly on the Danish kings, and has made the right exercise of royal power the recurrent theme of his work. As we shall see below, he even suggests, like Pontanus, that the Danish monarchy is quasi-hereditary. In these respects his work may well be said to point forward to absolutism. But what I think needs emphasizing is that these tendencies had made themselves felt ever since the Reformation.[138] As mentioned in connection with Pontanus, Erasmus Lætus had already spoken in favour of hereditary monarchy in 1577.

I have here drawn attention to the resemblances between Melanchthon's and Meursius's views on the role of the *magistratus*, the public officials. Perhaps it should be added that this agreement suits well with Meursius's ties to the Dutch Remonstrants, for whom Melanchthon was an important authority; he was (in the words of a modern scholar) a life-long theological hero of Hugo Grotius, one of the leading Remonstrants.[139] As to Luther, there may be a slight reservation in Meursius's reference to him in connection with the Reformation. Christianus III saw to it that the so-called *kirkeordinans* was approved by Luther – "whose name was in high esteem by that time".[140]

---

[138] In his essay on the concept of the *magistratus* in the sixteenth century, H. Bornkamm draws a line from Erasmus's and Melanchthon's notion (of medieval origin) of the Christian state with a Christian *magistratus* to the absolute monarchies of the seventeenth century (Bornkamm 1966, 291-315).

[139] Dam 1994, 38.

[140] *Ea vero postquam scripta, et probata a Theologis regni esset, Christiano oblata fuit; isque Wittenbergam mittit, ad Lutherum, cuius magnum, uti per id tempus nomen, ita quoque apud ipsum existimatio* (col. 898). Meursius's reservation is a little stronger than that of his source, Niels Krag's *Christianus III*: *Qvi* [i.e. Christianus III] *totus fere tum a Lutheri judicio dependens, eum Vitebergam miserat, ut Academiæ istius censuræ subjiceretur* (171).

8. The Hereditary Monarchy

By his many reflections on the monarch's position and his emphasis on God's rewards to virtuous and responsible kings, Meursius paints a picture of his ideal ruler, the powerful, pious, and morally upright king. The king's crucial role for the people's welfare is also highlighted. The legendary King Omundus is challenged to a duel by his Norwegian enemies. Saxo makes it clear that in those days it was very disgraceful for a king not to accept such a challenge, and Omundus at first refuses an offer from two of his men to fight the duel in his place, but finally agrees to leave the task to them (VIII, Ch. vii,7). In Meursius's version, the episode has been invested with another meaning. The king refuses the offer, "brave as he was" (*uti magno erat animo*) (I, 31), but the magnates find it unworthy to expose the king to this danger, since "in his safety rested the safety of the whole people" (*in salute cujus populi totius salus verteretur*) (I, 31). From Saxo's slight sarcasm on Omundus's behalf the episode has been turned into an example of the relationship between faithful subjects and their paternal monarch.[141]

After the death of Ericus IV in 1137, the royal family is almost extinct, and the magnates support different candidates to the throne. Christiernus, one of the magnates, sees to it that the young boy Valdemarus (later Valdemarus I, 1157-82) is designated as future king. In Saxo's version Christiernus argues that Valdemarus's father, having saved his country from many dangers, deserved to have his son on the Danish throne (XIV, Ch. ii, 1-2). Meursius develops this theme into abstract considerations on the benefits of one man's rule. Christiernus is here guided by a noble concern for the nation: if there is no king, internal strife and external attacks will be constant dangers:

> For this wisest of men reflected on the extent to which a kingdom, bereft of a king, was in constant danger; there was always the fear of civil tumults at home and enemy invasions from abroad.[142]

A similar strengthening of the monarchical theme is found when Valdemarus's little boy, Canutus (VI), is designated as his father's successor.

---

[141] Krantz gives another version and makes Omundus fight in spite of his men's protests (*Dania*, II, Ch. 13).

[142] *etenim vir prudentissimus apud animum reputabat, quanto regnum, rege orbatum, in discrimine versaretur; dum civiles domi motus, foris vero hostium irruptiones semper metuendæ essent* (I, 84b).

Saxo makes it clear that the magnates took the initiative out of concern for the country (XIV, Ch. xxxiii,1), and this is further elaborated in Meursius's account, where they explain their motives in a speech. They ask the king to accept the designation:

> if he were to succumb to mortality, there should be some individual on whom everyone's hopes might rest. Realms where there was no obvious successor were prone to many evils, a lesson which had been learnt during the former triumvirate; therefore he should grant their request, since it would be creditable to him and beneficial to the kingdom.[143]

Here the chaos of the recent triumvirate is contrasted with the peace and order which is characteristic of monarchy. – Like the former examples, the change is due either to Meursius himself or perhaps to Svaning.

The kings of the Oldenburg line, with the exception of Christianus II, embody this royal ideal. This is made clear right from the beginning of their rule, that is, in the introduction to the third part of Meursius's *History*. Like Pontanus at the very beginning of his *History*, Meursius introduces his Oldenburg section (written and published first) with allusions to a Roman historian. Having first echoed Tacitus's famous avowal at the beginning of the *Annals* that he will write "without anger and without partiality",[144] he shortly afterwards alludes to another Tacitean tag, when praising the Oldenburg kings for their ability to unite two apparently incompatible phenomena, freedom and monarchical rule:

> Qua re [i. e. the Danish wish that the kings of the Oldenburg line should be succeeded by their sons] factum, ut plus minus centum octoginta annis familia una Daniam omnem, et conjunctas regiones, sua in potestate habuerit; tanta quidem moderatione animi, ut res duas, vix conjungi posse creditas, libertatem, ac principatum, conjunxisse cum ingenti sua gloria visa fuerit (III, 1).

---

[143] *ut [...] si ipsi [ipso edd. 1638 & 1746] aliquid humanitus fieret, esset, in quo spes cunctorum acquiescerent. etenim obnoxia fere multis malis sine certo successore regna esse, atque id præterito triumviratu didicisse. itaque concederet, quod postularent; sibi honestum, regno utile* (I, 105). Cf. Saxo: *[...] ut haberent proceres, ad cuius nomen titulumque decurrerent, si quid de regis capite fortuna variaret* (XIV, xxxiii, 1).

[144] *HISTORIAM Daniæ scribere, consilium cepi; sine gratia, odioque: quorum causas, homo Batavus, nulli caritate obnoxius, aut offensa inimicus, procul habeo* (III, 1). Cf. Tacitus: *Inde consilium mihi pauca de Augusto et extrema tradere, mox Tiberii principatum et cetera, sine ira et studio, quorum causas procul habeo* (Tac. *Ann.* I, Ch. 1). On this allusion, see further Skovgaard-Petersen 1995. Meursius perhaps also had a contemporary "classic" in mind. Jacobus Thuanus (de Thou) introduces his *Historia sui temporis* (1604ff) with the same allusion to Tacitus: *Consilium mihi est res orbe toto gestas paullo ante excessum Francisci I repetitas ad hæc vsque tempora fide sincera procul ab odio et gratia posteris tradere.* In the Preface to the Oldenburg part (III), Meursius refers to Thuanus's praise of the French King Francis I.

(Thus it has come about that for around 180 years one family has ruled over the whole of Denmark and the regions attached to it – displaying such moderation, however, that, to its own immense glory, it has been observed to unite two things which had been regarded as hardly compatible, monarchy and liberty).

With similar words Tacitus, at the beginning of *Agricola*, describes the era which began with the emperors Nerva and Trajan:

> et quamquam primo statim beatissimi saeculi ortu Nerva Caesar res olim dissociabiles miscuerit, principatum ac libertatem [...] (Tac. *Agr.* Ch. 3).

> (from the first, from the very outset of this happy age, Nerva has united things long incompatible, empire and liberty [...]).

The overall effect of such an allusion is of course that Denmark is put on a par with Rome, just as Pontanus does with his Livian beginning. More particularly, Meursius here associates the period of the Oldenburg kings in Denmark with Tacitus's proclamation of a new, happy era under Nerva and Trajan. This is an appropriate allusion, since in both cases the author himself lives in that happy era, whose beginning he here dates. But Meursius does not, like Tacitus, say that freedom and one man's rule had been incompatible before (*olim dissociabiles*). Rather he claims that these two concepts had been *regarded* as incompatible, that is, instead of Tacitus's contrast between past and present government he introduces a contrast between theory and practice. What had so far (not in Denmark particularly, but generally) been regarded as hardly compatible, the Danish kings of the Oldenburg line have managed to unite. In this way he avoids associating the Danish rulers before the Oldenburg kings with Tacitus's gloomy picture of the early Roman principate.[145]

Apart from the connotations with imperial Rome at the height of its power, this introduction strikes the theme of hereditary monarchy. The Danish nobility, we are told, realized the eminent qualities of Christianus I and:

> regnum, quanquam electione semper solitum conferri, quasi hæreditarium facerent (III, 1).

> (they made the power which had hitherto always been conferred by election, almost hereditary).

---

[145] For a fuller discussion of Meursius's use of Tacitus in this introduction, see Skovgaard-Petersen 1995.

From the very outset, then, Meursius emphasizes the benefit of the quasi-hereditary monarchy of the Oldenburgs.

But the Danes' love of their kings had deeper roots. The election in 1439 of Christophorus III, who was related, though remotely, to both his immediate predecessors, Margareta and Ericus X (*Erik af Pommern*), had also proved that:

> the Danish magnates had such great affection for their kings that, when there was no male successor, even though they could have taken a foreigner, they preferred to elect a woman and the descendants of a woman rather than deviate from the family.[146]

One of the early kings, who had lost his only son, selected the neighbouring king Unguinus as his successor. Had his son lived, Meursius reflects, he would never have done this, nor would the magnates (*proceres*) have allowed it, since "they have always had a great love for the sons of the kings" (*qui amore semper summo regum filios sunt complexi*) (I, 26). In fact, Meursius carefully notes how son succeeds father from the very start, in many cases without support in Saxo. – In both Meursius's and Pontanus's works, then, we find suggestions of the hereditary nature of the Danish monarchy (cf. above, Chapter VI).

9. The Danish Empire

The Continued Rule over Neighbouring Countries in the Legendary Past
A peculiar feature of Meursius's description of early Danish history is his effort to describe Denmark and its relations to other countries in terms of organized politics. The chapter on the first king, Danus, is about his unification of the various provinces into one *regnum* ruled by one man, *unius sub imperio*, who is hailed as king, *rex creatur*. Saxo's corresponding chapter is basically about the same phenomenon, the unification of Denmark. But he, in fact, explicitly says that Dan did *not* bear the title of king (I, Ch. i,1). The alteration was not made by Meursius, though. Already in the late Middle Ages Danus was called king, e.g. in the *Annals of Ryd*, which was used and highly valued by Meursius. In the list of contents of Svaning's history, Danus is also counted as king, but Svaning may still

---

[146] *Tanta enim apud regni Daniæ proceres reverentia regum erat, uti, stirpe mascula deficiente, quanquam legere peregrinum quemvis possent, tamen foeminam maluerint, et ex foeminis prognatos, quam discedere a prosapia* (II, 129).

have noted that Danus was "without the name of king" (*regij nominis expers*), as Pontanus (12) does, echoing Saxo (and Krantz[147]). Meursius makes it clear that Denmark's history begins when the various provinces were united under one king.

Already from the beginning the kings were advised by a council, a *senatus*, if we are to believe Meursius. The son of Scioldus, the fourth king, was educated to take over the rule after his father, "at the bidding of the council" (*senatu sic jubente*, I, 2). The use of this term implies continuity: Denmark has always enjoyed a well-organized administration, and supreme power was already then shared between king and council. This body, the *senatus*, is itself invested with age-old legitimacy.[148]

Throughout the older period of history Denmark is described as a great power, having subjected many neighbouring countries to its rule. This general picture agrees with Saxo (and Krantz), but Meursius puts much more emphasis on the continuity of the neighbouring countries' dependency on Denmark. When a war between Denmark and a neighbouring country begins, it is typically described as a rebellion, a defection from Danish rule. Let me give some examples.

Both Saxo and Meursius relate how Hadingus, the eighth king of Denmark, conquered Sweden. Meursius sums up – with no parallel in Saxo – his achievement in these proud words: "when rule over the North had been restored to the Danish kingdom" (*restituta regno Daniæ boreali monarchia*, I, 6) – which not only emphasize the continuity of Danish monarchy but also its traditional position as the great power of Scandinavia.

Hadingus installed a deputy king, Hundingus, on the Swedish throne. Meursius here notes that the name of Hundingus gave rise to the saying that the Danes had installed a dog as king of Sweden (*Atque inde, cum Hundingus Canem, aut Caninum notet, dici coepit, canem Danos regem Suecis posuisse*, I, 5). As we saw in the chapter on Pontanus, Saxo himself has it that a Swede once made a dog ruler of Norway, a story which Johannes Magnus then adapted to his own purposes, making the Swedish king Attilus install a dog on the Danish throne (103-4). Meursius's remark, while dismissing the story as an anecdote, makes a further suggestion of Danish superiority. Interestingly, Meursius did not originally include the

---

[147] *Dania*, I, Ch. 2.

[148] Neither Krantz nor Pontanus refers to a senate in this connection (Krantz, *Dania*, I, Ch. 6; Pontanus, 13); Saxo never uses the term *senatus* about the king's councillors (I rely on F. Blatt's *Index verborum*, Kbh. 1957).

note. It was added at the suggestion of the nobleman who revised his manuscript.[149] Gram notes *ad loc.* that Meursius's version is due to Svaning, who made it up as an answer to Johannes Magnus,[150] and the nobleman's interference suggests that he, too, like Svaning, Lætus, Pontanus, Huitfeldt, and Stephanius regarded Magnus's story of the dog ruler as an unacceptable national insult.

Later, Hadingus's son and successor Frotho I is asked by his sister Suanthuita to recognize her marriage with the son of Hundingus, Regnerus, whom she has herself installed as king of Sweden while Frotho was in the East, and Frotho agrees. This is what Saxo tells us (II, Ch. ii, 10).[151] In Meursius's account, Frotho not only accepts the marriage but also makes him rule over Sweden as his deputy: "to be held henceforth with the title of viceroy, just as his father, Hunding, had received it from his own father, Hading" (*titulo clientis deinceps, sicut ab Hadingo patre pridem, Hundingus, eius pater, accepisset, possidendum*, I, 7). Meursius, in other words, highlights the fact that Sweden was still subject to the Danish king. Note again how he suggests a certain level of organized politics by using the term *titulo clientis*.

The theme of Danish supremacy is taken up again by Meursius shortly afterwards, when a war breaks out under Frotho I's grandson. In Saxo's account, the Swedish King Hotbrodus, confident after successful battles against eastern enemies, attacks Denmark. The king is the son of Suanthuita and Regnerus, whom Saxo simply presents as king of Sweden (II, Ch. iv, 3). Meursius, on the other hand, is at pains to emphasize the continuity of the Swedish dependency; and where Saxo's Hotbrodus is merely guided by a desire for conquests, in Meursius's version he finds the Danish supremacy intolerable:

> Meanwhile, when Regnerus departed this life, he bequeathed to his son Hotbrodus the Swedish kingdom, which he himself had gained through the favour of Frotho; he refused to acknowledge the name of viceroy under Roe and behaved as a king who was in no way subservient to Denmark, even going to the lengths of launching a hostile attack on it; Roe, striving to oppose him, was overcome in their third battle.[152]

---

[149] *monendum brevissime, e nomine hoc ortam fabulam de cane, quem Dani Regem Svecis dedisse dicuntur, Hundingus enim caninum, vel canem notat*, he says ('Anonymi auctoris in Historiam Danicam Io. Meursi priusquam publici iuris fieret observationes', col. 1121).

[150] Meursius 1741-63, IX, cols. 13-14.

[151] Krantz tells the story in two versions, *Dania*, I, Ch. 11, and *Svecia*, I, Ch. 17.

[152] *Inter ista, cum Regnerus, vita excedens, Sueciæ regnum, quod Frothonis beneficio obtinebat, filio Hotbro-*

Later, Amlethus's return from England is laconically noted by Saxo: "he sought his homeland with his wives" (*patriam cum coniugibus petit*, IV, Ch. i, 20; Krantz is similar, *Dania*, I, Ch. 19). But Meursius, taking the opportunity to sum up Amlethus's achievement, concludes that the Danish realm had been vastly extended:

> Once the whole of England had been recaptured, now enriched by two realms, Scotland and Britain, he shortly returned to Denmark [...] and so everybody was bathed in a double happiness, for their fatherland had long since been freed from Fengo's despotism, and now there was this huge expansion of the Danish empire.[153]

England is recaptured, that is, it had been conquered by Denmark before and was now regained (which must be a reference to Frotho I's victories in England). Denmark's supremacy is generally seen as the "normal" situation, the point of departure.

Later, Vermundus, son of Amlethus's successor, is threatened by the Swedish Atislus, of whom Saxo just says: "Atislus reigned in Sweden" (*regnabat apud Suetiam Athislus*, IV, Ch. iii,2; Krantz says *rex Suecia*, in *Dania*, I, Ch. 21). Meursius, on his side, makes it clear that Atislus was only *præfectus* of Sweden, that is, we are reminded that Sweden was subject to Danish rule and had no king of its own (I, 14). Of one of the following kings, Hugletus, we only learn from Saxo that he obtained a victory over two Swedish tyrants.[154] Again Meursius carefully reminds us that Denmark ruled over Sweden. In his version Hugletus managed to subdue the rebellious Swedes: "Indeed he soon subdued Sweden itself, which was undertaking a rebellion" (*Sueciamque adeo ipsam, nova inde molientem, mox represserit*, I, 15).

The next king, Frotho II, reconquered Norway which had defected long ago; Sweden again caused trouble, "but did not defect" (*sed in fide*

---

do traderet; atque is clientis nomen apud Roe profiteri detrectaret, ac pro rege, Daniæ nequaquam obnoxio, sese gereret, insuper lacesseret bello; ille obviam contendens, tertio prælio superatur (I, 8-9). Cf. Saxo: *Interea Regnero apud Suetiam defuncto, coniunx eius Suanhuita parvo post et ipsa* [...] *decedit* [...] *His filius Hothbrodus succedit, qui proferendi imperii studio Orienti bellum intulit* [...] *Nec Orientis victoria contentus Daniam petit eiusque regem Roe tribus proeliis provocatum occidit* (II, Ch. v,5). Krantz, *Svecia*, I, Ch. 18 is similar to Saxo, except for the fact that he underlines Hotbrodus's hereditary right to the Swedish throne.

[153] *redacta in potestatem tota Anglia, duplici jam regno auctus, Scotia, Britanniaque, mox in Daniam se recipit* [...] *adeoque universi duplici lætitia perfundebantur; cum ob patriam pridem a Fengone tyranno liberatam, tum ob ingens regni Danici incrementum* (I, 13).

[154] Saxo, IV, Ch. vii; cf. Krantz, *Dania*, I, Ch. 24.

tamen mansit, I, 15). These wars are seen as rebellions against Danish rule, while Saxo simply tells of the fight against the Norwegians and does not mention any Swedish conflict at all.[155] After Frotho's death, the Germans (*Saxones*) took advantage of his young son Dan's inexperience and demanded either war or taxes, says Saxo[156] – and Meursius again underlines Denmark's status as a great power by noting that the Germans had in fact paid taxes (*tributum*) to the Danes since the time of Uffo (I, 16); and when the Germans are defeated and forced to pay taxes to Denmark, he adds: "as they had been used to before" (*sicut ante consuevissent*, I, 16). The next king, Fridlevus Celer, unsuccesfully tried to subdue the English "who had once again rebelled" (I, 16), whereas Saxo simply makes him attack England.[157]

The conquest of Norway by Frotho III is also seen in a larger historical perspective: "which had been wrested away from Denmark by Frotho II's death, and was now once more drawn back into our power",[158] while Saxo just notes the victory over Norway (V, Ch. vi; cf. Krantz, *Norvagia*, I, Ch. 16); the same goes for England: "He then made for Britain, which had been subdued by his forebears, because he believed that it had defected once more" (*tum Britanniam, a majoribus subactam, defecisse item cogitans, eam petit*, I, 20), says Meursius. Saxo does not mention any rebellion but simply war, because England in his account was not "originally" part of Denmark (and the same is true of Krantz).[159]

The many victories over Norway, Russia, Ireland and other peoples by Sterchaterus (*Starkad*), one of Frotho IV's men and one of the great warriors of Saxo's legendary history, are described by Meursius as the results of rebellions against the Danish empire (I, 23-24). In this he may have been inspired by Saxo who mentions rebellion in two cases (VI, Ch. v, 14, 16). But already in the reign of the next king, Ingellus, a difference between Saxo and Meursius is evident. Sterchaterus, disgusted with Ingellus's depraved and luxurious manners, settled down at the court of the Swedish king, Saxo tells us (VI, Ch. vi,1). Meursius, in his heavily abbreviated account, left that out. But he does say that Sweden, along with the other dependencies, now began to defect as a result of Ingellus's

---

[155] Saxo, IV, Ch. viii; cf. Krantz, *Dania*, I, Ch. 25.

[156] Saxo, IV, Ch. ix; cf. Krantz, *Dania*, I, Ch. 26.

[157] Saxo, IV, Ch. x, 4; cf. Krantz, *Dania*, I, Ch. 27.

[158] *quod, a Dania avulsum, a Frothonis II. morte, denuo in potestatem nunc reductum* (I, 18).

[159] Saxo, V, Ch. xiv; cf. Krantz, *Dania* I, Ch. 31.

misrule (I, 24). This must be an inference from Saxo's mention of a Swedish king, since Saxo says nothing of any defection (nor does Krantz, *Dania*, I, Ch. 37); in fact, in this chapter he no longer refers to Sweden or any other nation as dependencies.

The last example to be mentioned here comes from the reign of Regnerus. He wages war against the Swedish king Frous, who, as Meursius carefully explains, had taken control in Sweden while the Danes were occupied with internal quarrels (I, 38). Saxo simply presents him as king of Sweden (IX, Ch. iv, 1). Later Meursius declares that, having successfully fought a new Swedish king, Regnerus again subjected the whole of Sweden to his rule (*Sueciamque universam denuo vectigalem facit*, I, 40), while Saxo again just says that Regnerus let his son rule over Sweden (and so does Krantz).[160]

In short, we can observe how in the early history Meursius stresses Denmark's continuous position as a great empire. Wars against neighbouring countries are more often than not described as suppressions of rebellions.

Saxo, like Meursius, also describes Danish power in imperial terms. In both works Denmark gradually loses its grandeur. The permanent loss of England in the reign of Magnus Bonus (1042-47) is solemnly noted by Saxo (X, Ch. xxi, 6), and this is repeated by Meursius (I, 58). Already earlier, after the reign of Regnerus, Meursius presents Swedish and Norwegian rulers simply as kings without reference to any former or "real" dependence on Denmark (I, 44).

Still, later kings also provided occasions for celebrating the great Danish empire; such were Canutus II Magnus (1018-35), (I, 55), Canutus Durus (1035-42), (I, 57), and Valdemarus I (1157-82), (I, 117). The reign of Valdemarus II (1202-41) saw impressive conquests, but was flawed by the king's matrimonial infidelity. Meursius sums up this ambiguity in his obituary:

> He was a prince who governed the most spacious domains, and who had made numerous conquests, for which he had been awarded the name Victorious; no previous Danish king might take precedence over him. He had reduced Estonia, Livonia, Kurland and Prussia, Pomerania, Mecklenburg, Holstein, Stormarn, Ditmarsken and Wagria, as well as the towns of Lübeck and Lauenburg. Yet he had sullied this vast renown by adultery and discovered that God took revenge in no uncertain manner.

---

[160] Saxo, IX, Ch. iv, 18; cf. Krantz, *Dania*, IV, Ch. 8.

For this immensely powerful king, together with his son, Valdemarus, now heir-designate, was captured through guile by the count of Schwerin, who could in no way be compared with him in strength, and, to his much greater shame, even in his own kingdom; moreover, after being abducted, he was kept in prison.[161]

The vast Danish empire was eventually diminished as a result of Christophorus II's disastrous rule (1320-32): "He had held on to none of his widespread dominions apart from Skanderborg in Jutland and Nyborg on Funen (*Nihil ex amplissimo regno retinuerat, præter Scanderburgum Cimbriæ, et Fioniæ Neoburgum*, II, 76). But still, on reaching Christianus II (1513-23) we learn that he was initially more powerful than any of his predecessors (III, 61).

Hand in hand with this imperial theme goes Meursius's emphasis on the kings' concern for peace. Frotho I's attack on Duna, a town on the Hellespont, was, as Saxo has it, motivated by a desire for new conquests. Not so in Meursius. Here Frotho goes to war because the king in Duna, who had been tributary to the Danish king since his defeat by Frotho's father, Hadingus, had not paid his taxes.[162] Later Saxo's Frotho, eager to extend his warlike fame to the West, fights a naval battle against the Frisian Witho and his men, who suffer total defeat (II, Ch. iii,1). Meursius, on the contrary, makes him act out of concern for Danish merchants. Vittho, in his version, threatens the Danish seamen, and Frotho, having defeated him, now sees to the proper organization of things there:

> When he had carried out these activities in Denmark, he set out to repress Vittho. This character was pursuing piracy across Greater Friesland and doing enormous damage to Danish merchants. To stop this nuisance and protect trade, he consequently led his troops against Vittho [...] In this way the victorious Frotho, having settled the situation there

---

[161] *Erat princeps, cum amplissimo dominatu, tum victoriis multiplicibus, propter quas Victoriosi cognomentum acquisiverat, nulli antea Daniæ regum postponendus. nam Esthoniam subjugaverat, et Livoniam, Curolandiam, ac Borussiam; insuper et Pomeraniam, ac Megapolin, cum Holsatia, Stormaria, et Dithmarsia, Vagriaque: etiam Lubecam urbem, et Louwenburgum. sed hanc tam ingentem gloriam adulterio offuscavit: cujus Deum satis manifestum ultorem est expertus. cum, rex longe potentissimus, filiusque Valdemarus, jam successor designatus, a Suerinensi comite, qui nequaquam viribus cum illo comparari poterat, suo etiam in regno, ad opprobrium multo majus, astu capitur; et abductus, sub custodia detinetur* (II, 24).

[162] *Rex illius, Handuanus, ab Hadingo pridem patre superatus, atque vectigalis factus, jam tributum recusabat: eaque bellandi causa* (I, 7). Cf. Saxo: *Urbe capta, Frotho spe Orientis imperium complexus Andwani moenibus admovetur* (II, Ch. i, 8).

according to his wishes, soon afterwards attacked Germany, which was refusing to pay the tribute formerly demanded by King Scioldus, and brought it to heel once again.[163]

– Frotho's attack on the Germans (*Saxones*), here motivated by their illegal refusal to pay their taxes to the Danish king, has no such explanation in Saxo, where again it seems to be sheer desire for conquest.

One of the important features of the praiseworthy legendary King Rolvo is his love of peace and disapproval of war. That is the first point of Meursius's final summing up of Rolvo's reign:

> Rolvo was a leader widely deserving the utmost praise, for he was adorned with a multitude of royal virtues. He shunned war and loved peace, knowing that this is how any realm prospers and the general safety of its citizens rests secure.[164]

– a point of view which Saxo nowhere connects with Rolvo, not even indirectly.

The history of Fridlevus Celer ends in Saxo rather abruptly with his successful encounters with Irish and English enemies (IV, Ch. x, 4). Evidently Meursius found it necessary to account for the rest of the reign. The lack of positive information is used to stress his concern for peace: "After that, cherishing his inclination for peace, he spent the remainder of his life calmly until he died, worn out by old age" (*Inde, amplexus pacis studium, in quiete reliquam ætatem agit: donec, senio confectus, diem obit*, I, 16).

The great conqueror king in Saxo's work, Frotho III, having brought a large number of countries under his rule, decides to include the northernmost areas as well, driven as he is by "human greed" (V, Ch. xi,2). Meursius, on the contrary, makes this war a result of some vague Norwegian rebellion: "After these accomplishments, since Norway was creating disturbances ..." (*Quæ cum ita gesta essent, et Norvagia turbas daret*, I, 19). The aggressive side of Frotho III has been removed. He is, in Meursius's version, first and foremost a responsible and energetic king.

Concern for peace is of course a virtue also praised in many of the later kings (such as Gormo Anglicus, Canutus III, Olaus, Christianus I,

---

[163] *Quæ in Dania cum gessisset, ad Vitthonem compescendum proficiscitur. is in Frisia majori cum piraticam exerceret, ingens Danis mercatoribus detrimentum afferebat. itaque, ut prohiberet, ac commercia vindicaret, copias in eum ducit [...] atque ita victor Frotho, rebus illic pro arbitrio constitutis, mox Saxoniam, quæ tributum, a Scioldo olim rege imperatum, recusabat, et aggreditur, et reducit ad obsequium* (I, 8).

[164] *Erat Roluo princeps longe laudatissimus; quem virtutes, rege dignæ, plurimæ condecorabant. belli fugiens, pacem amabat: qua florere regna quævis, et constare subditorum publicam salutem, sciret* (I, 10).

Johannes, Fridericus I). What is particularly interesting in the early legendary kings is the change of motives compared to those in Saxo. Their
warlike desire for conquests in the *Gesta Danorum* has in Meursius's history been replaced by concern for peace and people.

Svaning and the Danish Empire in the Legendary Past
The tendency in the early part to describe Denmark as a great empire ruling over other nations ultimately goes back to Saxo. But Meursius's presentation of this theme, as sketched above, is, in my view, likely to have
been strongly influenced by Svaning's *History of Denmark*. In the history of
Haraldus III, Meursius reminds us that England had belonged to Denmark since the time of Frotho III (I, 29), and Hans Gram here notes that
he had taken this remark from Svaning. Perhaps, then, many of Meursius's
notes on the continuity of Danish dominance go back to Svaning.

Sweden is constantly subdued. In view of Svaning's rather aggressive
emphasis on the Danish supremacy in the Union of Kalmar, which mirrors the hostile atmosphere at the time of writing, c. 1560-70, it is very
likely that Svaning would have described the relationship, in the earliest
history also, as one of Swedish inferiority. Of course we cannot rule out
that Svaning wrote his legendary part in the 1570s (he was presumably
working on his *History of Denmark* until he was forced to submit the manuscript in 1579), and that he toned down the anti-Swedish polemic as a
consequence of the prohibition against defamatory writings laid down in
the peace treaty of 1570. Even so, there are two arguments speaking in
favour of his having constructed a Danish legendary empire under which
Sweden was subdued time and again. One is Christen Friis's advice to
Meursius in 1629, after his having read a draft of the latter's Oldenburg
section, that the Swedes must be treated less aggressively. In this light it is
highly unlikely that Meursius later, when writing the early history, would
have added such consistently "imperialistic" touches. It was one thing to
take them over from Svaning; it would be quite another to invent them
on his own initiative.

But my primary reason for attributing the imperial theme to Svaning's
History of Denmark is the presence of the same theme, in reverse, in the
History of the Swedish Kings of Johannes Magnus (1554). Svaning wrote his
work in part as an answer to Magnus's denigrating picture of the Danes
as sly and unreliable and in every respect inferior to their Swedish neighbours. In the account of the legendary past given by Magnus we find
Sweden described as an empire ruling over several neighbouring coun-

tries; the normal situation is that Denmark is a Swedish dependency, except when the Danes from time to time succeed in temporarily liberating themselves. It is to my mind very likely that Svaning constructed his legendary past as a deliberate corrective to Magnus's; he may have been less insistent on Swedish unreliability than he is in his preserved accounts of Christianus I (1448-81) and Johannes (1481-1513), but he does seem to have adopted Magnus's idea of stressing the continuity of the neighbour's subordination.

Magnus, on his part, reacted against the celebration of the Danish past in Saxo's *Gesta Danorum*, and his legendary past constitutes, as pointed out by Kurt Johannesson, an inversion of Saxo's description of the relative strength of Denmark and Sweden. Johannesson exemplifies this inversion of Saxo in his survey of Magnus's treatment of the Danes.[165] But Magnus was much more consistent in his emphasis on the neighbour's moral inferiority and political subordination. Krantz's *Regnorum aquilonarium, Daniæ, Sueciæ, Norvagiæ chronica* (1548) should probably be seen as an important inspiration to Magnus, inasmuch as he, too, in the book on Sweden, constructed a legendary Swedish past on the basis of the scattered information in Saxo. Furthermore Krantz, writing as he did around 1500 when Denmark and Sweden were in constant conflict, seems to have paved the way for Magnus's (and, presumably, Svaning's) focus on the Danish-Swedish legendary rivalry: "This old contest between the kingdoms has lasted right up to our time, so that the inhabitants on both sides claim that they are nobler than the others. But by that time Sweden once again obeyed the Danish crown", he says after the Danish King Helgo's victory over the Swedish king Hotbrodus.[166]

But let us return to Meursius and his indirect reaction against Magnus via Svaning. I shall not attempt here to make an exhaustive comparison of the legendary parts of Magnus's and Meursius's *Histories*, but I shall illustrate the point with some examples.

Hotbrodus is, as we saw above, known from Saxo as a Swedish king who wanted to extend his rule eastwards and conducted many wars; not content with that, he looked for new victories and attacked Denmark.

---

[165] Kurt Johannesson 1982, 138-63.

[166] *Quæ vetus regnorum contentio vsque ad nos perdurauit, vt regnicolæ altrinsecus inuicem se nobiliores esse contendant. Sed tunc Suecia iterum Danicæ coronæ paruit* (*Svecia*, I, Ch. 18). (Magnus's view of Swedish-Danish relations in the earliest past was retained in Laurentius Paulinus's *Historiæ Arctoæ libri III* of 1636).

The Danish King Roe dies after three battles against the Swede, but his brother Helgo takes revenge and kills Hotbrodus. This is told very briefly by Saxo (II, Ch. v, 5), but Magnus makes a number of supplements and adjustments.

As Magnus tells the story, Hotbrodus is the twenty-fifth king of Sweden, a great ruler who conquers a number of neighbouring countries and establishes a large Swedish empire: "He extended his empire vastly and imposed laws and tributes on the nations he had subdued" (*imperiumque suum longe lateque proferendo, leges tributaque devictis a se nationibus praescripsit*, 98). Later he attacks Denmark out of a just desire to take revenge for earlier injuries. Three times in a row the Danish King Roe suffers defeat and is finally killed. Hotbrodus now brings Denmark under his rule:

> Advancing to the interior of Denmark the vanquisher Hotbrodus occupied the whole realm, set garrisons in the strongholds and laid laws and taxes on the defeated people. Following these exploits he returned to Sweden in no less triumph from the subjugation of Denmark than on another occasion after his conquest of Eastern lands; everyone applauded their prosperous fortunes, since through his bravery and diligence the Swedish empire had been enlarged, so that it now extended from the River Don in the East to the Elbe or Weser in the West.[167]

Meursius, on the contrary, carefully emphasizes that Hotbrodus was a Danish vassal king – for which he had no direct support in Saxo.[168] Hotbrodus here attacks Denmark because he does not want to recognize his subordinate status:

> he refused to acknowledge the name of viceroy under Roe and behaved as a king who was in no way subservient to Denmark, even going to the length of launching a hostile attack on it,[169]

---

[167] *Progressus ad interiora regni Daniae victor Hothebrotus, totum regnum occupat, arcibus praesidia imponit, leges et tributa victis praescribit. His gestis non minore triumpho ex subacta Dania, quam alias ex devictis Orientis regionibus in Suetiam est reversus, cunctis fausta et felicia acclamantibus, quod ejus fortitudine et industria Suetiae imperium a flumine Tanai versus Orientem, ad Albim fluvium, vel Visurgum in Occidentem extensum esset, et ampliatum* (Magnus, 99).

[168] Indirectly, Hotbrodus's dependent status may be deduced from Saxo, according to whom Hotbrodus's father, Regnerus, was installed on the Swedish throne by the Danish king (cf. above). But the crucial difference is that Meursius is explicit about Hotbrodus's inferior position, whereas Saxo simply refers to him as Regner's successor (II, Ch. v, 5). — Krantz merely refers to Roe's adversary as *Sueciae rex* (*Dania*, I, Ch. 14).

[169] *atque is clientis nomen apud Roe profiteri detrectaret, ac pro rege, Daniae nequaquam obnoxio, sese gereret, insuper lacesseret bello* (I, 8-9).

– and Meursius, of course, follows Saxo (and Krantz) in simply noting the Danish king Roe's death in battle without any hint of consequent subordination.

Of Hotbrodus's son Atislus (or Attilus, as Magnus calls him) we learn from Magnus that he, as the twenty-sixth king of Sweden, conducted his first war against the Danes when they rebelled ("his first and foremost employment in war was occasioned by the rebellion of the Danes"[170]) – whereas Meursius makes clear that Atislus ruled Sweden at the behest of the Danish King Helgo, who therefore exacted tribute from him: "Then he set Atislus, Hotbrodus's son, on the throne and demanded the tribute which he had earlier refused to pay" (*tum Atislum, Hotbrodi filium, imperato, quod is pridem recusaverat, tributo, regno imponit*, I, 9), and again a little later: "In order to free himself from the burden of tribute, Atislus, who possessed Sweden through Helgo's favour [...]" (*Atislus, Sueciam Helgonis beneficio tenens, ut tributi onere se liberaret* [...], I, 9). In this case, though, Meursius had support in Saxo and Krantz, who here refer, briefly, to Sweden as a Danish dependency.[171]

After various battles, in Magnus's version, the Danes realized their inferior strength and begged Atislus to place his brother Hotherus, known for his mild character, on the Danish throne (107); at Atislus's death, Hotherus then became king of Sweden, and for some time the Danes now accepted their subordinate status and paid their tributes: "Moreover during those same years the Danes, paying taxes with bowed heads, were subservient to the kingdom of Sweden" (*In eisdem etiam annis Dani submissis capitibus, et tributis, regno Suetiæ paruerunt*, 111).[172] Saxo, too, has it that Hotherus (who followed Helgo's son Rolvo) was brother to the Swedish king, Atislus; and he is referred to as king of both Denmark and Sweden,[173] but no word is spoken of Danish inferiority.

Nor, of course, does Meursius suggest any such inferiority. In fact, he even conceals the circumstance that Hotherus was the brother of the Swedish king. Instead Meursius presents him as great-grandchild of the old Danish king Hadingus through his daughter Suanthuita – which also

---

[170] *Huic primum et præcipuum belli negocium ex rebellantibus Danis procreatum est* (Magnus, 100).

[171] Saxo: *cum Danorum imperio Suetia subiaceret* (II, Ch. vi, 1); Krantz: *Atislus, Suecia regis filius, iam Danis subiectus* (*Dania*, I, Ch. 16); *Quumque Suecia, vt diximus, Danis pareret* (*Svecia*, I, Ch. 19).

[172] In fact, Krantz, too, had made Hotherus conquer Denmark: *Ita variante fortuna vices, commutauerat alterna sors regnandi: vt quomodo antea Suecia Danis sub tributo seruierat, nunc vicissim illa Daniæ imperaret* (*Svecia*, I, Ch. 21).

[173] Saxo, III, Ch. i, closely followed by Krantz, *Dania*, I, Ch. 17.

fits with his being brother of Atislus, but Meursius avoids bringing out the relationship. This manœuvre makes particular sense against the background of Magnus's exploitation of their being brothers.

Vermundus, a later Danish king, was threatened by Atislus of Sweden (the second of that name); we saw above that whereas Saxo simply says that he ruled the Swedes (IV, ch. iii,2), Meursius puts emphasis on his being a *præfectus*, dependent on the Danish king (I, 14). Turning to Magnus, however, we learn first that Atislus, son of the former Swedish king, Rodericus, was elected unanimously by his subjects.[174] Atislus realizes that the Danish Vermundus has unjustly taken power in Denmark disregardful of the fact that Atislus was Rodericus's legitimate successor (Rodericus, the former Swedish king, having, in Magnus's version also ruled over Denmark): he understands that "Vermundus was occupying the Danish throne by an unjust claim, while he himself, Rodericus's rightful successor, had been debarred from it" (*Vermundum injusto titulo Daniæ regnum occupare, secluso se legitimo Roderici successore*, 116). Of course he manages to defeat Vermundus in battle and now allows Vermundus to "administer" Denmark in subordination to the Swedes: "So, once victory over the Danes had been achieved, Vermundus was allowed to manage Denmark as a tributary nation" (*Itaque parta de Danis victoria, permissus est Veremundus Daniæ regnum sub tributo administrare*, 117). Shortly afterwards, still according to Magnus, the Danish King Hugletus takes advantage of internal Swedish discord, and lets the Danes attack Sweden, so that they finally have an occasion to gain their liberty. Meursius, on the contrary, makes Hugletus suppress a Swedish rebellion (*Sveciamque adeo ipsam, nova inde molientem, mox represserit*, I, 15) – and Saxo just says in one line that Hugletus defeated two Swedes.[175]

Thus we can observe how Magnus and Meursius, on the basis of Saxo, each construct a picture of the continued supremacy of Sweden and Denmark respectively. I think that Meursius's history here provides us with a clue to Svaning's handling of the legendary past, which seems to have been marked by the hostile atmostphere at the time of the Seven Years War (1563-70) and the appearance in print of Magnus's *History of the Swedish Kings*.

---

[174] He may have been inspired by Krantz: *quem proceres Sueciæ regem creauere* (*Svecia*, I, Ch. 22).

[175] Saxo, IV, Ch. vii; Krantz, *Dania*, I, Ch. 24.

10. Sweden and the Union of Kalmar

The history of the three first Oldenburg kings, Christianus I, Johannes, and Christianus II, which constitutes Part III of Meursius's work, is very much about the Swedes' attempts to liberate themselves from the Danish dominance of the Kalmar Union. Time and again the Swedes try to fool the Danish kings, who are prone to think too well of their Swedish neighbours, and are always bent on peace. These basic characteristics are found in both Svaning's and Meursius's versions, but the aggressively anti-Swedish tone of the former has been considerably toned down by his successor.

Svaning's *History of Denmark*, as far as we know it, is highly coloured by the strained tensions between Sweden and Denmark around 1560. His history of Johannes was, as we have seen, published together with his answer to some of the accusations put forward against Denmark by Johannes Magnus in his *History of Sweden* (1554). Meursius by various means removed the pamphlet-like aggressiveness. For one thing he dropped Svaning's many attacks on Johannes Magnus and other "recent Swedish historians."[176] Further, he either abbreviated or simply left out a number of passages in which Svaning launches attacks on Swedish unreliability and lack of respect for the *solenne foedus*, that is, the Union of Kalmar. When the Swedes in 1469 – not for the first time – failed to appear at the appointed peace negotiations with the Danes, Svaning finds occasion to burst into long accusations, placing the problem of the Swedes' reluctance to join the union in a wider perspective. History has later shown how God inflicted punishment on them, Svaning declares, with a hint at the massacre of Stockholm in 1520, and he also reminds his readers of the prophecies of the holy Birgitta who had foreseen future disasters for the Swedes.[177] This outburst was entirely left out by Meursius.[178]

It is not that Meursius leaves his readers in any doubt as to right and wrong. But he does not use quite as many words as Svaning to stress the

---

[176] Some examples from Svaning's history of Johannes (1481-1513), the *Chronicon Ioannis* (1561): Q1r, R4r, V1r-2r, Ee2r, Ll1v-2r, Pp4r.

[177] Svaning, *History of Christianus I*, 56v-60r (*Gl. Kgl. S.,* 2444, 4to).

[178] Other examples of Svaning's attacks on the Swedes, which have been softened or left out by Meursius: In the history of Christianus I: 44r, 63r-64v, 90r-v (*Gl. Kgl. S.,* 2444, 4to). In the *Chronicon Ioannis* (1561): O3r, P3r, P4v, Q1v-3r, R3v-4r, S4v, T2v-3r, Cc3v, Ee3v, Ff1r, Ff2v-3r, Ll2r-v.

treacherous nature of the Swedish rebel leaders. An example: in 1509 they wanted to renew peace-talks, but Johannes had learnt not to trust them. Svaning says:

> Rex toties a Suecis delusus, etsi parum lubricæ ac fluxæ fidei genti tribuere visus sit [...] (Kk4r).

> (The king had so often been cheated by the Swedes, and although he seemed to be giving rather little to this people, whose trustworthiness was lax and uncertain [...])

Meursius confines himself to the first part:

> Ac Ioannes, quanquam, toties rebellantibus, fidem habendam non censeret [...] (III, 50).

> (Now Johannes, although he did not believe he should put trust in those who were rebelling so frequently [...])

Similarly, Meursius almost laconically notes another rupture of a peace agreement made in 1512:

> quam [the peace], perfidia usitata, paullo post defuncto rege, denuo quoque violarunt [the Swedes] (III, 57).

> ([...] the peace which the Swedes with their usual dishonesty again violated shortly after the king's death).

This is his paraphrase of Svaning's indignant accusations of Swedish untrustworthiness (*Chronicon Ioannis*, 1561, Pp4r-v), in which Svaning also alludes to misrepresentations in Swedish historiography:

> Sed hæc omnia callide occultant Sueci, harum rerum nullam in descriptione rerum Sueticarum omnino mentionem facientes [...]

> (But all these matters are cunningly concealed by the Swedes, who make absolutely no reference to such events in their account of Swedish affairs [...])

– i.e. the Swedes will not recognize that they have still not paid a debt which they acknowledged in a treaty in 1512.

Sometimes Meursius toned down the aggressiveness of Svaning simply by substituting one word for another. Christianus I (1448-81) was induced by some Swedes to believe that the Swedish archbishop had conspired against him. These Swedish deceivers are described by Svaning as "spiteful", "sly", and "villainous" (*malevoli, astuti* and *scelerati*).[179] Meursius (III, 13) replaces the two first with "hostile" (*infesti*) and omits *scelerati*. He thereby avoids describing the Swedes as innately bad, "hostile" having more of an explanatory effect than the simple "wicked" and "astute". In the same vein he does not, like Svaning, refer to the Danes as *nostri*.

Carolus Canuti (*Karl Knuttsøn*), leader of the Swedish rebellion against Christianus I, is portrayed as deceitful and power-seeking, but Meursius gives an impression of balanced judgement by his recognition of one laudable deed on Carolus's part:

> He departed from the realm of his own accord; certainly he should be praised for this one act in the final stage of his life, for though his ambition was strong, he also made everyone understand that he could despise sovereignty.[180]

– an observation made neither by Svaning nor by Krantz.

Meursius's softened tone is probably, at least in part, the result of the chancellor's interference. As mentioned earlier Friis had read a previous draft of Meursius's *History* in 1629 and reacted against its anti-Swedish attitude. Presumably Meursius in this first version had conformed more closely with Svaning than in the next version, which was the one eventually published.

11. Christianus II, the Tyrant King

To demonstrate that the protagonists, pious and morally upright as they are, have God on their side, is a common historiographical strategy. Trouble arises when some of these protagonists in the earlier historiographical tradition are depicted as notoriously immoral individuals. Meursius faced this problem when dealing with Christianus II (1513-23).

Christianus II enjoyed a singularly bad reputation both in Swedish and Danish tradition, as a tyrant, comparable, in Svaning's opinion, to classical monsters like Nero and Caligula. His worst crime was the Stockholm massacre of 1520, where more than seventy Swedish noblemen

---

[179] This part of Svaning's *Christianus I* is preserved in the Ms., *Bartholiniana, Tome J, E don. var. 1, fol.*, 364sq.

[180] *sponte sua regno cedit: vel hoc uno in postremo vitæ actu celebrandus, quod, ambitionis potens, etiam contemnere sese regnum posse omnibus testatum faceret* (III, 14).

were executed. But many other crimes were attributed to him. Svaning has practically nothing to say in his defence. His treatment bears the marks of an already established tradition of superhuman evil, such as ominous portents of the king's nature already when he was a baby. Only towards the end of his life (still according to Svaning), when he had been imprisoned for many years, did the death of his beloved son make Christianus II realize the extent of his own crimes and passionately beg God for mercy.

Meursius does not try to conceal Christianus's tyrannical behaviour, and like Svaning, on whose account he based his own, he sees the king's fate as an illustration of God's punishment of arrogance and pride. Already in the introduction to Part III on the Oldenburg kings he makes clear that Christianus II formed an exception to the excellence of these rulers. But in various ways he softened the verdict. Christianus II in his description is not totally evil.

He changed the beginning. Where Svaning tells of all the bad omens of Christianus's future tyranny from his early infancy, Meursius instead presents the great size of his realm. We are informed that the unreliability of the Swedes and the Wendish towns prompted him to forge new foreign alliances, primarily through his marriage to the sister of the future Charles V. This is taken from the second chapter of Svaning, but in this introductory position it serves to underline the impressive power of Christianus II. Meursius concludes this theme on a majestic scale:

> And so, by a truly rare kindness from the Supreme God, he achieved a power which surpassed that of every single Danish king who had ever preceded him.[181]

To be sure, this all builds up to forming a contrast with his later crime and tragic fate, demonstrating the general truth that God sees to it that kings are punished particularly severely for their crimes, since they are like gods on earth. Nevertheless, Meursius focuses on the power and success of the Danish monarchy at the beginning of Christianus's reign instead of drawing the portrait of an archtyrant by tracing the causes of depravity in his childhood, as Svaning does.

One of Christianus's frightening acts was the execution of Torbernus Oxius, whom he suspected of having had an affair with his own mistress,

---

[181] *Atque ita, raro sane summi Dei beneficio, illud consecutus fuit, ut potentia reges Daniæ uniuersos, quotquot unquam ante ipsum exstitissent, superaret* (III, 61).

the recently deceased Columbula (*Dyveke*). The suspicion was loosely founded on accusations made by a secretary, whose execution the king had also brought about. Oxius's death seemed to most people to be quite out of proportion to the alleged crime. It seemed to be a cruel act of tyranny, unpredictable and much too harsh. So the story went, which Meursius found in Svaning. But Meursius adds his own interesting judgement. Oxius was executed for something he had not done, but he was in fact guilty in prompting the deaths of Columbula and, indirectly, of the secretary. The king was unaware of that – he was the unknowing instrument God used in procuring Oxius's punishment for the killings:

> Therefore God, ever a righteous judge of human affairs and from whom nothing whatsoever is hidden, incensed the king's mind and made him attack an innocent man; in this way Christianus was unknowingly executing His judgement, even though that punishment was to be dealt for no fault and was supremely unfair. But it is the custom for divine providence often to exert its own equity through mankind's injustice and to safeguard its honour through another's disgrace. Since human beings generally overlook the primary cause and give their attention to the secondary, this affair disturbed everyone profoundly, especially the noblemen of the realm; they, angry at this sudden harshness, felt that in future they must fear the most extreme measures with regard to themselves also, even for the lightest infringement. For this reason they began to harbour hatred [...][182]

The episode in Svaning's version[183] is just a plain illustration of Christianus II's tyrannical behaviour; Svaning does not make it as clear as Meursius that Oxius had killed Columbula and contributed to the death of the secretary. Meursius evidently strove to diminish Christianus's degree of tyranny. By emphasizing Oxius's guilt in the two deaths he is able to launch his own theological explanation of Christianus's apparent cruelty, viz. that the king was being used by God to bring about divine retaliation.

---

[182] *Itaque Deus, justus semper rerum humanarum judex, et quem nil omnino latet, efferavit mentem regis, ut invaderet innocentem; et judicium suum quamvis inscius exsequeretur; poena ea extra culpam summa cum iniquitate infligenda. Sed divinæ providentiæ usitatum, ut in hominum injustitia suum sæpe jus exerceat, et honorem in opprobrio alieno tueatur. Ea res, ut solent homines, prima causa præterhabita, in secundam intueri, movit vehementer omnes, et inprimis regni proceres: qui, abruptum hunc rigorem indignati, etiam sibi, vel levissimam ob offensam, extrema quæque metuenda deinceps esse existimabant. Ergo odia concipiunt* [...] (III, 65).

[183] Svaning, 1658, 98sqq.

Christianus II's massacre in Stockholm in 1520 was in the words of Meursius a crime of almost supernatural dimensions:

> Undoubtedly it was a detestable crime, which no age will ever cease to talk of, nor any remember without horror and denunciation.[184]

Having reached Stockholm after a successful campaign through Sweden, Christianus II promised to forgive all the harm done by the Swedes to his father and himself, and the Swedes believed him. But, sly as he was, he had not included in his promise their recent conspiracy against their own archbishop because of his support of Christianus, a crime which the Pope himself had ordered Christianus to punish. This deceitful behaviour on the king's part is severely condemned by both Svaning and Meursius.[185] As Meursius says, Christianus now committed the double sin of perfidy and cruelty. Like Svaning, and clearly inspired by him, Meursius concludes that Christianus II was punished by God for his cruelty.[186]

Even so, both Meursius and Svaning make it clear that Christianus had good reasons for attacking the Swedes – not only the many attempts at rebellion and their refusal to recognize him as king, but also the fact that they had conspired against the archbishop, which had resulted in a papal order to Christianus to subdue Sweden. But, as both Meursius and Svaning see it, this order from the Pope was seen by Christianus as an opportunity to execute his personal revenge.

To the emphatic condemnation of the king which he took over from Svaning, Meursius added a suggestion that a deeper divine meaning may be detected. The Swedes who were executed themselves suffered the violence which they had inflicted on the archbishop, Gustavus, and the mortal punishment which they had intended him to undergo:

> The violence they had inflicted on Gustavus they too suffered in their turn through a secret judgement of God, all receiving a public punishment of the sort they, ignorant of the future, had earlier wished to administer.[187]

---

[184] *Illaudatum certe facinus; et quod nulla unquam ætas conticescet: nulla etiam sine horrore, atque exsecratione, memorabit* (III, 78).

[185] Svaning, 1658, 330; Meursius, III, 78.

[186] As mentioned at the beginning of this chapter, Meursius, strangely enough, also made use of Jacob Ziegler's *Excidium Holmense* (1532, and later), which gives an even more elaborate account of the cruelty enacted by the Danes; Kurt Johannesson argues that Johannes Magnus, being an old friend of Ziegler, provided Ziegler with information on the massacre (Johannesson 1982, 33-38).

[187] *vim, Gustavo quam intulerant, occulto quodam Dei judicio, etiam vicissim passi: ac communi omnes poena; sicut ipsi, futurorum imprudentes, pridem voverant* (III, 78).

It would seem to be the same kind of explanation as in the case of Oxius. Christianus II is certainly to blame, but at the same time he was the instrument of God in bringing about the punishment of the Swedes. Again Meursius sees a divine meaning hidden in the fact that Christianus II, although imprisoned, was the only king left in Denmark at the time of his death in 1559, since his cousin, Christianus III, had died shortly before. This circumstance, the only king in Denmark being a king in prison, was in Meursius's opinion God's silent reproach for his expulsion. Having declared that the Danes hardly had enough reason to expel the king, Meursius goes on:

> Nor will anyone who properly weighs up the causes behind events believe that this happened entirely at random; by some hidden wish of God, at the time of his death, when his cousin, Christianus, had already died, like someone who was free, even though he was in custody, he recognized no one in the whole realm as being of higher rank; and at that moment, as if through some secret disgrace, Denmark had no crowned monarch other than this prisoner.[188]

By these theological reflections – which he did not find in Svaning – Meursius seems to have aimed at solving the problem of this indisputable tyrant in recent Danish history, a problem which must have seemed even greater inasmuch as he belonged to the family of Christian IV himself.[189]

12. Denmark and Germany in the Twelfth Century

Denmark's relations with her German neighbours in the twelfth century figure prominently in Saxo's work. He displays a marked distrust of the emperors' intentions regarding Denmark, a distrust fully shared by Meursius who in fact stresses this German unreliability even more than Saxo.

When Canutus (son of Magnus, who had murdered Canutus Slesvicensis) and Sueno (son of Ericus, king 1134-37) were struggling for the

---

[188] *neque, qui momenta rerum recte censeat, temere sane evenisse existimabit, quod, occulta quadam Dei voluntate, cum obiret, mortuo pridem Christiano, patruele, quasi liber, etiamsi in custodia, ampliori dignitate toto regno nullum agnosceret; Daniaque, velut tacito quodam opprobrio, regem id temporis coronatum, quam captivum, non haberet* (III, 86).

[189] Pontanus did not attempt to soften the verdict on Christianus II. He followed Huitfeldt, with some additions from Meursius, and his portrait is, like Huitfeldt's, without redeeming features.

throne in the 1140s and 1150s, Canutus turned to the Emperor (Frederik Barbarossa, 1152-90) for help, promising to declare Denmark a German fief. The Emperor, as both Saxo and Meursius tell us, is happy about this prospect of gaining control over Denmark, and persuades Sueno to travel to Germany where he is magnificently received. But soon the Emperor turns hostile. Sueno is faced with the unpleasant alternatives of acknowledging the Emperor as his superior and giving Zealand to Canutus, or being attacked by the Emperor's army in support of Canutus. Sueno is forced to accept the first alternative, but, in Saxo's version, later, on his return to Denmark, he refuses to recognize conditions which he had been tricked into. Saxo now focuses on the interplay between the unreliable Sueno and his two rivals, Canutus and Valdemarus (XIV, Ch. viii).

In Saxo's version the Emperor is indisputably deceitful. But Saxo also wants to suggest that Sueno's real motive for going to Germany was vanity; he wished to receive people's admiring acclamation and show off his riches. Meursius concentrates on the unfairness of the Emperor's treatment of Sueno (I, 89). First we hear that Sueno went in spite of his more prudent councillors (*senatores*), which agrees with Meursius's general favourable picture of this body.[190] Then, leaving out the problems between Sueno, Canutus and Valdemarus, Meursius relates how Sueno asked to have his case tried at the imperial court in order to demonstrate that the Danish king was subject to no one. This proud request is then described as rightful and fair. The long trial produced many statements in favour of Sueno, we are told. But the greedy Emperor finally cut it short by declaring his intention of having Sueno recognize him as his lord, or if he refused, to wage war against him, and Meursius describes Sueno's hopeless situation with sympathy. He had to accept subjection, but only if the senate approved. After his return it is not he but the senate who write a letter to the Emperor declaring the arrangement invalid.

Meursius does not, in this connection, mention any cunning plotting against his rivals on Sueno's part. Backed by the senate he stands firmly and proudly against the German Emperor, embodying the Meursian ideal of harmony between senate and king and their independence of

---

[190] Gram comments on the unlikelihood of anybody realizing the Emperor's intentions, ascribing this detail to Meursius himself or Svaning, *cuius vestigiis insistit* (Meursius 1741-63, IX, col. 276).

foreign nations.[191] Most probably Meursius here simply follows Svaning.[192]

The struggle for supreme power in Denmark between Sueno, Canutus, and Valdemarus ended in Valdemarus's favour. He reigned as Valdemarus I from 1157 to 1182. He also, as Saxo saw it, was the object of Barbarossa's attempts at deception. Under the pretext of wanting Valdemarus's advice in the current schism between Pope Alexander and Pope Octavianus, he asks Valdemarus to come to Germany, adding the promise to give him some regions in Italy and Wendland. Valdemarus agrees in spite of his bishop, Absalon's, warnings against the unreliable Emperor. After their arrival (in 1162) Valdemarus sends Absalon to meet the Emperor, who immediately confronts him with his claim on Denmark, denying that he has promised the king anything. Valdemarus and Absalon realize that escape is the only way to avoid accepting the Emperor's demands. But the Emperor succeeds in preventing that, by cunningly offering Valdemarus the whole of Wendland if he will accept him as his lord. It is agreed that Valdemarus's successors on the Danish throne should not be bound by his oath to the Emperor. Saxo further seeks to diminish the shame by pointing out that the king of England likewise ruled as vassal of the French king.[193]

Meursius adds extra emphasis on the fraudulent behaviour of the Emperor. The letter by which the Emperor persuades Valdemarus to go to Germany, merely mentioned by Saxo, is described by Meursius as "a verbal enticement" (*verborum lenocinia*), whose purpose is explained as follows:

> the Emperor, realizing that Valdemarus now held supreme authority after his two rivals had been killed, intended to draw him from his kingdom after deceiving him by guile, snatch away his old freedom, as he

---

[191] Krantz also suggests that Sueno benefited from the advice of the magnates. At least he lets Sueno write to the Emperor that they would not accept the agreement between himself and the Emperor. Otherwise he follows Saxo, though playing down, like Meursius, Sueno's vanity (*Dania*, V, Ch. 31).

[192] In Huitfeldt's very brief account (*Fra Kong Dan* [...], 222) there is no reference to Sueno's acknowledging the Emperor as his lord. Pontanus (221-222) abbreviates Saxo, with a minor addition about the Emperor's considerations.

[193] *Gesta Danorum* XIV, Ch. xxviii. Saxo's account of the relations between Denmark and the Holy Roman Empire (including the medieval German empire) is the subject of Friis-Jensen 1993a. Krantz abbreviates Saxo (*Dania*, VI, Ch. 14-17), and so does Pontanus (239-42).

had done with Sueno before him, and force him to swear an oath of allegiance.[194]

Valdemarus is so keen to go that he pays no attention to the advice of the *senatus*:

> so that no advice from his council nor even the quite recent example of Sueno could persuade him to withdraw from his purpose.[195]

Again Meursius here introduces the *senatus* on the scene, noting its wise and sober advice. In Saxo the arguments against the journey are presented first by Absalon and later by his brother Esbernus.

In his meeting with the Emperor, Absalon (still in Meursius's account), points out that the king had undertaken the journey out of pious motives, to assist in solving the schism. But Barbarossa – Cæsar, as Meursius calls him – will not let Valdemarus go until he has sworn an oath of allegiance, and the king now regrets that he did not listen to the advice of the senate. An envoy from the Emperor again bids him swear the oath, but Valdemarus answers him with a proud speech about the age-old freedom of Denmark, a speech which has no parallel in Saxo, and the Emperor cannot help admiring his constancy and courage. He does, however, succeed in obtaining Valdemarus's oath by donating Wendland to him (I, 102-3).

Meursius thus spells out the contrast between the dishonest Emperor and the freedom-loving and well-meaning Danish king, whose only fault was that he did not listen to his *senatus*. Following the *Annals of Ryd* (perhaps via Svaning), he lets Valdemarus strengthen the defensive wall, Dannevirke, as a protection against German invasions (I, 103).[196] Meursius further, unlike Saxo, concludes by pointing out that Valdemarus's subjection was not legally valid: "In this way he cheated Valdemarus and wrung from him by deception an allegiance he had no legal right to" (*Sic obsequium circumvento Valdemaro, quod non ullo jure posset, fraude extorsit*, I, 103). Interestingly, it seems that this statement was inserted at the request

---

[194] *uti dolo circumventum, quem in Dania iam potiri rerum summa, æmulis duobus cæsis intellexerat, et e regno evocaret, sicut antea Suenonem, et, erepta item prisca libertate, jusjurandum in verba sua dare cogeret* (I, 102).

[195] *uti nec consilio senatus ullo, neque etiam Suenonis admodum recenti exemplo retrahi se a proposito pateretur* (I, 102).

[196] The rebuilding of Dannevirke took place in 1158 according to Huitfeldt (*Fra Kong Dan* [...], 228). Huitfeldt, as in the case of Sueno, makes no reference to Valdemarus's submission to the Emperor (*ibidem*, 229).

of the anonymous nobleman who read Meursius's work before it was printed. He wanted Meursius to reduce the disgrace of Valdemarus's oath:

> I should like the author to point out here that the compliance insidiously forced from the king removed none of his sovereignty. Such allegiance was granted by the decision of the Estates, without whose consent submission could not have been made on any account. What the king did in his own person was due to the pressure of the moment and did not put his royal authority under obligation.[197]

As we have already seen, Pontanus also, in his *Chorographica descriptio*, tried to tone down this embarrasing dependent status of Denmark in the twelfth century. So did both Meursius in his original version and the nobleman, who called for further emphasis. Perhaps because of Bodin's influence (cf. above, Chapter VI), they (and their employers) apparently regarded it as a matter of some urgency to create an impression that Denmark was an independent country in the twelfth century as well.[198]

Shortly after Valdemarus I's son Canutus had acceded to the throne, he too was approached by Fredericus Barbarossa. According to Saxo[199] his alleged purpose was to strike up a friendship with the new king, and Meursius (and Krantz) even has it that he offered Canutus rule over Wendland as his vassal (II, 2). Saxo, Krantz and Meursius all now tell how Absalon indignantly rejects the proposal, arguing that the Danes had learned from Valdemarus's example that the Emperor's friendliness was not to be trusted. Unlike his father, Canutus follows the advice of his men and the Emperor is turned down.

Meursius now somewhat surprisingly advances the opinion that the addition of Wendland would have enlarged the Danish realm without damaging its royal dignity (*majestas*), just as Danish kings today rule over Holstein, Stormarn, and Ditmarsken as vassals of the German Em-

---

[197] *Vellem hic moneret auctor, fraude extortum obsequium Regis, regni maiestati nihil derogare. Illud electione deferri ab Ordinibus, sine quorum consensu submitti nullo modo potuit. Quodque Rex pro persona, et temporis necessitate fecit, regnum non obligavit* ('The anonymous nobleman [...]', Meursius 1741-63, IX, col. 1130).

[198] In his commentary on Meursius's descriptions of the German Emperor's attempt to have the Danish kings recognize him as their overlord, Gram argues at length against the German polyhistor Herman Conring (1606-81), who, on the basis of Otto of Freising, had tried to demonstrate Danish dependence on the German Emperor (Meursius 1741-63, IX, cols. 278-80, 304-6).

[199] Saxo, XVI, Ch. iii; cf. Krantz, *Dania*, VII, Ch. 3 & Pontanus 276-77.

peror.[200] His point is that Canutus would be vassal of the Emperor only with respect to Wendland, while he would still rule Denmark as an independent king, an arrangement similar to that of e.g. Holstein in his own day. The reflection, incidentally, is not Meursius's own, since it is also found in Huitfeldt (*Chron.* I, 16). It may go back to Svaning (of whom Huitfeldt, too, made extensive use), or Meursius may have it from Huitfeldt himself. But the following maxim is not found in Huitfeldt; no doubt this is Meursius's own addition – an observation, typical of Meursius, on the nature of power: "But it is generally the nature of kings and princes to prefer the loss of a dominion rather than to hold it in submission to another person" (*sed hoc fere regum, principumque ingenium est, ut mittere principatum, quam habere alteri obnoxium, malint*, II, 3).

13. The Anonymous Nobleman's Commentary on Meursius's Historia Danica[201]

On the previous pages we have had occasion to note some of the points raised by the anonymous nobleman who was entrusted with the task of going through the manuscript of Meursius's account of the early history. I shall here confine myself to pointing to some general tendencies of the commentary. First I would like to stress, in anticipation of the next chapter, that the nobleman was much impressed with Meursius's style, which he repeatedly finds occasion to praise.

The nobleman had – as we have already seen – a keen eye for possible threats to national honour. At a certain point in the earliest legendary history, as Meursius originally had it, Denmark suffered a major disgrace, being ruled by a king appointed "by Norway". No, says the nobleman, *Norway* should be erased and replaced with the name of the Norwegian king, *Svibdagerus*, "since now our relations with Norway are friendly, and it

---

[200] *Quanquam vero, si Canutus Imperatoris in Vandalia beneficium agnoscere non detractasset, quod illæsa in regno Danico majestate certe poterat; hodieque in Holsatia, et Stormaria, ac Dithmarsia, reges nostri non recusant, sine dubio ampliorem in Vandalia dominatum successores tenuissent, et pacatius ipse regnum habuisset* (II, 3).

[201] The nobleman's commentary is printed in Meursius 1741-63, IX, cols. 1115-30, where it is entitled: 'Anonymi auctoris in Historiam Danicam Io. Meursi priusquam publici iuris fieret observationes'. Then follows Meursius's response: 'Ioannis Meursi ad adnotationes viri illustris a Dn. Cancellario sibi communicatas Responsio' (cols. 1131-40). Both the commentary and Meursius's response are extant in three manuscripts in the Royal Library of Copenhagen, *Thott* 1552, 4to; *Gl. kgl. S.* 2429, 4to and 2430, 4to. I refer to the printed edition.

is an illustrious country".[202] Clearly even details in this legendary past were regarded as politically important. And Meursius did as he was told. In the printed version it says *Svibdagerus* (I, 3).[203]

Later on, in the history of Haraldus VIII (1074-80), Meursius in the first version took over from Saxo (XI, Ch. x, 7) a complaint that many people accused of some crime abused their privilege to reject the accusations by means of a false oath. This may well have been the case, the nobleman comments, but Johannes Magnus and other Swedes have used this passage in Saxo to claim that even according to their own historian the Danes are completely untrustworthy; though Saxo clearly speaks of some Danes in a certain period, he argues, it is better to leave the complaint out – otherwise the Swedes might find occasion to repeat their accusations.[204] Meursius accepted the suggestion (I, 63).

Similarly, it was on the nobleman's suggestion that Meursius included a declaration that the tragic love story of Hagabertus and Signe did in fact take place in Denmark and not in Sweden; those who claim that Signe's father Sigarus was Swedish are wrong, he declares, and points to the name of a village, Siarsted derived from Sigarsted as proof.[205] The nobleman had pointed out to Meursius that certain Swedish historians claimed that Danish historians lied when they made this take place in Denmark and regarded Sigarus as a Danish king.[206] As Gram in his notes to Meursius *ad loc.* points out, it was Johannes Messenius who had argued (on the basis of writings of Laurentius Nerecius, archbishop of Uppsala) that this was an episode of Swedish history.[207] Nerecius and Messenius point to the similarity between the names of Sigarus and the Swedish

---

[202] *Norvegiae] inducendum, eiusque loco, Svibdageri substituendum. Norvegia amica nobis iam; et illustris natio* (col. 1120).

[203] *ac vix unquam Dania majus passa dedecus, quam quod munere Suibdageri habere regem sit coacta* (I, 3).

[204] The nobleman comments: *Licet haec ita se habeant, tolli tamen malim. Saxo Grammaticus de sui seculi moribus loquutus, ait, homines tum deierare, et mentiri inter vitia non habuisse. Illud detorserunt Ioannes Magnus, et Sveci ad nationem Danicam, proprium illis, vel proprio Historico teste, hoc esse. Idem hic facerent, licet non isto fine scribantur* (col. 1127).

[205] *Exstat vero etiamnum ille pagus ad Ringstedium; et corrupte Siarstedium, nomen retinens Sigari, cujus regia tunc erat, nuncupatur. Errant autem, qui Sigarum Sueciae fuisse regem, ac de Hagaberto hoc supplicium in Suecia sumptum, sunt auctores* (I, 27).

[206] The nobleman's comment is in full: *Vellem hic addi loca prope Ringstadium, Sigersted regia Sigari, item locus ubi subspensus, et ceterae circumstantiae. Sveci enim in hac Historia mendacii Historicos nostros arguunt, statuuntque, Sigarum hunc Sveciae Regem fuisse, in Svecia peractam hanc tragoediam. Quum vero maxima styli Auctoris dignitas et elegantia sit, vellem nonnulla diductius, fusiusque traderet* (col. 1124).

[207] Messenius 1611, 61-64.

town Sigtonia, and, as we saw, it was the same kind of argument which the nobleman wanted Meursius to put forward. (Gram notes with discreet wonder that Ole Worm and Stephanius also found it worthwhile to discuss the question).[208]

As mentioned earlier, Meursius sees a punishment from God in the fact that all Sueno III's (1047-74) sons who followed him on the throne were born outside marriage. It was a disgrace to the people, and none of the sons was very successful. The nobleman, however, was not pleased when Meursius pointed out that Ericus IV (1134-37) was the sixth son of illegitimate origin on the Danish throne (his father was Ericus Bonus, *Erik Ejegod*, one of the sons of Sueno III). It is quite true, he admits, but it is too disgraceful. But in spite of the nobleman's suggestion, Meursius did not leave it out (I, 84a), and he even explained his reason to the nobleman. Ericus was not only son of a sinful father, he himself committed even worse crimes; it would be in his interest to leave it all out, but Ericus's history has something to teach later kings, since he may serve as a deterrent example.[209]

The nobleman's aristocratic point of view comes out in the suggestion that Meursius should make clear that Canutus Sanctus's (*Knud den Hellige*) legislation was the result of the combined efforts of the king and the magnates; laws were made, in the past as well as today, not by the kings but by the kings together with the magnates, he claims.[210] Instead of Meursius's *ipse statuisset* he wanted him to use the plural and write *ipsi statuissent*. But Meursius did not correct it – perhaps out of negligence or perhaps because he wanted to keep the focus on royal power (I, 63-64).

The nobleman was displeased with Meursius's omission of an introductory discussion concerning the origin of the Danes.[211] He wanted Meursius to declare that he, following Melanchthon, Anders Sørensen Vedel, Camden and others, regarded the *Dai* as ancestors of the Danes; and that these *Dai* according to Herodotus were related to the Germans, the Persians, and the Parthians; the similarities between modern Persian

---

[208] Ole Worm in the second book of his *Monumenta Danica* (1643), and Stephanius in his notes to Saxo, the *Notæ uberiores* (1645), *ad loc.*

[209] The nobleman's comment begins: *Dissimulari haec, licet verissima, malim. Nota enim quaedam Regibus nostris inuritur, et talia tegenda, quum ad Historiam parum faciunt* (col. 1128; Meursius's answer, col. 1133).

[210] *Semel ipse statuisset*] Nb. *leges olim, ut et hodie non Reges, sed Reges cum Optimatibus statuunt, ergo scribendum, ipsi statuissent* (col. 1127).

[211] Cols. 1116sq. (There is an error in the pagination, col. 1119 following col. 1116).

and Danish should, in the nobleman's view, be adduced as further support.[212] In many other connections the nobleman wants Meursius to discuss the possible links between the domestic tradition from Saxo and the
accounts of foreign (classical and medieval) historians. To mention just a
few examples: he wants Meursius to take up the possible identification
between some of Saxo's legendary kings and Homer's and Strabo's Cimmerians, and to argue, at least indirectly, against the pro-Swedish Gothic
fantasies of Johannes Magnus (col. 1120). He suggests an identification
between the legendary hero, Ericus Disertus, known from Saxo's Book V
(one of Frode V's men) and Ariovistus (cols. 1122-23).

Together with the nobleman's commentaries, Meursius's reactions to
some of the points have also been preserved. Here we find his attempts
to comply with the nobleman's request by writing small essays on the
origin of the Danes and the other matters whose inclusion in the historical narrative his critic had asked for. The decision not to include these
essays in the final work is in my view likely to have been made by the
chancellor, for the reason, probably, that such introductory discussion
would make the work less of a compendium. It would be longer and
more argumentative, and, moreover, it would move into an area already
covered by Pontanus. The nobleman, on this line of reasoning, was not
aware that Meursius's work was intended as a compendium, a brief presentation of Danish history, primarily (in the early history) based on the
domestic tradition from Saxo.

---

[212] We have already met this theory of close relationship between Persian and Danish, put
forward by Christen Friis in a letter to Pontanus (see above, Chapter VI). Ole Worm, in a letter to Arngrímur Jónsson, mentions another adherent, Johannes Elichmann (d. 1639), a doctor of medicine from Silesia, working in Leiden; he had argued that the Old Nordic language
was a Persian dialect, brought to Scandinavia with Odin, whose Asian followers were Persians (letter from Worm to Arngrímur Jónsson, written May 24 or May 25, 1635 (Worm 1751,
no. 332; Worm 1948, 38-39; Worm 1965-68, I, no. 555 (Danish trans.)).

Chapter VIII

Style

Introduction

1. Contemporary and Later Evaluations

It has sometimes been suggested in surveys of Danish history and literature – insofar as Pontanus's and Meursius's *Histories of Denmark* have
received any attention – that their lofty Latin style was their very *raison
d'être*. Carl S. Petersen talked of the elevated Latin of Pontanus and the
tasteful style of Meursius, the idea of their engagements being, he claims,
to present a Danish history dignified by elegant Latinity.[1] Ellen Jørgensen, in spite of her acknowledgement of Pontanus's achievement in
his attempts to rewrite early Danish history, nevertheless lumps them
together as empty rhetorical refinement without any impact on serious
historical research in Denmark.[2] In the latest surveys we are similarly
told, though without the slighting attitude towards rhetoric found in the
earlier works, that Pontanus and Meursius fulfilled the stylistic demands
of humanism.[3]

The implicit assumption seems to be that whatever is written in Latin
is written in an elevated style. In a way, this point of view is surprising,
considering that the use of Latin lasted longest in works of plain scientific prose. As to the style of Pontanus's and Meursius's works, there is in
fact a considerable difference. In Meursius's case I think it is fair to say
that the stylistic demands of humanism were fulfilled. His style may well
be described by the German word *Kunstprosa*, artistic prose, whereas
Pontanus writes a much plainer prose. Using another pair of stylistic
concepts, we may describe Meursius's style as uniform, or homogeneous,

---

[1] Carl S. Petersen 1929, 610-12.
[2] Ellen Jørgensen 1931, 122. She was echoed by Kay Schmidt-Phiseldeck 1945.
[3] Torben Damsholt 1992, 60, Erik V. Rasmussen 1983, 156. Rørdam, too, in his biography of
Pontanus, stressed the superiority of Pontanus over Huitfeldt regarding style, Rørdam 1898,
454.

and Pontanus's as heterogeneous. It is the purpose of this chapter to explore this difference, which in its turn reflects different conceptions of a work of national history.

In contemporary comments Meursius's *History of Denmark* is praised for its style. In a letter to Meursius shortly after the publication of his first volume, on the Oldenburg kings, Holger Rosenkrantz, as we saw, wrote of his "felicious style of writing" (*felicitas in scribendo*), and the following year Petrus Scriverius, in a letter to Pontanus, who had not yet seen the book, described it as being

> certainly not clumsily written, but exactly like the histories of the Netherlands and [William of] Orange, as far as I could discover by dipping into it.[4]

More detailed is the enthusiastic acclaim of Gerardus Vossius in a letter from April 1631:

> The style is wonderfully pleasing. Unaffected, compact and altogether Roman. Added to this it is very transparent, a feature I set in high praise.[5]

An element of flattery may be present, the recipient being Meursius himself, but we need not doubt that Vossius did admire Meursius's style for the reasons stated. So did the anonymous nobleman who, at the chancellor's request, looked through Part I, the pre-Oldenburg section, of Meursius's work before publication. He introduced his commentary with a similar description of the style (addressing himself not to the author but to the chancellor):

> concise, plain and sinewy, a style which will undoubtedly surpass everything he has ever written when he has given it its finishing touches; a work which will last for ever to accompany the immortal fame of its writer.[6]

---

[4] *Liber sane non ineleganter, eodemque prorsus modo quo Belgarum et Auriaci res gestæ, scriptus, quantum in gustu deprehendere potui* (letter from Scriverius to Pontanus, dated February 13, 1631 (new style) (Matthæus 1695, no. 71)).

[5] *Dictio mire placet. Candida est et tersa, penitusque Romana. Ad haec perspicua plane, quod ego in magna laude pono* (letter from Vossius to Meursius, dated May 12, 1631 (Meursius 1741-63, XI, no. 674; also printed *ibidem* no. 654 wrongly dated 1630; Vossius 1691, I, no. 119, also dated 1630)).

[6] *brevis, purus, et nervosus, et qui procul dubio omnia, quae umquam scripsit, excedet, ubi extrema manus accesserit, opus cum immortali auctoris gloria perpetuo duraturum* ('The anonymous nobleman [...]', (Meursius 1741-63, IX, col. 1116)).

Brevity, vigour, elegance, perspicuity, adherence to classical norms — these are the qualities that Vossius and the nobleman, in different words, focus upon. A hundred years later Hans Gram added similar praise in his reassesment of Meursius's use of Niels Krag's *History of Christianus III*:

> He wanted to owe nothing to Krag beyond the subject-matter and events. These he handled in his own style of writing, simple, unaffected, appropriate, and with a certain uniform elegance, so that he generally overlooked nothing that was essential, though he occasionally expressed some details in a more succinct manner and with more concise phraseology than Krag. Consequently, as Meursius presented himself in the other historical works which circulate in public view, so he can be recognized here too.[7]

Like Scriverius in the quotation above, Gram here notes the stylistic similarity of Meursius's historical works. Brevity, clarity and striving for classical Latin are recurrent features of his style. Stephanius, too, joined the chorus of admirers of Meursius's style. At least he commended the elegance of Meursius's final appraisal of the legendary King Lotherus.[8]

Pontanus's style does not seem to have elicited many comments from his contemporaries. I have found only three, two of which are made by our two authors themselves. Meursius was critical, as we shall see below. And Pontanus himself described his style in these words:

> I have related the actions of kings, keeping to chronological sequence, in a consistent style and also in a Latin that is ordinary, in other words, unpretentious, a feature of mine.[9]

This modesty may seem conventional. On the other hand, it was not, as such conventional claims usually are, made in the public context of a

---

[7] *Nihil enim Cragio debere, præter materiam et res, voluit. Quas quidem suo scribendi genere, quod ipsi simplex fuit et candidum, et concinna quadam æquabilitate decorum, sic tractavit, ut nihil fere ejus, quod necessarium esset, prætermiserit, interdum autem nonnulla pressius, quam ille, et breviore verborum ambitu sit complexus. Igitur, qualem in ceteris, qui in publica luce versantur, historiarum libris se præstitit Meursius, talis etiam hic agnoscitur* (Hans Gram, Preface to his edition of Krag 1737, 35). Gram explicitly declared that he preferred Meursius's style to that of Pontanus in the handwritten survey of historiography relating to Denmark, preserved in Jena (ms. in Jena, *Cod. Jen. Bud.* fol. 341 (photocopy in the Royal library of Copenhagen)).

[8] *Cæterum eleganti Epiphonemate Lotheri vitam concludit Cl. Meursius* [...] (Stephanius 1645, 30).

[9] *Regum res continuo stilo, eoque Latino et populari, id est, humili, et qualis est noster, servata ubique annorum serie, absolvimus* (letter from Pontanus to Lyschander, dated August 25, 1622, (Matthæus 1695, no. 101)).

dedication or a preface to the reader. It is found in a private letter to a colleague, the Danish historian Lyschander, who had apparently asked Pontanus for his opinion of his own Danish history, *Synopsis historiarum Danicarum* of 1622; Pontanus now informs Lyschander in this letter that he himself is engaged in a similar project, which he then describes (on this letter, cf. above Chapter III). In other words, he was not obliged to go into the question of style, let alone do it so emphatically, unless he did in fact regard it as a characteristic feature of his own work.

Stephanius, as we saw, was among those who praised Meursius's stylistical elegance. It is somewhat surprising to find that he claimed to find the same quality in Pontanus's *History*. Its style, he declared, was only surpassed by that of Saxo himself.[10] He wrote this brief but enthusiastic praise in a letter to the author himself (the letter mentioned in Chapter III in which he thanked Pontanus for three copies of the 1631 edition), and his wish to flatter his friend must surely be taken into account. Anyway Stephanius seems to have been alone in singling out Pontanus's style for praise.

A stylistic analysis potentially involves all aspects of language and the way it is used in a given text. However, it must be functional, pointing out significant elements of style in a text. A given stylistic element does not have one given meaning or value; rather its interpretation depends on the context. Stylistic analysis should focus on the interplay between form and content, on the way in which the overall "message" is reflected in linguistic and literary phenomena at all levels, or to put it the other way round, how formal elements contribute to shaping the overall message.[11] In what follows, then, I shall draw attention to some stylistic features of the two texts which seem to me to be relevant to the overall interpretation.

2. *Words and Syntax*

Let us begin by looking at some aspects of the two authors' choice of words and syntax. Leonardo Olschki once described the scientific Neo-Latin of the sixteenth century as a living language, based, of course, on classical Latin, but also influenced by the early ecclesiastical writers,

---

[10] *Nihil etenim rerum gestarum, saltem literis consignatum, post coelestem Saxonis eloquentiam, Daniam vidisse elegantius* (letter from Stephanius to Pontanus, dated April 16, 1632 (*Archief voor kerkelijke geschiedenis* 1833, 185-88)).

[11] Cf. Wolfram Ax 1976.

scholastic Latin and the vernaculars; as a result the vocabulary was immensely enriched. Of sixteenth-century men of learning Olschki says: "The grammatical and lexical eclecticism of their language corresponds to their characteristic passion for collecting, their encyclopaedic and polymathic interests".[12] This description fits Pontanus well – but not Meursius, who adheres closely to classical standards in his syntax and choice of words.

An instructive piece of evidence for their divergent views on these matters is found in the notes to Pontanus's *History* which Meursius made while composing his own history of the period up to 1448.

Pontanus's choice of words is the object of Meursius's frequent disapproval. Meursius displays a strong purism, recognizing only words and expressions which are known from classical authors. Here follow some examples[13] (the introductory numbers refer to page and line in Pontanus's 1631 edition):

> 183,54. *adhibuerunt lapidem*] debuisset dicere, *Moverunt*. Nam ita habet proverbium vetus: *omnem lapidem movere*, non, *adhibere*. (They turned the stone] He should have said *moverunt*. For the old saying has: *omnem lapidem movere* (to turn every stone), not *adhibere*).

> 233,27 *ad praesulatus*] Non est dictio latina; nam licet a Consul dicatur Consulatus, non tamen ab Exul, et Praesul, *Exulatus* aut *Praesulatus*. (To presidencies] This is not Latin vocabulary; for though *consul* gives *consulatus* (consulship), *exul* (exile) and *praesul* (president) do not form the derivatives *exulatus* and *praesulatus*).

> 238,8 *archego*] Est dictio graeca, non latina: nec latina civitate ex Auctoribus probatis quisquam hanc donavit hactenus. (Leader] This is Greek, not Latin speech; no approved author has so far granted this word Roman citizenship).

> 247,49 *militonum*] non est vocabulum hoc ulli probato Auctori usitatum; quanquam vox composita, Commilito, sit usitata. (Of soldiers] This is not a word used by any reputable author, although the compound *commilito* (fellow-soldier) is used).

> 250, 25 *annuatim*] non est vox latina. (Annually] This is not a Latin word).

> 368, 6 *resoluta in risum bucca*] Non est dictio latina. (The face dissolved into laughter] Not a Latin expression).

---

[12] *Ihrem charakteristischen Sammeleifer, ihren enzyklopädischen und polyhistorischen Interessen entspricht der grammatische und lexikalische Eklektizismus ihrer Sprache* (Olschki 1922, 69).

[13] Meursius's notes to Pontanus ('Ioannis Meursi animadversiones in Historiam Danicam Io. Isacii Pontani') are found in Meursius 1741-63, IX, cols. 1141-48.

Nor is Meursius prepared to accept a word which has only one classical occurence:

> 138,38 *esset offensui*] Vox Lucretio usitata, neque fere Auctorum alteri. (It would be an annoyance] A word used by Lucretius, but not generally by any other writer).

> 182,10 *potionatam*] Hoc vocabulo solus utitur Suetonius in Caligula cap. 1. (Having been given a potion] Only Suetonius uses this word in the first chapter of his *Life of Caligula*).

– It may even come from an unacceptable model:

> 240,2 *famigerabilis*] Apud solum Apuleium, haud bonum latinae linguae Auctorem, hoc vocabulum reperitur. (Famous] This word is found only in Apuleius, not a good writer of the Latin language).

In Meursius's view, it is no excuse that Pontanus borrowed a given expression from Saxo, if it has no classical origin. Saxo was not an acceptable model:

> 33,17 *Inde exertam crumena ... pecuniam*] Est phrasis Saxonis, sed auctoribus Latinis minus usitata. (Then the money drawn out of his purse] This phrase is from Saxo, but is little used by Roman authors).

In some cases Pontanus constructed the words wrongly, according to the classical norm:

> 264,57 *ope reservatum*] Immo, *servatum*, aut *conservatum*. Nam ad alia, sive fausta, sive infausta, reservamur. (Saved by assistance] He should rather write *servatum* or *conservatum*. We are preserved (*reservamur*) for other things, fortunate or unfortunate).

> 271,57 *exercitum construit*] potius, *instruit*; nam construere exercitum, non facile apud probatum linguae latinae auctorem reperitur. (He drew up his army] *Instruit* is preferable. *Construere exercitum* cannot easily be found in any reputable writer of the Latin language).

> 350,22 *regem sibi operuit*] Dicendum erat: *oppertus est*; vel ut Plautus loquitur, *opperitus est*. (He waited for the king] He should have written *oppertus est*, or, as Plautus says, *opperitus est*).

> 466, 29 *adpromisit*] Adpromittere est, rem aliquam cum altero promittere, eius nomine. (He promised] *Adpromittere* is to promise a thing in someone else's name).

Nor is Pontanus's syntax flawless in Meursius's view:

> 17, 1 *consumpserit*] consumpsit. (He ate it] *consumpsit*).

> 264, 25 *ire ac redire*] debebat dicere per futura, *iturum, ac rediturum*. (Would
> go and return] He ought to have written, referring to the future, *iturum ac
> rediturum*).

Sometimes Meursius, as Pontanus's compatriot, is able to uncover the
cause of the error:

> 222,3 *Imperatorem recognosceret*] Recognoscere, ea significatione Latini non
> dicunt, sed Agnoscere. Est idiotismus Gallicus. (He recognized the
> Emperor] The Romans do not write *recognoscere*, but *agnoscere* with this
> meaning. It is a Gallicism).

> 222,7 *ad plenum*] Est idiotismus Belgicus. Latine dixisset *plene*. (Fully] A
> Dutch idiom. He should have written *plene* in Latin).

> 228,19 *caput ei ense deverberat*] Est idiotismus Belgicus. (He struck the
> man's head off with his sword] A Dutch idiom).

> 243,30 *relicto, ut plurimum, foetore recedere*] Est idiotismus Belgicus. (Com-
> monly to withdraw, leaving the stench behind] A Dutch idiom).

Pontanus's violation of grammatical rules is met with open sarcasm:

> 211, 24 *exigiturum*] Vapula Prisciane. Docent Grammatici dicendum esse
> *exacturum*. (About to drive out] Priscian be hanged! The grammarians tell
> us to write *exacturum*).

> 258, 50 *quae supra aquas imminebant, stipitibus*] Stipes est masculini generis,
> non feminini. Inspice Grammaticam, Pontane. (With stakes that rose
> above the water] *Stipes* is masculine, not feminine. Examine your
> grammar, Pontanus).

Syntactical awkwardness is also castigated by Meursius. Quoting the following statement from Pontanus:

> 247, 54-55 *Erici Regis Chronicon, quod addit oculos ei effossos; et Albertus Abbas,
> qui aquis submersum a Valdemaro ait, apud Saxonem legere non memini*] (King
> Ericus's *History*, which adds that his eyes were dug out; and the abbot
> Albertus, who says that he was drowned by Valdemarus, I do not
> remember reading this in Saxo).

– Meursius simply comments: This is not a Latin construction (*non est con-
structio latina*).

These criticisms tell us something of both Pontanus and Meursius.[14] Pontanus did not bother to purge his language of non-classical Latin, and his syntactical constructions are occasionally awkward (many other examples than those singled out by Meursius could be adduced). Meursius, for his part, found this indifference noteworthy and reprehensible. In his view adherence to classical standards was a matter of importance, and as one would expect, he himself fulfilled this demand. With a few exceptions his vocabulary and syntax are classical, and his account is normally marked by clarity; this is no doubt what Vossius and the anonymous nobleman had in mind when they described Meursius's style as *Romana* and *purus*.

Meursius also displays a tendency to use Roman terms in titles. The *regni strategus* of Pontanus (440) is in Meursius a man *inter principes militiæ* (II, 70), and in the notes to Pontanus he suggests that the *archegus* should instead be *ductor*. Still, Meursius did not, as Gram approvingly notes, translate Danish place-names into Latin, as Krag had done in his *History of Christianus III*; he just adapted them to Latin usage.[15]

---

[14] Meursius's comments contain more corrections of his colleague's Latin than those quoted here. He also deals with matters of content. In Chapter IX below, a fuller presentation of these notes will be given. Another version of these comments is found in the copy of Pontanus's *History* preserved in the University Library in Lund. Apart from the notes also printed by Gram in the *Opera omnia IX*, several others are found here, mostly simple underlinings. The majority of these extra notes concern Pontanus's Latin. The same expressions are repeatedly underlined, many of them prepositions in adverbial functions, such as *in totum, de novo, ex commodo*, or certain words, such as *procinctus* and *salvusconductus*.

[15] *Atque hic non dissimulandum, rectius fecisse Meursium, quod plerumque in hac parte a Cragio prudens recesserit. Nam apud illum non Sliæviga, Collina, Svenopolis, ostium Dravi, Liberi mons, et similia, quæ Cragio adamata, sed eorum loco communia magis, Slesvicum, Coldinga, Svenoburgum, Travemunda, Lyberhoya, ubique fere posita cernuntur* (Hans Gram, Preface to his edition of Krag 1737, 71).

Meursius

1. Meursius's Adaptation of Pontanus

Meursius's *Historia Danica* is essentially a paraphrase of other narrative Latin histories. In determining the characteristic features of his style it is useful to inquire into his strategy of paraphrase. What changes does he make and what are the effects?

As Vossius notes in his letter, clarity, *perspicua dictio*, is one of the virtues of Meursius's style, characteristic of single periods as well as longer narrative units. In this respect also he clearly found Pontanus's work blameworthy, as one of his comments makes clear: Pontanus begins his chapter on Canutus (one of three rivals who shared royal power in the 1140s and 1150s) with his death in 1157; in the rest of the chapter (229-30) he names some of the supporters of the rival princes and relates a story of a Dane mentioned in the *Annals of Silesia*. He simply amplifies Huitfeldt's brief note about Canutus's death after his having ruled with Sueno and Valdemarus for ten years (*Fra Dan* [...], 224). Meursius (who did not treat Canutus as an independent king in his own work) made this comment:

> He places the beginning of the account of Canutus, who has already been killed, in a foolish position. And what he adds to this has nothing to do with Canutus. This is not the only time when one could rightly require some soundness of judgement.[1]

Throughout his reworking of Pontanus, Meursius's wish to achieve lucidity is apparent. The same striving can be observed in his reworkings of other texts. I shall here give examples of Meursius's use of Pontanus, Svaning, Krantz, Saxo, and Krag, with the emphasis on the two first, who were his most important sources.

Pontanus's *History of Denmark* served as Meursius's main source for the period c. 1157-1448. As noted earlier, he left out a considerable amount of material. He also displays a concern for stylistic brevity, for a condensed (and sometimes pungent) expression, as the following three examples will demonstrate. A simple case is this passage about the capture of two Danish clergymen in 1343:

---

[1] 229, 31 *Canutus igitur*] *Inepte hic initium Canuti ponit, qui iam ante interfectus: nec eorum, quae subiungit, quicquam ad Canutum pertinet. Merito iudicium quis, ut non semel, requisiverit* (from 'Ioannis Meursi Animadversiones In Historiam Danicam Io. Isacii Pontani', col. 1143).

> *Pontanus:* Eodem circiter tempore Sueno Arhusiensis episcopus, nec non Roschildensium Diaconus Iacobus Pauli cum iter Roschildiam instituissent, captivi Padebornam, (arx erat Zelandiæ) abducti sunt. Qua de causa confestim toti regno sacris interdictum, ex formula ac vi constitutionis ejus, quam superius Wedelæ olim concinnatam indicavimus (470).[2]

> *Meursius:* Per id tempus, Sueno, Arhusiensis episcopus, ac Iacobus item Paulus, diaconus Roschildiensis, in Roschildiensi via comprehensi, Padebornam, arcem quandam Sialandiæ, abducuntur: ac continuo hac de causa, ex statuto Vedelensi, toti regno sacris omnibus interdicitur (II, 80).[3]

The changes made by Meursius are few. Primarily the number of finite verbs has been reduced, Pontanus's *cum*-clause (*cum [...] instituissent*) having been changed into a prepositional group and the parenthetic explanation *arx erat Zelandiæ* into an apposition. Further the reference to *statutum Vedelense* is briefer. Very characteristic of Meursius's narrative is his use of the historic present tense (*abducuntur* corresponding to Pontanus's *abducti sunt* in the perfect tense), one of the means whereby he enlivens the narrative, as we shall see in later examples.

Meursius's narrative economy is well illustrated in the following instance. The subject is the Swedish dissatisfaction with the Danish administration under the reign of Ericus VIII, or as Meursius has it, Ericus X (*Erik af Pommern*, 1412-39):

> *Pontanus:* Cum enim diu ibi Dani Theutonesque præfecturas imperiumque a rege acceptum impotentius in subditos exercerent, nec juri aut

---

[2] "At about the same time Sueno, bishop of Århus, and Jacobus Pauli, deacon of Roskilde, had set off on a journey to Roskilde when they were carried off as prisoners to Padeborg (a fortress in Zealand). For this reason there was an immediate interdict on religious worship throughout the kingdom, according to the terms and nature of the regulation which I mentioned above as being produced at one time in Vejle".

[3] "During that period Sueno, bishop of Århus, and Jacobus Pauli, deacon of Roskilde, were seized on their way to Roskilde and carried off to Padeborg, a fortress in Zealand; and for that reason, a speedy interdict was put on all religious worship throughout the kingdom, in accordance with the statute of Vejle". Svaning's version of this account has been preserved: *Eodem die quo Slaulosiam Rex movit, Sveno Episcopus Arhusiensis et Jacobus Pauli decanus Roschildensis, Ringstadii Regem adeuntes, expeditis negotiis, cum inde Roschildiam peterent, in itinere a militibus Comitum Holsatiæ capti sunt, atque Padeburgi in vincula conjecti. Quamobrem brevi post summus Pontifex Romanus regno sacris interdicit* (Ms. *Bartholiniana, Tome J, E don. var. 1, fol.,* 356). Although Svaning's version resembles that of Meursius, it is clear that Pontanus and not Svaning served as Meursius's source. Among other things both Meursius and Pontanus mention that the interdiction was made *ex statuto Vedelensi*, which is not found in Svaning. And Svaning is the only one to mention the Pope. The similarity between Meursius and Svaning is due to Meursius's use of Pontanus, who built on Huitfeldt, who in his turn made use of Svaning.

æquitati apud multos, absente, ut plurimum, rege superesse locus videretur, tum et querelæ, quas ad regem ipsum in Daniam Suevi deferebant,
præcipue in Iessonem quendam Ericsenum ab Asdal, qui inter præfectos
regios veluti coryphæus eminebat, dirigerentur, ita semper ille conatibus
eorum, datis ad regem in contrarium literis, occurrit, ut parum ac-
cusatoribus fidei relinqueretur (595).[4]

Meursius: Dani illic, et Germani, quos rex passim imposuerat, potestate
nimium superbe usi, jus, et æquum, conculcabant. inter omnes Iesso
Asdalius, Vesterosiæ præfectus, excellebat; et querelas, quæ ad regem
deferrentur, contrariis ad ipsum literis eludebat (II, 116-17).[5]

Both have just stated, as a sort of heading, that a minor rising among the
Swedes turned into a serious rebellion; and Pontanus's *enim* points to the
whole of the following account of the rebellion. He arranged this presentation in one period, consisting of a three-membered *cum*-clause
(*Dani Theutonesque* [...] *exercerent; locus videretur; querelæ* [...] *dirigerentur*) and
one main clause (*ille* [...] *occurrit*) to which belongs a consecutive clause *ut
parum* [...] *relinqueretur*. To the third of the members of the *cum*-clause is
attached the relative clause *quas* [...] *deferebant* to which belongs another
relative clause *qui* [...] *eminebat*. With this rather intricate syntax comes a
further complication concerning the relation between the main clause
and the *cum*-clause: as the *ita* of the main clause suggests, its contents are
parallel to that of the *cum*-clause; it is not that the *cum*-clause gives a
reason for the contents of the main clause. The fraud of Iesso Ericsenus
(*Jens Eriksen*) from Asdal, which the main clause is about, was a reason
for the dissatisfaction just as the generally blameworthy Danish rule was.
(The *tum* which introduces the third part of the *cum*-clause suggests that
Pontanus at this point forgot that he had introduced the clause with the

---

[4] "For when the Danes and Germans there had for a long while been employing in despotic
fashion over their subjects the governorships and positions of command they had received
from the king, there seemed for many of the people to be no place left for justice and equity
while the monarch was absent, as was normally the case; the complaints that the Swedes
were bringing to the king in Denmark were particularly directed against a certain Iesso Ericsenus from Asdal, who stood out as foremost among the royal governors, but he always
countered their attempts by giving the sovereign a letter stating the reverse, so that there
remained too little belief in his accusers".

[5] "There the Danes and Germans whom the king had set in authority all over Sweden exer-
cised their power in far too arrogant a manner, trampling down justice and equity. Iesso of
Asdal, governor of Västerås, surpassed the rest, and the complaints which the countrymen
brought to the king he parried by sending a letter to Ericus proclaiming the opposite".

subordinating *cum*, and not the coordinating *cum* of a *cum-tum* construction).

Meursius's version is considerably briefer in spite of the fact that he left out only one substantial piece of information, namely the almost constant absence of the king. In agreement with the semantic structure, he arranged the material in parallel main clauses with the verbs *conculcabant, excellebat, eludebat,* and also avoided the staccato-like character of Pontanus's *nec, tum et, ita,* by the participial construction *potestate* [...] *usi.* Most importantly, Meursius gave the passage a clear sequence, the first period stating the brutal rule of the Danes and the Germans and the second giving an example, viz. Iesso of Asdal, the connection being established by *inter omnes.* Further he combined the complaints with Iesso's denials. Pontanus, on the other hand, first mentions the complaints, then the fact that they concerned Iesso in particular, to whom we are then introduced, and finally in the main clause Iesso's denials of the complaints. Meursius begins by introducing Iesso. Then we are informed of the complaints over him and that he forged the letters of complaint. In other words, he not only abbreviated but also made it much clearer. He avoids Pontanus's references to the complaints just mentioned (*conatibus eorum*) and to Iesso (*ille*), because he only has to mention the complaints once and keep Iesso as subject. Meursius's presentation of Iesso as *Vesterosiæ præfectus* is taken from Pontanus's next reference to Iesso, *cæperat jam Iesso Erici, Vesterosiæ præfectus, tributum singulis imperitare* (597). Meursius appropriately moved the presentation to the first time Iesso is mentioned. (Note also that Meursius instead of Pontanus's Greek *coryphæus* writes *inter omnes excellebat*).

In our final example Meursius's striving for brevity and clarity is connected with other characteristic features. The example concerns Ericus VIII's (Ericus X's, *Erik af Pommern's*) repeated attacks on Fehmarn (an island on the north coast of Germany) in 1419.

Pontanus: Hinc iterum navibus conscensis secundo Fimbrienses petiit. Sed et tum priore successu ferociores redditi posticas ei corporis partes obvertendo aliaque dictu ac visu fæda petulanter ostentando exscendere eum prohibuerunt, dum tandem repetito tertium impetu terram tenuit, amissis ex suis mille quingentis. Quam id temporis acrem vindicem egerit omniaque deplorata ibi fuerint, ostendit, præter cetera, Slavicum Chronicon ad eundem hunc annum, commemorans sacra prophanaque nullo discrimine habita, quidquid esset virilis sexus una propemodum strage sublatum, nec parcitum matronis virginibusque et has præcipue vel abductas aut stupro contaminatas, adeo ut ipse Rex, quod Crantzius addit, illachrimare sit solitus, quotiescunque illius diei ac cladis recordaretur. Reducta tum in potestatem regis arx Glambekensis [...] (564).[6]

Meursius: inde rursum Fimbriam aggredientem, iterum, qui propugnabant, rejecere; cum protervia, ac ludibrio. itaque invadit tertium, contumelia irritatus; et post prælium atrocissimum, amissis suorum mille, ac quingentis, tandem expugnat. tum, ut fere in talibus solet, victor miles, pro libidine sua agens, cuncta diripit; nec profani, neque sacri, ullam rationem habet: quicquid masculum, trucidat: muliebrem sexum stuprat. adeoque tristis rerum facies erat, ut rex ipse, quoties diei hujus, atque stragis, meminisset, lacrymas non contineret. verum est hoc ipsum exemplo; nunquam hosti, quamvis etiam profligato, aut depulso, insolenter insultandum; nec convitia in eum, quæ mulieres potius, quam viros, decent, jacienda: siquidem irrisa virtus iram capit, et ad contumeliæ vindictam accenditur (II, 108).[7]

Meursius is shorter and both clearer and more elegant. He has reduced the description of the Danes' second attack to one period (*inde* [...] *ludibrio*). By using first *rursum* then *iterum* Meursius creates variety, underlining at the same time the repeated course of events – new attack, new defeat. He has placed the main verb *rejecere* before the way they behaved when they beat back the Danes, viz. *protervia* and *ludibrio*, with the effect that the latter is given extra weight, a compensation for the lack of details, compared to Pontanus's description of the mockery. Besides, Pontanus's psychological explanation of the Fimbrians' behaviour (they were encouraged by previous success) has been left out by Meursius.

---

[6] "From here they boarded the ships and Ericus attacked the inhabitants of Fehmarn a second time. However, these people had been made fiercer because of their earlier success; turning their backsides towards him and impudently displaying other parts, unseemly to mention and to look upon, they prevented him from disembarking until, in the end, repeating the assault a third time, he gained dry land after losing fifteen hundred of his men. Apart from the other records the *Slav Chronicle* for that year reveals how on this occasion he acted the role of passionate avenger and how everything there was a cause for sorrow; it recalls that no distinction was observed between sacred and secular, and all the males were exterminated in what was virtually a single massacre; nor was there any exemption for married women and virgins, for the latter in particular were carried off or raped, so that the king himself, as Krantz adds, used to lament whenever he remembered the slaughter on that day. It was then that the fortress of Glambæk was brought back under royal control".

[7] "Thereupon he again attacked Fehmarn and once more its defenders beat him back with impudence and mockery. Aggravated by this insult he assailed them a third time and after a hideous battle, in which he lost fifteen hundred of his men, Ericus finally subdued them. Subsequently, as generally occurs in such situations, the victorious soldiery, behaving just as

After the victory the Danish soldiers went berserk, killing the men and raping the women, and the king, when recalling this episode later, would always start to cry. Pontanus begins by referring to the *Slavicum chronicon* and its chronological agreement with his own account. The soldiers' behaviour is described in indirect form, as a report of the chronicle. Syntactically, the main point is the reference to the chronicle. Touching then upon the king's lamentations, he informs us that he now follows another source, viz. Albert Krantz.

Meursius has concentrated on this third attack of the Danes, reducing the second to a prelude. Here he adds a motive: the Danish king was now *contumelia irritatus*. Instead of Pontanus's references to the sources, whereby the violence of the soldiers is reduced to something told as a paraphrase of the *Slavicum chronicon*, Meursius has, on the contrary, intensified the drama by various means. He creates suspense by inserting after the initial *tum* a generalization *ut fere in talibus solet*, and a vague description *pro libidine sua agens*, before the violent *cuncta diripit*, which in its turn is followed by a swift row of parallel main verbs in the historic present tense, *habet, trucidat, stuprat*, the two last being asyndetically connected; this lively description of the soldiers' brutality is then summed up with the emotional *tristis rerum facies erat*.

The episode is also, in Meursius's version, an illustration of a moral and political maxim: the victors should never, as the Fimbrians did, insult their beaten enemy, since the defeated party will always in the end succeed in carrying out their revenge (provided they are endowed with *virtus*). This conclusion shifts the focus from the Danish cruelty to the rudeness of the Fimbrians. They only had themselves to thank for the massacre. The generalization *ut fere in talibus solet* about the soldiers' violence has the same effect of reducing the crime of the Danish soldiers.

Such generalizing observations form, as we have seen above (Chapter VII), a typical feature of Meursius's *History of Denmark*. Another such characteristic, which we have had occasion to observe in the passages

---

they pleased, totally ravaged the island, showing no respect for sacred or secular; every male was butchered, the females raped. The overall sight was so miserable that whenever the king himself recollected that day and its bloodshed, he could not restrain his tears. However, this incident provides a lesson: one should never behave insolently towards an enemy, even if he has been overcome or driven back; nor should abuse be hurled at him, for this is more suited to women than to men; courage, when ridiculed, flies into a rage, and is incited into taking vengeance for the indignity".

quoted here, is his concern for a brief, clear, and lively narrative. These two aspects are interrelated in the sense that both concern the plot; a moral stands out more powerfully against the background of a clear and dramatic presentation of the plot. These are facets which we shall explore further in the last part (pp. 387 sqq) of the present chapter.

2. Meursius's Adaptation of Svaning

Meursius's wish to create brevity and clarity is also observable in his adaptation of Svaning. The following example is about the fatal influence on Christianus II (1513-23) of his mother-in-law, Sigbritta:

> *Svaning:* Hac amicitia Regis nimium confisa, eo demum audaciæ impotens mulier processit; ut authoritate Regia posthabita, contempto Regni Senatu, atque Ecclesiastico ordine illuso, quæ vellet, quæque cuperet, etiamsi ipsa turpis esset serva, ac vile mancipium, in libero tamen Regno omnia impune, ageret: atque insuper Senatui reliquisque Regni ordinibus omnibus, superbe insultaret, Rege adhæc connivente; atque incoepta hæc omnia procacis impotentisque foeminæ comprobante, non aliter quam si carminibus, magicisve artibus infatuatus, omnibus sensibus ipse destitutus fuisset. Ita posthabito regio nomine, ac neglecta Regni Majestate, totus ab ea pendebat (*Christiernus II. Daniæ rex,* 163-64).[8]

> *Meursius:* Tanta denique insolentia ejus fuit, uti cuncta pro libidine agitaret, ac proceribus quoque regni quibuscunque, et ordinibus, insultaret: omnia hæc probante rege, aut ferente, et connivente (III, 68).[9]

Although Svaning uses many more words, Meursius has not omitted any concrete piece of information apart from the references to her low class; consequently Svaning's rhetorical contrast between her servile back-

---

[8] "Far too assured of the king's friendship, the headstrong woman finally went to a level of boldness in which she spurned royal authority, despised the council of the realm, jeered at the ecclesiastical order and acted out all her wishes and desires, since even though she herself was a common servant, a worthless chattel, she could still do everything without fear of punishment in a free realm; on top of that she haughtily scoffed at the council and every other person of rank in the kingdom, and this with the sovereign's toleration; for in sanctioning all this shameless, unbridled woman's enterprises, he was exactly like a man bewitched by spells and magic arts, and totally deprived of his senses. So, in neglect of his royal title and indifferent to the dignity of his kingship he was wholly dependent on her".

[9] "Eventually she attained such a level of arrogance that she did everything according to her pleasure and would even taunt any of the chief personages of the realm, including those of noble rank; to all this the king lent his approval, or his sufferance and toleration".

ground and her present influence in a free nation is also absent from Meursius's version. Both stress the king's passivity and her contempt for the council and the Church, but Meursius has condensed the attitude of the king towards the power of Sigbritta in the final ablative absolute *omnia hæc probante rege, aut ferente, et connivente*, in which the *aut* further expresses the difference between acceptance and powerlessness: the king actively supported her (*probante*) – or he was simply incapable of intervening. Svaning just treats the two concepts (*connivente atque* [...] *comprobante*) more or less as synonyms. The passage thus illustrates a characteristic difference between Svaning and Meursius. Where Svaning uses repetitions and synonyms to emphasize a given matter, Meursius achieves a similar effect by his pungent wording.

In some cases Meursius adheres closely to Svaning's version, as in the following reflections on the partition of Schleswig between Johannes (1482-1513) and his brother Fridericus:

> *Svaning:* Sed quam prudenter nouo Regi ac regno Daniæ consuluerunt ij, qui id tum persuaserunt, vt Ducatus Slesuicensis qui sub Erico rege cognomento Pomerano, a regno separatus, nullis armis recuperari poterat, tunc post obitum Adolphi Ducis coronæ restitutus, iterum ab ea distraheretur, posteritatis esto iudicium (*Chronicon Ioannis*, N2v).[10]

> *Meursius:* Sed quam recte novo regi, et regno Daniæ, consuluerint, qui ducatum Slesvicensem, sub Erico Pomerano separatum, nec recuperari facilem, vixque per Adolphi mortem restitutum, iterum tunc disjungendum censuerunt, judicent prudentes rerum (III, 22).[11]

Meursius has used a number of the words found in Svaning and only to a limited extent substituted synonyms (*post obitum Adolphi* (Sv), *per Adolphi mortem* (M), *distraheretur* (Sv), *disjungendum* (M)). He has also retained the general structure, the *sed quam*-clause being object of the final "let others judge". Still, we can also observe his strategy of abbreviation and clarity.

---

[10] "But let posterity judge how wisely those men consulted the interests of the new king and the Danish realm, when they persuaded him to separate the duchy of Schleswig once again from Denmark; under King Ericus Pomeranus it had been severed in such a way that it could not be recovered by any armed force and had then been restored to the crown after the death of Duke Adolphus".

[11] "But let those with experience of affairs judge how correctly these men consulted the interests of the new king and the Danish realm, when they decided that once again the duchy of Schleswig should be separated after it had been severed under Ericus Pomeranus, with no easy means of recovery, and was only restored with difficulty after the death of Duke Adolphus".

The number of subordinate clauses has been reduced twice, first by replacing Svaning's *persuaserunt ut* [...] *distraheretur* by a gerundival construction *disjungendum censuerunt,* and then by using an adjectival syntagma *nec recuperari facilem* in place of the relative clause of Svaning *qui* [...] *nullis armis recuperari poterat,* thus also avoiding the repetition of a relative clause beginning with *qui.* And finally he has left out the correlate to *qui, ij.*

Svaning's account of the Oldenburg kings is, as mentioned, strongly coloured by the hostile atmosphere in Danish-Swedish relations around 1560, and also in rhetorical terms it bears the stamp of a pamphlet, a contribution to the on-going polemics. We have already observed how Meursius has softened the aggressive tone of Svaning (Chapter VII.10). Here I shall just add a single example of his more dispassionate style. Having described the contents of a Swedish edict against Archbishop Gustavus, Svaning addresses the reader with this exclamation:

> quanta autem miseria et calamitate, quanta denique sangvinis effusione hæc iniqua conjuratio Svecorum exundavit [...] (*Christiernus II. Daniæ rex,* 158).[12]

Meursius turns it into a more laconic statement:

> Hoc edictum maximæ calamitatis insecutæ causa fuit (III, 67).[13]

Meursius's abbreviations are often elegant, as we have already had occasion to note. When, in the history of Johannes (1481-1513), the Swedes are persuaded by Steno Sture to revolt against the Danes, Meursius discreetly suggests that his promises of freedom were false, while Svaning is more blunt:

> *Svaning:* Nam Sueci per tumultum ad spem libertatis opinione quidem ipsorum, sed reuera ad seruitutem a Stenone iterum vocati, rursus ad eum summam rerum deferunt (*Chronicon Ioannis,* 1561, Q2r).[14]

> *Meursius:* quippe animis iterum in spem libertatis, ut vocabat [sc. Steno], concitatis, rerum summam denuo deferri sibi procuravit (III, 25).[15]

---

[12] "With what wretchedness and harm and what shedding of blood this wicked conspiracy of the Swedes abounded [...]".

[13] "This edict was a cause of the utmost harm to follow".

[14] "In this rebellion the Swedes themselves believed that they had been called by Steno to the expectation of freedom, but in reality it was to subjection once more, and yet again they were granting him supreme power".

[15] "By exciting their minds once more to an expectation of freedom, as he called it, Steno again contrived that supreme power should be offered to him".

3. Meursius's Adaptations of Saxo and Krantz

For the period up to c. 1157, it was probably Svaning's adaptation of Saxo and not Saxo's text itself that served as Meursius's main source. Though it is a reasonable assumption that he consulted Saxo throughout, we can never rule out the possibility that Svaning functioned as an intermediary, however closely a passage in Meursius's text resembles Saxo's. The following example should therefore be taken to illustrate characteristic differences between him and Saxo rather than a strategy of adaptation on Meursius's part. It concerns Sivardus II, who after having spent a war-like youth became a peace-loving king:

> *Saxo:* Hic autem post editas late strages domestica claritate contentus, toga quam armis illustris haberi maluit, omissoque castrorum cultu ex acerrimo tyranno exactissimum pacis custodem agere coepit, tantum decoris in otio atque vacatione constituens, quantum ante in victoriarum frequentia repositum autumabat. Adeo autem studiorum eius mutationem fortuna favorabiliter prosecuta est, ut, sicut ipse neminem, ita nec ipsum quisquam hostiliter laceraret (IX, Ch. v, 7).[16]

> *Meursius:* Is, in juventute acer, et bellandi admodum amans, cum ad regnum pervenisset, animum ad pacem vertit, et tranquillam ætatem egit. Studiumque juvit Deus, qui amanti pacem dedit: utque ipse neminem bello lacessivit, sic vicissim neque lacessitus fuit (I, 44).[17]

Again brevity marks Meursius's text. Sivardus's change is expressed in three different ways by Saxo, and only in one way by Meursius. Saxo's *studiorum eius mutationem* corresponds to Meursius's *studium*, just as he has the simple *juvit* instead of Saxo's *favorabiliter prosecuta est*. Characteristic, too, is the last *ut*-sentence where Saxo changes subject (*ipse*, *quisquam*) and Meursius keeps the same subject by means of a passive construction. Meursius has brought God on the scene, corresponding to Saxo's imper-

---

[16] "After widespread slaughters he was happy to enjoy honour at home and now thought it better to be esteemed noble in civilian dress, not armour; abandoning camp-life, from being a ruler of great violence he began to act as a scrupulous guardian of peace, finding as much attractiveness in ease and tranquillity as he had previously thought rested in a string of victories. Fortune favoured his change in aims to such an extent that as he distressed nobody with hostilities, so no one harassed him".

[17] "In his youth he had been violent and a great lover of fighting, but when he attained the throne, his thoughts turned to peace and he lived a calm life. God favoured his inclinations by granting him the peace he loved, and as he challenged no one to war, so in his turn he was unchallenged".

sonal Fortuna, and on this one point he is more verbose than Saxo, inasmuch as he explains in what way God helped (*qui amanti pacem dedit*). As noted earlier, God's active interference is a feature of Meursius's work which he does not share with Saxo (cf. above, Ch. VII. 6).

In those rather few passages where Albert Krantz can be pointed to as the main source, Meursius has not made any drastic changes. One example is found in Christianus I's history, where the king suffers defeat in a battle against the Swedes after having attempted to quash a rebellion in Sweden. In the preceding passage Meursius, following Svaning, has told how supporters of the exiled Swedish rebel leader, Carolus Canuti (Karl Knutssøn), succeeded in persuading Christianus I that the Swedish archbishop was now plotting against the king; Christianus believed the false accusations and the bishop was captured. This incident is not mentioned by Krantz:[18]

> *Krantz:* Reperit autem rex maiorem quam putauerat in se factam coniurationem: nam prodire audebant in aciem, et conserere manus. Pugnatur acriter, et aliquandiu incertis alis volitante victoria: Suecis inde inclinauit. Cæsi ex regijs multi: rex in naues reducitur, capiuntur multi. Aliquot dum in naues refugiunt, trepidatione nimia, mari merguntur (*Dania*, VIII, Ch. 31).[19]

> *Meursius:* Iamque aperta rebellio erat, et in regem incursatur: qui, commisso acri prælio, diu ancipiti, tandem victus, classem repetit, et in Daniam enavigat. Ea in pugna multi ex regiis cecidere, multi capti: neque pauci, dum in naves fugam capiunt, trepidatione nimia, aquis mersi (III, 14).[20]

Again Meursius abbreviates. The course of the battle is condensed in two adjectives/participles and temporal adverbs, *diu ancipiti, tandem victus*, both

---

[18] Svaning, on the other hand, only mentions general rebellion among the Swedes as a consequence, not this particular battle. This part of Svaning's *Christian I* is not known from the Ms. *Gl. Kgl. S. 2444, 4to* (which contains most of the history of this king) but from the Ms. *Bartholiniana, Tome J, E don. var.* 1, *fol.*, 364sq. (Both in the Royal Library of Copenhagen).

[19] "The king discovered that the conspiracy formed against him was greater than he had imagined, for they were bold enough to march into battle and join in conflict. There was fierce fighting and for some time Victory flitted to and fro with hesitant wings, but then she veered towards the Swedes. Many of the royal troops were cut down; the king was brought back to the ships, but many prisoners were taken. While a number were fleeing back to their vessels in excessive panic, they were drowned in the sea".

[20] "Now there was open revolt and an attack was made on the king; he joined in a fierce battle, which for a long while remained undecided, but finally he was overcome, fell back to his fleet and sailed off to Denmark. In that engagement many of the royal troops fell, many were captured, and not a few, taking flight to the ships in excessive panic, were drowned in the waters".

belonging to the relative clause *qui [...] enavigat*, whose main verbs inform the reader that the king went back to Denmark (consequently Meursius later leaves out Krantz's reference to the king's seeking refuge in the ships). Not only does Meursius press much information into one relative clause, he also pushes the battle into the background and makes the king the grammatical subject. This is a common feature of his narrative, the grammatical correlate to his concentration on the actions of the kings.

Both authors also obtain an effect of liveliness by their use of the historic present, Meursius even more than Krantz. The structure of Krantz's account of the fates of the various groups has been preserved, but by Meursius's anaphoric repetition of *multi* the extent of the disaster is emphasized. Another characteristic feature of Meursius's syntactical brevity, also present in Krantz's *cæsi*, is the exclusion of forms of *esse* in the passive perfect forms *capti* and *mersi*.

Some of Krantz's words have been replaced with synonyms – *incertis alis volitante victoria* (K), *ancipiti* (sc. *prælio*, M), *cæsi* (K), *cecidere* (M), *aliquot* (K), *neque pauci* (M), *refugiunt* (K), *fugam capiunt* (M), *mari* (K), *aquis* (M). Others have been retained, though sometimes in variant forms: *acri, multi ex regiis, multi capti, dum in naves trepidatione nimia, mersi.*

4. Meursius's Adaptation of Niels Krag

Even closer is Meursius's adaptation of Krag's prose, which was his source for the period 1533-50. Here follow their accounts of the peace between Christianus III (1536-59) and Count Christophorus after a rebellion in 1534.

> *Krag:* Actum ibi de pace aliqva tolerabili, qvam Rex afflictæ reipublicæ omnibus modis præoptabat. Sed ubi ventum ad ferendas conditiones pacis, nimis qvam iniqvum Comes postulabat. Rex designatus æqvas conditiones haud abnuebat, pecuniam Comiti offerens, si regno cederet et provincias occupatas traderet: ratus enim satius jacturam facere pecuniæ, et bello defungi, qvam opes regni simul in militem erogare, et fuso sangvine humano tandem pacem qværere (*Historia regis Christiani III*, 69-70).[21]

---

[21] "Then discussion took place about some peace-treaty which would be acceptable, since the king wholly desired it for his distressed realm. But when it came to obtaining terms for this peace, the count demanded far more than was just. The monarch-elect was not denying him fair terms, for he offered the count money if he would withdraw from the kingdom and hand back the regions he had occupied, believing it preferable to bear the expense and have done with the war, rather than pay out the kingdom's resources to his soldiery as well as eventually seeking peace after the spilling of human blood".

> *Meursius:* Agitatum de constituenda pace, quam in primis Christianus, ut adflicto regno suo subveniret (si honeste id liceret) reparatam cupiebat. Sed Christophorus postquam ventum ad conditiones fuit, periniquas postulabat. Obferebat Christianus non exiguam pecuniam, ea pacem, quam humano sanguine, recuperare satius ducens (col. 847).[22]

Meursius here retains the syntactical structure as well as many words (*de pace quam, adflicto, ventum ad conditiones, (per)iniquas, postulabat, obferebat, pecuniam, humano sanguine, satius*). Others have been replaced with synonyms (*agitatum – actum, regnum – respublica, ducens – ratus*), and titles have been replaced by names. But again we can observe discreet alterations on Meursius's part. For one thing he abbreviates. He does not explain the contents of Christianus's offer, and simply establishes a pungent contrast between peace achieved by money and peace achieved by further bloodshed, while Krag explains these alternatives in more detail. Besides, Meursius, in the relative clause at the beginning, *quam [...]*, adds a little more emphasis on the king as agent; he wanted the peace in order that he could thereby come to the rescue of the country; and Meursius makes explicit the king's concern for his honour: *si honeste id liceret*. The contrast between Christianus and Christophorus is marked by the placing of Christophorus at the beginning of the *Sed*-clause: we know at once that he presented the problem suggested by *Sed*. Further, Meursius's replacement of the substantival *nimis qvam iniqvum* by the adjective *periniquas*, which points back to *conditiones*, adds to the smoothness of the period.

Sometimes Meursius is even more loyal to Krag's text, as in the following description of Christianus's actions after the conquest of Copenhagen in 1536:

> *Krag:* CHRISTIANUS, ne qvis publicum regni liberi statum injussu populi mutare eum criminaretur, indictis comitiis, ex plebe urbana ac rustica delectos, ex nobilitate superstites universos Hafniam vocat. Ordo ecclesiasticus, qvi captis antistitibus perturbatus erat, exclusus, ne dominari in comitiis assvetus, libertati suffragiorum officeret, qvia contra eum omnia fere tendebant. Qvum ergo ingens ex reliqvis duobus ordinibus hominum multitudo confluxisset, principio cum patribus actum de obligatione, qva jura nobilitatis et ordinum sacramento a Rege præstito

---

[22] "They conferred over the establishment of peace, which Christianus particularly wanted restored so that he might relieve his distressed realm (if he were allowed to do it honourably). But when it came to terms, those demanded by Christophorus were extremely unfair. Christianus offered no small sum of money, believing it preferable to recover peace by this means, rather than at the cost of human blood".

confirmantur, qvibus ea verbis conciperetur, ac qvæ jura, immunitatesve superioribus adjungerentur, de qvibus postqvam utrinqve convenisset, convocata in forum concione, Rex et Senatus in pegmate ad eum usum exstructo consistens, populum circumstantem ex scripto per interpretem affatur (*Historia regis Christiani III*, 152).[23]

Meursius: Porro, ne quid statum regni liberi, iniussu populi, immutare videretur, mox comitia indicit; et delectos ex urbanis, rusticisque ex nobilibus, omnes quotquot cladi publicae superessent convenire Hafniam iubet. Ordinem Ecclesiasticum, iam captivis antistitibus perturbatum, ne adsuetus in comitiis dominari, libertatem suffragiorum impediret, praetermittit. Ideoque, quum die dicto magna ex utroque ordine multitudo confluxisset, statim cum senatu actum de nobilitatis iure, populique, ad quod rex obstringebatur, sacramento confirmando. Item quibus illud verbis proferendum, aut quid etiam adiungendum videretur. In quae postquam convenissent, convocata concione, rex in pegmate, quod in foro ideo exstructum erat, cum senatu constitutus, hunc in modum per interpretem populum circumfusum adfatur (col. 889).[24]

---

[23] "In case anyone should charge him with altering the political status of a free realm without the authority of its people, CHRISTIANUS appointed bodies chosen from the population of the towns and countryside and summoned them along with all the surviving nobility to Copenhagen. The ecclesiastical order, who had been thrown into confusion after the bishops had been imprisoned, were excluded, to prevent them hampering these people's freedom of decision, for they had been accustomed to lord it over public meetings, seeing that everything tended to contradict their interests. When a large throng of men from the other two orders had flocked together, there was first of all a debate with the council on the royal pledge, in which the rights of the nobility and the other orders were established by the king's guaranteed oath; furthermore they discussed the words in which the pledge should be couched and the rights and exemptions that should be added to the preceding articles; when both sides were agreed on these, an assembly was called in the main square, where the king, attended by his council stood on a platform erected for the purpose and spoke from a script to the surrounding populace through an interpreter".

[24] "Furthermore, in case he should seem to be altering the status of a free realm without the authority of its people, he soon appointed representative bodies, comprised of chosen townsfolk and countrymen, and as many of the nobility as had survived the communal devastation; these the king commanded to gather in Copenhagen. He left out the ecclesiastical order, now thrown into confusion after the bishops had been imprisoned, to prevent them hampering these people's freedom of decision, for they had been accustomed to lord it over public meetings. And so, when a large throng from both orders had flocked together on the appointed day, there was an immediate debate with the council over the rights of the nobles and the people, to which the king was bound, confirming them with an oath. Likewise, they discussed the wording to be published and what additions appeared to be needed. After these had been agreed upon, an assembly was called and the sovereign, standing with the council on a platform specially erected in the main square, spoke in this manner to the surrounding populace through an interpreter".

The Krag-passage introduces a new book. This is not the case with the passage from Meursius, and so Meursius's transition is different; he just continues his account with Christianus as subject. A slight simplicification is evident in Meursius's replacement of *quis criminaretur* with *videretur*, where he keeps the king as subject. So he does in the next sentence (*prætermittit*), whereas Krag uses a passive construction (*exclusus*) with *ordo ecclesiasticus* as subject. The effect of Meursius's construction with the king as the only subject is both one of smoothness, inasmuch as he avoids a change of subjects, and one of emphasis on the king as agent. Smoothness, or perhaps rather clarity, is also recognizable in Meursius's placement of *assuetus* first in the syntagma *assuetus in comitiis dominari* where Krag begins with the infinitive. Here Meursius has left out the reason for the exclusion of the ecclesiastical order. The last period, which in Krag's version is complicated and a little awkward, has been made simpler. Krag's *actum de obligatione, qva jura nobilitatis et ordinum sacramento a Rege præstito confirmantur* is in Meursius's text reduced to *actum de nobilitatis iure, populique, ad quod rex obstringebatur, sacramento confirmando*; with this gerundival construction, it is clear (in spite of the confusing comma, which should be placed after *sacramento* and not after *obstringebatur*) that *iure confirmando* is the object of negotiation, whereas Krag's *de obligatione* may be seen either as the object of negotiation or merely as preparatory to the object-clauses *quibus ea* and *quæ iura*. Meursius distinguishes between the main point, *iure ... confirmando*, and the less important ones, introduced by *Item*, and they are bound together by *videretur* which applies to the two gerundives. (Further, the comma in Krag's text after *adjungerentur* prevents the reader from realizing at once that the *quibus*-clause is not a new point of negotiation; in Meursius's version there is a full stop instead).

In the case of Krag also, then, Meursius's changes are due to his concern for brevity, clarity, and correctness. But his adaptation of Krag is discreet. Krag's prose, it may be suggested, came close to Meursius's own ideals. Krag, too, displays a fondness for brevity, often, like Meursius, leaving out forms of *esse* (when used as an auxiliary verb) and using many participial constructions. Both enliven the account by an extended use of the historic present. And the similarities are not confined to the syntactical level. Neither of them brings in any quotations; they both paraphrase the contents of documents in their own words.

5. General Features of Meursius's Prose

In Chapter VII it was noted that Meursius's many general reflections on the nature of power should be seen in connection with contemporary Tacitism, especially as it appears in Lipsius's *Politica*. Tacitism has a stylistic side, sometimes referred to as the Attic movement, which I think also left its mark on Meursius's prose. Partly reacting against the humanists' cultivation of Cicero's prose as a stylistic ideal, the "Attic" writers of the seventeenth century took Seneca and Tacitus and other Roman authors of the so-called Silver Age as their models. Their prose is coloured by paradoxes, antitheses, pungent phrases, puns, and brevity – features which are all, though to a varying degree, found in Meursius.[25]

"Concise" is one of the adjectives used by the anonymous nobleman about Meursius's style. As we have already seen, he often uses participicial and adjectival constructions instead of the finite verbs of his sources, he leaves out auxiliary forms of *esse* and demonstrative pronouns and avoids repetitions and accumulations of synonyms.

Let me give some further examples. One of the men who took part in the murder of Ericus VI (1241-50), was an *eques Danus, sed Erico infestissimus, profugusque ad Abelum* ("A Danish knight, but a bitter enemy of Ericus, who had fled to Abelus", II, 30). Condensed as it is, with adjectives and substantives dominating at the expense of finite verbs, this construction may well be called Tacitean. The same is true of Meursius's many omissions of *esse* in the perfect passive; the fates of the Englishmen who suffered defeat against the army of Canutus Magnus in the eleventh century are described thus: *multi cæsi, plures capti; qui dimissi, præmio libertatis suæ persoluto* ("many were slain, many captured; the latter were released when the price of their freedom had been discharged", I, 53).

Meursius is fond of pungent and conspicuous expressions. A longer passage in Svaning is clearly and elegantly condensed into: *Qui, adventu intellecto, fugam capit, et evadit: indulgente Christiano, qui elabi, quam prehendi, fratrem mallet* ("perceiving the other's arrival, he took flight and made his escape; Christianus condoned this, preferring that his brother should slip away rahter than be seized", III, 15). Johannes's (1481-1513) declaration of war against Ditmarsken was too bold, as Svaning disapprovingly notes (*Chronicon Ioannis*, XIr); Meursius gives it a more positive and majestic

---

[25] I have discussed the stylistic aspect of Meursius's Tacitism in more detail in Skovgaard-Petersen 1995. The seminal work on the Attic writers of the seventeenth century is Croll 1921.

ring by this construction: *Ioannes, sumptis semel armis, et bellare, et vincere, suetus* ("Johannes, accustomed to fighting and winning once he had taken up arms", III, 31), and a little later Meursius adds rhetorical force to Johannes's declaration of war: *mox denuntiat: quando principem recusarent, hostem sese habituros* ("He shortly made this declaration: when they rejected their prince, they could consider him their enemy", III, 32).

Sometimes he takes advantage of the outward similarity between two words: *uti clarus, ita carus* ("he was as precious as he was prestigious", I, 54), *ut severitatis nimiæ serio tandem, quanquam sero, poenituerit* ("so that he finally repented of his over-severity, gravely, even if belatedly", III, 66). Or he creates an effect by combining one word with two concepts from different spheres: *Vermundus, plenus gaudii, et dierum, vita excedit* ("Vermundus departed this life full of joy and years", I, 15); or he uses the active and the passive forms of a word to make a condensed paradox: *cum huc usque formidabilis universis exstitisset, nunc formidans* ("Though hitherto he had been feared by all, he himself was now in fear", I, 34).[26]

Such condensed contrasts are frequent: *victoria, laudabiliter parta, turpiter utens; et infamiam gloria majorem referens* ("After a victory won praiseworthily, he now used it villainously; and his glory brought with it greater disgrace", I, 26), *Sivardus [...] meliore multo animo, quam fortuna* ("Sivardus, his spirits much brighter than his fortunes", I, 31). The point may be the contrast between one and many: *ne contra plures hostes uno tempore bellum habere cogeretur* ("lest he be compelled to wage war against several enemies all at one time", I, 53), *Neque principes una Dania duos caperet* ("Nor could a single Denmark contain two princes", I, 1), or he contrasts life-death, peace-war: *mortem nactus, qualem ante vitam habuerat* ("Meeting a death which resembled the life he had had previously", I, 3), *quam paraverat armis gloriam, pace universam amisit* ("The renown he had gained in war he lost entirely during peace", I, 34).

He also a few times borrows pungent expressions from Tacitus himself. Olo, one of the legendary kings, was, like Tacitus's Galba (*Hist.* I, Ch. 49), *regno dignus [...] ni regnasset* ("Worthy of rule [...] had he not ruled", I, 30). The conflict after the death of Frederik I in 1533 when the Catholic bishops gradually lost ground, is at one point described in these terms: *Cum in partes [...] itum, prout spes, metusve impelleret* ("When they had taken

---

[26] Another example: *Atque ita rex fortissimus, et clarissimus, restituta regno Daniæ boreali monarchia, toties victrices manus, animi dolore victus, sibi infert. quique vitam maxima cum laude egerat, cum opprobrio summo finit, morte neque viro digna, ne dum rege* (I, 6) (– here the contrast between the honourable life of the king, Hadingus, and his disgraceful death is further elaborated).

sides, just as hope or fear drove them", col. 812), taken from Tacitus's *Histories: ut quemque metus vel spes impulerat* ("as each had been driven by fear or hope", *Hist.* I, Ch. 19).

All these features suggest, as I mentioned above, an inspiration from contemporary Tacitism. It must be stressed, though, that syntactically Meursius's Tacitism is moderate. Unlike Tacitus and his imitators Meursius strives to achieve balanced periods and normally puts the main verb at the end of a period.

Meursius's use of verbal tenses follows a consistent pattern. The historic present is very often employed in action-packed contexts instead of the perfect tense, while the historic infinitive correspondingly replaces the imperfect though not as frequently. The present tense, moreover, is used for the general moral and political observations. The imperfect is also found in various kinds of summaries of the type: *Certe miser Daniæ tunc status erat* ("Certainly the condition of Denmark was wretched at that stage", I, 31), *ac Guthormus ideo plebi gratus erat* ("For this reason Guthormus was beloved of the common folk", I, 45).

Throughout Meursius follows the same principles in structuring syntactical periods in accordance with the contents, as the following examples will demonstrate. First let us take a look at his description of a battle in 1534:

> Christianus, qui Coldingae consistebat, quum Fionii, quamquam dubio rumore, defecisse nuntiantur, postquam vero Ioannes Frisius, aliique certiorem reddidissent, e vestigio copias adversus mittit laborantibus subventuras, ducibus Ioanne Rantzovio, Petro Ebbonio, Ioanne Iulio. Illi postquam in Fioniam traiecissent, obvios ad Farscoviae montem oppidanos, rusticosque habuere, qui armorum insolentes, ideoque nec sat gnari, quum ad manus ventum esset, loco facile cesserunt; et incondita multitudo sine mora dissipata. Multi caesi; quidam fuga evasere; regiorum vero pauci admodum desiderati; uno praelio res peracta, et recepti, qui defecerunt, Frisio, Rantzovioque nomine regis Christiani fidem suam iuramento obligarunt (col. 843).[27]

---

[27] "Christianus had stopped at Kolding when he was informed that the people of Funen had revolted, though the report was uncertain; but once Johannes Frisius and others had verified the rumour, the monarch immediately sent his troops against them under the leadership of Johannes Rantzovius, Petrus Ebbonius and Johannes Julius, so that they might bring help to those in trouble. Once they had crossed over into Funen, near the hill of Faurskov the soldiers encountered both townsmen and peasants; being inexperienced in handling weapons and therefore not sufficiently skilful when it came to grappling with their adversaries, they were easily removed from the field and disordered masses quickly dispersed. Many were cut

Christianus (III) learns of a riot in Funen and sends troops to put it down. This is the background, related in a period with many subordinate constructions (*Christianus* [...] *Iulio*). Hypotactic, too, is the description of the organization of the battle in the first part of the following period (*Illi* [...] *ventum esset*), which, however, ends in two paratactic statements on the result of the battle (*loco* [...] *dissipata*); and the parataxis continues in the final enumeration of the various fates of the losers (*multi* [...] *obligarunt*).[28]

A similar hypotactic description of the background of a battle followed by a swift, matter-of-fact account of its outcome is found in the description of the clash between the legendary King Sivardus and the Swedish King Gotharus:

> nam Gotharus cum mox sponsam per legatum eundem peteret, isque in via, in Hallandiæ quodam pago, a latronibus circumventus, pene interfectus esset; ac, periculo vix elapsus, et reversus ad Gotharum, rem narrasset; ille hoc Sivardi fraude factum ratus, bello vindicare injuriam, quam existimabat, statuit. itaque et bellum infert, et Sivardum, occurrentem in Hallandiæ finibus, sternit (I, 31).[29]

In the first long period, the course of events narrated in the *cum*-clause (*nam Gotharus cum* [...] *peteret, isque* [...] *narrasset*), provides the background for Gotharus's decision to wage war on the Danish king (*ille* [...] *statuit*). The resulting defeat of Sivardus then follows in two paratactic main clauses (*itaque* [...] *infert, et* [...] *sternit*).

Recurrent, too, are the "headlines" (in the perfect tense) with which Meursius sums up the next event to be related. They are usually followed by an explanatory conjunction such as *nam, enim* or *quippe*. One example will suffice:

---

down; some fled to safety; a very few of the king's men were lost; so, the affair was over and done with after a single battle and the rebels, accepted back, pledged their faith to Frisius and Rantzovius, swearing by the name of King Christianus".

[28] As usual, Meursius has abbreviated Krag's version (*Historia regis Christiani III*, 60). Although he has a similar shift from hypotaxis to staccato-like parataxis, the contrast is not as strong as in Meursius.

[29] "Shortly after, when Gotharus was having his betrothed fetched to him by the same envoy, the latter was beset by robbers in a village of Halland and almost killed; after escaping the peril with some difficulty he got back to Gotharus and told his tale; the latter, believing this treachery had been engineered by Sivardus, resolved to avenge the supposed wrong by warfare. He therefore launched hostilities against Sivardus and, meeting him on the borders of Halland, laid him low".

> Inter hæc Estritha [...] viro gratiam apud fratrem reparavit: quanquam ea minus diuturna fuit. nam Roschildiæ postquam ille in convivio temulentus cladem Danis [...] carmine a se composito nimis temere exprobraret, irritatus mox Canutus [...] (I, 55).[30]

This practice also contributes to the lucidity of Meursius's account. The reader is at once informed about the central point in the following exposition.

The stylistic unity of Meursius's work not only comes out in his choice of words, syntax and rhetorical figures. The numerous moral and political reflections also contribute to the general homogeneity. The same applies to another recurrent feature, the summing up and evaluation of the reign of each king. Unity and homogeneity mark the work, both in choice of subjects and in style. Meursius's own awareness of the virtue of stylistic unity emerges in his answer (mentioned above, p. 141) to the anonymous nobleman who had advised him to supply the dates of each king's reign, a practice Meursius only adopts at the beginning of Part II (i.e. from the year 1182). No, says Meursius, that would spoil the unity; without doubt Saxo himself could have added the years in the latter part of his history, but it is a sign of his sound judgement that he preferred to omit them altogether in order to preserve the unity of his work.[31]

Stylistic unity is a central concept of classical historiography. Nipperdey describes it in these words:

> So, in their national histories the ancients excluded every single word from foreign languages; in fact they also excluded all passages written in the language they themselves used but created by another person and therefore framed in another style. And for the same reason they did not introduce available speeches or letters into such historical works, but rather, insofar as they retained the content, adjusted the expression so that it harmonized with all the rest of their work.[32]

---

[30] "Meanwhile Estritha [...] restored her brother's friendship towards her husband, although it did not last very long. For when the latter had become drunk at a banquet in Roskilde and criticized a Danish disaster rather too thoughtlessly in a song he had composed himself, in a short time Canutus became exasperated".

[31] *Potuisset sine dubio Saxo noster in nonnullis postremorum etiam annos indicare, uti factum a Pontano. Sed profecto vir egregii iudicii, quod non posset in principio, illud nec in fine voluit: arbitratus, faciem historiae decoram magis, si a se differret nusquam, et ubique similis foret* (Ioannis Meursi ad adnotationes viri illustris a Domino Cancellario sibi communicatas responsio, (Meursius 1741-63, IX, col. 1131)).

[32] *Die Alten haben also in der Staatengeschichte durchaus alle Wörter fremder Sprachen ausgeschlossen; sie haben aber auch alles ausgeschlossen, was zwar in der Sprache, in der sie schrieben, aber von einer anderen*

With his consistent adaptation of his sources to a homogeneous style, Meursius is on a par with the classical historians. He never introduces a quotation, either from other authors or from documents. The words are his own throughout. Only very occasionally does he refer to other authors (name and sometimes title, no details of chapters and pages),[33] and interestingly, he never mentions his two main sources, Svaning and Pontanus. We shall return in the discussion of narrator and authority to Meursius's lack of quotations and his few references. But first let us take a look at the very different practice of Pontanus.

Person und darum in einem anderen Stil verfasst war. Deswegen haben sie vorhandene Reden oder Briefe anderer in solche Geschichtswerke nicht aufgenommen, sondern, indem sie den Inhalt beibehielten, den Ausdruck im Einklang mit dem ganzen Werk umgestaltet (Nipperdey: *Die antiken Historiographie*, Berlin 1877, 418sq. Quoted from E. Norden: *Die Antike Kunstprosa*, 89).

[33] E.g. I, 35, 36, 37, 43.

Pontanus

1. Introduction

At the beginning of this chapter I characterized the style of Pontanus as heterogeneous as opposed to the uniformity of Meursius. In this section I shall discuss the nature of this heterogeneity in more detail. Compared with Meursius, two aspects seem striking. For one thing Pontanus's *History* is filled with quotations; the texts quoted are primarily documents (which Pontanus in most cases found in Huitfeldt's work), classical and medieval Latin authors, and occasionally inscriptions and various kinds of verses. As mentioned earlier (Chapter V), the quotations take up about 130 of the total 636 pages of the chronological narrative in the 1631 edition.[1] All these quotations in themselves entail a certain abrupt character, the more so, since they are not all in Latin; English, German, Danish are all represented. Secondly, Pontanus's account alternates constantly between a narrative and a reasoning mode; now a course of events is set forth plainly, now the versions of various authors are discussed, the probability of a piece of information is considered, alternative versions are mentioned, etc. This argumentative mode is characterized by a prominent narrator. In Meursius's text such argumentative passages are few; or to put it in another way, the roles of the narrator in Pontanus's and Meursius's texts are quite different. (Another feature which contributes to the heterogeneous character of Pontanus's text, also graphically, is the numerous lists of kings and genealogical trees).

In this section I shall first discuss Pontanus's strategy of quoting and then the related topic of the way he paraphrases his sources. The second aspect, the role of the narrator, will be discussed with respect to both Pontanus and Meursius in a separate section, which will form a conclusion to the chapter on style.

---

[1] This figure (which is, of course, only approximate) only includes quotations which are graphically marked as such (by italics or quotation marks). I have not counted the many passages where Pontanus reuses the wording of another author without indication; nor have I included passages of this type: *Et author est Gulielmus Gemmeticensis, ut ejus verbis utar* (141), where the the wording of the source is adapted to the syntax of Pontanus's text.

2. *Indications of Sources and Quotations*

To a modern reader the number of quotations in Pontanus's work may seem formidable. Much of the material which in scientific literature of later periods has been reserved for footnotes, for the purpose of documentation or discussion, is here part of the text itself. Besides, Pontanus and his contemporary colleagues no doubt quote more extensively than historians of later times, their foot-notes included.

In many cases, though, Pontanus is content to refer to his sources and give a paraphrase of their contents. In that respect he also differs markedly from Meursius, as we just saw. Where Meursius, in Parts I-III, that is up to 1523, altogether refers to other authors fewer than fifty times, Pontanus in the first ten books, up to 1448, reaches a total of between 900 and 1000. Moreover Meursius's references are found together in clusters, in the few cases where he notes a disagreement between the sources.

Pontanus does not, however, refer to his informants with any degree of consistency. It was not a matter of principle to him that the reader should constantly be aware of the source of a given piece of information. Very often he follows a source without indication. But when he leaves the source to add some sort of information, he will often mention the new source. Moreover, a source may be referred to by various names. Huitfeldt is sometimes mentioned by name, sometimes his work is referred to as *annales domestici* (540), *annales* (280), *chronologi* (509), or similar designations, just as *Scotorum annales* (106) refers to George Buchanan, who is elsewhere mentioned by name.

References to other authors are always made in cases of doubt, whether Pontanus himself casts doubt on the information of a given source, or whether he informs the reader that several conflicting accounts of the same event are to be found. In his account of Canutus Durus (whom he dates 1037-45), he first follows "English annals", *Annales Anglici* (173-74), and then informs us that the Danes, among them Saxo, give another version: "However, our native writers, especially Saxo Grammaticus, whose word must in no way be rejected, have set out the history of these times far differently. For Saxo relates [...]"[2] – and then follows a summary of Saxo, in the accusative with infinitive. Apparently Pontanus thereby marks

---

[2] *Scriptores tamen domestici, et Saxo præcipue Grammaticus, cui fides nequaquam est abroganda, temporum horum historiam longe aliter digerunt. Tradit enim Saxo* [...] (174).

a certain scepticism towards Saxo as opposed to the English version, which he has just related in direct form. On the other hand, he explicitly claims in the above quotation that Saxo should not be doubted. It seems, then, that he does not make a decision as to who is right. Then he calls attention to a point on which Adam of Bremen differs from Saxo ("Although Adam of Bremen seems to imply" (*Quamvis Adamus Bremensis innuere videatur,* 174)), adding to that a piece of information from *Saxonici annales,* which seems to agree with Adam and not with Saxo, although Pontanus does not say so explicitly. He simply reports the contents of the various versions without taking a stand. Finally he mentions another Danish account, the *Annals of Ryd,* which, unlike the texts hitherto mentioned, is quoted and not paraphrased (174-75).

Why is this last version quoted? Why not Saxo or the English sources? One answer is that they are "almost" quoted, but without indication. At least in the case of Saxo, Pontanus has taken over most of his words and rendered them in an indirect form. It is often difficult to explain why Pontanus chose to quote some texts and paraphrase others. On the other hand, it is possible to enumerate a number of the functions which the quotations serve.

3. The Functions of the Quotations

In many cases Pontanus himself states a reason for his introducing a quotation. In trying to come to grips with their functions let us take his own explanations as a point of departure.

As for documents and inscriptions their status as direct testimonies is the central point. Having mentioned the tombstone of Haraldus (*Harald Blåtand,* dated 931-80) in Roskilde, Pontanus claims, in words that have a general bearing, that this inscription is more trustworthy than historical writing:

> His epitaph, which is still there today, despite its being rather unpolished and not particularly charming or graceful, a characteristic of that age, still evinces a truer record of the year in which he departed this life than do the calculations of the annalists.[3]

---

[3] *Epicedium ejus, quod ibi hodieque exstat, licet id, prout tum erat seculum, incultius minusque amoenum aut elegans sit, annum interim, quo vita excessit, multo, quam æræ chronologorum, certius annotatum subindicat* (136).

Similarly the numerous quotations of documents are often motivated by their particular worth as contemporary sources, as in the case of the agreement between Valdemarus III and the Swedish king, Magnus Smek, in 1343: "There were documents delivered in Latin on this matter, which I have added next, and in the identical form to that in which they were written",[4] and, to take an early example, as in the case of the Emperor Otto III's bestowing of privileges to four Danish churches: "because of the record they preserve of that ancient event, I have thought fit to add these next in the form and wording of that era, as they were conceived".[5]

The same awareness of the significance of age is displayed in connection with literary quotations, where Pontanus often notes the author's being contemporary or almost contemporary with the events. An example is the *Slavonic Chronicle* of Helmold, which Pontanus used extensively in dealing with the eleventh and twelfth centuries:

> I must not here leave out Helmold's mention of this matter; I have quoted his testimony several times already, inasmuch as he was a contemporary author who lived in those times,[6]

he declares when telling of the pact between Henricus Leo and Valdemarus I in the 1160s. Upon the death of Absalon, the influential counsellor of Valdemarus I, Pontanus similarly brings in the near-contemporary testimony of Arnold of Lübeck:

> It would be worth my while setting down here in his own words the thoughts about Absalon expressed by Arnold, the abbot of Lübeck, who flourished about this time and who wrote a continuation of Helmold.[7]

An attempt of the Pope to make the Norwegian king Emperor is also documented with a quotation from a contemporary author:

> Concerning him there is the account of Matthew Paris, who was not only an eye-witness but an ear-witness, and more important than any

---

[4] *Datis ea de re Latine literis, quas eadem quoque, qua tum conscriptæ sunt, formula proxime subjeci* (468).

[5] *quas ob antiquitatis ac rei memoriam, qua conceptæ sunt ævi ejus phrasi ac formula, proxime subjiciendas putavi* (137).

[6] *Non omittenda hoc loco Helmoldi, quem aliquoties jam, utpote temporum horum authorem coævum ac synchronum, ad testimonium citavimus, de re eadem commemoratio* (244).

[7] *De Absalone vero ipso quid senserit, qui hoc circiter seculo floruit, Abbas Lubecensis Arnoldus, qui Helmoldum continuavit, operæ pretium sit ejus hic verbis apponere* (293).

363

other inasmuch as he performed the duty of envoy to Haquinus during this period. In fact I shall next add his own words, just as they deserve, since they recall the fame of Denmark and Norway.[8]

In the earliest history the classical authors play a prominent role. The long quotations guarantee the truth of Pontanus's account of the Cimbrians and the Goths and their Scandinavian origin. These authors were almost contemporary with the events they relate, and furthermore they have a special authority. They are *en bloc* trustworthy authors (*certi authores*).

In some cases Pontanus allows the reader to follow his deliberations as to whether a given source should be quoted. That too much is better than too little seems to have been the decisive argument in favour of quoting a distich on the death of Christophorus III in 1448:

> At that time an elegiac poem of a single couplet was composed on his death; it was of rough artistry, reflecting the era in its quality and comprising almost nothing more than the year and day of his departure, which I stated above; for this reason I had decided not to put it in, but nevertheless I did so, so that nothing should appear to be missing.[9]

A similar striving for completeness is apparent in the reasons he gives for quoting a document in its entirety, as in this introduction to a document from 1425:

> However, in case it should appear that I had omitted something, I have added a copy of the regulation we are talking about, word for word as it was drawn up;[10]

similarly he is doubtful whether to quote a deed from 1303, which he found rather lengthy: "However, so that I do not appear to have left anything out, you can see that I have added it verbatim" (*Ne quid tamen omisisse videamur, en et ipsas verbotenus adjecimus*, 392).

---

[8] *De quo exstant Matthæi Parisiensis verba, testis non oculati modo, sed auriti quoque atque omni exceptione majoris, utpote qui per idem tempus ad Haquinum [...] legati munus obijt. Sed ipsa eius verba, quia id merentur ob Danici Norvagicique nominis memoriam, hic proxime subjiciam (347-48).*

[9] *Concinnatum per id tempus in obitum ejus Elegiacum rudioris Minervæ carmen ac seculi sui venam unico disticho referens, nec quicquid fere præter annum et mortis diem superius expressos complectens; quocirca nec adscribere constitueram: Adscripsi tamen, ne quid omissum videretur (635).*

[10] *Verum ne quid a nobis omissum videatur, ipsius hujus, de qua loquimur, Constitutionis, cujusmodi ea concepta verbotenus fuit, exemplum subjeci (579).*

It is characteristic of Pontanus that he displays uncertainty on the surface, so to speak, in cases of conflicting versions or inherent improbabilities. Then the quotations serve the purpose of documenting the single versions. A long quotation from the Norman historian, William of Jumièges (writing in the latter half of the eleventh century), is about Haraldus's (*Harald Blåtand*) stay in Normandy (tenth century). Pontanus observes that it contains information not found in Danish sources, and he goes on:

> Nevertheless I will bring in at some length the words of the old author, William of Jumièges, because he has described those events accurately and has added when incidents occurred.[11]

Here the emphasis on William's care and the antiquity of his work suggest that Pontanus regards this version as at least as probable as the Danish. But sometimes he indicates a discreet scepticism. In summing up the qualities of a later Haraldus (1074-80), Pontanus quotes Saxo's negative judgement, apparently because he will not himself guarantee this point of view: "That our own Saxo was rather unfair on him must be demonstrated by his rather than my words" (*Saxonem nostrum minus ei æquum fuisse, ejus potius quam meis verbis declarandum*, 196).

Quotations of old poems and inscriptions are often accompanied by a commentary on their old-fashioned Latin. A contemporary poem on the coronation of Christophorus III in 1443 is presented in these words:

> The verses written about this event at that time, speaking in the vocabulary and phraseology of their age, I have set down for the reader to see here, in case I should appear to have missed something out;[12]

the twelfth century funeral inscription of a Dane in Vratislava is written in verses "which smack of that age" (*qui seculum istud resipiunt*, 229). An eleventh century funeral inscription is, in Pontanus's eyes, downright clumsy, "with its syllables a mixture of iambs and choriambs in rough artistry, it was characteristic of its age" (*mixtis ex jambis et choriambis rudi minerva, ut tum erat seculum, syllabis*, 192), and in similar terms he criticizes the funeral inscription of Christophorus III (635, quoted above). These

---

[11] *Sed verba Gemmeticensis antiqui auctoris, qui eam historiam accurate, et additis rerum occasionibus, prosecutus est, plenius subjiciemus* (132).

[12] *Versus, qui eo tempore hac de re consignati, lexi ac seculi ejus phrasi loquentes, ne quid omisisse videamur, ecce ipsos adscripsi* (621)

declarations should probably be regarded as excuses for quoting medieval Latin, mirroring humanistic contempt. But there may also be a
more positive side to it. Introducing the poem *Plange primatus Daciæ* from
the 1220s, he does in fact use its old-fashioned form as one of the reasons for quoting it:

> Redolent as it is of the spirit of that period, it will serve as a demonstra-
> tion of the verses which Fauns and native bards once sang.[13]

Although there is no doubt an element of excuse, it is the cultural interest
of the poem that is explicitly emphasized. The song provides an example
of the poetry of our forefathers. The last part, *quales [...] canebant*, alludes to
the early Roman poet Ennius, who with these words referred to the less refined poetry of previous generations, as we know from Cicero's *Brutus*.[14]
Arguably Pontanus, by associating the medieval poem with old, primitive
Roman poetry invests it with a certain reverence. Perhaps, then, his many
other remarks about the old-fashioned language of medieval texts about
to be quoted should not just be seen as excuses. By drawing attention to the
fact that in earlier days language and style were different, less polished,
Pontanus may also want to suggest that these texts have a claim on the
reader's interest as cultural testimonies.

Huitfeldt in another context gives a similar reason for quoting a medieval Latin poem, viz. that it will illustrate the poetical taste of the day (and
he does not conceal that he finds it unpolished) (*Chron. II*, 397-401). The
poem is a lamentation over the state of Denmark in the reign of
Christophorus II (1320-32). Pontanus chose to leave this poem out and, interestingly, he explains why: in his opinion its attack on both the king and
the people was scurrilous; it read like a defamatory piece of writing (456).
So here his concern for the dignity of his work and its subject made him
depart from his usual practice of all-inclusive quotation (*Ne quid tamen omisisse videamur*, is a reason he often gives for introducing a quotation).[15]

In a couple of places Pontanus does in fact adduce the aesthetic qualities of a poem as a reason for quoting it:

---

[13] *quæ et seculi genium redolens indicio erit, quales tum versus Fauni vatesque canebant* (310).

[14] Cf. Cicero, Brutus, Ch. 18 (71): *quos olim Fauni vatesque canebant*. In the translation I have
borrowed from the Loeb version.

[15] A further note on songs: Pontanus was familiar with Anders Sørensen Vedel's collection of
old Danish ballads of 1591 (it is mentioned on p. 311). He refers to the ballad of the death
of Queen Dagmar (302) and a song which blamed Valdemarus III (1340-75) for having a
share in a murder (486); in connection with the small town of Vestervig, he mentions *Liden*

as its details are expressed more concisely, so they are stated more elegantly than in the long-drawn-out chronicles of many writers. Therefore
I considered it worthwhile to insert it at this point,[16]

he says of the funeral inscription of the eleventh-century King Sveno III.

Also in connection with documents, Pontanus frequently comments
upon their old-fashioned language: "This is the wording of a document
which the people of Funen published in Latin, in the diction of that era,
on this choice they had made" (*Literarum, quas Fionenses super eadem electione
Latinas et ejus seculi phrasi evulgarunt, hoc exemplum est*, 514), he says of a document in which the inhabitants of Funen recognize Margareta as their
queen in 1387, and similarly a document from 1413 is introduced with
these words: "Since we have all these particulars set out in Latin, compre-
hended in the phraseology normal at that time, it seemed a good idea to
append them" (*Sed hæc cuncta cum Latine concepta habeamus, phrasi et verbis eo
seculo usitatis, ea* [...] *subjicere visum fuit*, 548). Again, there is a definite element
of excuse in this emphasis on the dated Latin. But then it also serves to
underscore the antiquity of the documents and consequently their reliability – an aspect also present in the quotations of songs and inscriptions.

There is one further function of the quotations which deserves attention, namely that of prestige. Unlike the functions so far discussed, this
one is nowhere explicitly mentioned in the text. But I do not think we are
wrong in seeing an underlying message in the demonstration that so
many authors in the course of history have taken notice of the Danish
nation and its inhabitants (even when it was not for any laudatory purpose). It is an indirect testimony to the historical importance of Denmark, and it certainly adds to the prestige of Danish history to document
its influence on European affairs all the way from classical antiquity by
means of authentic quotations.

Summing up the functions mentioned so far, the keyword is documentation. Quotations serve to document, or to guarantee, that these
were the very words used. Even in the few cases where Pontanus quotes
a text only to express his own scepticism, the quotation guarantees that
these were the words used by the author. In the great majority of cases,
when Pontanus does not distance himself from the contents of the quo-

---

Kirsten in the *Chorographica descriptio* (663). He regarded these songs as contemporary testimonies and used them as sources of information.

[16] *ut brevius ita quoque venustius quam longis multorum annalibus exprimuntur. Itaque et apponendum hoc
loco pretium operæ existimavi* (192).

tations, they bestow authority, convincing us that Pontanus builds his account upon relevant material. Pontanus thereby invokes, or borrows, the authority of the authors, documents, and inscriptions he quotes. He builds up his own authority on the basis of all these earlier authorities. In a way, by incorporating their words into his work, he turns them into his own. And then it also works the other way round: by being part of Pontanus's work, a quotation is also invested with an extra authority, in the sense that Pontanus vouches for it as well.[17]

Documentation, then, is a basic function of the quotations in Pontanus's text. But they also perform another service relating to the process of composition: there is a time-saving side to quoting. Again, Pontanus does in fact sometimes hint at this aspect: "I thought I ought to add now a copy of this codicil, because it contains further material on inheritance, the guardianship of children and similar topics" (*Eorum codicillorum exemplum, quia et alia insuper de hæreditate et tutela liberorum similiaque continet, proxime subjiciendum putavi,* 450).[18] This is no doubt a very important reason for the many quotations in Pontanus's work. The long quotations from Livy, Florus and other classical authors at the beginning to some extent provide substitutes for his own composition of an account of these events.[19] This time-saving motive does not, of course, exclude the documentary aspect. In many cases they are probably both at work.

Pontanus's blatant rejection of the classical ideal of stylistic unity is noteworthy. In one sense he simply conformed to the practice of his time, inasmuch as quotations are a characteristic feature of learned Neo-

---

[17] In their investigation of a number of learned Neo-Latin texts, M. Benner & E. Tengström point out that the quotations in their material do not live up to modern standards of accuracy; not only have punctuation and spelling sometimes been changed without indication but words have also been omitted (Benner & Tengström 1977, 33). The same is no doubt true in Pontanus's case (although I have not, when I have had occasion to compare Pontanus's quotations with contemporary editions, come across such differences). Gertz notes in his critical edition of the *Plange primatus Dacie* (*Scriptores Minores I*, 476-79) that Pontanus corrected several errors found in Huitfeldt's version of the poem, without drawing attention to these corrections.

[18] Other examples: *Sed ipsæ hæ literæ, idiomate vernaculo evulgatæ, cum et alia non prætereunda propius cuncta exprimant, earum, quantum potuit, sensum atque exemplum hic subjiciendum existimavi* (464). A passage from William of Newburgh is introduced in these words: *Sed operæ pretium erit ipsius Neubrigensis verba, quod et alia ad rem spectantia contineant, his adjicere* (286), and similarly a quotation from the *Chronicon Norwegiæ*: *Cujus chronologi verba ipsa cum ob hoc tum alia, quæ interseruntur, ponenda verbotenus putavi* (202).

[19] Cf. the heading of the extract from Isidore's *Chronicon Gothorum*: *Isidori breve Chronicon Gothorum Ad uberiorem paulo enarrationem eorum, quæ superius de rebus præsertim Visegothorum in Hispania parcius sunt indicata, obiter additum* (70).

Latin prose. Their functions have been discussed by M. Benner & E. Tengström on the basis of a sample of Swedish seventeenth-century treatises of diverse disciplines, and they, too, point, *inter alia*, to time-saving and documentation as important factors.[20]

A glance at contemporary historical works reveals that Pontanus's habit of extensive quotation agrees with the practice adopted by writers of antiquarian descriptions in such productions as Beatus Rhenanus's *Res Germanicæ* (1531), Camden's *Britannia* (1586), Wolfgang Lazius's *Vienna Austriæ* (1546), and the antiquarian introduction of Buchanan's *Rerum Scoticarum historia* (1582); in these works we find numerous quotations, from other authors, documents and inscriptions, some Latin, some vernacular. Turning to chronological narratives, however, we find occasional quotations of documents or of other historians incorporated, e.g. in Johannes Magnus's *Historia de omnibus Gothorum Sveonumque regibus* (1554), Carlo Sigonio's *Historiarum de regno Italiæ libri quindecim* (1575), and Johannes Mariana's *Historiae de rebus Hispaniae libri XX* (1592). But these authors are all much more modest in their use of quotations than Pontanus and the antiquarian authors, being in this respect closer to the classical ideal of stylistic unity.[21] This is yet another indication of the affinity of Pontanus's *History* with the antiquarian branch of contemporary historiography.

4. Close Paraphrases and Quotations

It is not only in the form of quotations that the words of other texts recur in Pontanus's history. He often follows his sources so closely that the boundary between quotation and paraphrase seems blurred. I have here used a tangible criterion, viz. the graphical signs; only text graphically marked as quotation (by italics or inverted commas) has been counted as such. In these cases Pontanus always indicates the source of the words. That is not always the case when he merely paraphrases another text, even if he follows the wording meticulously.

---

[20] Benner & Tengström 1977, 32-36. Quotations were of course no recent invention. Although they had no place in classicizing artistic prose, they were found in less ambitious genres and became frequent in late antiquity and the Middle Ages (*ibidem*, 37).

[21] I have only seen one contemporary chronological narrative with a comparable amount of quotation, and that is Pontanus's own *Geldrian History*, which he composed in the 1630s.

As noted earlier it is hard to discern a principle as to when Pontanus chooses to quote and when he chooses to paraphrase.[22] Let us take a look at some examples of close paraphrases (*verbatim* agreements between Pontanus and his sources are marked in bold).

Ideological motives are clearly behind Pontanus's verbal changes of a passage from the *English History* of Polydore Vergil. It is about a battle in 857 (the date given by Pontanus) between Danes and Englishmen (the last part has already been quoted in Chapter VI).

> *Polydore Vergil:* Aluredus postridie illius diei, quam eo pervenerat, copias suas satis auctas in aciem eduxit: nec hostes extraxerunt pugnam, quam acriter coeptam viriliter tolerarunt, coactoque simul exercitu, nunquam alias tantis fere copiis, tantis animis dimicarunt: quippe tanto irarum certamine gesta res est, vt a neutra parte emissa sint tela: gladiis pugna coepit, et acerrime commissa, quæ adeo anceps fuit, vt non cum Dacis sæpe antea fusis, fugatis, atque etiam victis, sed cum aliqua noua gente videretur dimicatio esse (101).[23]

> *Pontanus:* **Aluredus postridie** ejus **diei quam eo**dem advenisset, **copias suas satis auctas in aciem eduxit; nec** Dani **extraxerunt pugnam,** sed **acriter coeptam viriliter tolerarunt; quippe tanto irarum certamine gesta res est, ut** neutra **a parte emissa sint tela**<;> **gladijs pugna coepit et acerrime commissa adeo anceps fuit ut non cum Danis** aut notis adversarijs **sed cum gente aliqua nova videretur esse dimicatio** (105).[24]

---

[22] In their investigation of stylistical characteristics of learned Neo-Latin prose in Latin from seventeenth-century Sweden, Benner & Tengström also observe that there seem to be no clear rules for the use of quotation as opposed to paraphrase.

[23] "On the day after Aluredus had arrived there, he led his troops into battle, with a fair increase in their numbers; nor did his enemies delay the strife, which began keenly and was borne manfully, for once their army had gathered, they contended with almost as many forces and with as high courage as on any earlier occasion. The action was fought with such rivalry in rage that neither side launched its missiles; the struggle began with swords, was engaged with the greatest ferocity, and was so equally matched that the contest did not seem to be waged against the Danes, whom they had often previously routed and sent fleeing, and vanquished, too, but with some unheard-of foe". (The first edition of Polydore Vergil's *Anglica historia* came out in 1534. The edition used here is from 1570 (Basel)).

[24] "On the day after Aluredus had arrived there, he led his troops into battle, with a fair increase in their numbers; nor did the Danes delay the strife, which began keenly and was borne manfully. The action was fought with such rivalry in rage that neither side launched its missiles; the struggle began with swords, was engaged with the greatest ferocity, and was so equally matched that the contest did not seem to be waged against the Danes or any well-known opponents but with some unheard-of foe".

Pontanus only made a few alterations. But they are significant. Towards the end he left out Vergil's pointed reference to the Danes as an enemy often defeated, placing them instead in the category of known enemies. At the beginning he changed Vergil's English point of view, referring to the Danes not as enemies but simply as Danes. At the end of the passage, however, he did not follow up this line; the Danes are here seen as adversaries, as in Polydore Vergil, since it is from the English point of view that the enemies seemed like a new people. Besides, Pontanus left out Vergil's remark that the Danes had never before fought as fiercely (*nunquam alias tantis fere copiis, tantis animis dimicarunt*). For one thing, since the fighting was indecisive, it was not a very flattering observation; furthermore, being about the heroes of Pontanus's work, it may have seemed too brief and general.

In his treatment of the Danish wars in England and Scotland in the ninth and tenth centuries Pontanus made extensive use of the Scottish history of George Buchanan, first published in 1582. The following example is about a battle between Scots and Danes at the beginning of Haraldus's (*Harald Blåtand*) reign:

> *Buchanan:* Edmundus prospiciens quanta belli moles instaret, Milcolumbum Cumbria et Vestmaria donat, ea lege, vt qui proxime in regnum Scotorum successurus esset, sacramentum Anglorum regi, ceu supremo eorum locorum domino, diceret. Deinde Danos variis calamitatibus afflictos, facile in suam ditionem redegit: nec ipse diu ei victoriæ superstes fuit. Angli in locum eius fratrem Eldredum regem creant. Aduersus hunc cum Dani, qui Nortumbriam tenebant, nec vnquam bona fide pacem cum Anglis fecerant, rebellassent, multaque loca munita de eo, in diuersa regni parte occupato cepissent: ac in primis Eboracum, decem milibus Scotorum in subsidium acceptis, Anglus eos magna clade compescuit (182).[25]

---

[25] "Edmundus, foreseeing the huge bulk of war that was threatening him, gave Cumberland and Westmoreland to Milcolumbus, with this provision, that inasmuch as he would be the next heir to the Scottish throne, he should swear allegiance to the sovereign of England as the supreme lord of those regions. Afterwards the Danes, who had suffered various disasters, were easily brought under Edmundus's sway; but he did not long outlive that victory. The English then elected his brother, Eldredus, king in his stead. The Danes, who held Northumbria and had never kept good faith when they concluded a peace with the English, had rebelled against him and taken many fortified towns, most notably York, while he was occupied in a different part of the realm; but after receiving the aid of ten thousand Scots, the English curbed them with massive slaughter". (I have used an edition from 1624 (Frankfurt am Main)).

> *Pontanus:* **Edmundus** vero, Adelstani frater, **prospiciens quanta belli moles instaret, Milcolumbum Cambria et Vestmatia donat, ea lege, ut qui proxime in regnum Scotorum successurus esset, sacramentum Anglorum regi, ceu supremo eorum locorum domino, diceret.** Atque inde **varijs calamitatibus obtritos Danos facile superavit,** licet ipse haud **diu victoriæ superstes fuerit.** Cuius **in locum** cum **frater Eldredus rex esset creatus** et **adversus** eum quoque **Dani, qui Northumbriam tenebant, nec unquam bona fide cum Anglis pacem fecerant, rebellassent multaque munita loca,** et in ijs **Eboracum cepissent,** tandem Eldredus **acceptis Scotorum** auxilijs, eos aliquatenus **compescuit** (130).[26]

The changes are few and can for the most part be ascribed to ideological and pedagogical considerations. Most interesting is the last one, where *magna clade* has been replaced by *tandem* and *aliquatenus*. The defeat of the Danes was not crushing as Buchanan has it; on the contrary, they were difficult to beat and only suffered a temporary set-back. Apart from that Pontanus added a clarification (*Adelstani frater*), he used synonyms in some cases, e.g. *atque inde* for *deinde*), changed an active construction into passive (*Eldredus rex esset creatus* for *Angli Eldredum regem creant*), probably just to reduce the number of persons, and he left out the number of Scottish auxiliary troops. He retained the syntactical structure, except in two cases: Buchanan's main clause *nec ipse diu ei victoriæ superstes fuit* has been turned into a concessive subordinate clause with *licet*, and Buchanan's following short main clause has been included in a *cum*-clause, with the effect that the English king is not so much in focus as in Buchanan's text. Otherwise Pontanus copied his Scottish colleague faithfully.

Even closer to the original is the following detailed description of a fight between Scots and Danes in 874; in fact only one word has been changed. Buchanan writes:

---

[26] "However, Edmundus, Adelstanus's brother, foreseeing the huge bulk of war that was threatening him, gave Cumberland and Westmoreland to Milcolumbus, with this provision, that inasmuch as he would be the next heir to the Scottish throne, he should swear allegiance to the sovereign of England as the supreme lord of those regions. Subsequently the Danes, who had been crushed by various disasters, were easily overcome, though he himself did not long outlive the victory. His brother Eldredus was elected king in his stead; the Danes, who held Northumbria and had never kept good faith when they concluded a peace with the English, had rebelled against him and taken many fortified towns, among them York, but eventually Eldredus, after receiving Scottish reinforcements, curbed them to a certain extent".

> Hi subito Leuini amnis incremento prohibiti cum suis vires co-
> niungere, facile victi omnesque cæsi, præter paucos, qui nandi
> periti, flumen transiere, atque ad Humbrum alterum ducem
> peruenere. Ad hos, fluuio iam permeabili, Constantinus tanquam
> ad prædam, non ad prælium ducens, eos est assecutus non procul
> a Caralia oppido, castris iam permunitis. Dani enim ab aduersæ
> pugnæ euentu magis in omnia intenti: super modicas et flexuosas
> rupes, prope littus, cumulis obiacentium passim saxorum
> aggestis, speciem valli obiecerunt. Ibi Constantinus eos adortus,
> loci iniquitate Danorum desperationem [Pontanus: *virtutem*] iuuante,
> multo cum suorum sanguine suæ temeritatis poenas luit. Magna
> enim exercitus parte amissa, ipse captus et in speluncam
> modicam tractus, occiditur. Extant adhuc eius pugnæ monu-
> menta, specus, et castrorum ambitus, non æquis spaciis dimen-
> sus, sed ad rupium flexus circumductus. Rei male gestæ culpam
> quidam in Pictos conferunt, qui a Constantino in fidem recepti, ac
> in commilitium asciti fuerant (Buchanan, 175-76; Pontanus, 106).[27]

Pontanus simply replaces *desperationem* with *virtutem* – a clearly ideological change, simple and significant. To be sure, such almost exact transcriptions of long passages without quotation marks and indication of source are few in Pontanus's work. But it highlights the question of the relationship between quotations and paraphrases in his text.

In the examples given here we can discern ideological and pedagogical motives in the small alterations. But as Benner & Tengström suggest, seventeenth-century authors did not shrink from making such simple changes when quoting other texts.[28] So we are not allowed to conclude

---

[27] "A sudden rising of the River Leven prevented them from joining forces with their fellow-soldiers, they were easily subdued, and all were killed apart from a few who were strong swimmers and crossed the river to reach their other leader, Humbrus. Constantinus led his troops towards them, the river now being passable, as if they were marching to their spoil and not to a broil; he caught up with them not far from the town of Crail, though not before the Danes had stoutly fortified their camp. After having come off worse in the fighting, the Danes were more attentive to everything; on top of some moderately high, winding rocks near the shore they erected a kind of rampart by piling up the heaps of stones which lay about everywhere. Constantinus attacked their position, but because the uneven terrain gave help to the desperate [Pontanus: valiant] Danes, he paid for his rashness with massive blood-shed among his own soldiery. Having lost a large proportion of his army, Constantinus him-self was captured and dragged to a smallish cave, where he was put to death. Memorials of that conflict still survive, namely the cave and the perimeter of the camp, which was not measured out symmetrically, but followed the winding rocks with its circumference. For the miscarriage of this operation some attribute blame to the Picts who had been taken into Constantinus's trust and enrolled as his companions-in-arms".

[28] Benner & Tengström 1977, 33.

that it was because of the change from *desperationem* to *virtutem* that Pontanus did not mark the passage above as a quotation. Even if it was the reason, it is noteworthy, seen from our modern perspective, that he did not mark any part of it as quotation.

Although, then, it is difficult to see a clear principle in his choice of paraphrase as opposed to quotation, it can at least be said that Pontanus did not refrain from taking over word for word whole periods from other texts without marking them as quotations. In this respect he differs from Meursius, in whose rewriting of other texts we could observe a number of recurrent features, such as extended use of participles and of the historic present tense, and omission of auxiliary forms of *esse*. Further it is clear that when Pontanus, as in these examples, chose not to indicate his *verbatim* borrowings and not even to refer to the author in question, he lost their documentary function. Close paraphrases, however, share with quotations the function of time-saving, and this is no doubt an important explanation of Pontanus's many such paraphrases.

It has become a commonplace in the study of Neo-Latin texts that the concept of plagiarism belongs to a later period; there was much wider scope for borrowing from other texts. After all, the idea of *imitatio* is based on the possibility of creative reuse. In our evaluation of Pontanus's transcriptions, we must, of course, be aware that literary property was by no means asserted as strictly as today. He obviously did not feel obliged to refer to his sources even when following them as closely as in the passages quoted. The works of George Buchanan and Polydore Vergil both enjoyed high status as standard works within their field. It seems likely that Pontanus's use of them was recognized at least by some readers – and that Pontanus himself was aware of that possibility and did not mind.

Pontanus's strategy was not unusual. In Albert Krantz's history of the Nordic countries (written shortly after 1500, 1st ed. 1548), for instance, long passages of Saxo's *Gesta Danorum* are included word for word, and the same is true of Johannes Magnus's *History of the Swedish Kings* (1554). None of them cared to draw attention to their *verbatim* borrowings with any degree of consistency. Other historians had different aims. One of Pontanus's successors as royal Danish historiographer, Vitus Bering (1617-75), declared that he would not reproduce a single word or a single rhetorical figure from the earlier Latin histories of Denmark from which he took his material.[29] To him stylistic independence was the primary

---

[29] Letter from Bering to an unknown addressee, written c. 1668; quoted in Rørdam's biography of Bering (Rørdam 1879, 72).

principle. Meursius, though less rigorously, displays similar ambitions – ambitions which are wholly alien to Pontanus.

In general Pontanus's prose is, as already suggested, plain and unadorned. As Meursius noted, he sometimes displays a certain stylistic awkwardness, a lack of concern; we have in passing noted a couple of examples and more will follow below. There are no recurrent rhetorical figures or effects which can be said to characterize his prose. But occasionally we meet a metaphor (*domi quoque exserere caput Bellona coepit,* "at home, too, Bellona began to stretch out her head", 102), a direct address to the reader in the form of a question (col. 766), and sometimes his use of alliteration is striking (*germane Germanum Germanis,* 94, *viros ac vires colligere,* col. 799).

Such figures, relatively few as they are, do not, as in Meursius's text, serve as a unifying factor. Among Meursius's recurrent rhetorical devices are the evaluations at the end of each chapter summing up the reign of the king treated. No such compositional pattern is adopted by Pontanus. Further, Meursius's general moral and political reflections have a unifying effect, interpreting events of Danish history along the same lines and by the same standards throughout all periods. Again, such reflections are few in Pontanus's account.

I shall discuss the connection between subject-matter and style in more detail in the section on the narrators of the texts. First I would like to close the present treatment of Pontanus with some notes on his use of Saxo and Huitfeldt.

5. Remarks on Pontanus's Use of Saxo and Huitfeldt

It was suggested above that since Pontanus takes over many passages from other texts word for word, or almost word for word, we cannot, in his case, point out a set of rhetorical devices by which he reworks his sources. This statement needs some qualification, however; I shall here limit myself to making a few observations on his adaptations of Saxo and Huitfeldt. In both cases it is possible to formulate certain principles.

Saxo

As to Saxo,[30] a tendency to "de-rhetoricize," to turn Saxo's intricate Latin into plainer prose, makes itself clearly felt. Saxo's text abounds in abstract nouns, accumulations of synonyms, parallelisms, paradoxes, and exclamations. In most cases Pontanus simplified the text of Saxo and left out these figures.

Let us take a look at some examples. In 1147 (the date is Pontanus's) the Pope sent out exhortations to the Christian world to fight barbarian neighbours. Saxo writes:

> Per eadem tempora Romanus antistes, barbaricæ tempestatis procella rem divinam pæne obrutam eversamque conspiciens, datis per Europam epistolis, universos Christianæ credulitatis hostes ab eius cultoribus oppugnari præcepit. Singulæ autem Catholicorum provinciæ confinem sibi barbariem incessere iubebantur (XIV, Ch. iii, 5).[31]

Pontanus here (among other changes) replaced the abstracts with concrete designations (*barbari* for *barbaricæ tempestatis procella*, *hostis* for *barbaries*). He shortened the papal exhortation by leaving out the first general statement that all the enemies of Christianity should be fought, and he replaced Saxo's classicizing *res divina* with the plainer *Christiana sacra:*

> **Per eadem tempora Romanus** pontifex animadvertens Christiana sacra a barbaris passim proculcari, principes per universam **Europam, datis** codicillis, adhortatur ut sumptis unanimiter armis quisque suæ **provinciæ** vicinum hostem invadat (218).[32]

Later Archbishop Absolon rebukes Valdemarus Magnus. Saxo describes Valdemarus's reaction in these words:

---

[30] Here as elsewhere I refer to the modern edition of Saxo (Olrik & Ræder 1931). But since I am here concerned with a comparison of his and Pontanus's wording, I have checked the passages from Saxo quoted below with the edition of the *Gesta Danorum* of 1576 (Frankfurt).

[31] "In this period the Pope, observing that religion was almost overwhelmed and destroyed by the tempestuous violence of the barbarians, sent letters throughout Europe directing the adherents of the Christian faith to assail all its foes. Individual Catholic states were instructed to invade the heathens across their borders".

[32] "In this period the Pope, seeing that Christian worship was everywhere being trampled down by the barbarians, sent letters to princes throughout the whole of Europe exhorting them to take up arms concurrently and urging each to attack the foe across their borders".

> Quamquam autem rex adversum dictorum eius libertatem acrius exar-
> sisset, tamen, ne monitorem impudentius avertere videretur, magni-
> tudinem iræ, quam vultu teste conceperat, moderatione sua ad leve et
> tolerabile responsum deflexit (XIV, Ch. xxiii, 8).[33]

Pontanus here replaced the abstracts *dictorum libertatem* and *magnitudinem iræ* with *liberius commonentem* and *iram*, respectively:

> Rex Absalonem recta quidem, sed liberius commonentem nonnihil aver-
> satus, iram tamen, quam vultus præferre videbatur, ad lenitatem re-
> ducens (234).[34]

In the following passage, which describes the impression made by Valde-marus Magnus on the Germans, Pontanus follows Saxo almost word for word; but he leaves out the abstract expression *sedendi humilitas obstaret* (and makes a few minor changes).

> *Saxo*: Illic exaudire erat Theutonum voces formam regis staturamque
> mirantium; quos tanta visendi eius cupiditas ceperat, ut, cum* sedendi
> humilitas obstaret, alter alterius conscensis humeris productis illum cer-
> vicibus inspectarent. Hunc regem, hunc dominum, hunc imperio
> dignum referre, Cæsarem regulum homuncionemque vocare (XV, Ch. v,
> 7).[35] *ut cum 1931; *ut* 1576.

> *Pontanus*: **Illic exaudire erat Theutonum voces formam regis statu-
> ramque mirantium, quos tanta visendi ejus cupiditas ceperat, ut
> alter alterius conscensis humeris** eum **productis cervicibus
> inspectarent, hunc regem, hunc imperio dignum, Cæsarem reg-
> ulum homuncionemque** referentes (272).[36]

---

[33] "Despite the fact that the monarch had been passionately incensed at the frankness of his speech, not wishing it to look as though he were blatantly cold-shouldering his admonisher, even while his face betrayed the extent of his anger, with characteristic restraint he switched to an easy, acceptable reply [...]"

[34] "When Absalon gave him sound but rather frank advice, the monarch reacted in no mean way against him, but then, restoring to mildness the anger which could be seen displayed in his face [...]"

[35] "There you could clearly hear the voices of Germans expressing amazement at the king's appearance and height; and they had been seized with such a strong passion to catch a glimpse of him that, if they were sitting too low, they would clamber on to one another's shoulders and crane their necks to stare at him. They kept saying that this was indeed a monarch, a lord, a man who deserved sovereignty, whereas the Emperor was a mere princeling, a little fellow".

[36] "There you could clearly hear the voices of Germans expressing amazement at the king's appearance and height; they had been seized with such a strong passion to catch a glimpse of him that they would clamber on to one another's shoulders and crane their necks to stare at him, repeating that here was indeed a monarch, a man who deserved sovereignty, whereas the Emperor was a mere princeling, a little fellow".

This passage, then, not only demonstrates Pontanus's tendency to leave out Saxo's abstracts but also his readiness, noticed above, to take over the wording of a whole period almost unchanged.

Still, although Pontanus generally adapted Saxo's prose to a plainer level, echoes of the latter's highflown rhetoric are sometimes heard. In the following passage Saxo's accumulations of synonyms recur in Pontanus's version:

> Ea tempestate Harthbenus quidam ab Helsyngia veniens, raptas regum filias stupro foedare gloriæ loco ducebat, illum perimere solitus, a quo peragendæ Veneris usu prohiberetur, illustres nuptias humilibus præferens, tantoque se clariorem existimans, quanto splendidiores concubitus per vim assequi potuisset (VII, Ch. ii, 11)[37]

– this is Saxo's presentation of the giant Harthbenus, and Pontanus takes over the three almost synonymous parts:

> Hic cum **raptas regum filias stupra**re **gloriæ duceret, illustres**que **nuptias humilibus præferret tantoque se clariorem** censeret, **quanto splendidiores concubitus per vim** assequeretur, id ei haud impune Haldanus esse voluit (28).[38]

Note also that Pontanus includes the wish on Haldanus's part to defeat the giant in this period, and that it is done at the expense of elegance. The contents of the *cum*-clause are picked up by *id* which is then object of the main clause.

Puns and pungent phrases, so characteristic of Meursius, are not frequent in Pontanus's text. But he took over some from Saxo. The legendary King Frotho IV died in combat with an enemy who had invited him on false pretences in order to burn him. As Saxo sums up: *Quo evenit, ut alterius scelus amborum interitus foret* ("So it came about that the crime of

---

[37] "At that time a certain Harthbenus, who came from Hälsingland, imagined it a glorious achievement to kidnap and violate princesses and would slay any man who hindered him from wreaking his lusts; because he preferred his brides aristocratic rather than humble, he calculated that the higher the rank of the women he managed to ravish, the greater credit it was to him".

[38] "As this individual imagined it a glorious achievement to kidnap and violate princesses, preferred his brides aristocratic rather than humble, and judged that the higher the rank of the women he ravished, the greater credit it was to him, Haldanus had no wish to grant him exemption from punishment".

one led to the death of both", VI, Ch. v, 19) – and this paradoxical conclusion is repeated by Pontanus (26).

Sivardus (ninth century) left behind him a little son, Ericus, who was at first prevented from following his father to the throne. Saxo's phrase is condensed:

> Idem fato functus Ericum admodum infantulum naturæ magis quam regni aut pacis heredem habuit (IX, Ch. v, 8)

> (When death took him, he left a very small child, Ericus, to inherit his nature rather than his kingdom or peace),

and Pontanus follows suit:

> jam **fato functus Ericum admodum infantulum magis naturæ quam regni hæredem** reliquerat (101)

> (now that death had taken him, he left behind a very small child, Ericus, to inherit his nature rather than his kingdom).

Olaus, king of Norway (c. 995-1000) was engaged to the Swedish king's mother, when he fell in love with the daughter of the Danish King Sueno, who would not, however, allow the marriage. Saxo exploits the paradox:

> Ita Olavus duobus splendidissimis coniugiis destitutus, dum alterum temere respuit, ab altero turpiter repelli meruit, utque hoc repulsa, ita illud insolentia perdidit (X, Ch. xii, 3)

> (That was how Olaus came to be robbed of two magnificent marriages; for rashly spurning one partner he deserved his slighting rejection by the other, and it turned out that his high-handedness with one and his repulse by the second meant he lost both),

and so does Pontanus, with a few changes:

> **Olaus ita**que, **dum alter**am stolide contemnit, **ab alter**a **turpiter repellitur, duobus** illustrissimis **conjugijs** destitutus (139)

> (Therefore, while Olaus spurned the one foolishly, he was rejected slightingly by the other, and so was robbed of two prestigious marriages).

After the English attack on the Danish army in the reign of Magnus (in the 1040s), Pontanus concludes on a solemn note:

> Eaque nox exiguo temporis momento vetustam Danorum domina-
> tionem ac longo multoque majorum sudore ac sanguine partum im-
> perium ita pessundedit, ut vix unquam Danos exinde fortuna respexerit
> (176).

> (A few brief moments of that night destroyed the Danes' ancient ascen-
> dancy and the supremacy gained through prolonged and profuse expen-
> diture of sweat and blood by their forebears; and so it was that Fate
> scarcely ever again looked kindly on them).

The solemnity is achieved by the personification of the night and the
contrast between the long Danish rule in England and the short time it
took to destroy it. Such figures are rare in Pontanus's text, and not surprisingly, they come from Saxo:

> **Ea nox** parvulo **temporis momento vetustam Danorum domina-
> tionem** diuque **maiorum** virtute elaboratum finivit imperium. Sed
> neque id postera nostris fortuna restituit (X, Ch. xxi, 6).

> (A few brief moments of that night put an end to the Danes' ancient
> ascendancy and the supremacy that had been painstakingly reinforced
> over the years by the valour of their forebears. Fate never afterwards
> restored that nation to our countrymen).

– But Pontanus strengthened the pathos by the alliterations *multoque
majorum* and *sudore ac sanguine*.

General moralizing reflections are also rare in Pontanus's work. But
again some have found their way from Saxo. Dealing with Frode IV's
generosity he observes that the jealousy of others is hard to fight by honourable means:

> dum ceteros largiendo præcurrere, omnes humanitatis officijs ante-
> venire, et, quod difficillimum est, virtute invidiam vincere curæ haberet
> (25).

> (while he made it his concern to surpass all others in bestowing largesse,
> to precede everyone in deeds of kindness and, most difficult of all, to
> overcome envy by his virtue).

This comes *verbatim* from Saxo, including the reflection that it is very difficult to conquer envy by means of virtue:

> **ceteros largiendo præcurrere, omnes humanitatis officiis
> antevenire et, quod difficillimum est, virtute invidiam vincere** con-
> tendebat (VI, Ch. iv, 14)

(He strove to surpass all others in bestowing largesse, to precede everyone in deeds of kindness and, most difficult of all, to overcome envy by his virtue).

Huitfeldt

Huitfeldt's text forms the basis of Pontanus's *History* from c. 1200 AD in a much more penetrating way than Saxo does in the preceding history (cf. above, Ch. VI).

One of the features of Huitfeldt's work most appreciated by later historians is the multitude of original documents transcribed in the text. From the fourteenth century they dominate large stretches of Huitfeldt's account. Most of them are in Danish and a smaller number in Latin. The latter recur unchanged in Pontanus's *History*, while those in Danish have been paraphrased in Latin. (In the Oldenburg history, 1448-1588, Pontanus has translated some of the Danish documents into Latin and not just paraphrased them). Quoted or paraphrased, the majority of the documents found in Huitfeldt thus recur in Pontanus's *History*. In other words, long stretches of his work, too, from the fourteenth century onwards, are taken up by reports or quotations of documents, including the long lists of signatories.

The documents aside, Pontanus's reworking of Huitfeldt's Danish text is often very close. Here follow their accounts of Saint Vinceslaus who in 1249 appeared to Ericus V (*Erik Plovpenning*) in a night-time vision:

Huitfeldt: Da Konning Erich haffde nu bestillet alting vel i Liffland / oc tenckte til at giffue sig ind vdi Rytsland / skeede det en Nat som hand lagde sig til Søffns / siuntis hannem at der kom en Guds Martyr for hannem / oc stod for hans Seng / oc sagde: Ver trøstig min Broder / Jeg er Vinceslaus, den du skalt ære / Oc kommer ieg nu til dig / oc forkynder dig / at du skalt dø / oc marteris lige som ieg / Dog vil ieg / at du skalt først opbygge oc stiffte it Kloster her vdi Landet / Gud til Loff oc ære / i mit Naffn / Oc den Siun strax forsuant. Huad heller det nu saa haffuer veret / eller er aff Muncke optenckt / som denne Konning Erich haffuer giort til en Helgen / Oc en heel Bog skreffuet / om hues Mirackle / effter hans Død skeed ere / maa Gud vide (*Chron.* I, 194).[39]

---

[39] "When King Erik had settled everything well in Livonia and intended to march into Russia, it so happened that one night when he had settled down to sleep, he imagined that a martyr of God came to him, stood by his bed, and said: "Be of good cheer, my brother. I am Vinceslaus, whom you shall venerate. I now come to you in order to announce that you shall die and suffer martyrdom like me. However, it is my wish that you first erect and found a monastery in my name, here in this country to celebrate God". At once the vision disap-

> *Pontanus:* Constitutis quaqua versum rebus, cum jam in Russos castra
> videretur moturus rex, accidit, ut nocte concubia sibi dormituro assistere
> martyrem quempiam putarit, inque hanc sententiam verba facere: Bono
> esto animo, mi frater, Ego Venseslaus sum, quem tu coles. Nunc autem
> te accedo, commonitumque venio, moriturum te, ac simili, quo ego fato
> ac martyrio periturum: Interim mando ut his in oris ad celebrandam Dei
> gloriam, ac nominis mei memoriam prius coenobium exædifices. Eoque
> dicto evanuit. Quod verum nec ne sit non affirmaverim, haud ignarus
> plurima hujusmodi pia fraude a monasticis præsertim confingi jam olim
> solita, qui et hunc ipsum Ericum in divos retulerunt, condito de mirac-
> ulis ejus, quibus post obitum inclaruerit, integro volumine (334).[40]

Here he sticks so closely to Huitfeldt, that he takes over the narrator's
opinion that the truth of this story cannot be confirmed. But even such
a close translation demonstrates that each language carries with it connotations of its own. Huitfeldt's *maa Gud vide* ("God only knows") is in Pontanus's translation *non affirmaverim* ("I should not like to maintain"),
which, with its suggestion of scepticism as to possibly supernatural phenomena, seems inspired by Livy's words of the Roman legendary past *nec
adfirmare nec refellere in animo est* ("It is not my intention either to confirm
or reject [these traditions]", Livy, Preface, 6).

Such alterations may be observed throughout. I shall here limit myself
to giving examples of one aspect of Pontanus's reworking of Huitfeldt.
He obviously strove to create from Huitfeldt's collection of material a
finished work of history. A brief note in Huitfeldt is typically expanded.
Huitfeldt's laconic list of prices of butter, honey etc. in 1478 has been
supplied with associations of a golden age:

---

peared. Whether it actually happened or whether it was invented by monks, who have made
a saint of this King Erik and composed a whole book about the miracles that took place
after his death, God only knows".

[40] "After matters had been settled in all quarters and the king was apparently intending to
march against Russia, it so happened that in the early part of the night, when he was on the
verge of sleep, he imagined that one of the martyrs stood by him and spoke to this effect:
"Be of good cheer, my brother. I am Venseslaus, whom you shall venerate. I come now to
your side in order to impress on you that you are going to die and suffer a similar fate and
martyrdom to my own. Meanwhile, before that, I command you to erect a monastery in this
region to celebrate God's glory and the memory of my name". Having delivered these
words, he disappeared. Whether this story is true or false I should not like to maintain, for I
am fully aware that for a long time now a good many pious frauds of such a kind have been
manufactured, especially by monks; such people have conveyed this same Ericus to the
divine sphere and compiled a complete volume of the miracles which rendered him famous
after his death".

Huitfeldt: Den tid galt Varene her i Danmarck / en Tønde Smør Sex Marck /en Tønde Hunning Otte Marck / en fed Oxe Sex Skillinge grot / it Lam Tre grot / en fed Ko Tre Skillinge grot (*Christian I*, 274).[41]

Pontanus: Felicem annum sive tempora hæc dicam rerum, omnium non ubertate solum, sed annonæ quoque felicitate. Proditum enim memoriæ, butyri tum tonnam-marcis <sex>, mellis octo, bovem perpinguem-schillingis, ut vocabant, grossis sex, agnum grossis tribus, vaccam item-schillingis grossis tribus venisse (col. 835).[42]

– but the repetition *felicem – felicitate*, which makes the latter explain the first, is perhaps less elegant.

In 1300 the dikes on the west coast of Holstein were breached, and twenty-eight parishes were flooded, Huitfeldt briefly notes:

Dette Aar indbrød Digerne vdi Lante Holsten / oc vndergick 28. Sogner (*Chron. II*, 45).

Pontanus elaborates:

Maxima eodem tempore Holsatis, et præsertim maritimis, oceani excessus damna intulit, perruptis passim ac dissipatis vi tempestatum aggeribus, adeo ut plana omnia ac vicos circiter viginti octo maris inun-datio oppresserit (389-90).[43]

His version is more dramatic, giving first, in the main clause, attention to the damage and its extent (*maxima damna*) and to the people harmed (*Holsatis, maritimis*); the concrete event, the breaching of the dikes, is then related by means of an ablative absolute; its violence is underlined by the details (*perruptis, dissipatis, vi tempestatum*), and its serious effects are marked by the *adeo*.

Another narrative feature in Pontanus's text is the occasional headlines announcing what is to come. Such headlines are not frequent in Huit-

---

[41] "At that time goods in Denmark were sold at these prices: butter six marks a cask, honey eight marks a cask, a fat ox six great skillings, a lamb three great, a fat cow likewise three great skillings".

[42] "I shall call this year (or these times) fruitful for commodities, not only because everything was plentiful, but because of the fruitfulness of the harvest. People recollect that butter was then <six> marks a cask, honey eight; a fat ox cost six great skillings, as they called them, a lamb three, and a cow the same amount".

[43] "At that time the ocean level rose excessively and inflicted enormous damage on the Holsteiners, particularly those living on the coast; everywhere dikes were breached and demolished by the violence of the storms, to such an extent that the sea-floods inundated all the flat countryside and about twenty-eight communities".

feldt. An example is Pontanus's declaration of Christianus I's troubles with his brother in 1473: *Detinebatur eo tempore haud leviter Christianus Rex importunitate fratris sui Comitis Gerhardi* ("At that time King Christianus was hindered in no small way by the churlishness of his brother, Count Gerhardus", cols. 820-21). Huitfeldt just says: *Anno 1473, kom Greffue Gert / Kong Christierns Broder / til Husem* ("In the year 1473 Count Gert, brother of King Christiern, came to Husem", *Christian I,* 232).

Pontanus often rearranges Huitfeldt's order of events within a single year in order to obtain a higher degree of coherence. In 1268, for instance, Huitfeldt first mentions the king's strengthening of the castle Koldinghus, then follow some meteorological phenomena (strong wind, hot and dry summer), and finally a meeting between the Danish and Swedish kings (*Chron. I,* 325). Pontanus relates the last point immediately after the first about Koldinghus, thereby retaining the king as subject (he built the new castle and he held a meeting with the Swedish king) (364). Similarly, in 1293, Huitfeldt notes that the Norwegian and Danish kings had conducted fruitless peace talks. Then follow some other events, and as the final item of the year we are informed that the Norwegian king on several occasions attacked Danish seafarers (*Chron. II,* 17). These two points, treated separately by Huitfeldt, were combined by Pontanus, thereby connecting the fruitless peace-talks and the many naval aggressions on the part of the Norwegian king (379).

Pontanus also creates coherence by other means. Marsk Stig, in 1288, goes to see the Norwegian king near Amager, Huitfeldt tells us (*Chron. II,* 6). Pontanus reminds us that we have already learnt of the king's presence close to the Danish island: *qui iuxta Amagum adhuc cum classe præcipua consistebat* ("who was still stationed with his main fleet off Amager", 375).

One of the events in 1293 related by Huitfeldt was the death of "King Valdemar [of Sweden] who was imprisoned in Nykøbing", as Huitfeldt laconically notes (*Chron. II,* 17). Pontanus elaborates the point:

> Finally Valdemarus, whom I reported earlier as having been humbled when he was king of Sweden by Magnus and ultimately imprisoned, at this point came to the end of his life; shortly before this his son, Ericus, had been seized in much the same way, according to Swedish history not so much for his own as for his father's offences, and held chained for some time in Stockholm, until he eventually underwent capital punishment.[44]

---

[44] *Valdemarus postremo, quem supra Sueonum rex cum esset a Magno in ordinem redactum ac carceri denique inclusum retulimus, hoc tempore supremum diem clausit, cum paulo ante filius ejus Ericus, non tam*

Here we are not only informed of Valdemarus's death, we are also reminded of his history, which both Huitfeldt and Pontanus had related earlier. What is the effect of this recapitulation? For one thing Pontanus makes sure that the reader is aware of the identity of this Valdemarus. Furthermore, he seems concerned about the emotional effect on his readers. By drawing attention to the tragedy of Valdemarus's son he invests the death of Valdemarus with a pathos absent from Huitfeldt's brief note.

Pontanus here refers to his own former treatment of these events: *quem supra* [...] *carceri* [...] *inclusum retulimus.* Such references to earlier (or future) mention of a given event are very frequent in his text (and very few in Huitfeldt's). This is another way of creating continuity, of emphasizing that the work is a unity, the result of conscious composition. The narrator here steps forward pointing to the work as a work.

The role of the narrator differs markedly in Huitfeldt's and Pontanus's texts. The Huitfeldt-narrator is distant, mostly stepping forward to voice his political judgements from time to time, while the Pontanus-narrator reflects explicitly over the reason for telling something, as we have already had occasion to note in connection with his motivations for quoting from documents and other authors. Thus Huitfeldt notes in the year 1296 that severe cold made it possible to walk from Oslo to Northern Jutland (*Chron. II*, 28). Pontanus explains why he brings this ephemeral piece of information: "an occurrence previously unparalleled and therefore one that I ought not to let pass unmentioned here" (*res* [...] *inauditi antea exempli adeoque hoc loco a nobis haud prætereunda*, 381).[45] Similarly, when only one event is told of the year 1297, the Pontanus-narrator draws attention to this scarcity: "I find this event the only one noted down by the chroniclers" (*hoc solum apud chronographos annotatum reperio*, 381); Christianus I's legate Marcellus was once attacked in Cologne on his way home from Rome. Huitfeldt begins by the statement: "In the previous year King Christiern sent a messenger to Rome ..." (*Vdi forneffnde Aar haffde Kong Christiern it Sendebud til Rom, Christian I*, 47), while Pontanus draws attention to his own efforts as researcher: "I discover that during this period King Christiernus had his own special legate in Rome" (*invenio peculiarem per ea tempora nuncium habuisse Romæ Regem Christiernum*, col. 746).

---

ob sua quam patris demerita, ut habet Suecorum historia, similiter comprehensus inque vinculis Stocholmiæ aliquandiu detentus, capitis tandem supplicium subierit (379).

[45] A similar example is mentioned above, p. 236.

The prominent narrator is a characteristic feature of Pontanus's work; it is one of the traits which distinguishes his account from Huitfeldt's. It contributes to giving the impression that the work is a result of energetic research and careful selection of material. The prominent Pontanus-narrator, however, is also a feature which distinguishes his work from that of Meursius. It is a significant stylistic difference between the two, which shall be discussed in the following section.

The Narrators in the Texts

In this section we shall look at Pontanus and Meursius together. Above I referred to the constant alternation between a narrative and a reasoning mode in Pontanus's text. Narrative passages relate events in the imperfect or the perfect indicative (or historic present). But Pontanus does not just relate events as past facts. The account is constantly interrupted by references to other authors, discussions of conflicting evidence, motivations for mentioning or quoting something, and so on. We have already encountered a number of instances in the preceding chapter.

The switch from narrative to reasoning mode is also a switch from a detached to a prominent narrator. In other words, since the argumentative mode is so often employed by Pontanus, the prominent narrator is a very characteristic feature of his text. This is a significant difference from Meursius, in whose work the narrative mode is close to universal and the narrator much more in the background. These features and their wider implications for the creation of authority will form the last chapter of my discussion of the style of Pontanus's and Meursius's *Histories*.

1. The Captivity of Valdemarus II

In analyzing the diverse roles of the narrators in Pontanus's and Meursius's texts, I shall concentrate on a single passage. It is about the captivity of the Danish king, Valdemarus II, in 1223. After a hunting expedition on Lyø, a small island south of Funen, he was captured by one of his vassals, the German Count Henricus. According to modern accounts the motive is uncertain. An older tradition regards Henricus's kidnapping as an act of revenge, because Valdemarus had seduced his wife while Henricus himself was on pilgrimage. This tradition is represented by Meursius, and mentioned by Pontanus. Whatever the motive, it is generally agreed, both in the older tradition, followed by Meursius and Pontanus, and in modern accounts, that this event marked a turning point in Valdemarus's reign. Previously he had controlled wide areas on the Baltic coast, but after his release he never regained this position. Pontanus, at the beginning of the passage, marks the significance by referring to a comet. Meursius, later summing up the whole reign of Valdemarus, notes that from that time his luck had vanished. In the following transcription of the two passages the division into paragraphs is my own.

310　　　　　　　**RERUM DANICARUM**

VOLDEMA-　duxisse in arcem Dannebergicam. Ita ferè Vitfeldius. Quamvis Abbas Stadensis Alber-
RUS II.　　tus, qui eo ævo superstes claruit, eadem plane cum Crantzio, aut potius cum Abbate
Rex.　　　Crantzius commemoret. Erici regis chronicon arcem, in quam deductus non *Danneber-*
A 6　　　*gam*, sed *Zuerinium* nominat. Et illud de regis etiam filio habet, quod nec apud Stadensem
　　　　　neque apud Crantzium reperias. Insula verò in quâ captus rex *Lythæ* eidem Erico dici-
　　　　　tur, & eam Fioniæ esse contiguam, nec à *Foburgo* longe dissitam existimat in glossis suis
　　　　　ad Rhytmos veteres Andreas Velleius.
　　　　　　Addam his threnum sive nœniam potius super eâdem hac regum captivitate eodem illo ævo Latine scriptam, quæ & seculi genium redolens indicio erit, *quales tum versus Fauni*　　　　10
vatesque canebant. Est autem ista:

　　　　　Plange primatus Daciæ, quondam clarus in acie.
　　　　　Sed nunc tua militia, vili torpet pigritiâ.
　　　　　Rex tuus furtim tollitur, sævus hostis extollitur.
　　　　　O maris acris spicula, cave mortis pericula.
　　　　　Mare piratis scaturit, fures spelunca parturit.
　　　　　Horret nemus latronibus, campus patet prædonibus.
　　　　　Pater inquam claustralium, pax exulat ruralium.
　　　　　Premit regnum impetus, rebus spoliatur penus.
　　　　　Omnis dolet relligio, novo stupens prodigio:　　　　　　　　　　　　20
　　　　　Deplorat infortunium, & infaustum augurium;
　　　　　Munus rusticorum coruit, totus orbis cobortuit:
　　　　　Detestans pseudocomitis scelus nefandi criminis.
　　　　　Novus Iudas invaluit, contra pias prævaluit.
　　　　　Invisus Christi nomine, seduxit Christus Domini.
　　　　　Venit pacis sub specie, fultus turba nequitiæ.
　　　　　Falsum fingens negotium, regis turbavit otium.
　　　　　Donativa subsequitur, sed gratia negligitur.
　　　　　Dolum ingratus gratiæ, blandâ celat sub facie.
　　　　　Invadit solitarium, nihil timentem contrarium.　　　　　　　　　　30
　　　　　Aggreditur in lectulo, quem non audet in prælio.
　　　　　Sic infelix vir Belial, alter Cam alter Nabal.
　　　　　Qui cruentas in proprias manus injecit dominos.
　　　　　Hunc Herodis impietas, quem nulla flectit pietas,
　　　　　Addicit noxæ sceleris, malis rerum præ ceteris.
　　　　　Hunc Neronis immanitas, & enormis crudelitas.
　　　　　Condemnant impiissimum. Videlicet plus impium
　　　　　Dum impios recenseo, nullum pejorem censeo
　　　　　Hoc Henrico nequissimo, vel Iudâ suo socio,
　　　　　Sed Iudas eo melior, quo nobis necessarior:　　　　　　　　　　　40
　　　　　Dum Christum morti tradidit, nobis ignorans profuit.
　　　　　Sed hic malorum pessimus, & latro nocentissimus,
　　　　　Nullis juvando consulit, sed damna multis intulit.
　　　　　Commovit statum seculi, turbavit pacem populi.
　　　　　Fit causa pugnæ principum, certus sudor militum.
　　　　　Regnum super regnum ruit, & hoc malum vulgus luit.
　　　　　Quod plectitur hic populus, asseverat philosophus:
　　　　　Quicquid delirant reges plectuntur Achivi.
　　　　　Væ mundo nunc à scandalis, væ pauperum piaculis.
　　　　　Quicquid plangit Dania, læta gaudet Saxonia.　　　　　　　　　50
　　　　　Eheu, heu perfidia, heu vetus invidia!
　　　　　Quod diu clam delituit, nunc in palam apparuit.
　　　　　Eheu reges tam nobiles, toti mundo spectabiles,
　　　　　Raptos regni fastigio, actos flemus exilio!
　　　　　Heu præclaros proceres, insigni fama celebres,
　　　　　Clausos dolemus carcere, insontes omni scelere!
　　　　　Vt quid obdormis Domine, & requiescis ab homine,

　　　　　　　　　　　　　　　　　　　　　　　　　Ab homine

FREDERICUS II. IMP.

The last part of Pontanus's account of the captivity of Valdemarus II. (Rerum Danicarum historia 1631, p. 310).

Pontanus, 309-10:

At nunc anno post millesimum ducentesimum vigesimo tertio, versis fatis, retro relabi cuncta cœperunt. Quarum calamitatum haud fallax nuncius etiam cœlum fuit. Nam per Augustum mensem anni superioris, terribile sidus, cujusmodi *Cometam* vocant, ad septentrionem spectandum se præbuerat, quasi fecialis ac caduceator, quæ, secuta sunt mala præcurrens.

Eorumque occasio non uno modo ab authoribus memoratur. Crantzius ait *Zuerini Comitem Henricum* gratiæ et reconciliationis cum rege ineunde avidum in Daniam fide publica accepta concessisse: Ac ei cum conditiones duriores rex proponit, consilium de rege clam abducendo cepisse: et mox capto sub serum diei tempore, dum regiæ excubiæ, utpote domi, et ab hoste nihil hostile metuentes, solutius agunt, aut more gentis, poculis vacant, regem forte fortuna e venatu venientem accessisse salutasseque humaniter, ac tandem in tentorium, quod ibi sub dio habebatur, fessum ac somnolentum deduxisse: et mox parata ad hoc navi assumtisque ex suo comitatu viris armatis papilionem ingressum ac regem ore occluso ad navigium, quod proximo littore in anchoris stabat, vinctum deportasse: ac statim datis vento velis, in Germaniam appulisse, atque ibi expositum regem, moxque in arcem suam *Danebergam* productum carceri mancipasse.

Vitfeldius, quo authore, domestico an extraneo, non addit, sed aliter multo occasionem hujus infortunij denarrat. Nam de controversia et reconciliatione inter Henricum et regem, quod ait Crantzius, si eam intelligit; quæ orta erat occasione viri nobilis *Iohannis Gans*, cujus arcem, ipso exturbato, Henricus et Gunzelinus sibi vindicare cœperant, ea jam ante constituta fuerat, ut est superius ad annum 1205 et 1210, memoratum. Vitfeldius itaque primam mali causam in adulterium regis rejicit, Valdemarum nimirum a Comite Zuerinensi Henrico, cum is in Palæstinam voti et religionis ergo abiret, tutelæ suæ commendatam accepisse et conjugem et ditiones ejusdem: atque ea occasione defuncta jam Berengaria, et absente Henrico, consuevisse cum uxore ejus: Idque reversum mox ad suos Henricum ubi intellexisset, subticuisse quidem, sed istud ulciscendi sui consilium haud multo post agitasse. atque ideo accepta a rege liberi accessus ac reditus fide, unica cum navi in Daniæ insulas proximas, ubi tum venationi rex vacabat, profectum, atque ibi cum filio Valdemaro, eum in modum, ut ante est memoratum, regem cepisse ac vinctum abduxisse in arcem Dannebergicam.

Ita fere Vitfeldius. Quamvis Abbas Stadensis Albertus, qui eo ævo superstes claruit, eadem plane cum Crantzio, aut potius cum Abbate Crantzius commemoret. Erici regis chronicon arcem, in quam deductus non *Dannebergam*, sed *Zuerinium* nominat. Et illud de regis etiam filio habet, quod nec apud Stadensem neque apud Crantzium reperias. Insula vero in qua captus rex *Lythæ* eidem Erico dicitur, et eam Fioniæ esse contiguam, nec a *Foburgo* longe dissitam existimat in glossis suis ad Rhytmos veteres Andreas Velleius.

Addam his threnum sive noeniam potius super eadem hac regum captivitate eodem illo ævo Latine scriptam, quæ et seculi genium redolens indicio erit, *quales tum versus Fauni vatesque canebant.* Est autem ista:
Plange primatus Daciæ, quondam clarus in acie [etc. 69 lines]

(But now, in the year 1223, his luck turned and everything began to decline. These adversities were also announced by trustworthy signs from heaven, since the year before in the month of August a terrible star, the kind known as a comet, had appeared in the North, proclaiming, like a fetial priest and a herald, the evils that were to come.

Our authorities do not report the reasons for these evils in the same manner. Krantz says that the count of Schwerin, Henricus, eager to be reconciled with the king and win his goodwill, went to Denmark after having received an official guarantee of protection. When the conditions offered him by the king were rather severe, he formed a plan to kidnap him; he chose a late time of day when the royal guard, being at home and fearing nothing hostile from any enemy, was relaxing or drinking (a national habit), to approach the king who, as it chanced, was just returning from a hunting expedition. With friendly greetings he then led the tired and drowsy king to his tent, which had been put up there in the open air. Soon after, with a ship ready for the purpose and assisted by some of his men, all of them armed, he entered the tent and carried off the king, gagged and tied up, to the boat which lay at anchor on the shore nearby. The sails were immediately set, and when they reached Germany, the king was put ashore and at once led to Henricus's castle, Dannenberg, where he was imprisoned.

Huitfeldt gives a very different account of the background of this misfortune, but he does not name his source, be that native or foreign. As to the controversy and reconciliation between Henricus and the king which Krantz mentions – if he refers to the one concerning the nobleman, Johannes Gans, whose castle Henricus and Gunzelinus had begun to claim for themselves after Gans himself had been evicted – then it had already been settled earlier, as mentioned above under the years 1205 and 1210. Huitfeldt, then, points to the king's adultery as the first cause of the mischief. He tells how the count of Schwerin, Henricus, had entrusted his wife and possessions to Valdemarus, when he himself went away to Palestine on a pilgrimage; and in this state of affairs, Berengaria being already dead and Henricus absent, the king had an affair with his wife; and when Henricus, on his return soon afterwards, found out about this, he said nothing at first, but shortly afterwards formed a scheme of vengeance; and so, having obtained a safe-conduct from the king, he went with a single ship to the nearest of the Danish islands where the king spent his time hunting, and there he caught the king, together with his son Valdemarus, in the way described above, and took him off in chains to the castle of Dannenberg.

This is more or less what Huitfeldt says. The abbot, Albert of Stade, however, who was a contemporary observer, writes exactly the same as Krantz, or rather Krantz agrees with the abbot. *King Erik's Chronicle* does not call the castle to which the king was taken Dannenberg but Schwerin. And it also mentions the part about the king's son, which you will neither find in Albert of Stade nor in Krantz. As to the island on which the king was caught, it is called Lyø by the same *King Erik's Chronicle*; and Anders Vedel, in his notes to the old songs, assumes that it is situated close to Funen, not very far from Fåborg.

I shall add to this a lamentation, or rather a dirge, about this same captivity of the kings. It is composed in Latin and dates from the same time. Redolent as it is of the spirit of that period, it will serve as a demonstration of "the verses which Fauns and native bards once sang". It goes like this: [...]).

Meursius, II, 17-18:

ubi [i.e. in Dania] dum defessum animum recreare paulum instituit [i.e. Valdemarus], et venationem agitat, ipse capitur, ab Henrico Suerinensi. Ille, cum in Palæstinam, voti reus, cogitaret, ditiones, conjugemque, Valdemaro commendaverat. qui, jam viduus, mortua pridem Berengaria, fæminæ amore captus, eâ abutitur ad libidinem. idque cum Henricus redux accepisset, animo offensam occultans, ultionem hunc in modum meditatur. Impetrato commeatu, ad Liutham, assitam Fioniæ insulam, ubi rex venationi intentus erat, unico navigio appellit. Et egressus, simulata animi demissione, regem accedit gratiasque ingentes agit, pro defensa per absentiam ditione. tum quotidie venatum exeuntem officiose comitatur: aliquando, ut suspicionem omnem insidiarum amoveret, etiam solus, parvo utentem satellitio.

Quod cum aliquoties jam factum esset, Valdemarus die quodam, parvo itidem progressus, uti ante, comitatu, circa vesperam, e labore multo fessus, in tugurio, non tam longe a portu sito, in quo navem suam Henricus applicuerat, locum pernoctandi capit. ac, nil minus, quam insidias, illic metuens, blande ipsum ad cænam invitat, et potationem quandam largiorem. ipse vero, qui occasionem eam exspectaret, datam sibi minime negligendam ratus, ocyus parare suos vela jubet: et ex his promptissimum quemque, manu pariter, animoque, ad id facinus præsto esse. cum potatio longiuscule processisset, rexque ipse, et qui circa eum erant, vino graves, lectum omnes petiissent, ille suis, ex insidiis evocatis, imperat, vincirent propere, somno altiore pressum; ac cum eo filium quoque Valdemarum, successorem designatum. Statim compedes utrique injicientes, ora etiam obturant, ne clamore auxilia excitare possent; et ad navem raptim abducunt. inde avehunt Suerinum, ac mox item Dannebergam.

Certe crimine detestando Valdemarus se obstrinxerat, qui uxorem Suerinensis, suæ fidei commissam, violaverat: et ostendit iram manifetam Deus, qui dynastam, multo sane inferiorem, contra eum excitavit; ut in suo eum regno, quando bello inferendo impar esset, astu adoriri auderet, et abduceret captivum, teneretque in triennium: nec dimitteret, ne in Cæsaris quidem gratiam, principumque aliorum, nisi magno liberationis pretio. Certe Deus, sicuti fortunam regum in fastigio excellenti collocavit, atque eo modo ipsos magis ad virtutem obstrinxit, ita etiam peccantibus multo gravius irascitur, et delicta severissime vindicare item solet.

(There [in Denmark], when [Valdemarus] wanted to relax his exhausted mind a little and engaged himself in hunting, he was captured by Henricus of Schwerin. The latter had entrusted his possessions and his wife to Valdemarus, when planning a pilgrimage to Palestine. Valdemarus who was now a widower, Berengaria having died some time ago, fell in love with the woman and seduced her. And when Henricus on his return was informed of that, he kept his hatred to himself and planned his revenge in this way. Having obtained permission to travel freely, he arrived with a single ship at Lyø, an island close to Funen, where the king occupied himself with hunting. He disembarked and approached the king with feigned humility and expressed his immense gratitude for Valdemarus's protection of his property in his absence. He then made a point of joining the king in his daily hunt, sometimes even alone while the king had only a small number of men, in order to remove all suspicions.

This went on for some time. One day Valdemarus returned home late, as usual followed by only a small escort. He was exhausted and decided to spend the night in a cottage, not far from the harbour where Henricus had landed his ship. And without the slightest fear of ambush from that side, he kindly invited him to dinner, including a considerable amount of drink. But Henricus, who had been waiting for this opportunity and would not miss it when it offered itself, told his men to prepare the ship in a hurry, and those most ready and eager to fight were told to be on the alert for the operation. When the drinking had gone on for rather a long time, and the king himself and those who were with him had all gone to bed drowsy from the wine, he summoned his men from their hiding-places and told them to tie up the king, who was fast asleep, and together with him his son Valdemarus, who had been designated as his successor. They immediately put them both in chains, stopping up their mouths to prevent them from calling for help, and led them in great haste to the ship. Then they sailed off to Schwerin and soon reached Dannenberg.

18   I O A N N I S   M E V R S I I

veret, etiam folus, parvo utentem fatelli-
tio. Quod cùm aliquoties jam factum
effet, Valdemarus die quodam, parvo itidem progreffus, uti antè, comitatu, circa
vefperam, è labore multo feffus, in tugurio, non tam longè à portu fito, in quo
navem fuam Henricus applicuerat,locum
pernoctandi capit. ac, nil minus, quàm
infidias, illic metuens, blandè ipfum ad
cænam invitat, & potationem quandam
largiorem. ipfe verò, qui occafionem eam
exfpectaret, datam fibi minimè negligendam ratus, ocyùs parare fuos vela jubet:
& ex his promptiffimum quemque, manu
pariter, animoque, ad id facinus præfto
effe. cùm potatio longiufculè proceffiffet,
rexque ipfe, & qui circa eum erant, vino
graves, lectum omnes petiiffent, ille fuis,
ex infidiis evocatis,imperat,vincirent pro-
però, fomno altiore preffùm; ac cum eo
filium quoque Valdemarum, fuccefforem
defignatum. Statim compedes utrique
injicientes,ora etiam obturant,ne clamore
auxilia excitare poffent; & ad navem raptim abducunt. inde avehunt Suerinum,
ac mox item Dannebergam. Certè crimine deteftando Valdemarus fe obftrinxe-
rat,qui uxorem Suerinenfis,fuæ fidei com-
miffam, violaverat: & oftendit iram ma-
nifeftam Deus, qui dynaftam, multo fanè
inferiorem, contra eum excitavit; ut in
fuo eum regno, quando bello inferendo
impar effet, aftu adoriri auderet, & abduceret captivum, teneretque in triennium:
nec dimitteret,ne in Cæfaris quidem gratiam, principumque aliorum, nifi magno
liberationis pretio. Certè Deus,ficuti fortunam regum in faftigio excellenti collocavit, atque eo modo ipfos magis ad virtutem obftrinxit, ita etiam peccantibus
multo graviùs irafcitur, & delicta feve-
riffimè vindicare item folet. Ad abducti
regis famam, ftatim fenatores regni, de
redemptione ejus confulturi, convenere.
placuitque per legatos petere ab Impera-
tore, ut auctoritate fuà id negotium adju-
varet. ifque ipfe, five filius Henricus,cum
Germaniæ principibus aliis, & in his anti-
ftite Colonienfi, Bardevicum, in vicinam
Pomeraniam, fe recipiens, cùm nequic-
quam rem tentaffet,mox receffit. etenim,
cum regem fibi, & Imperio, fubditum

VALDEMARVS II.

vellet; tum Henrico Suerinenfi ut Van-
daliam, Nordalbingiamque, traderet;
refpuens conditiones tam indignas Valdemarus, ut excelfo erat animo, maluit ma-
nere in carcere,falvo regno,ac majeftate,
quàm damnofam adeò fibi,ac probrofam,
liberationem admittere. Inter ifta Suerinenfis, ut res fuas ftabiliret, cum finitimis
principibus, urbibufque, fœdus init. infuper Adolphum quoque Scouwenburgi-
cum exftimulat,ut tam bonâ occafione ad
recuperandam Holfatiam, patri Adolpho
ante annos circitèr viginti & unum, per
captivitatem extortam,uteretur. qui,cùm
folus non fufficeret, ejus operâ adjutus, ac
Gerhardi,archiepifcopi Bremenfis,tum &
Henrici Verlenfis, aliorumque, rem aggreditur, & Alberto Orlemundio bellum
infert. quem, cum manu raptim armatâ
occurrentem,ftatim vincit; &, in vinculis
abductum, Valdemaro comiti cuftodiæ
addit. inde Holfatiam pervagatus,univer-
fam, adeòque ipfum Hamburgum, mini-
mo negotio in poteftatem fuam redigit.
Atque fic fubactâ Holfatiâ, & Stormariâ,
ceu jam nulla ultra metus caufa effet, arma Adolphus, & Henricus, deponentes,
militi dant miffionem. Sed nec hìc fortuna defiit Valdemaro adverfari. nam
Efthonii,ac Livoni,eodem tempore,poft-
quam captum audiviffent, milites Teuto-
nici ordinis, quos Enfigeros appellatos fu-
pra dixi, & epifcopus Rigenfis, Revaliæ
occafionem invadendæ fibi datam exifti-
mârunt. & exemplo quoque eorum Ofi-
lienfis excitatus, libertatem item vindi-
candam ftatuit. ad hos Vandali, Sclaviæ-
que populi, præfertim occidui, ditioque
Suerinenfium,ac Verlenfium,ab obfequio
difceffere. infuper Barnimus quoque, &
Vratiflaus, Pomeraniæ tunc principes,
Rugiam & Deminum, & Lofitium, aliaque quædam loca, extorferunt. denique
Danfvicum etiam Suentepoldus occupa-
vit. atque ita Sclavia tota, multis expedi-
tionibus difficillimis vix fubacta, facili
admodù negotio Valdemaro fe fubduxit.
Inter ifta proceres regni, ut captivum regem fuum liberarent, quidvis tentant. In
Germaniam aliquos fuorum mittunt,prin-
cipefque paffim prenfant; ac, muneribus
non exiguis inter illos diftributis, eò tandem

The last part of Meursius's account of the captivity of Valdemarus II. (*Historia Danica* 1638, p. 18 (part II)).

To be sure, Valdemarus was guilty of a terrible crime by his violation of the count of Schwerin's wife, who had been entrusted to his care. And God showed his wrath openly, by calling up a prince of much lower dignity against him and giving this prince the audacity to attack the king in his own kingdom by employing a ruse, since he was incapable of waging open war, and next to carry him off as a captive, keeping him for three years and not even releasing him at the wish of the Emperor or other princes except for a large ransom. To be sure, just as God has placed kings' lives in the highest position and in this way bound them to virtue, He is also much more enraged at them when they go wrong and usually inflicts very severe punishments on them).

2. *Composition*

The whole passage in Pontanus's version may be divided into five parts which I have marked by new paragraphs. The first tells us that everything now began to decline. The "headline" of the next states that the authors disagree about the course of events and we are then informed of the contents of Albert Krantz's version. Paragraph three reports the contents of another account by the Danish historian, Arild Huitfeldt. The following paragraph introduces us briefly to some other descriptions of the events, and in the last Pontanus announces his intention of quoting a poem, which then follows. As to the difference between Krantz and Huitfeldt, we can observe that Pontanus does not decide whether Krantz or Huitfeldt is right. He sees a problem in the reason given by Krantz for the count's grudge against the king: the old enmity had been settled long ago, he observes. And therefore, though he does not say so directly, he seems to prefer Huitfeldt's motive, the king's seduction of the count's wife. But on the other hand, he says (I think *quamvis* must be understood thus), the contemporary source Albert of Stade agrees with Krantz. So he leaves the question of motive there, unsettled.

Meursius's version falls into three main parts. The transition from one main part to another is not, as in Pontanus, a transition to a new version of another author. In Part two we simply reach a new phase in the story – the kidnapping itself. With the beginning of Part three the story has come to an end and the narrator now reflects on it; he points out the divine meaning: God punished Valdemar for his seduction of the count's wife (in this interpretation we are in fact given extra information on the story, namely that the captivity lasted for three years and that the count was paid a ransom).

3. *Verbal Tenses*

Let us take a look at the tenses of the main verbs. In Pontanus' case, the first short paragraph is the only one kept in a past tense (*cœperunt* etc). The others are all in the present tense: *memoratur, ait, addit, denarrat, rejicit, commemorat, nominat, habet, dicitur, existimat, addam* (present subjunctive or future) (exceptions are *constituta fuerat, est memoratum*). They are declarative verbs, whose subjects are the authors (Krantz, Huitfeldt etc). The bulk of the second and the third paragraphs comprises reports of what these authors say, cast in the accusative with infinitive construction. In other words, it is only the first paragraph which narrates the events directly. The rest is about the accounts of the various authors. What is presented as the main point, then, is the fact that different versions are found, and the way in which they differ, primarily Krantz and Huitfeldt. Finally, we have the narrator's own person as agent in *addam*, describing what he is about to do in his composition of the work.

In Meursius's version most of the main verbs in the two first paragraphs are, like the main verbs in Pontanus, in the present tense. But it is the historic present (the subordinate verbs are all in past tenses), that is, it is equivalent to a past tense. It is a narrative tense. They are not, as in Pontanus, declarative verbs introducing the reports of some other authors, or verbs which focus on the narrator's present intention, like Pontanus's *addam*. It is a narrative tense that maintains a relation exclusively to the events being related. In the third paragraph of Meursius's text, the "interpretive" paragraph, the whole episode is first summed up in the perfect (and pluperfect) tense. Finally, we then meet another use of the present tense, the general statement at the end about God's design: he punishes (always, at all times) princes more severely than other human beings.

4. *The Narrators*

These observations on tenses provide us with clues about the role of the narrators, the "I"'s of the texts. Pontanus's shift, after the short introductory part, from the past to the present tense also marks a change in the narrator's prominence. Instead of the impersonal distance in the first paragraph, things are now told as reports of *his* readings of the various authors. The present tense of the main (declarative) verbs refers to *his* studying these accounts. It is he, for instance, who observes that the authors do not relate the events in the same way; *he* notes that Huitfeldt does not name his sources; it is *he* who argues against Krantz concerning the motive of the kidnapping; *he* is aware of the agreement between Krantz and Albert of Stade and their disagreement with Huitfeldt, *he* has noticed the supplementary details of the story provided by *King Erik's Chronicle* and Vedel's notes. Finally, and emphatically, the narrator stands out declaring his intention of quoting a song, *addam*.

Contrary to Pontanus's version, the longest part of Meursius's account (the two first of the three main parts) is characterized by a distanced and impersonal narrator, who simply sets forth the course of events. Then a shift takes place, and the narrator becomes prominent. The shift is strongly marked by *Certe*, which indicates that we are now about to read the judgement of the narrator. The whole paragraph is subordinated to this *Certe* (repeated towards the end). The narrator stands out saying: "it is certain that [...]". Semantically *certe* is also in the present tense.

We have, then, a prominent narrator in the last third of Meursius's text and in the whole of the passage from Pontanus, except the first paragraph. But these narrators are very different. The narrator in Pontanus's text gives us both Krantz's and Huitfeldt's versions of the story because they differ, and presents his arguments for and against them. The Pontanus-narrator is openly reasoning, concerned about finding out what was the real motive. In this case, paradoxically, his desire for finding the truth is expressed by his being content to leave the question of motive open; he will not, on the basis of these arguments pro and contra, venture to settle the matter. Further, the Pontanus-narrator calls attention to the process of his composition by the verb in the first person sing. *addam*, "I shall now add". The relationship to the reader is also marked by *reperias*, "you will find". The reader is invited to participate in the process of research.

In Meursius's text, a very different narrator appears. He gives us no hint of his own wrestling with the sources, of his striving to find out what really happened and why. The course of events is simply told as facts. We are offered no glimpses of the historian in the process of composition, such as Pontanus's *addam*. So how, then, should the Meursius-narrator be characterized? The first word of the last paragraph, *Certe*, is, as I said, his (discreet) way of stepping forward. It announces an indisputable judgement. The narrator who becomes prominent in the last paragraph sets himself up as a moral judge concerned about the eternal truths to be extracted from this particular event.

Seen from this angle it makes good sense for the Meursius-narrator not to betray any doubts as to the course of events itself. If the point is the moral judgement and the general rule to be deduced, there should be no uncertainty about the premises on which these judgements rest. We must not doubt (as we are asked to do by the Pontanus-narrator) that the king really did seduce the count's wife. That must be stated as a simple fact.

To put it briefly, one narrator discusses and debates and one passes his moral judgements. The difference may also be described in terms of concreteness. The Pontanus-narrator is placed temporarily in relation to the events described. The song he quotes was composed, he tells us, at the same time (*eodem illo ævo*) as the events took place. By that time Latin poetry was composed in a different manner, different, that is, from Latin poetry in the narrator's own time. Further, the mere mention of the various sources for these events contributes to our perception of the Pontanus-narrator as some one *like* these other authors, some one, that is, writing at a particular time in history.

This may sound obvious, but still, it is not the case with Meursius's text. The narrator here is not expressly placed at a particular point in time. He refers to no other points of time than the events themselves. There is no parallel to Pontanus's *illo ævo* which would imply the narrator's own position at a particular point in time. And no references are given here, in Meursius's text, to other authors. This narrator is not presented as yet another of the authors who have written of these events. He is less concrete, less personal than the Pontanus-narrator.

5. Selection of Material

This difference between the types of narrator, the one who argues and discusses and the one who stands aloof and passes his judgements, is also reflected in the inclusion in the works of foreign events. Meursius, as we know, keeps to his Danish subject. He does not include foreign matters unless they have an obvious bearing on Danish history. Pontanus, on the other hand, often informs us of significant events on the European scene. Danish history is placed in the larger context of world history. What is interesting in this context, is that all these digressions from Danish history contribute to focusing our attention on the narrator, they make him stand out. It is he who singles out a given foreign event from the mass of world history, he who connects it with some point of Danish history or simply finds it worth noticing.

The same effect is manifest in Pontanus's many comparisons between persons and events of Danish history and similar phenomena of the classical world. It is the narrator who notes a given parallel. The prominent narrator, in short, reflects the broad range of subjects in the work and, more fundamentally, this narrator reflects the fact that Danish history is constantly placed within the larger context of world history.

Let me give another example of Pontanus's comparisons with the classical world. Around 1260 a German prince, he tells us, wrongly invaded Denmark and suffered a well-deserved death at the hand of a woman. Pontanus notes the parallel to the woman who murdered Pyrrhus (of Epirus in 272 BC):

> However, when a little later he was pursuing a hasty return through Scania and was engaged in attacking and plundering a local village, he died as the result of a stab from a knife, driven into his belly by some woman of manly spirit, one who loathed the arrogance of such a robber; undoubtedly he thereby won a reward commensurate with his deeds. Besides, as such courage is worthy of more admiration in a woman than in a man, so also must she be considered a rare instance among her sex and truly deserves comparison with that heroine who slew Pyrrhus with her own hand.[1]

The narrator here stands out with the observation of the likeness between the two women, expressed as an admonition to compare them. The effects of such a parallel are several. The event itself, by its being worthy of a comparison, gains weight; and since this comparison involves an event of classical history, Danish history, producing examples just as memorable, is made its equal. Further, we are confirmed in our impression of the learned character of the work.

While parallels from classical literature are frequent in Pontanus's history, Meursius never draws such a parallel. In fact he only once mentions one classical name (cf. note below). Characteristically, he replaced this comparison with Pyrrhus with a moral consideration, pointing to the exemplary value of the woman's deed from a religious stance:

---

[1] *Verum reditum haud multo post per Scaniam maturans, ac vico cuidam ibidem invadendo diripiendoque occupatus, a foemina quapiam virilis animi, quæ execrabatur grassatoris insolentiam, cultello intra abdomen ejus adacto, perfossus interijt; pretium scilicet hoc ipso factis dignum reportans. Talis autem ut in foemina quam viro admirabilior virtus, ita quoque rari exempli hæc in sexu suo habenda, et quæ cum illa, quæ Pyrrhum sua manu interfecit, viragine haud immerito comparanda* (357-58).

Plainly he was killed because God was exacting revenge for his villainy
and treachery; and in a degrading manner, too, since it was at the hand of
a woman, who drove a knife into his belly.[2]

6. *Authority*

What is the effect of this impersonal aloofness of the Meursius-narrator? I think it enhances the impression of the narrator's infallibility as
moral judge. He is presented as standing above history, so to speak,
passing the same kind of timeless moral judgements on persons of
Danish history from the earliest times to the sixteenth century, and
deducing from these judgements general truths about the nature of
power and about God's ways with men.

We now touch upon the question of authority: how do Pontanus and
Meursius convince us of the truth of what they tell us? As I have just
suggested, the narrator of Meursius's text is suited to confirm our trust
in the moral message of this text. Similarly in Pontanus: here the narrator, prominent, arguing, and personal as he is, is suited to contribute to
the impression of painstaking research on the part of the implied author,
and a striving to find out what really happened. Further, the energetic
historian, which the narrator impersonates, is suited to make us trust that
he has indeed had access to information about so many varied topics and
foreign events with which the text deals.

By the expression "the implied author" I mean the writer of the text as
we infer him from the text. In the words of the literary critic Wayne
Booth: "we infer him as an ideal, literary, created version of the real man;
he is the sum of his own choices".[3] The speaker of the work, the narrator, then, is only one of the elements from which we infer the implied
author. In analogy with the implied author, we may also speak of an
implied audience, that is the audience as we may infer it from the text.
The implied audience of Pontanus's text are his equals. They are furnished with documentation and arguments and thus in a sense invited to
participate in his research. Not so with Meursius. Rather than speaking to
his audience as his equals he speaks down to them. They are his inferiors
whom he is determined to teach. From him they shall learn about Danish

---

[2] *clare Deo latrocinium, ac perfidiam, vindicante, interficitur: idque ignominiose, manu fæminæ, adacto in abdomen cultro* (II, 41).

[3] Booth 1983 (1st ed. 1961), 74-75.

history, and they shall learn about the fundamental moral principles by which God directs the course of history.

Authority is, of course, also based on other elements than the type of narrator. In Pontanus's text our confidence is strengthened by the display of knowledge about the relevant sources of Danish history. We trust that Pontanus does indeed know what he is talking about, and we trust that he has striven to obtain as much information as possible about what really took place. Thus, from his unwillingness to decide the motive of the count in the passage quoted above, we infer that a decision is not possible.

Throughout the work he is portrayed as a diligent and energetic researcher and analytical historian – a feature which also distinguishes his account from Huitfeldt's, as we saw; for instance, where Huitfeldt merely mentions how in 1456 a Swedish nobleman and some other magnates surrendered a castle, Pontanus refers to his own research efforts: *eundem* [...] *convenisse cum regiis præfectis* **invenio** [...], ("I find that this man [...] came to terms with the royal prefects [...]", col. 752). Unlike Meursius, who depicts Danish history in a vacuum, so to speak, Pontanus constantly relates it to European history, to older history, to his own time (sometimes in the form of personal remarks, such as "my old friend Ubbo Emmius", 657). Meursius only relates it to his own time when occasionally drawing attention to the connection between modern place-names and historical events.[4] And only a few times does he refer to classical and Biblical antiquity.[5]

In Meursius's case the display of learning is more indirect. We are seldom given any direct impression of his knowledge of the relevant sources of Danish history. But we are shown that Meursius is very well versed in the Latin of the classical Roman authors. His vocabulary and syntax is throughout in accordance with them. In particular he displays his awareness of the stylistic principles of classical historical writing. Unlike Pontanus, who displays his learning on the surface, so to speak, constantly referring to other authors and constantly quoting from them,

---

[4] E.g. I, 28 (Haderslev), 29 (Slesvig). Meursius's most emphatic break of narrative distance is the following celebration of Christian IV (with an allusion to his motto), made in connection with Christophorus III (1440-48): *cujus* [i.e. Christian I's] *nunc prosapia, continuata diu serie, ad ducentos fere annos, floret; ac florebit porro, quoad PIETATEM colet, unam omnium REGNORVM FIRMAMENTVM validissimum* (II, 129).

[5] I have noted four such references. At the suggestion of Saxo (V, Ch. xv, 3) (and probably made more explicit by Svaning) he compares Augustus to the Danish king, Frotho III (I, 21). A parallel is drawn between the change of Canutus Sanctus's name from *Cnutus* to *Canutus* and the change of the name of *Abraham* from *Abram* (I, 68). The other two references are more vague (*tota Antiquitas*, I, 62; *ecclesia antiqua*, I, 64).

Meursius, like the classical historians, rarely mentions any sources and never quotes them. Throughout, the words are his own. This classicizing style is an important ingredient in Meursius's authority. To put it generally, we might say that such stylistical imitation of the classics is a typically humanistic way of creating authority. It has to do with the status of Latin as the eternal language, as the language of antiquity as well as the language in which future generations could be addressed.[6] This notion of eternity, or immortality, applies most forcefully to a Latin untainted by neologisms, apparently unaffected by change. I think, therefore, we may see a connection between Meursius's striving for a pure classical Latin and his particular kind of authority, the authority of a moral judge. By cultivating the eternal language in his Danish history, he added weight to his timeless moral judgements.

---

[6] I owe this notion to Minna Skafte Jensen 1991, 60.

Chapter IX

Meursius's Notes to Pontanus's
Rerum Danicarum historia

Pontanus's and Meursius's References to
Each Other in their Histories of Denmark

We saw in the biographical presentations of Pontanus and Meursius that there are indications of disapproval by both men of their colleague's achievements in the field of Danish history. The previous chapters have, I hope, demonstrated how different their contributions within this field are. I shall here give a brief presentation of Meursius's view of Pontanus's *History of Denmark*, as it is expressed in his notes to his colleague's work; but first I shall make a note, also quite briefly, on their ways of referring to each other in their *Histories of Denmark*.

It is a conspicuous fact that neither of them in the course of his *History* refers by name to the colleague, although both have profited from the other's work. It may seem most striking in the case of Pontanus, who is usually so generous in his references to his sources. But then his use of Meursius is limited to single passages in the Oldenburg section. Meursius, on the other hand, based his account of the period c. 1182-1448 on his colleague's work without ever mentioning him by name. This is surprising considering that he occasionally names sources of much smaller significance. However, he never mentions Svaning either, whose *History of Denmark* must be regarded as his most important source.[1] We cannot, then, take this lack of mutual acknowledgement in the works themselves as an indication of jealous rivalry; rather they may have been instructed not to refer by name to their colleague. But perhaps it is significant that they both found occasion to reject details of their colleague's account in the course of their histories, even though no names are mentioned. Pontanus's points of indirect criticism concern the early Oldenburg kings, 1448-1523, the only part which he wrote after Meursius's version of the

---

[1] He was well aware that Svaning was the author of the manuscript history of Denmark on which he based his work. That is clear from his letters and from his notes to Pontanus.

same period had been published. In connection with the election of Christianus I as future king of Denmark, he writes:

> Others have it, without indicating the author they follow, that when Christianus's father, Didericus, had been approached by the delegates, he first of all answered that he had three sons, who were, however, of different characters; of the two younger, one was dedicated to gambling and feasting, the other to warfare whether just or unjust; but the third was led rather by exercise of judgement than by impulse.

This refers to Meursius:

> When the delegates had addressed Didericus, he answered that he had three sons who were, however, of different characters. One was quite as much interested in gambling as in sumptuousness; the second ready for warfare whether just or unjust; the third estimated everything by the standard of reason and never acted without consideration ...[2]

By pointing out that these "other authors" do not indicate their sources Pontanus suggests a slight scepticism – and perhaps a disapproval of Meursius's lack of source references.

In another case Pontanus disagrees with Meursius's judgement of Johannes's (1481-1513) rule in Sweden. Echoing Svaning's *Chronicon Ioannis*, Meursius had criticized Johannes for having placed non-Swedish men as governors in Sweden. Significantly, Pontanus here polemicizes against Petrus Parvus Rosefontanus (Svaning's pseudonym) and then, vaguely, "those who follow him". Meursius is not named, but he is clearly the target.[3]

---

[2] Pontanus: *Tradunt alii, auctore, quem sequuntur, non addito, patrem Christiani Didericum a delegatis hoc nomine conventum, omnium primo respondisse, esse sibi tres filios, sed ingenio dispares, et quidem juniorem utrumque hunc ad aleam et commessationes, illum ad justa injusta bella æque promptum paratumque: At tertium consilio magis quam impetu duci* (col. 720).

Meursius: *Hac de causa cum legati Didericum adiissent, is respondet: tres se filios habere, sed ingenio differentes. Vnum enim, aleæ pariter, ac luxuriæ, studiosum; alterum, ad bella justa, aut injusta, animo, et manu, promptum: tertium, metiri ratione cuncta, nec quid inconsulto gerere* (III, 2). Pontanus's hint at Meursius is noted by Gram in his commentary on Meursius, *ad loc.*

[3] Meursius had written: *Sed in eo etiam in regnandi legem deliquisse merito censeri potest, quod subactis a se Suecis, contra pacta, Danos suos, ac Germanos, peregrinos, potius præficiendos, quam indigenas Suecos, duxerit: nec eorum in dominatu non ferendam impotentiam tempestive compescuerit* (III, 59). Cf. Svaning, (Ff3, Z4v-Aar).

Pontanus's wording is similar: *Petrus Parvus Rosefontanus auctor ipsemet domesticus ac eques Danus, et si qui eum seqvuti, deliquisse eo vel impegisse, vel, ut clarius dicam, contra pactum, inter cetera cum Suecis initum fecisse existimant, quod Danos Germanosque, homines peregrinos, non indigenas, Suecis imposuerit.* (Then follows his own point of view) (col. 973).

Again when Stockholm surrenders to Christianus II in 1520, Pontanus distances himself from authors who claim that the inhabitants had been driven to surrender by their sufferings:

> Some claim that the beleaguered only surrendered after having suffered extreme hardships, but in the domestic documents and those followed by the most noble Huitfeldt nothing of this is found.

The criticism is levelled at Meursius, who writes that the king prevented food supplies from being imported into the town, and when nothing was left, "the beleaguered suffered extreme hardships", whereupon they persuaded the queen to surrender.[4]

These must be some of Meursius's many errors to which Pontanus refers in the letter to Stephanius quoted earlier.[5] Meursius, on his side, hints, in his own *History*, at errors found in Pontanus's 1631 edition. Queen Margareta ruled, he says, for thirty-six years; but others wrongly reduce the number to thirty-two (II, 103-4). Surely he has Pontanus in mind here, who like Huitfeldt (*Chron.* III, 216) states that her rule lasted thirty-two years (544). Similarly, Meursius corrects those who say that Valdemarus III in 1354 saw Pope Urbanus V in Avignon, when it was in fact, he says, Innocens VI (II, 85). Again this must be aimed at Pontanus (482), who follows Huitfeldt (*Chron.* II, 519). Perhaps we may also see an allusion to Pontanus when Meursius a few times in the older history emphasizes the fact that he finds the national historical tradition more trustworthy than foreign authors' information on Danish affairs. Having related, in the tradition from Saxo, the death of Regnerus, Meursius adds: "I am aware that others recount these things differently, but I do not see the reason why I should believe a foreign author rather than a native one concerning the affairs of Denmark's kings".[6] These words were probably aimed at Pontanus who tells a quite different story, identifying Saxo's Regnerus with Regenarius, known from Aimoin of Fleury (c. 1000) as a

---

[4] Pontanus: *Sunt qui obsessos ad extrema redactos deditionem fecisse memorant, quorum in actis domesticis, et quæ secutus nobilissimus Witfeldius fuit, nihil occurrit* (cols. 1027-28).

Meursius: *Rex Stockholmum ita arcte obsidebat, ut omnino commeatus importari nullus posset, quo deficiente tandem, cum obsessi ad extrema adigerentur, adeunt Christinam proceres [...] ac deditionem suadent* (III, 76).

[5] Letter from Pontanus to Stephanius, dated July 1st, 1638 (Matthæus, 1695, n. 122). Cf. Chapter III.

[6] *Non ignoro alios hæc aliter commemorare; sed, in rebus Daniæ regum, cur extraneo scriptori potius credam, quam indigenæ, causam equidem non video* (I, 43).

warrior who plundered Paris in 845 (100). Meursius also emphatically professes his trust in the native tradition shortly before, in connection with Olaus III, a king mentioned by Saxo but not by foreign sources (I, 37). He is mentioned by Pontanus, though with scepticism, since, as he says, neither Albert of Stade, nor the *Frankish Annals* refer to him (95). In this case also, Meursius's outburst is probably aimed at Pontanus.

The most significant reference to Pontanus's history in Meursius's work is found in the latter's very first lines (I, 1). Here Meursius explains why he will not go into certain matters (the origin of the Danes, Danish geography etc.) because it has been done by others. The passage has been discussed above (Chapter VII. 2), and we shall return to it in the Conclusion (Chapter X).

Meursius's Notes to Pontanus's Rerum Danicarum historia

Only by a few hints, then, do Pontanus and Meursius refer to their colleague's work. On Meursius's view of Pontanus's achievement , however, we have more detailed information in the set of notes he made to Pontanus's 1631 edition, probably as preparations for his own treatment of the history before 1448. The notes were printed by Gram as an appendix to his edition of Meursius's *History* (*Opera omnia IX*, cols. 1141-48).[7] They went back to a copy of Pontanus's work owned by the nobleman Ove Juul (1615-86), who had added them in the margin on the basis of Meursius's own notes. They were then transcribed from Juul's copy, according to Gram's edition by Thomas Bartholin (1616-80).[8] Another transcription of the notes found in Juul's copy was made by another nobleman Laurids Ulfeldt (1605-59); they are extant in a manuscript in the Royal Library of Copenhagen.[9] A third copy of Meursius's notes is found in a

---

[7] 'Ioannis Meursi Animadversiones in Historiam Danicam Io. Isacii Pontani editam Amstelodami M. DC. XXXI. Cum adspersis pauculis Steph. Stephanii notis, quibus Pontanum vindicatum ivit. Apud Ioannem Iansonium'. I refer to Gram's edition in the following.

[8] This seems to be the meaning of the following statement which concludes the notes in Gram's edition of the notes: *Communicatae mihi* ab Illustrissimo Viro Domino Owenio Iul Serenissimi Regis Vice Cancellario, Qui eas ad marginem sui libri <ex> autographo Meursiano adnotaverat.* And to *mihi*, Gram notes: **Fil. Thomae Bartholino Sen. Medicinae Professori, Anatomico et Polyhistori: cujus ex autographo hoc descriptum.* (I assume this refers to Thomas Bartholin the elder and not to his son in spite of the introductory *Fil.*).

[9] The signature of the ms. is *Gl. kgl. Saml.* 2428, 4to. It ends with the same note as the one found in the printed edition: *Communicatæ mihi ab Illustrissimo viro Dn. Owenio Jul. Serenissimi Regiæ Majestatis Vicecancellario, qui eas ad marginem sui libri ex autographo Meursiano annotaverat.* According to Gigas, most of the manuscript is written in Laurids Ulfeldt's hand (E. Gigas:

copy of Pontanus's *Rerum Danicarum historia* in the University Library of Lund. This copy belonged to the famous book collector and nobleman, Jørgen Seefeldt (1594-1662). On the inside of the binding Seefeldt informs the reader that all the handwritten notes and corrections found in this copy have been transcribed from Meursius's own book (*e libro Clarissimi Viri Joannis Meursii*), which he had been given by Meursius's son at the beginning of 1641.[10]

We have already had occasion to deal with Meursius's criticism of Pontanus's Latin. From these notes we get the distinct impression, confirmed by the two texts themselves, that Meursius paid much more attention to clarity and literary elegance than did his colleague. Questions of correct Latin loom large, but Meursius is also aware of matters of disposition and internal inconsistencies. "These passages contradict each other" (*Hæc sunt contraria*), he observes when Pontanus hints at the low birth of a man whom he has shortly before placed "amongst the elite" (*inter primarios*, 248). A considerable part of his commentaries concerns factual details, e.g.:

> 454,31. *Ringstadii*] Immo, Sorae. (At Ringsted] On the contrary, at Sorø).

> 476,24 *insula Dragorae*] Dragora non est insula, sed Amagriae insulae pagus. (The island of Dragør] Dragør is not an island, but a village on Amager).

> 482,39 *Urbanum V.*] Innocentium VI. Nam is hoc tempore pontificatum tenebat, adeptus biennio ante; ac possedit usque ad annum MCCCLXII. quo demum successit Vrbanus V. (Urbanus V] Innocentius VI. He held the papacy at this time, having attained it two years earlier; and he occupied it until the year 1362, when Urbanus V finally succeeded him),

– this last correction also found its way into Meursius's *History* itself, as we saw. Sometimes Meursius's comments seem irrelevant, as when he adds to Pontanus's account of Valdemarus I's sons (274) a third son,

---

Katalog over det store Kongelige Bibliotheks Haandskrifter vedrørende Norden, særlig Danmark (Kbh. 1903-15), III,10. *Mihi*, then, must here refer to Ulfeldt, whereas according to Gram it referred to Bartholin. Either Bartholin or Ulfeldt, it would seem, transcribed the other's copy of the notes from Juul without changing the *mihi*.

In this copy some extra notes are added as an appendix from a copy possessed by Stephanius; these notes, apparently, also go back to Meursius (they are introduced with these words: *Easdem codici suo adscripsit Stephanius, qui in Bibliotheca Muleriana asservatur, paucissimis additis*).

[10] I was made aware of the existence of Seefeldt's copy by Walde 1916-20, 408.

Christophorus. Pontanus deals with the sons who survived Valdemarus, and Christophorus, as Meursius himself says, died before his father.

Meursius's comments only concern Pontanus's faults. We cannot tell from them whether he also found features of Pontanus's *History* worthy of admiration. But in a number of cases Meursius does not confine himself to noting an error (*debebat dicere*, "he ought to have said"), he also stresses its seriousness or stupidity with exclamations such as *Magna akurologia, Magnus error, Inepte, Male, Erras graviter, Pontane, Ergo hic est crassus error, Est haec itaque magna akurologia.*[11] Sometimes, as we have seen in the preceding chapter, there is an unmistakably sarcastic tone. An example is this demonstration of Pontanus's confusing of Roman dates (col. 1146):

> 454, 32 *xi. nonas Maii*] Crassus error. Maius enim, uti sciunt, qui vel medi-ocriter docti, sex duntaxat Nonas habet. Posset mendum typographicum putari, nisi etiam Witfeldius, quem verbo tenus sequitur auctor, ad eundem modum haberet.

> (*xi nonas Maii*] A stupid mistake. As those who are even moderately well educated know, May has only six days of 'nones'. It might have been thought a printing error, had not Huitfeldt, whom this author follows word for word, also put it the same way).

Of course one must be careful in evaluating the significance of such expressions of opinion. But the evident sarcasm of many of these comments does seem to suggest that Meursius took a certain pleasure in listing the shortcomings of his colleague, and that he regarded the latter's work with no warm feelings. – One of the existing versions of Meursius's notes, though, the one found in Jørgen Seefeldt's copy of Pontanus, strikes a friendlier note. Here we do not find sarcastic addresses to Pontanus, such as those quoted above. Presumably Seefeldt simply left them out. Otherwise Seefeldt's version contains material not found in the other two: printing errors in Pontanus's text are corrected and many words are underlined, presumably words and expressions of which Meursius disapproved on stylistic grounds (cf. above pp. 335 sqq).

One of Meursius's commentaries deserves special attention, since it has wider implications for our understanding of his view of historiography. From Saxo's account we learn that during Svibdagerus's reign a

---

[11] "A great inaccuracy"; "a great mistake"; "absurd"; "bad"; "you are seriously wrong, Pontanus"; "so this is a silly mistake"; "so this is a great inaccuracy".

giant took care of the children of the previous king. Saxo then, in a small digression, describes the three different kinds of soothsayers in those days (I, Ch. v). This piece of cultural history obviously inspired Pontanus. Having reeled off Svibdagerus's history in just eight lines, he then devotes one and a half folio pages to pointing out that Saxo's three types of fortune-tellers have their close parallels in classical antiquity. His aim is to demonstrate that these magicians were not exclusively Nordic, and he calls attention to a number of classical authors, such as Martianus Capella, Cicero, Caesar, Ammianus Marcellinus, Tacitus, and Lucan (13-15).

In Meursius's view, this demonstration is completely out of place. "This whole chapter is philological rather than historical", he tersely comments, "and it has nothing to do with Svibdagerus".[12] By describing Pontanus's digression as "philological" he seems to mean that Pontanus here discusses the interpretation of classical texts – and this was simply not appropriate in a work of history. Similarly he later on criticizes Pontanus's attempt to emend the text of Saxo: "He should not pose as 'critic' in a work of history"[13] – again, in a historical work matters of textual criticism should not be discussed.

Here Meursius explicitly disapproves of Pontanus's broad range of subjects. These criticisms, in fact, apply to the antiquarian branch of historical writing as a whole. They testify to Meursius's sense of historiographical *decorum*, so clearly evidenced in his own *History of Denmark*.[14]

But they should not, of course, be taken as a disapproval of philological enterprise as such. About the same time that he wrote his comments on Pontanus's history, Meursius gave proof of his ability as a philological and antiquarian historian in his edition of the English monk Ailnothus's description from c. 1120 of the life and martyrdom of Canutus Sanctus (1080-86) together with a contemporary, anonymous account of the martyrdom of Canutus's son, Carolus of Flanders.[15] He furnished the texts with elaborate commentaries, in which he discusses not only textual and linguistic questions, such as the meaning of rare words, but also

---

[12] *Totum hoc caput potius Philologicum est, quam historicum; neque ad Svibdagerum pertinet* (col. 1141).

[13] *Non recte in Historia Criticum agit* (col. 1143).

[14] I have presented these observations on Meursius's censure of Pontanus's account of Svibdagerus in Skovgaard-Petersen 1998b.

[15] Meursius 1631.

problems of chronology and instances of conflicting evidence in other sources. In short we here find the kind of material which is so often taken up by Pontanus in his *History of Denmark* and which Meursius kept out of his own history. Correspondingly, the "I", the narrator of the commentaries, is here very much like the "I" of Pontanus's work, prominent, openly discussing, concerned about finding the truth. The narrator steps forward with verbs in the first person singular (*video, ostendi*), he discusses and argues (*verum ego mendum esse ubique existimo*, "but I think there is error everywhere", 103), even describing his own research: Caspar Bartholin himself, we learn, showed him the fountain from which Roskilde has its name, when he came to visit him shortly after having arrived in Denmark (100-1).

Meursius, I think we can conclude, paid attention to the demands of diverse genres. In his view a national history demanded a different kind of rhetoric from a commentary; and, as his notes to Pontanus's *History of Denmark* show, he disapproved of Pontanus's confusion in these matters.

Chapter X

Conclusion

As a point of departure for the examination of Pontanus's and Meursius's *Histories of Denmark*, I took the observation that both authors were told to write a full history each. Assuming that the two histories were meant to supplement each other, I set out to make a comparative study. In the following pages I shall first confine myself to summing up the main results of the examination of the two texts themselves, and then discuss whether it is possible, on the basis of these results, to form an idea of the instructions Pontanus and Meursius received from the Danish government.

The Texts

In the Introduction I singled out three areas on which the investigation would focus, one ideological, one historiographical and one stylistic. In the historiographical and stylistic areas – which, as I have tried to argue, are closely interrelated – we were able to note remarkable differences between Pontanus's and Meursius's *Histories*.

Meursius's *History* is classicizing. Unity is a key concept, stylistically as well as thematically. All the Danish kings, from Danus to Christianus III, exemplify timeless maxims on the nature of power and the obligations of the prince, a theme which seems to be inspired by contemporary Tacitism and more particularly by Lipsius's *Politica*. The will of God is seen as the active governing principle in the course of history, even in pagan times. (Sometimes a disillusioned, almost Machiavellian, realism makes itself felt, in descriptions of the egoistical and greedy nature of princes, but the first of these trends is dominant). The kings are judged along moral lines by the narrator, and we learn that their crimes were punished by God. Royal matrimonial infidelity is a sin which, in Meursius's description, has always had severe consequences for the whole nation. Kings derive their power directly from God, they are God's vicars on earth, and the good king realizes that his exalted position gives him a singular responsibility. These themes seem – with the exception of the Machiavellian cynicism – to place Meursius's *History of Denmark* in the tradition of Melanchthon, whose chronicle of world history, *Carion's Chronicle*, likewise depicts the course of history, in pagan times also, as governed by God's rewards for virtue and punishments of crimes. The notion of the worldly authorities being God's vicars on earth and the strong condemnation of marital infidelity as a threat to the order of society are Melanchthonian. So is Meursius's criticism of the medieval bishops' partaking in warfare and other worldly activities and his description of the Reformation as a restitution of the primitive Church.

Meursius focuses, rather narrowly, on the subject of Danish kings and their reigns. Foreign events are seldom, if ever, mentioned unless they are directly related to Danish history. In the early history Meursius basically follows the legendary tradition from Saxo, beginning with Danus. He has not included any considerations about the inhabitants of Denmark before Danus.

The thematic unity is matched by a unity of style. Meursius confined himself to a vocabulary authorized by classical Latin authors. Throughout, his striving for a brief, clear, and lively narrative is evident. He displays an awareness of the stylistic principles of classical historiography by reworking the Latin of his sources into a uniform prose, by avoiding quotations, and by referring to his sources only occasionally. Such stylistic imitation of the classics is a typically humanistic way of creating authority. Furthermore, since the narrator's voice of Meursius's text is that of a moral judge, I suggested a connection between the timeless moral outlook and the classicizing Latin, the "eternal" language which was, apparently, untainted by change. The use of this "eternal" Latin added weight to the narrator's authority as moral judge. This timelessness is emphasized by the lack of references to foreign affairs and to events of classical history.

Pontanus's *History* was placed within the category of antiquarian historiography. With its broad range of subjects, particularly in the *Chorographica descriptio*, it is an example of the tendency to "historicize" more and more areas of human life, which has been emphasized by Donald R. Kelley. It lacks the thematic unity found in Meursius's *History*, its explicit moralizing being rare and scattered. Pontanus rarely makes general observations or deduces moral and political maxims from the events narrated. Foreign affairs receive considerable attention, even when they have no direct bearing on Danish history. Throughout, Danish history is related to world history by the indication of the contemporary Roman emperor at the bottom of each page. Further, he draws a number of parallels between events or persons of Danish history and similar phenomena known from classical literature, and these parallels serve to present the Danish past as equal to the Graeco-Roman. In short, Pontanus, unlike Meursius, depicts Danish history as part of a greater whole. In the early history Pontanus made an innovation by omitting the legendary tradition from Saxo and instead beginning Danish history with the migrations known from classical and early medieval writers.

Stylistically Pontanus's work – and, I would suggest, the Latin antiquarian historiography of the period in general – is characterized by a prominent narrator, by discussions, by many quotations from other authors, by the transcribing of inscriptions and documents, and by a mixture of languages in the quotations, and occasional use of non-classical words and expressions. On the basis of observations of the narrators's voices in Pontanus's and Meursius's texts, I described the difference between them in terms of authority. Briefly put, Pontanus's authority lies in his many discussions, quotations and references to other texts, by which we are convinced of his learning and energy as a researcher. His learning is displayed on the surface. Meursius's authority, as mentioned above, is humanistic in the sense that his learning is displayed through the classicizing Latin and the uniform prose; and by these stylistic means he adds further to his authority as moral judge.

The difference between the two histories may also be expressed in terms of their relationship to the classics. For Pontanus they are sources of information possessing great authority, while for Meursius they are stylistic models. But the very orientation towards the classics is common to them. Above I have used the term 'humanistic' to denote Meursius's way of establishing authority through his classicizing style. 'Humanistic' may, however, also be used in a broader sense to denote the orientation towards the Greek and particularly the Roman classics. In this sense both Pontanus's and Meursius's works are, in their different ways, humanistic, and so is the greater part of medieval and early modern national historiography in Western Europe.

In the third main area of interest in this book, the ideological, there is reason to stress the basic agreement between Pontanus's and Meursius's histories. In both works Denmark is depicted as a powerful nation, particularly in the early history. In Pontanus's case this greatness is secured by placing the migrations of Late Antiquity and the Early Middle Ages and later the Norman expeditions in a heroic light. The Cimbrians, the Goths, the Anglo-Saxons, and the Normans are described as coming from Denmark (or sometimes more broadly from Scandinavia), and they are, primarily, seen as impressive warriors. We can often observe how Pontanus changed the condemnatory tone of a foreign source in order to heroize the Danish forefathers (but he is not quite consistent; sometimes he retains the foreign perspective of suffering and cruelty). The basic message of this part of Pontanus's work is Denmark's decisive contribution to European history. Denmark's influence on Europe is also demonstrated, though on a much smaller scale, in the later parts of Pontanus's work.

While Pontanus, in the early history, concentrates on Danes outside Denmark, Meursius is primarily concerned with internal affairs. But he, too, conveys an impression of strength and victories. Denmark is depicted as a power under which several neighbouring nations are subdued. Wars with neighbours are normally described as defections, revolts against rightful Danish rule.

Meursius manages to convey an impression of an organized society right from the earliest kings. Not only is the monarchy an institution which goes back to the very beginning, or rather which constitutes the very beginning, but also the council (*rigsråd*), the *senatus*, has been there from the earliest times. Pontanus, too, makes it clear that the early Danish forefathers were not barbarians. This is most clearly emphasized in the thematic treatment in the *Chorographica descriptio*, where the monarchy, together with certain legal traditions, is traced back to the Cimbrians on the basis of classical testimonies. But he also draws attention to the high civilization of the Cimbrians in the chronological narrative. In the summary of Saxo's legendary history he sees a connection between Frotho III's (*Frode Fredegod*) law-making and Tacitus's description of the old German moral codex, a connection which apparently makes him trust this piece of Saxo's legendary history and thus ascribe a legal system to early Danish society.

The celebration of Denmark as an independent monarchy is a main theme of both Pontanus and Meursius. They stress the great age of monarchical government. In Meursius the institution of monarchy constitutes the beginning of Danish history. Following the tradition from Saxo, he makes Danish history start with Danus, the first king. For Pontanus it was not as simple because of his declared distrust of Saxo's legendary part, but he did, in fact, dispense with his scepticism by concluding the summary of the earliest part of Saxo's *Gesta Danorum* with a survey of the kings whose reigns he had just recapitulated. The survey is arranged both in a list and in a genealogical tree, with no indication of mistrust; on the contrary Pontanus here makes it clear that family relations exist between all the Danish kings, right up to the Oldenburgs. Moreover, he took care to emphasize, in the *Chorographica descriptio*, that the old Cimbrians were governed by kings; also within this new paradigm, then, where classical authors formed the basis instead of Saxo, he found room for celebrating the old Danish monarchy.

The Danes have always loved their kings and with good reason. This is another common theme of Pontanus's and Meursius's works. Time and again Pontanus, in connection with royal celebrations, has it that everybody supported the king. He also, in a couple of general reflections, praises monarchical rule as the best kind of government. In Meursius's work, though, the monarchical focus is stronger. Meursius, as I said, made the exercise of power the recurrent theme, depicting the pious and morally upright king, who is first and foremost concerned about his people, as the ideal ruler. In the course of history various Danes in Meursius's work realize that without a king chaos is likely to fall upon the country.

Particularly noteworthy is both historians' suggestion that the Danish monarchy comes close to being hereditary. Pontanus, in his survey of kings, points out that the Danish throne has been occupied by very few families ever since the first king, Danus – accepting, as we saw, Saxo's legendary version without comment. Leaving out most of Huitfeldt's references to Denmark as an elective monarchy, he finds instead occasion to suggest the genealogical continuity of the kings on the Danish throne. Meursius declares at the beginning of the Oldenburg section (beginning in 1448) that now the Danish monarchy, which had hitherto been elective, became *quasi hæreditarium*, "almost hereditary". But in fact, in the earlier history also he is careful to point out how son almost always followed father on the throne, an arrangement which was also preferred by the magnates of the realm. Both convey the impression that the old Danish monarchy has always been *quasi hæreditarium*.

Danish relations with Sweden were a delicate topic. A prohibition against defamatory writings had been in effect since the peace treaty in 1570 (except in periods of open war), and the Danish government had taken care to respect it, although relations between the two countries were always tense during the reigns of Frederik II and Christian IV. The governmental cautiousness is reflected in both Pontanus's and Meursius's works. The most sensitive part of history with respect to Sweden was during the Union of Kalmar (1397-1523), when Denmark, Norway and Sweden had been united under Danish rule. Against Johannes Magnus's *History of Sweden* of 1554, which contrasted Swedish love of freedom, high morals, and occasional naivety with Danish unreliabilty and greed, Hans Svaning had stressed, in his *Refutatio* of Magnus and the *Chronicon Ioannis* (1561), the Danes' striving for peace as opposed to the recurring breaches of agreements on the part of the Swedes. Huitfeldt had likewise (in his Danish *History of Denmark*, 1595-1604) praised the Union and in general underlined that the Danes had right on their side, but he was much less aggressive than Svaning. Pontanus retained this balanced point of view. But both he and Huitfeldt found it necessary to establish a defence against some of the attacks on Denmark made by Johannes Magnus in his *History of Sweden*. Most important – and a recurrent issue in Magnus's work – was the question of Scania. Pontanus follows Huitfeldt in his argument against Magnus's claim that the region rightfully belonged to Sweden. Pontanus also found occasion to refute Magnus on other points of his polemics against the Danes, to which Huitfeldt had not reacted. In the *Chorographica descriptio*, moreover, he launched a serious attack on the whole Gothicist construction, on which Magnus based his account of a high Gothic civilization in Sweden a long time before Greece and Rome. Pontanus argued that nothing is known of the Goths before the second century AD. Magnus was defeated with learned weapons.

Similarly, Meursius in his treatment of the Union of Kalmar creates an impression of not being unduly polemical, while at the same time making it clear that Denmark, both in terms of power and morals, had the upper hand. His source for this period was Hans Svaning's *History of Denmark*, which (judging from the preserved parts) was clearly designed as an answer and a parallel to Johannes Magnus, with a strong emphasis on Swedish slyness and unreliablity as opposed to the high morals of the Danes. Meursius, in his first version, seems to have retained this anti-Swedish aggressiveness to the point that the chancellor, after having read a draft, asked Meursius to adopt a more polite attitude towards the Swedes. The result, the printed version which is known today, is considerably less aggressive than Svaning's. Besides, Meursius, as we saw, describes Denmark in the earliest times as a great power ruling over several neighbouring nations, among which is, of course, Sweden. In Meursius's account of these earliest times it is the normal situation that Sweden is subject to Denmark and then occasionally defects from its rightful master. The fact that this version of Danish-Swedish relations in the early past did not, apparently, cause the chancellor concern, but was allowed to be printed, suggests that freer rein was given in the depiction of the remotest past than in the treatment of the recent Union of Kalmar.

Thus we can note a considerable agreement on these ideological and political points in Pontanus and Meursius. But their different approaches also offered each of them particular opportunities for panegyric. Pontanus's history contains a presentation of Denmark which has no counterpart in the work of his colleague. He appended to his chronological narrative a topographical description of Denmark, in which, *inter alia*, the fertility of Danish soil, its rich trade, the many historical monuments, the excellent organization of Danish society, and the long traditions of learning are described. For this rich and detailed thematic presentation of Denmark Pontanus had models in several recent works of national history, and such a thematic presentation of a country belonged, as earlier mentioned, to the antiquarian branch of early modern historiography. Another standard topic of these thematic presentations was the origin of the nation and people on the basis of classical and biblical testimonies. Following contemporary convention Pontanus claims that the first settlement in Denmark goes back to the arrival of Noah's son Japhet in Scandinavia. He further connects this theory with Tacitus's statement in the *Germania* that the Germans were *indigenæ*: Danish ways of life, he concludes, have remained untainted by foreign influences since the arrival of the first inhabitants. In this way antiquarian studies provided possibilities for celebration of a nation which were not available to the writer of a more narrowly scoped political history.

Meursius on his side was able to pass explicit moral judgements on the kings; though not all of them were without faults, they almost invariably came out morally superior in external conflicts. They had God on their side. In this moral universe where the good cause wins, success is a sign of high morals and divine grace. As to the origin of the Danes Meursius, like Saxo, simply starts with Danus without further suggestions of what came before. In fact, this procedure was just as unusual in the sixteenth and seventeenth centuries as Pontanus's radical rewriting of the earliest history. Other accounts of the earliest past would enquire into the period before Danus. Meursius does not, like Saxo, convey the impression that the Danes were autochthonous, inasmuch as he refers to other treatments of the origin of the Danes as the reason for his own omission of this topic; but his procedure is a strong monarchical statement to the effect that Denmark's history began when Danus united the various regions under one king.

Pontanus's and Meursius's histories were shaped by many factors – personal inclinations and talents, available sources and governmental instructions – and the interplay between these factors cannot be reconstructed in detail today. But some conjectures can be made. As to personal inclinations, for instance, I think Meursius's commentaries on Pontanus confirm our impression from the stylistic analysis that he disapproved of his colleague's stylistic carelessness; that he, adhering to classical ideals, regarded unity of style as an indispensable ingredient of a national history. Similarly, some conjectures about the instructions they received from the government mandates can be made.

The Governmental Instructions

Pontanus's and Meursius's *Histories of Denmark* must be regarded as official statements about Danish history. The authors were engaged and paid by the government, and their status as royal historiographers comes out clearly in the printed books. In the dedicatory letters to Christian IV the authors present themselves as historiographers engaged by the king, just as Pontanus, on the title page of the 1631 edition, is called *regius historiographus*, and Meursius, on the frame of the portrait of him in the 1638 edition is presented as "royal historiographer", *serenissimi Daniæ regis historiographus*.

The official status of the works is reflected in the concern displayed by the chancellor, Christen Friis, about the contents of the works. The government wanted to be able to subscribe to what was said. From the letters written to him by Pontanus it is clear that he himself read the samples which Pontanus sent to him and commented upon them in letters to the author. His own interest in the migrations of Late Antiquity and the Early Middle Ages is seen in this correspondence. In Meursius's case we know that he himself read a draft of the period 1448-1523 (which was published in 1630), and that he engaged both the anonymous nobleman, whose comments have survived, and the secretary, Niels Eggebrecht, to read through Meursius's pre-1448 history.

In Chapter II I tried to reconstruct the process which led to Pontanus and Meursius being both engaged to compose a full history of Denmark. The course of events is not quite clear, but my main intention was to point out that the Danish government (whose architect behind the engagements of the historiographers was Christen Friis) was prepared to spend considerable resources to have Denmark's history, from the earliest times to the present day, composed and published in Latin. In the last half of the 1620s it planned to have three historiographers engaged at the same time to reach this goal. From 1618 Pontanus was engaged on a work covering the whole of Danish history. Then from 1624 Meursius was employed to deal with the Oldenburg kings, from 1448 onwards, including the ruling king, Christian IV. This plan was then changed, and there is evidence to suggest that towards the end of 1626 Johan Jacob Grasser in Basel was contacted with a request to compose a history of Christian IV; he refused and a couple of years later, in 1629, another Dutchman, Nicolaes Wassenaer, was hired to write about Christian IV's deeds, but he died shortly after his appointment.

It was probably around this time, 1630, that it was decided that Meursius, instead of proceeding with the Oldenburg kings – he had now covered the period 1448-1523 – should write his own version of the earlier history up to 1448, which had already been covered by Pontanus (this part of Pontanus's work was published in 1631); further it was decided that Pontanus should go on with the three first Oldenburg kings, 1448-1523, already treated by Meursius (in the 1630 edition). In other words, two complete histories were now aimed at. This does not seem to have been the plan all along. At least Meursius, in a couple of letters, seems to express surprise at the idea that he is now expected to go over the ground already covered by Pontanus. (On the other hand, Pontanus did not, apparently, receive instructions to stop at 1448, when Meursius entered the scene). Even though, then, we cannot say when this idea was formed, it seems likely that the chancellor realized, after having seen specimens of both men's works, that they would be too different to function as parts of a whole.

I put forward the hypothesis (still in Chapter II) that Friis now projected two versions of Danish history, a compendium (the work of Meursius) and a longer version (that of Pontanus). I would now like to address the question of whether we can come closer to forming an idea of Friis's intentions and expectations of Pontanus and Meursius. Do the analyses conducted in this book permit us to form an opinion of the instructions they received?

To some extent I think they do, although, of course, most of it must remain hypothetical. What we do know is that the chancellor told Meursius to soften the tone in the treatment of Sweden's role in the Union of Kalmar. Meursius's first draft, it seems, had retained more of Svaning's aggressiveness than the version which was printed after Friis's admonition. Friis's interference suggests the importance which was attached to the question of Sweden. It seems safe to assume that the balance observed in both Meursius's and Pontanus's *Histories* between stressing pro-Danish views and avoiding insults was the result of governmental instructions. Pontanus's destruction of Johannes Magnus's Gothicist basis may well have been discussed beforehand between him and the chancellor. Magnus's claims on Scania had been echoed by Swedish politicians during the reign of Christian IV, and Huitfeldt's and Pontanus's restating of the Danish position reflects the contemporary relevance of the question. It is quite possible, then, that Magnus's arguments in favour of Sweden's right to Scania in the government's view needed a refutation. Anyway, Pontanus refutes Magnus on enough points to suggest that he was told to do so, either on specific questions or in general. Just as Magnus's *History of Sweden* kept serving as an inspiration for national self-assurance and propaganda in seventeenth-century Sweden, Pontanus's arguments against it are a testimony to its lasting ability to cause concern in Denmark.

H.F. Rørdam suggested, in his biography of Pontanus, that his works on the late classical and medieval migrations in connection with the Franks had drawn Friis's attention to Pontanus as a possible royal historiographer (besides, they had met in person at least once, and Pontanus would also have been known to Friis through his family ties with Denmark). This is a reasonable assumption judging from the prominent part the migrations play in Pontanus's *History of Denmark*. The Cimbrians, Anglo-Saxons, Goths and Normans receive ample treatment and their expeditions are seen as great Danish enterprises. Friis himself took an interest in these matters and probably saw the scholarly and ideological prestige to be gained from a thorough treatment of these peoples as early Danes. Huitfeldt, moreover, had only given a brief account of the Early Middle Ages. He had, it is true, paid attention to the Normans, but taken over the attitude of the foreign sources with their emphasis on aggression and plundering. Considering that Pontanus based his later history (after c. 1185) on his work, it is easy to assume that he was told to adopt a different strategy from Huitfeldt on this point, by giving a thorough treatment of the migrations and by placing the Normans – as well as their Cimbrian, Anglo-Saxon, and Gothic predecessors – in a heroic light.

But why did Pontanus, in spite of his declared lack of confidence, include the summary of Saxo's legendary past after having already given his alternative version of the beginnings of Danish history? I suspect that it was due to governmental instructions – that a complete omission was regarded as too drastic and disrespectful a step. Pontanus managed to place the existence of the old myths in a heroic light by his Livian insistence on the right of great nations to boast of a mythical past. But the coexistence of the two versions in the *History of Denmark* is not altogether happy, and a possible explanation is that it was the result of Friis's intervention. This view gains support from Pontanus's ideological use of Saxo's legends. On the basis of the summary he points out that Danish kings from Danus onwards have belonged to a very small number of families, in other words that Denmark has had long traditions of hereditary monarchy. This is a point which clearly bears upon contemporary politics, and so it is tempting to see it as imposed upon Pontanus (the more so since it is also found in Meursius's *History*). He may have been instructed to include the earliest part of Saxo in order to bring home this point about hereditary monarchy.

Another argument to the effect that Pontanus was told to include the summary of Saxo is the fact that Meursius later gave a fuller account. Meursius's version shows us that the traditional legends could not simply be discarded. But at the time Pontanus wrote his early history it had not been decided that Meursius should write another account of this period. If Pontanus's version was to be the only one, the tradition from Saxo had to be represented.

With his loyalty to the tradition from Saxo and his consequent focus on internal history, Meursius adopts a strategy clearly designed to supplement Pontanus's early history. In fact, he himself suggests as much at the very beginning: "Others have given diligent accounts of the origin of the Danes, their great age, and the geographical situation of Denmark, and therefore I will not go into these matters; instead I will turn to the kings and their deeds at home and abroad", he declares (I,I). This statement relates his work to that of Pontanus (who is not named): because the latter had given ample treatment of the origin of the Danes, their earliest past and the geography of the country, Meursius will not do it. And – we could add, I think – because Pontanus had only paid a little attention to the tradition from Saxo, Meursius will do it here. This division of labour was no doubt devised by Friis. I suspect that the whole idea of having Meursius engaged to go over the pre-1448 history was partly inspired by Pontanus's irreverent treatment of Saxo's earliest part. They were to supplement each other by dealing with early Danish history (up to around 1100) in different ways.

Meursius's task was to rewrite Saxo's version of Danish history. It is a reminder of the force of tradition. Even though Pontanus (and before him Anders Fos, Venusin and others) had regarded the early part of Saxo as too fanciful to count as proper history, there was still nothing to substitute for it. Pontanus made an attempt, but it was probably seen as a drawback that his alternative did not go back earlier than c. 100 BC. At least we can note that the legendary tradition from Saxo was retold once again by Vitus Bering in his *Florus Danicus* (1698) and, partly, by Ludvig Holberg in his *Danmarks riges historie* (1732-35).

Having read a draft of Meursius's account of the period 1448-1523, the chancellor expressed his satisfaction with its stylistic elegance and its small scale. It seems likely that he instructed Meursius to cultivate these two qualities when he told him to go on with an account of the earlier history. Many of the features which we have noted as being characteristic of Meursius's work – narrative brevity and clarity, lack of quotations, few references and discussions – contribute to the impression of a clear and lucid compendium; and in this sense they may be said to have been part of the mandate. To what extent the other characteristics of Meursius's account – the many general reflections on politics and power, the Christian moralism and the specifically Protestant features – were explicitly recommended we cannot tell. But we can at least observe that they were approved and accepted for publication.

The two histories advocate the same political values. They stress Denmark's long and strong royal traditions and the advantages of monarchical rule. Meursius's approach permitted him to focus on the kings, right from the start, and this was, I assume, regarded as an advantage. The kings are the agents of Danish history in his version, whereas Pontanus's strategy implied collective agents, viz. the *Cimbri, Gothi, Normanni, Dani*, in the first millennium. It may have been felt, from a governmental point of view, as another setback of Pontanus's *History*.

The notion of hereditary rule is found in both works and is likely to have been part of the mandate. We have observed (Chapter VI) how Pontanus left out Huitfeldt's references to Denmark's being an elective monarchy (though not all of them); in connection with Christianus II

(1513-23), who was removed from power and followed on the throne by his uncle, Fredericus I, he inserted the reflection that the Danes on similar occasions had always taken a new king from the same family; further, he claimed a hereditary status for Norway, in contrast to what he could have read in Huitfeldt. As mentioned above, Pontanus's inclusion of the earliest Saxo may in part have been motivated by a governmental wish to have him make the point about the few families on the Danish throne.

In the introduction to his Oldenburg section Meursius makes the statement that Denmark has since 1448 been "an almost hereditary kingdom", *regnum quasi hæreditarium* (III,1). In the sections on the preceding period (which he wrote afterwards) he demonstrates that this description also suited the rule before the Oldenburg kings. He is careful to point out how son followed father on the throne; this was the practice, with a few exceptions, from the very beginning. All these manoeuvres suggest that they had been told to describe Denmark as *quasi hæreditarium*.

Denmark was to be presented as a strong monarchy, whose stability was secured by its being, in practice, hereditary. The notion of the hereditary kingdom is noteworthy, inasmuch as Denmark was an elective monarchy, but as earlier mentioned, statements to the same effect had been made already in the reign of Frederik II (1559-88). Something similar can be said about Meursius's theocratically-coloured phrases about kings being God's vicars on earth. Though such phrases were probably not the result of direct instructions, they must have been approved by the government's representatives before publication. I suspect that these censors did not object to Meursius's occasional strongly royalistic language, because it had been part of the discourse of kingship since the Reformation.

Pontanus and Meursius were engaged to celebrate an idealized version of the *status quo*. In a way of course, their emphasis on the strong, hereditary monarchy may be said to point forward to the introduction of absolutism in 1660. But they also both depict the *senatus*, the council, as a powerful body, Pontanus by explaining the sensible division of power (in the *Chorographica descriptio*), Meursius by demonstrating, from time to time in the course of history, the prudent advice of the council.

Significantly, with the advent of absolutism Pontanus's and Meursius's interpretations of Danish history were no longer regarded as adequate. Once again Danish history was now rewritten by a royally commissioned historiographer. In the new work, the *Florus Danicus* (published in 1698, but written in the 1660s) by Vitus Bering, the demonstration that Denmark has always been a hereditary monarchy constitutes the main theme. What was only suggested in the works of Pontanus and Meursius now becomes the central issue. These three Latin histories of Denmark, written as they are within 30-40 years, thus reflect, in their interpretations of the past, the intervening change of political system.

The observations on the characteristic features of Pontanus's and Meursius's *Histories* and the considerations put forward above on the possible governmental instructions invite further reflections on audience. Whom did the government want to influence, whom were Pontanus's and Meursius's *Histories* written for? This highly interesting problem of their reception is a subject, however, which I have not taken up. A broad examination of seventeenth-century historiography and of letters dealing with history and politics would no doubt reveal information on the actual use of Pontanus's and Meursius's *Histories* and thereby enhance our understanding of the functions of official historiography. I shall just make a single general point. From the correspondence of Meursius and Pontanus we learn that they both took care to distribute the fruits of their labours among their circle of academic friends and colleagues. These were no doubt among the intended readers, as also seen from the point of view of the Danish government. The connections between the academic world and the world of diplomacy and politics were close in early modern Europe; academics of non-noble stock would often function as diplomats, and noblemen in the service of the state would have received an education which enabled them to consult a Latin work of national historiography – and appreciate its learning and methods. We can be fairly certain that one of the functions of Pontanus's and Meursius's *Histories* was to serve as current sources of information for diplomats and politicians, foreign and Danish alike. To an educated diplomat Pontanus's and Meursius's works, with their status as authoritative and official statements on Denmark, would serve as reliable sources of information. He would be able to appreciate the scholarly achievement of Pontanus and the lucid narrative of Meursius. I have noted the existence of Pontanus's and Meursius's *Histories of Denmark* in several European libraries. A systematic investigation would, I believe, confirm my impression that they became widely spread.

I have stressed the difference between the two histories. But still, as will appear from the considerations above, I think they were designed to be read by the same European élite of politicians, intellectuals, and diplomats. They were not written for different audiences but for different uses; Meursius's work would offer an easily read survey of Danish history, while Pontanus's would be consulted for more thorough information on history, geography and society. By their different kinds of authority they were designed to convince and impress the same educated group of society.

A new Latin history of Denmark had been a long-cherished wish on the part of Danish intellectuals and politicians. The massive efforts in the reign of Christian IV under Christen Friis's leadership – *auspiciis Serenissimæ Regiæ Majestatis, ductu vero Nobilissimi ac Magnifici viri Christiani Frys, magni Cancellarii*, as Pontanus wrote to Lyschander in 1622 – to accomplish the goal resulted in no less than two works. These two histories of Denmark, then, form an example of the time-honoured distinction in Western historiography between two approaches: Pontanus's work is erudite and learned with much information and many discussions, while that of Meursius is stylistically polished, focused on kings and with an emphasis on moral utility. In the course of the following centuries, with the increasing sophistication of historical scholarship, the Meursius-model lost status, authority no longer being conferred on historiography by means of stylistic imitation of the classics. Conversely the well-documented, argumentative type of historiography gained in esteem. The fact that both kinds were represented at the court of Christian IV could perhaps be said to mirror a certain phase in the history of Western historiography when equal prestige was attached to these two approaches.

Bibliography

The bibliography comprises texts referred to in the book, with the following exceptions:
– Classical texts (which I have used in modern standard editions).
– Texts which are referred to at second hand.
– General works of reference.

Sources (written before c. 1800)
Adam of Bremen. *Historia ecclesiastica.* Ed. A.S. Vedel. København 1579. [Modern ed. in *Quellen des 9. und 11. Jahrhunderts zur Geschichte der Hamburgischen Kirche und des Reiches*, edd. W. Trillmich *et al.* Darmstadt 1978: 160-503.].
Ailnothus. *Ælnothus, monachus Cantuariensis, De vita, et passione Sancti Canvti, Regis Daniæ. Item Anonymus, De passione Sancti Caroli, Comitis Flandriæ, eius Filii.* Ed. J. Meursius. København 1631. [Modern ed. by M.Cl. Gertz in *Vitæ sanctorum Danorum.* København (1908-12): 42-53 (preface), 77-147 (text)].
Albert of Stade. *Chronicon Alberti, Abbatis Stadensis, a condito orbe vsqve ad avctoris aetatem, id est, annum Iesu Christi M. CC. LVI. deductum et nunc primum euulgatum.* Ed. R.R. Steinhemius. Helmstadt 1587. [Modern ed. by J. Lappenberg in *Monumenta Germaniae historica 16*, 1859: 382-378 (extracts)].
Althamerus, A. *Commentaria in P. Cornelii Taciti* [...] *libellum De situ, moribus et populis Germani.* Amberg 1609. [First ed. 1536].
Amerinus, J. *Carmina varii generis.* Wittenberg 1576.
Annales Ryenses (Rydårbogen, Chronicon Erici). In *Danmarks middelalderlige annaler.* Ed. Erik Kroman. København 1980: 149-76. [First ed. 1603].
"The Anonymous Nobleman". 'Anonymi auctoris in Historiam Danicam Io. Meursi priusquam publici iuris fieret observationes'. Ed. H. Gram. (In Meursius, *Opera omnia IX* (1746), cols. 1115-30). (The nobleman's notes are extant in three mss., The Royal Library of Copenhagen: *Gl. Kgl S.* 2429, 4to, *Gl. Kgl S.* 2430, 4to, *Thott* 1552, 4to).
Archief, see Stephanius.
Arngrímur Jónsson. *Opera Latine conscripta I-IV.* Ed. Jakob Benediktsson. København 1950-57.
Arngrímur Jónsson. *Chrymogæa sive Rerum Islandicarum libri III.* In *Opera Latine conscripta II*: 1-225. [First ed. 1609].
Aventinus, J. *Annales ducum Boiariae.* In *Sämmtliche Werke II-III.* Ed. S. Riezler. München 1884. [First complete ed. 1580].
Barlæus, C. *Epistolarum liber pars prior.* Amsterdam 1662.
Bering, Vitus. *Florus Danicus.* Odense 1698.
Bodin, Jean. *Methodus ad facilem historiarum cognitionem.* Paris 1572. [First ed. 1566].
Boxhorn, Marcus Z. *Epistolæ et poemata.* Amsterdam 1662.
Buchanan, George. *Rerum Scoticarum historia libris XX descripta.* Frankfurt am Main 1624. [First ed. 1582].
Camden, William. *Britannia sive Florentissimorum regnorum, Angliæ, Scotiæ, Hiberniæ, et insularum adiacentium ex intima antiquitate chorographica descriptio.* London 1590. [First ed. 1586].

Camden, William. *V. Cl. Gulielmi Camdeni et illustrium virorum ad G. Camdenum epistolæ*. London 1611.

Chytræus, David. *De lectione historiarum recte instituenda*. Rostock 1563.

Chytræus, David. *Saxonia, ab anno Christi 1500. vsque ad annum M. DC. Nunc tertium recognita, et integri decennij accessione ad præsentem usque M. DC. XI. annum continuata*. Leipzig 1611. [First ed. 1585].

Cilicius Cimber, C. *Belli Dithmarsici [...] descriptio*. Basel 1570.

Cochlaeus, Johannes. *Brevis Germanie descriptio*. Ed. Karl Langosch. Darmstadt 1960 (Third ed. 1976). [First ed. 1512].

Dudo. *De moribus et actis primorum Normanniæ ducum*. Ed. J. Lair. *Mémoires de la société des antiquaires de Normandie 23*. Caen 1865. [Previously ed. by A. Duchesne 1619].

Einhard. *Vita Karoli*. In *Quellen zur karolingischen Reichsgeschichte I*. Ed. R. Rau. Darmstadt 1968; rep. 1980: 163–211.

Emilio, Paolo. *De rebus gestis Francorum*. Paris 1555 (First ed. 1516 sqq).

Emmius, Ubbo *Rerum Frisicarum historia*. Leiden 1616.

Encomium Emmae Reginae. Ed. A. Campbell. *Camden Society, 3rd series, 72*. London 1949. (*Camden Classic Reprints 4*, Cambridge 1998). [First ed. by A. Duchesne 1619].

Ens, Caspar. *Rervm Danicarum Friderico II. inclitæ memoriæ, rerum potiente, terra marique gestarvm historia: bella Ditmarsicvm et Svecicvm maxime memorabilia complectens*. Frankfurt 1593.

Erasmus Roterodamus. *Institutio principis Christiani*. Ed. G. Christian. *Ausgewählte Schriften V*. Darmstadt 1968: 112–357. [First ed. 1515].

Flores historiarum. Ed. H.R. Luard. In *Rerum Britannicarum medii ævi scriptores 95*. 1890. (Published under the name of Matthias Westmonasteriensis in 1567, 1570, 1601).

Fos, Anders. 'Censura de Saxone Grammatico.' Ed. H.F. Rørdam. In *Monumenta historiæ Danicæ I. 2*. København 1875: 568–79.

Frankish annals. In *Quellen zur karolingischen Reichsgeschichte I*. Ed. R. Rau. Darmstadt 1968; rep. 1980: 9–155.

Galt, Peder. *Peder Galts depescher 1622-24*. Ed. Nils Ahnlund. Stockholm 1920.

Gram, Hans. *Historici Daniæ et Norvegiæ præcipui* (ms. in Jena, *Cod. Jen. Bud.* fol. 341 (photocopy in the Royal Library of Copenhagen)).

Grasser, Johann Jacob. *Itinerarium historico politicum, quod ... Per celebriores Heluetiæ, et Regni Arelatensis urbes in uniuersam extenditur Italiam, varijs ad Prudentiam Politicam, et verum peregrinationis usum, Hypomnematibus exornatum*. Basel 1624.

Grasser, Johann Jacob. *Schweitzerisch Heldenbuch darinn Die Denckwürdigsten Thaten und Sachen: Gemeiner Loblicher Eydgnossschafft / auffgezeichnet und beschrieben. Schön und lustig zu lesen*. Basel 1624.

Helgesen, Povl. *Compendiosa et succincta regum Daniæ historia*. Edd. M. Kristensen & H. Ræder. In *Skrifter af Paulus Helie VI*. København 1937: 4–50. [First ed. 1595 (anon.)].

Helmoldus. *Chronica Slavorum*. Ed. B. Schmeidler. *Monumenta Germaniae historica. Scriptores rerum Germanicarum 32*. 1937.

Holberg, Ludvig. *Danmarks riges historie I-III*. København 1856. [First ed. 1732-35].

Huitfeldt, Arild. *Danmarks riges krønike*. København 1595–1604. [Facs. Kbh. 1977].

(Single volumes:)

Christian III (1595).

Christian II (1596).

Frederik I (1597).

Christian I (1599).

Kong Hans (1599).

Chronologia I (Fra Knud VI til Erik Glipping) (1600).

Chronologia II (Fra Erik Menved til Valdemar Atterdag) (1601).

Chronologia III (Fra Oluf Håkonsson til Christoffer af Bayern) (1603).

Fra Kong Dan indtil Knud VI (1603).

Den geistlige histori (1604).

Kancelliets brevbøger vedrørende Danmarks indre forhold. Edd. C. F. Bricka *et al.* København 1885ff.

Kolding, Jon Jensen. *Daniæ descriptio nova*. Frankfurt am Main 1594. (Danish transl. by Allan A. Lund, Århus 1980).

Krag, Niels. *Annalium Libri VI: Quibus Res Danicæ ab excessu Regis Friderici I ac deinde a [...] Christiano III gestæ ad annum usque 1550 enarrantur [...]* Ed. Hans Gram. København 1737. (Danish transl., Kbh. 1776).

Krantz, Albert. *Regnorum aquilonarium, Daniæ, Sueciæ, Norvagiæ, chronica*. Ed. J. Wolf. Frankfurt am Main 1583. (Reprint of edition of 1575, Frankfurt am Main). [First ed. 1548]. (Publ. 1575, 1583, 1587 with Cilicius Cimber's *Belli Dithmarsici descriptio* and J. Ziegler's *Schondia* and his *Excidium Holmense*). The work is divided into three parts: *Dania, Suecia, Norvagia*.

Langebek, Jacob (ed.). *Scriptores rerum Danicarum*. København 1772–1834.

Lazius, Wolfgang. *Vienna Austriæ*. Basel 1546.

Lipsius, Justus. *Politicorum sive civilis doctrinæ libri sex*. Antwerpen 1596. [First ed. 1589].

Lyschander, Claus C. *Synopsis historiarum Danicarum [...] Danske Kongers Slectebog*. København 1622.

Lyschander, Claus C. 'Udtog af Lyschanders Fortale til sin store utrykte danske Krønike'. In *Samlinger til den danske Historie* I, 2. Ed. P.F. Suhm. København 1780, 57-88.

Lyschander, Claus C. *Lyschander's digtning I-II*. Edd. Fl. Lundgreen-Nielsen & E. Petersen (København 1989).

Lætus, Erasmus. *Margaretica*. Frankfurt am Main 1573.

Lætus, Erasmus. *Res Danicæ*. Frankfurt am Main 1574.

Lætus, Erasmus. *Erasmus Lætus' skrift om Christian IVs fødsel og dåb (1577)*. Edd. K. Skovgaard-Petersen & P. Zeeberg. (Det danske Sprog- og Litteraturselskab). København 1992.

Macrobius. *Aur. Theodosii Macrobi [...] opera*. Ed. J. Pontanus. Leiden 1597.

Magnus, Johannes. *Gothorum Sueonumque historia*. S.l. 1617. [First ed. Rome 1554: *Historia de omnibus Gothorum Sueonumque regibus*].

Mariana, Johannes. *Historiae de rebus Hispaniae Libri XX*. Toleto 1592.

Masius, H. G. *Epistola ad [...] Dn. Bartoldum Botsaccum [...] qua Daniam orthodoxam, fidelem et pacificam, licet a professore qvodam Marpurgensi impugnatam, nulla apologia indigere ostendit*. København 1691.

Matthæus, Ant. (ed). *Andrea Alciati ad Bernardum Mattium epistol. Accedit Sylloge epistolarum Giphani, Vulcani, Tychonis Brahe, Scriverii, Pontani, Vossi [...]* Leiden 1695.

Matthæus, Ant. (ed.). *Veteris ævi analecta I-V*. den Haag 1738.

Matthew Paris. *Matthæi Parisiensis [...] Chronica majora*. Ed. H. R. Luard. (*Rerum Britannicarum medii ævi scriptores 57*) (1880; rep. 1964): vol. 5.

Melanchthon, Philipp & Caspar Peucer. *Chronicon Carionis expositum et auctum multis et veteribus et recentibus historiis, in descriptionibus regnorum et gentium antiquarum, et narrationibus rerum ecclesiasticarum, et politicarum, Græcarum, Romanarum, Germanicarum et aliarum, ab exordio mundi vsque ad Carolum quintum Imperatorem*. Wittenberg 1580. [First ed. 1572].

Melanchthon, Philipp. *Chronicon Carionis*. In *Corpus Reformatorum XII*. Ed. C.G. Bretschneider. Halle 1844: cols. 711–1094. [First ed. 1558].

Melanchthon, Philipp. *Loci praecipui theologici*. In *Corpus Reformatorum XXI*. Ed. H. E. Bindseil. Braunschweig 1854: cols. 601–1106. (The work was published in several versions during Melanchthon's life. This edition is based on the last edition from Melanchthon's hand, 1559).

Melanchthon, Philipp. *Enarratio epistolae Pauli ad Romanos*. In *Corpus Reformatorum XV*. Ed. C. G. Bretschneider. Halle 1848: cols. 797-1052. [First ed. 1556].

Messenius, Johannes. *Sveopentaprotopolis*. Stockholm 1611.

Messenius, Johannes. *Theatrum nobilitatis Svecanæ*. Stockholm 1616.

Meursius, J. *Meditationes Christianæ in psalmum CXVI. et tres priores partes CXIX*. den Haag 1604.

Meursius, Johannes. *Athenae Batavae*. Leiden 1625.

Meursius, Johannes. *Historiæ Danicæ libri III*. København 1630.

Meursius, Johannes (ed.). *Ælnothus* [...], 1631, see Ailnothus (Sources).

Meursius, Johannes. *Historica; Danica pariter et Belgica; uno tomo comprehensa* [...] *Operum omnium tomus primus*. Amsterdam 1638.

Meursius, Johannes. *Historia Danica*. Amsterdam 1638.

Meursius, Johannes. *Opera omnia*. Ed. J. Lamius. Firenze 1741–63. (12 volumes).

Meursius, Johannes. *Historia Danica* [...] *Omnia a viro clar. Ioanne Grammio* [...] *scholiis perpetuiis illustrata. Iohannes Lamius recensuit*. Edd. Hans Gram & G. Lami (In Meursius, *Opera omnia* IX (1746), cols. 1–992).

Meursius, Johannes. 'Animadversiones in Historiam Danicam Io. Isacii Pontani'. Ed. Hans Gram. (In Meursius, *Opera omnia* IX (1746), cols. 1141–48). (Meursius's notes to Pontanus are also extant in a ms., The Royal Library of Copenhagen, *Gl. kgl. S.* 2428, 4to, and as handwritten notes in a copy of Pontanus's *Rerum Danicarum historia* (1631), in the University Library of Lund).

Meursius, Johannes. 'Ad adnotationes viri illustris a Dn. Cancellario sibi communicatas responsio'. Ed. Hans Gram. (In Meursius, *Opera omnia* IX (1746), cols. 1131–40). Meursius's *Responsio* is extant in three Mss., The Royal Library of Copenhagen: *Gl. Kgl S.* 2429, 4to, *Gl. Kgl S.* 2930, 4to, *Thott* 1552, 4to)

Meursius, Johannes. (*Letters to and from Johs. Meursius*). Ed. Hans Gram. Meursius, *Opera omnia* XI (1762).

(Meursius, Johannes). *Epistolæ Mss. ad Jo. Meursium*. Ms., The Royal Library of Copenhagen, *Thott* 1843, 4to.

(Meursius, Johannes) 'Breve til Joh. Meursius'. In H. F. Rørdam. *Historiske samlinger og studier I*. København 1891: 276–88.

(Meursius. Catalogues of his books:).

1. (ms.) *Gl. kgl. S.* 2120, 4to (The Royal Library of Copenhagen).

2. *Pars librorum rarissimorum tam Græcorum, quam Latinorum viri nobilissimi D. Joannis Meursii, quorum auctio habebitur Lugd. Batav. in ædibus Francisci Hackii, die ultimo Septemb. stilo novo, hora octava matutina*. Leiden 1642.

Mollerus, D. G. 'Dissertatio de Io. Meursio'. In Meursius, *Opera omnia I* (1741), 100–108.

Müller, Georgius. *Oratio funebris de vita atque obitu* [...] *D. Ioh. Iacobi Grasseri*. Basel 1627.

Paulinus, Laurentius. *Historiæ Arctoæ libri tres*. Strängnäs 1636.

Plange primatus Dacie. Ed. M. Cl. Gertz. In *Scriptores minores I*. København 1917-18: 476-79. (Rep. 1970).

Polydore Vergil. *Anglica historia*. Basel 1570. [First ed. 1534].

Pontanus, Johannes. 'Album amicorum' (ms., Paris, Bibl. Nat., Coll. James Rotschild, no. 3371. Microfilm in The Royal Library, Copenhagen, ms. micro 2027).

Pontanus, Johannes. *Apologia pro historia Amstelodamensi adversus Franciscum Sweertium ad Arnoldum Buchelium*. Amsterdam 1628, 1634.

Pontanus, Johannes. *Rerum Danicarum Historia. Libris X unoque tomo ad domum usque Oldenburgicam deducta*. Amsterdam 1631.

Pontanus, Johannes. *Poemata*. Amsterdam 1634.

Pontanus, Johannes. *Discussionum historicarum libri II, quibus præcipue quatenus et quodnam mare liberum vel non liberum clausumque accipiendum, dispicitur expenditurque*. Harderwijk 1637.

Pontanus, Johannes. *Historiæ Gelricæ libri XIV. Deducta omnia ad ea usque tempora nostra, quibus firmata sub ordinibus respublica*. Amsterdam 1639.

Pontanus, Johannes. *Vita Christiani III*. Ed. J. Hubnerus. Hannover 1729.

Pontanus, Johannes. *Vita Friderici Secundi*. Ed. G. Krysingus. Flensburg 1735.

Pontanus, Johannes. 'Historia rerum Danicarum qua res post excessum Christophori Bavari [...] sub regibus e domo Oldenburgica [...] gestæ continentur.' Ed. E.J. v. Westphalen. In *Monumenta inedita rerum Germanicarum præcipue Cimbricarum et Megapolensium II*. Leipzig 1740:

cols. 713–1230. (Pontanus's *History of Denmark 1448–1588* is extant in two mss. in The Royal Library of Copenhagen: *Gl. Kgl. S.* 839 fol. and *Gl. Kgl. S.* 840 fol.).

Pontanus, Johannes. *Brieven van en aan Jo. Is. Pontanus 1595–1639.* Edd. P.N. v. Doorninck & P.C. Molhuysen. Haarlem 1909.

Pontanus's letters, see also Matthæus (1695), Matthæus (1738), and Stephanius *et alii* (1833).

Regino of Prüm. *Regino, Chronik.* In *Quellen zur karolingischen Reichsgeschichte III.* Ed. R. Rau. Darmstadt 1969; rep. 1982: 179–319.

Reinboth, F. A. (Collection of material on Pontanus). Ms., The Royal Library of Copenhagen, *Thott 1957, 4to.*

Resen, P. H. *Kong Frederichs Den Andens krønicke.* København 1680.

Rhenanus, Beatus. *Rerum Germanicarum libri III.* Basel 1531.

Rhenanus, Beatus. *In P. Cornelium Tacitum annotationes Beati Rhenani, Alciati, ac Beroaldi. Eiusdem B. Rhenani Thesaurus constructionum, locutionumque et uocum Tacito solennium.* Lyon 1542. [First ed. 1533].

Rosenkrantz, Holger. 'Breve til og fra Holger Rosenkrantz.' In *Kirkehistoriske samlinger III.* København 1887-89: 1 (114-64), 5 (714-63), 6 (24-77, 292-338, 516-58, 609–53).

Sascerides, Johannes. *Epicedium in obitum* [...] *Christiani Tertij* [...] *Historia de coronatione* [...] *regis Friderici.* København 1559.

Saxo Grammaticus. *Saxonis Gesta Danorum.* Edd. J. Olrik & H. Ræder. København 1931. [First ed. 1514]. (I have also consulted the edition of 1576, Frankfurt am Main).

Saxo Grammaticus. *Den Danske Krønicke som Saxo Grammaticus screff / halfffierde hundrede Aar forleden: Nu først aff Latinen vdsæt / flittelige offuerseet oc forbedret / Aff Anders Søffrinssøn Vedel.* København 1575.

Saxo Grammaticus. *Den danske krønike oversat af Anders Sørensen Vedel. Trykt på ny og tilligemed Vedels levnet af C. F. Wegener.* København 1851.

Schramm, J. V. *De vita et scriptis Io. Meursii patris dissertatio.* Leipzig 1715. (Also in Meursius, *Opera omnia I* (1741), 109-16).

Sigonius, Carolus. *Historiarvm de regno Italiæ libri quindecim.* Basel 1575.

Stephanius, St. J. (ed.). *De regno Daniæ et Norwegiæ insulisque adjacentibus juxta ac de Holsatia, Ducatu Slesvicensi, et finitimis provincijs tractatus varij.* Leiden 1629.

Stephanius, St. J. *Notæ uberiores in Historiam Danicam Saxonis Grammatici.* Sorø 1645; København 1978 (facsimile).

Stephanius, St. J. *Historiæ Danicæ libri II* [...] *ab anno Christi MDL. ad annum MDLIX. Opus posthumum.* Ed. Hans Svaning. Sorø 1650. (Re-edited by Hans Gram in his edition of Niels Krag's *Christianus III* (Krag, 1737, 331-401), and in his edition of Meursius's *Historia Danica* (Meursius 1741-63, IX, cols. 993-1056).

Stephanius, St. J. *et alii.* 'Bijlage A. Petri Scriverii, Gerhardi Joh. Vossii et Steph. Johannis Stephani ad Joh. Isaaci Pontanum epistolas'. In *Archief voor kerkelijke geschiedenis* [...] *vierte deel.* Edd. N. C. Kist & H. J. Royaards. Leiden 1833: 181-88.

Størssøn, Mattis. *Den norske krønike.* Ed. Mikjel Sørlie. Oslo, Bergen 1962. [First ed. 1594].

Suhm, P. F. 'Tanker om de vanskeligheder, som møde ved at skrive den gamle danske og norske historie'. In *Peter Friderich Suhms samlede skrifter* 9. København 1792: 5-112. (First ed. in *Videnskabernes Selskabs skrifter* 9, 1765).

Svaning, Hans. *Refutatio calumniarum cuiusdam Ioannis Magni* [...] *huic accessit Chronicon sive Historia Ioannis Regis Daniæ.* S.l. 1561. (Published under the pseudononym Petrus Parvus Rosefontanus and dated 1560).

Svaning, Hans. *Christiernus II. Daniæ rex.* Frankfurt 1658.

Svaning, Hans. Christianus I (ms. in The Royal Library of Copenhagen. *Gl. kgl. S.* 2444, 4to).

Svaning, Hans. 'Commentarii rerum Danicarum' (extracts from Svaning's *History of Denmark*) (ms. in The Royal Library of Copenhagen: *Bartholiniana, Tome J, E don. var. 1, fol.*, 346-75 (previously: *Additamenta* Fol. 89).

Thuanus, Jacobus: *Historia sui temporis*. Paris, Orléans 1604-20.

Vedel, Anders Sørensen. 'Commentarius de scribenda historia Danica'. (The Latin version, written 1578) (ms. in the Royal Library of Copenhagen, *Gl. kgl. S.* 2437, 4to). Revised version in Danish, written 1581: ms. *ibidem*, 2435, 4to). (Modern edition of the Danish version in G. Albeck, *Humanister i Jylland*, 1959, 130-52).

Vedel, Anders Sørensen. 'M. Anders Wedels fortale til sin utrykte danske krønike'. In *Samlinger til den danske historie 1*. Ed. P. F. Suhm. København 1779: 144-62.

Vedel's translation of Saxo, see Saxo (1575) (Sources).

Vedel's edition of Adam of Bremen, see Adam (1579) (Sources).

Venusin, Jon Jacobsen. *De historia*. København 1604.

Venusin, Jon Jacobsen. *De fabulis*. København 1605.

Vinstrup, Peder. 'Det genfundne originalmanuskript til Peder Vinstrups kroningstale 1596'. Ed. Sebastian Olden-Jørgensen in *Danske magazin*, 9.rk, 1. 1999: 245-70. Previously publ. by F. P. Jensen. 'Peder Vinstrups tale ved Christian 4.s kroning. Et teokratisk indlæg' in *Historisk tidsskrift* 12. rk., 2. 1967: 375-94.

Vita et obitus Pontani. *Vita et obitus Johannes Isacii Pontani medicinæ doctoris, et in illustri gymnasio Gelro-Velavico philosophiæ ac historiarum professoris: serenis. Daniæ regis et ducatus Gelriæ historiographi*. Harderwijk 1640.

Vorstius, A. 'Ioanni Meursio Ioan. [...] F. Adolfus Vorstius S. D.' (dat. Leiden 1640). In Meursius, *Opera omnia 1* (1741), 118. (Addressed to Meursius's son, Johs. Meursius the younger).

Vossius, G. J. *Gerardi Joan. Vossii et clarorum virorum ad eum epistolæ*. Ed. Paulus Colomesius. Augsburg 1691.

William of Jumièges. *Gesta Normannorum ducum I-II*. Ed. E. M. C. van Houts. Oxford 1992.

William of Malmesbury. *De gestis regum Anglorum*. Ed. W. Stubbs. *Rerum Britannicarum medii ævi scriptores 90* (2 vols). London 1987, rep. 1964. [First ed. 1596].

Worm, Ole. *Olai Wormii et ad eum doctorum virorum epistolæ*. Ed. Hans Gram. København 1751.

Worm, Ole. *Ole Worm's Correspondence with Icelanders*. Ed. Jakob Benediktsson. København 1948.

Worm, Ole. *Breve fra og til Ole Worm I-III*. Transl. by H. D. Schepelern. København 1965-68.

Ziegler, J. 'Schondia' & 'Christierni Secundi [...] crudelitas'. Ed. J. Wolf. In A. Krantz. *Regnorum aquilonarium [...] chronica*. Frankfurt am Main 1583: 473–97 & 498–505. (Rep. of ed. 1575). [First ed. 1532].

Secondary Literature

Ax, Wolfram (1976). *Probleme des Sprachstils als Gegenstand der lateinischen Philologie*. Hildesheim, New York.

Bagge, Sverre & Knut Mykland (1987). *Norge i Dansketiden*. Oslo.

Benner, Margrethe & Emin Tengström (1977). *On the Interpretation of Learned Neo-Latin. An Explorative Study Based on Some Texts from Sweden 1611-1716*. Göteborg.

Bennich-Björkman, Bo (1970). *Författaren i ämbetet. Studier i funktion och organisation av författarämbeten vid svenska hovet och kansliet 1550-1850*. Uppsala.

Birket Smith, S. (1882). *Om Kjøbenhavns Universitetsbibliothek før 1728*. København.

Booth, Wayne (1983, first ed. 1961). *The Rhetoric of Fiction*. Chicago.

Borchardt, Frank L. (1971). *German Antiquity in Renaissance Myth*. Baltimore, London.

Bornkamm, H. (1966). *Das Jahrhundert der Reformation. Gestalten und Kräfte*. Göttingen.

Burke, Peter (1969). 'Tacitism'. In *Tacitus*. Ed. T. A. Dorey. London: 149-71.

Christensen, Charlotte (1988). 'Christian IVs renæssance. Billedkunsten i Danmark 1588-1648'. In *Christian IVs verden*. Ed. S. Ellehøj. København: 302-35.

Christensen, Karsten (1978). *Om overleveringen af Sven Aggesens værker*. København.

Christensen, William (1913). 'Steffen Hanssøn Stephanius's Designatio variorum documentorum et antiquitatum'. In *Danske Magazin 6. rk. 1.* København: 5-8, 176-77.

Croll, M.V. (1921). 'Attic Prose in the Seventeenth Century'. In *Studies in Philology 18:* 79-128.

Dam, H.-J. v. (1994). 'De imperio summarum potestatum circa sacra'. In *Hugo Grotius Theologian.* Edd. H.J.M. Nellen & E. Rabbie. Leiden, New York, Köln: 19-39.

D'Amico, John F. (1988). *Theory and Practice in Renaissance Textual Criticism. Beatus Rhenanus between Conjecture and History.* Berkeley, Los Angeles, London.

Damsholt, Torben (1992). 'Den nationale magtstat 1560-1760'. In *Historiens historie (Danmarks historie 10).* Ed. S. Mørch. København: 53-104.

Degn, Ole (1988 [1987]). *Christian 4.s kansler. Christen Friis til Kragerup (1581-1639) som menneske og politiker.* Viborg.

Eisenstein, Elizabeth (1979). *The Printing Press as an Agent of Change: Communications and Cultural Transformations in Early-Modern Europe.* Cambridge.

Erslev, Kristian (1928). *Svaning-Hvitfeld.* København.

Fabricius, Knud (1920, rep. 1971). *Kongeloven. Dens tilblivelse og plads i samtidens natur- og arveretlige udvikling.* København.

Fraenkel, Peter (1961). *Testimonia patrum.* Genève.

Friis, Oluf (1945). *Den danske litteraturs historie.* København.

Friis-Jensen, Karsten (1988-89). 'Humanism and Politics: the Paris Edition of Saxo Grammaticus's Gesta Danorum 1514'. In *Analecta Romani Instituti Danici 17-18:* 149-62.

Friis-Jensen, Karsten (1991). 'Historiography and Humanism in Early Sixteenth-century Scandinavia'. In *Acta Conventus Neo-Latini Torontonensis.* Edd. A. Dalzell *et al.* Binghamton, New York: 325-33.

Friis-Jensen, Karsten (1993a). 'Middelalderens Danmark og det romerske imperium'. In *Imperium Romanum. Realitet, ide, ideal.* Edd. J. Isager & O. Due. Århus. II: 187-203.

Friis-Jensen, Karsten (1993b). *Vedels Saxo og den danske adel.* København.

Friis-Jensen, Karsten (1996). 'Versification and Topicality. Two Encomiastic Poems Written during the Seven Years War'. In *Reformation and Latin Literature in Northern Europe.* Edd. Inger Ekrem *et al.* Oslo: 179-92.

Fruin, R. (1900-5, 1. ed. 1872). 'Meursius' Geschiedenis van het bestand'. In *Verspreide geschriften.* Gravenhage: VII, 449-53.

Fueter, Eduard (1911). *Geschichte der Neueren Historiographie.* München, Berlin.

Fussner, Frank S. (1962). *The Historical Revolution: English Historical Writing and Thought 1580-1640.* London, New York.

Grobecker, Manfred (1964). *Studien zur Geschichtsschreibung des Albert Krantz.* Hamburg.

Grundtvig, Johannes (1872). *Meddelelser fra Rentekammerarchivet.* København.

Haitsma Mulier, E.O.G. & G.A.C. van der Lem (1990). *Repertorium van geschiedschrijvers in Nederland 1500-1800.* Den Haag.

Heesakkers, Chris L. (1994). 'Te weinig koren of alleen te veel kaf? Leiden's eerste Noordnederlandse filoloog Joannes Meursius (1579-1639)'. In *Miro fervore. Een bundel lezingen & artikelen over de beoefening van de klassieke wetenschappen in de zeventiende & achttiende eeuw.* Leiden: 13-26.

Heiberg, Steffen (1988). *Christian 4. Monarken, mennesket og myten.* København.

Hentschke, Ada &. Ulrich Muhlack (1972). *Einführung in die Geschichte der klassischen Philologie.* Darmstadt.

Herendeen, W. H. (1988). 'William Camden: Historian, Herald, and Antiquary'. In *Studies in Philology 85:* 192-210.

Huschke, Rolf B. (1968). *Melanchthons Lehre vom Ordo politicus.* Gütersloh.

Hørby, Kai (1962). 'Skolen og akademiet gennem 400 år'. In *Academia Sorana. Kloster, akademi, skole.* Ed. Soransk Samfund. København: 9-136.

Ilsøe, Harald (1963-66). 'Håndskriftet H 112 og de danske historikere. En studie i overlevering'. In *Historisk tidsskrift 12. rk. 1:* 399-435.

Ilsøe, Harald (1967). 'Arild Huitfeldts krønike konfronteret med Anders Sørensen Vedel og eftertiden'. In *Fund og forskning 14:* 24-58.

Ilsøe, Harald (1972). 'Omkring Hans Svanings Refutatio og Chronicon Ioannis'. In *Historisk tidsskrift 12. rk. 6:* 21-58.

Ilsøe, Harald (1973). 'Historisk censur i Danmark indtil Holberg'. In *Fund og forskning 20:* 45-70.

Ilsøe, Harald (1984). 'Svaning, Vedel, Huitfeld og Krag. Omkring spørgsmålet om den første historiografudnævnelse'. In *Tradition og kritik. Festskrift til Svend Ellehøj den 8. september 1984.* Edd. G. Christensen *et al.* København: 235-58.

Ilsøe, Ingrid (1979-80). 'Boghandleren Joachim Moltke og hans virksomhed 1626-1664.' In *Fund og forskning 24:* 63-92.

Jensen, Minna Skafte (1991). 'The Language of Eternity. The Role of Latin in 16th-Century Danish Culture'. In *Acta conventus Neo-Latini Torontonensis.* Edd. A. Dalzell *et al.* Binghamton, New York: 41-61.

Joachimsen, Paul (1910, rep. 1968). *Geschichtsauffassung und Geschichtsschreibung in Deutschland unter dem Einfluss des Humanismus.* Leipzig, Berlin.

Johannesson, Kurt (1982). *Gotisk renässans. Johannes och Olaus Magnus som politiker och historiker.* Stockholm. (English translation (1991): *The Renaissance of the Goths in Sixteenth-Century Sweden,* tr. J. Larson. Berkeley and Oxford).

Jørgensen, A. D. (1884). *Udsigt over de danske Rigsarkivers Historie.* København.

Jørgensen, Ellen (1917). 'Stephanus Johannis Stephanii manuskriptsamling'. In *Nordisk tidskrift för bok- och biblioteksväsen,* årg. IV, 19-28.

Jørgensen, Ellen (1924). 'Hans Grams Vurdering af Holbergs historiske Arbejder'. In *Holberg aarbog,* edd. Francis Bull & Carl S. Petersen. Kjøbenhavn og Kristiania: 137-41.

Jørgensen, Ellen (1931). *Historieforskning og historieskrivning i Danmark indtil aar 1800.* København.

Jørgensen, Jon Gunnar (1993). 'Sagaoversettelser i Norge på 1500-tallet'. In *Collegium medievale 1993/2:* 169-98.

Kanstrup, Jan (1973). 'Huitfeldts fremstilling af Christoffer II's tilbagekomst til Danmark'. In *Historisk tidsskrift 12. rk. 6:* 93-121.

Kelley, Donald R. (1970). *Foundations of Modern Historical Scholarship. Language, Law, and History in the French Renaissance.* New York, London.

Kelley, Donald R. (1991). *Versions of History from Antiquity to the Enlightenment.* New Haven, London.

Kelley, Donald R. (1998). *Faces of History from Herodotus to Herder.* New Haven, London.

Klatt, Detloff (1908). *David Chytraeus als Geschichtslehrer und Geschichtsschreiber.* Rostock.

Klempt, Adalbert (1960). *Die Säkularisierung der universalhistorischen Auffassung. Zum Wandel des Geschichtsdenkens im 16. und 17. Jahrhundert.* Göttingen, Berlin, Frankfurt.

Kongsrud, Helge (1984). *Den kongelige arveretten til Norge 1536–1661. Ide og politisk instrument.* Oslo, Bergen, Tromsø.

Kongsted, Ole (1988). 'Den verdslige "rex splendens"'. In *Christian IVs verden.* Ed. S. Ellehøj. København: 433–64.

Lausten, Martin Schwarz (1987). *Christian d. 3. og kirken (1537-1559).* København.

Leroy, P. B. & H. Bots (edd.) (1987). *Claude Saumaise & André Rivet. Correspondance echangée entre 1632 et 1648.* Amsterdam & Maarssen.

Mackeprang, M. (1924). 'Christian IVs Ridderakademi og Skolen 1623-65'. In *Sorø. Klostret, skolen, akademiet gennem tiderne.* Ed. Soransk Samfund. København: 374–502.

Martin & Woodman (edd.) (1989). *Tacitus, Annals IV* (Cambridge).

Metcalf, George J. (1974). 'The Indo-European Hypothesis in the 16th and 17th Centuries'. In *Studies in the History of Linguistics. Traditions and Paradigms.* Ed. D. Hymes. Bloomington, London: 233–57.

Mohlin, A. (1960). *Kristoffer II av Danmark I-II.* Lund, København.

Momigliano, Arnaldo (1966, first ed. 1950). 'Ancient History and the Antiquarian'. In Momigliano, *Studies in Historiography*. London: 1–39.

Momigliano, Arnaldo (1990). 'The Rise of Antiquarian Research'. In Momigliano, *The Classical Foundations of Modern Historiography*. Berkeley, Los Angeles, Oxford: 54–79.

Mortensen, Lars Boje (1987). 'Saxo Grammaticus' View of the Origin of the Danes and his Historiographical Models'. In *Cahiers de l'Institut du Moyen-age Grec et Latin 55:* 169–83.

Mortensen, Lars Boje (1991). 'Den latinske version af Anders Sørensen Vedels historiografiske programskrift (Gks 2437 40)'. In *Latin og nationalsprog i Norden*. Edd. M. Alenius *et al.* København: 34-44.

Mortensen, Lars Boje (1995). 'Anders Sørensen Vedel. The Latin Writings of a Vernacular Humanist'. In *A History of Nordic Neo-Latin*. Ed. M. Skafte Jensen. Odense: 267–79.

Mortensen, Lars Boje (1998a). 'Andreas Velleius's Commentarius de scribenda historia Danica (1578) and its European Background'. In *Acta conventus Neo-Latini Barensis*. Edd. J. F. Alcina *et al.* New York: 401-10.

Mortensen, Lars Boje (1998b). 'François Bauduin's De institutione historiæ (1561): a primary text behind Anders Sørensen Vedel's De scribenda historia Danica (1578)'. In *Symbolae Osloenses 73:* 188-200.

Muhlack, Ulrich (1991). *Geschichtswissenschaft im Humanismus und in der Aufklärung: die Vorgeschichte des Historismus*. München.

Munck, Thomas (1990). *Seventeenth Century Europe* (Macmillan History of Europe). Basingstoke, London.

Mund-Dopchie, Monique (1992). 'L'"Ultima Thule" de Pythéas dans les textes de la Renaissance et du XVIIe siècle. La Réalité et le rêve'. In *Humanistica Lovaniensia 41:* 134–58.

Neddermeyer, Uwe (1988). *Das Mittelalter in der deutschen Historiographie vom 15. bis 18. Jahrhundert. Geschichtsgliederung und Epochenverständnis in der frühen Neuzeit*. Köln, Wien.

Norden, Eduard (1971). *Die antike Kunstprosa I-II*. Stuttgart. (1st ed. 1898).

Nordman, V. A. (1936). *Die Chronica Regnorum Aquilonarium des Albert Krantz*. Helsinki.

Nordström, Johan (1934). 'Götisk historieromantik och stormaktstidens anda'. In *De yverbornes ö*. Stockholm: 53–76.

Norvin, William (1924). 'Undervisning og Studieliv'. In *Sorø. Klostret, skolen, akademiet gennem tiderne*. Ed. Soransk Samfund. København: 548–632.

Nyenhuis, J. T. B. (1840). 'Levensbijzonderheden van den Nederlandschen geschiedschrijver Johannes Isacius Pontanus'. In *Bijdragen voor vaderlandsche geschiedenis en oudheidkunde II* (Arnhem): 81–109.

Olschki, Leonardo (1922). *Bildung und Wissenschaft im Zeitalter der Renaissance in Italien*. Leipzig, Firenze, Roma, Genève.

Petersen, Carl S. (1929). *Illustreret dansk Litteraturhistorie I*. København.

Petersen, Erling Ladewig (1973). 'Norgesparagraffen i Christian III's håndfæstning 1536'. In *Historisk tidsskrift 12 rk. 6:* 393–464.

Postumus Meyjes, G. H. M. (1984). Hugo Grotius as an Irenicist. In *The World of Hugo Grotius (1583-1645)*. Ed. Koninklijke Nederlandse Akademie van Wetenschappen. Grotius-Commissie. Amsterdam: 43–63.

Rasmussen, Erik V. (1983). 'Adelskulturen'. In Hougaard *et al. Dansk litteraturhistorie 3*. København: 135–88.

Ridé, J. (1977). *L'Image du Germain dans la pensée et la littérature allemandes de la redécouverte de Tacite à la fin du XVIème siècle*. I-III. Lille, Paris.

Rørdam, H.F. (1857). *Mester Anders Christensen Arrebos Levnet og Skrifter*. København.

Rørdam, H.F. (1867). *Historieskrivningen og Historieskriverne i Danmark og Norge siden reformationen*. København.

Rørdam, H.F. (1868). *Klavs Christoffersen Lyskanders Levned*. København.

Rørdam, H.F. (1868-77). *Kjøbenhavns Universitets Historie fra 1537 til 1621*. København.

Rørdam, H.F. (1874-77). 'Jon Jakobsen Venusinus'. In *Kirkehistoriske Samlinger III, 1:* 241–310.

Rørdam, H.F. (1879). 'Den kgl. Historieskriver Vitus Bering'. In *Historisk Tidsskrift 5. rk. 1:* 1-115.

Rørdam, H.F. (1891). 'Den kongelige Historiograf Steffen Hansen Stephanius'. In *Historiske Samlinger og Studier I.* København: 1-74, 193-275.

Rørdam, H.F. (1896). *Historieskriveren Arild Hvitfeldt.* København.

Rørdam, H.F. (1898). 'Den kongelige Historiograf, Dr. Johan Isaksen Pontanus'. In *Historiske Samlinger og Studier III.* København: 1–24 & 440–92.

Schellhase, Kenneth C. (1976). *Tacitus in Renaissance Political Thought.* Chicago, London.

Schepelern, H.D. (1971). *Museum Wormianum. Dets forudsætninger og tilblivelse.* København.

Schepelern, H.D. & Ulla Houkjær (1988). *The Kronborg Series. King Christian IV and his Pictures of Early Danish History.* København.

Schmidt-Phiseldeck, Kay (1945). 'De humanistiske Videnskaber'. In *Holland – Danmark I-II.* Edd. Knud Fabricius *et al.* København 1945: 2: 251-85.

Schück, Henrik (1920). *Messenius. Några blad ur Vasatidens Kulturhistoria.* Stockholm.

Schück, Henrik & Karl Warburg (1927). *Illustrerad svensk Litteraturhistoria II.* Stockholm. (third ed).

Seaton, E. (1935). *Literary Relations of England and Scandinavia in the 17th century.* Oxford.

Sellin, Paul R. (1968). *Daniel Heinsius and Stuart England.* London, Leiden.

Sepp, Chr. (1872). 'Prof. Meursius als geschiedschrijver der Leidsche hoogeschool'. In *Geschiedkundige nasporingen I.* Leiden: 1-21.

Skovgaard-Petersen, K. (1987). 'Erasmus Lætus' Margaretica — et bidrag til den dansk-svenske pennefejde i det 16. årh.' In *Historisk tidsskrift 1987(2):* 209-37.

Skovgaard-Petersen, K. (1988). *Erasmus Lætus' Margaretica. Klassisk epos og dansk propaganda.* København.

Skovgaard-Petersen, K. (1994). 'The Beginnings of Danish History in the *Rerum Danicarum historia* of Johannes Pontanus'. In *Acta conventus Neo-Latini Hafniensis.* Edd. Ann Moss *et al.* Binghamton, New York: 907-16.

Skovgaard-Petersen, K. (1995). 'Tacitus and Tacitism in Johannes Meursius' *Historia Danica* (1630-38)'. In *Symbolae Osloenses 70:* 212-40.

Skovgaard-Petersen, K. (1995). 'Norges plads i den officielle historieskrivning under Christian IV'. In *Nordica Bergensia 7:* 55-68.

Skovgaard-Petersen, K. (1996). 'Den største zirat udi fædernelandets historie? Om folkevandringerne i Pontanus' og Holbergs danmarkshistorier'. In *Hvad tales her om? (Festskrift til Johnny Christensen).* Edd. Mette Sophie Christensen *et al.* København: 389-99.

Skovgaard-Petersen, K. (1996). 'Universal History and Early National Past – the *De historia* (1604) by Jon Jakobsen Venusin'. In *Reformation and Latin Literature in Northern Europe.* Edd. I. Ekrem *et al.* Oslo: 226-36.

Skovgaard-Petersen, K. (1998a). 'Carion's Chronicle in Sixteenth-century Danish Historiography.' In *Symbolae Osloenses 73:* 158-67.

Skovgaard-Petersen, K. (1998b). 'Two Trends of Historiography at the Court of King Christian IV (1588-1648). The Latin Histories of Denmark by Johannes Pontanus and Johannes Meursius'. In *Acta Conventus Neo-Latini Bariensis.* Edd. J.F. Alcina *et al.* Tempe, Arizona: 541-48.

Skovgaard-Petersen, K. (1998c). 'A Safe Haven for the Church – on Melanchthon's Influence on Historical Discourse in Sixteenth-Century Denmark.' In *Philipp Melanchthon und seine Rezeption in Skandinavien* (Kungl. Vitterhets Historie och Antikvitets Akademien, konf. 43). Ed. B. Stolt. Stockholm: 113-35.

Sorø. Klostret [...], see Mackeprang and Norvin.

Svennung, J. (1967). *Zur Geschichte des Goticismus.* Stockholm.

Sørensen, Peer E. (1983). 'Reformpoesi og sprogpatriotisme'. In Hougaard *et al. Dansk litteraturhistorie 3.* København: 95-113.

Tauber, E.G. (1827). *Udsigt over Sorøe Academies Forfatning under Kongerne Chrstian den Fjerde og Frederich den Tredie, 1623-1666 med Bilag af utrykte Actstykker.* København.

Wade, Mara (1992). 'Festival Books as Historical Literature: The Reign of Christian IV of Denmark (1596-1648)'. In *The Seventeenth Century 7,1*: 1-14.

Walde, O. (1917). 'Stephanii Bibliotek och dess Historia'. In *Nordisk Tidskrift för Bok- och Biblioteksväsen*, årg. IV: 29-65 & 261-301.

Walde, O. (1916-20). *Storhetstidens litterära Krigsbyten. En kulturhistorisk-bibliografisk Studie I-II.* Uppsala, Stockholm.

Wegener's life of Anders Sørensen Vedel, see Saxo Grammaticus (1851) (Sources).

Historiographical Initiatives during Christen Friis's Period as Chancellor

(The survey is intended both as a summing up of important dates mentioned in the present book and as a general survey of historiographical initiatives during Friis's period as chancellor. Not all the points are mentioned on the preceding pages. I owe several suggestions to Harald Ilsøe).

1616   C.C. Lyschander is engaged as royal Danish historiographer.
Christen Friis becomes chancellor.

1617   Re-edition of Johannes Magnus's *History of Sweden* (first ed. 1554).

1617/   Daniel Heinsius is engaged as royal Swedish historiographer (but not
1618   subsequently paid).

1618   Pontanus is engaged as royal Danish historiographer.

1620   Publication of Swedish translation of Johannes Magnus's *History of Sweden*.

1622   Publication of Tegel's history of Gustav Vasa and of Lyschander's *Synopsis historiarum Danicarum*.
Pontanus is admonished by Christian IV to finish his *History of Denmark* as soon as possible.
On Ole Worm's initiative Christian IV orders the bishops in Denmark and Norway to obtain information from their vicars about local antiquities.

1624   Meursius is engaged as royal Danish historiographer.
Lyschander dies (around New Year 1623/24).

1625 Meursius moves to Denmark to become royal historiographer and professor at the Academy of Sorø.

Christian IV orders the professors of the University to prepare those historical documents that seem suitable for print; likewise it must be found out what kind of historical documents Johannes Kirchmann in Lübeck is said to have discovered.

Jesper Brochmand is engaged to see to the re-edition of Huitfeldt's *History of Denmark* and the edition of Lyschander's *History of Frederik II*.

The professors of the University arrange that Svaning's History of Denmark shall be published in Frankfurt.

Johannes Narssius is engaged by Gustavus Adolphus to compose a history of Sweden in verse.

1626 A Danish delegation addresses, as it seems, Grasser in Basel asking him to become royal Danish historiographer. Grasser does not accept the offer and dies soon afterwards.

Pontanus is once again told to finish his work soon – this time by the chancellor.

Publication of Worm's *Fasti Danici*.

Christoffer Heidman, professor at the Academy of Sorø, is engaged to search for accounts of Danish and Norwegian history in the University library.

1627 Holger Rosenkrantz is admonished by Christian IV to send him information on the histories of Norway discovered by Johannes Kirchmann in Lübeck.

1629 Wassenaer is engaged as royal Danish historiographer but dies in the same year.

Publication of Stephanius's anthology of texts concerning the history of Denmark, *De regno Daniæ et Norwegiæ insulisque adjacentibus* [...].

1630 Publication of Meursius's *Historia Danica* (covers 1448-1523, i.e. the three first kings of the Oldenburg line).

1631 Publication of Pontanus's *Rerum Danicarum historia* (covers beginnings-1448).

Publication of Meursius's edition of Ailnothus.

1632 Peder Clausen (Friis)'s description of Norway is published by Ole Worm.

1633 Peder Clausen (Friis)'s reworking of Snorre's sagas is published by Ole Worm.

1636 Publication of Worm's *Runir seu Danica literatura antiquissima*. Publication of Laurentius Paulinus's *Historiæ Arctoæ libri tres*.

1638 Publication of Meursius's *Historia Danica* (covers beginnings-1523).

1639 Pontanus, Meursius, and Christen Friis die. Stephanius becomes royal historiographer.

1643 Publication of Arngrímur Jónsson's *Specimen Islandiæ*, in which he argues against Pontanus on the question of ancient Thule.

1740 Publication of Westphalen's edition of Pontanus's *Rerum Danicarum Historia*, second part (covers 1448-1588).

1746 Publication of Gram's edition of Meursius's *Historia Danica* (covers beginnings-1550).

Index of Personal Names
and Anonymous Works

Mythological figures are included. Modern scholars (after c. 1800) are not included. Note occurences are marked with (n).

Acknowledgements

This book is a revised version of a doctoral thesis submitted at the University of Bergen in 1998. The main part of my studies was conducted in Bergen in the years 1993-96, and I am grateful to the The Carlsberg Foundation for supporting me with a generous grant during these years. Likewise I would like to thank the University in Bergen and the Department of Greek and Latin for accepting me as a visiting fellow in this period.

My research required consultation of many old books and manuscripts. The staffs at the University Library in Bergen and at the Royal Library in Copenhagen were always efficient and ready to comply with my numerous and sometimes obscure requests. Thanks also to the University Library in Lund.

When it finally came to the production of the book, I had the pleasure of working together with the staff at the Museum Tusculanum Press. The book received financial support from the Danish Research Council, the Norwegian Research Council, and the Hielmstierne-Rosencroneske Stiftelse, for which I am very grateful.

During my work I have received substantial help and advice from friends and colleagues. I am indebted to the members of the committee Sverre Bagge, Tomas Hägg, and Minna Skafte Jensen. In particular I would like to thank Minna Skafte Jensen for thorough comments on the manuscript. Likewise Chris Heesakkers and Sebastian Olden-Jørgensen undertook to read the manuscript at this stage and provided me with valuable advice. Jørgen Steen Jensen and Thelma Jexlev gave me much-needed information on specific fields.

A special thank goes to Harald Ilsøe, who not only commented upon the manuscript but also generously, throughout my studies, shared with me of his profound knowledge of early modern Danish intellectual history and historiography in particular. The present book bears witness to his contribution on this field during four decades.

Acknowledgements

Peter Fisher took it upon him to correct my English. Not limiting himself to matters of language he subjected the manuscript to close scrutiny, pointed out inconsistencies, and offered me insightful suggestions.

Throughout my studies Peter Zeeberg has been an invaluable support. The inconvenience of living far away from the Royal Library of Copenhagen has been greatly relieved by his helpfulness and his ability to solve bibliographical riddles.

My parents Inge and Vagn Skovgaard-Petersen have followed my studies with unfailing interest, encouragement, and active support. My husband Lars Boje Mortensen lived with this project all along and has contributed to it with hours of inspiring conversation, patient listening and critical scrutiny of the manuscript. Thanks to all of them.

Bergen/Copenhagen 2000/2001   *Karen Skovgaard-Petersen*